CASTLES, CUSTOMS, AND KINGS

TRUE TALES BY ENGLISH HISTORICAL FICTION AUTHORS

Castles, Customs, and Kings

True Tales by English Historical Fiction Authors

Edited by

Debra Brown & M.M. Bennetts

MADISON STREET
PUBLISHING

LCCN: 2014939266

Paperback ISBN: 978-0-9836719-6-1
Hardback ISBN: 978-0-9836719-5-4
Publisher: Madison Street Publishing

3 5 7 9 10 8 6 4

CONTENTS

INTRODUCTION

BY DEBRA BROWN

CASTLES, MANSIONS, BANQUETS AND BALLS. DUNGEONS, ARMIES AND KINGS. DOES BRITISH history sound boring to you? Suppose there was a way to encounter history without the frustration of cramming for a test, a way to learn about the past that filled you with interest instead of indifference?

Have you ever heard the phrase "stranger than fiction"? Do strange-but-true stories fascinate you? The goal of this book is to provide a wide range of absorbing historical information about the lands and peoples of the Isles of Britain.

The greatest tourist attraction of Northern England is Hadrian's Wall, now a length of ruins from Roman times. We can stand looking at it, trying to comprehend the time that has passed since workmen put those stones together nearly two thousand years ago. We can imagine the travelers that passed near them over the centuries, the children that climbed over them—all of them grown up, grown old, grown silent.

Almost all of those people have been forgotten. Yet each of them had a life, achievements, and a story. Some of those stories have been retrieved from sources long hidden away and shared in this book.

Through the millennia, eras came and went. Each had its rulers, its heroes, and its unfortunate poor. Its left-behind structures stand—or fall. Its art, music, and dances have passed down to us, and with those, sometimes we imitate the lives of those before us.

The authors of this book are, for the most part, historical fiction writers. To craft good historical fiction, we have studied the times about which we write and the events that came before. We would like to share some of the fascinating things we have learned.

The true tales found in this book originated with the English Historical Fiction Authors Blog (http://englishhistoryauthors.blogspot.com/) which was founded on September 23, 2011. Every day, one of our member authors posts a historical article on a subject he or she has studied. Reading the daily post is a way to keep ablaze your ancient English, Scottish, Welsh, or Irish fancies. You may want to bring along a cup of your favorite tea.

The articles in this book have been collected from the first year of the blog's existence, and are presented here in a new format for easier enjoyment.

This book will also introduce you to our authors and their work. There is a section following this introduction with a short biography of each of the authors and links to their websites, blogs, and books. There is also a list of novels arranged by era so that you can find historical fiction from whatever time most strikes your fancy. Some authors are blog members, posting on a regular basis, and others are guests who post occasionally.

We hope you will be captivated by each and every historical tale we offer in this book and that you will join us on the blog for our daily post. Perhaps you will find a new favorite author who can whisk you away to times past or a new stack of books to fill up your rainy days with tales of yesteryear.

CONTRIBUTING AUTHORS

ANDERSEN, MAGGI

An Australian author with a BA in English and an MA in Creative Writing, Maggi Andersen lives with her lawyer husband in a pretty, historical town in the Southern Highlands with their spoiled Persian cat, plus the assorted wildlife they love to feed: the chickens wandering in from next door, the ducks swimming in their pool, and the parrots and possums lining up for bananas and seed. Maggi writes historical romance, contemporary romantic suspense, and young adult novels.

ARNOPP, JUDITH

Judith Arnopp's historical novels are written from a female perspective. *The Song of Heledd* is set in 7th century Powys, *Peaceweaver* and *The Forest Dwellers* in the years encompassing the Norman Conquest, and *Dear Henry* and *The Winchester Goose* in the Tudor period. She is currently working on *The Kiss of the Concubine*, a novel of Anne Boleyn.

ASHE, KATHERINE

Katherine Ashe is the author of *Montfort*, a four volume novelized biography of Simon de Montfort, who founded England's Parliament in 1258 and died on the battlefield of Evesham in 1265. He was believed to be the Angel of the Apocalypse. The speaking of his name was made a hanging crime.

ASHWORTH, ELIZABETH

Elizabeth Ashworth is a UK author who writes historical fiction and local interest books about Lancashire. A published writer since her early teens, she has also written articles and short stories for a wide range of publications. Her first published novel was *The de Lacy Inheritance*. This was followed by *An Honourable Estate*. 2013 will see publication of *By Loyalty Bound* from Pen and Sword Fiction. It tells the story of the mistress of King Richard III.

BAGWELL, GILLIAN

Gillian Bagwell's richly detailed historical novels bring to vivid life England in the sixteenth and seventeenth centuries. *Venus in Winter* chronicles the life of the formidable Bess of Hardwick at the court of Henry VIII. *The Darling Strumpet* charts Nell Gwynn's meteoric rise from the grimy slums to triumph as a beloved comic actress in the arms of the king. *The September Queen* (U.K. title *The King's Mistress*) gives the first fictional accounting of Jane Lane, who risked all to help the young Charles II, saving his life and the future of the English monarchy. Gillian uses her years of experience in theatre as an actress, director, and producer to help authors give effective public readings, through workshops and private coaching.

BARDEN, JENNY

Jenny Barden has had a love of history ever since an encounter in infancy with a suit of armour at Tamworth Castle. Training as an artist, followed by a career as a city solicitor, did little to help displace her early dream of becoming a knight. Impelled by a fascination with the Age of Discovery, she has travelled widely throughout the Americas, and much of the inspiration for her novels has come from retracing the steps of early adventurers in the New World. Jenny has four children and now lives in Dorset with her long suffering husband and an ever increasing assortment of pets.

BATTEN, PRUE

A former researcher/journalist with the Australian Broadcasting Corporation (the Australian version of the BBC) Prue Batten majored in history at university. She finds it a gentle irony to be moving back to the era she found most fascinating then, the Middle Ages. Prue spends as much time as she can by the water and with her dogs, has a huge affinity with gardens and embroidery, and takes pleasure and contentment in The Small Things.

BEARD, J. A.

J.A. Beard is a history-loving restless soul married to an equally restless soul and has two very restless children. He's tried his hand at several careers, including intelligence analysis, programming, and research science. Though he likes to declare himself the Pie Master, he's yet to prove his worth in the brutal baking show-downs of Celebration, Florida.

BENNETTS, M.M.

A former book critic for the Pulitzer Prize-winning *Christian Science Monitor*, M.M. Bennetts is an historian specialising in early 19th century Europe and the author of two best-selling novels set amidst the turbulence of the Napoleonic wars: *May 1812* and *Of Honest Fame*. An avid cross country rider, Bennetts is also an accomplished pianist and accompanist. She is now at work on a third novel, *Or Fear of Peace*. She blogs regularly about history.

BILYEAU, NANCY

Nancy Bilyeau is a novelist and magazine editor who has worked on the staffs of *InStyle*, *Good Housekeeping*, and *Rolling Stone*. She graduated from the University of Michigan and lived in the American Midwest and Toronto, Ontario, before moving to New York City. She is descended from Pierre Billiou, the Huguenot settler who built one of the first stone houses in New York in 1665. Her Tudor-era mystery thriller *The Crown* was short-listed for the CWA's Ellis Peters Historical in the 2012 Dagger Awards. The second book in her series, *The*

Chalice, was published in North America and the United Kingdom in March 2013. Nancy is currently writing her third mystery novel, *The Covenant.*

BRANT, LUCINDA

Lucinda Brant writes bestselling Georgian historical romances with wit and adventure, and crimances—crime with lashings of romance. All her books are set in the 18th century, spanning 1740 to early 1780s Georgian England, with occasional crossings to the France of Louis XV.

BROWN, DEBRA

Debra has enjoyed varied creative pursuits and has worked in the interior design field. While making jewelry, she watched all the period dramas she could find. Her Victorian story *The Companion of Lady Holmeshire* was written when they ran out. She is now working on The Dante and Evangeline Series. Its first novel, *For the Skylark*, was inspired by the Dickens' character Miss Havisham. Debra runs the English Historical Fiction Authors blog and the Goodreads group Historical Info for Historical Fiction Readers.

BROWN, PHILLIP

Phillip Brown is a retired computer consultant who has been collecting and researching Victorian art for nearly 40 years, particularly the Pre-Raphaelites. He has always found it fascinating how art of the time reflects social life and attitudes and the lives of the artists. It's an exciting time for Victorian studies and exhibitions, and they can lead to so many exciting discoveries.

BYRD, SANDRA

Bestselling author Sandra Byrd has now published more than forty books, recently focusing especially on England-set historicals. Her novels *To Die For: A Novel of Anne Boleyn* and *The Secret Keeper: A Novel of Kateryn Parr* were selected by Library Journal as Best Books Picks for 2011 and 2012. *Roses Have Thorns: A Novel of Elizabeth I* published in April, 2013. Please visit www.sandrabyrd.com to learn more and for the most up-to-date information on her forthcoming series, *Daughters of Hampshire*, also set in historic England.

CALKINS, SUSANNA

Susanna is the author of *A Murder at Rosamund's Gate* and *From the Charred Remains (*St. Martin's Press /Minotaur Books), a historical mystery series featuring Lucy Campion, a crime-solving chambermaid in plague-ridden 17th century London. Susanna received her PhD in early modern English history from Purdue University.

CAMPBELL, JOHN

As a classically trained musician, John B. Campbell developed an interest in history while touring Europe in his youth. An interest in creative writing came along with his mid-life crisis. Campbell's debut novel, *Walk to Paradise Garden*, earned an editor's desk review wherein Harper Collins described his book as, "compulsively readable." The author lives north of Milwaukee, WI with his wife Pamela and their two dogs.

COLLISON, LINDA

Linda Collison's novel, *Star-Crossed*, was published by Knopf in 2006 and chosen by the New York Public Library to be among the *Books for the Teen Age—2007*. Her fiction has won awards from the former Maui Writers' Conference, the Southwest Writers, and *Honolulu Magazine*. Her short stories, essays and articles have appeared in *Ladies Home Journal, Skydiving, American Baby, Parachutist, Sailing Magazine, Cruising World, and RN*. Her nautical historical novels include *Barbados Bound* and *Surgeon's Mate*.

COWELL, STEPHANIE

Born in New York City, Stephanie Cowell fell in love with history, music, Shakespeare, and art almost at once. She started to write stories very young, and by the age of twenty had won prizes twice in a national story contest. Stephanie is married to the poet and spiritual director Russell Clay and they make their home on the Upper West Side of New York City where they live in an apartment with thousands of books. To Stephanie, being an historical novelist is one of the best things in the world!

DAVISON, ANITA

Born in London, Anita began writing 17th century historical family sagas, then tried out Victorian romance. She now feels she has found her niche with 17th century historical biographical novels with her latest book, *Royalist Rebel*, released by Claymore Books in early 2013 under the name Anita Seymour. She writes reviews for Romantic Historical Lovers and the Historical Novel Review Blog.

DENNING, RICHARD

Richard Denning is a historical fiction and fantasy author. He works as a GP in the West Midlands. He has always been fascinated by historical settings as well as by horror and fantasy. Other than writing, his main interests are games of all types. He is the designer of a board game based on the Great Fire of London. His most popular book is *The Amber Treasure*—Dark Ages historical fiction.

DENVIL, BARBARA GASKELL

Barbara Gaskell Denvil was born in Gloucestershire, England. Moving to London, she built up a career publishing numerous short stories and articles while also working as a critic and editor, television scriptwriter, and publishers' reader. She then spent many hot and colourful years sailing the Mediterranean and living in various European countries. Finally, she has moved to rural Australia where she lives amongst the parrots and wallabies and writes historical fiction.

ELLIOT, GRACE

Grace Elliot leads a double life as a veterinarian by day and author of historical romance by night. She is addicted to cats and is housekeeping staff for five adorable moggies—Wallace, Gromit, Pilchard, Widget, and her daughter Noni. Grace started writing as an escape from an emotionally demanding job and believes all intelligent people need romance in their lives—as an antidote to the modern world.

ENGLISH, CHRISTY

After years of acting in Shakespeare's plays, Christy English is excited to bring the Bard to Regency England in her recent romances published by Sourcebooks Casablanca (*How To Tame A Willful Wife, Love on A Midsummer Night*). Christy indulged her obsession with Eleanor of Aquitaine and 12th century England and France in her historical novels *The Queen's Pawn* and *To Be Queen*.

GILBERT, LAUREN

Lauren Gilbert lives in Florida with her husband. Lauren obtained a degree in English and Art History, and is a member of JASNA. An avid reader, she has always dreamed of writing, and has a stockpile of notes and manuscripts started and laid aside. *Heyerwood: A Novel* is her first published novel.

GRACE, MARIA

Though Maria Grace has been writing fiction since she was ten years old, those early efforts happily reside in a file drawer and are unlikely to see the light of day again, for which many are grateful. She has one husband, two graduate degrees and two black belts, three sons, four under-graduate majors, five nieces, six cats, seven Regency-era fiction projects and notes for eight more writing projects in progress. To round out the list, she cooks for nine in order to accommodate the growing boys and usually makes ten meals at a time so she only cooks twice a month.

HIGGINBOTHAM, SCOTT

Scott Higginbotham is the author of *A Soul's Ransom, For a Thousand Generations*, and *A Matter of Honor*, novels which complement one another. All the books are historical in nature and are populated with characters and contexts that connect with modern readers. He believes that books should serve as a means of escaping the trials of daily living, where the impossible becomes possible, and where readers are refreshed and left with good and enduring truths.

HIGGINS, MARIE

Marie Higgins is a best-selling, multi-published author of sweet romance—from refined bad-boy heroes who make your heart melt to the feisty heroines who somehow manage to love them regardless of their faults. Visit her website/blog to discover more about her.

INBINDER, GARY

Gary Inbinder is a retired attorney who left the practice of law to write full time. Gary holds a J.D. from the University of La Verne (California) where he received an American Jurisprudence Award for Legal Writing and a B.A. in English Literature from the University of Illinois, Chicago. Gary is a member of the Historical Novel Society and the Bewildering Stories Editorial Review Board. His short fiction, articles, and essays appear in *Bewildering Stories, Halfway Down the Stairs, Morpheus Tales, Humanitas, Touchstone Magazine* and other publications. Fireship Press published his novels *The Flower to the Painter* (2011) and *Confessions of the Creature* (2012).

JONES, SHERRY

Internationally best-selling novelist and award-winning journalist Sherry Jones has been writing professionally since the age of 18, when she landed her first newspaper reporting job in her hometown. She says, "I strive for beautifully written page-turners that explore relationships and power, especially women's power in a man's world. My novels portray women in history who have achieved power over others as well as—especially—over their own lives, in spite of patriarchal limits. I hope that, in telling their stories, I can inspire others to dream big, to aim high, to dare to make a difference no matter how impossible doing so might seem."

KEYWORTH, PHILIPPA JANE

Known to her friends as Pip, Philippa Jane Keyworth has been writing since she was twelve in every notebook she could find. Add to this her love for reading, history, and horse-riding, and you have the perfect recipe for writing Regency romances. Pip's debut novel, *The Widow's Redeemer* (Madison Street Publishing, 2012), brings to life the romance between a young widow with an indomitable spirit and a wealthy viscount with an unsavory reputation.

KYLE, BARBARA

Barbara Kyle is the author of the acclaimed Tudor-era "Thornleigh Saga" novels *The Queen's Lady, The King's Daughter, The Queen's Captive, The Queen's Gamble* and *Blood Between Queens* and of contemporary thrillers. Her books have been published in seven countries, with over 400,000 copies sold in North America. Barbara is known for her dynamic workshops for writers. Before becoming an author Barbara enjoyed a twenty-year acting career in the U.S. and Canada. She and her husband live in Ontario.

LEWIS, DIANE SCOTT

Diane Parkinson (Diane Scott Lewis) writes book reviews for the *Historical Novels Review* and worked at The Wild Rose Press from 2007 to 2010 as a historical editor. She has three published historical novels: *Elysium* and *The False Light*, and her sequel to *The False Light*, *Without Refuge*, which was released in March 2012. Her debut novel, *The False Light*, will be re-released by Books We Love, re-titled *Betrayed Countess*.

LOFTING, PAULA

Paula Lofting works as a psychiatric nurse and writes in her spare time. She lives in Sussex and is an active member of Regia Anglorum re-enactment society. It was always her ambition to write a novel. In her forties, she began on the journey that has led her to her first book, *Sons of the Wolf*, the first in a series of books about the Norman conquest of England. She is currently working on the sequel *The Wolf Banner*.

LORTZ, ROSANNE E.

Rosanne E. Lortz is a medieval enthusiast, a book addict, and a native of Oregon. She taught high school history for several years before "retiring" to stay at home with her four boys and write historical fiction. Her debut novel, *I Serve: A Novel of the Black Prince*, is a fourteenth century adventure/romance. Her second book, *Road from the West: Book I of the Chronicles of Tancred*, begins a trilogy set during the First Crusade.

LUCE, WANDA

Wanda Luce's great passion for British Literature was born in the stories spun by Charles Dickens and Jane Austen. The old-world vocabulary and sentence construction as well as the historical settings of their books hold a strong enchantment for her and propelled her into a love of writing Regency-era novels. At present, she resides with her husband and two sons in Utah.

MCGRATH, CAROL

Carol has a degree in Russian Studies and English from Queens University, Belfast, where she was taught by Seamus Heaney. She took an MA in Creative Writing at QUB in 2003 and followed this with an MPhil at Royal Holloway (University of London in English and Creative Writing). She currently reviews for the HNS Review. Carol's debut novel, *The Handfasted Wife*, first in the trilogy *The Daughters of Hastings*, is published by Accent Press and can be purchased for all e-readers and as a paperback from Amazon.

MOSS, TOM

Tom Moss is a textile technologist by profession and currently manages a specialist weaving concern in north Cumbria, England, just a few miles south of the border between England and Scotland. Fascinated by its turbulent history, Tom's passion is the Border Reivers—a people whose history is replete with theft, murder, and family feud; a people who had no love for either monarchy or authority. Tom's blog has more than 100 posts about the Border Reivers at http://wwwborderreiverstories-neblessclem.blogspot.com/.

O'BRIEN, ANNE

Anne O'Brien lives in the Welsh Marches, indulging her love of history by writing about medieval women, their lives, loves, and the influences that shaped them. Anne Neville, wife of Richard III stars in *Virgin Widow*, splendid Eleanor of Aquitaine in *Queen Defiant*. *The King's Concubine* features Alice Perrers, mistress to Edward III, and Katherine de Valois relives her marriage to Henry V and affair with Owen Tudor in *The Forbidden Queen*.

PARRILLO, VINCENT

Professor of Sociology at William Paterson University, Vincent is author of the historical novel *Guardians of the Gate* and a dozen college textbooks, as well as General Editor of the two-volume *Encyclopedia of Social Problems*. Writer, narrator, and producer of three PBS documentaries, his latest, *The Sculptor Laureate of Paterson*, premiered in April 2013. A Fulbright scholar and senior specialist, he has been a guest lecturer at dozens of universities in Asia, Europe, Canada, and the United States.

PYM, KATHERINE

Katherine Pym is the author of historical novels set in 1660s London with one novel of the French Revolution. She lives in the Seattle area with her husband and puppy dog.

QUEENEY, TIM

In addition to writing books, Tim is a magazine editor, filmmaker, celestial navigation instructor, a dad, and an offshore sailor. He also writes a news satire site called Height of Eye (timqueeney.com) which provides the latest in nonsensical news and curdled current events. He lives in Maine and can hear the fog horns of three lighthouses when the fog rolls in.

RENDELL, MIKE

Mike Rendell is author of a book *The Journal of a Georgian Gentleman*, based on the array of diaries, journals, accounts—even shopping lists—left by his 4xgreat grandfather, Richard Hall. It tells the story of everyday life in the eighteenth century, seen through the eyes of his ancestor who had a haberdashery shop at Number One London Bridge. Details of the book appear on his website.

RUSSELL, ARTHUR

Arthur Russell is a native of County Meath, Ireland. He is a professional in Agro-Industry and has worked in Ireland, Eastern Europe, and Central Asia. When he is not on assignments abroad, he lives with his family in Navan. His interests include history, especially local history, photography, and music. *Morgallion*, his first book, is a historic novel based on actual events during the Bruce Invasion of Ireland in 1315.

SIMONSEN, MARY LYDON

Mary Lydon Simonsen is the author of several *Pride and Prejudice* and *Persuasion* re-imaginings. She is also the author of the Patrick Shea mystery series.

SKEA, MARGARET

Margaret Skea grew up in Ulster at the height of the "Troubles", but now lives in Scotland. Her passion for Scotland's turbulent history and her own Ulster-Scots heritage led to *Turn of the Tide*—Historical Fiction Winner, Harper Collins People's Novelist Competition 2011— judged "outstanding" by Jeffrey Archer. An award-winning short story writer, Margaret has been published in a range of magazines and anthologies in Britain and the USA.

ST. JOHN, PETER

Peter St. John is best known for his six "Gang" books about children's gangs during World War II. These novels spring from adventures in an English village as an evacuee from the London Blitz. Two other novels draw on his career as a chartered engineer in aerospace research, as well as from experience within parliamentary and governmental organizations. He lives in France where he is president of a cultural association.

SWIFT, DEBORAH

Deborah Swift is the author of *The Lady's Slipper*, *The Gilded Lily*, and *A Divided Inheritance* (St Martins/Pan Macmillan). She used to work in the theatre and at the BBC as a set and costume designer, and later became a lecturer in theatre and art history. She took an MA in Creative Writing in 2007 and now divides her time between writing and teaching. She lives in a historic village of 17th century houses and enjoys exploring the varied landscape of Cumbria—the lakes, mountains, and coast.

THOMAS, SAM

Sam Thomas teaches history at University School, an independent day school outside Cleveland, Ohio. Before coming to US he taught at the college level for seven years and received research grants from the National Endowment for the Humanities, the Newberry Library, and the British Academy. He lives in Shaker Heights, Ohio with his wife and two sons. You can find him on the web at: http://www.samthomasbooks.com. *The Midwife's Tale* is his first novel.

VICARY, TIM

Tim Vicary is an author and teacher at the Norwegian Study Centre at the University of York, England. He's written three crime/legal thrillers, three historical novels, two children's books, and twenty graded readers for foreign learners of English in the Oxford Bookworms series. In 2010, one of these, *Titanic*, won in its category for the Language Learner Literature Award for the Extensive Reading Foundation, and another, *The Everest Story*, won the same prize in 2011.

WAINWRIGHT, BRIAN

Brian Wainwright has had a deep interest in the Middle Ages for most of his life. His first published novel, *The Adventures of Alianore Audley*, was produced by way of light relief during a lull in the long task of researching and writing *Within the Fetterlock*, a novel born of his obsession with Constance of York. Brian owes a debt to many writers, living and dead, who have influenced his work and admits to a particular fondness for Jane Austen, Robert Graves, and Geoffrey Chaucer.

WASYLOWSKI, KAREN V.

Karen V. Wasylowski is the author of two *Pride and Prejudice* sequels, *Darcy and Fitzwilliam: The Tale of a Gentleman and an Officer, Book One*, and *Sons and Daughters: Book Two of Darcy and Fitzwilliam*. These novels follow cousins Fitzwilliam Darcy and Colonel Fitzwilliam from young manhood, through marriages, children, and then on into middle age. Their adventures are never predictable and far from dull. Karen's blog, The League of British Artists, follows the finest in British acting and music.

WHEATLEY, JOHN

A writer, teacher, and plumber, John Wheatley taught English for many years, then trained to fix boilers! He started writing novels when inspired by the story of the wreck of the *Royal Charter* on the coast of Anglesey. John spends a lot of time on the Isle of Anglesey, and his books are all historical novels set on this beautiful island!

WILKIN, DAVID WILLIAM

Mr. Wilkin is a student of the English Regency. He has written several books in the genre. A student of history, Mr. Wilkin graduated with a Bachelor's degree from UCLA. In later years he continued his studies after college and applied himself as a reenactor of history. Along with his research, he also has become a teacher of the dances of our bygone years. Look for scenes in all of his writings where dance plays a part.

WILSON, LYNNE

Lynne Wilson is the author of several historical true crime books. Born in Stirling, Scotland, Lynne studied Chemistry at Edinburgh Napier University and worked mainly in scientific and research work. However, she always had a strong interest in the subject of Victorian history, and after combining this with a Diploma in Criminology, Lynne decided to start writing, concentrating on historical true crime in Scotland's cities. Lynne also works as an article writer and a historical researcher.

List of Novels by Contributing Authors

ROMAN BRITAIN AND EARLY MEDIEVAL PERIOD (55 B.C. - A.D. 1000)

The Song of Heledd, by Judith Arnopp

The Amber Treasure, by Richard Denning

Child of Loki, by Richard Denning

Princes in Exile, by Richard Denning

Shield Maiden, by Richard Denning

The Jewel of Medina, by Sherry Jones

The Sword of Medina, by Sherry Jones

Triple Agent, by Peter St. John

LATE MEDIEVAL PERIOD (1001-1485)

Peaceweaver, by Judith Arnopp

The Forest Dwellers, by Judith Arnopp

Montfort: The Early Years 1229-1243, by Katherine Ashe

Montfort: The Viceroy 1243-1253, by Katherine Ashe

Montfort: The Revolutionary 1253-1260, by Katherine Ashe

Montfort: The Angel with the Sword 1260-1265, by Katherine Ashe

The de Lacy Inheritance, by Elizabeth Ashworth

An Honourable Estate, by Elizabeth Ashworth

By Loyalty Bound, by Elizabeth Ashworth

Gisborne: Book of Pawns, by Prue Batten

Gisborne: Book of Knights, by Prue Batten

Fair Weather, by Barbara Gaskell Denvil

Satin Cinnabar, by Barbara Gaskell Denvil

Sumerford's Autumn, by Barbara Gaskell Denvil

The Queen's Pawn, by Christy English

To Be Queen, by Christy English

A Soul's Ransom, by Scott Higginbotham

For a Thousand Generations, by Scott Higginbotham

Four Sisters, All Queens, by Sherry Jones

Sons of the Wolf, by Paula Lofting

The Wolf Banner, by Paula Lofting

I Serve: A Novel of the Black Prince, by Rosanne E. Lortz

Road from the West: Book I of the Chronicles of Tancred, by Rosanne E. Lortz

The Handfasted Wife: A Story of Edith Swan-Neck, by Carol McGrath

The Virgin Widow, by Anne O'Brien

Queen Defiant (US) / *Devil's Consort* (UK), by Anne O'Brien

The King's Concubine, by Anne O'Brien

The Forbidden Queen (to be released in US Feb. 2014), by Anne O'Brien

Morgallion, by Arthur Russell

Within the Fetterlock, by Brian Wainwright

The Adventures of Alianore Audley, by Brian Wainwright

TUDOR PERIOD (1485-1603)

The Winchester Goose, by Judith Arnopp

Dear Henry: Confessions of the Queens, by Judith Arnopp

Venus in Winter, by Gillian Bagwell

Mistress of the Sea, by Jenny Barden

The Lost Duchess, by Jenny Barden

The Crown, by Nancy Bilyeau

The Chalice, by Nancy Bilyeau

To Die For: A Novel of Anne Boleyn, by Sandra Byrd

The Secret Keeper: A Novel of Kateryn Parr, by Sandra Byrd

Roses Have Thorns: A Novel of Elizabeth I, by Sandra Byrd

Nicholas Cooke: Actor, Soldier, Physician, Priest, by Stephanie Cowell

The Players: A Novel of the Young Shakespeare, by Stephanie Cowell

The Queen's Lady, by Barbara Kyle

The King's Daughter, by Barbara Kyle

The Queen's Captive, by Barbara Kyle

The Queen's Gamble, by Barbara Kyle

Blood Between Queens, by Barbara Kyle

Fire the Braes, by Tom Moss

Turn of the Tide, by Margaret Skea

Nobody's Slave, by Tim Vicary

STUART PERIOD (1603-1714)

The Darling Strumpet, by Gillian Bagwell

The September Queen (US) / *The King's Mistress* (UK), by Gillian Bagwell

A Murder at Rosamund's Gate, by Susanna Calkins

The Physician of London, by Stephanie Cowell

The Last Seal (board game), by Richard Denning

Viola, a Woeful Tale of Marriage, by Katherine Pym

Twins, by Katherine Pym

Of Carrion Feathers, by Katherine Pym

Royalist Rebel, by Anita Seymour

The Lady's Slipper, by Deborah Swift

The Gilded Lily, by Deborah Swift

A Divided Inheritance, by Deborah Swift

The Midwife's Tale, by Sam Thomas

The Harlot's Tale (to be released 2014), by Sam Thomas

The Monmouth Summer, by Tim Vicary

The Weeping Sands, by John Wheatley

EARLY GEORGIAN ERA (1715-1800)

Noble Satyr: A Georgian Historical Romance (Roxton Series #1), by Lucinda Brant

Midnight Marriage: A Georgian Historical Romance (Roxton Series #2), by Lucinda Brant

Autumn Duchess: A Georgian Historical Romance (Roxton Series #3), by Lucinda Brant

Salt Bride: A Georgian Historical Romance (Salt Hendon #1), by Lucinda Brant

Salt Redux: Sequel to Salt Bride (Salt Hendon #2), by Lucinda Brant

Deadly Engagement: A Georgian Historical Mystery (Alec Halsey Crimance #1), by Lucinda Brant

Deadly Affair: A Georgian Historical Mystery (Alec Halsey Crimance #2), by Lucinda Brant

Barbados Bound, by Linda Collison

Surgeon's Mate, by Linda Collison

Marrying Mozart, by Stephanie Cowell

Betrayed Countess, by Diane Scott Lewis

Without Refuge, by Diane Scott Lewis

George in London, by Tim Queeney

The Journal of a Georgian Gentleman (nonfiction), by Mike Rendell

Bristol Blue: The Story of a Remarkable Cobalt Blue Glassware (nonfiction), by Mike Rendell

18th Century Paper Cutting: How Richard Hall Illustrated His World (nonfiction), by Mike Rendell

LATE GEORGIAN AND REGENCY ERA (1800-1837)

A Woman of Proper Accomplishments, by J.A. Beard

May 1812, by M.M. Bennetts

Of Honest Fame, by M.M. Bennetts

A Dead Man's Debt, by Grace Elliot

Eulogy's Secret, by Grace Elliot

Hope's Betrayal, by Grace Elliot

Verity's Lie, by Grace Elliot

How to Tame a Willful Wife, by Christy English

Love on a Midsummer Night, by Christy English

Heyerwood: A Novel, by Lauren Gilbert

VICTORIAN ERA (1837-1901)

CASTLES, CUSTOMS, AND KINGS

TRUE TALES BY ENGLISH HISTORICAL FICTION AUTHORS

Falling in Love with England and Its History

BY **STEPHANIE COWELL**

IT BEGAN WHEN I WAS VERY YOUNG; I FELT I DID NOT BELONG IN NEW YORK CITY WHERE I WAS born but somewhere across the sea in that land called England. But what was England to me? Any place for which we long is formed from fragments which mysteriously arrive and become part of us.

My first sense of England was literature, of course: Sara Crewe in *A Little Princess* and Mary Lennox in *The Secret Garden* in beautifully illustrated editions. I read them until the words almost wore away. I was Sara coming from her attic to be discovered at last as the little girl everyone had been looking for. I was Mary exploring the deserted rooms of the manor house on the moors. In my early teens it was the poetry (all of Shakespeare) and the great Victorian novels. I told myself, "That is where I belong; that is where I must be." England had formed in my mind as the place where I could find my true self.

I painted a picture of "this earth, this realm, this England," as Shakespeare calls it. It was a mixture of lovers running over the moors, a beautiful young queen, London attics, hot milky tea and servants always on hand to make it, and a great mysterious line of kings described as "the Unready" or "the Confessor" and queens who always looked ready to have their portraits painted and who each possessed a far more glamorous wardrobe than that within my schoolgirl closet; tombstones, ancient churches, an orderly way of being and doing things. (I was looking for the orderly; I passed by Henry VIII and his disorderly coterie of marriages. I am glad others felt differently! What would we do without Anne Boleyn?)

And so I saved and saved and finally went to England, and the England I expected was waiting for me. I walked all over London. I visited the Tower on an overcast day when it was not crowded and was properly awed by the tiny rooms and thick walls. Still, the heart of *my* England was literature not royalty even though I love the stability and ceremony of a monarch, a world in which everyone had their place.

I looked for writers—the new Globe had not been built, but I walked where Shakespeare had walked and found the old streets he had known: Cheapside, Love Lane. I visited Dickens' House. I found and touched what was left of the London City Walls.

I went to Haworth and walked in the parlor where Charlotte Bronte had walked with her sisters. I climbed about the moors and heard the wind wuthering. I went to Oxford where my great heroes had studied and heard the choirboys sing in the little cathedral as they had done for hundreds of years. I longed for medieval houses, for London fog, for wonderful names of villages. (I shall not forget my first bus ride to Yorkshire and passing the signs for the town of Giggleswick.)

I was looking for something that I felt had been waiting for me. I believe it was.

My husband came with me as I visited the places I love. When we stood in the old city, though, he saw the tall financial buildings and I saw the long-gone, half-timbered houses. Upon taking a tour bus, I became increasingly emotional at every sight, and when we finally passed Temple Bar where Fleet Street, City of London, becomes the Strand, Westminster, and where the City of London traditionally erected a barrier to regulate trade into the city (and traditionally the Lord Mayor of London must meet and allow entry to the monarch), I burst into a flood of tears. My husband was patient, comforting, and bewildered; he has often repeated this story to friends of how his wife could cry because someone walked a street in London three hundred years ago.

All of us who write on this blog or read it are English or have longed for England so intensely that we have made it a major part of our creative and emotional lives. Its present and past are rooted in us in a way we cannot fully explain; it calls to each of us in a slightly different way. How has it called you and for what reasons?

> *"This royal throne of kings, this sceptered isle…*
> *This happy breed of men, this little world,*
> *This precious stone set in the silver sea…*
> *This blessed plot, this earth, this realm, this England."*
>
> —*Richard II* (Shakespeare)

Roman Britain and Early Medieval Period (55 B.C.—A.D. 1000)

THE FIRST WORD IN ENGLISH

BY RICHARD DENNING

IN 1929 AN RAF CREW TOOK AERIAL SHOTS OF THE SITE OF THE OLD ROMAN TOWN OF VENTA Icenorum around the church of Caistor St. Edmund near Norwich. The photographs revealed an extensive road network and soon the archaeologists moved in. During their excavations they came across a large early Anglo-Saxon cemetery with burials dating from the 5th century.

In the cemetery, they found some cremation urns as well as pots with possessions inside. One of these was full of bones—but they were not human remains. Most were sheep knuckle bones and probably dice or other game pieces. But amongst them was a bone that was and still is of historical importance.

It was a bone from a Roe deer and upon it there were runic inscriptions. The runes were Old German/Old English runes and spelt this word: RHIHFt

Which means *Raihan*.

What is Raihan? Well the "an" in old German meant "belonging to or from," and the "Raih" is believed to be a very early version of the word "roe". So this inscription which has been dated to circa 420 A.D. means "from a roe".

It is not uncommon in the Saxon period to find similar bones from other animals with writing telling us which beast it is from.

So what we have here are the possessions of a man or woman from the very first years of Anglo-Saxon settlement of East Anglia buried in a cemetery that would have been very new, within or close to a decaying Roman town. What we also have is the very first word written in the country that would one day become England in the language which would one day be called English.

What we see here are the scrapings of one of the first of the mercenaries who crossed the North Sea on hearing the call from the Britons for fighters to help protect Britannia from the Picts and Irish. He and thousands like him stayed on to carve out a nation.

There is more on this word and 99 other ones that form part of our history in *The Story of English in 100 Words* by David Crystal. It's a fascinating book and I very much recommend it.

I find this evidence of the first written word in English fascinating and quite romantic really. I write novels about the early Anglo-Saxon period, always striving to bring back to life people who died fourteen centuries ago. This to me is a tangible relic of one of those people.

DEGSASTAN: A LOST BATTLEFIELD

BY RICHARD DENNING

Ethelfrid, king of the Northumbrians, having vanquished the nations of the Scots, expels them from the territories of the English, [a.d. 603.] At this time, Ethelfrid, a most worthy king, with ambitions of glory, governed the kingdom of the Northumbrians, and ravaged the Britons more than all the great men of the English...whereupon, Aedan, king of the Scots that inhabit Britain, being concerned at his success, came against him with an immense and mighty army, but was beaten by an inferior force, and put to flight; for almost all his army was slain at a famous place, called Degsastan. In which battle also Theodbald, brother to Ethelfrid, was killed, with almost all the forces he commanded.... From that time, no king of the Scots durst come into Britain to make war on the English to this day.

—from the chronicler Bede

IN THE YEAR 603 AN IMPORTANT BATTLE WAS FOUGHT SOMEWHERE IN THE SCOTTISH BORDERS. It probably brought together several nations and races—Scots, Picts, Romano-British and English—in a showdown that determined the future of the region for a hundred years and propelled the Northumbrian Kingdom into a dominance that led to its golden age as recorded by Bede in the 8th century.

It was so well known a location that Bede even says it was *"a famous place, called Degsastan."* Yet today we do not know with any certainty where it may lie. So what do we really know?

The nations of Deira, Bernicia, Rheged, Strathclyde, Manau Goddin, Dál-Riata, Mercia, and the lands of the Picts are the players in this drama and frequently entered into conflicts and alliances with each other.

Coming from the east, the tribes of Anglo-Saxons were expanding their holdings in Northumbria and moving west. They came into conflict first with the Romano-British or Welsh. The Battle of Catraeth—fought around 597 A.D. between the fledgling English Kingdoms and the Romano-British natives of Rheged (Cumbria), Strathclyde (Dumbarton area) and Manau Goddodin (around Edinburgh)—weakened the British to the extent that Aethelfrith's Bernicians were able to move on into the lands "between the walls," that is, to threaten that area between Hadrian's Wall and the Antonine Wall.

This seems to have provoked the Scots under Aedann Mac Gabrhrain into becoming interested in Bernicia. The Scots were actually an Irish tribe from Ulster who in about 500 to 600 settled the west coast of Scotland. They came into conflict with the Picts and the British too. But in c. A.D. 601 a diplomatic mission from the Scots to the Angles appears to have occurred.

All we know is that the Scots princes Bran and Domanghast died at that meeting, or shortly afterwards, and that Aethelfrith was held to blame. The Scots' response was not immediate however—not, in fact, for two years. There are references to a plague in the *Annals Cambriae* about the same time which might explain why the Scots took two years to respond to the loss of two princes. Eventually, they gathered an alliance and marched under King Aedann to Degsastan where, as Bede describes, the Scots were beaten by the much smaller forces of Aethelfrith and his brother Theobald, the one who perished in the battle.

The actual location of the battle is not known. Historians have suggested that it occurred at Dawstone in Liddesdale. But others have criticized this, saying the only reason for believing it is Dawstone is because of similar sounding words. Degsastan might come from Degga's stone—perhaps corrupting to Dawstone in time. Equally, there has been a lot of discussion about stones and monoliths—of which there are hundreds in the region including the Lochmaben stone not far away in the Solway Firth and itself a location often used for mustering armies and militia in later centuries.

As a writer of historical fiction, a moment comes when you have to decide which way to jump. I was content to go with Dawstone when researching *Child of Loki*. I visited this place with my family when writing the novel. It is a remote location and, at first glance, seems an unlikely place for a great battle. It does, however, have some supporting evidence. Geographically, it occupies the watershed where rivers and streams flow away west and east and gives access to routes through the hills of the Scottish borders and Northern Pennines. Thus an army heading for Carlisle might just go that way.

Furthermore, archeological digs on the site in the early 20th century found evidence of iron weaponry and arrowheads in the area. There is even today in the southern valley the outlines of a circular fort, a settlement as well as a shallow ditch cutting across Dawstone Rig (the plateau). The top of the rig is littered with the vague remnants of stone cairns—possibly raised over the bodies of the fallen.

In the very old papers of a local archaeological society there is a record of a rather interesting monument which is now lost. There is a photo—of poor quality—of a black tombstone. It was supposed to be found in the south valley near the remains of old fortifications and a settlement. Could this indeed be the place where Theobald died as recorded by Bede?

The Battle of Degsastan features in *Child of Loki* which is the second in my *Northern Crown Series* which follows the history of the late 6th and early 7th centuries.

Anno Domini and the Venerable Bede

by ROSANNE E. LORTZ

IN THE YEAR OF OUR LORD
ANNO DOMINI

OVER TWENTY CENTURIES OF HISTORY HAVE THIS PHRASE APPENDED TO THEM, BUT IT HAS only been fifteen centuries since the system of dating was first devised, and only twelve centuries since the work of the Venerable Bede made it common usage in the Western world.

The Romans used the founding of Rome by the legendary figure Romulus, the year we now know as 753 B.C., as *year one* of their dating system. As the Roman Empire spread, this system of ordering time spread with it.

If Rome still ruled the world, the date on this essay would be the year 2765 *ab urbe condita* (and these paragraphs would probably be written in Latin). But Rome went the way of the tyrannosaurus rex, and somewhere in that muddle we know as the Middle Ages, someone decided that time needed to be re-ordered. Someone decided that the founding of a little city on the banks of the Tiber would no longer be the focal point of history.

In A.D. 525, an abbot named Dionysus Exiguus, which translates as Dionysus the Humble, began transferring dates from the Roman system into a new system centered around *"the incarnation of our Lord Jesus Christ."* Dionysus originated in Scythia (modern day Bulgaria or Romania), but had come to Rome to translate works of theology and compile collections of canon law.

Interestingly, Dionysus was no historian. His purpose for this new method of dating was to correctly calculate the date of Easter for the Christian calendar. Easter, unlike Christmas, is a moveable feast day and, according the First Council of Nicaea, was supposed to be celebrated on the Sunday after the first full moon following the spring equinox.

Dionysus' goal was to write out yearly tables so that churches all around the world would know which Sunday to celebrate the holy day. To do this, he re-ordered time to begin year one with the birth of Christ—or what he thought was the birth of Christ, since we now know that Jesus of Nazareth was born in 3 or 4 B.C.

The Roman church adopted the tables but did not yet see how useful Dionysus' system of dating could be for other things. Historians continued to use the regnal dates of Roman emperors to measure time and still counted up the years since the founding of the city of Rome.

Two hundred years later, a Northumbrian monk known as the Venerable Bede also became preoccupied with the question of when to celebrate Easter. It had been a subject of great dispute in Britain. The adherents of the Celtic church (those who had been evangelized by Columba and the monks from Ireland) often observed the holy day at a different time than the adherents of the Roman church (those who had been evangelized by the Roman missionary Augustine of Kent).

This might seem like a minor point of religious practice to us today, but imagine what it could mean for a kingdom when the king and his courtiers were celebrating the highest holy day of the church year while the queen and her followers were still fasting for Lent. It was a troubling mark of disunity, both religiously and politically.

The Synod of Whitby in 664, which occurred ten years before Bede's birth, had ruled in favor of the Roman practice (the tables and method of calculation devised by Dionysus Exiguus). By Bede's death in 735, almost the entire British church had accepted this method. But the controversy was still current enough in his lifetime for him to devote extensive portions of his *Ecclesiastical History of the English People* to it.

Somewhere in his historical studies on the Easter controversy, Bede developed a keen interest in Dionysus Exiguus' method of ordering time. He decided to use the new Anno Domini dating system for his *Ecclesiastical History*, and with this decision, he created a precedent for historians everywhere in the Western world.

It is a difficult matter to convert an entire society from one dating system to another. The numbers we have assigned to the past don't like to pack up their tents and leave.

Several years ago, when I taught history to high school students, I asked them to pick the most important date in American history and make it year one. Most chose the Declaration of Independence, and with that as the focal point, they had to use their math skills to draw up a timeline of other important dates B.D.o.I and A.D.o.I (Before the Declaration of Independence and After the Declaration of Independence). It is a little mind boggling to realize that the numbers that were drilled into your head all your life (1066, 1215, 1776, 1914) don't actually mean anything except in relation to the chosen focal point of history.

Despite the difficulty, Bede did a marvelous job of moving the Anglo-Saxon society from the old system of dating to the new one. In the *Ecclesiastical History* he initially used both systems side by side until his readers become acclimated to the change. In the second chapter of his book, Bede wrote:

> *Now Britain had never been visited by the Romans and was unknown to them until the time of Gaius Julius Caesar who, in the year of Rome 693, that is, in the year 60 before our Lord, was consul with Lucius Bibulus...*

In the third chapter, Bede once again cited the Roman system and then followed it up with a time marker from the new system.

> *In the year of Rome 798 the Emperor Claudius, fourth after Augustus, wishing to prove that he was a benefactor to the State, sought to make war everywhere and to gain victories on every hand...He brought the war to an end in the fourth year of his reign, that is in the year of our Lord 46.*

But by the fourth chapter, Bede had fully implemented the new system of Anno Domini and expected the reader to catch on accordingly.

In the year of our Lord 156 Marcus Antoninus Verus was made emperor...In the year of our Lord 189 Severus...became emperor...In the year of our Lord 286 Diocletian, the thirty-third after Augustus, was elected emperor...

Bede's new use of the Anno Domini dating system spread gradually throughout Europe. By the beginning of the 800s, Alcuin had introduced it to Charlemagne's court, and in 1422, Portugal became the last Roman Catholic country to adopt this system of reckoning time.

In 1700, Russia discovered that adopting the Anno Domini system was a requirement for westernization. In 1949, the People's Republic of China jettisoned the old Chinese calendar in favor of the Western and international system.

To accommodate people from other religions, some recent historians have tried to alter the nomenclature of the Anno Domini system to B.C.E. (Before Common Era) and C.E. (Common Era). I suspect that Dionysus Exiguus would have been amused by this effort since even if the names change, the focal point still remains the same.

And once the focal point has been established, it is no easy thing to alter. Until we have a historian as enterprising and influential as the Venerable Bede, year one will stay exactly where it is—at the birth of Jesus of Nazareth (give or take a few years).

SOURCE

Bede. *The Ecclesiastical History of the English People.* New York: Oxford University Press, 1969.

Monarchy: The Early Middle Ages—House of Wessex

by DEBRA BROWN

WHEN CONSIDERING THE MONARCHS OF ENGLAND, WE WILL START WITH THE ANGLO-Saxon kings of the Early Middle Ages—since most of the Romans left and King Arthur may or may not have existed. The earliest works mentioning Arthur are from centuries after he would have lived, and they do not call him a king. There is a stone from Tintagel Castle upon which is carved "*Artognou descendant of Patern*[us] *Colus made* [this]." Some have said that this may speak of Arthur, who it was claimed (again, centuries later) was conceived in Tintagel. A battle in which he is said to have fought has been recorded, but there is no mention of him in the writing. The most substantial evidence of Arthur's existence is that where there is smoke, there must have been a fire. Yet, fictional characters can yield the same smoke.

At the turn of the 6th century, the area now known as England was divided into various kingdoms. Of note is pagan King Æthelberht of Kent who married Bertha, a Frankish Christian princess. This marriage brought Christianity to the Anglo-Saxon royal houses. Pope Gregory sent the monk Augustine. Æthelberht converted and thereafter claimed the divine right of kings.

King Offa of Mercia (who likely killed his predecessor) ruled 757-796 and brought Mercia to power over the other six kingdoms. He was ruthless and brought an end to their dynasties, including that of Æthelberht. He did claim to be Christian, though he was in conflict with the Church when his rulership or wishes were hampered.

Though Offa had a role in unifying England, his goal was his own personal power. Coins were struck with his image and were of better quality than the Frankish coins of the time. Offa's Dyke was built, possibly by King Offa and probably to create a barrier and establish commanding views into Wales. The builder had considerable resources.

In the 780s King Egbert of Wessex was forced into exile by Offa of Mercia and Beorhtric of Wessex, but on Beorhtric's death in 802 Egbert returned and took back the throne. He took Northumbria and defeated the Danes at Hingston Down. He reigned until his death in 839 when he was succeeded by his son Æthelwulf.

Within twenty years of Offa's death, England had reverted into smaller kingdoms and Viking invasions had begun. By the 860s, the Vikings had decided to stay.

King Æthelwulf of Wessex died in 855, leaving the throne to his four sons, one after the other. Æthelbald, Æthelberht and Æthelred all ruled for short periods of time, fighting the Danes. Their youngest brother became known as Alfred the Great; he was King of Wessex from 871 to 899.

Alfred took the throne at age twenty-two. He endured difficulties with the Vikings for some time, but in May 878 he rallied a force of men and won a brilliant victory at the Battle of Ashdown on the Berkshire Downs. He then trapped the Danes in their stronghold at Chippenham and their king Guthrum fulfilled his promise to leave Wessex.

Alfred reorganized the army to be ready at any time and built the first English Navy. He took London and its mint.

Alfred established a long law code which he determined to be just, taking parts of the Bible into account, and he considered judicial matters with care. He built *burhs*—fortified communities in which, rather than being a place of protection for a lord, the people lived under his patronage and protection. (The suffix "-bury" and the word "borough" come from *burh*.)

Alfred became the King of not just the West Saxons, but of the Anglo-Saxons. He translated a letter from Pope Gregory into the vernacular and sent it to his bishops, establishing himself as the religious head of the country.

Edward I the Elder succeeded his father Alfred in 899. His eldest sister Æthelflæd married Æthelred of Mercia and ruled in his place when he became ill. After her death, her daughter ruled for a short time before being supplanted by Edward. This union helped Edward to recapture the Midlands and Southeast of England from the Danes and drive them out. The princes of West Wales acknowledged Edward as their overlord, but he died in a Welsh-Mercian uprising against him.

Æthelstan succeeded Edward and reigned from 924 or 925 to 939. He was the first English king of several to be crowned on the King's Stone at Kingston. In 927, he was recognized as overlord by the rulers of Northern England, some of which now includes southern parts of Scotland. Ten years later he defeated Scots, Welsh, and Viking forces at the Battle of Brunanburh and claimed the title "King of all Britain". He never had a son, but his sisters married five European monarchs, adding to England's wealth and prestige.

In 939, he was succeeded by his half-brother Edmund I, who subdued the Norse Vikings. The story goes that Edmund was murdered by Leofa, a thief whom he had once exiled. Leofa was instantly killed thereafter.

Eadred, another brother, ruled from 946 through 955, taking the throne at age sixteen. He faced off with former Norse king Eric Bloodaxe, so named after he'd bloodied his axe on his seven brothers—his people drove him into exile for the act. The Vikings had been ruling within the Roman walls of York since the 870s. Eadred threatened all of Northumbria, who then sided with him and drove out Bloodaxe, killing him in the war. Eadred died at age 25 from a digestive malady without a wife or children.

Eadwig (or Edwy), the sixteen year old son of Edmund I lived to the age of twenty, ruling from 955 to 959. The thanes of Mercia and Northumbria switched their allegiance to Eadwig's younger brother Edgar. Edgar, who took over Mercia and Northumbria at age fourteen, doubted Eadwig's qualifications. In 957, rather than see civil war, an agreement was reached by which the kingdom would be divided along the Thames, with Eadwig ruling Wessex and Kent in the south and Edgar ruling in the north.

Eadwig's marriage was annulled by powerful church officials, although that was against the will of both husband and wife. On the day of the king's Coronation Feast, Bishop Dunstan dragged King Eadwig away from the young woman. Dunstan claimed that they were too closely related, but they were less so than today's Queen Elizabeth II and Prince Phillip.

After Eadwig's death, Edgar ruled from 959 to 975 as king of a united England. He was the first to be crowned with a crown rather than a military style helmet. Though not a peaceful man himself, his rule was free of war and he came to be called Edgar the Peaceful. His rule unified England to the extent that it never again broke up into sovereign kingdoms. He founded forty religious houses and helped instigate a monastic revival.

Edgar was succeeded by his twelve-year-old son, Edward II, though Edgar's third wife claimed that her son Æthelred should have the throne. In 978, young Edward went to visit his ten-year-old half-brother and was killed by Æthelred's agents. He has since been called Edward the Martyr.

Æthelred II "The Unready" ruled from 979 to 1013 and 1014 to 1016. He was the pawn of those who brought him to the throne. He paid the Danes to leave him alone, but it failed. He fled from them to Normandy where he was protected by Duke Robert the Good while the Danish King Sweyn ruled. In just a few months, however, the Danish king fell off his horse and died, and Æthelred returned to rule for two years more. His wife was Emma of Normandy, the sister of Robert the Good who was eventually the grandfather of William the Conqueror.

Edmund II "Ironside", Æthelred's son, was king from April to November of 1016. He thwarted the son of Danish King Sweyn, Cnut, who tried to take London. Edmund foolishly agreed to a deal where Cnut would get Mercia and Northumbria while he ruled Wessex, and after one of them died, the other would get the rest of the country. Edmund somehow died shortly thereafter.

Cnut "The Great" reigned from 1016 to 1035. He had Edmund's younger brother Eadwig murdered and Edward's sons exiled to Hungary. Cnut had sons by his English mistress Ælfgifu of Northampton, who was acknowledged as Queen of Denmark. He also had a son, Harthacnut, by his new wife, (whoa!) Emma of Normandy, widow of Æthelred II. Emma's son by Cnut was regarded as the heir in England.

Cnut was the first Dane to rule England in the sense of being able to collect taxes and mint coin. He poured out his English wealth on Danish supporters while still a teenager. In time, though, he was said to become more English than the English—he loved Emma. She married him because it would help to neutralize British claims on the throne and the claims of her own older sons once she had a child by Cnut.

Cnut endorsed the code of laws by Æthelred I and was deemed Cnut under Heaven. He severed his Nordish roots and was remade as a Christian king. He was seen as a good and just ruler and was buried in Winchester Cathedral when he died.

Harold Harefoot, son of Cnut and Ælfgifu, contended for Harthacnut's throne as did Alfred, son of Emma and Æthelred II. (What a mess.) Alfred was killed by Earl Godwin of Wessex. Harold Harefoot, the name referring to his swiftness, became Regent from 1035 to 1040 while rightful heir Harthacnut was busy as King of Denmark. They were to be joint monarchs, but in 1037, Harold was elected king by the English. Harthacnut had made preparations to invade and claim his throne, when Harold died, childless.

Harthacnut, 1035 to 1042, should have been happy. The throne was his. However, he had spent a great deal of money preparing to fight for it, and he was displeased. He blamed it on the English, who had voted for his half-breed brother as king, and so he imposed a "fleet tax" on them. His popularity suffered. They shed no tears when he died with no wife or children of convulsions at a drinking party in 1042.

Edward "The Confessor" ruled from 1042 to 1066. The eldest son of Æthelred II and Emma, he had stayed in Normandy through the reign of Cnut. He attempted the throne in 1035, and helped by Harthacnut and Earl Godwin of Wessex (who wanted political favor), he succeeded in 1042. He married Godwin's daughter Edith.

Godwin later decided that he wanted his own son on the throne instead of Edward. Since he had been involved in the murder of Edward's brother Alfred, Godwin was sent into exile, and Edith was banished to a monastery.

In 1051, Godwin returned with the people's support and the king was forced to restore him to favor. Edward also had to expel his Norman friends and have Godwin's son, Harold Godwinson, as his chief advisor. However, he announced that upon his death he would have his cousin William, Duke of Normandy, as his successor, unless he had children. William came to him and pledged his loyalty.

Edward built the original Westminster Abbey. Most monarchs have been crowned there (or in the newer model) since. Too sick to attend its consecration, he died the next January. On his deathbed, he named Harold Godwinson to be the next king. However, the right actually belonged to Edgar, the grandson of his half-brother Edmund Ironside.

Harold II Godwinson ruled from January to October, 1066, as the last Anglo-Saxon King of England. Harold was the first of only three English kings to die in warfare. He was killed at the Battle of Hastings by Norman invaders during the conquest by William, Duke of Normandy.

After the battle, Edgar the Ætheling was declared King of England, but never crowned. He was born in Hungary where his father, Edward the Exile, had lived since being sent there when Cnut became king. Edward the Confessor had learned of his (Edward's) existence and sent for him to take his place in court as heir to the throne. (That makes three people to whom he promised it—I wonder what history would have been if he had not put the idea into William's heart!) Edward the Exile died in strange circumstances shortly after arriving.

Edgar was six years old at the time. Edward the Confessor made no attempt to make him the heir, but after the death of Harold II, the Witanagemot assembled and elected Edgar king. However, as William of Normandy began his invasion, they brought the child to William at Berkhamsted Castle where the Crown of England is said to have been handed over to William by nobles including Edgar the Ætheling. Later in his life he struggled for the throne but never succeeded. He was still known to be alive in 1126.

Athelstan: The Secrets
of a Dark Ages King

BY NANCY BILYEAU

"*HOLY KING ATHELSTAN, RENOWNED THROUGH THE WHOLE WORLD, WHOSE ESTEEM FLOURISHES and whose honour endures everywhere,*" said a 10th century Latin poem.

In his own lifetime, Athelstan, the grandson of Alfred of Great, was praised as "the English Charlemagne." By defeating the combined armies of Danes, Scots, and Welsh in the Battle of Brunanburh in 937 A.D., Athelstan could rightly claim the title of "King of all Britain." In his 15-year reign, he also established laws, financed Catholic monasteries, and made key alliances with European royalty.

Yet today, Athelstan is mostly forgotten.

While researching this Anglo-Saxon king who plays a crucial role in my historical thriller *The Crown*, I puzzled over why Athelstan dissolved into obscurity. It's not all attributable to the time in which he lived—those ill-documented, striving, brutish, yet sporadically dazzling centuries between the Roman Occupation and the Norman Conquest. Everyone has heard of Alfred the Great. Why not Athelstan, who arguably accomplished just as much?

I concluded that it was the mysteries surrounding Athelstan—ones that the most determined historians have not been able to solve—that made him too blurry for easy familiarity. His secrets make him tantalizing. But they also prevent his life from hardening into the simple outlines that propel a legend through time.

1) WAS ATHELSTAN'S MOTHER A CONCUBINE?

This is hotly disputed, with biographer Sarah Foot convinced that Athelstan's mother was an obscure but highly born young woman who had a child or two and died. Sort of a Dark Ages version of a starter wife.

Yet the story persists that Athelstan's father, Prince Edward, fell in love with a beautiful young shepherdess while visiting his former wet nurse and conceived Athelstan that very night. It's quite the erotic tale, putting to rest that stereotype of 10th century men only caring for their swords.

More practically, if there were any truth to Athelstan being illegitimate, it would explain why he did not have strong support when he succeeded his father to the throne at age 30—and it would also explain a serious problem he had with one of his half-brothers….

2) DID ATHELSTAN HAVE A HALF-BROTHER KILLED?

The story goes that Athelstan suspected young Edwin, the son of his father's undoubted queen, of conspiring against him with disaffected nobles. As punishment, Edwin was put in an oarless boat without food or water and set out to sea. He threw himself overboard rather than continue to suffer.

Later, Athelstan is said to have expressed remorse and performed penance. This whole story is far from confirmed, but it's persistent—and historians believe that it flung a shadow across the character of Athelstan.

3) WHY DID ATHELSTAN NEVER MARRY OR HAVE ANY CHILDREN?

Thanks to chronicler William of Malmesbury, we know what Athelstan looked like: handsome, slim, and blond. He was well educated. He was personally brave—Athelstan *"won by the sword's edge undying glory in battle."* In short, the man is King Arthur material. So why wasn't there a Guinevere?

Historians struggle to explain it: *"Athelstan's decision to remain unmarried seems more readily explicable as a religiously motivated determination on chastity as a way of life."* Still, the concept of celibate warrior monks—such as the Knights Templar—did not come along for another two centuries. A king was expected to marry and beget heirs, in Athelstan's time and throughout the succeeding dynasties (see Henry the Eighth). Lacking a Dark Ages Dr. Phil—which is perhaps for the best—we'll never get to the truth of this one.

4) WHERE DID THE BATTLE OF BRUNANBURH TAKE PLACE?

Athelstan's enemies, determined to put an end to Wessex domination, drew him north for a cataclysmic encounter. Winston Churchill, as only he could, summed up the odds against Athelstan in *The Birth of Britain*: *"The whole of North Britain—Celtic, Danish and Norwegian, pagan and Christian—together presented a hostile front under Constantine, king of the Scots, and Olaf of Dublin, with Viking reinforcements from Norway."* And yet…Athelstan won. Where this battle was fought, no one knows, though Yorkshire is a solid guess. Most of our information about Brunanburh comes from a rapturous Anglo-Saxon poem. There is a great deal of *"they hewed the battle shafts with hammered weapons,"* but no identifiable landmarks.

5) WHY DID ATHELSTAN REQUEST BURIAL AT MALMESBURY ABBEY?

Almost every king of the House of Wessex was laid to rest in Winchester, the family's seat of power. But Athelstan arranged to be buried at Malmesbury Abbey in Wiltshire. The king had *"such a veneration for the place that he thought nowhere more desirable or more sacred."* Whatever his reasons, Malmesbury rose to the occasion and dedicated itself to the memory of the great king. Today you can visit Athelstan's tomb and glimpse his effigy, though his corpse is long gone. Some say it disappeared a few decades after his death, others that it was removed shortly before the Dissolution of the Monasteries.

6) DID ATHELSTAN POSSESS THE MOST SACRED RELIGIOUS RELICS OF HIS TIME?

This was the age of relic collecting, and no one pursued them with greater passion than Athelstan. He was so famous for his love of relics than when Hugh Capet, descendant of Charlemagne, was interested in marrying Athelstan's most beautiful sister, he is said to have delivered an amazing amount of treasure to England—as well as relics that dated back to Golgotha. The most famous one was the Spear of Destiny, also known as the Lance of Longinus, that pierced Jesus's side. But Athelstan is said to have possessed other objects of mystical value, too, and that is what I delve into in my novel, *The Crown*....

Late Medieval Period (1001-1485)

WILLIAM BEFORE HE WAS THE CONQUEROR

BY **ROSANNE E. LORTZ**

He was born William the Bastard, illegitimate son of Duke Robert of Normandy, but history knows him as William the Conqueror, first Norman king of England and compiler of the Domesday Book. Many historians focus on the year 1066 and the legitimacy of William's claim to the English crown. But how did an illegitimate boy across the Channel become powerful enough to make that claim in the first place? What did he accomplish before he invaded England? What did he win before the Battle of Hastings?

France during the eleventh century was not a unified country as it was in the earlier Carolingian period or in the later Middle Ages. It was split up into lots of little areas, which I will call counties—not because they were anything like modern day counties, but because they were typically ruled by a count.

Some of Normandy's most important neighbors were Brittany, Maine, Flanders, Anjou, Blois, and Burgundy. And let us not forget the most important neighbor of all: the Isle of France, where the Capetian king Henry I had his court.

The first duke of Normandy, Rollo the Viking, had sworn a reluctant fealty to the king of France (a very droll story that would take too long to tell here), but there is some question as to whether the duchy of Normandy, during William's time, was still considered a vassal of the French king.

When William's father, Robert, died in 1035, on the return trip from a pilgrimage to Jerusalem, his only son and heir was seven years old. Robert had never taken the trouble to marry Herleva, William's mother, but he had also never taken the trouble to marry anyone else, so there were no legitimate sons to dispute William's claim to the dukedom of Normandy.

In the age of robber barons, a seven-year-old duke was hardly able to rule his demesne with the requisite strength of arm. William's childhood was marked at times by fighting between his various guardians and, at other times, by outright anarchy. But through it all, the boy was learning, and when he came of age he took steps to teach not only Normandy but also the lands around him to fear and honor his iron sword and iron will.

William of Poitiers (yes, we're talking about a different William now) was a Norman chronicler who provides one of the most thorough pictures of Duke William's early exploits. This chronicler was one of the duke's biggest fans and also proposed his own version of the just war theory: whatever Duke William did was *just* fine.

In 1043, when the duke was about fifteen years of age, his neighbor Geoffrey Martel, the Count of Anjou, was having a spat with another neighbor, the Count of Blois. In the process, the Count of Anjou *accidentally* captured Alençon, one of the Norman castles. William didn't think it was an accident. He took back Alençon and chased off the Count of Anjou, making a bitter enemy in the process.

Guy of Burgundy presented the next problem. Realizing that Normandy was quite a nice vacation spot, Guy began to subvert various Norman barons in an attempt to take over the dukedom. William got wise to the situation and marched out to fight Guy.

This was the Battle of Val-es-Dunes in 1047. In this battle, William had the support of King Henry (who had not yet developed his later fear and hatred of the Norman duke), and with this help, William carried the day and defeated Guy.

A couple of years after this, William formed a marriage alliance with the mighty Baldwin of Flanders by marrying his daughter Matilda. The county of Flanders was one of the more significant territories in France, and William's connection with Baldwin increased both his power and his prestige.

There are many interesting legends about William and his bride. Later sources record that when William asked for Matilda's hand in marriage, she refused on the grounds of his illegitimacy. She was too high born to marry a bastard.

Undeterred, William rode to her father's domains, grabbed her by her braids, threw her to the floor, and beat her until she changed her mind. Whether the story is true or not, it indicates how William was perceived by posterity—a man who would stop at nothing in order to get his way.

William of Arques was the next French nobleman to test William's mettle. Unhappy with his feudal obligations to Normandy, Arques renounced his vassalship and began to pillage Norman territory. Incensed by these depredations, William drove the brigand back into his castle and besieged him until he was forced to surrender. With these actions William made it abundantly clear that vassals of Normandy were not allowed to renounce their obligations.

At this point, King Henry decided William was getting too powerful and too cocksure. The chronicler from Poitiers writes thus:

> *The king bore it ill and considered it an affront very greatly to be avenged, that while he had the* [Holy] *Roman emperor as a friend and ally…and while he presided over many powerful provinces of which lords and rulers commanded troops in his army, Count William was neither his friend nor his vassal, but his enemy; and that Normandy, which had been under the kings of the Franks from the earliest times, had now been raised almost to a kingdom. None of the more prominent counts, however great their aspirations, had dared anything of this sort.*

King Henry realized that he needed to put William in his place before it was too late. What he didn't realize was that he had already delayed too long. Supported by Theobald of Blois, William of Aquitaine, and Geoffrey Martel of Anjou, King Henry attacked William in 1054 at the Battle of Mortemer. Even these combined powers could not crush the might of Normandy. William drove their armies from the field, taking many prisoners.

With victory achieved, William showed how insolent he could be. In the middle of the night, he sent a herald to King Henry's camp, instructing him to climb the tallest tree and there declaim in full detail the sad news of Henry's defeat. It wasn't the happiest thing for the king to wake up to.

Because of this defeat, Henry was forced to make concessions to William. The chief concession was this: that William could do anything he wanted to Geoffrey Martel, Count of Anjou, without fear of reprisal from the king.

Extremely pleased by this green light, William began to construct a castle in the region of Maine. This county was under the governance of Geoffrey of Maine, but (in the complicated web of feudal relationships) owed homage to Geoffrey Martel of Anjou. Maine sent Martel an urgent cry for help.

Martel, joined by William of Aquitaine and Eudo of Brittany, began to attack the stonemasons at the castle site. William, who had been expecting some resistance, soon arrived with his formidable army and put the counts' collective forces to flight. Then, in the words of the chronicler, William *"turned his attack against Geoffrey of Mayenne* [Maine]...*and in a very short time he reduced him to the point of coming into the heart of Normandy, to put his conquered hands into William's own, swearing the fealty which a vassal owes his lord."* In this way he stole the county of Maine from Anjou and extended the reach of Normandy.

With one last burst of energy, King Henry gathered another army against William. (Geoffrey Martel, who didn't know when to cry uncle, was part of it.) This led to the Battle of Varaville in August 1057. As you probably expected, William defeated Henry who *"realized in consternation that it would be madness to attack Normandy further."*

King Henry I died three years later, in August of 1060, and was soon accompanied into the afterlife by Geoffrey Martel of Anjou. Philip I assumed the throne in France, but by this time the lesson had been well learned: don't mess with Normandy.

When Edward the Confessor died in 1066, the Duke William of Normandy who laid claim to the throne of England was far more than some petty nobleman across the Channel. He was a man who had risen through the force of his will and his arm, maintained and increased the lands left to him by his father, and proven himself the equal (or superior?) of the King of France.

The character that William displayed during his rise in Normandy would continue during his reign in England. His new subjects found him a harsh master in many things, and the *Anglo-Saxon Chronicle* records that he was *"severe beyond measure to those who withstood his will."* When he forbade hunting in the king's forest, *"the rich complained and the poor murmured, but he was so sturdy that he took no notice of them; they must will all that the king willed, if they would live, or keep their lands...."*

The Battle of Hastings may be the one that we remember William for, but it was all the battles before Hastings that paved the way for his victory. And while we call him the Conqueror for his exploits in England, the eleventh century counts and kings of France had good reason to call him by that name as well, a nickname born not from affection, but from the bitterness of the vanquished.

SOURCES

"Medieval Sourcebook: The Anglo-Saxon Chronicle: Assessment of William I." Fordham University. From the *Anglo-Saxon Chronicle*, sub anno 1086, as it appears in F. A. Ogg, *A Source Book of Medieval History* (New York, 1907). http://www.fordham.edu/Halsall/source/1186ASChron-William1.asp.

William of Poitiers. *The* Gesta Guillelmi *of William of Poitiers*. Trans. Marjorie Chibnall. USA: Oxford University Press, 1998.

MONARCHY: WILLIAM THE CONQUEROR

BY **DEBRA BROWN**

Edward the Confessor had in his younger days fled to Normandy with his parents. He later, as king, put Norman friends in high places in England, and promised that his cousin, William, Duke of Normandy, would succeed him—according to William.

Edward, though, changed his decision upon his deathbed, and he now left the throne to Harold Godwinson, who had no blood ties to the succession.

William was having none of that, and he made plans to invade England. Winds did not permit the duke to sail across when he had first intended to do so, and he left later, but this turned out to be in his favor.

Despite realizing that William was finally on his way, Harold II was forced to pull away from southern England to ward off an attack in the north by even more powerful forces, his own brother Tostig along with the King of Norway. When Harold II was asked by Tostig how much land he was prepared to yield to the King, he replied, *"Six feet of ground or as much more as he needs, as he is taller than most men."*

Harold successfully routed that attack at the Battle of Stamford Bridge.

Only three days later, the Normans landed at Pevensey the 28th of September, 1066. Harold headed south, obtained fresh troops in London, and set off to meet the advancing Duke.

William had but seven thousand men to England's two million. They met six miles north of Hastings. Though Harold II had the upper hand much of the day, when the ten-hour battle ended, he and his brothers lay dead. He was the last monarch of England to be defeated by a foreign invader. William went on to devastate a large circle of land to establish his authority and then swept into London to claim the throne.

The Witanagemot had assembled and elected young Edgar the Ætheling, the grandnephew and rightful heir of the Confessor, king after the death of Harold Godwinson. Edgar was never crowned, however, and a group of nobles met the invading Duke of Normandy and handed over the Crown of England—as well as young Edgar. William took him in.

Edgar lived to attempt the crown, but never gain it. He was still known to be alive in 1126.

William had some ruling experience from his duchy in Normandy, and set about organizing England his way. He took estates away from English owners, kept much for himself, and gave some to his supporters from France.

These nobles (who also had interests in France) built castles, following the lead of William with his start on the Tower of London, to protect themselves from the angry English.

Over the next 600 years, this trend continued and some 2,000 castles appeared. The French barons divided their land into *fiefs* and handed them out to *vassals* who organized men under them, knights, for military service to the king.

William was an administrative genius and commissioned a national survey of belongings—his Domesday Book records the possessions of all his subjects for taxation purposes. It was said that there was *"not an ox, cow, or swine that was not set down in the writ"*.

William also took firm action against criminals, even castrating rapists. There was, therefore, less crime in the country under his rule. He introduced trial by jury. However, he was far from just.

William was an avid deer hunter, and he cleared the New Forest of its buildings and inhabitants to create game reserves for himself. His forests came to cover a third of English land. Poachers were killed or mutilated.

When rebellions reared he reacted firmly, even burning entire villages and their crops. Much of Northern England was devastated, its economy ruined for decades after a rebellion. In this way, he kept firm control.

He spent much of his time in France, as did his new English knights and his English tax money. He was, after all, first and foremost, the Duke of Normandy.

William was the illegitimate son of Norman Duke Robert I and a tanner's daughter. Though he succeeded to his father's duchy, he had grown up with the nickname William the Bastard. Perhaps this is why the great conqueror was such a faithful and devoted husband to Matilda of Flanders, by whom he had four sons and five daughters.

The former English ruling class disappeared when William conquered England, and French speech and customs thereafter heavily influenced the English. French fashions, manners, art, and architecture made a permanent mark. He built great cathedrals, which were to give the impression that he was, indeed, ordained by God to rule England.

William, a calculating and brutal invader, deemed his eldest son, Robert, too generous and easygoing, and while he left his Norman holdings to him, just before his death he willed the rule of rebellious England to his second son, William Rufus. He then died a day after having been thrown from his horse, who had stepped on hot coals following William's capture of the French town of Nantes.

His body was looted by those who had been taking care of him, and he was left nearly naked. His corpse broke in half as it was being forced into a too-small coffin.

He was buried in Caen. In time, his body was dug up and parts of it taken, but a thigh-bone remained to be reburied in dignity. Even this bone was disinterred and stolen during the French Revolution. The long-missed thigh-bone was found, however, and confirmed to be authentic in the 1980s, and it was finally laid to rest under a new tombstone.

CHRISTMAS 1065

BY **CAROL MCGRATH**

CHRISTMAS 1065 WAS ONE OF THE MOST SIGNIFICANT CHRISTMASES IN ENGLAND'S HIStory. Thanes and their families, bishops and two Archbishops gathered in Westminster for the king's Christmas feast and for the consecration of the newly built Cathedral Church of St. Peter (Westminster), close to the king's palace on Thorny Island.

However, during the twelve days of Christmas, the childless King Edward died, setting in motion a not unexpected succession crisis.

The day after King Edward's death, Harold Godwinson was crowned king, thus leading to invasions of England from two usurping contenders, William of Normandy and Harold Harthrada of Norway.

The story of that Christmas is recorded in both Norman and English writing from the period. William of Poitiers, a Norman historian, refers to Harold Godwinson as *"a mad Englishman who seized the throne of England while his people were in mourning for Edward the Confessor."* This is, of course, opinionated. Such comments as that of Poitiers are part of the Norman justification for the invasion of England. Whilst historians may not invent incidents, they do not necessarily tell the truth but rather a version of it.

Yet the story of King Edward's death varies little within the main contemporary sources.

The *Anglo-Saxon Chronicle* contains a poem which speaks of the dying king's visions. He envisioned a green tree, with the prophecy that within a year and a day of his death God would punish the kingdom for its sins by delivering it into the hands of its enemy, that devils would go through the land with fire and sword and the chaos of war. The vision is repeated in another contemporary source, the *Vita Edwardi*, commissioned by the royal widow, Queen Edith.

The anonymous author reports Edward's last words to those around him. The king said to Edith, his wife and Harold's sister, *"May God be gracious to this wife for the zealous solicitude of her service; for certainly she has served me devotedly and always stood by my side like a loving daughter."* He commended her into Harold's protection and also commended to Harold all his servants. It is not a straightforward nomination by Edward of Harold as his heir because it really concerns his direct court of Edith and those close to the king.

The Bayeux Tapestry seems to illustrate the *Vita's* text. In the presence of an Archbishop, a second man helps the king to sit up in bed and a woman is weeping at his feet. Edward appears to stretch out his right hand so as to touch a third man's right hand. Fingers are fully extended but only the tips of the fingers are in contact. They do not clasp hands. The meaning is ambiguous. However, at that time, a dying king's wish was sacrosanct.

The death of King Edward is the pivotal scene in the Tapestry. In the eleventh century, artists, historians, and writers used older traditions to tell events. The poetically beautiful *Song of the Battle of Hastings* of 1068, written for Queen Matilda's coronation, harks back to Carolingian praise poetry. William of Poitiers was deeply influenced by classical literature and depicts Duke William as a latter-day Julius Caesar.

The visual context for the Bayeux Tapestry existed somewhere between liturgical drama of the eleventh century performed in minsters and vernacular plays of the twelfth century performed at court.

Eleventh century religious plays contained a strong sense of procession. At various points in the drama, static scenes occurred in open places in the church, by altars and sepulchres. Often a two-tiered structure was used to bring the story alive.

Plays were like informative picture books. They were layered with symbolism. For instance, the actors were able to show visually the medieval notions of hierarchy. The actors used hand gestures and facial expressions to relay emotion and the story's progress. There would have been a narrator.

The two-tiered structure also provided symbolic opportunity. In the earthly space below, an angel or a devil might wander out amongst the audience. Often the notion of paradise was portrayed above this earthly space. In the Tapestry, in a procession, the events of 1065-6 also move through staged pieces.

The influence of drama is clear, and it is not impossible that it actually initially accompanied performance of some of its scenes. King Edward's death is a pertinent example. The two-storey structure of Edward's death scene shows figures on the upper level cropped at the waist. King Edward is about to ascend into heavenly paradise. Below is associated with more earthly activity.

In performance art of the period, Heaven appears on the viewer's left and Hell to the viewer's right which can also indicate Christ's sinister side. Take now the long view of Edward's death scene. To the left Edward is enthroned in his palace where Harold is addressing him. Edward looks displeased. The long view is completed with Harold enthroned over ghost ships. This is to the right of the central scenes concerning Edward's death and Harold's coronation.

The funeral procession is also interestingly to the left of the death itself. This too can be interpreted symbolically. Seen this way, Edward is placed in the privileged position but it is the folly of Harold's claim and his illegal coronation that the viewer sees to the right. The central scenes correspond to the acting space of a two-tiered stage depicting symbolically and in fact King Edward's death and Harold's coronation.

Facial expressions and hand gestures guide the viewer through the drama of the Tapestry as do props for a play with doors, steps, and gateways of buildings, palaces, castles, and a cathedral providing portals, entrances, and exits from one vignette into the next. This is not unique to this event but follows on throughout the Tapestry. The Latin inscriptions correspond to the Norman French words and could even be prompts spoken by a scene's narrator.

The most interesting narratives concerning the events of Christmas 1065 are to be discovered in the exquisite language of the poem in the *Anglo-Saxon Chronicle*, the thrillingly beautiful *Song of Hastings*, the pompous account of William of Poitiers and, most of all, in the dramatic depiction of King Edward's death on the Bayeux Tapestry. All these accounts contribute to helping the fiction writer recreate the atmosphere of King Edward's death during the days of Christmas 1065-66.

Two Men, One Crown: Harold Godwinson and William of Normandy

by PAULA LOFTING

O**N A COLD JANUARY DAY IN 1066, KING EDWARD LAY DYING IN HIS CHAMBER, SURROUNDED** by his closest advisors: Earl Harold, his kinsman Robert FitzWymarch, and Stigand, Archbishop of Canterbury.

His dutiful wife, Edith Godwinsdottor sat at the bottom of his bed, warming his feet as she had been wont to do throughout most of their married life. They were waiting with bated breath, as those who were gathered in the Great Hall of the palace of Westminster no doubt were also, to hear who their dying sovereign would finally announce as his successor.

They had been waiting for many years for Edward to confirm for them whom he would nominate. He had been dangling the crown in front of various faces for roughly 16 years—first to Swein of Denmark, although he was no relation to Edward but a nephew of Cnut, then to William of Normandy, next to perhaps his favourite Tostig Godwinson, and also to his great-nephew Edgar, the last surviving of the line of Edmund Ironside, the only one amongst them who was ever referred to as the *Atheling*.

Edward, it seemed, had a penchant for using his need for an heir in order to gain men's support.

At the time his great-uncle was lying close to death in his newly built palace next to his life's work, the new minster of St. Peter, Edgar was still only a young lad of roughly fourteen or fifteen. Not too young to wear a crown—however, he was not heavily supported by any earldoms or lands and lacked the leadership experience one would have looked for in a potential king.

He may have been undergoing some military and administrative grooming perhaps, being educated at court with his mother Agatha and two sisters, Christina and Margaret, but his vulnerability and lack of resources would not have made him a favourable choice from the nobles' point of view. He had the best claim through lineage, but most likely it wasn't enough for Edgar to secure their support.

Seeing that there were others hoping to gain the crown for themselves, men like William of Normandy and Harald Hardrada, it stands to reason that the English would have preferred a strong man like Harold Godwinson, Earl of Wessex, to lead them against these enemies.

To most of the English, Harold was the man. Harold was crowned with unseemly haste the next day in Westminster. It seems likely that the Witan had already decided that he would take the crown; Edward's permission had just been a formality for in those times, in the days of the "Anglo-Saxons", the king's nominee would have to be approved by the Witan. Kings in pre-Conquest England were elected, in theory.

Across the Channel in the old Viking enclave of Normandy, William was told of the news that Harold had "usurped" his throne when he was out hunting. He was said to have gone stony cold and remained silent for some time before he would speak again.

When he did speak again, he raged that Harold had broken his oath to him! Harold had promised to support his claim to the crown that Edward had offered to him years ago during a visit to England in the early 1050s. How dare this English noble betray his lord and rightful "King" in this way, breaking the oath that he had sworn to him in Normandy. The Duke had saved him from Guy de Ponthieu's dark dungeons and treated him as an honoured guest in his palace with all the luxuries befitting a great noble. This was an outrage—the man had stolen his crown!

William was not a man to dismiss such a crime against his person and plotted his retaliation. A full scale invasion to retrieve what was his was the only option.

Harold Godwinson was a liar and an oathbreaker, a stealer of crowns. William vowed that he would wrest the crown from the usurper. He called a council and according to Poitiers, there was a great debate as to whether or not an invasion was viable, given the extraordinary lengths he would have to go to organise such a feat.

Boats would have to be built, bought, or commandeered; horses gathered, men conscripted and trained; provisions stocked and plans agreed upon amongst the commanders of such an undertaking. Then there was the task of selling such a plan, of waiting for a good wind for the ships to sail, the cost and practicalities of keeping a large force fed while they waited it out.

Would the men whose skills and support he was trying to harness be willing to risk their lives, their fortunes, and their equipment for an expedition that might not work? What if it didn't? There were many things that could go wrong.

The boats might be wrecked in a storm. There might be a landing party waiting for them when they arrived, to slaughter them. What if they were defeated in some great battle, taken as prisoner and blinded, as Harold's father had done to Prince Alfred, King Edward's younger brother?

There must have been many doubtful men attending that council that day. Still, they agreed to follow him, landless knights, the youngest sons of fathers whose wealth might only extend to the first sons, lured by promises of land and wealth.

William was going to conquer a far greater land than their little corner of France. There would be plenty for all those who would follow him and fight loyally by his side. Of course, there would be those who already had their own baronies—Guy of Ponthieu; Odo, his brother, with the wealth of Bayeux; William Fitz Osborne, his closest advisor; a younger brother Robert, Count of Mortain; and many more—their hearts full of desire for more wealth to add to their own, for English lands, lush and prosperous, yielding a good and relatively safe living, away from the threats of the French King and the Angevins and the Bretons who closed in on them like vices, squeezing them inwards.

Also William, it was said, had been received by the Pope and endowed with blessings and a Papal Banner. Divine right was on his side. What more could they ask for than approval from God's advocate on earth?

That's if the story of him receiving a papal banner and the Pope's approval was indeed true. Later, the Pope would demand penance from those who fought at Hastings, so maybe the approval came later when the Pope received Harold's personal banner of the fighting man. There are some differing opinions on this.

And so it began—William's preparations for the invasion of England. If we study the scenes in the Bayeux Tapestry, we will see that ships were built, weapons honed, and armour made for those who were to accompany him on his mission to win the crown, rightfully his, that the man he had once thought his friend had stolen from him.

HAROLD GODWINSON

Harold Godwinson, Earl of Wessex and then King of England for only 10 months, was born the second son of Godwin Wulfnothson and his wife Gytha, a woman of noble Scandinavian blood. Godwin, as recent research has turned up, was able to trace his ancestry back to the earlier Kings of Wessex. Contemporary sources have not mentioned this fact and so there may be some doubt about it; however, it seems quite plausible given the evidence.

In 1042, Harold and his older brother, the somewhat rebellious Swegn, were given earldoms; Swegn was endowed with lands in the West Country and Harold was given charge of East Anglia.

In 1051, the whole family was exiled and their sister Queen Edith put into a nunnery. Within a year they forcibly restored themselves to their former glories. Swegn died in 1052 after a long career of insubordinate behaviour, abducting an Abbess and holding her hostage for a year, murdering his cousin Beorn, and accusing his own mother of adultery with Cnut by stating that he was not the son of Godwin, but of the Danish King himself.

Harold was thus able to take his place as head of the family when a short while later Godwin also died, leaving him to step into his father's shoes in Wessex. This was not necessarily an inherited position, but for practical reasons, these offices often went to the son of the predecessor.

By 1058, Harold's younger brothers, Tostig, Gyrth, and Leofwine, were also Earls, making the Godwinsons the most powerful family in England with collective wealth that rivalled the King. In 1062/3, Harold's actions in Wales brought him military success when the troublesome Welsh leader Gruffydd ap Llewelyn was murdered by his own men and his head brought to the Earl. Harold's actions had brought the beleaguered Marcher settlements some peace with the death of their greatest enemy, the man the Welsh revered as the *Shield of the Britons*.

In 1064, Harold decided to make a journey to Normandy to seek the release of his kinsmen who had been held as hostages at Duke William's court for some years. The Norman historians make no mention of Harold requesting his kinsmen's return. This story was told later by the chronicler Eadmer and has since been accepted as a possible reason for Harold venturing to Normandy. It is not entirely clear how or why the boys went to Normandy, but it is thought that Edward had agreed to them being sent there as a way of controlling Godwin's behaviour in the years before Godwin's death.

For William, they were his surety, a down payment for the promised Kingdom. By going to Normandy to seek their release, Harold was about to play into William's hands.

Things did not quite go to plan for Harold. He returned with only one of the boys, Hakon, Swegn's son; Wulfnoth remained, probably to be released when William was King.

He also returned having being coerced to pledge an oath to support William upon Edward's death, swearing on holy relics. Did he mean to do this? Many think not. He was simply put in a dangerous position by William who knew that he could not let him go without him vowing his allegiance to him. For Harold, this was probably his only way of going home.

Harold's career ended with his life on the bloody field of Senlac, butchered by William's henchmen and possibly even by William himself. He was most likely not shot with an arrow in the eye as the Bayeux Tapestry shows, but cut down toward the end of the battle after the Normans had broken through the English shieldwall. He and those who died with him lost their lives courageously fighting for their lands and the right to choose their own King.

DUKE WILLIAM OF NORMANDY

Duke William of Normandy's career started when he was around seven years old. His father was Duke Robert I of Normandy and his mother was a low born woman called Herleve, probably from a family who served in the Duke's household. Being born out of wedlock didn't necessarily mean that he was initially out of the running as heir of Normandy, for previous dukes had also been illegitimate.

In around 1034, Robert made all his followers swear fealty to his son before he left on a pilgrimage to Jerusalem. He never returned, dying on the way back in Nicea.

Upon his father's death, William was thrust into a cutthroat world of a military society where it was "dog eat dog" attitude, not exactly a safe world for a seven-year-old boy. Luckily for William, he was given support from his great uncle Robert, Archbishop of Rouen, and the King of France, Henry I. Without their support, I am sure that William would have encountered problems from relatives also in the line of descent from the earliest ruler, Rollo.

However in 1037, the death of his great uncle was to plunge Normandy into anarchy which would last until around 1054. During those years, the young William was given into custody of various guardians who protected him from those trying to gain control over him. Many of those guardians were killed, including one who was slain whilst the young adolescent Duke slept in his chamber. His maternal uncle Walter was supposed to have hidden William in peasant homes to keep him safe.

Such a traumatic upbringing would have fashioned William into the man he was to become. One can imagine him vowing to himself that he would never forgive treachery lightly...and he didn't.

Henry continued to support him and fought with him in his victorious campaign in 1046/7 when they returned triumphant from the Battle of Val-ès-Dunes. However, this was not indeed the end of his troubles, and more wars ensued as William struggled to contain his nobles, with continuing crises tapering off until 1060.

During this time, William fell out with Henry who began to side with William's enemies.

William was struggling to fight pockets of rebellious barons within the duchy, the king— his one-time friend and supporter—had turned upon him, and he found himself facing threats from Geoffrey Martel of Anjou also. It is hard to think of William as being anything but an extraordinary man who survived the worst kind of intimidation on all fronts.

In 1057, Geoffrey Martel and Henry led their forces against William when they tried to invade the duchy and were defeated by the Norman forces at Varaville. That was the last time William would have to fight off an invasion of Normandy in his lifetime. By 1060, the deaths of Henry and Martel were to see him stabilised in his duchy, and at last William could think about Project England.

In 1064, a chance visit from Harold to Normandy gave William the opportunity to seal a deal with the man who he was sure would be his number one upon his ascent to the throne.

He coerced Harold into allowing himself to be knighted, which was a very clever move because as such, Harold, Earl of Wessex, was now his vassal. William might have had some nerve doing this, for Harold was his equal, not someone he could make his vassal, but it was a very astute manoeuvre, and Harold was now in a difficult position.

In 1066, William was to embark on a mission that would settle things for once and all. The Battle of Hastings victory over the English meant that the Normans were now running England.

FURTHER READING

Barlow, Frank. *The Godwins: The Rise and Fall of a Noble Dynasty*. Longman Publishing Group, 2002.

Howarth, David. *1066: The Year of the Conquest*. New York: Viking Press, 1978.

Stenton, Frank. *Anglo-Saxon England (Oxford History of England)*. Reading: Oxford University Press, 1971.

Walker, Ian W. *Harold: The Last Anglo-Saxon King*. Stroud, Gloucestershire: The History Press, 2010.

THE TOWER OF LONDON

BY DEBRA BROWN

Officially Her Majesty's Royal Palace and Fortress, the Tower of London was founded during the Norman Conquest of 1066. The White Tower within was the first stone keep built in England, begun by William the Conqueror in 1078.

Although the Tower is often thought of as a prison, it was built to be a royal residence and was strongly fortified as such. Early protection was afforded by the River Thames, ditches, and ancient Roman town walls. Over the first few centuries of its being built, the fortress became all but impossible to enter without permission.

The White Tower came to be surrounded by double concentric walls, the outer being fifteen feet thick, and a moat, ten feet wide and ten feet deep, on all but its south side which overlooks the Thames. Visitors had to cross a drawbridge which could suddenly be pulled up by counterweights, leaving unwelcome callers to drop into pits.

If an intruder could get through the first formidable doors, he was likely to be killed traveling across a courtyard to the second by sharpshooters who were well protected behind stone walls. The riverside walls were also supplied with arrow-slits. Each door had its dangers, such as holes through which boiling oil could be poured from above, and there were even lions and other animals inconveniently placed, though the Lion Tower is now demolished. Over the centuries, modifications such as gun ports were made to address the development of offensive weaponry.

The Tower was broken into by violence only once, during the Peasant's Revolt in 1381. Anger over the poll tax, at the time, was directed at Simon of Sudbury, the Archbishop of Canterbury, who was within the Tower walls. He was also unpopular with the Warders of the Tower or the peasants could never have entered. He was dragged out and killed, beheaded with a lack of skill as his skull reveals. His body was given proper burial as the Archbishop—though without his head, which remains at the Tower.

Once, in the year 1340, the king arrived via the Thames unannounced and found the Water Gate open and unguarded. There was punishment at hand, and, ever since, there has been rigidly structured attention to locking the gates. Even today, every night of the year, the Queen's Keys are carried in great ceremony to lock up the gates of the Tower. The Chief Yeoman Warder at 9:53 meets his escort warders and they walk to the gates.

They arrive at 10:00 p.m. exactly and are challenged by a sentry with a bayonet who cries loudly, *"Who comes here?"*

The reply by the Chief is, *"The Keys."*

"Whose keys?"

"Queen Elizabeth's keys."

"Pass, Queen Elizabeth's keys, and all is well."

The party passes through the Bloody Tower Archway into the fortress and halts at the

Broadway Steps. At the top of the stairs, the Tower Guard presents arms and the Chief Warder raises his hat and proclaims, *"God preserve Queen Elizabeth."*

The sentry replies, *"Amen!"*

Afterward, the keys are taken to the Queen's House for safekeeping and the Last Post is sounded.

This ancient ceremony was interrupted only once since the 14th century. During World War II there was an air raid on London. Bombs fell on the Victorian guardroom just as the party was coming through the Bloody Tower Archway. The noise knocked down the Chief Yeoman and one of the Warder escorts.

In the Tower is a letter from the Officer of the Guard in which he apologizes to King George VI for the ceremony finishing late, as well as a reply from the King which states that the officer is not to be punished since the delay was due to enemy action.

The Tower is the oldest fortified building still in occupation, and it was built to protect the Norman William the Conqueror from the angry people he had conquered. But for centuries there were many people living therein, including archers, men-at-arms, groomsmen, masons, carpenters, warders, gaolers, the executive and administrative staff, roadmenders, domestic servants, cooks, barmaids, tradesmen, messengers and prisoners (who at times exceeded a thousand in number).

1) THE FIRST KNOWN PRISONER

The first known prisoner was also a Norman, Rannulf Flambard, chief minister to William II (Rufus). He was a churchman whom Rufus later appointed Bishop of Durham. He was of humble origins but worked his way up to his positions by flattery and treachery. He was dishonest, unscrupulous, and arrogant.

Londoners cried out against him for his practice of extortion, an endless succession of taxes, and heavy fines. The clergy learned that he was selling church appointments to the highest bidder, and they joined in against him.

Rufus was benefiting from the money brought in and did not listen. His successor Henry I, however, wanted to allay the people's anger and charged Flambard with simony. He was imprisoned in the White Tower, and all England rejoiced greatly.

Flambard was allowed great privileges as a prisoner, including chaplains, servants, and a plentiful supply of food. Many casks of wine were brought in.

Interestingly, he was imprisoned in the Banqueting Hall. One night he invited his guards to dine with him. In one of the casks, rope had been hidden by his friends. He made sure that the warders drank plenty, and as they slept it off he tied the rope to a pillar by a window. Though he barely could squeeze his great girth through it, he managed. The rope was short and he fell part of the way to the ground, but, merely bruised, he succeeded in escaping. Friends took him by boat and then ship to Normandy.

2) JEWISH PRISONERS

Because the Church did not allow its followers to loan money on interest, the Jews came to be the country's sole moneylenders. Traders, craftsmen, landowners, noblemen, and even the King himself would borrow from them. Often the interest was high, goods and land were given as surety, and the Jews inevitably profited. Resentment began to develop against them.

The Jews were regarded as aliens who dressed differently, talked with accents, and took no part in Christendom's ceremonies. Soon growing anti-Semitism was fanned over the killing of Jesus, and the Jews were accused of ritually slaughtering Christian children.

A massacre of Jewish elders occurred when they brought gifts for the coronation of Richard the Lionhearted. To prevent such incidents, the Jews were made to live in separate walled sections of towns. A part of the city of London is Old Jewry.

Richard greatly disapproved of the anti-Semitic outbreaks, for the Jews brought considerable profit to the Crown in taxes and fines. Henry III allowed them to move into the Tower of London to escape persecution.

However, his son had a different viewpoint. Edward I had borrowed heavily from Italian bankers, who later moved into England. The Jews were no longer indispensable. In 1278 Edward arrested them all on the charge that they were clipping precious metals off the coins of the realm.

He moved the Mint into the Tower, and he imprisoned six hundred Jews in its rat-infested vaults. After some months, 267 of them were taken out and hanged. In 1290 they were banished from the country and did not return for four centuries.

3) WELSH AND SCOTTISH KINGS

Welsh chieftain Llewellyn the Great took two-thirds of Wales back from the Norman Marchers. His son Griffith was captured and taken to the Tower along with his own son, also named Llewellyn. Though Griffith died in an attempt to escape, his son was allowed to rule the northwest corner of Wales on the condition that he did homage to the English King. Llewellyn, titling himself Prince of Wales, declined to pay homage to Edward and even married Simon de Montfort's daughter. His head was impaled upon a pike above the White Tower. His brother David was also executed, and the title Prince of Wales was bestowed upon Edward's eldest son, who was born at Caernarvon. The title has been given to the eldest son of the monarch ever since.

In 1295, John Baliol, King of Scotland, allied himself with France and marched his troops across the border into England. Edward retaliated. Baliol's rivals for the throne, the father and son both named Robert Bruce, supported Edward. Edward captured Edinburgh Castle and Baliol surrendered. He and his son went to the Tower along with other Scottish prisoners. His life there was luxurious, paid for by the English King who now had Baliol's personal estate. At the Pope's intercession, Baliol was pardoned and given a home in England and a pension.

4) "FALSTAFF"—LORD COBHAM, SIR JOHN OLDCASTLE

During the reign of Henry V, the Lollards were a religious group who advocated the teaching of John Wycliffe, who had denounced the great wealth of the Church. They were greatly opposed by the Archbishop of Canterbury as well as by rich barons and merchants who feared that popular criticism might be directed against their wealth as well.

The Lollards went underground for a time, but they were supported by parish priests, the middle classes, and many of the gentry.

An assault was finally launched against them by the Church and high ranking nobles. They were called heretics, laws were passed against them, and many were martyred, burned at the stake. Young King Henry V at first opposed the Archbishop who instigated the conflagration and would not permit the man to crown him king.

A good friend of Henry's from earlier years, Sir John Oldcastle, had commanded a section of the King's army, was elected to Parliament, and married the heiress of Cobham, becoming Lord Cobham and moving to the Upper House of Parliament.

Oldcastle joined the Lollards in Herefordshire and was accused of heresy in the last days of Henry IV, but his friendship with the Prince of Wales prevented any action from being taken against him. The new king protected him from recurring charges, though he did attempt to dissuade him from his Lollard association. Oldcastle refused, saying that he would give all his wealth to the King, but could not abandon his religious convictions.

Henry at last allowed the Church to take action. Oldcastle was arrested and taken to the Tower of London. He was convicted of heresy, but his death decree was delayed by Henry for forty days. Perhaps the King still hoped for his friend to recant.

Somehow, Oldcastle escaped from the dungeon, was smuggled across the heavily guarded enclosure of the Tower, taken through the Bloody Tower gate, and brought over the Outer Wall and across the wide moat. It is thought that the King must have colluded in the escape.

Oldcastle, however, was not about to change his viewpoints, and he zealously plotted with the Lollards to seize the King and his brothers during a Twelfth Night celebration. His purpose was to abolish the monarchy and set up a Commonwealth.

The King was warned and escaped with his brothers and the Archbishop of Canterbury. Henry and his men-at-arms captured the Lollards that had conspired against him. Some were killed, others taken to the Tower.

Oldcastle managed to escape and hide in various places for nearly four years. He continued to hatch plots against the King. Finally he was "sore wounded" and brought again to the Tower. Now he was accused of treason as well as heresy, and was hanged and burned, "gallows and all".

Shakespeare's play, *Henry IV,* initially had Oldcastle portrayed under his own name, but the family objected, and the name in the play was changed to Falstaff.

5) EDMUND DUDLEY AND SIR RICHARD EMPSON

Henry VIII had great autocratic power because powerful barons were dead and their heirs were too young to contend against him when he took the throne. His authority was not strongly challenged as had been that of his predecessors who failed and were forced to sign away power or were deposed or murdered or lost their supporters to rivals. The country wanted peace when he came to the throne, which helped him as well.

Edmund Dudley and Sir Richard Empson had been crooked at procuring money for

Henry VII. They charged innocent people with crimes and then allowed them to pay their way out of the legal proceedings. They were highly unpopular.

After Henry VII's death, the Council arrested them and threw them into the Tower, though Henry VIII kept the moneys that had been extorted.

The Council, to gain popularity for the new reign, decided to execute the two men. There was no death penalty for extortion, so they were charged with "constructive treason"—the assembling of their friends for a discussion was interpreted as *"an armed conspiracy to overthrow and murder"* the new King, though it was likely organized to discuss how to protect themselves from the wrath of the people after Henry VII's death.

Dudley wrote a treatise about the advantages of having a monarchy, hoping to impress the new king, but it was never read by Henry VIII.

The two were executed on Tower Hill in 1510.

6) SIR THOMAS MORE

Sir Thomas More, Lord Chancellor, was not in favor of Henry VIII's divorce from Katherine of Aragon, but he did defend the King's motives in Parliament. More also supported the reform of the Church, but could not accept rejection of the Pope's authority or that Henry should become Supreme Head of the English Church.

More resigned as Lord Chancellor and was living on a low income with his family when he received an invitation to the coronation of Anne Boleyn, along with a fifth additional of his annual income to buy himself a new suit for the occasion. Opposed to the divorce and remarriage, he declined the invitation and returned the money. When he was later required to take an Oath of Supremacy, accepting the King as the head of the Church, he would not.

He was taken to the Tower by boat and confined in the Bell Tower on 17 April 1534.

His cell had a very high ceiling with one small window high in the wall, and so he lived in near darkness. He was denied pen and ink, so he wrote to his daughter with coal. He was allowed no books and was given an illiterate attendant, while a constant flow of visitors sought to persuade him to take the Oath of Supremacy.

After a year of illness and pain in the Tower, he walked, leaning heavily on a staff, the four miles to Westminster Hall, where he had previously sat as judge.

Fifteen specially commissioned judges sat there—among them Anne Boleyn's father, the First Earl of Wiltshire, her brother, Lord Rochford, and the Duke of Norfolk. There was also a jury of the King's known supporters. More's successor as Lord Chancellor, Sir Thomas Audley, sentenced him to be hanged, drawn, and quartered.

He returned by boat to the Tower. His daughter, Margaret Roper, rushed past the guard on the Wharf, flung her arms around him and kissed him, crying. He and others nearby also broke down. He spent five days in his cell composing prayers.

On the morning of his execution, he was told that the King had shown mercy and would, rather than hang, draw, and quarter him, have him beheaded on Tower Hill. He replied, *"God forbid the King shall use any more such mercy on any of my friends."*

After his death, his elderly wife, Lady More, was turned out of their house. His property and effects were settled by Henry on his own infant daughter, Princess Elizabeth, who kept it throughout her reign.

FURTHER READING

Minney, R.J. *The Tower of London.* Prentice Hall, 1974.

Monarchy: The Normans— William Rufus and Henry I

by DEBRA BROWN

The Normans that followed the Duke of Normandy, William the Conqueror, provide an interesting historical story. William left Normandy to his eldest, whom he considered to be too generous and easy-going to manage England. England he left to his second son, William, called William Rufus for his red complexion. He was crowned on September 26, 1087.

Rufus came to be known as cruel, ruthless, greedy, and crude. He was always looking for ways to obtain more money, and when he couldn't get it from the Norman barons or the English townsfolk, he taxed the Church heavily.

When the Archbishop of Canterbury Lanfranc died, the irreligious Rufus did not replace him, but kept the revenues normally allotted to the post for himself. He did the same when other bishops and archbishops died. When fearing death, he finally replaced the Archbishop with a Benedictine monk, Anselm of Bec, but upon recovering, he exiled him to Rome and seized his assets. This was a very different method of rule than that of his famously pious Norman predecessor as well as the English kings Alfred the Great and Edward the Confessor.

Rufus built the Great Hall of Westminster according to his grand scale ambitions. It was the largest secular space north of the Alps, used for feasting and entertainments. He would sit on an elevated plane, crowned, robed, and enthroned. The choirs would sing in Latin, wishing him long life and victory.

The gap between rich and poor increased, and those with money began to dress extravagantly. Men wore flamboyant, puffed-up tunics and curved, pointy-toed shoes. Women wore more and more extravagant jewelry. Rufus himself, or William II, surrounded himself with "half-naked", long-haired young men according to contemporary accounts.

England's French-speaking barons often owned estates both in England and Normandy—thus, they owed some of their allegiance to William's older brother, Duke Robert. Robert was staking his claim to the English throne, and some of the barons united in his support just a year after William's coronation.

William crushed the revolt, and in 1090, he invaded Normandy to subdue Robert. He also repelled attempts by Malcolm III of Scotland and an uprising by barons in Northumberland.

William, like his father, loved hunting. William I had taken over huge areas of countryside, 90,000 acres, for his own use; Rufus took 20,000 more and made the rules of the oppressive Forest Law even harsher. Killing a deer was punished by death. Men were maimed just for shooting an arrow at one. The punishment for simply disturbing a deer was blinding. These rules were considered un-English and were a constant reminder that William Rufus was a foreigner, ruling and oppressing England.

After only thirteen years of rule, in a superstitious age, it appeared that Rufus received punishment for his ways. While out hunting deer in the New Forest with a party which included his younger brother Henry, he was hit by an arrow and died "without repentance". His body lay neglected for several hours and was finally carried to Winchester in a charcoal-burner's cart. He was buried there beneath the cathedral tower. Imagine the thoughts of the superstitious people who hated this king when a year later the tower came tumbling down!

Who killed William Rufus? It has never been proved.

One account says that he accidentally killed himself. Others state that a Norman lord named Walter Tirel shot him. Tirel fled the country but always maintained his innocence.

Interestingly, as soon as the king was dead, his brother Henry seized power with suspicious ease. He wasted no time mourning his brother. He rushed to Winchester, secured the treasury, seized the royal crown and rode off to London to have himself crowned. His claim to the throne was dubious. Rufus and his older brother Robert, still Duke of Normandy, had agreed to be heirs to each other. Robert was known to be on his way home from the Crusades with a reputation for chivalry and a young wife who could bear him sons. There was no time to waste.

Henry turned to the English people for support. He was "born in the purple", the only one of William the Conqueror's sons to be born in England while his father was the English king rather than just the Duke of Normandy. Unlike his father and brother, he could read, write, and speak some English.

Rather than just swear to rule justly, as was normal at a coronation, Henry had his promises written down and widely circulated. He promised to bring back the laws of Edward the Confessor. He would rule with consent, like an Anglo-Saxon king, and not with force and extortion. He vowed to remove the tyrannical rule of the oppressed people that his father and brother had practiced. He was crowned in Westminster Abbey on August 5, 1100.

Henry's Charter of Liberty was followed by all the kings up until the Magna Carta in 1215, and was copied fairly closely therein. He also set up the *Curia Regis*, or King's Council, to settle disputes between the monarch and the people. He married a Scottish princess, Edith, who was descended directly from Alfred the Great and Edward the Confessor, which helped him to placate both the Scottish and Saxons to some degree. She did, however, adopt the Norman name Matilda, and their two children were named Matilda and William.

However, a problem arose. Galloping inflation set in when the silver money began to be mixed with tin. England's stable currency had been the envy of Europe for three centuries. Henry arrested the one hundred and fifty men who had worked in the mint and put them on trial. Ninety-four of them were found guilty and were punished with barbaric severity. Even though these men were not Normans, but Englishmen of high status, the people were behind Henry in the matter. The coinage must be protected at any cost.

For Henry, the greatest problem of all was the death of his young heir William at age seventeen. William was returning to England from Normandy in a ship. It crashed against rocks because of the drinking on board, and though William was safely put into a boat, he insisted on returning to the area to save his illegitimate sister. The only survivor was a butcher.

William's sister Matilda was, at the time, living as Empress Consort of the Holy Roman Empire in Germany.

King Henry is said to have never smiled again, and he was now faced with the need to choose a new heir to the throne. His nephew Stephen had no Saxon blood, something that had been important to Henry for his heir, and so he chose instead his daughter Matilda, a descendant of Alfred. We'll see how well that went in the next post of the series!

SOURCES

Buskin, Richard. *The Complete Idiot's Guide to British Royalty*. Alpha Books, 1997.

Monarchy with David Starkey. Directed by David Hutt and Mary Cranitch. 2006. Acorn Media. DVD.

Ross, Josephine. *The Monarchy of Britain*. William Morrow & Co., 1982.

THE MYSTERIOUS DEATH OF KING WILLIAM THE SECOND

BY JUDITH ARNOPP

THE NEW FOREST IS A TIMELESS PLACE, WITH MANY AREAS REMAINING UNCHANGED SINCE medieval times. If you venture away from the tourist spots you will find ancient woodlands, rusty-coloured streams, and vast areas of heath that seem to belong to another era.

As a child, I spent so much time in the New Forest that it became like a second home. Even now, forty-odd years later, the aroma of heather, the tang of the pine, the vague hint of the salty Solent evoke those wonderful days.

The tales of William Rufus and the "Rufus Stone" were familiar, repeated over and over until they became part of my psyche. I could easily imagine him riding out to hunt with the hounds baying and the pennants casting an unnatural splash of colour on the woodland.

A few years ago when I was looking around for ideas for my next novel, the name William Rufus seemed to jump from nowhere into my head, and I quickly determined that the New Forest would provide an ideal setting for my story, a story that was already embedded in the British consciousness—the mystery surrounding the death of William Rufus.

The early Norman period is very much neglected in fiction. Perhaps the events were too long ago for to us to properly engage with, or maybe publishers are just not prepared to take the risk of straying too far from their beloved Tudors.

As a lover of early British history, I think there is a place for fiction set earlier in the calendar and so I went ahead regardless. *The Forest Dwellers* is not just the story of Rufus, but the early Norman regime and the mysterious deaths of the Conqueror's sons form the backdrop to the fiction of Ælf and Alys.

The Domesday Book tells us that in 1065, before the invasion, the villages cleared for the main part of the forest consisted of an estimated five hundred families, possibly two thousand men, women, and children. This estimate does not allow for slaves, personal retainers, or men working under villains; it only represents the landowners or occupiers. It is not a huge number when compared with devastation caused elsewhere by the conquering Normans but enough, I think, to generate a considerable amount of resentment.

The defeated Saxon population of England did not welcome the Normans; all over Britain there are accounts of uprisings and dissent. There were Saxons who fought and lost, those who retired into obscurity to die in poverty and want, and there were those that collaborated, pretended to accept Norman authority.

In the forest, new rules meant that making a living was impossible—punishment was harsh and frequent, but life went on. People lived and died in oppression while memories of the old way of life slowly faded. The thing that remained unchanged was hatred and resentment for the Norman interloper.

Like the Saxon kings before them, the Normans were lovers of the hunt, but whereas Harold and his predecessors were content to share the forest with the commoners, the Normans were less tolerant.

King William I had four sons: Robert (known as Curthose, later to become Duke of Normandy); Richard, who died young; William (known as Rufus, his father's successor who became King William II); and Henry (known as Beauclerc, later to become Henry I). The king's second son, Richard, should have inherited the English throne, but he predeceased his father. Records of Prince Richard's death are scarce; most simply relate that he was killed during a chase in the New Forest.

Fatal hunting accidents were not uncommon, but losing his heir to the English throne was King William's first major blow. The people of the forest would undoubtedly have seen it as divine retribution, and there would certainly have been no mourning or pity among the commoners. It occurred to me that, perhaps, twenty years later, the memory of the first royal death in the forest gave life to the more mysterious demise of his brother, King William Rufus.

According to William of Malmesbury, William Rufus was *"well set; his complexion florid, his hair yellow; of open countenance; different coloured eyes, varying with certain glittering specks; of astonishing strength, though not very tall, and his belly rather projecting."*

Not a very flattering picture and, all in all, William seems to have been a complex fellow.

He was popular among his companions but his relationship with his brothers was volatile and the church regarded the king almost as an anti-Christ. Rufus was a very luke-warm Christian and not above selling church positions to the highest bidder rather than filling them by appointment. He left many positions empty, depriving the church of revenue and pocketing the income himself.

The most recorded characteristics of the king seem to have been his love of hunting, his delight in rich cuisine (particularly eels), a predilection for young male companions, and excessive monetary greed. He was a man of eclectic tastes; his companions at court were reported as effeminate, adopting ridiculous fashions and wearing their hair long.

Some say he was homosexual, some that he was not, but there are no recorded offspring, either legitimate or otherwise. This does not mean that he did not father any children. A man like Rufus would be more than capable of ignoring his responsibilities. In *The Forest Dwellers*, which is a fictional tale, he is an amiable but selfish man whose sexual impartiality eventually leads to his downfall.

On the day of his last hunt, Rufus had been taken ill and the outing was postponed, but quite late in the evening the king, deciding he was well enough after all, called up the horses and the party rode off into the forest. The company consisted of many powerful magnates that were close to the king, among them his brother, Henry Beauclerc, and Rufus' friend, Sir Walter Tyrell.

The Peterborough manuscript of the *Anglo-Saxon Chronicle* states that *"on the morning after Lammas Day, the king William was shot with an arrow in hunting by a man of his"* (*Anglo Saxon Chronicle (E) 1099*).

Another chronicler, Geoffrey Gaimer stated, *"We do not know who shot the king,"* and Gerald of Wales wrote, *"The King was shot by Ranulf of Aquis."* Research into Ranulf of Aquis draws a blank. There is no clear indication of who he was, but what is clear is that Rufus' death was as much a mystery then as it is now.

The *Anglo-Saxon Chronicle* goes on to say what a wicked fellow Rufus had been, but it must be remembered that the church had many grievances against Rufus. In fact, all contemporary accounts written of William Rufus are the work of those with an agenda against him, so the picture we have of him is distorted.

At the time there seems to have been little fuss made about who shot the fatal arrow. Rufus was dead, his body abandoned in the forest while his erstwhile companions fled to secure their holdings and their place in the court of the new king.

Tradition has it that Rufus' body remained where it fell until it was picked up by a charcoal burner named Purkiss, and taken to Winchester for burial.

Rufus' brother Henry, being in the right place at the right time, became the next monarch and perhaps had a reason for not pursuing the truth—perhaps he was complicit in his brother's death, perhaps not.

Later historians and fictional representations of the tale point the finger at Sir Walter Tyrell, Lord of Piox de Picardie in France and friend of the king. The night before the hunt Rufus is said to have presented Tyrell with two rather splendid arrows with the words *"to the good archer, the good arrows."* It was one of these arrows that was later found embedded in the king's heart. Allegedly, Tyrell shot at a stag but the arrow deflected and lodged in the king's chest. Tyrell, on seeing what he'd done, fled to France.

Tyrell was never pursued for his crime—perhaps it suited the new king that he was never found and questioned, perhaps he housed dangerous truths. Some say he was Henry's man, paid well for his services, but, although Henry undoubtedly had the best motive, Tyrell spent his remaining years exiled in France, receiving no reward and never speaking out against the English king. Therefore, his involvement seems unlikely and one chronicler, Abbot Suger, maintained until he died that,

> It was laid to the charge of a certain noble, Walter Thurold, that he had shot the king with an arrow; but I have often heard him, when he had nothing to fear nor to hope, solemnly swear that on the day in question he was not in the part of the forest where the king was hunting, nor ever saw him in the forest at all.

The fact remains that almost a thousand years have passed since that day and during those centuries, historians have been over and over the story, seeking a culprit, patching together fact and fiction, mismatching truth with legend until the real story is totally lost in speculation.

I suppose the main message I want to make in *The Forest Dwellers* is this: the forest was teeming with people that day—it could have been anyone! *The Forest Dwellers* is an action-packed adventure, peopled with plausible characters. You will find no "goodies" and no "baddies", just complex humans, struggling to survive in an unkind world.

Monarchy: The Normans— Stephen and Matilda

by DEBRA BROWN

Following the early death of the only legitimate son of Henry I, William, few of the English and Norman barons were prepared to stand by their oath to him to support his daughter's claim to the throne. Matilda was, after all, a woman, and was said to have been arrogant and unpopular. She was also married to the Count of Anjou. He was the ruler of Anjou—England and Normandy's traditional enemy.

When Henry died in 1135, the barons met to choose a king. Despite Matilda's having an infant son, they chose Count Theobald of Blois, the grandson of William the Conqueror by his daughter, Adela.

Negotiations were in progress when Stephen, Theobald's younger brother, made himself King of England.

Stephen had been brought up by Henry I, who had loved him and made him one of the richest men in England. Stephen now pointed to this as evidence that Henry had been grooming him to become the next king, despite Henry's having obtained Stephen's oath to support Matilda.

As soon as Henry was dead, Stephen sailed for England. He obtained the support of his brother, whom Henry had created Bishop of Winchester, as well as the citizens of London. The Archbishop of Canterbury crowned him king on 22 December 1135.

Stephen was charming, courageous, and chivalrous. He became the first English king to allow jousting. He had humbly earned the people's affection and was generous toward the church. Most of the barons and even Henry's favorite illegitimate son, Earl Robert of Gloucester, swore allegiance to him.

Stephen was a brave soldier, but a failure as a king and commander. Because of it, Robert turned against him, and many followed. Matilda's uncle, David I of Scotland, invaded England, and though Stephen defeated David, Matilda could see that Stephen's support was bleeding away and that it was time for her to act.

In an attempt to weaken King Henry's bureaucracy, which might support Matilda, Stephen arrested bishops and councilors, some of whom were his own family. This lost for him the vital support of the church.

He made strategic mistakes in battle defending his rule, not the least of which was to decide not to besiege Arundel, the castle where Matilda had taken up residence after arriving from France with Robert, and to allow her safe passage to join Robert in Bristol.

Chivalrous it was, but foolish, and the result was full-scale civil war. Barons built illegal castles and plundered. They sold their allegiance to the highest bidder and then changed sides at will. Anarchy existed and no one felt safe.

Finally, Stephen was a prisoner in chains at Bristol, and Matilda rode to London to claim her throne with the help of Stephen's brother, the Bishop of Winchester. She was called Lady of the English by her supporters, but she had imposed high taxes and was still a woman, and the people would not have her. They drove her out of the city.

Stephen's wife, also named Matilda for the sake of confusion, was rallying *his* forces. Robert was captured, and the Matildas made an exchange. Henry's daughter was forced to release Stephen in exchange for her main supporter. The Bishop of Winchester had by now realigned himself with Stephen.

Matilda sent Robert to Anjou to request help from her husband. The count was, however, engaged in a successful invasion of Normandy and could not leave. Stephen had become reconciled to the clergy, and Matilda's supporters were under threat of excommunication.

Stephen laid siege to Matilda in Oxford Castle.

On a frozen, snowy night Matilda and four knights dressed in white (she was in a nightgown) climbed down from a tower. They slipped through Stephen's lines and ran to London. The war dragged on, but five years later Robert died and Matilda was forced to give up. She left for Anjou.

Since the Count of Anjou had taken over Normandy, some of the English barons who owned Norman estates felt their only hope of retaining their possessions across the Channel was to support Anjou in England. They threw their support to the son of Matilda, Henry, the heir to the house of Anjou. And the war dragged on.

Stephen attempted to secure the succession of his line by having his son and heir, Eustace, crowned during his own lifetime. The Archbishop of Canterbury, however, with the Pope's backing, refused to perform the coronation.

Young Henry returned to England in 1153. He was now the most powerful feudal prince in Europe. Through inheritance and marriage, he was now Duke of Normandy and Aquitaine. He landed with a small army, and barons flocked to join him.

Fear of reprisals caused the barons to conclude a peace agreement, but Stephen remained adamant that his son should succeed. When Eustace died, however, in 1153, Stephen gave up interest in the succession. Peace through the Treaty of Westminster meant that Stephen would rule till his death and that Henry was acknowledged as his heir instead of his own second son, William. Stephen did not enjoy the peace for long—he died the next year.

Henry II was crowned in 1154. Matilda lived till 1167, long enough to know of her son's succession, though she did not attend his coronation in Westminster Abbey, and she never returned to England.

WHY I LOVE ELEANOR OF AQUITAINE

BY CHRISTY ENGLISH

I LOVE TO WRITE ABOUT ELEANOR OF AQUITAINE BECAUSE SHE ALWAYS SURPRISES ME. EVEN though she is an historical figure and the events of her life are set in stone, the character of Eleanor as she comes to life in my novels always teaches me something new.

On the pages of history books her life was dynamic enough—Duchess of Aquitaine at the age of fifteen, Eleanor finished brokering her own marriage to Louis VII of France.

Years later, Eleanor rode at her husband's side on Crusade, and on her way home, sick of being married to Louis, she began working to annul her marriage. Only months after she earned her freedom, Eleanor married her second husband, Henry of Normandy, who became King of England two years later…and that is just the first half of her life. So you see what I mean when I say Eleanor of Aquitaine was a dynamic woman.

Nothing stopped Eleanor from achieving her goals. For decades, she wanted the County of Toulouse back under the control of her family. After sending both husbands out to reclaim it through warfare (and after both men failed), she simply arranged her daughter's marriage to the Count of Toulouse, effectively putting her family in line to inherit that county and thus to take control of it once more.

Eleanor would wait for years for what she wanted. Tenacious and single minded, she was an amazing politician—much to both her husbands' annoyance. Louis would have been perfectly happy if Eleanor had settled down to raise her princesses quietly, if she had left the political machinations of the day to him. Her second husband, King Henry II of England, married her for her brains and beauty as well as her land, but even he came to regret her brilliance as the years wore on. For after years of partnership, Eleanor began to want more power of her own.

In 1173, she reached out for that power, setting her sons against their father so that she might gain indirect control of the duchies of Brittany and Normandy, in addition to the duchy of Aquitaine.

Henry locked Eleanor away in 1174 to keep his crown and to keep his sons at bay. Henry always knew that if he set Eleanor free she would stop at nothing to take his Continental holdings from him. And she was the one person on earth who had a fighting chance of doing it, so he kept her locked away until his death.

Once Henry was dead, Eleanor ruled through her favorite son, Richard. Richard the Lionheart rode off to Crusade to seek the Holy Grail of Jerusalem, leaving the Continental holdings inherited from his father in Eleanor's hands.

She was technically regent of England, too, while Richard was on Crusade, but she had spent more than enough time locked away in England during the last fifteen years of Henry II's reign. She left that cold, rainy land to the tender mercies of her youngest son, John, for she finally had what she wanted—control over most of what is now modern France.

Eleanor was unstoppable. She was brave and beautiful and so full of fire that both her critics and her admirers agreed: she was stronger than any woman they had ever seen. She is the strongest woman I have ever had the pleasure to write about, and the most dynamic. She is a woman who would be renowned in any age. Which is why, over 800 years later, we still remember her.

HENRY II AND THOMAS BECKET

BY CHRISTY ENGLISH

Henry II of England and Thomas Becket were two of the greatest rivals for power in English history. We remember them even today, over 850 years later. Their struggle for power ended as do so many battles when one of the protagonists is the ruling king, with death—in this case, with Thomas Becket slain in his own cathedral.

The king and Thomas Becket began as friends and allies. Becket served Henry well as his Chancellor and was trusted so deeply that he was given the guardianship of the king's eldest son, young Prince Henry. This alliance was so strong, and so strongly based in personal friendship, that King Henry II was certain that Thomas Becket would be the answer to his troubles with the Church.

Though we associate the clash between Church and State in England with Henry VIII of the Tudor dynasty, the seeds had been sown much earlier, and this battle for power came to a head during Henry II's reign. In 1154, Henry II reclaimed the throne of England from the usurper, Stephen of Blois, after decades of civil war which left the lands of England devastated.

Henry believed all his life that rule of law and the strength of the King's Peace could extend protection to the common man. Of course, while this goal is lofty, it also served the political purpose of allowing the people to receive justice not just from their barons and local ruler, but from the king himself.

One aspect of extending the King's Peace was to deal with the members of the lower clergy who broke the law. As things stood, if a clergyman or priest committed rape or murder, he would not be called on to stand trial as any other man would; rather, he would be given over to the Church for trial and punishment in the Church courts. The Church did little but chastise their brethren even for crimes as hideous as thievery, rape, and murder.

Since Henry II was working so hard to keep the peace in the land, this loophole was one he could not allow to continue. So he began trying lower clergymen in secular court, much to the Pope's fury.

In 1162, Henry made Thomas, his friend and ally, the next Archbishop of Canterbury, certain that the man who had served him so well as Chancellor would continue to help him uphold the law of the land, and would allow the secular courts to punish those clergy who broke the law. This was not the case.

Once Thomas became archbishop, he did a complete turnaround in his attitude toward the law. As a prince of the Church, he served the Church first and Henry second. He fought Henry at every turn in an effort to protect his own power as well as the power of the Church in England.

By 1170, this conflict had become such a burden to Henry II that he made a snide remark in company at a Christmas feast—the famous line, *Will no one rid me of this turbulent priest?*

Four of Henry's knights, Hugh de Morville, William de Tracy, Reginald Fitz Urse, and

Richard le Bret, were among those who listened to Henry's furious outburst. They took ship for England at once, and on December 29th, murdered Thomas Becket at the foot of the altar of Canterbury Cathedral.

Scholars are divided as to whether or not these men were acting on direct orders from the king. The king was stricken with grief when he heard the news of his old friend's death, and Pope Alexander III later absolved him of involvement in this crime.

Though Thomas Becket lost his life, the Church retained its power through the sympathy gained by his death. In exchange for forgiveness and absolution of Thomas Becket's murder, Henry II agreed that law-breaking clerics would continue to be tried by the Church courts.

Alais of France:
Forgotten Princess

by CHRISTY ENGLISH

In my first novel, *The Queen's Pawn*, Princess Alais, a little known French princess from the 12th century, is my protagonist and the linchpin of the story. The historical Alais was the daughter of Louis VII of France and Constance of Castile, a pawn of politics and alliance, as most highborn women were during her lifetime. Born in 1160, Princess Alais was betrothed to Prince Richard of England (later Richard the Lionheart) in 1169.

Though she came to the court of Henry II and Eleanor of Aquitaine as a child, her marriage to Richard never took place, and she returned to France years later at the age of thirty-five.

We do not know what Alais looked like, nor do we even know for certain the correct spelling of her name. She is mentioned by the chroniclers of the time as Alys, Alix, and Alais.

In the modern parlance, she is often called Alice, the young princess portrayed in the film *The Lion in Winter,* starring Peter O'Toole in the role of Henry II, Katherine Hepburn in the role of Eleanor of Aquitaine, and Anthony Hopkins as Prince Richard. This modern brush with fame was fleeting, because for the most part, no one remembers Princess Alais at all.

We know that she was held by her father's enemies from the time she was nine years old. While she never married her intended, Prince Richard, Alais was said to have been one of Henry II's many mistresses. Whether or not she actually became the mistress of the king has been questioned by modern historians, but I believe she did.

Different chroniclers speak of Alais only in relation to the men in her life, as the daughter of Louis VII, as the mistress of Henry II, and as the spurned betrothed of Richard I. Primary sources differ on the number of children that she and Henry might have had during their supposed liaison, but no one mentions the fate of these children. If they lived, their fate is forgotten, as so much of Princess Alais' life has been.

We know for certain that Richard the Lionheart refused to marry Alais, though in every other instance, he always kept any oath he made. This alone is evidence to suggest that King Richard believed that Alais had been his father's paramour.

Instead of marrying Alais upon his ascension to the throne, Richard arranged his own marriage to Berengaria of Navarre and went on Crusade with the hope of freeing Jerusalem from the Turks. While Richard was away, Princess Alais remained in the Norman city of Rouen, for though King Richard refused to honor their betrothal, he also did not send her home.

Alais languished in Rouen for almost five years until she was returned to her brother, King Philippe Auguste of France in 1195.

Her brother arranged a second marriage for Princess Alais to William, Count of Ponthieu. Once married to Philippe Auguste's vassal, Alais disappeared from the historical record. It is unknown how many children she had with her husband or when she died. She was once again forgotten, as she was during most of the years she spent trapped at the courts of Henry II and Richard I, waiting to complete a political alliance which never took place.

KNIGHTS TEMPLAR: THE BEGINNING

BY SCOTT HIGGINBOTHAM

THE KNIGHTS TEMPLAR OCCUPY A UNIQUE NICHE IN THE CHRONICLES OF HISTORY, AND those who write historical fiction have no shortage of fodder for their novels as there is a wealth of information—sometimes conflicting. The Templar order was feared, hated, respected, hailed, and coveted across a wide spectrum of medieval society, both in Europe and the Holy Land. To be certain, this order of knights had few equals; they forged a new path and formed their bond upon a foundation like no other. They were true originals.

In modern times they are speculated upon in countless ways—the Templars control the banking system, the stock market, are behind every uprising around the globe, wear strange hats and drive jalopies in parades. Their secret symbols are on currency, and if a scapegoat is needed then look no further than the *The Order of the Poor Fellow Soldiers of Christ and the Temple of Solomon.*

There is much speculation, informed and otherwise, concerning the Knights Templar, but this piece will briefly touch upon their humble genesis and those facts which are undisputed by historians.

After Jerusalem was captured during the First Crusade in 1099, religious zeal swelled as the news of the Crusaders' victory spread across Europe. Pious pilgrims trekked to the Holy City. However, they were beset on the perilous roads of Palestine, suffering the loss of their belongings and even their lives. Nine knights later formed an armed brotherhood to protect the pilgrim roads of which Charles Addison puts it nicely:

> *To alleviate the dangers and distresses to which these pious enthusiasts were exposed, to guard the honour of the saintly virgins and matrons, and to protect the gray hairs of the venerable palmer, nine noble knights formed a holy brotherhood in arms, and entered into a solemn compact to aid one another in clearing the highways of infidels, and of robbers, and in protecting the pilgrims through the passes and defiles of the mountains to the Holy City.*

Moreover, their brotherhood was unique and original owing to the fact that these knights were warriors, but ones that embraced the same vows as those of monks—poverty, chastity, and obedience. The ideal of a dashing knight astride a pawing destrier, begging a lady's favor to wear on his arm had taken an odd turn. Troubadours and bards had lost a portion of the deep, chivalrous well upon which to draw their verse. Addison writes further:

> *They renounced the world and its pleasures, and in the holy church of the Resurrection, in the presence of the patriarch of Jerusalem, they embraced vows of perpetual chastity, obedience, and poverty, after the manner of monks.*

In 1118, these nine knights, led by Hugues de Payens, the order's first Grand Master, were granted usage of a portion of the King of Jerusalem's quarters, which was part of the al-Aqsa Mosque, believed to be built over King Solomon's temple. The Temple of Mysteries writes that, *"It was from this place that the Order took its name—the Order of the Poor Fellow-Soldiers of Christ and the Temple of Solomon (Ordo Pauperum Commilitonum Christi Templique Salominici); Templars for short."*

It took a little time before the fledgling movement became a force to be reckoned with. The Temple of Mysteries writes that:

> *Until they were officially recognized, the Knights Templar remained a small and obscure force for about the first decade of their existence. They operated largely upon their own initiative, but with the blessing and support of the King of Jerusalem and its Patriarch. They initially wore no distinctive devices that proclaimed this new order, but their actions piqued the interest of Bernard of Clairvaux, head of the Cistercian monks, for it was Bernard who organized the Council of Troyes in 1129 thus giving the order official papal recognition. This council transformed this small band that simply protected pilgrims into the army of Christendom and the interests of the Church.*

The Order would soon grow to be one of the most formidable fighting forces in medieval Europe, transcending borders and drawing some of the most skilled knights into their ranks. They were fighting men, but they were also monks, adhering to a strict Benedictine rule. The red cross pattée on their surcoats (with minor variances) and the black and white Beauseant shield and banner were soon adopted as part of their distinction—many knights during the crusading era had crosses etched into the pommel of their swords.

Much more can be said upon their rise, their nuances, and their ultimate demise, but even this short introduction shows that their legacy lives on as an interesting footnote in history and fuels much conjecture for novelists, theorists, and the curious.

SOURCES

Addison, Charles G. *The History of the Knights Templars, the Temple Church, and the Temple.* Kindle Edition: 2012. Kindle Locations 211-215, 216-218.

Temple of Mysteries. *The Knights Templar.* Kindle Edition: Temple of Mysteries, 2010. Kindle Locations 116-118, 148-149.

A Bad Rap for Henry and Eléonore

by SHERRY JONES

Never had I found myself disagreeing so thoroughly with an historian. In fact, Thomas B. Costain's *The Magnificent Century* (first published in 1951) rubbed me the wrong way so completely that I had to put it down and walk away more than once.

My issue? His portrayals of England's King Henry III and Queen Eléonore of Provence, lead characters in my historical novel *Four Sisters, All Queens*.

I didn't have to read far before the author's sniping began. After one hundred pages or so of background, Costain launches into the royal wedding—and soon thereafter is exclaiming over the extravagance of the affair as if such a thing were unheard of, as if extravagance were not expected of a king for such occasions.

"Fatuous," he writes. "Spendthift." For the rest of the tale, poor King Henry never gets a break. Costain paints a portrait of a mercurial, petulant, impulsive, and weak ruler, even giving Henry a "high neighing laugh." Talk about historical fiction!

Eléonore fares even worse. "England's Most Unpopular Queen," she was one of those high-faluting snobs from Provence. *"A most superior lot,"* Costain sniffs, for whom *"the English people conceived a hatred...which grew with every day."*

"The Queen," he informs us, *"was never happy unless surrounded by her relatives and favorites from Provence."* They were unhappy with her failure to give birth to an heir four years after her marriage, he tells us, failing to point out that she was but thirteen on her wedding day. Eléonore even falls short as a mother in his assessment; she "scandalized" the monks at Beaulieu, he sneers, by insisting on staying to nurse her son—the king's heir—Edward back to health when he fell ill there.

We historical novelists deal with this all the time. Historians are humans and have points of view. Whom to believe? *The Magnificent Century* is more obvious than most in its approach, being a blatant hagiography with no pretensions toward objectivity.

Costain falls squarely on the side of Simon de Montfort, Henry's seneschal, who instigated a revolution that is credited with establishing British Parliament as it exists. Costain portrays him as a democratic visionary. My research gave me a view of Montfort that is decidedly more ambivalent—he acted as much out of ambition for himself and his sons as for the good of the common people.

I found in Henry and Eléonore a royal couple who, although far from perfect, possessed a vision for England no less valid. They might have propelled the kingdom into superpower status had their reign not followed that of Henry III's father, the tyrannical King John.

John lost some of England's greatest landed possessions on the European continent to

France's King Philip Augustus. Weakened by unrest at home over his cruelty and corruption, he never reclaimed those lands. Losing Normandy, with all its riches, dealt a particularly harsh blow to the kingdom's treasury. In true Oedipal fashion, Henry strived for years to regain the duchy, but could not muster support from his barons.

Costain is one of a number of historians who have portrayed King Henry III as a weak and ineffectual king and Eléonore as favoring her own family's interests over those of the people she ruled. In my opinion, they get a bad rap. Eléonore and Henry were intelligent, ambitious rulers who might have done much for England. Their misfortune lay in Henry's being the son of John and inheriting his father's messes—corrupt bailiffs whose corruption bred resentment among the people, protectionist barons loath to spend any more money on ventures overseas, and a general distrust of "big government" at a time when big government was sorely needed.

Together, Henry and Eléonore refurbished Westminster Abbey, creating a splendid work of art. They created an alliance with the young Scottish king, Alexander, with his marriage to their daughter, Margaret, and kept the aggressive Prince Llewellyn from reclaiming their barons' lands in the Welsh Marches.

They held onto Gascony, of which Henry was Duke, in spite of constant uprisings there. They might have gained not only Normandy but Sicily, too, had their barons supported their empire-building vision. They squelched the Montfortian campaign to end the Plantagenet reign—Simon had already planned to award lands and castles to his sons and place himself on the throne—and they produced instead a son who would become Edward I, one of England's great kings...unless you were Scottish, Welsh, or Jewish.

Simon de Montfort and Simon de Montfort

by KATHERINE ASHE

IN FEBRUARY OF THE YEAR 1230—OR 1229 BY THE WAY THEY CALCULATED YEARS THEN, starting at Easter—a French youth appeared at the Court of Henry III of England claiming the title of Earl of Leicester, and its companion honor, Steward of England. He was jettisoned from the Court and later offered insulting pay as a mercenary.

Yet, a few months after his ignominious visit to Westminster, with the support of his cousin Ranulf, the Earl of Chester, he did manage to persuade King Henry to pay him the earldom's rents. Later, he would indeed be Earl of Leicester, and later still, he would make Parliament a reality, harnessing the powers of King Henry.

The youth was Simon de Montfort, and the name already was famous by 1229. His father, for whom he was named, was a leader of the Fourth Crusade. He had refused to become entangled with the politics of Constantinople and took his forces on to Palestine, while the rest of his fellow-crusaders covered themselves with shame in the imperial upheavals. For his single-mindedness, Simon de Montfort Pere was looked upon as a hero.

Today he's looked upon as a ruthless opportunist.

In the France to which Simon Pere and his Normandy knights returned, there was a new religion rising which the papacy condemned as heretical. Named for the southern French city of Albi, a center of their preaching, the Albigensians were gaining converts from conventional Catholicism by the virtuous lives they lived and the astute reasoning of their market-square preaching. Their religion entailed a forty-day fast and a celebratory meal, followed by another forty day fast. Those who survived this regimen were confirmed as Cathars: Pure Ones.

Pope Innocent III commissioned Dominic Felix de Guzman (Saint Dominic) to found a preaching order to counter this increasingly popular diversion from standard Christianity.

But when the papal legate Pierre de Castelnau was murdered, the Pope took military measures. A knight who went on crusade to the Holy Land received forgiveness of his debts and of his sins; now those highly desirable gifts were offered for a far less costly crusade merely to southern France.

Thousands of northern French knights responded, converging on the south with a holy license to destroy. They entrapped six thousand Albigensians in the church at Bezier, piled wood around the building, and roasted to death every man, woman, and child within.

Recovering from this bout of blood-lust, the crusaders realized they needed a leader. But no one much wanted the dubious honor of making the murderous roisterers into a proper fighting force. Simon de Montfort Pere eventually accepted the command and, of course, has been blamed for the Bezier horror.

Fighting a lengthy war against the lords of southern France who harbored the Albigensians, Simon Pere was forced to hire mercenaries at his own expense. He conquered most of the strategic cities, setting up for himself a dukedom that included Foix, Toulouse, and Carcassonne.

Then, during his absence from the city, Toulouse managed to rebel. Simon found the outer walls held against him. When he attacked, he was killed by a stone hurled from a mangonel mounted on the wall and operated by a woman.

Toulouse still celebrates the event with an image of a lamb skewering a toppled lion with the point of a flagpole. (In a taxi in Toulouse I made a favorable remark about Simon de Montfort. The driver stopped the car, fished in the trunk, found a tire-iron and came at me. I escaped through the car's farther door.)

Normal medieval practice usually included providing a virtual hostage to ensure the contact-giver's commitment to the agreement. The obvious choice available for Amaury to offer to the Crown of France was his little brother Simon, whose mother was also dead by 1221, and hence unable to object. But such hostages in Paris enjoyed considerable advantages of education in the most scholarly and devout court in Christendom.

There is no record of young Simon's childhood, but his excellent education, as attested by the letters of his Franciscan friends who were among the foremost scholars of the era, and the great fondness and trust repeatedly placed in him by King Louis IX of France (Saint Louis) and his mother Queen Blanche, who was regent for Louis, suggest that Simon—as I propose in my book—probably served as that hostage and was the little King of France's childhood companion.

Queen Blanche even saw fit to betroth this title-less, virtually landless, and penniless orphan to Johanna, the Princess of Flanders, another child-hostage at her court, but one with immense wealth and power as her dowry. (Johanna eventually wed Thomas, the Count of Provence.)

That betrothal, and every other connection with the Court of France, collapsed for Simon after he pledged his liege to Henry III to obtain his earldom's rents. Gossip of the period had Blanche cursing Simon and his fleeing from France.

What was the dispute about?

Simon's brother Amaury repeatedly had petitioned Henry III for the Leicester titles and had been refused—understandably. Amaury was Marshall of France. He was responsible for providing mounts and pack-animals for the French Crown's military campaigns, and England and France were at war, though in a desultory sort of way. Simon first appears in England after Amaury's efforts irrevocably had come to naught, and at a time when France feared an English invasion.

Queen Blanche was noted for her network of spies. Was she hoping to place an agent in Henry's Court? A man who could inform her of Henry's plans, and possibly could influence the young and inept king away from military actions? Was Simon sent to be that agent, in his brother's stead? And once he had pledged his solemn and holy oath of liege to Henry, as was required of him, did he then consider it would be an act of disloyalty to his pledged lord to serve Queen Blanche as her spy? My belief is that something along these lines was the cause of young Simon's early rift with the French royal family.

That rift was mended in the years to come—though probably not by his being a secret agent for France. In 1252, when the Queen Regent was dying and Louis was on crusade in Palestine,

Blanche named Simon Regent of France, a position he held with such success that the English chroniclers claim the French were temptingly considering that he would be a better king than Louis. Simon did not remain in France to seize power for himself, but fled, returning to the service of King Henry and England. And Louis hurriedly returned from Palestine, where he was being offered a sultanate if only he would convert to Islam.

SOURCES

Bemont, Charles. *Simon de Montfort*. Oxford: Clarendon Press, 1930.

Excerpta e Rotulis Finium in Turri Londdinensi Asservatis Henry III, 1216-1272. Edited by C. Roberts. Public Record Office, 1835-36.

Labarge, Margaret Wade. *Simon de Montfort*. London: Eyre and Spottiswood, 1962. (Page 22 indicates that author's leaning to my theory of Simon's childhood at the Court of France.)

Luard, H.R. Rolls Series, Vol. III.

Matthew Paris. *English History from 1235 to 1273*. Translated by the Rev. J. A. Giles. London: Henry Bohn, 1852.

Please see K. Ashe's Volume One, Montfort The Early Years 1229 to 1243, for a full bibliography, and discussion of these points in the Historical Context section of the book.

An Alchemist, an Earl, and the Stupor Mundi: The Cannon and Gunpowder in 13th Century Europe, with a Nod to *Tess of the D'Urbervilles*

BY KATHERINE ASHE

ROGER BACON IS CONSIDERED TO HAVE INTRODUCED THE FORMULA AND USE OF GUN-powder to Europe in an article in his encyclopedic *De Secretis Operibus Artis et Naturae*. He illustrates a vase-shaped bronze vessel and offers a practical compounding of what is now called black powder. How did this 13th century Oxford scholar and alchemist come to have the secret of China's explosive substance and its use in artillery?

The trail of evidence is sometimes circumstantial but the facts are these:

Gunpowder and cannons were known in China by the twelfth century. The first recorded use in the West appears to have been by Islamic forces battling Christians on the Iberian Peninsula in the early thirteenth century. Arab trade with China at that time, with dhows sailing to Canton and junks sailing to Aden, was quite active, and most likely was the means of bringing the technology to Arabic domains. But cannons and gunpowder remained very secret weapons.

The Holy Roman Emperor Frederic II, known as the Stupor Mundi for his breadth of education and his insouciance toward Christianity, was educated by Arab scholars, attended by Arab physicians, and remained close to Arabic intellectuals and informants all his life.

At his siege of Milan in 1238, Frederic's army deployed a strange weapon that reportedly lofted missiles amid smoke and a thunderous roar.

This same Milanese siege, at which Simon de Montfort was serving while in Italy—applying to the Vatican for the lifting of his wife's vows as a nun—was commanded by Henry D'Urberville, on loan to Frederic from England and Simon's former commander in Wales. D'Urberville would have seen Frederic's secret weapon in operation.

D'Urberville was also Simon's immediate predecessor as governor for Gascony, England's dukedom in southern France. Incidentally, this is that same Henry d'Urberville whose empty tomb appears in *Tess of the D'Urbervilles* to inspire the country girl with her great ancestry. Henry died on crusade in the Holy Land at King Louis' battle at Mansourah.

Before going to govern Gascony for King Henry, Simon de Montfort served as ambassador for England at King Louis IX's court in Paris (1246-48). During the time of his stay there, the university brought charges against a young alchemist named Roger Bacon who was annoying everyone by making foul smells in his room. The university authorities applied to King Louis to have him evicted.

Roger Bacon next turns up established at Oxford, which is then under the care of Robert Grosseteste's protégé, Adam Marsh. Grosseteste's and Marsh's existing letters to Simon show an extraordinary degree of familiarity with the Earl; they undoubtedly were his closest friends. It would seem likely that Simon was the link between Bacon and Oxford, and it was probably through his initial patronage that Bacon found a home there—on a bridge where his malodorous matter could be conveniently dumped into the river.

In his *De Secretis Operibus Artis et Naturae*, published in 1248, Bacon describes explosives and includes a drawing of a bronze vase-like vessel, the prototype of the European cannon.

Commissioned to suppress the Gascon lords' rebellion against English rule, Simon de Montfort defeated the mountain fortress of Mauleon in 1248 so swiftly that the deed was attributed to supernatural agency and brought about a fairly prompt surrender to the new governor. Might Simon have been using the cannon that Bacon describes?

The next record of what seems to have been the use of a cannon was in 1253, when King Henry was trying to raise funds from his English barons for a war—again to subdue Gascony. The king displayed to the lords steel arrows, quarrels which had been lobbed at him amid thunderous noise from the roof of the fortress of La Reole—which previously had been supplied and used as headquarters by Montfort. The butt ends of the arrows were blackened as from a fiery explosion.

A cannon, very similar to the one Bacon illustrated in his writings of 1248, appears in *De Nobilitatibus, Sapientii, et Prudentiis Regum*, by Walter de Milemete in 1326. But the use of cannon and gunpowder by the English is not widely recognized until the Battle of Crecy in 1346.

WILLIAM WALLACE, THE HERO?

BY ROSANNE E. LORTZ

WHENEVER I STUDY HISTORY, I HAVE AN INNATE BIAS IN FAVOR OF THE UNDERDOG. WHEN the Britons face the invading Angles and Saxons, I root for King Arthur's warriors at Badon Hill. When the Anglo-Saxons bear the iron yoke of the Normans, I rally with Robin Hood's men in Sherwood Forest. And when the Scots thwart Edward I's ambition to rule the entire island, I look to William Wallace as the hero of the hour.

My first introduction to William Wallace was in *The Scottish Chiefs*, a nineteenth century novel by Jane Porter. The highly romanticized story, strewn with N. C. Wyeth's poignant illustrations, appealed to my young teenage self. My second encounter with Wallace was in the 1995 movie *Braveheart*. The much grimier, but still highly romanticized story appealed to my older teenage self. Both stories made me want to cry "Freedom!" with the Scottish warrior and shed tears for his patriotic martyrdom.

Later, when I was curious enough to sift fact from fiction, I discovered that both of these retellings were about as accurate as a perjurer's deposition. But, even with all the embellishments discarded, I had no doubts where my loyalty lay. I was still committed to William Wallace, and taking Edward I's side was unthinkable.

This certainty was sorely shaken when I encountered the *Flores Historiarum*, a Latin chronicle written by several English hands during the twelfth to fourteenth centuries. It was begun at St. Alban's Abbey, continued at Westminster Abbey, and today there are approximately twenty manuscripts extant.

The *Flores Historiarum* presents a much less romanticized view of William Wallace; it presents an English opinion of the Scottish hero:

> About the time of the festival of the Assumption of the Blessed Virgin Mary, a certain Scot, by name William Wallace, an outcast from pity, a robber, a sacrilegious man, an incendiary and a homicide, a man more cruel than the cruelty of Herod, and more insane than the fury of Nero…a man who burnt alive boys in schools and churches, in great numbers; who, when he had collected an army of Scots in the battle of Falkirk against the King of England, and had seen that he could not resist the powerful army of the king, said to the Scots, "Behold I have brought you into a ring, now carol and dance as well as you can," and so fled himself from the battle, leaving his people to be slain by the sword.
>
> He, I say, this man of Belial, after his innumerable wickedness, was at last taken prisoner by the king's servants and brought to London, as the king ordained that he should be formally tried, and was on the eve of St. Bartholomew [23 August 1305] condemned by the nobles of the kingdom of England to a most cruel but amply deserved

death. First of all, he was led through the streets of London, dragged at the tail of a horse, and dragged to a very high gallows, made on purpose for him, where he was hanged with a halter, then taken down half dead, after which his body was vivisected in a most cruel and torturous manner, and after he had expired, his body was divided into four quarters, and his head fixed on a stake and set on London Bridge. But his four quarters thus divided, were sent to the four quarters of Scotland. Behold the end of a merciless man whom his mercilessness brought to this end.

For the William Wallace of this story, the punishment fits the crime. For the William Wallace of this story, the reader has no tears.

The portrayal of William Wallace in the *Flores Historiarum* is certainly as yellow as a jaundiced eye can make it. Some could argue that it is as far removed from truth as the whitewashed hagiographies of several centuries later.

But whether it is accurate or not, for me, this passage has always illustrated an important lesson: there are two sides to every story.

As a historical novelist concerned about my craft, I can't always follow my innate biases. I can't just root for the underdog, or the man with the most glamorous legends. If two voices deserve to be heard, I must let them both speak.

What if Edward Bruce Had Succeeded in Ireland?

by ARTHUR RUSSELL

The early years of England's King Edward II's reign were dogged by many difficulties. First, he had to fight his barons who wanted to increase their own power at the expense of Royal power. Of even more significance, he had inherited a disastrous war with Robert Bruce in Scotland, arising from the claim of his father (Edward I, nicknamed "Longshanks") to the throne of Scotland. This was effectively ended with the decisive battle of Bannockburn in 1314, which was a defeat for English arms.

But King Edward's Scottish troubles did not end with Bannockburn. The victorious Bruce had been invited by an alliance of Irish chieftains to take over the vacant throne of Ard-Rí. And Bruce felt strong enough to do just that in hopes of opening a second war front against the English. He wanted to form a pan-Celtic alliance which he hoped would attract support not just from Ireland but from dissident elements in Wales. There was much talk of a "Celtic Empire of the West" which potentially would have created a strong counterbalance to the still embryonic power of London and a future British Empire.

On May 26, 1314, a huge army of Scottish soldiers (gallowglasses) landed at Larne in Co Antrim under the leadership of Bruce's younger brother Edward, the man chosen to assume the title of Ard-Rí (High King).

For over three years, the Scottish invasion defeated every effort of the English colonists to resist them. Among the English who fought Edward Bruce were Justiciar Edward deBoteler and Sir Roger Mortimer, Earl of Wigmore, who was also Lord of Trim by virtue of his marriage to a scion of the deLacy family.

Mortimer was lucky to escape from the Scots after the decisive battle of Kells in November 1315 which left the whole of Ireland—with the exception of the city of Dublin and a few castled towns—under the control of the invader.

Edward Bruce was crowned Ard-Rí of Ireland at Knocknamellan, near Dundalk, in May 1316.

The weather played a vital role in the progress of war. Not for the first or last time, northwestern Europe was hit by a succession of wet and windy summers which impacted the ability of the land to produce enough to feed the population. Add to this the impact of a hungry, invading army intent on starving all opposition into compliance, and you have the ideal environment for famine and famine-related pestilence to ravage Ireland during those turbulent years.

It meant that Bruce could never move too far away from his northern base which was supplied from Scotland. It also caused many Irish allies to blame the Scots for the damage that was being done to Ireland's food supply and to withhold their support for his cause. Bruce's Gaelic allies also failed to win Papal recognition for the newly crowned Ard-Rí, which further eroded support for the invasion.

The war dragged on until 1318 when the English King finally put together the men and resources to roll back the Scottish advance. Sir Roger Mortimer landed with a huge army at Youghal and succeeded in pinning the Scots back into Ulster where they awaited the arrival of promised reinforcements from King Robert later in the year.

The next battle would decide the fate of the invasion and of Ireland for centuries. Against all the advice of all his own commanders as well his remaining Irish allies, Bruce insisted on taking to the field at Faughart near Dundalk on October 14, 1318, days before his brother's army, which had by then arrived in Ireland, could help him. Due to the rivalry that existed between the brothers, Edward wanted to win this last deciding battle without Robert's help.

Seriously outnumbered, the Scots were defeated. Edward Bruce and many leading Scottish nobles were killed at the battle of Faughart. This battle was the end of Scotland's interest in Irish affairs and the dream of a strong alliance of Celtic nations that could challenge England's hegemony.

Sir Roger Mortimer, who is rightly credited with being the main architect of the defeat of the Bruces' invasion of Ireland, subsequently went on to play a significant part in England's history. (See *The Greatest Traitor*, by Ian Mortimer.)

THE GREAT "WHAT-IFS?"

What if Edward had waited for his brother at Faughart? What if he had won and succeeded in establishing a strong Irish Royal dynasty allied to Scotland? How different would subsequent Irish, Scottish, and English history have been?

GAELIC IRELAND

The Bruce invasion of Ireland provides the historical backdrop to my novel *Morgallion*, which takes its title from the marchland barony of the same name. It was here that the remains of an ancient lake or "crannóg" settlement was uncovered 20 years ago beside Moynagh Lough in Co Meath. This site was the subject of an extensive archaeological excavation led by John Bradley from the National University of Ireland Maynooth who traced its origins to Neolithic times and its continued development right into the Middle Ages. Moynagh's crannóg Gaelic community was therefore on the frontier of Norman-English and Gaelic cultures after the Norman invasion and inevitably had to endure all the inherent dangers and traumas that living in such a precarious location entailed.

It is also on record that Edward Bruce's invading army occupied the nearby caput town of Nobber for several weeks on his way to his victory over Sir Roger Mortimer at the battle of Kells in November 1315. In common with every other district in the front-line of the invading army's advance, its people suffered dreadfully from famine, disease, and the ravages of war.

These are some of the "pegs" of historical fact on which the story of *Morgallion* hangs. While it is fiction, it portrays how the lives of ordinary people might have been impacted by events that washed over and around them. The book is an attempt to put some "flesh on the bones" of what scant historic records tell us. The research and writing of the book began twenty years ago and was finally brought to completion in April 2012.

Two Legends, Two Outlaws: Robin Hood and William Bradshaigh

by ELIZABETH ASHWORTH

Probably the best known of all the medieval outlaws is the English folk hero, Robin Hood. The stories of his exploits have been told many times over the centuries from *A Lyttell Geste of Robin Hood* which was printed in the early 1500s to the more recent BBC television series and the film starring Russell Crowe.

One popular version of the Robin Hood legend begins in the year 1193 and names Robin as the Earl of Huntingdon, the trusted friend of Richard the Lionheart. Whilst King Richard was away fighting in Palestine, Prince John outlawed Robin and seized his lands, forcing him to live in Sherwood Forest with his band of "merry men" and possibly "Maid Marion". Though ruthlessly pursued by the Sheriff of Nottingham, Robin spent much of his time robbing from the rich to give to the poor and became the hero of the Saxon peasants against their Norman overlords. Or, so the story goes.

The *Geste* records the story of an outlaw who lived in the forest at Barnsdale and who had many adventures. He gave money to an impoverished knight who was in debt to the monks of St. Mary's Abbey in York, and later in the story Robin takes back twice as much from a monk who is travelling with some of the abbey's wealth. He later enters the service of the king, but pines for the Greenwood and returns without permission to the forest.

The story ends by telling how Robin dies at Kirklees Priory. He goes there in old age, possibly because he is ill, and the prioress, who may be his cousin, bleeds him. Bleeding was a well-known medical procedure at that time, but because Robin has criticised the corruption within the church, this prioress, in cahoots with her lover Red Roger of Doncaster, allows him to bleed to death. But before he dies, he manages to summon Little John by blowing his hunting horn, and then he shoots an arrow from the window of the gatehouse and asks to be buried where it lands.

Although there is no compelling evidence that a real Robin Hood ever existed, one of the most popular searches on my website is for "Robin Hood's Grave" and, a short walk from what remains of the priory gatehouse of Kirklees, there is a grave hidden amongst the yew trees. It is inscribed:

> *Here underneath dis laitl stean*
> *Laz Robert Earl of Huntingtun*
> *Ne'er arcir ver as hie sa geud*
> *An pipl kauld im Robin Heud*
> *Sick utlawz as him as iz men*
> *Vil England nivr si agen*
> *Obit. 24. Kal Dekembris, 1247.*

The gravestone was placed here in 1850 by Sir George Armytage II who was then the land-owner and is based on an earlier inscription from 1631. The grave was originally discovered by John Leland, Henry VIII's librarian and chief antiquarian, who visited Kirklees in 1542 during the Dissolution of the Monasteries. He saw the grave and recorded that: "*Resting under this monument lies buried Robin Hood that nobleman who was beyond the law.*"

However, the earliest stories about Robin Hood are not set in the reign of Richard the Lionheart at all, but mention "Edward, our comely king" which may point to these events taking place in the reign of Edward II when there was also unrest across England. A succession of very wet summers from 1315 to 1317 led to crops rotting in the fields. There was widespread famine as food shortages and high prices led to starvation. There were accusations of bad government, and in Lancashire some of the local knights decided to take the law into their own hands.

Sir Adam Banastre and Sir William Bradshaigh led a local rebellion against their overlord, Thomas, Earl of Lancaster. In preparation for what is now called the Banastre Rebellion, these leaders and their confederates rode around Lancashire seeking supplies. This resulted in a man named Sir Henry de Bury being killed and his horse and other goods stolen.

Sir William was accused of sheltering the perpetrators of these crimes and was summoned to court. He didn't attend because by this time the rebels had faced a battle at Preston, on the banks of the River Ribble, against the deputy sheriff of Lancashire, Sir Edmund Neville, where they were defeated and had to flee for their lives.

Accused of treason and also wanted in relation to the murder inquiry, Sir William was declared an outlaw. His lands at Haigh, which were his wife Mabel's inheritance, were confiscated by the king, and he was forced to go into hiding, probably in the forest around Charnock. If you ever travel on the M6 motorway you will pass a service station named Charnock Richard which is near to this area.

However, a document dated at Westminster on 21 May 1318 records that William received a pardon:

> *Pardon to William de Bradeshagh, knight, of his outlawry in the county of Lancaster, for non-appearance before Robert de Lathom and his fellows, justices, assigned to enquire touching the death of Henry de Bury, knight, killed by Stephen Scallard and John de Walton, as is alleged, when charged with assenting thereto.*
>
> (Cal. Pat. 1317-21, p.145)

Whether he was still outlawed for his part in the rebellion is unclear, but he did not return home, and in 1319, his wife Mabel declared that he was dead. The story of Lady Mabel and Sir William has been handed down over the years and is known as the legend of Mab's Cross, which records that William was fighting in Palestine rather than being an outlaw.

It also tells that Lady Mabel remarried, although there is no documentary evidence for this, and that when her husband eventually returned home she performed a penance for her adultery by walking barefoot from her home at Haigh Hall to a wayside cross in Wigan. The remains of the cross can still be seen outside Mab's Cross Primary School in the town.

And, like Robin Hood, Sir William also has a marked grave, although it is more likely that this one is genuine and he is really buried in Wigan Parish Church where his effigy can be seen.

A Brief but Very Satisfactory Wooing: Edward III and Philippa of Hainault

by ANNE O'BRIEN

The only true representation we have of the appearance of Philippa of Hainault is taken from her tomb in Westminster Abbey next to that of Edward III.

Some five years before her death she gave orders for it to be carved specifically to show her as she was in advancing age, not as she had been in her youth. She was about 55 years old at this time. It shows her as stout and maternal with broad features. She had no claim to beauty but without doubt Edward loved her.

In July 1326, when the future Edward III was fourteen years old, he and his mother Queen Isabella visited Valenciennes in the state of Hainault on a mission—to find the youthful Edward a bride. They had been sent a description of one of the Hainault daughters, of which there were four: Margaret, Philippa, Jeanne, and Isabella.

The description we have of the prospective bride was always thought to have been of Philippa, written by Bishop Stapledon who had visited Hainault twice and reported back. The young girl was described in 1319 as having dark hair, deep-set brown eyes, a large forehead, and a large nose, but not snubbed. Her body and limbs were well formed but some of her teeth were discoloured. It does not sound to be the stuff of high romance, but the proposed bride was considered to be an attractive proposition for the young prince.

It has to be said that Isabella, in conflict with her husband Edward II, had her eye on a troop of Hainaulter mercenaries, which might have swayed her in her choice of a Hainault bride for her son. A contemporary writer further suggested that Philippa had been chosen because of the quality of her hips for childbearing—not the first or the last time such an attribute was to play a part when the provision of an heir was of paramount importance.

Recent research suggests that the description was not in fact Philippa, but more likely her eldest sister Margaret, chiefly because of the correlation of birth dates with Stapledon's visit. By the time that Edward visited Hainault, however, Margaret was not available for marriage, being already married to Ludwig of Bavaria.

The decision that Edward and Philippa would marry was made by Isabella and Count William of Hainault, Philippa's father; thus, the young people had no say in the matter. Philippa was about twelve years old and the wedding, it was agreed, would happen within the next two years. Edward's visit lasted for only eight days, at the end of which, when Edward left, Philippa is said to have wept bitterly.

Edward met Philippa again in January 1328 at the gates of York, and they were married the next day in York Minster. Thus began a marriage that lasted for forty years until Philippa's death in 1369.

In character, they matched each other perfectly. They enjoyed books—Philippa read romances while Edward enjoyed tales of the heroic feats of King Arthur. They enjoyed hunting, celebrations, and extravagant festivities. They also enjoyed their family life—Philippa producing twelve children, Edward being an indulgent and generous father. Edward was the flamboyant one; Philippa had a strong streak of common sense and loyalty to Edward, both of which he needed to put his reign on a firm footing.

So what happened in those eight days in Valenciennes in July 1326 between Edward and Philippa that caused Philippa to weep when her young suitor left? We have no idea. But whatever attraction there was between the two young people, it laid the foundation for one of the most important and successful marriages—and one of the most definitive reigns—in English history.

A (Possible) Page from the London Gazette: September 1331

BY ANNE O'BRIEN

CHEAPSIDE DRAMA

QUEEN IN NEAR-DEATH DISASTER...

Today at Cheapside, in the very centre of our fair city of London, we expected to celebrate the birth, one year ago, of Edward of Woodstock, the heir to our illustrious King Edward III. Instead we witnessed a drama that could have had fatal results.

NOBLE EDWARD

It began with the magnificence of all our King's celebrations. As we know, Edward enjoys every opportunity to put the royal family on display with extravagant feasts and dressing up. Who can forget his astonishing caperings as a gigantic golden bird to mark the feast of Twelfth Night? He is a master of festivities, warming our hearts with his energy. We wish him long life and every success in his campaigns to subdue the villainous French and bring our lands across the Channel back under our rightful dominion.

ENGLAND'S GLORY

The tournament to celebrate the glory of England and England's King is planned to thrill us over four days. This morning King Edward and his knights, who were intending to participate in the lists and the melee, were arrayed as fierce Tartars from the wild steppes of Muscovy. Clad in sumptuous robes of velvet and damask, lined with rich fur, our brave lads led in procession the most noble and the most beautiful women of the realm, all tricked out in red velvet tunics and white hoods—the King's own colours. King Edward led his fair sister Eleanor in the procession.

OUR RADIANT QUEEN...

It was planned for our Queen and her damsels, in regal splendour, to watch the display of knightly valour from a wooden gallery constructed for the occasion, all hung about with red and white silk, swagged in banners and pennons. The crowds cheered her and our noble King, as he saluted her in true chivalric manner, and then rode towards the lists. Queen Philippa looked radiant and smiled at her loyal subjects, before seating herself on golden cushions.

DISASTER!

Hardly had Chester Herald blown the blast to summon all competitors than a harsh grinding of wood could be heard by all present. The hangings on the Queen's gallery shivered, the banners dipped and swayed. Before our horrified eyes, without more warning, the whole construction collapsed in a cloud of dust and debris. The cries of the Queen's damsels made our blood run cold. Knights and servants ran from all sides to rescue our dear Queen. King Edward was the first to be there at Philippa's side, lifting the wood and canvas from her with his own hands.

THE NATION'S RELIEF

We are delighted to be able to report that Queen Philippa is unharmed, although some of her ladies were seriously injured. The whole country should give thanks in special Masses for her happy restoration to health. King Edward was noticeably overcome at the prospect of his dear wife's possible injury or even death. An eye-witness reported that he kissed and hugged her when she was capable of standing on her own feet. It was a tender moment and moved our hearts.

EDWARD'S FURY

Our King was justifiably furious at the shoddy workmanship that caused the gallery to collapse, and demanded to know the workmen involved. His anger was terrible to see. Craftsmanship is not what it used to be! Even the Queen feared for the workmen's lives, for we know that our King has a temper when he is roused. If he is challenged, he will face force with force, which we have found to be a good thing in our dealings with the despicable French.

OUR QUEEN'S BRAVERY

Despite her obvious shock, brave Philippa fell to her knees before her irate husband and begged his mercy for the hapless carpenters since she was not harmed. An eye-witness said she spoke soothing words in his ear. Her tears of compassion melted his anger. Our King lifted her up and promised to have mercy. The crowd cheered at his magnanimity and the Queen's care for her subjects and for justice. The craftsmen grovelled in the dust in relief, as they should.

THE SHOW GOES ON!

Reassured of his wife's escape, in true English character, Edward saw to her comfort and then ordered the tournament to proceed as normal. He might be persuaded to spare the carpenters— but a tournament he must have! The French should take note of our King's determination and mental strength when under pressure. The nation rejoices at Queen Philippa's restoration to good health and King Edward's victory over all comers in the tournament. We give thanks to God.

⚜

This may be a fictitious newspaper account, but the events at the Cheapside tournament in 1331 are all true. What an astonishing reign was Edward III's, for colour and for drama.

THE ELUSIVE HISTORY OF THE ORDER OF THE GARTER

BY **ROSANNE E. LORTZ**

"*H*ONI SOIT QUI MAL Y PENSE—SHAMED BE THE ONE WHO THINKS EVIL OF IT." SO READS THE motto of the famous Order of the Garter, a society of knights established by Edward III, the English king who began the Hundred Years' War with France.

But what does the motto refer to and why did Edward choose it? That question is just one of the many surrounding the foundation of the Garter Order.

According to historian Elizabeth Hallam, the inspiration for chivalric orders like the Order of the Garter came from *"the imagination of a 12th-century Norman churchman, Wace, who added the story of the Round Table to Geoffrey of Monmouth's fictional history of King Arthur."* The stories of the Knights of the Round Table spread far and wide as other writers took Wace's idea and elaborated on it. *"During the 13th century knights in tournaments adopted the roles and fictional coats of arms of Arthur and his knights. 'Round Tables' were set up at many English tournaments,"* and this playacting eventually *"led to knights forming more regular tourneying brotherhoods: the golf clubs of their age."*

Edward III, who was fond of holding these "Round Table" tournaments, eventually moved to create an official society that would mimic King Arthur's legendary brotherhood of knights.

The Order of the Garter was founded in 1344 (if we are to believe Jean Froissart), in 1350 (if we are to believe Geoffrey le Baker), or in 1348 (if we piece together some of the expenditures in the Royal Exchequer). This discrepancy in sources may seem amusing at first, until you realize that the date of establishment is only one of many knots historians must untangle as they weave together a history of the Order.

Froissart, a contemporary of King Edward's, gives us this glimpse of the establishment:

> At that time King Edward of England conceived the idea of altering and rebuilding the great castle of Windsor, originally built by King Arthur, and where had first been established the noble Round Table, from which so many fine men and brave knights had gone forth and performed great deeds throughout the world. King Edward's intention was to found an order of knights, made up of himself and his sons and the bravest and noblest in England. There would be forty of them in all and they would be called the Knights of the Blue Garter and their feast was to be held every year at Windsor on St George's Day. To institute the feast, the King called together the earls, barons and knights of the whole country and told them of his intentions and of his great desire to see them carried out. They agreed with him wholeheartedly, because they thought it an honourable undertaking and one which would strengthen the bonds of friendship

among them. Forty knights were then chosen from among the most gallant of them all and these swore a solemn oath to the King always to observe the feast and the statutes, as these were agreed and drawn up.

Geoffrey le Baker, also a contemporary chronicler, gives his own description of the establishment of the Order and highlights the importance of the garter in their knightly regalia: *"All these men, together with the king, were dressed in robes of russet and wore garters of dark blue on their right legs. The robes of the order were completed by a blue mantle, embroidered with the arms of St George."*

Nowadays, the garter is associated almost exclusively with women's lingerie. How did it come to be the symbol of a chivalric order for an English king and his knights? Here we find yet another confusing tile in the mosaic of the Order's history.

One legend, written down by Polydore Vergil in 1534, gives this romantic rationale:

> *[P]opular tradition nowadays declares that Edward at some time picked up from the ground a garter from the stocking of his queen or mistress, which had become unloosed by some chance, and had fallen. As some of the knights began to laugh and jeer on seeing this, he is reputed to have said that in a very little while the same garter would be held by them in the highest honour. And not long after, he is said to have founded this order and given it the title by which he showed those knights who had laughed at him how to judge his actions. Such is popular tradition.*

The romantic elements of the story continued to grow over time.

By the end of the sixteenth century, Joan of Kent, the Countess of Salisbury (she who would later marry the Black Prince), had become the celebrated beauty whose garter fell to the floor while dancing with the king. And the chivalrous Edward responded to his jeering courtiers with the same words which he would make the motto of the Order: *"Honi soit qui mal y pense*—Shamed be the one who thinks evil of it."

How much stock should be put in this story is difficult to say. Some historians partially accept it, but state that the woman referred to was actually Joan of Kent's mother-in-law (another Countess of Salisbury for whom King Edward was reputed to have a violent passion). Others discount the story altogether as a tale too fantastical and too anachronistic. Richard Barber, a historian of the latter school, writes:

> *The word 'garter' is extremely rare, and indeed only appears once before the foundation of the Order…here it is applied to an item of apparel worn by fashionable squires to keep up their hose…. I have found only one piece of evidence of ladies wearing garters before the fifteenth century: in 1389, the prostitutes of Toulouse were to wear a badge of a garter by royal decree—once again, there is a suggestion of political mockery and propaganda* [i.e. the French making fun of Edward III and his already-established Order].

After arguing that the garter was not commonly worn by women during the fourteenth century, Barber goes on to say that the garter of this time period was a much different item of dress than we would think of as a garter today.

> *The form of the garter, as shown in the earliest known representation, is also unusual: it is a miniature belt, with buckle and perforated tongue, hardly a purely practical item of clothing. Later garters were usually a strip of cloth or silk, tied in a knot. I would tentatively suggest that the design is connected with the knight's belt, one of the insignia used in the ceremony of knighthood.*

Those who accept Barber's opinion, that the symbol of the Garter was a masculine one, a piece of equipment typically worn by knights, must still find an explanation for the Order's motto: "*Honi soit qui mal y pense*—Shamed be the one who thinks evil of it." If the episode of a lady dropping her garter never occurred, then what motivated Edward to choose this phrase?

A plausible answer to this question can be found in Edward III's claim to the French throne.

In 1328, the last son of the French king Philip IV died, leaving no male heir. Edward III of England, as the son of Philip IV's daughter Isabella, considered himself next in line for the French crown. The French, however, had already chosen Philip VI, nephew to Philip IV and grandson to Philip III, to be their ruler.

The laws of inheritance during this time period varied by country and were hotly disputed within France itself, but suffice it to say that there were more quibbles with Edward's claim than the fact that he was English. In 1337, he invaded France in an attempt to take the French crown by force and began the conflict now known as the Hundred Years' War. The Order of the Garter, whether it was founded in 1344, 1348, or 1350, came onto the scene during the first phase of this war, and all of its founding members were English nobility who would take part in the fight against France. Its motto—"Shamed be the one who thinks evil of it"—could very well be a gauntlet thrown at those naysayers who denied Edward's claim to the crown.

Although the real events surrounding the founding of this Order may never be totally proved, it is indisputably acknowledged that the Order of the Garter is the most famous and longest lasting society of chivalry in the world. On April 23, 2008, Prince William was appointed the one thousandth member of the group. Some of the vestments have changed to accommodate the more modern clothing of our own time, but at the ceremony where Prince William was invested one can still see the blue mantle described by Geoffrey le Baker. And if you look closely at the circular badge attached to that mantle, you will see that enigmatic motto still in use: "*Honi soit qui mal y pense*—Shamed be the one who thinks evil of it."

SOURCES

Barber, Richard. *Edward, Prince of Wales and Aquitaine: A Biography of the Black Prince*. Great Britain: The Boydell Press, 1978.

Froissart, Jean. *Chronicles*. Translated and edited by Geoffrey Brereton. London: Penguin Books, 1978.

Hallam, Elizabeth, ed. *Chronicles of the Age of Chivalry*. London: Salamander Books, Ltd., 2002.

THE PLAGUE

BY BARBARA GASKELL DENVIL

THE NURSERY RHYME "RING A RING O' ROSES" HAS A LOT TO ANSWER FOR.

As far as can be ascertained, this emanates from 19th century America, but the popular modern supposition is now that it refers to the sufferings of the Plague, thus describing the common symptoms (rings of roses and a-tishoo), followed by falling down dead. Cheery! But entirely erroneous.

Indeed, one of the greatest catastrophes ever to alter England's history was neither war nor dynastic challenge. The bubonic plague which first arrived in England in the 14th century and is now known as the Black Death, originally also the Great Mortality and the Pestilence, changed the whole country and its population, the politics and almost every aspect of everyday living conditions. The absolute terror which this first sudden visitation wreaked on the whole of Europe can barely be imagined.

But outbreaks of this dreadful disease reappeared sporadically and frequently over the next few hundred years until its final catastrophic visitation in England in 1665, after which it appears to have quite mysteriously died out. The bubonic plague has revisited some other countries, however, with occasional outbreaks even in the recent past, yet the actual sufferings of the people are now persistently misunderstood.

Indeed, plague victims did not sneeze and quickly die. The rash did not consist of large florid circles, and actually the word posies in past history did not refer to small bunches of flowers, but to short poems. There are many firsthand contemporary references to this terrible disease and its effects, and also modern accounts both scientific and colloquial. Therefore, researching this particular subject is not too difficult.

There are several related forms of the plague, and recently some experts have suggested that the original Black Death was not the bubonic but another similar kind, or even a combination of infections. Others argue that the affliction was indeed the bubonic type, but of a more lethal and unpleasant strain than is presently in existence. However, the symptoms are all sufficiently identical.

The bubonic plague was not passed directly between humans and was contagious only via the rodent flea, but the flea was numerous in most human habitations, so the specific cause of infection mattered little. Besides, if the bacteria affected the lungs, this became pneumonic plague, and the sputum was then contagious human to human. Indeed, those thus infected, those desperate souls now dismissed by some writers as suffering from sneezes and the occasional bubo, did instead suffer from some of the most hideous and agonising symptoms I can imagine.

Once the infected rats had died in large numbers, the fleas carrying the bacteria inevitably looked for other hosts. Humanity, living in close proximity and with generally poor standards of hygiene, was the next step.

It seems there was a four to six day incubation period from the moment of actual infection, during which time this horrible condition, usually localised, occurred virtually every 15 to 20 years in some area or another. Where this occurred in highly populated areas (such as London) the death toll could still be alarmingly high.

The threat of this appalling disease therefore continued and must have haunted people, especially those who saw it as a punishment from God. Throughout the final epidemic in 1665/6, definitely the worst since its very first arrival in the country in 1348, great pits were dug on the outskirts of towns to take the piled corpses. Many of these plague pits have later been uncovered in England, sometimes unearthed due to the subsidence of a building's foundations unknowingly erected on this unsound ground.

No one knows why the plague then died out in England. Hygiene did not noticeably improve for some time afterwards, and the supposition that the Great Fire of London in 1666 was the cleansing miracle is not supported by experts. But the plague has never devastated England since.

Researching and writing about this dreadful suffering is heartbreaking. I cannot possibly contemplate the utter terror and hopeless misery caused throughout plague-affected areas during those 400 relevant years from the 14th to the 17th centuries, and the confusion, terror, and bitter loss experienced by both those poor souls afflicted, and by those left alive to mourn the mass deaths of their loved ones.

And not a sneeze in sight.

Scourge of Europe: The Religious Hysteria Created by the Black Plague

by ROSANNE E. LORTZ

DEATH HAS ALWAYS BEEN ONE OF THE MOST FRIGHTENING PROSPECTS FACED BY MANKIND. The fear of death even has its own word to describe it—thanotophobia.

In a society where a third to a half of the people around you have succumbed to death *within the past year*, the terror of knowing that you might be next can become overwhelming. It can drive a person to bizarre and unthinkable acts as he tries to ward off death's icy grip from descending on his own shoulder.

This is what happened in the mid-fourteenth century, during the years of the Black Plague. The world went wild with thanotophobia, and the country of England was no exception.

Monty Python to the contrary, the Black Plague was no joking matter. The medieval chronicler Geoffrey le Baker wrote:

> Men who had been one day full of life, were often found dead the next. Some were afflicted with abscesses which erupted in various parts of their bodies, and which were so hard and dry, that even when they were cut with a knife, hardly any liquid flowed out.... Others had small black sores which developed all over their bodies. Only a very few who suffered from these survived and recovered their health.
>
> Such was the great plague which reached Bristol on 15 August [1348], and London around 29 September. It raged in England for a year or more, and such were its ravages, that many country towns were almost emptied of human life.

For some, the proximity of the plague created the pernicious attitude of "*eat, drink, and be merry, for tomorrow we die.*" Immorality, excess, and crime became rife in towns and cities, especially in the metropolis of London, as despairing people grasped after every last piece of self-gratification before death should come for them.

Others, however, still nourished the hope that the plague might be avoided. Doctors tried the normal remedies of bleeding and laxatives and prescribed more outlandish cures such as drinking one's own urine. It soon became obvious, however, that medicine had failed to find the answer. As corpse after corpse was thrown in the common burial pits, the only course left to the living was to repent of their sins, cast themselves on divine mercy, and entreat the angel of death to forbear.

The fourteenth century, like the rest of the medieval period, was quick to consider any sort of disaster (natural or manmade) as a judgment from God. Earthquakes, fires, Viking invasions, Muslim conquests—all these things came about because of the sinful backsliding of God's people. When the Black Plague, the greatest disaster in human memory, beset Europe, it was not hard for the deeply religious and deeply frightened populace to believe that God was exceptionally wroth with the world. Someone must intercede with the Almighty and prevail upon Him to stay His hand.

The early Church had understood Christ to be the intercessor between His people and God the Father. But somewhere, in between the age of the Church Fathers and the era of the Hundred Years' War, Christ, the "shepherd of tender youth," had metamorphosed into Christ, the stern and implacable Judge. With Christ seen as the author of the plague itself, the desperate looked for a mediator in His kinder, gentler mother Mary.

Across Europe, a sect known as the Flagellants began to gain followers. Wearing a uniform of a white robe marked with a red cross—much like the Knights Templar surcoat seen in so many period films—the Flagellants were a society of ascetic laymen determined to atone for the sins of the world. They gathered in groups of anywhere from 50 to 500 men, traveling around the towns of Europe and performing the ritual of publicly scourging themselves.

The Catholic Encyclopedia offers this description of the Flagellants' activities:

> *Twice a day, proceeding slowly to the public square or to the principal church, they put off their shoes, stripped themselves to the waist and prostrated themselves in a large circle. By their posture they indicated the nature of the sins they intended to expiate, the murderer lying on his back, the adulterer on his face, the perjurer on one side holding up three fingers, etc. First they were beaten by the "Master", then, bidden solemnly in a prescribed form to rise, they stood in a circle and scourged themselves severely, crying out that their blood was mingled with the Blood of Christ and that their penance was preserving the whole world from perishing.*

After the Flagellants had gathered a crowd to watch their bloody performance, the Master would read aloud from a "heavenly letter," trying to terrify the onlookers with its apocalyptic contents. Matthew of Neuenberg wrote:

> *In this* [letter], *the angel said that Christ was displeased by the depravities of the world, and named many sins: violation of the Lord's day, not fasting on Friday, blasphemy, usury, adultery. The letter went on to say that, through the intercession of the Blessed Virgin and the angels, Christ had replied that to obtain mercy, a man should undertake voluntary exile and flagellate himself for thirty-three and a half days....*

The number was a symbolic one, standing for the thirty-three and a half years that Christ had dwelt in human form upon the earth. By identifying themselves with Christ, and taking on his sufferings as it were, the Flagellants could redeem the world from the death and destruction that had come in the form of the Black Plague.

At first, the Church did not know what to make of this new sect. The clergy appreciated the Flagellants' calls for repentance but also feared that this parachurch organization would provide a rival to the Roman Church's authority. When the Flagellants began to speak out against the Church, blaming it for allowing the corruption that had brought God's judgment, and also began to embellish their own teachings with flagrant heresy (e.g. denying the sacraments, professing their own ability to grant absolution), the Church reacted violently. Pope Clement VI commanded that the brotherhood be suppressed in whatever country they appeared throughout Europe.

The Church's antagonism toward the Flagellants, however, did not necessarily reflect the popular perception of them. The fear of death that had overshadowed Europe created a ripe breeding ground for the Flagellants' fanaticism. The movement grew quickly in Germany and the Netherlands.

Matthew of Neuenberg remarks that after the Flagellants proceeded through the city of Strasbourg, about a thousand men joined their brotherhood. France, also, had many converts to the sect until, in 1349, King Philip VI forbade public self-flagellation on pain of death; this decree effectively nipped the movement in the bud throughout his domains.

Interestingly enough, England was one of the countries where the Flagellants made the fewest inroads. In 1349, a group of fanatical Frisians came across the Channel hoping to gain converts in London. They put on a dramatic public display outside of St. Paul's Cathedral. But although their bloody flails and eerie chants unnerved the crowd, the chroniclers record that not a single Englishman wished to don their red-cross robes and take up the scourge himself.

In my book, *I Serve: A Novel of the Black Prince*, the hero Sir John Potenhale encounters this group of Flagellants making their demonstration in London. His mother has already been carried off by the plague, his father has been driven insane by it, and Potenhale himself is in a spiritually fragile condition. The Flagellants' bloody ceremony fills him with horror and makes him wonder whether it is indeed the sins of the world that have brought this punishment upon the land. Although he is not impelled to join the brotherhood, their ceremony does make him question his own calling as a knight, a quandary central to the plot of the novel.

Fortunately for Europe, this movement did not last. The fuel of the Flagellants' fanaticism had always been the terror created by the Black Plague, and when the pestilence began to abate in the early 1350s, the numbers of the sect diminished significantly.

Although it was not eradicated entirely, the Flagellant brotherhood disappeared from public view and into the void of obscurity. Throughout the next couple centuries, pockets of it would crop up here and there, but the brotherhood never again gained the same following that the Black Plague had brought them. The scourge of Europe had disappeared, and there was no longer any need to scourge oneself in an attempt to avoid it. The thanotophobia had receded, and with it the religious hysteria that had turned the fourteenth century on its head.

How Joan of Kent Became Princess of Wales

BY ROSANNE E. LORTZ

E DWARD, THE BLACK PRINCE, AND JOAN OF KENT—A PAIR OF STAR CROSS'D LOVERS THAT eventually came together in one of history's true love matches. It took three marriages and over thirty years before Joan finally became the Princess of Wales, but if the chroniclers are to be believed, it was worth the wait.

Joan, who later became known as "The Fair Maid of Kent," was the daughter of Edmund of Woodstock, half-brother to King Edward II of England. Edmund supported the king in the bitter battle against his wife Queen Isabella, pejoratively known as the "she-wolf of France."

When Isabella and her lover Roger Mortimer triumphed, Edward II was deposed, placed in prison, and later murdered. Edmund Woodstock, for the crime of remaining loyal to his brother, was sentenced to death for treason in 1330. As the story goes, Edmund had to wait nearly half a day for the authorities to find an executioner willing to do the deed since no one wanted to be responsible for his unjust death. Edmund of Woodstock was survived by his wife and four children. Joan, the third of Edmund's progeny, was a little less than two years old at the time.

Young Edward III had been placed on the throne by Isabella and Mortimer, but he was more filial to his father's memory than to his mother's commands. When he came of age, he organized a coup to remove the adulterous pair from power. Mortimer he executed, Isabella he imprisoned, and in a kindly gesture, he took Edmund Woodstock's widow and her brood into his household to be provided for.

As these events were transpiring, Edward III's wife Philippa gave birth to their oldest son, another Edward, to whom history would give the appellation, the "Black Prince of Wales." This Prince Edward and his cousin Joan were raised in close proximity to each other, and later events indicate that they grew to be fast friends. A marriage between the two was never considered, at least not by the one person who mattered.

King Edward III was determined to secure for his eldest son a matrimonial alliance that would benefit the country of England. During the Black Prince's early years, his father attempted at various times to betroth him to the daughter of the French king, the daughter of the Duke of Brabant, and a Portuguese princess. None of these marriage alliances materialized, however, and the prince was destined to remain a bachelor until the age of thirty, winning great glory on the battlefields of Crecy and Poitiers.

Joan, on the other hand, was in the unenviable position of having too many marriages materialize. When she was twelve years of age (fifteen or sixteen, according to other sources), she contracted a secret marriage with Thomas Holland, a man twice her age and seneschal to the house of Salisbury. Her royal family, it is certain, knew nothing of this marriage to Holland, for a few years later they betrothed her to William Montacute, the Earl of Salisbury.

What happened next is unclear, whether Joan actually did go through with the marriage to Salisbury or whether the news of her earlier marriage came out first and prevented the ceremony. Holland, it is thought, must have been overseas at the time or he would have spoken up to prevent the polyandrous relationship. One fact at least is certain: there were now two Englishmen claiming Joan of Kent as their wife.

Joan's opinion on the matter was that her first marriage to Thomas Holland was binding and ought to be recognized. But Joan's opinion was also of little consequence.

One story, perhaps apocryphal, describes the Earl of Salisbury locking the lady up in a tower and refusing to let her go to her first husband. An appeal was sent to the pope asking him to rule on the situation. Even though it had been undertaken without her guardians' permission, Pope Clement VI decided in favor of the first marriage, and Joan took her place in Holland's home as his wife.

Joan's marriage to Thomas Holland produced two sons and two daughters. Her oldest son, Thomas, was privileged to have the Black Prince stand godfather to him at his baptism, a sign of the mutual regard between his mother and her cousin Edward.

Holland, although his first appearance on the scene was as a lowly seneschal, rose swiftly in the world. He became Earl of Kent in right of his wife, and shortly before his death in 1360 was named captain-general of all of England's holdings on the continent.

At Holland's death, Joan—fabulously wealthy, still young, and still beautiful—was the most eligible widow in all of England. A French chronicler tells how many of the English lords sought her hand in marriage, asking the Black Prince to be the go-between and make the match. Here is historian Henry Dwight Sedgwick's delightful summary of the story:

> *The widow, as I say, was a great catch, and, as in those martial days there was little time for the more delicate hesitations and diffidences of life, suitors very soon gathered round. Many gentlemen, knowing that she and the Prince were not only cousins but good friends, went to him and asked him to say a few words to her in their favor. The most importunate of these was Lord Brocas, a very gallant nobleman of high rank, who had served the Prince well both in war and peace. The Prince, accordingly, accepted the commission and went to see the Countess of Kent several times on the suitor's behalf.*
>
> *The chronicler states that he went very willingly; for which, apart from the commission, there were reasons enough. First, she was his cousin; second, he took notice of her very great beauty and of her gracious manner that pleased him wonderfully well; and third, the time passed agreeably.*
>
> *On one occasion, when the Prince was speaking to her of the said gentleman, she answered that she should never marry again. She was* moult soubtille et sage *and repeated this to the Prince several times. The Prince replied, "Heigh ho! Belle Cousine, in case you do not wish to marry any of my friends, the great beauties, of which you are compact, will be wasted. If you and I were not of common kin, there is no lady under*

heaven whom I should hold so dear as you." And the Prince was taken unawares by love for the Countess. And then, like the subtle woman, and skillful in ambush, that she was, the Countess began to cry.

Then the Prince tried to comfort her; he kissed her very often, and felt great tenderness for her tears, and said to her: "Belle Cousine, I have a message for you from one of the gallant gentlemen of England, and he is besides a very charming man." The Countess answered, still weeping: "Ah, Sire, for God's sake forbear to speak of such things to me. I have made up my mind not to marry again; for I have given my heart to the most gallant gentleman under the firmament, and for love of him, I shall have no husband but God, so long as I live. It is impossible that I should marry him. So, for love of him, I wish to shun the company of men. I am resolved never to marry."

The Prince was very desirous to know who was the most gallant gentleman in the world, and begged the Countess insistently to tell him who it was. But the Countess the more she saw his eagerness, the more she besought him not to inquire further; and, falling on her knees, said to him: "My very dear Lord, for God's sake, and for His mother's, the sweet Virgin, please forbear." The Prince answered that, if she did not tell him who was the most gallant gentleman in the world, he would be her deadly enemy. Then the Lady said to him: "Very dear and redoubtable Lord, it is you, and for love of you no gentleman shall lie beside me." The Prince, who was then all on fire with love for her, said: "Lady, I swear to God, that as long as I live, no other woman shall be my wife." And soon they were betrothed.

A less colorful, and probably less embroidered version of the story is given in the *Life of the Black Prince* written by Chandos Herald:

The prince, very soon after this [the Treaty of Bretigny in 1360], *married a lady of great worth, with whom he had fallen in love, who was beautiful, pleasing and wise. He did not wait long after his marriage before going to Gascony to take possession of his lands. The prince took his wife with him, whom he loved greatly.*

Because the two were closely related, they needed to receive a dispensation from the pope allowing the marriage. They had no trouble obtaining it. The historian Richard Barber writes: *"Innocent VI, like all the Avignon popes, favoured the French cause, and the prince's proposed marriage eliminated an important diplomatic weapon for the English."* The French wanted nothing better than to see Edward III's son make a politically useless marriage.

But although an alliance with Joan offered no political advantage, the prince never appeared to regret his choice. Seven years later, the romance was still alive, as evidenced by a letter written to Joan after the Battle of Najera. The prince's salutation reads: *"My dearest and truest sweetheart and beloved companion."*

Although sickness and time would harden the prince's character, making him capable of committing the massacre at Limoges in 1370, we never hear of anything but felicity betwixt him and Joan. Together Edward and Joan had two sons, the youngest of whom would become Richard II of England.

Edward died in 1376 at the age of 45. He had instructed that his body be laid to rest in the crypt of Canterbury Cathedral, in the Chapel of Our Lady, with a space nearby for his dear wife. He even had carvings of her face added to the ceiling there. The crypt, however, was not deemed worthy enough, and so his body was moved upstairs to be placed by the shrine of the famous Saint Thomas Becket. Joan lived nine years longer to see the accession of her son to the throne, the rise of the Lollards, and the Peasants' Revolt. When she died, her body was laid to rest in Lincolnshire beside the tomb of Thomas Holland, her first husband. And so, despite the prince's dearest wishes, in the end he and his "beloved companion" were separated.

As wife to Edward, the Black Prince, Joan became history's first English Princess of Wales. But there was more to remember about Joan than just her title. She was, in the words of the chronicler Froissart, "*la plus belle de tout le royaume d'Engleterre et la plus amoureuse*—the most beautiful woman in all the realm of England, and the most loving." Or to use Henry Dwight Sedgwick's translation: "*the prettiest girl and greatest coquette in England.*"

SOURCES

Barber, Richard. *Edward, Prince of Wales and Aquitaine: A Biography of the Black Prince*. Great Britain: The Boydell Press, 1978.

_____, trans. and ed. *The Life and Campaigns of the Black Prince: from contemporary letters, diaries and chronicles, including Chandos Herald's Life of the Black Prince*. Great Britain: The Boydell Press, 1979.

Froissart, Jean. *Chronicles*. Translated and edited by Geoffrey Brereton. London: Penguin Books, 1978.

Sedgwick, Henry Dwight. *The Black Prince*. New York: Barnes and Noble Books, 1993.

ALICE PERRERS: A NOTORIOUS WOMAN

BY ANNE O'BRIEN

ALICE PERRERS, MISTRESS OF KING EDWARD III AT THE SAME TIME AS SHE WAS A DAMSEL (lady-in-waiting) to Queen Philippa, has had an astonishingly bad press. Her reputation is black with no redeeming features. *"There was...in England a shameless woman and wanton harlot called Ales Peres, of base kindred...being neither beautiful or fair, she knew how to cover these defects with her flattering tongue...."*

Modern historians have been hardly less damning than her contemporaries. Here she is, in all her notoriety, as seen in the fourteenth century:

1) ALICE THE LOWBORN USURPER OF ROYAL POWER

Did Alice know her place in society, or did she step outrageously beyond it? As far as we know, Alice had neither breeding nor wealth nor significant family connections, but was she the reputed bastard of a labourer and tavern whore? Perhaps not.

Recent evidence suggests that she may have had a brother with whom she did business, and that she engaged in a brief marriage to Janyn Perres, a Lombardy merchant and moneylender, during which she made her first purchase of property. She could read and write and figure. Somewhere she learned this—if not with her invisible family, then in a convent. And royal mistress to Edward III? Alice would not be the first lowborn woman to share a King's bed, nor the last.

We do not know how she came to the attention of Queen Philippa but it is unlikely that she would have done so if she had been born in the filth of the gutter. Perhaps Alice does not deserve her notoriety based on her stepping beyond her birth.

2) ALICE THE UNATTRACTIVE WOMAN

Alice was not merely a plain woman but "famously ugly". How could an ugly woman rise to such pre-eminence? Using supernatural powers—she was accused of witchcraft—she gained a foothold in the Queen's household and lured the unsuspecting King into a sexual liaison from which she never allowed him to escape.

Much can be forgiven a beautiful woman but not an ill favoured one. Alice was reputed to be the inspiration for Chaucer's Wife of Bath. He gave her a bold face, a gap-toothed smile, broad hips, a wide hat, and red stockings. I'm sure he enjoyed writing this description, but is it true? He also gave her five "legitimate" husbands. It may be that Chaucer's physical description of Alice/the Wife is as scurrilous as the rest of it.

Alice was said to be graceful and possess a pleasing, seductive voice. Certainly she had enough attractions to please the King. Could it be that she was dark rather than fair, the fashionable trend for the day? Perhaps she did not have mere beauty but rather a lively, striking countenance. How unfortunate that there are no representations of this famously ugly woman. We might decide that she was not ugly at all.

3) ALICE THE RAPACIOUS ROYAL MISTRESS

Alice beguiled and manipulated King Edward until he neglected his wife and his country. Because she seduced him while Philippa was still alive, Alice was the cause of King Edward committing the sin of adultery. So great was her power over the King that he could refuse her nothing. So corrupt were her morals that she entered into a clandestine marriage with William de Windsor without Edward's knowledge.

It is true that Alice became Edward's mistress during the lifetime of the much loved Queen Philippa, and for this she was condemned. How interesting that on such occasions (even in modern royal scandals) the blame is placed very firmly on the shoulder of the non-royal woman involved. Edward was not to blame: it was Alice who seduced the King! Hard to believe that Edward, a true Plantagenet, had no part in this sexual chemistry, even in his later years.

How did Philippa react to her damsel sleeping with her husband? Certainly she must have known, yet she made no move to dismiss her. Interestingly, during Philippa's lifetime, the scandal was kept under wraps at court as if there was a conspiracy of silence to protect the Queen from humiliation. It was only on her death that Alice's position was widely acclaimed. Despite the liaison between Edward and Alice, there is no evidence that the King neglected his wife. To the contrary, when Philippa died, Edward was heart-broken. It was a very strange ménage-a-trois. I regret that we know so little about it—but it is a gem for a writer of historical fiction.

4) ALICE THE GREEDY EMBEZZLER OF WEALTH

It is impossible to deny Alice's desire for wealth. Alice dipped her hands into the royal treasury at the same time as she amassed jewels worth more than £200,000. After Queen Philippa's death, Alice demanded that Edward give the Queen's jewels, placed by Philippa into the keeping of her senior lady-in-waiting, to her as a gift. Alice wore them ostentatiously as if she were queen, flaunting her power. At the same time, together with Windsor, her new husband, an equally unprincipled courtier, she was embezzling funds set aside by the King to deal with the uprisings in Ireland.

And the most heinous crime of all? When Edward lay on his death bed, Alice stripped the rings from his fingers. All difficult to defend? So it would seem, and Alice was without doubt guilty of a degree of embezzlement, but as a writer of historical fiction I have allowed Alice to give her own reasons. Read *The King's Concubine* to discover more.

5) ALICE THE GRASPING LAND-GRABBER

Alice persuaded Edward to give her land. So successful was she that she controlled 56 manors, castles, and town houses stretching over 25 counties of England.

Perhaps surprisingly, out of the 56 manors in her possession, only 15 came from royal grants. All the rest—45 of them—were gained by her own initiative and efforts, and most of them in prime locations in the counties surrounding London.

Alice made use of her clerk William Greseley and a group of male business associates to acquire and manage the manors for her. Sometimes she made the purchases herself, showing a knowledge of business and the law. When she came under legal attack from men whose toes she trod on, Alice sat in court, next to the judge, to ensure that he considered her interests first and foremost. (What a wonderful scene this would make!) If a man had shown such acumen, he might have been accused of gross self-interest, but he might equally have been admired for his achievements. He would not have been denigrated to the extent that Alice was.

6) ALICE THE ARCH-MANIPULATOR OF THE KING AND QUEEN

The government of England in the final years of Edward's life when he was at his most vulnerable fell into the hands of Alice, in alliance with John of Gaunt, Edward's son, and a group of royal ministers appointed by her and loyal to her. Edward was unable to prevent her from usurping royal power that was not hers to take. This cannot be argued against.

It was said of her by Thomas Walsingham, a monk at St. Albans: "*no one dared go against her*". And no one did, until Edward became too weak to protect her. When the Good Parliament in 1376 finally set its sights on Alice, intent on dismissing her from court, stripping away all her property and jewels, and even banishing her from the country, we are left with the impression that she deserved everything she got.

One thing that should be mentioned, however, is that in these years Edward suffered from increasing dementia. Perhaps it was Alice's duty, as she saw it, to save the King from humiliation in the sight of his subjects. She created a façade to protect him. There is no evidence that she had any influence on the direction of royal policy during these years.

7) SO WHAT AND WHO IS THE REAL ALICE PERRERS?

Alice was neither bad nor good. Certainly she was no angel. She was opportunistic and seized every opportunity that came her way to feather her nest against the bad times. But Alice was a realist. She was a survivor. She was aware, first and foremost, that when Edward died, she would be alone and vulnerable to attack. She must prepare for an uncertain future, both for herself and her four children. And this is what she did, acquiring land as a very permanent form of wealth. Perhaps this explains Alice's less-than-wise clandestine marriage to William de Windsor. When Edward was sinking into dementia, as he was in 1373, she saw in Windsor some security for her future.

Alice was smart and clever and a formidable opponent. Intelligent and ruthless, she set out to make her way in life, and much of what she did would have been forgiven if she had been a man. If a man had acquired her wealth and standing with the King, he would have been entitled to high praise and an earldom, a degree of respect if not outright popularity. Alice, as a woman, was condemned as a mercenary and immoral swindler.

Alice struggled constantly against her lack of connection, making her way in the world in one of the few ways open to women without family or influence. I believe that she deserves some admiration for her strength of character under adversity. She was even accused of witchcraft in her seduction of the King—always a useful weapon to use against a powerful woman.

We never hear Alice's voice raised in her own defence. I hope in some small way in *The King's Concubine* I have given her back her voice and a measure of respect.

EDWARD, 2ND DUKE OF YORK

BY BRIAN WAINWRIGHT

Edward was born sometime in 1373, the eldest child of Edmund of Langley, Earl of Cambridge, fourth surviving son of King Edward III, and his wife Isabella of Castile. Edmund was by some way the least rich of his brothers, of whom he was the only one *not* to marry an heiress.

Isabella was the younger sister of Constance of Castile, who had married Edmund's brother, John of Gaunt, Duke of Lancaster, as his second wife. Constance claimed to be the rightful heiress to the throne of Castile, a claim which her husband was to pursue, unsuccessfully, over the next few years.

Edmund and Isabella were merely pawns in this game and were in fact required to renounce any rights in Castile. It was a very poor deal for the Earl of Cambridge, but he seems to have been an amiable cove without the excessive and distasteful ambition of most of his family.

Edmund and Isabella's son Edward is sometimes known to historians as "Edward of Norwich" although there is no evidence he was born there or had any connection with it. As his father was created Duke of York in 1385, it is more appropriate to refer to him as Edward of York. He was knighted at the coronation of his first cousin, King Richard II, when only four years old.

It was not long before young Edward became involved in English diplomatic manoeuvres. In 1381, he was taken by his parents to Portugal, Edmund having been placed at the head of an English expeditionary force which was intended, with the aid of Portuguese allies, to attack Castile. Edward was "married" to the Princess Beatriz of Portugal, and if his father had not made such a mess of the expedition Edward might eventually have become King of Portugal, because Beatriz was her father's heiress.

Instead, with Edmund's army in a state of near-mutiny, her father had second thoughts and married her to the son of his enemy, the King of Castile. He also paid to send Edmund of Langley, his wife, son, and attendant unruly army back home.

Back in England, the York family was to receive increasing favour from Richard II, not least because they were loyal to a fault and gave him far less trouble than his other relatives. Edward was created a Knight of the Garter in 1387 (just when Richard was starting to have serious political difficulties) and was then made Earl of Rutland in 1390 (once Richard was back in full control of his affairs).

By late 1391 he was also Lord Admiral of England, one of the great offices of state, despite the fact that he was not yet of full age. As the 1390s progressed, Edward of York gradually acquired more offices and more gifts of land, and despite his relative youth was clearly one of Richard II's most favoured advisers, being chosen to represent the King on a number of key diplomatic missions abroad, including those to negotiate Richard's marriage to the (very) young French princess Isabella of Valois. He accompanied the King on the successful military expedition to Ireland in 1394, and enjoyed an independent command during operations against Richard's Irish enemies.

Edward was one of those selected to "appeal" the Duke of Gloucester and the earls of Warwick and Arundel in the Parliament of 1397—in other words publicly to accuse them of treason. This process led to the deaths of Gloucester (uncle to the King and to Edward) and Arundel, and the imprisonment of Warwick.

All their lands and offices were forfeited and Edward received a handsome share of the proceeds. Not least of his rewards was to be made Lord High Constable of England in succession to Gloucester. He was also created Duke of Aumale.

Gloucester seems to have been murdered (or privately executed, if you prefer) at Calais, and it was later alleged that Edward sent one of his squires across the Channel to see to it that the deed was done.

A few months later, Edward's cousin, Henry Bolingbroke, the son and heir of John of Gaunt, Duke of Lancaster, accused Thomas Mowbray, Duke of Norfolk of treasonable words. Both these men had sided against Richard in 1387-1388 and with him in 1397. It seems likely that despite fresh honours (dukedoms) laid upon them they were both worried that Richard might at some point take revenge against them for their earlier actions.

Edward was one of those who stood surety for his cousin, Bolingbroke.

Since the quarrel could not be resolved by normal legal processes, because of a lack of witnesses, it was eventually referred for trial by mortal combat. Edward, in his role as Lord High Constable, presided over the trial, but as is well known, the King decided to stop it before it came to blows, and instead banished both men.

Before this event Edward had made what was (for a man in his position) a most unusual marriage. Given that he was at the peak of his political power, and had lately been suggested as a husband for another very young French princess, the most likely explanation for his choice is that he fell in love.

His bride, Philippa Mohun, was at least ten years his senior and had already been widowed twice. She had only a life-interest in modest dower lands and no history of successful childbearing. As it happens, she was destined not to give Edward children either. The matter of children apart, some may see a congruence with the decision of Edward's great-nephew, Edward IV, to marry Elizabeth Woodville.

When John of Gaunt died in 1399, Richard decided to extend the term of Henry Bolingbroke's exile to life and took the Lancastrian inheritance into his own hands. Although many nobles, including Edward and his father, received custody of elements of the Lancastrian estates, there is no evidence that Richard intended the confiscation to be permanent. He continued to send his exiled cousin handsome sums of cash for his maintenance, apparently unaware that Henry (currently based in France) was planning to invade England.

On the other hand, Ian Mortimer, in *The Fears of Henry IV,* sets out the theory that Richard II intended to exclude the Mortimers and the Lancastrians from the succession, and appoint Edward of York as his heir. There is some evidence to support this, quite apart from the strange fact that Richard referred to Edward in his grants as "the King's brother" and not, as was correct, "the King's kinsman."

Anyway, such was the King's confidence in his security that he now undertook a second expedition to Ireland. Edward of York, having been given certain tasks on the Scottish March, was late to join this expedition, and it has been suggested (particularly in the French chronicles) that he was already plotting against the King. This seems unlikely.

Edward's father, Edmund of Langley, Duke of York, was left in charge as Keeper of England, and when Henry landed in Yorkshire, Langley's attempts at resistance were feeble. It is true that many of the nobility, and perhaps even York himself, sympathised with Henry and were reluctant to fight him.

York's forces eventually capitulated at Berkeley Castle, in Gloucestershire, with scarcely a blow struck. (The Bishop of Norwich, Henry Despenser, was among those who *did* fight, but they had no chance against the formidable force Henry had gathered.)

Meanwhile, Richard had landed in Wales. He made no urgent effort to advance and seems to have waited for news. When it reached him, it was to the effect that York had gone over to his rebellious cousin. The King seems to have been struck by panic and misled by rumours of plotting. He abandoned his army and made his way to North Wales at the head of a small, picked band of followers. Edward was one of those left behind, doubtless because of his father's surrender.

Edward promptly made his way eastward and submitted to Henry in his turn. As a result, when King Richard was eventually run to earth at Flint Castle, Edward was in the victorious Henry's company. Nevertheless, he immediately lost several of his most important offices, including that of Lord Constable, and it must have been clear to him that he did not enjoy Henry's trust.

A Royal Love Story: Richard II and Anne of Bohemia

by ANITA DAVISON

WHEN AQUITAINE BELONGED TO ENGLAND, RICHARD WAS BORN IN BORDEAUX, BECOMING King Richard II as a child of ten. He was the son of the Black Prince and Joan of Kent. William Shakespeare portrayed him as a cruel, vindictive, and irresponsible king who leaned toward madness. However, many more enlightened historians believe he suffered from a personality disorder, even schizophrenia.

Richard was a patron of Chaucer and a cultured man who loved beauty, described by a contemporary thus:

> King Richard was of the common stature, his hair yellowish, his face fair and rosy, rather round than long, and sometimes flushed; He was prodigal in his gifts, extravagantly splendid in his entertainment and dress, timid as to war, very passionate toward his domestics, haughty and too much devoted to voluptousness...yet there were many laudable features in his character: he loved religion and the clergy, he encouraged architecture, he built the church of Westminster almost entirely, and left much property by his will to finish what he had begun.

Richard did have principles; he did not condone Christians killing Christians and sought a way to end the Hundred Years' War with France, not least because it was turning against the English.

Michael de la Pole, a favourite of Richard's, arranged his marriage with Anne of Bohemia (Czechoslovakia), the eldest daughter of the Emperor Charles IV by his fourth wife, Elizabeth of Pomerania.

The union was unpopular, for not only was Anne poor and therefore brought no dowry, her brother, Wenzel of Bohemia also demanded 20,000 florins (around four million pounds in today's money) for her.

Her arrival in England was postponed by the Peasants' Revolt, when, under the leadership of Wat Tyler, John Ball, and Jack Straw, the populace gathered at Blackheath in London to air their grievances and demand the end of serfdom. Tyler's followers sacked the Tower of London and murdered the archbishop of Canterbury, burning John of Gaunt's Savoy Palace to the ground.

The fourteen-year-old King Richard rode out to meet the rebels at Mile End, and his apparent courage in facing the mob contributed to the failure of the revolt, although Richard's magnanimous offer of mercy for the leaders was rescinded later by his council.

Anne was sixteen when she left Bohemia for England in December 1381, accompanied by a large train of attendants under the charge of the Duke of Saxony and his wife. Described as a Godly, intelligent young girl with an inquiring mind, Anne was renowned for her love of reading and her command of the Scriptures in three languages, an unusual skill for a woman, even a noble one.

Anne was received by the Duke and Duchess of Brabant, Anne's aunt and uncle, in Brussels, from whence she was to proceed to Calais by water, thus avoiding travelling through French-held lands. Here they heard that the King of France had sent twelve armed vessels of Normans to intercept her. After a month's delay and negotiations in Paris, the French king yielded to the Duke of Saxony's request, *"out of kindness to his cousin Anne, but not out of regard to the King of England."*

Anne reached Dover on the nineteenth of December, and had only just landed when a heavy ground swell caused the ships to collide, and the ship in which she had sailed broke up. The destruction of her fleet was deemed a disastrous omen.

In Canterbury, Anne was received by Richard's uncle, Thomas, Duke of Gloucester, with a large retinue, then at Blackheath by the lord-mayor of London, the scene of the Peasants' Revolt the previous year.

In London, the bride was welcomed by young girls at the top of a castle and tower throwing a shower of golden snow, with fountains at the sides flowing with wine and pages offering the princess wine from golden cups.

The royal couple married in Westminster chapel in January 1382. King Richard, a year younger than his bride, appeared delighted with Anne, and after a week spent with her and the court in festivities and celebrations, they left for Windsor by barge, accompanied by Richard's mother, Joan of Kent.

The aftermath of the Peasants' Revolt was still evident, and the culprits were still being sought out for punishment. Their conditions distressed the young queen, who begged the king to grant a general pardon on the occasion of her coronation, which he allowed.

Anne became a peace-maker, interceding for those who offended the king as she travelled all over the country with him, some reports saying that on several occasions she prostrated herself before him in the great hall to plead for those he would punish.

In the fourteenth century, women rode astride, or pillion (i.e. seated sideways on a cushion behind the male rider's saddle). Anne was reputed to have introduced sidesaddles, a seat made of wood strapped to the horse's back with a pommel for a hand grip. A wooden plank, wide enough for both feet hung along the left side of the animal. This method of riding was considered necessary for high-born women to preserve their hymen and thus ensure their purity.

Anne also introduced new fashions into England, including the long-pointed shoes called Cracows (from Cracow, in Poland), which her attendants apparently wore, and horned caps for ladies, often two feet high, and just as wide, arranged on a frame of wire and pasteboard, covered with muslin or gauze. Anne was also reputed to have brought pins into England, as gowns in those days were fastened with tiny skewers made of wood or ivory.

Because of Richard's high-handed behaviour as an adolescent and the extravagance of his household, he was forced to accept a controlling council. Tired after years of their control, he asked his uncle, Gloucester, at the council table to tell him how old he was. When the duke replied that he was twenty-two, Richard declared: *"Then I must be able to manage my own affairs as every heir in my kingdom can do at twenty-one."*

In celebration of having received the great seal and the keys of the exchequer, he arranged a round of celebrations which rivalled his coronation. At a tournament at Smithfield, Anne presented the prizes, which consisted of a richly jewelled clasp and a crown of gold. The tournament was followed by a banquet at the palace of the Bishop of London, with music and dancing, jugglers and acrobats which continued into the night.

Richard kept many establishments in palaces round the country and enjoyed living well, which was yet another characteristic that enraged his impoverished subjects. His entertainments and banquets were magnificent, and three hundred scullions worked in his kitchens.

Anne did not bear the king any children, but this did not appear to affect his devotion to her. Nor did the king take other mistresses as it appears he did not father any illegitimates children either.

In 1394, when Richard was preparing for an expedition into Ireland to quell a rebellion, the queen fell ill at Shene Manor, purportedly of the plague. The king rushed to her side and was with her when she died. Inconsolable at the loss of his beloved wife, Richard ordered Shene to be partially dismantled. He never occupied it again.

Richard summoned all the nobles and barons of England to an extravagant funeral that took two months to prepare, and instructed them to arrive the day before and escort the body from Shene to Westminster Abbey.

A long procession escorted the queen, accompanied by a large number of torch-bearers—so many that wax had to be imported from Flanders expressly for the purpose. Anne was buried in the Confessor's chapel behind the high altar in Westminster Abbey, where Richard had ordered a double tomb made for them both.

The Earl of Arundel absented himself from the procession, arrived late at the abbey, and then requested permission to leave early on urgent business. Richard was deeply offended and appears to have drawn his sword and struck him. He ordered the presumably injured earl to the Tower and kept him there for a week. For a year after Anne's death, the grief-stricken king refused to go into any room she'd been in.

Coppersmiths crafted effigies of gilded copper and latten in a canopy above the crowned figures of Richard and Anne, their right hands joined and their left hands holding sceptres.

Anne's epitaph mentions her as having been kind to "pregnant women". The Evesham chronicler said, "*this queen, although she did not bear children, was still held to have contributed to the glory and wealth of the realm, as far as she was able*". She was referred to as "Good Queen Anne". Her tomb bears this inscription in Latin.

> *Under this stone lies Anne, here entombed,*
> *Wedded in this world's life to the second Richard.*
> *To Christ were her meek virtues devoted:*
> *His poor she freely fed from her treasures;*
> *Strife she assuaged, and swelling feuds appeased;*
> *Beauteous her form, her face surpassing fair.*
> *On July's seventh day, thirteen hundred ninety-four,*

All comfort was bereft, for through irremediable sickness
She passed away into interminable joys.

Queen Anne's tomb was opened in 1871, when many of her bones were found to have been stolen via a hole in the side of the casket.

The rest of Richard's life wasn't exactly happy. Richard's authoritarian approach and his increasing dependence on his favourites provoked resentment. A group of lords headed by his uncle, Gloucester, executed many of Richard's favourites and forced him to renew his coronation oath.

In the interests of state, he married the six-year-old Isabella of Valois two years after his wife's death, though he became openly fond of her. He persisted in calling himself king of France and refused to give up Calais; thus, the last two years of his reign were a period of tyranny with the government levying forced loans, carrying out arbitrary arrests, and murdering his rivals.

John of Gaunt died in February 1399, and Richard seized his vast Lancastrian estates, which would have passed to John's son, Henry Bolingbroke. In May, Richard left to campaign in Ireland, and in his absence Bolingbroke invaded England with support of the barons. When Richard returned that summer, he was captured. Forced to abdicate, he was imprisoned in Pontefract Castle, where he died, allegedly starving to death. Bolingbroke, Richard's cousin, assumed the throne as Henry IV.

Isabella grieved for Richard deeply, remaining in England while Henry IV quibbled about returning both her and her £83,000 dowry. She returned to France where she married Charles of Angouleme (later Duke of Orléans), but died in childbirth at the age of nineteen.

RICHARD II AND HIS DOUBLES

BY BRIAN WAINWRIGHT

THE "OFFICIAL" VERSION OF RICHARD II'S DEATH IS STRAIGHTFORWARD. AFTER HIS DEPOSI-tion in the autumn of 1399 in favour of his cousin Bolingbroke (Henry IV) he was impris-oned in Pontefract Castle. Following a rebellion of his supporters against his successor in early January 1400, he was starved to death. The date of death is usually given as 14 February 1400.

His body was subsequently taken by stages to London, being publicly exhibited (as was the tradition for deposed, dead kings in England), culminating in a final display in St. Paul's Cathe-dral prior to a relatively obscure burial at King's Langley, Hertfordshire. However, rumours per-sisted that he was still alive, and the promise of his return was often, if not invariably, attached to the various conspiracies of Henry IV's reign.

Although Richard's body was put on display, only part of his face was actually visible and he was presented on a high catafalque. This may have led to some suspicion that his corpse had been substituted as it would have been impossible for anyone to study the King's features with any degree of thoroughness.

Richard II had a known "double"—his clerk, Richard Maudelyn, supposedly the son of no less a person than Hawise Maudelyn, sometime waiting woman to Katherine Roet-Swynford, mistress and later third wife of John of Gaunt, Duke of Lancaster, the eldest of Richard's sur-viving uncles and father of Henry Bolingbroke. The family resemblance suggests that Richard Maudelyn's father may well have been John of Gaunt or one of the other royal uncles, and it is reasonable to assume that Maudelyn was at least a cousin to Richard II and maybe rather closer in blood to Henry IV.

Maudelyn was used by the January 1400 conspirators to impersonate Richard II in the hope of drawing out support. This suggests the resemblance was at least strong enough to deceive country gentlemen and the like, if not people who knew Richard really well.

Maudelyn was captured and executed by the usual means of hanging, drawing, and quar-tering. It seems unlikely his body could have been used as a substitute for Richard's unless this was decided upon immediately and his remains embalmed. One might expect the bones of Maudelyn to be severely damaged by his violent execution, but when Richard II's (presumed) remains were examined in the 19th Century no such evidence was found. It seems certain that whoever was buried in the official tomb, it could not have been Maudelyn.

The "Scottish Richard II" was found wandering about on the island of Islay, of all places. He was "recognized" by a woman who claimed she had seen the King while visiting Ireland the previous year and, following this incident, was conveyed to the Scottish Court, where he was treated as an honoured guest for the rest of his life.

Islay is a small and relatively remote island off the west coast of Scotland, nowadays best known for the production of the incomparable *Laphroaig* whisky. Assuming Richard escaped from Pontefract, is it likely that he would make his way to such an obscure place? Surprisingly, the answer is—yes, he might.

Richard saw himself primarily as emperor of the British Isles, and his complex diplomacy in the 1390s had as one of its principal objectives the detachment of Scotland from the Franco-Scottish alliance and its subordination to England. This proved impossible because of the attitude of the French, and the Scots were included in the 28-year truce concluded in the autumn of 1396.

However, as part of his diplomacy, Richard had secured an alliance with the semi-independent Lord of the Isles, valuable in strategic terms for both his Scottish and Irish pretensions. (Since the Lord of the Isles came close to breaking the Scottish Crown's forces at Harlaw, 1411, it seems likely that the combination of his forces with those of England would have been formidable in this context.)

Therefore, Richard had some reason to expect help in the Western Isles. That the supposed imposter should turn up on Islay may well be significant.

The Grey Friars in England were persistent in spreading the rumour that Richard II was alive, and several were executed for their trouble. Several nobles received letters from "Richard II" bearing one of his authentic seals, which had somehow found its way to Scotland.

In 1403 the Percys—in effective alliance with the Scots—rose in rebellion against King Henry and promised the men of Cheshire that Richard would appear at their rendezvous at Sandiway, Cheshire. Needless to say, he did not, and the Percys were defeated, but the rumours of his survival went on.

Bolingbroke claimed that the "Scottish Richard II" was one Thomas Warde of Trumpington, Cambridgeshire, and continued to execute those foolish enough to spread the word that Richard was alive. (It is not explained how Thomas Warde came to be on Islay.)

As late as 1415, the Southampton Conspirators were still talking of bringing back "Richard II" from Scotland while in December 1417 Sir John Oldcastle, Lord Cobham, refused to recognise the authority of his judges *so long as his liege lord King Richard was alive in Scotland.* It may be that one of the motives for Henry V's reburial of the official corpse of Richard II at Westminster was a desire to squash the belief that his father's predecessor on the throne was still living.

Thomas Warde was a real person. His few acres of land in Trumpington were forfeited in 1408. However, the evidence to prove he was the same individual as the "Scottish Richard II" no longer exists, supposing that it ever did.

It appears the man responsible for many, if not all, of the rumours of Richard II's survival was William Serle who had been a minor member of Richard's household. When captured, he admitted he had stolen Richard's seal at Flint (where the King had fallen into Bolingbroke's hands) and forged a number of letters. Of course, it should be borne in mind this admission may well have been extracted by torture and is not necessarily reliable. Bolingbroke was sometimes generous to high-born traitors, but for those of lower birth he had no mercy at all. Serle was half-hanged in a number of towns before his ultimate execution.

When the "Scottish Richard II" died at Stirling in 1419, he was buried with full honours close to the High Altar of the Blackfriars. Whether he was the "real Richard" we shall probably never know, but it remains a fascinating possibility.

An All-Consuming Passion: The Love Affair that Changed the Course of English History

BY **ANNE O'BRIEN**

OWEN TUDOR AND KATHERINE DE VALOIS

He was a servant. She was the Queen-Dowager of England. He was a dispossessed Welshman. She had royal Valois blood in her veins and was the widow of England's glorious hero of Agincourt, King Henry V. She was the King's Mother; he was the Keeper of the Queen's Wardrobe.

Such a liaison would be unthinkable, and yet they fell victim to a passionate romance.

A WINDSOR ROMANCE

It all happened at Windsor since Katherine was bound by law to live in her son's household after her politically disastrous near-marriage to Edmund Beaufort. She was considered to be a woman "*unable fully to curb her carnal passions*" and so she must live a carefully controlled life.

So how did Katherine and Owen manage to fall in love? The record of the occasion of the romance has been described as "*a pot pourri of myth, romanticism, tradition and anti-Tudor propaganda.*" It is certainly a gift to writers of historical fiction—although it brings its own problems.

A MIXED BAG OF HISTORICAL TRADITION

One strong tradition, written in a poem in 1361 at the time of Owen's death, was that he first caught Katherine's attention when he over-balanced and fell into her lap at a Court ball. Too much alcohol? Or clumsy dancing? Impossible to tell.

A mid-16th century chronicler tells a quite different story. Katherine saw Owen and his friends swimming in the river on a summer's day. Overcome by his sheer masculinity, Katherine changed garments with her maid and arranged to meet Owen in disguise. He was too ardent, she struggled and, escaping his embrace, received a wound to her cheek.

Serving her at supper that night, Owen saw the bruise and realised who the "maidservant" had been. Ashamed, he begged her forgiveness. Katherine forgave him readily, they professed their love and were duly married.

Sadly, there is no historical proof for either version. But what vivid scenes these sources paint for us. The difficulty for a novelist is of course producing something half-way realistic. If Owen was Katherine's personal servant, how could he not recognise her face, her voice, even in disguise? Unless she was mute and they met in a dark cupboard, it would seem impossible. As for the drunken mishap...it makes writing a credible version highly entertaining.

A PRIVATE MARRIAGE

Whatever the truth of their meeting, their love was strong enough to encourage the unlikely pair to flout the law of the land. Katherine was forbidden to marry without the permission of the King who was not yet ten years old. Any man foolish enough to wed her without permission would find all his lands and possessions declared forfeit. Here Katherine was fortunate for Owen had no assets to lose. Penal statutes against the Welsh after Owen Glendywr's rising in the reign of Henry IV dispossessed many, as well as prohibiting them from carrying arms, meeting in gatherings, owning land east of the ancient border of Offa's Dyke, and holding government office. When Owen married Katherine, he had nothing to forfeit.

The clandestine affair was no secret at Court—Katherine had no compunction in taking the law into her own hands and challenging the Council to do its worst. She would be wed and be damned to them! Perhaps this suggests that Katherine was not the mindless beauty that she has sometimes been described as, but a woman of considerable audacity and courage. The marriage was conducted privately, and the happy couple left Windsor to live out the years of their marriage quietly in Katherine's dower properties.

A RIGHT ROYAL REVENGE

It was obviously not a popular marriage but Owen was untouchable during Katherine's lifetime. If the Royal Council took action against them, it would simply create a scandal around the Queen-Dowager which they were keen to avoid. Owen was actually given letters of denizenship to allow him English rights before the law. But Humphrey, Duke of Gloucester, uncle to the young king and brother to Henry V, never forgave Owen for his presumption in marrying the Queen and simply bided his time.

As soon as Katherine was dead in 1431, Gloucester set out for revenge. It became a cat and mouse story, Gloucester intent on punishment, Owen equally intent on proclaiming his innocence. Gloucester summoned Owen to London to appear before the Royal Council under a safe conduct. Wisely, Owen sought sanctuary at Westminster. Although no action could be taken against him, for there was no evidence of any guilt of any crime, Owen was arrested and incarcerated in Newgate prison.

Managing to escape, he was recaptured and returned to Newgate before being transferred to Windsor in 1438 where he was kept under lock and key for at least a year before finally receiving a pardon for all offences. Gloucester had been thwarted.

Owen might have remained reconciled with the Lancastrian court but the Wars of the Roses put him once again in danger. After the battle of Mortimer's Cross, where his son Jasper's Lancastrian army was defeated by Edward, Earl of March, Owen was taken prisoner by the Yorkists.

THE END OF OWEN TUDOR

Owen was beheaded in Hereford. His head was placed on the base of the market cross in the

High Street, where it is said that "a madde woman" combed his hair and washed away the blood from his face, and then set 100 candles about his head.

Owen, because of his royal connections, did not expect to die. When he realised that this would be his fate, moments before his execution he is recorded as saying *"that head shall lye on the stock that was wont to lye on Queen Katherine's lap."*

A sad end. A stone marks the place of Owen's execution in Hereford High Street. It is hardly remarkable, and most shoppers walk over it without noticing that it is there.

Owen's body was taken to be buried in the chapel of the Greyfriars Church in Hereford. Unfortunately, Greyfriars suffered badly at the Dissolution, the building was demolished, and the land sold off for other purposes. There is no lasting trace of Owen Tudor today. The only record of the site of the Greyfriars is the name of the modern bridge over the River Wye and the blue plaque on the site of the old gate.

In the early 20th century, excavations were made where the church would have been, which discovered three skeletons, one of them a man of six feet three inches tall, but there was no evidence that they were the remains of Owen Tudor, once husband of the Queen of England. So all trace of Owen has vanished.

AND THE TUDORS

The circumstances of the astonishing marriage between Owen and Katherine is my primary interest since I have been engaged in writing a novel of Katherine de Valois in *The Forbidden Queen*, but for aficionados of the Tudors it is the descendants of this marriage who take all the attention. Their eldest son Edmund married Margaret Beaufort, the Beaufort heiress, who passed enough royal Plantagenet blood to their son to enable him to claim the crown of England as King Henry VII.

A bust of Henry VII based on his death mask can be seen in the Victoria & Albert Museum in London. We have no contemporary portrait of Owen Tudor. Did he look anything like his grandson? Would Katherine have fallen in love with this man?

Who knows?

BLOODY DEEDS AT TEWKESBURY

BY ANNE O'BRIEN

IN MAY OF 1471, THE LITTLE TOWN OF TEWKESBURY IN GLOUCESTERSHIRE—TODAY A peaceful place of half-timbered buildings, a magnificent Abbey, and lovely surroundings that make it a lure for visitors—witnessed a terrible battle.

It was a momentous victory for the Yorkists under King Edward IV and his brother Richard of Gloucester, played out over the water-meadows of Tewkesbury where the rivers Avon and Severn meet. The Lancastrian Army was attempting to cross the River Severn when King Edward ordered an attack. It was a devastating and final defeat for the Lancastrians with wholesale carnage on what is still known today as "Bloody Meadow."

The Lancastrians went into full scale retreat, many drowning when attempting to cross the river, many cut down as they ran. Lancastrian soldiers who sought refuge in the Abbey were hunted down and mercilessly hacked to death within the building itself. The Lancastrian leaders were dragged from the Abbey and summarily executed in the market place. It was a truly bloody event with over 2000 Lancastrians killed, the church and churchyard so polluted that King Edward had to arrange for its re-consecration by the Bishop of Worcester.

In the Abbey today a wooden door bears witness to the bloodbath: it is completely covered with plates of armour stripped from the dead and dying, perforated by gunshot and arrow holes.

One of those to meet his death at Tewkesbury was Prince Edward of Lancaster, son and heir of King Henry VI and Margaret of Anjou. But how did he die, and where exactly? There is considerable debate about it.

The Duke of Clarence, brother to Edward and Richard, recorded that the Prince "*had been slain in plain battle.*" Many contemporary writers also noted that he "*died in the field.*" The *Arrivall*, the official Yorkist account, recorded—as might be expected—that the Prince was "*taken fleeing to the townwards and slain in the field.*" There would appear to be no doubt that the Lancastrian Prince died in the fighting and there was no direct culpability on the part of King Edward and his brothers.

But was this so? The historian Croyland in 1486 after the death of King Edward and Richard III is more ambiguous, recording that the Prince died "*either on the field, or after the battle by the avenging hands of certain persons.*"

Tudor historians were also keen to implicate Richard of Gloucester. According to them, the Prince was taken during the rout and brought before King Edward when the battle was over. The King struck the Prince with his gauntlet in retaliation for an insolent remark, after which Clarence, Gloucester, and Hastings cut the Lancastrian heir down with their swords.

This might, of course, simply be a Tudor attempt to bloody Yorkist hands, but an illustrated French version of the *Arrivall*, perhaps dating to the actual year of the battle, shows a scene very like the one where the Prince was forced to face King Edward and was ultimately slain.

So perhaps there was more to Prince Edward's death than contemporary reports made clear. Certainly the Prince as a future Lancastrian King was too dangerous to be allowed to live. King Edward and the leading Yorkists might have seen it in their best interests not to leave the Prince's death to chance. Wherever Prince Edward was killed it was the death of the hopes of Lancaster to retrieve the Crown of England.

Legend says that the brutal confrontation and murder took place in the chancel of Tewkesbury Abbey. Today, the brass that marks the official place of the Prince's death in the chancel is a Victorian addition and thus cannot be used as proof of the site of the deed. It bears the words:

> *Here lies Edward prince of Wales,*
> *cruelly slain while a youth.*
> *Anno Domini 1471.*
> *Alas the savagery of men,*
> *Thou art the sole light of thy mother,*
> *the last hope of thy race.*

Whatever the truth of it, the Abbey is a place of wonderful atmosphere, and since ultimate proof is lacking, I make no excuse for choosing the Abbey as the scene of Prince Edward's death in *Virgin Widow*. It seemed very fitting that Prince Edward should, at the end, be forced to face the King he had tried to overthrow.

A Short—but Heartfelt— Valentine from the Fifteenth Century

by ANNE O'BRIEN

In the fifteenth century, England was torn apart by the Wars of the Roses. Between 1455 and 1485, four kings lost their crowns, more than forty nobles lost their lives, and thousands of those who fought on both sides met a violent death.

Meanwhile, in Norfolk, the members of the Paston family were writing letters. They were a family who rose rapidly up the social scale from Clement, being a *good plain husbandman* in 1378, to John III the King's *trusty and well-beloved knight,* invited by Henry VII to the marriage of his heir Arthur to Catherine of Aragon.

So what did this ordinary yet remarkable family write about? The conflict, of course, particularly their dispute with the Duke of Norfolk over the ownership of Caister Castle which ended in a full-blown siege. But they also wrote about politics, business, shopping, and love, chattering endlessly over the decades, one member of the family to another.

And one of these letters is believed to be the oldest Valentine.

For this we have to thank John Paston III and Margery Brews.

In 1476 John III was thirty-three years old and unmarried and was desperate enough for a wife to ask his brother to keep an eye out for "*an old thrifty alewife*" for him. Not the stuff of romance.

But early in 1477 he met Margery Brews, a girl probably in her late teens, daughter of a Norfolk knight. She was not an heiress, but the family was well thought of, and John fell passionately in love with her. And she with him.

The marriage seemed doomed to failure because of bitter disputes over the size of Margery's dowry—she had three sisters for whom her father must also provide—but their love held true. During their prolonged betrothal, Margery wrote to John, addressing him as her "*right well-beloved Valentine.*" She pleaded with him not to leave her because of the dowry difficulties.

> *If you love me, as I trust verily you do, you will not leave me therefore. My heart bids me ever more to love you, truly over all earthly thing.*

Then Margery added her initials in the shape of a heart.

They wed eventually and it seems lived happily ever after. They had three children. From their letters it would appear that their love lost none of its romance. Margery sometimes wrote to John as "*Right Reverend and Worshipful Sir*" but on other occasions as "*mine own sweetheart.*" Even when the letters were full of the detail of ordinary life and for the most part very decorous, the post script often was not.

Sir, I pray you, if you tarry long in London that it will please you to send for me for I think [it] *long since I lay in your arms.*

This is the John Paston who was invited to the royal wedding. Sadly, Margery did not live to enjoy the occasion for she had died in 1495.

Caister Castle, the fifteenth century moated manor house, took the family into war against the forces of the Duke of Norfolk. The Pastons were successful in keeping it in the family.

What a remarkable resource the Paston letters are to medieval historians, and what a miracle that so many of them have survived. Five hundred years on, the voices of this stalwart family still ring out loud and clear. And how good to know that love blossomed for John and Margery even in the years of upheaval and death.

Richard III vs. Henry VII: Naughty or Nice?

by JUDITH ARNOPP

I HAVE ALWAYS BEEN INTRIGUED BY THE MYSTERY OF THE PRINCES IN THE TOWER. Most people are aware that, on the sudden death of their father Edward IV, the two boys were ensconced in the Tower, as was tradition, to await the coronation of the eldest boy as Edward V. But, although preparations for his coronation were underway, it was suddenly claimed that Edward IV's marriage to Elizabeth Woodville had been bigamous and, therefore, all their children illegitimate.

Since illegitimacy barred the young Edward from the throne, his uncle, Richard III, was, by a statute known as the *Titulus Regius,* proclaimed as the rightful king and crowned in his stead.

After his coronation in 1483, accounts of the boys' whereabouts begin to dwindle from the historical record, and many believe they never left the Tower alive but were murdered there, suffocated in their sleep with a pillow.

Richard reigned until August 1485 when Henry Tudor landed at Milford Haven to claim the throne for himself.

After the Battle of Bosworth, Henry Tudor (and his subsequent heirs) did their best to damage Richard's reputation, and since that date it has been widely believed that Richard III was responsible for the boys' deaths. Thomas More was the first to blacken his name and William Shakespeare, also writing for a Tudor monarch, twisted Richard's character further. Consequently, many later histories are based on a literary play rather than on historical record, and historians now agree that many of the heinous crimes attributed to Richard were, in fact, committed by others.

Tudor propaganda ensured that the surviving accounts of the years surrounding Bosworth are murky to say the least. Early in his reign Henry Tudor ordered all copies of the *Titulus Regius* to be "utterly destroyed" for reasons which may, or may not, appear obvious. You have to dig deep to find unbiased accounts, but they do exist, and there are several other candidates that fit the "murderer" tag just as well as Richard.

Richard was crowned king in 1483 and would have been aware that his nephews provided a potential target for those wishing to supplant him. A prudent king would have removed them from the picture. Richard was by all accounts a religious man, and killing his nephews would have been sinful, even in those days. It would also be disloyal to his brother to whom Richard had been devoted in life.

The act would also be a Godsend to any enemy that wished to turn the kingdom against him and, therefore, foolish. Chronicles prove that Richard was neither imprudent, sinful, nor foolish. So why, when rumours of the death began circulating, did he not just produce the boys? A lot has been read into this, and it does seem to suggest that he could *not* produce them. But that doesn't necessarily mean they were already dead—they *could* have been sent out of harm's way.

Many believe Richard ordered that the boys be removed to safety, but there are now so many conflicting accounts and theories as to where they may have been moved to, that it is difficult to sift the good from the bad.

During Richard's reign there was a royal nursery at his castle at Sheriff Hutton where his brother George of Clarence's children, Margaret and Edward of Warwick, resided, along with Richard's legitimate son, also named Edward, and his two illegitimate children, John and Catherine. On Henry's accession to the throne, one of his first acts was to secure the persons of the children therein.

If the boys were found there then, when you consider Henry's treatment of other surviving Yorkists, their fate seems sealed. Richard's legitimate son Edward died of natural causes during his father's reign, but the other children were still living at the time of Bosworth.

Richard's illegitimate daughter Catherine was no longer surviving as early as Elizabeth of York's coronation in 1487, and her brother John's fate is less clear but records show that a *"base sone"* of Richard's was executed by Henry in 1491.

Clarence's children were also both executed by Tudors, Warwick was immediately incarcerated in the tower where he remained until accused of plotting with Perkin Warbeck. He was executed in 1499, an act made worse by the fact that the boy appears to have suffered from learning difficulties. His sister Margaret, Countess of Salisbury, managed to survive Henry VII's rule, but under Henry VIII, at the age of approximately sixty-eight, she was executed. But I digress. I will leave that story for another day.

True or not, I like the idea that the princes escaped, not least because of the wonderful array of "survival" theories that it has provoked. Such imaginings are a real gift to historical novelists whichever way they care to play it.

Henry Tudor's claim to the throne was tenuous to say the least, based upon his descent from Edward III, but through his mother's *illegitimate* Beaufort line. His title was Lancastrian and the House of Lancaster had long been regarded as usurpers and the direct line extinguished. He could never have won the victory nor ascended to the throne as heir of the House of Lancaster if his promise to marry Elizabeth of York, the daughter of Edward IV, had not won him the support of a few disaffected Yorkists.

It was imperative that Elizabeth's illegitimacy be reversed in order to bolster Henry's position, but in legitimising *her*, Henry also legitimised her brothers, thus placing them before himself in the line of succession. So, *if* the boys were still living at this time, they would have been much more of an obstruction to Henry than they ever were to Richard, who already legitimately held the position of king. This, in my view, provides a motive.

Of course, it's a big *if*. In my opinion, a study of the characters of Richard and Henry, make the latter more likely to resort to infanticide. Not that he would have wielded the axe himself, or in this particular case, the pillow.

Far from being the personification of evil as depicted by Shakespeare, Richard did have some qualities that Henry lacked. While Richard, having fought on numerous battlefields since his teens, was an undisputed warrior, Henry was not. At Bosworth he waited on the sidelines and let others do his dirty work for him.

While Richard's life is, with the exception of the puzzling execution of William Hastings, full of loyalty and honour, Henry's is not. If Richard had wanted the boys killed, he would probably have done the deed openly, or wielded the "pillow" himself. Underhanded infanticide does not seem to have been his style.

Henry's character was far more secretive and underhand. Henry never felt secure on his stolen throne. His court is famous for its intrigue and spies, and I believe his reign suffered more uprisings than any other. People just didn't like Henry, and it's easy to see why.

The first vengeance that Henry Tudor took as monarch was upon the body of the late King. After the battle, in an unprecedented act, the body of Richard III, an anointed king, was slung naked over a horse, arms and legs dangling, a halter tossed around his neck in symbolism of his defeat. In this indignity, he was taken to the Franciscan Priory church of the Greyfriars at Leicester where, for two days, his body was exhibited for all to see. He was buried at the friary with no ceremony. The church does not exist today—like so many others, it was destroyed when Henry's son ordered the dissolution of the monasteries in the 1530s—though as many will have heard, Richard's bones were recently found there, in what is now a car park, and with the help of modern forensic science, questions about him are now being answered.

Henry's next act as King was to date his reign from the day *before* Bosworth thus rendering as traitors all those who had loyally fought for King Richard, so that they could then be attainted for treason.

England lost much of its nobility during the battle, including men of great wealth like John Howard, the Duke of Norfolk. Henry appropriated their lands and kept the revenue for the crown. Some he executed for treason, among them William Bracher, Sir John Buck of Harthill, and William Catesby of Ashby St. Legers. Some, like Thomas Howard, Earl of Surrey, and Henry Percy, Earl of Northumberland, he imprisoned in the tower.

Those of Richard's supporters that did survive the battle were attainted and their estates confiscated; this effectively disarmed them and kept them from raising arms against the king.

Henry then forbade all nobles to retain their own armies to prevent them from being more powerful than himself and also to deter them from rebelling against him. It was an effective policy, and, although Henry did not manage to subdue all opposition, it is a fact that the English nobility, already in decline during the Wars of the Roses, fell rapidly from influence under the Tudors. By the reign of Queen Elizabeth I, England had just one remaining duke, that of Norfolk, and, after plotting to marry Mary Queen of Scots and restore Catholicism to England, he too was executed for treason in 1572.

It was not just the nobility that Henry targeted; indeed, they seem to have been lower down on his list than those descended directly from the bloodline of Plantagenet. During the next three reigns, the heirs of York were systematically wiped out.

I have tried to be objective in this brief overview, but possibly I have failed. I cannot help it. Every time I consider this argument it seems to me that Richard was the guy with the nobler tendencies. While Henry spent his youth skulking around Europe, living off others, emptying gaols in order to come and steal a crown to which he had no right, Richard was aiding his brother, King Edward, and proving almost unbelievably loyal despite disagreeing with his policies. In the short years that Richard was king, he showed promise of becoming a just ruler, championing the rights of the poor against the rich (imagine that!) and inspiring loyalty in his subjects in the north, who knew him well. He may have been a violent man by our standards, but he lived in violent times.

Killing on the battlefield was honourable; off the field it was not. He abhorred disloyalty, as is made apparent by his reaction to Hastings' betrayal, and, given the chance, I believe he would have made a better king than Henry who exploited rich and poor alike to bolster his own bulging coffers.

Throughout his life Henry resorted to devious methods. He lied and cheated his way to the throne, and, even once he had won it, his insecurities continued to dog him and his unscrupulous practices continued.

The Tudor regime may have put an end to the tumultuous years of the Wars of the Roses but the dying didn't stop. In Henry VIII's reign alone, it has been *estimated* that 72,000 people were executed. In 1485 the honourable ferocity of the Plantagenets was replaced by the deceit of the Tudors who, although they brought security and wealth to Britain, did so dishonourably.

You can probably tell which banner I fight under, but the subject is just as fascinating from the other side. The years surrounding the Battle of Bosworth have got to be the most intriguing in British history. If my rather biased view of the issues has inspired you to read more, there are countless books on the subject, and you will find that historians just cannot remain impartial. There is something about the Wars of the Roses that, even today, forces you to take sides.

MYSTERIES, MIRACLES, AND TABLEAUX: EARLY THEATER IN ENGLAND

BY **KATHERINE ASHE**

THEATER, IN ENGLAND AS IN ANCIENT GREECE, ORIGINALLY WAS AN EXPRESSION OF RELIgion. Scholars pin the beginning of English theater at about 960 and identify the *Quem Queritis* as the first play. An Easter presentation, it's an enactment of the Three Marys coming to Jesus' tomb and finding the Angel. A priest, dressed in white, sat on the church's altar as three enactors approached: monks or priests dressed as women, or, in a convent, nuns played the Marys.

Here's the whole text of the play:

"Quem queritis in sepulchro, o Christicolae?—Whom do you seek, O Christians?"

The women respond, *"Ihesum Nazarenum crucifixum, o Coelicola.*—Jesus of Nazareth, who was crucified, O Celestial."

He replies, *"Non est hic: surrexit sicut preadixerat. Ite, nuntiate quia surrexit de sepulchro.*—He is not here: He has risen, as he predicted. Go, announce that he has risen from the tomb."

That's the whole thing. The play was soon adapted for Christmas, the seekers coming to Christ's manger. The great popularity of such enactments led to their proliferation, but in the thirteenth century Pope Innocent III banned the clergy from performing or permitting such enactments within the church building itself.

Church performances merely moved to the porches and outer steps or to freestanding stages in public marketplaces, where they were displayed on feast days and performed by honored members of the parish. Interestingly, women seem to have performed the female roles, although, when professional theater developed in the 16th century, female roles were performed by adolescent boys and women were banned from the stage.

Early on, these theatricals took two forms, scripted enactments and tableaux or "living pictures." We know of an Adam and Eve in Paradise tableau from its mention in the *Chronica Majora*, which tells us that in January 1236, King Henry III's wedding procession passed through the play's Gate of Paradise, complete with nearly naked Adam and Eve greeting him and his bride, and no doubt shivering in the snow. This play apparently was lent to Henry's festivities by Saint Paul's Cathedral.

The mouth of Hell was particularly popular, possibly also for its theatrical nudity of both sexes. Somehow the fact that the people don't move seems to have made nudity in tableaux acceptable.

Separately, the London Guilds began their own forms of theatricals. The guilds, which were religious as well as mercantile and craft organizations, produced plays and tableaux of their patron saints. These, in contrast to the performances belonging to the churches which were called Mystery Plays, have come to be known as Miracle Plays. Less is known about the early development of the tableaux as they had no scripts, and the ledgers that would have recorded their costs probably were lost in the various conflagrations London suffered.

The guilds' theatricals were mounted on what are now referred to as pageant wagons, which were paraded through city streets during religious festivals. There are abundant illustrations of the later pageant wagons: sometimes quite elaborate vehicles with settings as backdrops for costumed players frozen in poses associated with each guild's patron saint, or enacting a significant moment in the saint's life. Occasionally the saint's "play" was combined with a tableau of the Life of Christ.

Simultaneous to the flowering of the tableaux were the guilds' Miracle Plays, centered upon the guilds' various patron saints. To name just a few of the subjects: Saint Eligious had begun his career as a goldsmith and was patron of all metalworkers including blacksmiths. The caterers favored Saint Lawrence—because he died on a grill and always was shown being roasted. Saint Apollonia, who suffered the torture of having her teeth pulled out, was of course the patron of dentists. Violence has been popular in theater for a very long time.

As the tableaux were becoming more elaborate, so were the Mystery Plays dealing with scenes from the New Testament. The Coventry cycle consisted of ten plays depicting the life of Christ, one scene showing Christ being judged by Pontius Pilate.

The York Cycle apparently consisted of forty-eight plays. The plays continued as popular entertainment during appropriate church holidays until they were banned in the late 16th century.

By then a variety of Mystery Play had developed that suggests a bawdy forerunner of Shakespeare's scenes designed to appeal to the "groundlings." The surviving Second Play of the Shepherds of the Wakefield Cycle serves as an example. Here the central characters are a husband and wife, Mac and Gill, who are thieves. Three shepherds come to Mac's cottage searching for their stolen lamb. Mac tells them his wife has just given birth and mustn't be disturbed, but the shepherds find their lamb wrapped up as the "newborn" in Gill's cradle. After punishing Mac by tossing him in a blanket, the shepherds return to their flocks, and an angel announces to them the birth of the Savior in Bethlehem. To a modern sensibility this takeoff on the Virgin Birth of the Lamb of God is rather stunning, and perhaps explains in part why the Mystery Plays eventually were closed down.

OF CAMELEOPARDS AND LIONS:
THE MEDIEVAL BESTIARY

BY **ROSANNE E. LORTZ**

THROUGHOUT HISTORY, FROM *AESOP'S FABLES* TO THE ANIMAL PLANET NETWORK, THE human imagination has been captured by the scaly, furry, four-footed, scurrying, slithering, swimming, and winged creatures of the animal world. Not only have the characteristics of animals provided endless fascination, but also the lessons that can be drawn from those characteristics.

The *Physiologos*, a Greek book written in the second or third century A.D., was the first book to take brief descriptions of animals and add to them Christian allegories. This book was translated into most of the European languages and is said to have been the second most popular book in Europe (after the Bible).

In the seventh century, Isidore of Seville wrote an extensive encyclopedia of animals (Book 12 of his *Etymologies*), attempting to describe every animal in the world. Eventually, someone had the bright idea of combining the allegorical interpretation of the *Physiologos* with the detailed descriptions from *Etymologies*. The medieval bestiary was born—part encyclopedia, part self-improvement, part doctrinal treatise, and especially popular in the country of England.

Richard Barber, in his translation of a thirteenth century bestiary, gives this succinct description of the genre:

> *Bestiaries are a particularly characteristic product of medieval England, and give a unique insight into the medieval mind. Richly illuminated and lavishly produced, they were luxury objects for noble families. Their three-fold purpose was to provide a natural history of birds, beasts, and fishes, to draw moral examples from animal behaviour (the industrious bee, the stubborn ass), and to reveal a mystical meaning—the phoenix, for instance, as a symbol of Christ's resurrection.*

The medievals believed that animals had a wonderful capacity to reveal truths about this world and the world beyond it. The Old Testament book of Proverbs had its own examples of morals learned from animals (e.g. Proverbs 6:6—*Go to the ant, thou sluggard; consider her ways and be wise*), and the book of Job supported the idea that mystical meanings could be gleaned from a study of the natural world:

> *"But ask now the beasts, and they shall teach thee;*
> *And the fowls of the air, and they shall tell thee:*
> *Or speak to the earth, and it shall teach thee:*

And the fishes of the sea shall declare unto thee."

—Job 12:7-8

An example of the mystical meanings placed in the bestiaries can be seen in this entry about a lion from a twelfth century bestiary.

> *Scientists say that Leo* [the Lion] *has three principal characteristics.... The Lion's third feature is this, that when a lioness gives birth to her cubs, she beings them forth dead and lays them up lifeless for three days—until their father, coming on the third day, breathes in their faces and makes them alive.*
>
> *Just so did the Father Omnipotent raise Our Lord Jesus Christ from the dead on the third day. Quoth Jacob: "He shall sleep like a lion, and the lion's whelp shall be raised."*

T. H. White, the twentieth century English author most famous for his King Arthur series *The Once and Future King*, was deeply interested in bestiaries and published his own translation of one. In the appendix he discussed the worldview that made this kind of literature possible:

> *In the ages of faith, people believed that the Universe was governed by a controlling mind and was capable of a rational explanation. They believed that everything meant something.... Every possible article in the world, and its name also, concealed a hidden message for the eye of faith.*

For modern readers, it often seems that these "hidden messages" or mystical meanings take precedence over reality. (A lion's offspring are born dead and come to life after three days—you're joking, right?) Many of the fantastic animals described in the bestiary also stretch the imagination to the point that one could consider the medievals insanely gullible or outright liars.

T.H. White, however, was not deterred by the seemingly false or the sublimely fantastic. *"It can hardly be repeated too often that the bestiary is a serious scientific work."* Many of the bizarre claims were honest mistakes made by naturalists from earlier centuries and repeated by others who drew on their work. Many of the animals that we would immediately classify as "mythical" return to the realm of reality upon closer examination. White noted that:

> *A Cameleopard...is a genuine animal, and by no means a bad attempt to describe an unseen creature which was as big as a camel while being spotted like a leopard, i.e. a giraffe...the real pleasure comes with identifying the existing creature, not with laughing at a supposedly imaginary one.*

In the passage quoted above, White expressed something very important, both for the study of bestiaries and for the study of the past in general. Instead of immediately dismissing the medievals as unintelligent or laughable, he extended them the courtesy of assuming them sensible and found a pleasure in puzzling out what they meant. By reading the bestiary on its own terms, White—an agnostic himself—was finally able to conclude that:

The Bestiary is a compassionate book. It has its bugaboos, of course, but these are only there to thrill us. It loves dogs, which never was usual in the East from which it originated; it is polite to bees, and even praises them for being communists…the horse moves it, as Sidney's heart was moved, 'more than with a trumpet'; above all, it has a reverence for the wonders of life, and praises the Creator of them: in whom, in those days, it was still possible absolutely to believe.

Food for Thought: Medieval Feasts

by BARBARA GASKELL DENVIL

By the final fading years of the English late Medieval period, just before the Tudor onslaught, the huge gap between rich and poor which had existed since 1066 had started to wane with the emergence of a new Middle Class, the expansion of trade, the regrowth of the population, and the development of new businesses.

But the initial narrowing of the poverty gap with the virtual end of the so-called feudal system really came about as a result of the Black Death (1348-1353 and onwards) when labour became harder to purchase and the working man discovered his real value. Another of those somewhat uncomfortable situations where great disaster brings great benefit in its wake!

Where food was concerned, however, the gap was still distinctive and no one was going to get excited about being invited to dinner at the local crofter's cottage. But a medieval feast—now that was a different matter.

For the majority, dinner was traditionally eaten at midday or some time earlier. Especially for those who rose at first light and took no breakfast, then dinner could be taken as early as 9 in the morning. Breakfast was not entirely unknown of course—breaking the fast of a long English evening and a long cold night was sensible, but it was unlikely to involve much more than bread and ale, or possibly porridge.

Farm labourers took food with them as they tramped out to the fields, something cold wrapped in their shirts or hats. This was, for instance, the origin of the Cornish pasty. Many took a little ale and bread after early morning Mass, but many others took nothing at all.

There were two qualities of bread—cheat for the poor and manchet for those who could pay for better. Manchet was baked with white flour and was considered more refined. Bread rolls were the most common (as loaves were more likely to be made of sugar at that time!), bought ready made from the bakers where a baker's dozen really did mean thirteen.

Cheat, on the other hand, was made with dark flour, either rye or a mixture of oats and barley, less refined in taste but more filling. Those with only rudimentary kitchens in their own homes often utilised communal ovens in cook houses or the village square.

Supper was likely eaten shortly before sundown, but the hour would depend on the working habits of the family. For the poor, this would likely comprise bread and cheese, a vegetable pottage, or what had been left over from dinner. For the wealthy, supper could be anything from a light snack to a full scale feast. Eating well was a proof of status, and, in any case, a rich man was likely to have a huge household to feed.

Thanks to the imagination of many and a few old films, there still appears to be a misunderstanding of medieval table habits. In fact, they were likely to be far more strictly tidy than our own modern more casual practises. The use of clean linen, including a very large starched napkin placed across the left shoulder, was essential.

Since the fork had not yet been introduced into general English usage in the late 15th century, cutlery meant spoon and knife only. The knife was often each man's own property brought to the table. The use of fingers was therefore necessary, but this did not mean bad manners. Hands were wiped on the napkin, washed before and after meals, and only used where the spoon and the knife were insufficient.

Grace would be pronounced first by the head of the family (or the chaplain in a large household), the first course would be laid, and there was supposed to be consideration for others at the table where communal bowls and platters were concerned. Someone taking more than his share would be frowned upon. The position of the salt cellar could be an important part of accepted etiquette, and generally behaving with discreet decorum was important. A child was taught table manners. His elders would be judged by theirs.

Light ale was the most common drink, also for children. It was weak by our standards but many beers were stronger. Wine was most likely to be imported from Flanders, France, Italy, or Spain, although some was produced in England.

The famous Malmsy was a sweetish Greek wine. Burgundy was highly favoured and there were various qualities, with Beaune perhaps the best. There was Claret, Cabernet from Brittany, Vernaccia and Trebbiano from Italy, Sack (sherry from Jerez) and many, many more. If spiced and possibly gingered, and then maybe heated, the wine became Hippocras and was supposedly medicinal—certainly very pleasant on a chilly evening by the fire.

Very sweet wines from the Levant were favoured by some ladies. Verjuice, made from unfermented and often unripe English grapes, was used in cooking. Mead was often bought from the monasteries where honey from the locally kept beehives was used, or sold, by the monks. So there was certainly no lack of good lubrication to help the digestion.

Water was, after all, completely undrinkable. It was dangerously polluted in almost all areas of the country and was used mainly for washing, though also in cooking where it was hopefully sufficiently boiled for safety. Dysentery was, however, common.

Fruit and vegetables were not particularly favoured, especially by the rich. Fresh fruit was considered extremely bad for you, and too much of any fruit could prove fatal! Death from a surfeit of berries was sometimes a doctor's diagnosis. Fruit was used in cooking, but more commonly for brewing. Cider and Perry were popular in country areas. Vegetables were given to farm animals, but also eaten by the poor. A vegetable pottage (slow cooked stew) or a cabbage soup was both filling and easily produced.

But for the rich it was protein all the way. Meat, fish, and dairy were favoured. Fish was not always popular, but the Church insisted on no meat being eaten on Fridays, religious fasts, and many saints' days. Abstention from these strictures could be bought or pleaded, but the rules were fairly strict and, it seems, usually upheld. Although a great variety of fish and seafood was available, the boredom of a fishy diet could be alleviated by the addition of duck, beaver, and other water or sea birds, usefully classified as fish by the helpful and hopeful clergy.

Meat was the staple diet of those who could afford it. Roasting was the favoured cooking method, meat slowly turned on a spit over a roaring open fire. Boiling in stews and soups was also common, as was frying, and smoked bacon was much utilised. Since there was no method of refrigeration available, meat and fish were preserved out of season by smoking and drying. Rich dishes of meat stuffed with onions, herbs, and raisins were popular, and apples were more often used in stuffings than as fresh fruit.

Those unable to afford such regular luxuries would still eat meat as often as was possible, but would frequently be reduced to eating simple stews of beans, barley, oatmeal, lentils, and peas.

The use of spices in cooking was considered important—not to disguise the taste of rotten meat which is another of the many myths regarding medieval affairs which still persists—but to add flavour and to pronounce wealth and status. Spices were, on the whole, enormously expensive. Therefore, the more spice added to your guests' platters, the more they knew and respected your importance. So a fair dose of cinnamon, nutmeg, anise, caraway seeds, cloves, and even the monstrously expensive saffron might be liberally spread across your dinner.

Dishes could be either simple or complicated—roast boar crusted in mustard; pickled lampreys; buttered crabs on a bed of smoked eels; calves' testicles filled with onion, minced lambs' kidneys and nutmeg; capon studded with cloves and served on salad greens, clams, and beans; a galantine of three dark meats in aspic; baked pike in burned cream; larks bound in leeks in a red wine sauce; boiled tripe and sweated onions; stewed rabbit in a pastry pie…the list goes on and on—both the amazing and the horrifying.

For feasts in grand houses, three courses were normally served (there could be more), but each course was comprised of many separate dishes. Depending on how lavish the host wished to appear, twenty or more different platters might be set across the table for each course.

And even more confusing to us, each of these courses could include both sweets and savouries. Custards, spit-roast apples, creamed almonds with marzipan berries, jellies, tarts, and fruity dumplings in syrup could be served right amongst the roast meats, stews, meat pies, and fish.

The third and last course, however, often contained only wafers and a huge sugar sculpture, known as a subtlety. This could be amazing and a chef could boost his reputation by producing something to make the guests gasp.

For Christmas celebrations a whole nativity scene might be carved from sugar loaves. Swans, peacocks, angels, crowns, palaces, and many other gorgeously elegant and fragile creations made of nothing but sugar, would be carried out to the table by the chef and his assistants, greeted by clapping and cheers. All in all, not a particularly healthy diet but not, perhaps, as pernicious as English eating habits became over the following centuries.

And, of course, in those days the great chandelier swinging from the huge medieval beams was true to its name and held only candles, their light dancing across the platters and gilding meat juices golden, highlighting the tips of pastry crust, flickering over the gleaming jellies, and blurring those magnificent subtleties until the swan truly seemed to be swimming in its pool of reflections. The candlelight, and the surging light of flame from the hearth, would also shimmer across the satins, the damasks, taffetas, and jewellery of the guests. Those were the days of dressing suitably for the occasion.

The poor rarely tasted sugar, which was dreadfully expensive. They did not lack sweetening, however, as honey was plentiful. But a humble meal did not aspire to contain sweet meats or custards, and a modest sufficiency to control hunger was frequently all that could be expected.

During these final years of the medieval period, particularly during the reigns of Edward IV and Richard III, the country prospered and the poor were rarely so poor. But only the extravagant rich aspired to a three course feast, or needed to announce their reputations with the massive expense of hosting one. Aldermen, city mayors, guild dignitaries, prosperous traders, and wedding parties where one side needed to impress the other—all these spread their tables heavily until the table legs groaned.

Some guests ate to do justice to such a feast (King Edward IV is reputed to have become an overweight glutton in his later years) but many of these sumptuous dishes were afterwards relegated to the kitchens, and were then shared out to the scullions, to local alms houses and charities, and to the beggars at the doors.

The new foods discovered by the Spanish in the New World (1492/3) had not yet been introduced into the European diet, so there were no potatoes or tomatoes or the many other originally American delights we now take for granted. But what was lacking was made up for by the enormous energy and ingenuity of the cooks and their imaginative adherence to inventing new recipes and enriching old ones.

There are many fascinations to discover during this long gone age of 500 years past, but my historical novel *Sumerford's Autumn* is not much concerned with the parties of the nobility, though some of this is mentioned. Set in 1497 it is more concerned with the poor, the disadvantaged, and those suffering the displeasure of the new Tudor king. Sumerford Castle is grand but damp, and the earl and his family are neither as rich nor as comfortable as they seem.

Rather than descriptions of feasts, there are descriptions of imprisonment, torture in the Tower, treachery, piracy, and misfortune. But the research on this time period, which I have been following with a passion for many years, covers all aspects of this remarkable era.

Dinner as It Might Have Been at Kenilworth 760 Years Ago

by KATHERINE ASHE

ELEANOR, COUNTESS OF LEICESTER, IS ENTERTAINING ROBERT GROSSETESTE, THE BISHOP of Lincoln, and Peter de Montfort, her husband's cousin from Gloucestershire, at her castle of Kenilworth. As is often the case, her husband is away from home. Trubody, her major d'omo, presides over the servants and will carve the principal roast meats as the sons at home, Guy, Amaury, and Richard, are still children.

It's early afternoon. The Countess sits on the turf seat with the Bishop in her rose garden. Peter is playing at battle with young Guy with wooden swords while Amaury reads a passage in Latin for the Bishop as his tutor Geoffrey de Boscellis hovers proudly. Richard, still an infant, is suckled by his wet nurse in the nursery where, from her corner tower room, she can look down on the garden as she munches her rich, bland meal of beef and blancmange.

From the thatch-roofed bake-shed beyond the garden's wattle wall the scents of baking savory pies and sweets perfume the breeze. Onto the crust of a chicken puree and custard pie the cook is grinding a sprinkle of white sugar from a hard, conical sugar loaf imported from Palestine. To give the custard a golden glaze she puts the big pie back under the inverted kettle that serves as oven in the hearth.

Herbs from the vegetable garden hang in bunches from the roof beams of the cook shed, beside strings of onions and medicinal garlic. Crocks of spring peas packed in lard are stacked along the walls, waiting to be winter treats. Barrels of cherries, quinces, and medlars soaked in honey and wine wait winter's feasts as well.

Finishing with the sugar, Cook hands the cone back to Trubody, the major d'omo, who puts it into Slingaway's basket with several boxes of spices, almonds, figs, and dates to go back to the hall where they're kept locked in the aumbry, the serving cupboard near the main door and the cellar door.

Before he leaves the cook shed, the major d'omo lights a candle lantern; it's full daylight and early afternoon, but he'll need it.

Climbing the foyer steps to the castle, Trubody takes the basket and sends Slingaway to tell the household servants to bring the board and trestles for the Countess' dining table—it's time to set them up on the raised dais at the end of the hall. After setting his lantern on the aumbry and putting the costly "groceries" securely away behind the aumbry's sturdy, iron-bound doors, the major d'omo checks the linens as the table is assembled, smoothing the white table cloth, seeing the napkins are at each place.

The dais' permanent furniture, the heavy, carved oak chairs for the Countess (and the Earl when he's at home), are adjusted at the center of the table where the Countess and the Bishop will sit. Cushioned stools are brought for the cousin and the tutor, and for young Amaury and Guy. The seating, facing out into the hall, is arranged with space enough from the rear wall for the diners and servants to pass, but most serving will be from the open side of the table.

Trubody nods now to Slingaway for the long trestle tables to be set up on the main floor of the hall for the castle's upper staff: Lady Mary, the Countess' principal lady-in-waiting, the almoner, the manor steward, the Countess' treasurer, the verger of the castle's chapel, the armorer and captain of the castle's guards, the chief huntsman and equerry, Lady Mary's own maids. The kitchen, household, and serving staff will take their places at the long tables when the first seating, of those who outrank them, is done and the diners at the high table have left for vespers in the chapel.

Taking up his lantern from the aumbry and selecting the cellar key from the great bunch of keys that hang from his belt, Trubody opens the door to the cellar. By the light of his lantern, he climbs down the ladder into the dark, moist pit. Gobehasty, the footman, hurrying from the kitchen with two large pewter pitchers, climbs down behind him.

In the dark, damp pit there in the cool darkness of the cellar are stacked the great casks of Bordeaux brought home when the Earl was viceroy in Gascony. Here also are iron chains and manacles fixed by massive iron staples to the wall—a reminder of King Henry's renovations when the master, the Earl Montfort, was in exile.

Trubody finds the cask pierced by an oak spigot and fills Gobehasty's pitchers. The lower household staff at the second seating will have beer, brought in wooden buckets from the brewster's shed.

In the kitchen, Cook sends Garbag to tell Trubody that all is ready.

Clambering up the cellar ladder, with Gobehasty close behind, the major d'omo hurriedly unlocks the aumbry's doors again and gives Garbag three silver goblets to set on the high table at the center places for Peter de Montfort, the Countess, and the Bishop. Treen goblets from the kitchen shed will be sufficient for everyone else.

But also for the high table, the major d'omo takes from the aumbry a fine pewter ewer shaped like a knight on horseback, the spout emerging from the horse's mouth. Gobehasty carefully pours wine from a pitcher to the ewer as Trubody hastens to the rose garden to inform the Countess that dinner is ready.

Peter stops his play with little Guy. With the Countess and the Bishop leading, Amaury, tucking his book into the blousing of his robe, follows his tutor, and the six go up the foyer steps to the hall.

As the Countess takes her place at the center of the table, with the Bishop to her right and Peter to her left, Boscelis and Amaury to the Bishop's right, Guy, coached by Trubody, brings a towel and bowl of rose water for the diners to dip and dry their fingers.

The Countess' staff seat themselves on the benches at the long tables along the walls, and Slingaway, at the high table, sets a large, square-trimmed, thick slice of four-day old bread, a "trencher," on the tablecloth at each diner's place.

The Countess asks the Bishop to say the blessing. Never perfunctory, Grosseteste prays at length for the well-being of the Countess and for the Earl, absent in France and from whom there is no news, for the king and for the outcome of the harvest—which can never be taken for granted even in a mild and moist year.

The staff members at the long tables sit, politely silent in the presence of their lady and a priest who's said to have second sight—some no doubt wondering if this means the harvest, so near ripening, will fail? The kitchen servants wait restively in line down the steps of the foyer, beyond the hall door. At last the Bishop makes the sign of the cross and says, "Amen," and the meal may begin.

Servant after servant comes briskly in and offers the dish he's bearing first to the Countess, then to the Bishop, then to Peter, last to tutor Boscellis and the boys. At the low tables Lady Mary presides and carves the trencher loaves, holding each round loaf cradled under her arm with the long knife sawing perilously toward her bosom.

Kitchen boys bring in a roast of beef and another of ham and a round of cheese. The left-overs of the dainty dishes of the high table may be offered here in the second course, and sometimes the Countess sends special samples down to Lady Mary. The cups that the staff carry tied to their belts are brought forth and filled by Garbag from the second pitcher of wine.

Non-meat dishes first are served at the high table since the Bishop will not eat red meat. A footman offers eels, caught in the abbey pond next door and baked in a crust with diced onion, ginger, currants, raisins, and vinegar. Next comes a charger of carp from Kenilworth's Mere, served in a pond of sauce galantine (see Recipe 1 below). Then come fritters of parsnips cooked with almond milk; baked eggs with mint, parsley, fennel, rue, and tansy; bowls of pease pottage with saffron and pepper (see Recipe 2 below).

Frowning at such extravagance, Grosseteste helps himself only to the pottage, eggs, and the parsnip fritters, while Boscellis happily accepts large servings of the rich eel and carp. Countess Eleanor smiles; she's fond of Boscellis and has told the cook to always have some fine dish for the tutor monk whose one indulgence is good food.

Peter de Montfort and the Countess herself have a taste of everything, and Peter summons back the carp for a larger serving, his trencher well soaked in sauce galantine. The boys poke at small servings of the carp, waiting for the roasts in the next course.

At the lower tables, Trubody carves the roasted meats. The staff members pass the wooden chargers laden with sliced ham or beef, pricking their choices with their dining knives. Like the diners at the high table, each has a knife case, hung with whatever other implements they need—keys, stylus, needle case, or hoof pick—from their belts.

Now at the high table the second course begins. Gobehasty brings a magnificent pastry-covered roast. On the platter, surrounding the golden dome that encases the meat, are spiced apples and pears. Into the honey-laden juices, the poured batter that covers the meat has flowed and crisped into crinkled bits, special treats for the children.

As Trubody carves and a servant takes the slices round the table, more dishes are run (coursed) from the kitchen: a pie of the spiced innards of the deer that was the main course yesterday; a capon stuffed with almonds and figs; a mawmenye of lamb with lentils, turnips, and currants (see Recipe 3 below).

Since the Earl is away and there are few guests today, the meal is not extensive. The diners at the high table spear the cut meat with the points of their dining knives, as Peter does, or delicately carry them from trencher to mouth with thumb and forefinger—or thumb and index finger—as the Countess does, with fingers not in use daintily splayed to keep them free of sauce. The wash basin and towel is brought round again.

When the second course is finished, the course of sweets is served. Dishes of home-grown sugared violets and rose petals, imported almonds, and dried cherries from the orchard are set upon the cloth as the sauce-soaked trenchers are removed.

Being thick and very dry, the undersides of the bread trenchers have left little on the table but crumbs. The poor of the manor's village, gathering at the castle gate, will receive the sauce-laden bread from the almoner this evening.

Cook has prepared a special sweet in honor of the Bishop, a *faun tempere*—carnation flower pudding (see Recipe 4 below). Small bowls, each garnished with carnations and roses, are set at each place at the high table.

The Countess, her guests and family, Lady Mary, and the Bishop leave the hall for evening prayers in the chapel. The diners at the low tables vacate the benches, and the kitchen, serving staff, and lesser servants of the castle take their places. Garbag and Slingaway bring wooden buckets of beer from the brewing shed and the copious remains of the roast meats and cheese are heaped on the trencher slices as quickly as Cook can slice the loaves.

In the kitchen shed the hearth's fire has been banked, the inverted kettles used for baking are cleared from the coals. The hanging kettle used for the pottage has been lifted from its trammel to the stone wash tub where, with fasces of twigs, it was scrubbed, along with the big forks and ladles, griddles and pots, in hot water from the great kettle that never leaves the hearth.

In a bucket of clean water Trubody himself carefully washes the silver goblets and the pewter ewer shaped like a knight on horseback, then he dries them and returns them to safety in the aumbry in the hall.

RECIPES

1) *Sauce galantine, to serve with fowl, meats, or fish*: 1/3 cup very dry bread or bread crusts ground to a fine grain, 1 cup stock (vegetable, chicken, fish, or meat depending upon the dish to be sauced), 1 tsp ground galingale, ¼ tsp each cinnamon, ginger, and cloves, 2 tbsp vinegar for fish or vegetable dishes, 3 tbsp sherry for fowl or meats. Combine bread crumbs with the spices. Add remaining ingredients and simmer gently until sauce thickens. Season with salt and pepper to taste and serve. About 1 ½ cups.

2) *Pease pottage*: 3 cups vegetable broth, 3 lb. shelled green peas, 1 large onion, minced, 2 tbsp brown sugar, ¼ tsp salt, ¼ tsp saffron, ¼ tsp of pepper, ¼ tsp dry ginger powder. Bring broth to a boil; add all the other ingredients, cook covered over medium heat for 12 to 15 minutes, turn out and puree the pottage and

return to the pot to reheat. Garnish with a slice of toasted, crusty bread for each bowl. Serves 6.

3) *Mawmenye of lamb and lentils*: 1¼ lb of lamb cut into small bite-size chunks, 1 cup chicken or vegetable broth, 4 cups beef broth, 1 cup dry lentils washed and cleansed of stones and blemished lentils, 1 cup diced turnips or parsnips, 1/3 cup chopped figs, 1 cup currants, 1/3 cup raisins, ¼ tsp cinnamon and ¼ tsp ginger (powdered), ¼ tsp pepper, ½ tsp salt, 2 tbsp butter, pale celery leaves, or yellow nasturtiums. Mix the ¼ tsp of pepper and ½ tsp of salt with the chunks of lamb and then sauté the lamb in the butter. Add chicken broth and simmer gently until lamb is cooked and tender (45 min. to an hour). Meanwhile bring lentils to boil in the 4 cups of beef broth; when boil is reached reduce heat and simmer for 15 minutes. Combine spices (additional salt may be added sparingly here, to taste) and add to turnips/parsnips, tossing to mix well. Add the turnips/parsnips, figs, and currants to the lentils and continue to cook for 10 to 15 minutes or until the lentils are tender. Stir the cooked lamb into the lentils and place in a large serving bowl. Distribute the celery leaves or flowers decoratively and serve. Serves 6 if offered with other main course dishes.

4) *Faun tempere—carnation flower pudding:* ½ cup beef or chicken broth, 2½ cups milk, ¼ cup white flour, ½ cup white sugar, 5 egg yolks, 9 or 10 carnation flowers (violets or rose petals may be substituted if carnations aren't available, but nasturtiums have too sharp a flavor), ½ cup skinned and grated almonds, ¼ tsp each cinnamon, galingale, mace and ginger powder. In a pot set into a kettle of gently boiling water (you can use a double boiler) heat milk and broth gradually. Mix the flour, sugar, and spices and gradually add to the milk and broth, stirring constantly for 12 to 15 minutes. Beat the eggs. Put ½ cup of the heated milk, flour, spices and stock into a separate bowl and gently stir in the beaten egg yolks. Add to the main pot, stirring continually as pudding thickens. Pour the pudding into separate bowls and allow to cool. Strew the top with the flowers and serve.

FURTHER READING

Aresty, Esther B. *The Delectable Past*. Bobbs-Merrill, 1964.

Cosman, Madeleine Pelner. *Fabulous Feasts*. George Braziller, 1976.

Sass, Lorna, S. *To the King's Taste*. The Metropolitan Museum of Art, 1975.

Tannahill, Reay. *The Fine Art of Food*. New York: A.S. Barnes, & Co., 1968.

Wilson, C. Anne. *Food and Drink in Britain*. Penguin Books, 1984.

LIFE IN A MEDIEVAL VILLAGE

BY KATHERINE ASHE

When Julius Caesar arrived in Albion, what we call Briton, he reported to the Roman Senate that here was a land completely under cultivation. A thousand years later, when William of Normandy conquered England he had to eradicate numerous villages to plant what is still known as the New Forest to create a future supply of oak for ships.

What did this long sustained agriculture look like and how was it maintained?

We don't know if the "three field system" was already in place in Caesar's time—it certainly was well before the arrival of the Normans, who were using it on their home fiefs as well.

Picture a land wide open, dotted with villages here and there, a manor house, often fortified and with a bit of woodland, a hunting chase that would also supply wood for heat and cooking and occasionally a few large timbers for a crook-built building the walls of which, between the supporting timbers, would be woven willow wands—a sort of basketry—wadded with clay and horsehair (a building material called wattle and daub).

The single village street would be lined with wattle and daub "half timbered" cottages, each set on its own little "toft", usually planted with a vegetable garden at the back and surrounded by a willow "wattle" fence to keep in the chickens. The cottage would also possess a "croft", another small piece of land probably planted with a few fruit trees—apple, pear, quince, cherry—and here pigs might be kept.

These cottages were not the property of the cottagers but belonged to the fief, the whole of the estate that included the village, the manor house, the fields, and the chase. Before the Conquest in 1066 these fiefs belonged to whatever Briton, Saxon, or Dane happened to hold it as overlord from time immemorial or as the results of war and apportionment to the dominant power's friends.

With the arrival of the Normans, the fiefs were granted to William's followers under the feudal system through the King's direct gift of a multitude of fiefs to his most useful followers, who then apportioned the fiefs under their control to their knights to supply them with a living through specific taxes so that they were free and well supplied when their services were called upon for war.

But regardless of who might be living in, or rebuilding the great house to suit his tastes, the life of the villagers, or "villeins" as they were properly called with no disparagement intended, remained the same. Even what they paid in duties to the holder of the fief remained the same according to ancient custom.

For each village had a "wittenmote," a group of elders who knew the customs of the place: what was owed to the lord of the manor and when, how the cultivated land was apportioned and to whom, what the penalties were for crimes, etc. Thus the wittenmote provided a continuity for village life regardless of who was the dominant force politically at any given time.

In the 13th century the royal judge Henry de Bracton made a compilation of these customary laws of the wittenmotes, and that collection lies at the foundation of the British and U.S. legal systems based upon precedent, rather than a code of law as is the practice in most of the rest of the world.

But who were these villagers who had been occupying the cottages from time out of mind?

Each cottage was held by its "house-bondsman," the eldest son, or in the counties under the Danelaw, the youngest son. One must suppose this Scandinavian practice of making the youngest son the inheritor, on the idea that the older ones would certainly be old enough to fend for themselves long before their father died, encouraged the expansionary practice of going a-viking—from which nearly everyone in reach of Scandinavian ships suffered.

The house-bondsman, or "husbandman," inherited the bond for the cottage and all that pertained to it: the toft, the croft, and a right to a certain number of rows, say three rows for example, in each of the three great fields surrounding the village. Since the land was not of equal quality in all of its rows, the rows were not permanently allotted to specific cottages.

Each year the fief's husbandmen drew straws for which set of rows would be theirs to cultivate that year. The unfortunate ended up with that "short straw" and "a hard row to hoe," but the misfortune would probably be rectified the following year.

The fields, and the rows in them, were demarcated by posts—palings or "pales." To trespass on someone else's row was to "go beyond the pale." Don't picture these rows as the little scraping of the soil you might do in your veggie garden—these rows were huge, and S shaped, giving the fields something of the look of a sea ruffled with waves as high as a man's waist and sometimes wider than one might be able to jump over. The S shape was the result of the wide turning radius of the ox drawn plows in use.

Though the Minoans apparently had huge bulls and the Romans had what look like the beautiful modern, good-sized, and cream colored Charolais, England's oxen in the Middle Ages were not very big at all, their backs reaching only to about the height of a man's chest.

For those not familiar with cattle raising, oxen are castrated bull calves. Since a cow, to be milk-able, must bear a calf, and since half the calves born are likely to be male and useless as milkers, it is these bull calves that supply the meat—as of course do the old cows past milking age. When needed, a strong bull calf would be kept for breeding, or castrated and trained to the heavy wooden oxbow that would couple him to another ox and enable him to be hitched to a plow or wagon.

These little cattle were not very strong; a team for plowing would require six of them, a heavy wagon might require a team of ten or more. So the husbandman would share his two oxen with his neighbors who had rows of a sufficient distance from his that the team, wending its way through the row's S curve, would take up the neighbor's row at the right place in the curve.

Where were all these oxen kept when they weren't plowing? Here we come to the three field system. The oxen lived on that year's fallow field, helpfully manuring it. The three fields in which the principal manor lands were divided followed a regular three year cycle.

The Fallow Field, on which nothing was planted, rested and was renewed with manuring by the village animals. The next field in the cycle, known as the Spring Field, was planted with oats, peas, beans, and barley—all nitrogen-fixing plants. Because these four plantings required different growing conditions regarding moisture, the slope of the row was used like a little hillside with the four different kinds of plants each in its own row along the incline. After harvesting, these plants would be plowed into the soil, enriching it even further.

The third field was planted with wheat (called "corn" but not at all the Indian corn we designate by that name now), which requires a great deal of nutrients. Grains will exhaust the soil in a short time if those nutrients are not replaced—and that is why modern farmers are so dependent upon chemical fertilizers. The three-field system, because of its cycle of two years of nutrient replacement before a piece of land was planted again with grain, was endlessly sustainable.

A certain number of rows in the field belonged to the manor house although, managed by the lord's steward, it took its chances in the row selection along with everyone else in many places. The husbandmen, in part payment of the "bond" for their holdings in the fief, gave service by plowing, seeding, and harvesting the lord's crops. They also might owe a hen or eggs every now and then, especially at Christmas time.

How their debt of labor was paid was specific to the customs of each fief and was well known to the wittenmote. Much distinction was made between a water "bidreap" and a beer "bidreap" when the steward of the manor was required to serve the plowmen beer when they rested.

Regarding local law and order, the principal person responsible in the village was the husbandmen's chosen "reeve." The reeve had a horn that he blew whenever there was an emergency, such as when the sheep had gotten into the meadow or a cow into the corn—Little Boy Blue was a typical reeve.

For crimes, there was a system of fines. Even murder was squared with a fine, a very heavy one that economically crippled not only the perpetrator but his entire family. The amount of fine for a murder depended upon the social status of the victim, fundamentally his lifetime's worth in earning ability, his value to the community. Except of course for aristocrats, who might be seen as having very little value to the local community but whose murder commanded so high a fine that the convicted, or a relative taking his place, would languish a lifetime in prison for the unpayable debt.

If the husbandman was the eldest, or youngest son in the Danelaw, what became of his brothers and sisters? Some migrated to the cities, learning crafts, becoming a new middle class of merchants and artisans. Some became servants in the manor house.

Many of the excess population of the fiefs peopled the enormous religious houses with their vast communities of low level monks and nuns, and some of these rose through education to become priests, and even bishops, as in the case of the brilliant Robert Grosseteste, Bishop of Lincoln, author of the standard published work on manor management of his time, translator of the Old Testament from Hebrew, mathematician, scientist, theologian, and author of "On Kingship and Tyranny" and hence instigator of the movement that resulted in the first Parliament with power over the Crown.

One of Grosseteste's acts as bishop was to establish a system for legitimizing bastard children. By the old system, only the husbandman (husband) could marry, for only he could provide a stable living for a family. It was a system that just about guaranteed a goodly supply of bastards.

Grosseteste's solution was to perform marriages for those who weren't husbandmen, to cover the couple's children with a sheet until the end of the wedding ceremony, then to whisk away the sheet, revealing the couple's children as "new-born" in legitimacy.

One wonders if Grosseteste, whose name is not a surname but means "the fat-head," was himself illegitimate, though such a history might impair a person's qualifications for the priesthood.

Each fief's village would have a church, and the lord of the manor would have the right, called "advowson," to designate whom the priest would be. With the appointment went a modest "living" charged against the local husbandmen.

Since the "living" might be given as an income to someone who didn't live in the village, indeed never showed up to preach or otherwise, there was a need for some currency. This was solved by fairs held in the nearest town. The husbandman's wife (which word incidentally means "carver of the loaf") would take the fruits and vegetables from her toft and croft, or a hen or eggs, in a basket and would walk to the nearest fair. If more money was needed she might have her child come with her to drive along some geese or a pig.

If these images of the Goose Girl or Little Boy Blue the reeve, and phrases such as "going beyond the pale" ring deep in our psyches, it's not only because we saw illustrations in books when we were very small, but because, if they dwelled in Europe, this was the life that most of our ancestors lived.

And on inspection at this remove, it seems not such a bad life, given they had no expectations of plumbing, heating, or modern means of travel and communications. There were, actually certain advantages, certain absences of stress regarding expectations of achievement—life would be what it had always been.

FURTHER READING

Homans, George Caspar. *English Villagers of the Thirteenth Century*. New York: Russell and Russell, 1960.

MEDIEVAL BATHING FOR CLEANLINESS, HEALTH, AND SEX

BY KATHERINE ASHE

THERE IS A QUITE ERRONEOUS NOTION THAT MEDIEVAL PEOPLE DIDN'T BATHE. Some Tudors may have been proud of bathing once a month whether they needed to or not, but their ancestors had looked upon bathing as one of the sensual pleasures of life. King Henry III even had a special room for the purpose of washing his hair.

True, the poor had little access to bathing facilities other than the local well, and hefting buckets of water home for cooking purposes was probably quite enough of a burden. What personal washing was to be done could be done with a bowl of water.

Laundry might be done in a village washhouse where once in the spring and once in the autumn stream water could be diverted to large stone tubs. Pounded lavender and soapwort made the washing compound, for soaps were not invented until the mid-thirteenth century. Soap was then imported from Spain and was only for the rich. Note, however, the shared linguistic root of "lavender" and "laundry," shared with the French word *lavande* and the Latin, heard in the Mass as the priest says, "*Lavabo*—I will wash." Not too bad, having your laundry smell of lavender—even if it's only twice a year.

In cities the early mornings began with the water sellers wheeling their barrow-like barrels through the streets and selling door to door. Few houses, even of the wealthy, would have their own tubs for the immersion of a full grown person.

Personal washing would be accomplished with a bowl, filled by a servant with one pitcher with very hot water from a cauldron in the hearth and another pitcher of unheated water from a barrel or stone tank in the kitchen or cellar. The desired temperature was achieved by mixing the water from the two pitchers. This arrangement would prevail for most people until the mid-nineteenth century.

So much for washing, but what of bathing? To bathe, medieval men and women went to a bathhouse.

Picture a vast cellar, an undercroft with broad columns supporting the building, or multiple buildings, up above. The ceiling is low and groined and there are no windows. Iron chandeliers or candle stands, rusted to a mellow brown, bear numerous fat, white wax candles giving off a scent of honey. At one end of the room is a huge hearth hung with several cauldrons, each giving off a different perfume: attar of rose, mossy vetiver, musk or the haunting sweet aroma of civet (refined from the chokingly foul odor of the civet cat's spray to make one of the loveliest of perfumes). The atmosphere in the low, dim room is dense with mists and laden with seductive aromas.

Arranged in aisles between the sturdy columns are curtained booths, their drapes hung from tall stands to provide total privacy—or, for parties of a racy nature, the curtains could be drawn back. Within each booth is a standing rack for clothing, a small table equipped with fruit, sweets, a carafe of wine and goblets, and soaps, oils, and strigils (which we will discuss below).

The central feature of the booth is, of course, the tub, made of wood like a huge bucket and equipped with seats inside so that the bathers may be immersed up to their necks when sitting. A friend of mine recently bought just such a tub from Russia, where apparently such bathing has continued in some places, sans plumbing, to this day. Such a tub will accommodate at least two people.

If this sounds a bit like the modern "hot tub" and the pleasures of the "fast set" in places like Las Vegas, you've got it about right. While such bathhouses were where one went to seriously wash, they were also popular with married couples with sensual tastes, were notorious trysting places for clandestine lovers, and were a favored workplace for courtesans.

Priests and street corner preaching monks inveighed against them as halls of sin and depravity, and seem to have succeeded in reducing their presence until their reincarnation (with plumbing in place of hot and cold running servants) in modern times. Most illustrations from medieval manuscripts disapprovingly depict the bathhouse of the brothel variety.

What of bathing for health? Spas developed all over the Roman empire, wherever there were hot springs and waters with minerals thought to heal or restore health and vitality. Many of these spas have never been out of business since Roman times. Probably everyone knows of Bath and its Pump Room, made the height of fashion by Beau Nash in the mid-18th century. So I'm going to describe a somewhat less grand, and more close to ancient usage, spa—that of Dax, in England's medieval dukedom of Gascony in southwestern France.

In medieval times Dax was especially busy, as it was located on the pilgrim route to Santiago de Compostella. Hence, it was richly supplied with jewelers' shops to make settings for the seashells which were the proud souvenirs of anyone who had reached Compostella.

Today the elegant shops lining Dax's main streets offer a wonderful array of toys for grannies to bring back to their grandchildren and the most beautiful candy shops perhaps in the world—row after row of footed crystal dishes heaped with chocolates wrapped in gold foil, each variety labeled with a tiny reproduction of a painting by Vermeer, Rubens, Rembrandt, etc. Dax, as it always has been, is a place for the rich and elderly to recover, indulge themselves, and think pleasantly of those back home.

And the bathing there? The bathers, monkishly sandaled and bundled in hooded white robes as they always have been, hurry through the streets to the bath. Which could hardly be more different from the undercroft bathhouse.

Along the main street is a marble trough the rear wall of which has a row of Roman bronze lion heads with open mouths, each spewing a stream of hot water. Above the wall of these small but magnificent public spigots rise the weathered columns of the Roman bath, at the street front of a rectangular, roofless, temple-like structure.

Where the floor of this temple of health would be is the pool, steaming with water from natural hot springs. A crowd of bathers, immersed amid the wreathing steam, soak in hopes of curing everything from rheumatism to varicose veins. Pilgrims too are still there, soaking their blistered feet after their trudge across the Pyrenees and back again.

Strigils? I mentioned that soap was a Spanish invention of the mid-thirteenth century, so it was probably available at Dax very soon after its first appearance in Spain.

But how did people wash before that? They rubbed themselves with scented oils and then scraped off the oils, dirt, and shedding skin with a strigil, which looks rather like a marriage of an old-fashioned straight razor with a butter knife—with the sharpness of the latter. The heat of the bath caused pores to open, helping to expel dirt, and the strigil scraped it away, leaving the skin smooth, clean, oiled and scented.

This was how people bathed in ancient Rome, this was how they bathed in Europe—until the invention of soap, in Spain, which may or may not be an improvement when dry skin is taken into consideration. However, the new Spanish luxury took over and made the strigil obsolete.

Other means of hygiene associated with Spain were not so universally embraced. Gaius Valerius Catullus, in about 50 BC, pokes a jibe at a Spanish customs of cleanliness in a poem addressed to Egnatius, a young Iberian gentleman overly given to flashing his brilliant smile. Catullus claims he would not be offended by such smiles from people of any of a number of other nationalities, but Egnatius is a Spaniard, and in Spain, according to Catullus, bright, clean teeth were achieved through the use of one's urine. If this seems shocking, we might take note that synthetic urine (urea) is an ingredient in many modern compounds. No doubt the synthetic variety is to be preferred.

Cleanliness has meant different things to different peoples at different times. It has always been considered a virtue, in whatever form was current, except of course when it was pursued with excessive sensual gusto. Then it could be a sin. The spa has two-thousand years of history as a treat for the rich and a hope for the sick. And lavender still scents some of our laundry detergents.

Boundaries: Medieval Women in Medieval Gardens

by JUDITH ARNOPP

Most of my novels feature at least one scene with a woman in a medieval garden. It may not be a key moment in the book but I like to illustrate how intricately linked high status women were to their gardens.

While I was at university I wrote a paper tracing the evolution of the medieval garden motif from its biblical roots through medieval art and on to Chaucer's development of the garden as a literary device.

The ideal of the garden was initially evoked in King Solomon's *Song of Songs,* and it is there that we see the first links between the enclosed garden and womanhood. The tradition slowly expanded to incorporate the story of the Fall from Paradise and the Cult of the Virgin Mary, until the motif expanded into secular love poetry.

Medieval literature depicts noblemen striding about the world, galloping into battle in the service of the king, embarking upon arduous pilgrimage and living and breathing upon a vastly dangerous, stimulating stage. These men are shown to be invincible, self-assured, and in control, and there were few limits placed upon them.

The women in this literature are portrayed very differently; they rarely travel, they never fight and are usually to be found within the vicinity of the castle walls. Their role is to marry, provide heirs, and be an asset to their husband. Life for most medieval woman was closeted; we see them safe within the walls of the castle, sewing, strumming musical instruments, listening to minstrels' songs or to tales of courtly-love.

The favoured place for these activities was the garden, and many manuscripts illustrate this. We see women sitting among the flowerbeds, sometimes planting and maintaining the gardens or, more often, we find them in a lovers' tryst. Other times they are shown sitting in the shade of a tree listening to a minstrel's tales and, paradoxically, the stories they are listening to are of other women also dwelling within the safety of their own gardens.

But these fictional women were not always as ordinary as they seemed, and many of them faced complex difficulties. They were invariably highborn, young and fair, and most of them expressed a personal desire that, because they were subject to male authority, could not be fulfilled.

Chaucer managed to depict the plight of these women so empathetically that there can be little doubt that he was conscious of their predicament. Even when projecting patriarchal prejudices through the mouths of his male narrator, he managed not to indoctrinate but to reveal how flawed male expectations were.

In *The Merchant's Tale,* May is married to a decrepit, selfish old man of higher status than herself. Her needs and wishes are not considered by anyone, and only the narrator takes the time to reflect upon what her reaction may have been to the consummation of her marriage. Her husband, Januarie, builds an idyllic garden in which to make love to her, and the following scenes are a horrific inversion of the story of Eden. The walls that enclose May in the pleasure garden lead her to make dramatic and hair-raising choices, but, instead of condemning her infidelity, Chaucer chooses to ultimately reward her with the "maisterie" that, according to the tale told by the Wife of Bath, all women desire.

Emelye in *The Knight's Tale* is similarly captive within a garden, and its walls serve as a prison cell. She expresses the wish to follow the goddess Diana, to run freely through the woods, to hunt and remain chaste forever, but she is not given the choice to do so. Hotly pursued by Palamon and Arcite who fight in mortal combat for her hand, Emelye is instead given as a prize in the male game of war.

Throughout *The Canterbury Tales*, the garden becomes a place of imprisonment; the lovely grounds in *The Franklin's Tale* and *The Shipman's Tale* become places of sexual transaction and solicitation. In *The Merchant's Tale* the garden becomes a place of sexual violence and adultery. Also *The Parlement of Foules* revisits this idea of feminine entrapment and the question is: why does Chaucer pick the garden, a place of peace and beauty, as the scene for feminine suffering?

In every way the woman and the literary garden are parallel; they are both fertile, they are both fragrant and decorative, and they are both controlled by a male gardener. Left to their own devices, they will go wild. In both art and literature, the garden wall sometimes encompasses an area so vast that the garden is more like a park. This is a metaphor for the wider boundaries placed upon medieval women, even those that seem to have escaped male rule.

Eve, the first female transgressor, was sent from the safe walls of Eden on a journey that was to lead her female children to other gardens. The Virgin Mary, made perfect by the idealisation of man, is painted within her wattle walled garden, a perfect flower of femininity, the fertile, unflawed mother of the perfect child. Wherever we look in medieval art we find women and gardens, walled gardens that secure and encumber the feminine tendency to stray from the path of moral rectitude.

Women must remain in the garden and those few that do escape into the world, perhaps to go on pilgrimage like the Wife of Bath, the Prioress, and the second nun, can only do so because they have managed to escape from the bounds of matrimony.

Even these empowered women, the female pilgrims, are subject to limitations upon their freedom. The nuns are answerable to the male authority of the church, and the lusty, unrepentant Wife of Bath must, unless she wishes to lose her independence by remarrying, remain chaste.

A medieval woman was monitored for signs of wildness just as a garden was, and this provided Chaucer with the perfect allegory. A garden, cultivated like May and Emelye, is a controlled environment where the gardener maintains constant vigilance in case his flourishing flower beds should run rampant and wild seeds take hold.

There is a wonderful example of a medieval garden at Tretower in Powys, and it is well worth a visit.

A SEER, A PROPHET, OR A WITCH?

BY SANDRA BYRD

And it shall come to pass in the last days, saith God, I will pour out of my Spirit upon all flesh: and your sons and your daughters shall prophesy, and your young men shall see visions, and your old men shall dream dreams....

—Acts 2:17 (KJV)

FIVE WOMEN IN THE BIBLE ARE EXPRESSLY STATED AS POSSESSING THE TITLE OF PROPHetess: Miriam, Deborah, Huldah, Noahdiah, and Isaiah's wife. Philip is mentioned in Acts as having four daughters who prophesied, which brings the number of known Biblical prophetesses to nine. There is no reason to believe that there weren't thousands more, undocumented throughout history, then and now. According to religious tradition, women have often been powerful seers, and that is why I've included them in my novel *The Secret Keeper: A Novel of Kateryn Parr*.

Hundreds of years before the renaissance, which would bring about improved education for women, Saint Hildegard of Bingen (1098-1179) wrote medicinal texts and composed music. She also oversaw the illumination of many manuscripts and wrote lengthy theological treatises. But what she is best known for, and was beatified for, were her visions.

Hildegard said that she first saw "The Shade of the Living Light" at the age of three, and by the age of five she began to understand that she was experiencing visions. In her forties she was instructed by God to write them down. She said:

> *I set my hand to the writing. While I was doing it, I sensed, as I mentioned before, the deep profundity of scriptural exposition.... I spoke and wrote these things not by the invention of my heart or that of any other person, but as by the secret mysteries of God I heard and received them in the heavenly places. And again I heard a voice from Heaven saying to me, 'Cry out therefore, and write thus!'*

Spiritual gifting is not given for the edification of the person receiving it, but for the church at large. Hildegard wrote three volumes of her mystical visions, and then biblically exegeted them herself. Her theology was not, as one might expect, shunned by the church establishment of the time, but instead Pope Eugenius III gave her work his approval and she was published in Paris in 1513.

Several centuries later, Julian of Norwich continued Hildegard's tradition as a seer, a mystic, and a writer. In her early thirties, Julian had a series of visions which she claimed came from Jesus Christ. In them, she felt His deep love and had a desire to transmit that He desired to be known as a God of joy and compassion and not duty and judgment. Her book, *Revelations of Divine Love*, is said to be the first book written in the English language by a woman. She was well known as a mystic and a spiritual director by both men and women. The message of love and joy that she delivered is still celebrated today; she has feast days in the Roman Catholic, Anglican, and Lutheran traditions.

It had been for good cause that Hildegard and Julian kept their visions to themselves for a time. Visions were not widely accepted by society as a whole, and women in particular were often accused of witchcraft.

This risk was perhaps an even stronger danger in sixteenth and seventeenth century England when "witch hunts" were common. While there is no doubt that there was a real practice of witchcraft occurring in some places, the fear of it whipped up suspicion where no actual witchcraft was found. Henry VIII, after imprisoning Anne Boleyn, proclaimed to his illegitimate son, among others, that they were all lucky to have escaped Anne's witchcraft. The evidence? So obviously bewitching him away from his "good" judgment.

In that century, the smallest sign, imagined or not, could be used to indict a "witch". A gift handling herbs? Witchcraft. An unrestrained tongue? Witchcraft. Floating rather than sinking when placed in a body of water when accused of witchcraft and therefore tested? Guilty for sure. Women with "suspicious" spiritual gifts, including dreams and visions, had to be particularly careful. And yet they, like Hildegard and Julian before them, had been given just such a gift to share with others. And share they must.

One woman in the court of Queen Kateryn Parr is strongly believed to have had a gift of prophecy. Her name was Anne Calthorpe, the Countess of Sussex. One source possibly hinting at such a gift can be found at Kathy Emerson's terrific webpage of Tudor women: Emerson says that Calthorpe,

> was at court when Katherine Parr was queen and shared her evangelical beliefs. Along with other ladies at court, she was implicated in the heresy of Anne Askew. In 1549 she was examined by a commission 'for errors in scripture' and that 'the Privy Council imprisoned two men, Hartlepoole and Clarke, for lewd prophesies and other slanderous matters' touching the king and the council. Hartlepoole's wife and the countess of Sussex were jailed as 'a lesson to beware of sorcery.'

According to religious tradition women have often had very active prophetic gifts; we are mystical, engaging, and intuitive. I admire our sisters throughout history who actively, risk-takingly, used their intellectual and spiritual gifts with whatever power they had at hand.

Money Lending in the Middle Ages, or You Think Your Visa Card's Rates Are Bad?

by KATHERINE ASHE

> *"His lord answered and said unto him, 'Thou wicked, slothful servant, thou knewest that I reap where I sowed not, and gather where I have not strawed: Thou oughtest therefore to have put my money to the exchangers and then at my coming I should have received mine own with usury.'"*
>
> –Matthew 25:26-27

THAT IS THE PARABLE OF THE TALENTS, JESUS' TEACHING REGARDING MONEY LENDING. Granted, he was using this story as a parallel of what he expected of his followers in terms of making things of the spirit known and not hiding them. But he hardly would have used the example of usury if he opposed it—though he didn't think it a proper activity in the Temple itself, obviously.

There is an impression abroad that money lending was forbidden to Christians during medieval times. It certainly was not. In fact, the principal bankers to the lordly class were the knightly Orders, the Hospitallers and the Templars, and the Church itself was not above acting as collection agent for even the worst of usurers.

Regarding the knightly Orders, this business of theirs came about naturally in the course of their leadership in crusades to the Holy Land. A lord, leaving home for a venture to the Middle East that would last several years in all likelihood, needed to be able to draw funds in Palestine. Secured by his rents back home, he took a loan, payable at the Templars' or the Hospitallers' headquarters at Acre.

The loan entailed interest, for the knightly bankers took risks: would or could the properties entailed actually be able to repay the debt? Like any anxious banker, the knights charged what interest the business could support, sometimes 20% to 30% per annum.

The lord, upon signing for the loan before leaving home, received a written receipt cashable for silver or gold coin at Acre. This was not the beginning of notations of debt standing in the place of actual money. For that one must look back to ancient Egypt and temple credits and debits for the faithfuls' contributions to Ra, or taxes owed and paid to pharaoh. (See David Graeber's *Debt: The First 5000 Years* for an intriguing summary of the subject by an instigator of "Shut Down Wall Street.")

Apart from the Templars and Hospitallers, one could, in the 13th century, take a loan from the bankers in the French city of Cahors. Let's have a look at one such debt.

In the year 1232, Ranulf, the Earl of Chester, died, leaving a note for a debt of 200 marks, owed him by his young cousin Simon de Montfort. The note went as payment of a debt Ranulf owed to Piers Mauclerc, the Count of Brittany, and Piers sold the debt for quick cash to a money lender of Cahors—though the interest rate with this banker was 60% per annum.

The Cahorsine banker did nothing to inform Montfort of his receipt of the debt and application of the 60% interest rate to it, but let it accumulate that monstrous interest for five years, at which point the debt amounted to 2,080 marks. Even then he did nothing to collect but instead, at considerable profit to himself, sold the interest-heavy debt to the Bishop of Soisson—and left him to collect the full amount.

The Bishop wrote to Montfort, informing him of the debt and demanding payment of 2,080 marks. Montfort, under the impression that this interest rate was ludicrous—and that Ranulf had lent him money interest free in the first place (he had already repaid most of what his cousin had lent)—refused to pay anything more than the originally owed 200 marks. At which the Bishop of Soisson excommunicated this debtor.

An excommunicated person was cast out of the company of fellow Christians and bound over to hell. Now that is debt-collection clout.

The antidote was to go on crusade, which Montfort did. And that not only lifted excommunications but cleared all debts as well.

That Jews did survive, and even prospered, under such living and working conditions as these in England during the Middle Ages is cause for awe, and deep respect for their business capabilities.

SOURCES

Ashe, Katherine. *Montfort the Early Years 1229 to 1243.* Wake Robin Press, 2010 (p. 120 and note, p. 307).

Bemont, C. *Simon de Montfort.* Translated by E. F. Jacob. 1930, (p. 60).

Calendar of Patent Rolls, 1232-47 (p. 185).

Shirely. *Royal Letters*, Vol. II (p.16).

King Lear's Town: A Little History of the City of Leicester

BY **KATHERINE ASHE**

In the so-called "dark" and "middle" ages, Leicester was not a happy place. In 1173, by order of King Henry II, the city was besieged, razed, and depopulated as punishment for the support its earl, Robert "White-Hands," had given Queen Eleanor (of Aquitaine) and her son, Richard the Lionheart. On Richard's ascension to the throne, the Earl of Leicester was forgiven and rebuilt his hall. But the town recovered very slowly and sporadically, being still sparsely populated within its walls as late as 1722.

The situation was so bad that White Hands forgave any taxes the townspeople owed him. Of course, it was his fault they had suffered at all, so renouncing his taxes was the least he could do.

But Leicester had a prominent past. In the early Christian era, Leicester had been a major Roman town at the crossing of two of the most important of the Roman legions' roads in Britain. Fine mosaic floors in costly Roman villas have been excavated near the city. Endearing objects may be seen in Leicester's museum, such as a bowl inscribed from a centurion to his lady love.

Massive stone arches, perhaps a part of the Roman baths, still stand.

In the Middle Ages, those thick walls with their gaps served as the Jewish district, with shacks built against the walls, using the gaps as part of the shelter. Jews were not permitted to own land. But since no one owned the ancient stretch of wall and arches, the Jews remained there undisturbed—at least until the shameful incident of Simon de Montfort's youth, when he evicted them from the city.

Montfort had no title, and no knights or henchmen at the time, so he probably didn't accomplish that eviction single-handed. It's most likely the people of Leicester joined in the rout, thus cancelling their debts to the Jews who were chiefly money-lenders. Similar attacks against Jews in London and elsewhere occurred and seem to have been motivated by a desire to not pay back loans, rather than for any religious reasons. Being a Jew in England in the 13th century was hazardous.

It may not be coincidence that when young Simon drove out the Jews of Leicester, his mentor, Fr. Robert Grosseteste, had just founded a refuge for homeless Jews, in London—later the site of the Public Record Office. However, the Jews Simon drove from the old Roman wall probably knew that the local priest (Dean of Lincoln Cathedral) was offering not just hospitality, but an attempt at conversion. They simply crossed the River Soar to Simon's great-aunt's house, where they found sympathetic shelter.

From there they spread all over England the news of their mistreatment by the would-be Earl of Leicester. It made a very bad beginning for a young Frenchman hoping to redeem an English title.

Another instance of the impact of the youthful Simon de Montfort on Leicester appears in the royal court's legal records. The villeins of the Leicester fief brought suit against Simon for fencing their fields. He had done more than fence the fields—he had tried to persuade them away from the age-old three-field system of cultivation and toward the raising of sheep and cattle.

It may be that the depopulation of Leicester had made the three-field system too unproductive, with too many of the field rows going uncultivated. It is well to remember Montfort's mentor again, the ubiquitous Robert Grosseteste, who had published the then most respected "modern" work on manor management.

It is unlikely Montfort ventured such a change without Grosseteste's advice. As for the future of Leicester, woolen processing became its chief industry and remained so until after WWII.

But let's go further back in time.

After the conquest of Britain by the Angles and Saxons and the division of Britain into the heptarchy, the "seven kingdoms," in 753, Leicester became the capital city of the kingdom of Mercia.

The name "Leicester" derives from "Legre-caestre." Lyger, or Legre, was the old name of the River Soar, which encloses two sides of the old city. If King Lear is not to be looked upon merely as mythical, then Leicester was the site of his castle.

There is a mysterious conical mound with a door set in it on the castle grounds. A fairy hill? My inquiries when I was there only gained the answer, *"It was where m'lord kept his wines."* Well, that too—probably.

In 874, Leicester fell to the Danes. Its Roman walls protecting its perimeter (not the walls of the baths that became the Jewry) were destroyed, and the city became incorporated in the Danish "five boroughs," which included Nottingham, Lincoln, Derby, and Stamford.

In 920, Ethelfloeda, the daughter of King Alfred, succeeded in raising an army and driving the Danes from Leicester, Derby, and Nottingham. She caused the Roman walls to be rebuilt, with an assortment of stone and Roman tiles cemented together with an extraordinarily sturdy mortar that adhered in clumps, making any subsequent reuse of the building materials all but impossible.

City and castle walls were knocked down and rebuilt regularly in medieval times. The Palestinian castle at Caesaria was disassembled and reassembled with every passing phase of Moslem or Christian crusading success. To not be able to reassemble the cut stones of a city or castle wall was an unusual and serious problem.

After Ethelfloeda's death at Castle Tamworth in 922, Leicester passed back and forth between the Anglo-Saxons and the Danes, resulting in further demolition—no longer repairable thanks to Ethelfloeda's mortar.

In 1068, the Saxon Earl Edwin of Coventry and Leicester (grandson of the minimally covered Lady Godiva of Coventry and Leicester—one always hopes that notable ride was in summertime) surrendered and did homage to William the Conqueror. Leicester passed to William's follower Hugh de Grantmesnil as Norman governor.

After William's death, Hugh supported Robert of Normandy, rather than William's heir, William Rufus, or his brother Henry. When Henry succeeded as Henry I, Hugh retired to a monastery in France, and the king created his friend, Robert de Beaumont, the first Norman Earl of Leicester. After him came Robert de Bosso, who enjoyed the earldom for fifty years.

Then there was Robert "White Hands." His son and heir, Robert FitzParnel, died without heirs and the inheritance of the earldom of Leicester passed to Father White Hands' surviving sisters. One of those ladies was Margaret, the Countess of Winchester, the very one who welcomed the fleeing Jews—she already had complaints of her own against her grand-nephew for putting up his fences and encroaching on a corner of her lands. But Margaret only got twelve of the seventy-eight fiefs belonging to the earldom.

The other sister, who inherited the earldom's titles and sixty-six fiefs, was the mother of Simon de Montfort Pere, the crusader and harrier of Albigensians. There was a prediction, in his time, that the people of England would rise up and elect Simon de Montfort their king. The crusader announced he would "*never set foot in a land given to such prophecies.*" And he never did.

Chartres window has roused a great deal of confusion regarding the arms of Simon, the Earl of Leicester, whose blazon, as depicted by his friend Matthew Paris in his *Chronica Majora*, shows a two-tailed, *red* lion rampant on a *white* ground—suitably differenced from his father white-lion-on-red arms as a younger son's would be.

Simon Pere might have been disappointed if he had claimed his titles. Of those sixty-six fiefs, sixty were held by the knights whom the earl was expected to lead in battle. Most of those knights paid no rent, giving military service instead, although one of them was compelled, in lieu of rent, to deliver to the earl each year a single red rose. (This has echoes of *Beauty and the Beast*, but it's true. One wonders how commonly acceptable a single rose was for the clearing of a debt. There were certain advantages to living in the Middle Ages.)

Simon de Montfort's son and namesake, after the father's death and the family's relative bankruptcy, not only set foot in England, but did everything he could to gain the titles.

But fighting the Welsh for King Henry III accomplished little for him. It was when he fell in love with the King's sister, who was a nun, and entered into a secret and hasty marriage with her—followed by a successful effort at bribing the Pope to lift the nun's vows—that King Henry finally granted Simon the title Earl of Leicester and its companion honor, Steward of England.

A few decades later, much to Henry's chagrin, the people of England did elect Simon de Montfort to be their king. Luckily for Henry, he refused the Crown.

With Simon's death at Evesham, and the stripping from his sons of all of their claims of inheritance in England, Leicester passed to the Crown and became a bonus for royal relatives, enjoyed by a series of Lancastrians until John of Gaunt's heir ascended the throne as Henry IV.

The earldom then remained in the Crown's keeping again until Queen Elizabeth's favorite, Robert Dudley, was granted the title in 1564.

With the fall of Dudley from royal favor, Leicester went back to the Crown—to be lobbed like a tennis ball out to the Sidney family in 1618, where it bounced happily for the next hundred and fifty years before a royal serve sent it to Thomas Coke. Strangely, Coke's descendants didn't receive the earldom after his death in 1795, but it was lobbed back to them in 1837, and has remained with the Coke family ever since, the Seventh Coke Earl of Leicester receiving the title in 1994.

Leicester's chief industry, from the time of Earl Simon on, was the processing of wool. Prior to WWII, a major business was the lindsey-woolsey works, where a sturdy fabric of wool and linen was manufactured. During the war the factory was taken out of private hands for the war effort.

In recent years, Leicester has blossomed as an academic center, with Montfort University perhaps the largest and fastest growing educational institution in England. Earl Simon, whose statue is one of four ringing the base of the town clock, would be pleased.

SOURCES

Hollings, James Francis. *Roman Leicester*. The Literary and Philosophical Society, 1851.

Nichols, John. *History and Antiquities of the Town and County of Leicester*. 1795.

Staveley, Thomas. *History and Antiquities of the antient Towne and once Citte of Leicester*, MS. 1679 .

Stenton, F.M. "Documents Illustrative of the Social and Economic History of the Danelaw," *British Academy* 347 (1920).

Thompson, James. *History of Leicester from the Time of the Romans to the End of the Seventeenth Century*. 1849.

Throsby, John. *History and Antiquities of the Town of Leicester*. 1791.

Miniature Cathedrals: England's Market Crosses

by DEBORAH SWIFT

There is a wonderful market cross at Kirkby Lonsdale, a town near to where I live, where I sometimes go to shop or enjoy a pot of tea with friends. Seeing it made me curious to find out about other market crosses which are wonderful examples of miniature architecture, reflecting their time and the style of the day.

The primary purpose of wayside crosses was to remind the traveller that he was there but for the Grace of God:

> *for this reason ben Crosses by ye waye that whan folke passynge see the Crosse, they sholde thynke on Hym that deyed on the Crosse, and worsyppe Hym above all thynge*
> —Wynken de Worde, 1496

In Norman times crosses were often put up to define boundaries, particularly of a place of sanctuary. Within a mile of St. Wilfrid's church in Ripon a man was safe, no matter what crime he had committed. Crosses were therefore erected on each of the five major roads leading into the town to show the boundaries of the sanctuary.

However, as time went on, these crosses developed a more secular use as landmarks, meeting places, and points of trade. They also became places where punishment was meted out under the eye of God as represented by the cross. Stocks and pillories are often to be found at their bases. In Oakham, the market cross, used to trade butter and other produce, has its stocks right up next to the cross.

In Wales, the market cross was used to hang the heads of foxes and wolves captured in the vicinity as well as to punish thieves—foxes and wolves being considered a type of thief. A reward was offered for the capture of a wolf which was the same price as that of the reward for a robber; dog foxes were worth 2s 6d and vixens 1s 6d as late as the middle of the nineteenth century. Examples of these crosses can be seen at Eglwyscummin and Amroth.

As time went on, the cross grew a roof, and the covered areas beneath the crosses were used for trade, particularly after the Reformation, when people were unsure whether they were still to be used as "places of worship" or whether these old monuments would be against the edicts of the King. But even as early as 1337, the market cross at Norwich was large enough to house a chapel and four shops—the early equivalent of the modern shopping mall!

The finest of these is at Chichester. Built in 1501, it is octagonal in shape, features eight flying buttresses with matching arches, and above it the pinnacle is a lantern spire, originally lit at night. Salisbury has a similar one but hexagonal. It is known as the Poultry Cross, presumably because poultry was sold there. There are other examples at Leighton Buzzard and Shepton Mallet.

One of the most famous "preaching crosses", ones from which open air sermons were delivered, was Paul's Cross, erected in the early 13th century near the wall of old St. Paul's, London. Before it was pulled down in 1641, it was the scene of many historic events—mayors were elected under its shadow, heretics excommunicated there, and in 1588, the first news of the Armada's defeat was announced from it to the public. Today few preaching crosses remain, except the Black Friar's Preaching Cross in Hereford and the one at Iron Acton Gloucestershire.

In 1643, under Puritan rule, Parliament passed an act ordering all crosses in churches, chapels, and churchyards to be taken away, as "Monuments of Superstition and Idolatry". This led to the destruction of many fine crosses including Charing Cross in London, although stones from this cross were later used to make the pavements in front of the Palace of Whitehall.

Enterprising sympathisers who wanted to retain their connection with the cross also made souvenirs by cutting and polishing the stone and using it as knife handles. This is the period that interested me when writing *The Gilded Lily*, which features some Puritan characters alongside the libertines of London.

My explorations into these crosses led me to explore what are known as "The Eleanor Crosses", twelve crosses erected between 1291 and 1294. This became a whole separate interest, quite apart from the research I was doing for my books, and you can find out more about these beautiful monuments on my blog.

RELIC IN THE VALLEY: ST. MARTIN'S AT CWMIOU

BY **JUDITH ARNOPP**

At the time of the crucifixion, when darkness swallowed the world, a great earthquake struck the Vale of Ewyas, ripping a chunk from the side of the mountain above Cwmiou.

Today, nestled among ash, alder, and beech, the church of St. Martin seems to erupt from the undergrowth, the gravestones heaving and swaying in waves of bending grass. From the top of the graveyard, where the ancient stones stagger like an old man's teeth, it looks as if the church has come to life and is lumbering off down the hill. And the feeling of disorientation does not end when you push open the heavy oak door and step inside.

The silence swallows you, the aroma of mildew and a thousand years of Christian faith seep from yellow internal walls that twist and buckle like a living thing, making your feet run off of their own accord as you progress along the Welsh flag-stoned aisle. As your brain battles to make sense of the odd angles, it is uncannily like being aboard ship. I expect you are wondering why.

The name "Cwmiou" or "Cwmyoy" translates as "the valley of the yoke" and refers to the shape of the mountain above, which resembles an oxen's yoke.

The nature of the geology of the Honddu valley has caused the land to slowly shift and slide, and it is this land slippage, upon which the church was built, that has endowed St. Martin's with its matchless charm.

There are no right angles at St. Martin's. The tower lurches north (5.2" out of perpendicular), while the chancel arch and east window tilt alarmingly to the right. Consequently, it confuses the mind, confounds the senses—but there are other reasons besides this for visiting.

The church itself is a simple structure, consisting of nave, chancel, tower, and porch, dating from the 13th to 16th centuries. An original 15-16th century window bears some wonderful scrollwork, and a small stone stairway in the chancel leads to the remains of a rood loft, which was destroyed during the Reformation. (Just a little drive up the road at St. Issui's church at Patricio there is a superb example of a 15th century rood loft and screen that you should really not miss if you ever make this journey.)

19th century restoration work saw some of the windows at St. Martin's replaced, and it is believed that the plaster ceilings were removed at that time, but some examples of the original survive in the porch. To prevent further slippage, the church is now buttressed at the west end and large iron stays were added in the 1960s.

The church houses examples of the work of the Brute family, master masons from Llanbedr, who were active from the 1720s through to the 1840s. Thomas, Aaron, and John Brute worked in a distinctive style of artisan Rococo, and there is a fine collection of tombstones and memorials in this local tradition. Some examples are painted as well as carved, the fat little cherubs surrounded by Rococo wreaths of leaves and flowers.

Look out for some memorable epitaphs too, like the one on the grave of Thomas Price, who died in 1682.

> *Thomas Price he takes his nap*
> *In our common mother lap*
> *Waiting to heare the Bridegroome say*
> *"Awake my dear and come away."*

Also of interest at St. Martin's is a medieval stone cross that was dug up on a nearby farm in the 19th century. The cross is believed to be post-Norman, possibly a copy from an earlier cross or the design taken from a manuscript. It may well have been a cross marking the pilgrim's route along the valley to Brecon and on to the cathedral at St. David's. The font is also early medieval and the marks of the mason's chisel still plainly to be seen.

In this area of unspoiled medieval churches, Cwmiou would be unremarkable were it not for its structural irregularities. I have never experienced a building like it, and it really *is* an experience.

The journey to Cwmiou is a pilgrimage in itself. Although it is not far from the busy market town of Abergavenny, you will need to watch out for stray sheep as you drive through sleepy hamlets and along corkscrewing, almost perpendicular lanes. As the sunlight flickers through the trees and you turn the last bend and glimpse the staggering walls of St. Martin's peeking from the woods, you will know in that instant that you were right to come.

Welsh Idylls: St. Gwenog's Church

BY JUDITH ARNOPP

JUST A STONE'S THROW FROM MY HOME IN THE PARISH OF LLANWENOG IS ST. GWENOG'S church. I have only recently found the time to go and have a close look and thought I would share my visit with you.

The Church of St. Gwenog is delightful, and anyone in love with ancient churches and planning a trip to the area should put it on their list of places to visit. It is only a small building and does not take long to explore, but entering the church is like stepping into another world.

A memorable battle was fought in Llanwenog in 981, between the Dane Godfrid and the native Welsh chieftain, Eineon ab Owain, a battle in which the Danes were totally defeated. Nearby, there is a field on a farm named Ty Cam where the engagement is believed to have occurred. The field is called Cae'r Vaes, or roughly translated, "the battle field," although whether the story has its root in fact or legend is open to debate.

In ancient, pagan times the word "Llan" was used to denote an enclosure or sacred place. Early Christians built their churches in such places in an attempt to displace older religions. By utilising ancient religious sites, Christian priests thought to encourage pagan worshippers to abandon the old gods and adopt the new teachings.

There are many such sites in Wales, and Llanwenog is possibly one of the oldest for, although most of the extant building dates back to the 13th century, the foundation of the earliest church dates to the 6th. As I circumnavigate the graveyard, it is still just possible to detect that the original enclosure or "Llan" was circular, or oval, in shape although it has now been extended and squared off at one end.

We know almost nothing about St. Gwenog. She is mentioned in the Laws of Howell Dda copied in the 15th century, and in the 18th century an annual local fair, held in January, was known as Ffair Gwenog's.

Links have also been made with St. Gwennlian who was active locally, but it is a link that is difficult to establish. Even St. Gwenog's Well, once famous for its healing properties, has long since disappeared. Its existence points to the reason for the site being allocated as a "Llan" in pagan times as water was the earliest form of worship, followed by that of the sun, until Christianity incorporated elements of those older religions into its own.

Inside the church, I see thick whitewashed walls and, at the altar, an early stone carving of Mary and St. John at the foot of the cross. It is very badly weathered, having originally been built into the exterior end of the side chapel. Now it is safe and sound in the new altar, the figures barely discernible. I turn away and spy an early wall painting of the Apostles and the Ten Commandments; the faces peer out at me through the fog of time while, above me, the beautiful ceiling rafters smile down. Richly carved pews escort me to the door, and I climb a few worn stone steps while the tiny carved heads of the saints watch me as I pass.

Outside, the battlemented tower draws my eye from the older, softer parts of the church. It is an imposing feature, providing protection for the village in times of strife. It was a later addition to the building, built in the 15th century by Sir Rhys ap Thomas whose heraldric shield is displayed above one of the windows. The building was to commemorate Henry VII's victory over Richard III at Bosworth in 1485. Many men from Llanwenog parish fought and died for Henry in his quest for the throne, but, once established, the Tudor dynasty did little to enhance the fortunes of their Welsh countrymen.

I sit for a while among the markers of the dead and think about what I have seen. I am touched by the peace and the great age of the place and love every inch of it. But for me, the best thing about the visit is the font. I slip back inside for another look.

It used to sit near the western doorway but has been moved to the south side of the lady chapel. Today it is filled with a tacky flower arrangement totally out of keeping with the awesome antiquity of the piece.

I take away the flowers and with the tip of one finger trace the marks where the cover once sat. It dates from the Norman period and is showing its age. The stone is carved with the heads of the twelve Apostles, worn from centuries of visitors drawn to touch the primitive features as I am doing now.

I have seen these carved faces described variously as "crude", "grotesque", and "rough", but to me, they are beautiful—the tracks of the ancient chisel giving voice to the long dead craftsman. I wish I could spend longer here. I run my fingers over the surface and feel as if I am clasping the gnarled hand of the mason that worked it.

TRETOWER COURT AND CASTLE

BY JUDITH ARNOPP

I HAVE LIVED IN WALES FOR ALMOST TWENTY YEARS NOW, AND, ALTHOUGH I AM STILL STUM-bling upon new treasures, there are some places that I find myself returning to time and time again. One of my favourite places is Tretower Court. It sits in the green Usk Valley between Abergavenny and Brecon, seemingly untouched, timeless.

When compared with the tourist hot spots like Pembroke and Conwy castles, the site is small, but for me, the lack of gift shop and tearoom simply adds to the atmosphere. The noise of the traffic dwindles, and all you can hear is birdsong and the sporadic bleating of sheep. Best of all, as the place is little known, there are occasions when you can find yourself there completely alone, with the ghosts of the past whispering in your ear.

Tretower marks the period when castles were abandoned in favour of more comfortable, less fortified homes. There are two distinct sites at Tretower, each as valuable in their own way as the other: the later medieval house and, two hundred yards to the north-west, the remains of the 12th century castle stronghold, the round tower being added later in the period.

Although the more domestic court building was erected early in the fourteenth century, later additions to the Tower suggest that the stronghold was not entirely abandoned at this time. Should the house have come under attack, the inhabitants would simply gather up their possessions, round up the livestock, and head for the impregnable walls of the tower.

The earliest part of medieval *house* is the north range, which dates from the early fourteenth century. The masonry and latrine turret on the west end may even have been built as early as 1300. The four major phases of building can clearly be seen from the central courtyard as can the later modifications added as late as the seventeenth century.

As you move through the building from room to room, duck through low doorways, climb twisting stairways, and creep into the dark recesses of the latrine turrets, you will know you are not alone. So much has happened here, so many people have passed through, so much laughter has rung out, and so many tears have fallen. A very brief history of the place reveals a wealth of stories waiting to be told.

The first building on the site was a motte and bailey raised by a Norman follower by the name of Picard. The property passed through the family's male line until the fourteenth century when it moved, via the female line, to Ralph Bluet and then, again through the marriage of another daughter, to James de Berkeley.

His son, also James, became Lord Berkeley on the death of his uncle. Tretower was later purchased from James by his mother's husband, Sir William ap Thomas. Sir William's second wife, Gwladys, gave him a son, William Herbert, later the earl of Pembroke, who inherited both Tretower and Raglan Castle on his father's death. Tretower was later gifted to William's half-brother, Roger Vaughan the younger, around 1450.

Herbert and Vaughan both played an important role during the Wars of the Roses with William Herbert becoming friend and advisor to Edward IV. His career continued to prosper until he was executed in 1469, following the Yorkist defeat at Edgecote.

Roger Vaughan, who was responsible for most of the major reconstruction of Tretower Court, was knighted in 1464, was present as a veteran at Tewkesbury, and was finally captured at Chepstow. There, he was beheaded by Jasper Tudor in an act of vengeance for beheading his father, Owen Tudor, ten years previously. Tretower remained in the possession of the Vaughans until the eighteenth century when it was sold and became a farm.

Years of neglect and disrepair followed, and it was not until the twentieth century that preservation and repair work began.

I am not a great fan of reconstructions, although I do realise their value. Too often historic buildings are Disneyfied and their historic role trivialized, but the restoration at Tretower Court is not like that at all, or not yet anyway. The work is totally sympathetic, and the building maintains an elegance and integrity. At the risk of spouting clichés, it is like stepping back in time—one can almost hear the laughter of children from the orchard, the sound of a minstrel singing, or the murmur of women's voices from the gardens.

The garden is as beautiful and as authentic as any I have seen is this country. Laid out and designed by Francesca Kay, it has a covered walk to keep the sun from the ladies' cheeks. Tumbling red and white roses, lavender, aquilegia, foxgloves, and marigolds sprawl beside a bubbling fountain in the midst of a chequered lawn.

I spent a long time here on a Sunday morning in July, wandering through the rose arbour, lingering in the orchard before returning to the house. As I progressed along the dim corridors, I could almost hear the skirts of my gown trailing after me on the stone floors. I paused, and time was suspended as I looked through thick, green glass to the courtyard and garden below.

If you should have the good fortune to visit Wales, make the time to call in at Tretower, and don't forget to bring a picnic and a blanket, for I guarantee you will want to stay a while.

Buried Treasure: St. Mary's in Burford

BY **ANNE O'BRIEN**

A pilgrim's heart, a much loved son, and a forgotten Plantagenet princess....

St. Mary's in Burford is a village church, isolated in its churchyard, surrounded by green fields and trees, all within a short distance of the dark and secretive River Teme in the Welsh Marches county of Shropshire.

Far away from any major towns—the nearest market town is Tenbury Wells—it is a beautiful and peaceful place to spend an hour or two. The church is small, perfect in its rural setting, and visitors, I imagine, are few compared with the likes of Worcester Cathedral and Tewkesbury Abbey, both fairly close.

Inside, it is dark and full of history. The chancel goes back to the 12th century, the nave and tower to the 14th. Stepping inside, one gets the impression that very few changes have been made over the centuries, even though we know that it was extensively restored in 1889. The restoration has been very sympathetic.

But the most compelling reason for a visitor to leave the beaten track and go to Burford is to see the astonishing collection of tombs in this little church, the most important connected with the Cornewall family who were medieval Lords of Burford.

In the chancel there are three in particular not to be missed.

To the left of the altar, set in the wall under a carved arch is what looks like the base of an old brightly-painted altar. Now it is the memorial to Sir Richard Cornewall. He died in 1436, in the reign of Henry VI, in Cologne, possibly when returning from a pilgrimage to the Holy Land. He left instructions for his body to be buried in Cologne, but his heart to be returned here to his home in Burford.

In the centre of the chancel, directly before the altar, is the fully painted, wooden effigy of Edmund Cornewall. Wooden effigies are quite rare in this part of the world. Edmund died in 1508 at only 20 years of age. He is shown in full plate armour with angels supporting his head and his feet resting on a splendid little dragon wearing a golden crown, crudely carved but with much charm. There is nothing sophisticated or elegant about the carving of Edmund, but this life-sized portrayal of the young man resonates with a sense of tragic loss and grief. His distraught parents must have felt his death keenly to place his tomb in the very centre of the chancel before the altar. It takes the eye, as it was intended to.

And then, the most surprising tomb of all. Set in the wall of the chancel is the life-sized figure and tomb of Elizabeth Plantagenet. Younger daughter of John of Gaunt and Blanche of Lancaster, her governess was, of course, Katherine Swynford. She is beautifully painted as she lies under the arch—the rich red and blue looks to me as if it was restored in the 1889 renovations—with angels at her head, her cloak lined with ermine. Her face is young and serene in repose, even though she was about 61 years old when she died in 1426. She looks truly royal. Who would have expected such a Plantagenet treasure here, far from a major town?

Elizabeth was buried here because her third husband was Sir John Cornewall, Lord of Burford. Perhaps it was her choice to be brought here after death because she loved the place. We will never know. Interestingly, her husband is not buried at Burford beside her, but in Ludgate in London.

And finally, the ceiling is a true treasure. Above the tombs is a splendid late 19th century barrel vault, carved with angels with their wings outstretched, as if watching over the pilgrim, the much-mourned son, and the Plantagenet princess.

Shropshire is a beautiful county to lure the tourist who wishes to enjoy rural seclusion, and this little church at Burford with its memorials (and there are others not even mentioned here!) is an unexpected jewel in its crown.

Tudor Period
(1485–1603)

AN INCONVENIENT PRINCESS

BY NANCY BILYEAU

ON NOVEMBER 11, 1480, A CHILD WAS BAPTIZED IN THE PALACE OF ELTHAM WITH ALL solemnity and grandeur, as was fitting for a royal princess of the House of York. The child was named Bridget, after the 14th century Swedish saint who wrote of personal visions of Christ and founded a religious order.

On baptism day Lady Margaret Beaufort, the Lancastrian heiress who was nonetheless in high standing at court, carried the one-day-old princess, a singular honor. Designated godparents were Bridget's oldest sister, the 14-year-old Elizabeth, and Bridget's grandmother, Cecily, duchess of York and mother of King Edward IV. No one could have foreseen how profoundly this trio of women would influence the destiny of Bridget of York.

After the Bishop of Chichester completed the baptism, the party carried the tiny princess to her waiting mother, with "great gifts" borne before her in procession. Bridget was the tenth and last child of Elizabeth Woodville, now 43 years of age.

History has not been kind to the consort of Edward IV. She is seen as an icily beautiful conniver who ensnared a love-struck king into a mismatch. There is another side to Elizabeth Woodville, that of a pious and diligent queen who produced a bevy of heirs as she did her best to ignore her husband's continual infidelities. But no one could deny her stubborn devotion to her own family, the Woodvilles, a myopia that cost her the trust of the kingdom's nobility.

During the first years of Bridget's life, her parents were much occupied with matchmaking diplomacy for their older children in the courts of Europe. Everyone assumed glittering futures for the two princes and six princesses.

The family's Christmastide in 1482 awed chroniclers. Like his grandson Henry VIII, the strapping King Edward loved fashion and splendor. He was *"clad in a great variety of most costly garments, of quite a different cut to those which had usually been seen hitherto in our kingdom,"* said one. The king presented a *"distinguished air to beholders, he being a person of most elegant appearance, and remarkable beyond all others for the attractions of his person."* The beauty of the daughters who surrounded him was "surpassing."

Less than four months later, King Edward caught a chill and died of his illness. Bridget's golden future darkened. She was now set on a path of troubling obscurity, tinged with rumors of madness and even, far in the future, sexual scandal.

It all happened very fast. A few weeks after the death of the king, the Prince of Wales was seized by Edward's younger brother, Richard of Gloucester, and Queen Elizabeth fled with the rest of her children to the sanctuary of Westminster. There she was observed "all desolate and dismayed." The most powerful in the land supported Richard, not Elizabeth. Conditions were not comfortable for the new widow and her children. But she refused to leave the Church-sanctified protection of sanctuary.

Bridget stayed with her mother through this harrowing time. After months of pressure, the queen broke down and turned over her younger son, Prince Richard, to men who promised he would be kept safe. The two princes disappeared from view shortly after; their fate is one of history's saddest and most tantalizing mysteries.

Richard III proclaimed the marriage of Edward IV and Elizabeth Woodville invalid because of an obscure pre-contract to another English woman. All the children were now illegitimate. On March 1, 1484, Elizabeth Woodville finally emerged with her daughters from sanctuary and appeared to be amenable to the new king. But in reality she was deep in conspiracy with Lady Margaret Beaufort to marry her oldest daughter to Margaret's son in exile, Henry Tudor.

In 1485, Henry Tudor claimed the throne after winning the Battle of Bosworth. He revoked the illegitimacy of the children, including Bridget, now five years old. He married the oldest girl, Elizabeth of York, as he'd promised.

But the status of the entire York family was uneasy in the infancy of the Tudor reign. In the court and country, grumblings turned to conspiracy. Pretenders emerged. Rebellions flared.

Rather suddenly, Elizabeth Woodville retired from public life to a suite of rooms in Bermondsey Abbey, a Benedictine order in the London borough of Southwark. Some believe her son-in-law forced the duplicitous queen dowager into monastic life because he thought she was plotting against him, though there is no evidence of it.

Said one biographer, *"Nineteen years as queen had cost her three sons, a father, and two brothers sacrificed to the court's bloody politics. Elizabeth Woodville now sought solace and peace in service to her God."*

But what about Bridget? Did she go with her mother to the abbey—or find a place with her sister the queen or another sibling? No one knows. The next time Bridget appears in historical record is in 1490, when she, too, left the public arena for religious life. But the youngest child of Edward IV was sent to live not at Bermondsey but at Dartford Priory, a Dominican order in Kent. No one knows if this was because of her own piety, her mother's wish to devote a child to God, or the sad fact that Bridget had become an inconvenience to her family.

There were no ten-year-old nuns, not even in the late medieval age. Only adults could take vows. But abbeys accepted boarders, and this might have been what happened to Bridget.

There is a theory to Bridget's rustication. Perhaps an unhappy childhood had unbalanced her. Ponders a historian: *"Bridget was excluded because she had mental incapacities and was hidden away to save the royal family any embarrassment."* However, a priory such as Dartford was far from a mental hospital. The sole Dominican convent in England was known for its library and its members' intellectual achievements. To be considered, a woman must be able to read or be capable of learning.

Another more probable explanation is that Bridget's grandmother, Cecily of York, had a hand in choosing Dartford. The priory attracted women of aristocratic background, often connected to the House of York. Prioress Joan Scrope, who oversaw Dartford in the 1470s, was the granddaughter of Cecily's sister, Margaret Neville. Cecily also bequeathed three beautiful devotional books to Bridget, including a tome of the life of Catherine Siena, a Dominican mystic. These seem unlikely gifts to a young woman with "mental incapacities."

Elizabeth Woodville died in her sleep on June 8, 1492. Her youngest child, twelve-year-old Bridget, attended the funeral, a simple one at the express wish of the queen. She was buried beside her beloved husband Edward at Windsor.

The Tudor regime continued to gain strength. Bridget's sister, the new queen, gave birth to four children who survived childhood.

Elizabeth of York quietly did what she could to protect her sisters and promote their interests. She supported Bridget with funds from her own privy purse:

> On the 6th July, 1502, 3l. 6s.8d. were paid by her sister the Queen to the Abbess of Dartford, towards the charges of Lady Bridget there; and in September following, a person was paid for going from Windsor to Dartford to Lady Bridget, with a message from her Majesty.

At some point Bridget took vows and became a sister of Dartford. One writer says: "Her whole adult life had been dedicated to God, within the walls of the nunnery, where her family had made little or no effort to see her." However, this is something of a misunderstanding of life in an enclosed order.

Visitors, family or otherwise, are rare; the sisters form a sealed-off community dedicated to prayer and intercession for the souls of the dead, with time set aside for study, embroidery, gardening, music, and the more menial tasks of the priory.

Elizabeth of York died in childbirth in 1503; her husband died in 1509, to be succeeded by young Prince Henry. It is not known if Henry VIII ever met his Aunt Bridget. Certainly he gave no thought to sparing Dartford Priory in the break from Rome. It was demolished along with all of the other monasteries of England in the late 1530s.

But Bridget did not live through the Dissolution; she did not suffer yet another wrenching change in her fate wrought by others. Sister Bridget of York died of unknown causes in 1517. She was only 37.

A new theory has come to light. One source believes she gave birth to an illegitimate child, a girl named Agnes, in 1498. Pregnancies were obviously very unusual at a priory and the cause of great scandal, though they did happen. There are no confirmed births to any of the nuns of Dartford.

Still, this girl supposedly became a ward of the priory, her expenses paid by the queen. She was called Agnes of Eltham, a reference to the palace where Bridget was born. According to Wikipedia: "Agnes later left the Priory and was married to Adam Langstroth, the head of a landed family in Yorkshire (the ancestral home of the Yorks and refuge of York loyalists in the early Tudor period) with 'a considerable dowry.'"

The leading book on the priory, Paul Lee's Nunneries, Learning and Spirituality in Late Medieval English Society: The Dominican Priory of Dartford, contains no mention of a child of Bridget. Instead, the book says: "Sister Agnes Roper, daughter of Henry VIII's attorney general John

Roper of Eltham…was a nun at Dartford from the 1520s until the time of Dissolution." Were there two women named Agnes, or have historical records become muddled?

I traveled to Dartford while researching my novel, *The Crown*, a historical thriller whose heroine, Sister Joanna Stafford, is a fictional nun of the priory. On a quiet afternoon I walked north of the town's center and discovered the site of the ruined convent. All that remains is a large gatehouse built by Henry VIII from the rubble in 1540—now, ironically, used for wedding receptions—and a long, low wall that ran the perimeter of the Dominican sisters' home. This wall kept Bridget of York in—and the world out.

Did she find peace and fulfillment in her vocation? Perhaps Bridget created a family for herself, to replace the one she lost to death and political strife, the last violent cataclysms of the Wars of the Roses. Or did she rebel against the strict, chaste life of a Dominican sister and take a secret lover and give birth to her own baby?

Six hundred years later, as I lingered by the crumbling medieval wall that now hugs a modern road, there is no way for me to know what happened to Bridget of York, what her life was like. But in that moment, I sensed a lingering sadness.

THE WORST MARRIAGE OF THE 16TH CENTURY

BY NANCY BILYEAU

ON NOVEMBER 23, 1511, AT THE AGE OF THIRTY-SIX, ANNE OF YORK, BORN A PRINCESS, died, possibly of consumption. She had outlived not only her parents, Edward IV and Elizabeth Woodville, but her two brothers, the tragic Princes of the Tower, her oldest sister, Queen Elizabeth of York, and, saddest of all, her own four children who died at birth or not long after.

We don't know how fervently the widower of Anne of York, Lord Thomas Howard, mourned her passing. It had been a prestigious match for Howard, not least because his father, the Earl of Surrey, fought on the wrong side of the Battle of Bosworth and the newly minted Tudor monarch, Henry VII, consigned him to the Tower of London as punishment. But after Surrey, the son of the first Duke of Norfolk, was released a few years later, he dedicated himself to playing the new game in town. With success.

Thomas and Anne's union was definitely not the last time a Howard married (or attempted to marry) royalty—the 16th century is littered with the carnage of ambitious Howards. Time and again they struggled to climb that final rung of the dynastic ladder but slipped and fell. Decapitation sometimes followed or, if they were lucky, a stint in the Tower. In fact, through a century of Tudor rule, the Howards cycled in and out of the Tower of London more than any other clan.

But to return to the premature passing of Anne of York, the most significant aspect of her death is how it cleared the way for a disastrous marriage, one that, if it weren't for the truly over-the-top Henry VIII and his "ill conditioned wives," would take a leading place on a hall of marital infamy.

With apologies to Jane Austen, a childless man who stands to inherit a dukedom must be in want of a wife. Proud Thomas Howard would settle for nothing less than the best, and so he zeroed in on the children of the man who was at that time the sole duke in England: Edward Stafford, duke of Buckingham. (Charles Brandon had not yet been elevated, nor had Howard's own father.) Stafford was rich and had three daughters. The oldest, Elizabeth, was of marriageable age: fifteen. Howard was old enough to be her father. But her own father was not bothered by the age gap—Buckingham approved of the marriage.

The young woman in question did not.

For the rest of her life, the word that would be used most often to describe Elizabeth Stafford was "willful," and she definitely wanted to exercise her own will in marriage. She had a husband in mind already: her father's ward, Ralph Neville, her own age and the future earl of Westmoreland. She wrote in a sad letter, years later: *"He and I had loved together two years, and I had married him before Christmas, if the widowed Thomas Howard, the earl of Surrey's heir, had not made vigorous suit to my father."*

Her wishes were ignored. Elizabeth married Howard on January 13, 1513.

In the early years, it must have seemed to most observers that the marriage succeeded. Elizabeth gave birth to a son within the first year, Henry, the future poet and earl of Surrey; three healthy children followed. Elizabeth traveled with her husband, including two military campaigns to Ireland. She was a success at the court of Henry VIII, becoming a trusted lady in waiting to Katherine of Aragon.

In the late 1520s, two things happened. First, Howard, by then the third Duke of Norfolk, the Lord Treasurer of England, and more than fifty years of age, humiliated his wife by trying to move his mistress, Bess Holland, into official apartments in one of their homes.

And second, Elizabeth and Norfolk took opposite sides on the matter of the king's divorce. Anne Boleyn was half-Howard, and Norfolk supported his niece's tireless quest to be queen. But Elizabeth, devoted to Katherine, was outraged by the king's affair with Anne Boleyn. She tried to smuggle foreign messages of support to the spurned queen in a basket of oranges. It was discovered, and Norfolk was embarrassed.

Politics may have strained the marriage, but infidelity destroyed it. Most wives suffered in silence when their husbands took mistresses. Not Elizabeth. Outraged, she complained to everyone, loud and clear. Bess Holland, she said, was a "churl's daughter." She wrote: *"But because I would not be content to suffer the harlots…therefore, he put me out of doors…. He locked me up in a chamber and took away all my jewels."*

Elizabeth said that her husband ordered women who served in his household to bind her and sit on her *"until I spat blood and he never punished them."* (Elizabeth also later claimed that her husband had assaulted her days after she gave birth to their daughter, but he furiously denied it.)

She had no support. Her father, the Duke of Buckingham, had been executed for treason years ago; his son, Lord Stafford, would not agree to his sister's return to the family home because of her "sensual and willful" nature. Stafford wrote to his brother-in-law Norfolk: *"Her accustomed wild language does not lie in my power to stop."*

For his part, Norfolk claimed his wife was unbearable, that she told *"false and abominable lies and has obstinacy against me."* He desperately tried to get her to shut up. She wouldn't. He offered her a divorce, which she refused (at that time divorces were difficult to obtain).

At certain points, intermediaries went back and forth, suggesting reconciliation. But the couple's mutual hatred ran too deep. They permanently separated in 1533. Elizabeth lived alone in a house in Hertfordshire her husband leased for her; their children did not visit, taking the side of the powerful duke, now the earl marshal of the kingdom. She wrote angry letters for years to Thomas Cromwell, the king's chief minister, and even to the king himself, protesting her ill treatment. Elizabeth wrote Cromwell: *"Though I be left poor, yet I am content with all, for I am out of danger from my enemies and of the ill life that I had with my husband since he loved Bess Holland first…she has been the cause of all my troubles."*

Norfolk, freed of his hostile wife, had his ups and downs. He turned against Anne Boleyn after she married Henry VIII and was not damaged by her fall. He even presided over her trial. Four years later, when another niece, Catherine Howard, married the king of England, he did not fare as well. The family suffered from the scandal of Catherine's adultery. They seemed to have righted themselves but the eldest son of Norfolk and Elizabeth, the earl of Surrey, was executed for treason shortly before Henry VIII died.

The duke himself was imprisoned in the Tower and was thought to have been spared the axe only by the death of the king. During Norfolk's long imprisonment through the following reign of Edward VI, the duke's daughter, Mary, petitioned for his release. At one point the Privy Council said that Norfolk's *"daughter and wife may have recourse to him."* The duke naturally recoiled from the prospect of visits from his long-estranged duchess.

When Mary took the throne, Thomas Howard, then an incredible eighty years of age, emerged from the Tower of London and plunged into organizing the queen's coronation and wreaking revenge on his various enemies. He even led a command against the rebels in the Wyatt uprising. But in 1554, the old warrior and schemer died. There was no mention of his surviving spouse in his long will.

Elizabeth seems to have found a place in the family again. She was, after all, on good terms with Queen Mary, the daughter of her friend, Katherine of Aragon. In June 1557, she served as godmother for her great-grandson, Philip Howard, named after Mary's husband, Philip of Spain. (In 1595 this same Philip Howard would die of dysentery following a hunger strike in the Tower of London, accused of treason against his second-cousin Elizabeth I.)

But four years later, it was Elizabeth's turn, and she died in London at the age of sixty-four. Amazingly, she asked to be buried in a Howard chapel. This wish, finally, was not ignored. Elizabeth and Thomas Howard are not buried together but they are joined in a chapel effigy. Reunited at last.

For Sale: Rich Orphans—The Tudor Court of Wards

BY BARBARA KYLE

In the late 1400s a young woman named Jonet Mychell was abducted. Her step-father, Richard Rous, wrote to the Chancellor of England asking for help.

According to Rous, Jonet had been living with her uncle in London when some "evil disposed" people led by one Otis Trenwyth took her away so that *"neither father nor mother, nor kin nor friend that she had could come to her, nor know where she was."* She was subsequently forced to marry against her will to *"such a person that was to her great shame and heaviness."*

To modern eyes, the crime of a man abducting a young woman is a sexual one. But Tudor eyes saw things differently.

The main dispute in Jonet Mychell's abduction was about wardship and marriage, and what those two things entailed, above all, was money. What concerned Tudor bureaucrats was the abduction of young women who were heirs to property.

Abduction of heiresses was not uncommon. Certainly it occurred frequently enough to necessitate a statute passed in 1487 under Henry VII, the first Tudor monarch: *"An Act Against Taking Away of Women Against Their Will."* A stolen heiress meant lost revenues for the Crown.

The revenue stream went back for centuries. The wardship of minor heirs of any tenant-in-chief was one of the king's ancient feudal rights, a royal prerogative dating back to the feudal principle of seigneurial guardianship. It entitled the king to all the revenues of the deceased's estate (excluding lands allocated to his widow as dower) until the heir reached the age of majority: twenty-one for a male, fourteen for a female. The king generally sold the wardships to the highest bidder or granted them *gratis* to favoured courtiers as a reward for services.

In other words, all orphans, male and female, who were heirs to significant property became wards of the king, who then sold the wardships. Gentlemen bid for these sought-after prizes because control of a ward's income-generating lands and their marriage was a significant source of revenue. The guardian pocketed the rents and revenues of the ward's property until the young person came of age, at which time the guardian often married the ward to one of his own children.

When Henry VIII, the second Tudor monarch, came to the throne, he fully exploited the royal right of wardships. Monarchy had to be a money-making business and wardships provided an excellent way to replenish the royal treasury.

Surveyors were appointed to search for potential royal wardships throughout the realm. Managing all of this was a Master of the King's Wards who supervised royal wardships and administered the lands and revenues of wards during the period of crown control, and sold those not to be retained. The revenues went into the king's private funds.

In 1540, Henry VIII replaced the office of Master of the King's Wards with the Court of

Wards, which assumed complete control of wards and the administration of their lands and the selling of the wardships. Eventually, the Court of Wards became one of the Tudor crown's most lucrative ministries.

In the reign of Elizabeth I, the last Tudor monarch, the Court of Wards was supervised by Sir William Cecil (later Lord Burghley) who exerted enormous control over this court, keeping several lucrative and important wardships for himself.

I became familiar with the situation of royal wardships when I wrote *The Queen's Lady*. My book features Sir Thomas More, Henry VIII's chancellor, who famously went to the execution block rather than swear the oath that Henry was supreme head of the church in England, a title Henry created in order to divorce Catherine of Aragon and marry Anne Boleyn.

Sir Thomas More had two wards, Anne Cresacre and Giles Heron. He brought them up in his household where they were educated alongside his children. Eventually, Anne married More's son John, and Giles married More's daughter Cecily. The marriages seem to have been happy ones.

Anne Cresacre's story inspired me to create another ward for Sir Thomas More: Honor Larke, the heroine of my novel *The Queen's Lady*. Honor grows up revering More and becomes a lady-in-waiting to Catherine of Aragon. Forced to take sides in the religious extremism of the day, Honor fights to save the church's victims from death at the stake, bringing her into conflict with her once-beloved guardian. She enlists Richard Thornleigh, a rogue sea captain, in her missions of mercy, and eventually risks her life to try to save Sir Thomas from the wrath of the King.

THE EXECUTION OF SIR THOMAS MORE

BY **BARBARA KYLE**

A *MAN FOR ALL SEASONS*, THE 1966 FILM BASED ON ROBERT BOLT'S PLAY AND STARRING Paul Scofield, imprinted on a generation a glowing picture of Sir Thomas More as a warmhearted humanist: a loving family man, a brilliant lawyer and writer, and a steadfast friend of Henry VIII until the rift over Henry's break with the Roman church brought More to the execution block.

A child of the '60s, I was drawn to More the humanist when I began to write my novel *The Queen's Lady*, the first in what became the seven-book *Thornleigh Saga*. What I discovered in my research was a complex and conflicted man. As Henry's Chancellor, More banned books and burned men at the stake. He was a child of *his* time, of course, and his time—the Reformation— terrified him.

Deeply conservative, More loathed and feared the radicalism of the German Lutherans. He was shaken by the news of the sack of Rome, a barbarous rampage by a mixed brew of Spanish, Italian, and German mercenary troops who, unpaid after fighting for the Emperor Charles, mutinied and stormed the city.

They massacred a third of the population, prodded cardinals through the streets to be butchered, auctioned off nuns who were then raped at their altars, and shredded precious man- uscripts of the Vatican library to use them for horses' bedding. The carnage stunned Europe.

As Chancellor of England, More was vigilant at upholding the church's authority as the supreme pillar of the state. At that time Bibles printed in English were illegal (the church allowed only Bibles in Latin), and More authorized raids on secret gatherings of people who had smuggled in English Bibles. He destroyed the books and sent the criminals, if they did not recant their heresy, to the stake to be burned.

Like complex ideologues of our own time, More, while condemning others to death, was also a caring and loving father. He wrote affectionate letters to his children whenever he was away on his business for the king, and, quite unusually for the period, he educated his daugh- ters on an equal footing with his son. He was so proud of his daughter Margaret's erudition he encouraged her to correspond regularly with his friend, the great Dutch intellectual humanist, Desiderius Erasmus.

More himself was eventually and famously forced to choose sides in the religious extremism of the day and a horrifying choice it was, when his friend Henry, the king, demanded that all men swear an oath acknowledging him as supreme head of the church in England. Henry's break with the Roman church was the result of his implacable drive to get the Pope to annul his marriage to Catherine so he could marry Anne Boleyn. The penalty for refusing to take the oath was death. The vast majority of Henry's subjects complied. But Sir Thomas More believed that no king was, or could ever be, the supreme head of the church, and that if he swore the oath he would perjure his immortal soul. Along with several Carthusian monks and Bishop John Fisher, More chose death.

On the scaffold, as the executioner stood ready with his axe, More's last words were true to his complex nature: *"I die the king's good servant, but God's first."*

LITTLE EASE: TORTURE
AND THE TUDORS

BY NANCY BILYEAU

O N A MARCH NIGHT IN 1534, A MAN AND WOMAN HURRIED PAST A ROW OF COTTAGES ON the outer grounds of the Tower of London. They had almost reached the gateway to Tower Hill and, not far beyond it, the city of London, when a group of yeomen warders on night watch appeared in their path, holding lanterns.

In response, the young couple turned toward each other in what seemed a lovers' embrace. But something about the man caught the attention of Yeoman Warder Charles Gore. He held his lantern higher and within seconds recognized the pair. The man was a fellow yeoman warder, John Bawd, and the woman was Alice Tankerville, a condemned thief and prisoner.

So ended the Tower's first known escape attempt by a woman.

But Alice's accomplice and admirer, the guard John Bawd, was destined to enter the Tower record books too, and for the grimmest of reasons—he is the first known occupant of a peculiar torture cell used during the reigns of the Tudors and early Stuarts.

The windowless cell measured 1.2m (4 square feet) and bore the faintly prim name of Little Ease. The prisoner within it could not stand nor sit nor lie down but crouched over, in increasing agony, until freed from the suffocating, dark space.

Torture and the Tower of London have long had an uneasy relationship. The echoes of those screams are part of the walled fortress' allure, along with the X marks the spot of Queen Anne Boleyn's and the Lady Jane Grey's decapitations and the tales of the travails of inmates Ralegh, Cranmer, Fisher, and More.

Today's visitors see for themselves, in well-curated exhibits, the replicas of the rack and other devices fashioned for pain. Tower publications are emphatic: torture only took place during a brief span in its near 1,000-year history. Which is true. But it happened, and with an intensity that cannot be denied.

In 1215, England outlawed torture through the passage of Magna Carta, except by royal warrant. The first king to authorize it, reluctantly, was Edward II. He submitted to intense pressure from the Pope to follow the lead of the king of France and demolish the Order of the Knights Templar, part of a tradition begun during the Crusades.

King Philip IV of France, jealous of the Templars' wealth and power, charged them with heresy, obscene rituals, idolatry, and other offenses. The French knights denied all, and were duly tortured. Some who broke down and "confessed" were released; all who denied wrongdoing were burned at the stake.

Once Edward II had ordered imprisonment of members of the English chapter, French monks arrived in London bearing their instruments of torture. In 1311, the Knights Templar *"were questioned and examined in the presence of notaries while suffering under the torments of the rack"* within the Tower of London as well as the prisons of Aldgate, Ludgate, Newgate, and Bishopgate, according to *The History of the Knights Templar, the Temple Church, and the Temple,* by Charles G. Addison. And so the Tower—principally a royal residence, military stronghold, armory, and menagerie up until that time—was baptized in torture.

Did the instruments remain after the Knights Templars were crushed, to be used on other prisoners? We cannot be certain as there is no record of it.

The next mention of a rack within the Tower is a startling one—an unsavory nobleman made Constable of the Tower pushed for one to be installed. John Holland, third duke of Exeter, arranged for a rack to be brought into the Tower. It is not known if men were stretched upon it or if it was merely used to frighten. In any case, this rack is known to history as the Duke of Exeter's Daughter.

It was in the 16th century that prisoners were unquestionably tortured in the Tower of London. The royal family rarely used the fortress on the Thames as a residence; more and more, its stone buildings contained prisoners. And while the Tudor monarchs seem glittering successes to us now, in their own time they were beset by insecurities: rebellions, conspiracies, and other threats both domestic and foreign. There was a willingness at the top of the government to override the law to obtain certain ends. This created a perfect storm for torture.

"It was during the time of the Tudors that the use of torture reached its height," wrote historian L.A. Parry in his 1933 book *The History of Torture in England.*

> *Under Henry VIII it was frequently employed; it was only used in a small number of cases in the reigns of Edward VI and of Mary. It was whilst Elizabeth sat on the throne that it was made use of more than in any other period of history.*

Yeoman Warder John Bawd admitted he had planned the escape of Alice Tankerville *"for the love and affection he bore her."* Unmoved, the Lieutenant of the Tower ordered Bawd into Little Ease where he crouched in growing agony. The lovers were condemned to horrible deaths for trying to escape. According to a letter in the State Papers of Lord Lisle, written on March 28, Alice Tankerville was *"hanged in chains at low water mark upon the Thames on Tuesday. John Bawd is in Little Ease cell in the Tower and is to be racked and hanged."*

Today no one knows exactly where Little Ease was located. One theory: within the nooks and crannies of the White Tower. Another: in the basement of the old Flint Tower. No visitor sees it today; it was torn down or walled up long ago.

Besides Little Ease, the most-used torture devices were the rack, manacles, and a horrific creation called the Scavenger's Daughter. For many prisoners, solitary confinement, repeated interrogation, and the threat of physical pain were enough to make them tell their tormentors anything they wanted to know.

Often the victims ended up in the Tower for religious reasons. Anne Askew was tortured and killed for her Protestant beliefs; Edmund Campion for his Catholic ones. But the crimes varied. *"The majority of the prisoners were charged with high treason, but murder, robbery, embezzling the Queen's plate, and failure to carry out proclamations against state players were among the offenses,"* wrote Parry. The monarch did not need to sign off on torture requests, although sometimes he or she did. Elizabeth I personally directed that torture be used on the members of the Babington Conspiracy, a group that plotted to depose her and replace her with Mary, Queen of Scots. But usually these initiatives went through the Privy Council or tapped the powers of the Star Chamber. It is believed that in some cases, permission was never sought at all.

Over and over, names pop up in state papers of those confined to Little Ease:

> *On 3 May 1555: Stephen Happes, for his lewd behavior and obstinacy, committed this day to the Tower to remain in Little Ease for two or three days till he may be further examined.*

> *10 January 1591: Richard Topcliffe is to take part in an examination in the Tower of George Beesley, seminary priest, and Robert Humberson, his companion. And if you shall see good cause by their obstinate refusal to declare the truth of such things as shall be laid to their charge in Her Majesty's behalf, then shall you by authority hereof commit them to the prison called Little Ease or to such other ordinary place of punishment as hath been accustomed to be used in those cases, and to certify proceedings from time to time.*

After the death of Elizabeth and succession of James I came the most famous prisoner of them all to be held in Little Ease—Guy Fawkes. Charged with plotting to blow up the king and Parliament, Fawkes was subjected to both manacles and rack to obtain his confession and the names of his fellow conspirators. After he had told his questioners everything they asked, Fawkes was still shackled hand and foot in Little Ease and left there for a number of days.

And after that final burst of savagery, Little Ease was no more. A House of Commons committee reported the same year as Fawkes' execution that the room was "disused." In 1640, during the reign of Charles I, torture was abolished forever; there would be no more forcing prisoners to crouch for days in dark, airless rooms, no more rack or hanging from chains.

And so, mercifully, closed one of the darkest chapters in England's history.

"The Rack Seldom Stood Idle…"

by NANCY BILYEAU

In 1588, more than halfway into the reign of Elizabeth I, a man named John Gerard, English by birth, returned to his homeland, setting foot on the coast at Norfolk. He was arrested six years later, in a London house he had rented.

The government officials disbelieved Gerard's story that he was a gentleman fond of gambling and hunting. And they were right to do so. Gerard was actually a Jesuit priest, educated in Douai and Rome and leading a covert and highly dangerous life in Protestant England.

Father Gerard was conveyed to the Tower, accused of trying *"to lure people from the obedience of the Queen to the obedience of the Pope."* His interrogators demanded to know who had assisted him in England. He refused to name names.

In a book Father Gerard wrote years later, he reported being one day *"taken for a second examination to the house of a magistrate called Young. Along with him was another…an old man, grown grey."* Young began the questioning—what Catholics did Father Gerard know? *"I answered that I neither could not nor would make disclosures that would get any one into trouble, for reasons already stated,"* said the Jesuit.

Young turned to his silent colleague and said, *"I told you how you would find him."* The older man looked at Father Gerard "frowningly" and finally spoke. *"Do you know me?"* he asked. *"I am Topcliffe, of whom I doubt not you have often heard."*

Sir Richard Topcliffe then led the interrogation, and Father Gerard was tortured by use of manacles for more than six hours. A friar said, *"Twice he has been hung up by the hands with great cruelty…the examiners say he is exceedingly obstinate."*

Topcliffe, a lawyer and Member of Parliament, began serving the queen in the 1570s and seems to have reported to Sir Francis Walsingham. He hated Catholics with great intensity and boasted of having a chamber in his home containing devices "superior" to the ones in the Tower. The government allowed him to make official use of this home chamber. When a prisoner must be "put to the pain," it was time to send for Topcliffe. His favorite methods: the rack and the manacles.

Of all the mysteries of Elizabeth I, few are as baffling as the humane queen's favor toward the inhuman Sir Richard Topcliffe, chief torturer of the realm. An undoubted sadist, he was the dark blot on her golden age.

When researching an earlier blog post on "Little Ease" in the Tower of London, I came across the 1933 book *The History of Torture in England,* by L.A. Parry. The 16th century was when torture reached its height in England. Parry quotes the historian Hallam: *"The rack seldom stood idle in the latter part of Elizabeth's reign."*

More recent historical works confirm this grim record. Prisoners were tortured and some were later executed. Anne Somerset in *Elizabeth I* said, *"one-hundred and eighty-three Catholics were executed during Elizabeth's reign; one-hundred and twenty-three of them were priests."*

Elizabeth Jenkins, author of *Elizabeth the Great,* shudders over the "unspeakable Richard Topcliffe" and says, *"The whole process of hunting down priests and examining them under torture was quite outside the domain of the law courts."*

How could the erudite Elizabeth who said she had *"no desire to make windows into men's souls"* officiate over these horrors? Two people seem to have triggered this change in the queen. One was Pope Pius V who excommunicated the queen in 1570, branding her as a "servant of crime." This act encouraged her subjects to rise up.

The other was the Catholic Mary, Queen of Scots, a focus of possible rebellion the entire time she was held in the kingdom after she was driven out of her own land.

Elizabeth's secretary Walsingham became her spymaster. The indefatigable Puritan was convinced that the Jesuits and other priests who secretly practiced in England were part of an international conspiracy to destabilize the realm and eventually depose the queen. Many of the interrogated priests, such as Father Gerard, insisted they were loyal to the queen, that they led secret lives because Mass was illegal. But some unquestionably were drawn into dangerous conspiracy against Elizabeth, such as those involved in the Babington Plot which sought to replace Elizabeth with Mary.

In fact, the embattled queen, no doubt frightened as well as enraged, ordered that the guilty Babington conspirators be executed in ways so horrible it would never be forgotten. And so the first ones were. But the crowd of spectators, presumably hardened to such sights, were sickened by the hellish castratings and disembowelings. When the queen heard of this, she ordered the next round of traitors be hanged until they were dead.

Elizabeth realized she had gone too far. It's regrettable that she did not realize that more often.

THE WILL OF THE PRIORESS

BY **NANCY BILYEAU**

IN THE TOWN OF DARTFORD, A 40-MINUTE TRAIN RIDE SOUTH OF LONDON'S CHARING Cross, stands a building called the Manor Gatehouse. Inside you will find a registration office to record the births, marriages, and deaths that occur in Kent. This handsome red-brick building, fronted by a garden, is also a popular place for weddings. *"It looks amazing in the official pictures,"* gushed one satisfied bride in a website testimonial.

But when I first walked up that path to the Gatehouse, I was filled with awe, and definitely not because I was planning a wedding. I was thinking of who stood on this same piece of ground six centuries ago. Because it was then a Catholic priory—a community of women who constituted the sole Dominican order in England before the dissolution of the monasteries—and it is where I chose to tell the story of my first novel, *The Crown*.

This is where Sister Joanna Stafford, my half-English, half-Spanish protagonist, prayed, and sang, and wept, and struggled.

I didn't create a Catholic novice as a protagonist for my book because of a religious or political agenda. A lifelong Tudor fanatic, I felt I had no choice but to set a story in the 16th century. I wanted to write about someone different, and so I plunged into researching the life of a young nun at the most tumultuous time in the Dissolution of the Monasteries. What would it be like to have your way of life taken from you—would you try to stop the destruction, or accept the inevitable?

At one time, like many others, I accepted a series of "truths" about life in the time of Henry VIII: people did not often live to old age; women were rarely educated outside of the royal family or high aristocracy; women outside of the court of the king, and the carnal grasp of the king, were not as interesting to our modern sensibilities; the monastic life was in decline, most likely corrupt, and deserved to be ended; and nuns were either forced to take vows or ended up in convents because they were not as "good" as the women who married—i.e., they were rejects.

My years of research revealed to me how wrong all of those stereotypes were.

The true story of one woman's life, Prioress Elizabeth Cressner, illuminates some of the complex truths. A "good and virtuous woman," she was the leader of the priory in Dartford for 50 years; she died in December 1536 at somewhere between 75 and 80 years of age, just as Henry VIII was putting intense pressure on the monasteries to submit to his will.

Dartford Priory had been founded with great care by Edward III, although the idea of establishing a house for Dominican sisters is attributed to Edward II. Did he feel some obligation to carry out the wish of his deposed father? Impossible to know. Once the pope approved the founding of the order, four Dominican sisters were recruited from France, for whose expenses 20 pounds was paid from the Exchequer.

The English priory soon established a reputation for *"strict discipline and plain living."*

Dartford was known for the value put on education and contained a library of books. It also drew aristocratic nuns, even royalty, most famously Princess Bridget of York, the daughter of Edward IV and Elizabeth Woodville.

Prioress Elizabeth Cressner took on her tasks with great energy and a bold temperament. She executed wills for people in the community and appointed priests to celebrate Mass in the parish church and masters to oversee the local almshouse for the poor. She administered much of the property owned by the priory, even though it was technically the job of the friars assigned there.

In the 1530s, Thomas Cromwell was turning a speculative eye on the monasteries. Undaunted, Prioress Elizabeth sent Henry VIII's minister a series of firm letters over a recent appointment of a certain Friar Robert Stroddel as president at the Dartford community. The prioress found him unkind and even dishonest.

The prioress wrote Cromwell:

> And now of late I understand [Stroddel] hath purchased letters of your good lordship under our most gracious founder's seal to be president here the term of his life, by feigned and untrue suggestion, for as much as he hath governed the office so well, as he himself reporteth.

Despite her fiery letters, the prioress was unable to dislodge Friar Stroddel. When Elizabeth Cresssner died, the convent at Dartford was still intact. There was no corruption found at the priory by the king's investigators.

But her successor, Joan Vane, was forced to surrender it just the same to the king, and all of the nuns were expelled with small pensions and no place to go. The king did not award the priory to a favored courtier, as he usually did. He took the priory for himself, ordered it demolished and a luxurious manor house raised on the property. Henry VIII never slept there, though his ex-wife, Anne of Cleves, lived there for a time.

The manor house was given to Sir Robert Cecil by King James I, and passed through various hands before being demolished by the 19th century. All that remains is the red-brick gatehouse, although that was built by Henry VIII. Nothing is left of the priory itself, except for the stone wall that ran along its perimeter.

On a cloudy afternoon, I walked the perimeter of the centuries-old wall as the cars whizzed by. There are no Dartford Priory gift shops, as exist at the carefully preserved Tower of London. No mugs for sale bearing the face of Prioress Elizabeth Cressner. But her life was significant all the same.

I paid her homage on my solitary walk.

THE LAST NUN

BY NANCY BILYEAU

ONE SPRING DAY IN 1539, TWENTY-SIX WOMEN WERE FORCED TO LEAVE THEIR HOME—the only home most had known for their entire adult lives. The women were nuns of the Dominican Order of Dartford Priory in Kent. The relentless dissolution of the monasteries had finally reached their convent door. Having no choice, Prioress Joan Vane turned the priory over to King Henry VIII, who had broken from Rome.

What the women would do with their lives now was unclear. Because Dartford Priory surrendered to, rather than defied, the crown, some monies were provided. Lord Privy Seal Thomas Cromwell, the architect of the dissolution that poured over a million pounds into the royal treasury, had devised a pension plan for the displaced monks, friars, and nuns.

According to John Russell Stowe's *History and Antiquities of Dartford*, published in 1844, Prioress Joan received *"66 pounds, 13 shillings per annum."* She left Dartford and was not heard from again—it's thought she lived with a brother.

Sister Elizabeth Exmewe, a younger, less important nun, received a pension of "100 shillings per annum." This was the amount that most Dartford nuns received. The roaring inflation of the 1540s meant that such a pension would probably not be enough to live on after a few years—but there was never a question of its being adjusted.

Some of the thousands of monks and friars who were turned out of their monasteries in the 1530s became priests or teachers or apothecaries. But nuns—roughly 1,900 of them at the time of the Dissolution—did not have such options. *"Those who had relatives sought asylum in the bosom of their own family,"* wrote Stowe with 19th century floridity. Marriage was not an option. In 1539, the most conservative noble, the Duke of Norfolk, introduced to Parliament "the Act of Six Articles," which forbade ex-nuns and monks from marrying. The act, which had the approval of Henry VIII, became law. The king did not want nuns in the priory but he did not want them to marry either. There was literally no place for them in England.

Sisters who could afford it emigrated to Catholic countries to search for priories that would take them in. Others lacking family support sank into poverty. Eustace Chapuys, the Spanish ambassador, wrote:

> *It is a lamentable thing to see a legion of monks and nuns who have been chased from their monasteries wandering miserably hither and thither seeking means to live; and several honest men have told me that what with monks, nuns, and persons dependent on the monasteries suppressed, there were over 20,000 who knew not how to live.*

Such wandering through England would not be the fate of Elizabeth Exmewe. Enough is known of her life from various sources to gain a picture of a determined woman.

Dartford Priory, founded by Edward III, drew women from the gentry and aristocracy, even one from royalty. Princess Bridget Plantagenet, youngest sister of Elizabeth of York, was promised to Dartford as a baby. She lived there from childhood until her death in 1517. Elizabeth Exmewe was typical of most of the other nuns—she was the daughter of a gentleman, Sir Thomas Exmewe. He was a goldsmith and "merchant adventurer," serving as Lord Mayor of London.

It was common for brothers and sisters to enter monastic life together, though at separate places. Elizabeth's brother, William Exmewe, was a Carthusian monk and respected scholar of Greek and Latin at the London Charterhouse. He was also one of the monks who in 1535 refused to sign the Oath of Supremacy to Henry VIII, despite intense pressure. The king had broken from the Pope because he could not get a divorce from Catherine of Aragon and marry Anne Boleyn.

Once the king became head of the Church of England, it was imperative that all monks shift their loyalty to him. But Exmewe would not compromise his beliefs, and he was punished with a horrifying death—he was hanged, disemboweled while still alive, and quartered.

No nun in England was executed besides Sister Elizabeth Barton, a Benedictine who prophesied against the king's marriage to Anne Boleyn. Barton was arrested, tortured, tried, and hanged for it. Elizabeth Exmewe did not publicly criticize the king or seek martyrdom. Four years after the death of her brother, she was turned out from Dartford Priory.

Historians studying the dissolution have noted a remarkable fact: in several cases, nuns attempted to live together in small groups after being forced from their priories. They were determined to continue their vocations, in whatever way they could. Elizabeth Exmewe shared a home in Walsingham with another ex-nun of Dartford. *"They were Catholic women of honest conversation,"* said one contemporary account.

A half-dozen other Dartford refugees tried to live under one roof closer to Dartford. Meanwhile, Henry VIII had their priory demolished. He built a luxurious manor house on the rubble of the Dominican Order, although he's not believed to have ever slept there. It became the home of his fourth wife, Anne of Cleves, after he divorced her in disgust in 1540.

Following the reign of Henry's Protestant son, Edward VI, his Catholic daughter, Mary I, took the throne in 1553. Mary re-formed several religious communities as she struggled to turn back time in England and restore the "True Faith." Elizabeth Exmewe and six other ex-nuns successfully petitioned Queen Mary to re-create their Dominican community at Dartford, which was vacant after the death of Anne of Cleves. They moved into the manor house, built on the home they had left 14 years earlier, with two chaplains. The convent life they loved flourished again: the sisters spent their days praying, singing and chanting, gardening, embroidering, and studying.

But the restoration didn't last long. When Mary died and her Protestant half-sister took the throne, one of Elizabeth's goals was extinguishing the monastic flames. In 1559, Elizabeth's first Reformation Parliament repressed all the re-founded convents and confiscated the land.

And so the Dartford nuns were ejected again, this time with no pensions. Mary's widower, King Philip of Spain, heard of their plight and paid for a ship to convey the nuns of Dartford and Syon Abbey to Antwerp, in the Low Countries. Paul Lee, in his book *Nunneries, Learning and Spirituality in Late Medieval Society*, has charted the sisters' poignant journey after leaving their native land.

After a few months, a new home was secured for them. For the next ten years Elizabeth Exmewe lived *"in the poor Dutch Dominican nunnery at Leliendal, near Zierikzee on the western shore of the bleak island of Schouwen in Zeeland."* Several of the English nuns were entering their eighties, with Elizabeth being the youngest. All suffered from illness and near poverty.

The Duchess of Parma, hearing of their hardships, sent an envoy to the Dartford nuns. He wrote:

> *I certainly found them extremely badly lodged. This monastery is very poor and very badly built.... I find that these are the most elderly of the religious and the most infirm, and it seems that they are more than half dead.*

Despite his dire observances, the nuns themselves expressed pride in their convent. Their leader, Prioress Elizabeth Croessner, wrote a letter to the new pope, Pius IV, saying they strove to remain faithful to their vows and were interested in new recruits!

In the 1560s the nuns died, one by one, leaving only Elizabeth Exmewe and her prioress, Elizabeth Croessner. Destitute, the pair moved to Bruges and found another convent. They lived through a bout of religious wars, with Calvinists marching through the streets.

The onetime prioress of Dartford, Elizabeth Croessner, died in 1577. Now Elizabeth Exmewe, the daughter of a Lord Mayor and the sister of a Carthusian martyr, was the only one left of her Order. In 1585, she, too, perished in Bruges and was buried by Dominican friars with all honors. Elizabeth Exmewe is believed to have lived to 76 years of age.

OUR TUDOR SISTERS

BY SANDRA BYRD

Historical novelists are sometimes suspected of importing twenty-first century values into sixteenth century novels. While it's true that most authors seek to connect their readers with their novel's women of the past, it isn't necessary to ascribe new values to past women. While we cannot know what conversations between persons sounded like with certainty, we can draw upon what we do know to extrapolate their emotions, desires, and life goals.

They valued education. Although medieval women's education was often limited to gentler feminine arts such as dance, needlework, and playing of the lute or virginals, by the beginning of the Tudor era women were much more interested and involved in intellectual education. Queen Catherine of Aragon ensured that her daughter Mary had a strict regimen of demanding studies in accordance with the queen's own upbringing. Sir Thomas More is often credited with putting into practice the idea that non-royal women deserved as much education as noble or highborn men. His daughters undertook an education complete in classical studies, languages, geography, astronomy, and mathematics.

Queen Kateryn Parr's mother Maude educated her own daughters in accordance with More's program for his children, eventually running a kind of "school for highborn girls" after she was widowed. Eventually, educating one's daughters was seen as a social necessity, and men expected their wives to be able to play chess with them, discuss poetry and devotional works, and be conversant in the issues of the day.

They knew they couldn't marry for love—the first time—but desired it anyway. Most historical readers understand that women in the Tudor era were chattel, legally controlled by their fathers and then their husbands. They married for dynastic or financial reasons; marriage was an alliance of families and strategy and not of the hearts. And yet, these women, too, had read Solomon's *Song of Songs* wherein a husband and wife declare their passion for one another. Classically educated as they were, Tudor women had surely come across the Greek myths, including Eros and Psyche, and perhaps had even read the medieval French love poem, *Roman de la Rose*.

If a woman was left widowed—and that happened quite often—she was free to remain widowed and under her own authority or to marry whom she wished. Henry VIII's sister Mary married first King Louis XII of France, for duty. When he died, she married Charles Brandon, for love. After Mary's death, Brandon married his ward, Katherine Willoughby, her duty. Later, she married Richard Bertie for love.

They were working women. High born women were often ladies-in-waiting to the queen, a demanding, full-time job with little pay or time off. They ran the accounts for their husbands' properties and juggled household management. Some highborn women, such as Lady Bryan, became governesses. Lower born women were lady's maids, seamstresses, nurses, servants, or baby maids in addition to helping their husbands as fishmongers or in the fields.

Although there are some notable differences, we have much more in common with our highborn sisters of five hundred years ago than one may think!

THE ART OF COURTLY LOVE: HENRY VIII AND ANNE BOLEYN

BY SANDRA BYRD

THE ART OF COURTLY LOVE AND CHIVALRIC ROMANCE SO POPULAR DURING THE EARLY medieval period saw a revival during the Tudor era. Because the majority of noble marriages were arranged, with the focus being on financial, familial, or political gain, courtly love was a gentle, parrying game of flirtation wherein people might express true, heart-felt affections.

According to historian Eric Ives,

> *The courtier, the 'perfect knight', was supposed to sublimate his relations with the ladies of the court by choosing a 'mistress' and serving her faithfully and exclusively. He formed part of her circle, wooed her with poems, songs and gifts, and he might wear her favor and joust in her honor…in return, the suitor must look for one thing only, 'kindness'—understanding and platonic friendship.*

Many of the plays and entertainments in Henry VIII's court reflected these values, and Henry himself, early in his reign, was very chivalrous and courtly indeed.

The longest game of courtly love, played out before all of Europe, was undoubtedly between Anne Boleyn and Henry VIII. The relationship started out as courtly flirtation but as sometimes happened, it then progressed to a more serious, deeper connection with a significant goal in outcome and purpose.

Andreas Capellanus, in his definitive twelfth century book *The Art of Courtly Love*, set out to inform "lovers" which gifts could be offered (among them a girdle, a purse, a ring, or gloves) and to clarify the signs and signals that indicated such a love game was underway—or on the wane.

Although Anne and Henry's courtly relationship did not follow each of the thirty-one rules Capellanus lists from the *King of Love*, it did dovetail with some of them—a few of which have been examined below.

Rule II. He who is not jealous cannot love. This rule immediately brings to mind the incident between Henry and Thomas Wyatt during a game of bowls. Thomas Wyatt used one of Anne's ribbons and a bauble to mark distance, and he meant to use it to provoke or test Henry's jealousy. Henry, predictably, flew into a possessive bluster. Anne recovered nicely from Wyatt's foolishness, but there was no further doubting that she was Caesar's and not to be touched.

Rule IV. It is well known that love is always increasing or decreasing. One of the most extraordinary things about Henry's affection for Anne is that she was able to not only capture it but build upon it over a remarkable period of time—seven years from 1525 when it was clear he had fallen for her, to 1533 when their public marriage took place.

He did not become bored or disinterested in her companionship. This was no mean feat when one considers Henry's short attention span. He wrote tender love letters to Anne, some of which still exist, a powerful demonstration of his growing love as Henry loathed writing.

Rule XI. It is not proper to love any woman whom one would be ashamed to seek to marry. Much has been made of the fact that Anne "held out" sexually from Henry for personal reasons, and that Henry wanted his heirs by her to be legitimate, two among other valid reasons why they did not simply have an affair. But there is strong evidence to suggest that Henry found Anne worthy of marriage—he crowned her—and took great pride in displaying her before all the court. In Anne it is clear that for some time Henry believed he'd found a spirited soul mate who was as vibrant as he was, and he desired for her to be his wife.

Rule XIV. The easy attainment of love makes it of little value; difficulty of attainment makes it prized. We're often reminded that Henry left his first wife and broke away from the Roman Catholic Church during his pursuit to marry Anne, courting war and ill will in the process.

But Anne, too, made sacrifices. Her child-bearing years were quickly slipping by; there was a rush to judgment as she was reviled by much of the populace as a usurper; she had no official role nor position; and, finally, there was no guarantee that she would even have her marriage. Both of them risked much.

Only one of them, in the end, lost everything.

Rule XXVIII. A slight presumption causes a lover to suspect his beloved. In the end, it took very little to convince Henry that Anne had betrayed him, a ridiculous acceptance of circumstances that demanded Anne be in places she clearly was not and act in ways that would never have gone unnoticed and that were in stark contrast to her character. One must ask, why?

Cappellanus answers that question for us, too. "*...when love has definitely begun to decline, it quickly comes to an end unless something comes to save it.*"

At the point when the King's affections began their precipitous drop, long after their game of courtly love was over and well into their marriage, the only thing that could have saved Anne was the son she miscarried. Chivalric values included integrity, protecting the vulnerable, and acting with self-sacrificing honor. Sadly, Henry did not turn out to be the "perfect knight" Ives speaks of.

The King, the Archbishop, and the Bear

by JUDITH ARNOPP

Bishop Burnet, writing a century after the event, relates a bizarre incident that took place in Henry VIII's reign during the aftermath of the Six Articles. The Six Articles was an act that set out quite clearly and reinforced six points of medieval doctrine which Protestants at that time had begun to undermine. The act also specified the punishments due to those who did not accept them and was known by many Protestants as *"the bloody whip with six strings."* As a married man, Archbishop Cranmer must have taken particular exception to Article Three which stated that priests should not be allowed to marry.

He set down his objections quite strongly, making detailed notes, all backed up with citations from the Bible and learned scholars, and it is believed he planned to present his findings to Henry. His secretary, Ralph Morice, duly copied the notes into a small book and set off with it to Westminster.

The king, meanwhile, was attending a bear-baiting across the river at Southwark, and, just as Ralph Morice and company were passing in a wherry, the bear broke loose from the pit and with the dogs in hot pursuit, leapt into the river and made straight for the boat. Bishop Burnet goes on to relate that:

> those that were in the boat leaped out and left the poor secretary alone there. But the bear got into the boat, with the dogs about her, and sank it. The secretary, apprehending his life was in danger, did not mind his book, which he lost in the water.

You can just picture it, can't you? Dripping wet bear, soaked dogs, terrified clerk, wildly rocking boat?

When Morice reached the shore, he saw his book floating and asked the bearward (who was not perhaps as "in charge" of the bear as one might hope) to retrieve it for him. But before he could get his hands on it, the book fell into the hands of a priest who, realising what it contained, declared that whoever claimed it would be hanged.

Burnet says that, *"This made the bearward more intractable for he was a spiteful papist and hated the archbishop, so no offers or entreaties could prevail on him to give it back."*

In no little panic, Morice sought the immediate assistance of Cromwell who, on discovering the bearward about to hand the book over to Cranmer's enemies, confiscated it, threatening him severely for meddling with the book of the privy councilor—thus saving the life of the Archbishop.

This all sounds rather like a scene from the film *Carry-on Henry*, a farce, far too unlikely to be true. I cannot help but wonder what Henry made of the spectacle.

THE DEATH OF HENRY VIII: DEMOLISHING THE MYTHS

BY NANCY BILYEAU

N O ONE WOULD HAVE CALLED SIR ANTHONY DENNY A BRAVE MAN, BUT ON THE EVENING of January 27, 1547, the Gentleman of the Privy Chamber performed a duty the most resolute would recoil from: he informed Henry VIII that *"in man's judgment you are not like to live."*

The 55-year-old king, lying in his vast bed in Westminster Palace, replied he believed *"the mercy of Christ is able to pardon me all my sins, yes, though they were greater than they be."* When asked if he wanted to speak to any "learned man," King Henry asked for Archbishop of Canterbury, Thomas Cranmer, *"but I will first take a little sleep. And then, as I feel myself, I will advise on the matter."*

Cranmer was sent for, but it took hours for the archbishop to make his way on frozen roads. Shortly after midnight, Henry VIII was barely conscious, unable to speak. The faithful Cranmer always insisted that when he asked for a sign that his monarch trusted in the mercy of Christ, Henry Tudor squeezed his hand.

At about 2 a.m. Henry VIII died, *"probably from renal and liver failure, coupled with the effects of his obesity,"* says Robert Hutchinson in his 2005 book *The Last Days of Henry VIII: Conspiracies, Treason and Heresy at the Court of the Dying Tyrant.*

It was a subdued end to a riotous life. The sources for what happened that night are respected, though they are secondary, coming long after the event: John Foxe's *Acts and Monuments* (1563) and Gilbert Burnet's *History of the Reformation of the Church of England* (1679).

Yet there are other stories told of the death and funeral of Henry VIII. He was perhaps the most famous king in English history, and so it is no surprise that in books and on the Internet, some strange or maudlin words and ghoulish acts have attached themselves to his demise.

It is time to address them, one by one.

1) MYTH: "MONKS, MONKS, MONKS"

Henry VIII broke from Rome and made himself the head of the Church of England, dissolving the monasteries. The monks and friars and nuns faithful to the Pope lost their homes and were turned out on the road. Those who defied the king and denied the royal supremacy, such as the Carthusian martyrs, were tortured and killed.

Did the king regret it at the end? *"He expired soon after allegedly uttering his last words: 'Monks! Monks! Monks!'"* says the *Wikipedia* entry for Henry VIII. It's a story that has popped up in books too.

The major source for it seems to be Agnes Strickland, a 19th century poet turned historian who penned the eight-volume *Lives of the Queens of England from the Norman Conquest, and Lives of the Queens of Scotland, and English Princesses.* Strickland writes that the king *"was afflicted with visionary horrors at the hour of his departure; for that he glanced with rolling eyes and looks of wild import towards the darker recesses of his chamber, muttering, 'Monks—monks!'"*

More on Strickland later. But when it comes to visions of cowled avengers glowering in the corner, it seems certain that this is an embellishment, an attempt at poetic justice but not something that happened. Most likely at the final hour Henry regretted nothing.

2) MYTH: "CRIED OUT FOR JANE SEYMOUR"

Another story is that while dying Henry VIII cried out for his third wife, the long dead Jane Seymour. It supports the idea that Jane, the pale lady-in-waiting who rapidly replaced Anne Boleyn, was the love of Henry's life. He did, after all, request to be buried next to her. And whenever a family portrait was commissioned after 1537, Jane was shown sitting beside him, rather than one of the wives he was actually married to. But Henry VIII does not quite deserve his reputation for being impossible to please when it comes to women. He actually had a low bar for marital success: birth of a baby boy. Jane produced the son who became Edward VI—doing so killed her—and thus moved to the top of the pecking order.

Whether he actually loved Jane more than the five other spouses (not to mention those alluring mistresses) is best left to screenwriters. But one thing seems certain: Henry VIII did not cry for his third wife while expiring. There is no historical source for it.

3) MYTH: "AND THE DOGS WILL LICK HIS BLOOD"

The most macabre story of all supposedly happened weeks after the king died but before he was lowered into the crypt next to Jane Seymour in St. George's Chapel. The king's corpse was transported in a lead coffin from Westminster to Windsor; the procession of thousands lasted two days. There was a large funeral effigy on top of the coffin, complete with crown at one end and crimson velvet shoes at the other, that, one chronicler said fearfully, was so realistic *"he seemed just as if he were alive."*

At the halfway mark, the coffin was housed in Syon Abbey, once one of England's most prestigious religious houses. That is fact. But the rest is suspect. Because of an accident or just the undoubted heaviness of the monarch's coffin—Henry VIII weighed well over 300 pounds at his death—there was supposedly a leak in the night, and either blood or "putrid matter" leaked onto the floor. When men arrived in the morning, a stray dog was seen licking under the coffin, goes the tale.

This hearkened to an unforgettable Easter Sunday sermon in 1532 before the king and his soon-to-be-second-wife, Anne Boleyn. Friar William Peto, provincial of the Observant Franciscans and a fiery supporter of first wife Katherine of Aragon, compared Henry VIII to King Ahab, husband of Jezebel. According to Scripture, after Ahab died, wild dogs licked his blood. Peto thundered that the same thing would happen to the English king.

Gilbert Burnet is the main source for the coffin-leaking story. A Scottish theologian and bishop of Salisbury, he is today considered reliable—except when he's not. One historian, while praising Burnet's book as an *"epoch in our historical literature,"* fretted that *"a great deal of fault has been found—and, no doubt, justly—with the inaccuracy and general imperfection of the transcripts on which his work was largely founded and which gave rise to endless blunders."* One of Burnet's most well-known contributions to Tudor lore was that a disappointed Henry VIII described fourth wife Anne of Cleves as a "Flanders mare." Author Antonia Fraser, in particular, writes sternly that Burnet had *"no contemporary reference to back it up"* in her book *The Six Wives of Henry VIII*.

What seems undeniable is that the foundation Burnet created, Agnes Strickland built on. Indeed, she raised a whole Gothic mansion in her own description of that night in Syon:

> *The King, being carried to Windsor to be buried, stood all night among the broken walls of Syon, and there the leaden coffin being cleft by the shaking of the carriage, the pavement of the church was wetted with Henry's blood. In the morning came plumbers to solder the coffin, under whose feet—'I tremble while I write it,' says the author—'was suddenly seen a dog creeping, and licking up the king's blood. If you ask me how I know this, I answer, William Greville, who could scarcely drive away the dog, told me and so did the plumber also.'*
>
> *It appears certain that the sleepy mourners and choristers had retired to rest, after the midnight dirges were sung, leaving the dead king to defend himself, as best as he might, from the assaults of his ghostly enemies, and some people might think they made their approaches in a currish form. It is scarcely, however, to be wondered that a circumstance so frightful should have excited feelings of superstitious horror, especially at such a time and place; for this desecrated convent had been the prison of his unhappy queen, Katherine Howard, whose tragic fate was fresh in the minds of men; and by a singular coincidence it happened that Henry's corpse rested there the very day after the fifth anniversary of her execution.*

Putting aside Strickland's Bram Stoker-esque prose, there's the question of whether such a ghastly thing could even occur. Sixteen-century embalmment did not call for completely draining a corpse of blood, it is true. And medical experts say it is possible that fluids circulate 17 days after death.

But Strickland's fervent connections to not only Friar Peto's sermon but also Syon's monastery past—echoing the "Monks, monks, monks" poetic justice—and the (near) anniversary of Katherine Howard's death make it seem likely that this was a case of too good a story to resist.

No one disturbed the coffin of the indomitable King Henry VIII—not even ghosts in "currish form."

THE BIRTH OF "BLOODY MARY"

BY NANCY BILYEAU

BLOODY MARY IS THE NAME OF A DRINK THAT ALWAYS CONTAINS BOOZE AND TOMATO juice and sometimes contains a dash of Worcestershire sauce, cayenne pepper, lemon, salt, black pepper, or a vigorous celery stalk. In 1939, the newspaper *This New York* reported breathlessly, *"George Jessel's newest pick-me-up that is receiving attention from the town's paragraphers is called a Bloody Mary: half tomato juice, half vodka."*

Bloody Mary is also the name of a macabre children's game. Find a mirror, turn out the lights, and call out her name three times. When you switch on the light, Bloody Mary herself will appear in the mirror—the ghost of a woman wrongly accused of killing her own children.

And, most significantly, Bloody Mary is the moniker for Mary Tudor, the oldest child of Henry VIII. At the age of 37, she courageously took the throne by force after her half-brother Edward altered the act of succession.

Young Edward wanted his Protestant cousin, Lady Jane Grey, to follow him, not his Catholic sister. But Mary raised an army and overthrew Jane's fragile government.

However, Mary's five-year reign is not considered a success. She married a Hapsburg prince—the marriage was very unpopular—and had a phantom pregnancy (maybe two). England experienced bad harvests every year during her reign. A war with France ended in disaster: the loss of Calais.

Those new to the 16th century sometimes have trouble keeping the "Mary's" straight. There is Mary, Queen of Scots, the beauty who married three times, lost her throne and was eventually executed by Elizabeth I. She was romantic. The Mary that I write about in this post is the other one—the "Bloody" one who, in her zeal to turn England back into a Catholic nation, had 284 Protestant martyrs burned at the stake over a period of just five years. While more than 300 Catholic martyrs died during the reigns of Henry VIII and Elizabeth I, Mary is the one who carries the reputation of being a merciless, bigotry-filled killer.

How that reputation evolved over the centuries is very interesting.

Mary Tudor was a woman of her time. While that may seem obvious, she was followed by a half-sister who was in some ways ahead of her time. Mary took a husband to secure the succession by having children, as every monarch was expected to do. Elizabeth refused to marry. Mary upheld the Catholic religion and did not recognize the opposing point of view. Elizabeth famously said, *"There is only one Christ, Jesus, one faith, all else is a dispute over trifles."*

Mary and Elizabeth, while close when young, distrusted each other by the time Mary took the throne. The relationship went downhill from there. When Elizabeth succeeded to the throne, she did not honor Mary's request to be buried with her mother, Katherine of Aragon, and rarely spoke well of her older sibling.

But it wasn't Elizabeth who ensured that Mary would be detested for centuries. The first person to push her toward infamy—hard—was John Foxe, the Protestant author of *The Book of*

Martyrs. Most English people did not witness the burnings of condemned heretics. But thanks to Foxe's widespread book, first published in 1563, the horror of being burned at the stake was made starkly clear. These descriptions make for harrowing reading, then and now.

It was Foxe who wrote, *"The next victim was the amiable Lady Jane Gray, who, by her acceptance of the crown at the earnest solicitations of her friends, incurred the implacable resentment of the bloody Mary."* But the nickname did not take hold then—in fact, it did not spring up until a century later.

The succession crisis in the late 17th century over James, Duke of York, directly led to the vilification of Mary Tudor. Fear that James, who had converted to Catholicism, would succeed his brother, Charles II, gripped much of England. Should a Catholic become king, one politician warned, the kingdom would see persecutions as *"bloody or bloodier than the ones in Mary's reign."*

An anonymous ballad in 1674 declared that after Edward VI died, *"Then Bloody Mary did begin / in England for to tyrannize."* She was used as a threatening memory of tyranny and death and slavish devotion to the Pope. This was the genesis of Bloody Mary.

The Glorious Revolution of 1688 put a Protestant on the throne and the Act of Union in 1707 ensured that a Catholic could never rule England. But paranoia about Jacobite risings led to more and more denunciations of Mary I.

Today historians agree that, no matter what one thinks of her later reign, Mary was an attractive young woman, well-educated and exceptionally talented in music. She loved fine clothes, jewelry, and gambling. She was a devoted godmother and generous friend right up until her death. But in the lowest point of Mary's historical reputation she was depicted as not only bloodthirsty and tyrannical but also stupid and hideous.

Here is how an 18th century historian describes the Tudor queen:

> *Mary was not formed to please, she had nothing of the woman in either her history or her behavior; she was stiff, formal, reserved, sour, haughty and arrogant, her face plain and coarse, without any soft features to smooth its roughness or any insinuating graces to shade its defects. Everything in her looks, her air, her carriage and manner, was forbidding...scarce ever was there a person so utterly void of all the agreeable qualities.*

A century later, no less a figure than Charles Dickens attacked Mary with ferocity. In *A Child's History of England*, Dickens ranted:

> *As BLOODY QUEEN MARY, this woman has become famous, and as BLOODY QUEEN MARY she will ever be justly remembered with horror and detestation in Great Britain. Her memory has been held in such abhorrence that some writers have arisen in later years to take her part and show that she was, upon the whole, quite an amiable and cheerful sovereign! 'By their fruits ye shall know them,' said OUR SAVIOR. The stake and the fire were the fruits of this reign, and you shall judge this Queen by nothing else.*

It is not until the 20th century that attempts were made to draw a more balanced portrait of Mary. Last year saw the publication of *Mary Tudor: Old and New Perspectives*, a collection of scholars' essays co-edited by Susan Doran and Thomas S. Freeman. On the first page, the editors say, the purpose of the book is to reveal an *"educated, resourceful and pragmatic queen."* One of the essays (bravely) takes on the issue of the martyrs:

> *The burning of 284 religious dissidents is morally unjustifiable from a twenty-first-century perspective. It is important to remember, however, that the values of the 21st century are not the values of the 16th century, and that in the 16th century the execution of obstinate heretics was almost universally regarded as a necessary duty of a Christian ruler.*

Will the real Mary Tudor finally emerge from the shadows, thanks to books like this one? I look forward to new perspectives on the oldest daughter of Henry VIII. The screams of the dying martyrs of the 1550s can never be silenced. But the time may have come for Mary's name to stand alone—and for "Bloody" to be no more.

Elizabeth Tudor's First Crisis: Enter Mary Queen of Scots

by BARBARA KYLE

When Elizabeth Tudor, at the age of twenty-five, inherited the English throne from her half-sister Mary in November of 1558, the country was on the brink of ruin. Mary had bankrupted the treasury through her disastrous war with France, which she had lost, leaving Elizabeth burdened with massive loans taken out in Europe's financial capital of Antwerp and a grossly debased coinage that was strangling English trade.

Danger threatened Elizabeth on every side. Spain, having ruthlessly established dominion over the Netherlands, eyed England as a possible addition to its empire that already spanned half the globe.

French power, too, was dangerously close in Scotland, a virtual French province under Marie de Guise who ruled in the name of her daughter, Mary Stuart, whose kingdom it was; Mary had married the heir to the French throne and by 1558 was Queen of France and, as Elizabeth's cousin, a claimant to Elizabeth's throne. Scotland's government was dominated by French overlords, and its capital was garrisoned with French troops, providing an ideal bridgehead for the French to launch an attack on England.

Meanwhile, at home Elizabeth faced seething discontent from a large portion of her people, the Catholics, who loathed her act of Parliament that had made the country officially Protestant. France and Spain sympathized with, and supported, the English Catholics.

If overtly threatened by either of those great powers, England would be vastly outmatched. The English people knew it and were frightened. Officials in the vulnerable coastal towns of Southampton, Portsmouth, and the Cinque Ports barraged Elizabeth's council with letters entreating aid in strengthening their fortifications against possible attack.

Unlike the European powers, England had never had a standing army. Her monarchs had always relied on a system of feudal levies by which local lords, when required, raised companies of their tenants and retainers to fight for the king, who then augmented the levies with foreign mercenaries. England was backward in armaments, too; while a revolution in warfare was happening in Europe with the development of artillery and small firearms, English soldiers still relied on pikes and bows. Even Elizabeth's navy was weak, consisting of just thirty-four ships, only eleven of them ships of war.

Ten months after Elizabeth's coronation, people throughout Europe were laying bets that her reign would not survive a second year. One crisis could destroy her.

That crisis came in the winter of 1559. In Scotland.

John Knox's Protestant rebel army, backed by several leading nobles including Lord James, the late king's illegitimate son, went on a country-wide rampage to oust Marie de Guise, the

Queen Regent, and they won much of Scotland to their cause. The Queen Regent's response was to bring in thousands of French troops.

This huge French military build-up on Elizabeth's border deeply alarmed her and her council (prompting the Spanish ambassador in London to write to his king, "*It is incredible the fear these people are in of the French on the Scottish border*").

Elizabeth sent clandestine financial support to Knox's rebels. She also sent Admiral Winter's small fleet into the December gales to intercept French ships bringing more troops. Knox captured Edinburgh. The momentum was with the rebels.

But the Queen Regent successfully counterattacked, forcing Knox's army to retreat to Stirling. Word reached Elizabeth that Philip of Spain had ordered thousands of Spanish troops in the Netherlands (a Spanish possession at the time) onto ships to sail to Scotland to help France put down Knox's "heretic" rebels.

Had the Spanish arrived, the fate of Scotland, and of England, could have been very different, but just then Philip's army in the Mediterranean battling the Turks suffered a devastating setback that made him halt his northern troops about to sail to Scotland and re-route them to fight the Turks. On such surprising hinges history often swings.

Elizabeth finally sent an English army into Scotland. Results were disastrous at first when they attacked the French at Leith, but eventually they laid a long siege that resulted in the surrender of the French and total victory for the English. John Knox, having secured the Scottish Reformation, had changed the course of Scotland.

Elizabeth's victory over the French in Scotland was a turning point in her fledgling reign, and its significance cannot be overemphasized. Her decision to defy the great powers of France and Spain, and to gamble on intervention, destroyed French domination in Scotland and made English influence there permanently predominant. Furthermore, it elevated Elizabeth's status at home and in the eyes of all Europe, whose leaders had to acknowledge her as a formidable ruler. She did this at the age of twenty-six, in just the second year of her reign.

Marie de Guise, unwell throughout the war with Knox's rebels, did not survive her troops' surrender; she died in Scotland in June 1560. Her daughter, Mary Stuart, Queen of France at the time, refused to sign the Treaty of Edinburgh, one article of which was her relinquishing her claim to the English throne. Her refusal infuriated Elizabeth, and thus began their nineteen-year feud.

Eleven months after the French surrender in Scotland, Mary Stuart, after less than two years as Queen of France, was widowed at age eighteen when her young husband, King Francis, died. With little status in the new court of her brother-in-law King Charles, Mary left France for her birthplace, Scotland, arriving at Leith by sea in August 1561, and took up her birthright, the Scottish throne.

Elizabeth's problems with Mary, her cousin and fellow queen, had just begun.

ELIZABETH & MARY, RIVAL QUEENS: LEADERSHIP LOST AND WON

BY BARBARA KYLE

SHOULD WE ACT FROM THE HEAD OR FROM THE HEART? DELIBERATION OR PASSION? IN fiction, the Dashwood sisters in Jane Austen's *Sense and Sensibility* personify this choice in matters of love. Elinor carefully considers her desires, weighing them against her responsibilities, holding her deepest feelings in check. Marianne scoffs at such reserve and acts boldly on her passions.

When it comes to ruling a country, with stakes infinitely higher, two queens have immortalized this crucial choice. Elizabeth Tudor of England planned her moves with Machiavellian care, keeping her ambitious nobles in line and her kingdom safe from foreign attack. Her peaceful reign spanned over forty years. Mary Stuart, Queen of Scots, followed her desires, making impetuous decisions that enraged her nobles. She ruled for less than seven years, created turmoil and civil war, boldly gambled her kingdom by hazarding all on the battlefield, and lost.

The two women were cousins. Yet they never met.

When Mary fled to England to escape the Protestant lords who had deposed her, she begged Elizabeth for protection and an army to fight her enemies. Elizabeth, however, needed Protestant Scotland as a bulwark against possible invasion by Catholic France or Spain, and so decided it was prudent to keep Mary in England under house arrest. Mary's captivity continued for nineteen years—a comfortable captivity befitting her status as a queen—during which she plotted ceaselessly to overthrow Elizabeth with the help of Spain and take her crown. Elizabeth waited out those nineteen years and finally, after the last plot almost succeeded, executed Mary.

It's a story that has enthralled the world for over four hundred years, sparking plays, operas, an endless stream of biographies, novels (including my own), and several movies. In 1895, one of the first movies ever made was an 18-second film of Mary's execution produced by Thomas Edison.

In Edison's brief film, the actress playing Mary lays her head across the executioner's block. He raises his axe. An edit occurs during which the actress is replaced by a mannequin. The mannequin's head is chopped off and the executioner holds it high in the air. It was filmdom's first special effect.

What is it about these two queens that so perennially fascinates us? I think it's that primal divide of head vs. heart, of sense vs. sensibility. Elizabeth, though passionate, acted with forethought. Mary, though intelligent, acted on her desires.

Partly, it stemmed from their upbringing. Mary became queen of Scotland just days after her birth. Her French mother, Mary of Guise, ruled in her daughter's name and sent Mary at the age of five to France to join the French king's family in preparation for marriage to his son and heir, Francis.

Growing up in the most glittering court in Europe, Mary was pampered and petted and loved by the French royal family. She married Francis when they were both in their teens, and when his father died a year later the young couple became king and queen of France. At age sixteen Mary had reached the pinnacle.

Elizabeth's upbringing could not have been more different. Hers was a childhood of uncertainty and fear.

Her father, Henry VIII, beheaded her mother, Anne Boleyn, for adultery when Elizabeth was three. He disinherited Elizabeth. Her half-sister Mary came to the throne when Elizabeth was twenty-one and sent her to the Tower where Elizabeth, terrified, fully expected to be executed. But Mary died, and Elizabeth, who had never thought she would rule, became queen at the age of twenty-five. In those perilous years she had learned to watch and wait, and never to act rashly.

It was a lesson Mary never learned.

These two queens, raised so differently, had very divergent outlooks on three aspects of monarchy. The first is what we today might call patriotism.

Mary, formed by France, was not much interested in Scotland, which she considered an unsophisticated backwater. In 1560, her husband, the young King Francis, died and so did her mother, who had ruled Scotland in Mary's name. Mary was therefore free to return to her homeland and take up her birthright as its reigning queen. Instead, she chose to stay in France where life was pleasant and spent many months casting about for a new European husband. Finding none to her liking, she grudgingly returned to Scotland.

Elizabeth, on the other hand, loved her country and its people with a sincerity in her words and actions that rings to us down the centuries. She was proud of being "mere English" ("mere" in those days meaning "purely"). She enjoyed meeting common people on her journeys through the shires and bantering with them with a familiarity that shocked the European aristocracy. She said often that her people were her family. Her people loved her in return.

Second, nowhere was the head-or-heart divide more apparent than in the choices these women made about marriage. For a queen, marriage was a crucial matter of state. After four years on the Scottish throne, Mary fell passionately in love with an English nobleman, Lord Darnley, and despite the vociferous disapproval of her nobles she hastily married him. She even used her power as monarch to name him king.

This splintered her court into factions—for and against Darnley—a situation that diminished much of Mary's power and led to a simmering civil war. Mary bore a son, James. But the marriage quickly soured when Darnley proved to be an arrogant, charmless wastrel.

Mary turned to a tough military man on her council, the Earl of Bothwell, and there was gossip that they were lovers. Seventeen months after marrying the queen, Darnley was murdered. (The house he was sleeping in was blown up.) Bothwell was accused of the murder, tried, and acquitted. Three months later, Mary took him as her third husband. The people suspected her of having colluded with him to murder Darnley. When she rode back into Edinburgh, the townsfolk hissed at her and called her "whore."

Elizabeth, famously, never married. She knew the danger if she did: her husband would be considered king, creating warring factions in her realm and eclipsing her power. For two decades foreign princes vied for her hand in marriage, and Elizabeth used them to negotiate alliances and to disrupt foreign alliances that endangered England. She frustrated her councilors, who constantly urged her to marry to produce an heir.

Elizabeth was acutely aware of the succession problem: a monarch who left no heir consigned her realm to likely civil war. And, with no heir of her body, her throne would pass to none other than Mary, her cousin. Elizabeth's decision to stay single was a hard one that brought her considerable personal anguish. She was heard to say, when Mary's son was born, that she envied Mary the baby "*while I am barren stock.*" But she knew her decision was wise.

Third, the head-or-heart divide had its greatest impact in how the two women ruled. The business of governance did not interest Mary. She rarely attended the meetings of her council, and when she did, she sat and sewed. She enraged Darnley and her nobles by ignoring them and spending her time with her young Italian secretary, Rizzio.

Elizabeth was what we would call a "hands-on" leader, involving herself in every aspect of governance. Furthermore, on the eve of a possible invasion by the terrifying Spanish Armada she rode out to her troops assembled at Tilbury and inspired them to face the foe, giving an address so stirring that in World War II Winston Churchill quoted it in the House of Commons to steel England's people to face a possible invasion by the Nazis.

> *Let tyrants fear...I have placed my chiefest strength and safeguard in the loyal hearts and good-will of my subjects. And therefore I am come amongst you...being resolved, in the midst and heat of the battle, to live and die amongst you all.*
> —Elizabeth I at Tilbury

Mary Stuart is to be pitied. She spent nineteen years under house arrest and died a gruesome death, beheaded at Elizabeth's order. But before she reached England it was her incompetence as a ruler in Scotland, her disastrous decisions in leadership, that led to her downfall there.

If peace, prosperity, religious tolerance, and increased international respect are the fruits of successful leadership, Elizabeth Tudor remains one of England's greatest rulers.

BORDER REIVERS: KINMONT WILLIE ARMSTRONG

BY TOM MOSS

KINMONT WILLIE WAS, WITHOUT DOUBT, ONE OF THE MOST NOTORIOUS SCOTTISH BORDER Reivers of the 16th century. His raids into England, in particular Tynedale in Northumberland, are particularly well documented. The primary sources from his day speak of big, organised raids involving hundreds of the Scottish Border Reiver fraternity intent on theft, spoil, and destruction south of the Border in England.

As such, Kinmont was well prized by the English.

Some of the raids into England in which Kinmont took part resulted in complete penury for the English families, but he was never brought to justice even though the English hotly demanded that he should be made to answer for his crimes. Yet for all his infamous notoriety and his successful and uncontested raids into England, Kinmont was to suffer the greatest of indignities when he was captured by the English at a time when he thought he was protected by the law of the Border at a "Day of Truce".

On 17 March 1596, a "Day of Truce" was held at the Dayholme of Kershope. The Dayholme was an area of flatland adjoining the little Kershope burn. It was a place traditionally used to hold "Days of Truce", a time when felons and miscreants were brought to the Border Line to answer for their crimes against the Border Law.

Written into Border Law was an "Assurance" that all who attended to witness fair play did so on the understanding that they were immune from confrontation with any enemy from the opposite side of the Border who might also be attending or, indeed, fellow countrymen with whom they might be at feud.

The "Assurance of the Truce" was thus the vehicle which gave all confidence that they could attend with impunity. The "Assurance" lasted not only for the time that the trials were in session but until the following sunrise, so that all who had attended would have time to return to their homes in safety. Kinmont attended the "Day" only as a witness.

The "Day of Truce" at the Dayholme of Kershope was over before sunset. Kinmont with a few compatriots from the Scottish West March rode down the Scottish side of the river Liddel whilst his English counterparts made for home down the English side. All were confident that the "Assurance" of the Truce still held and would do so until sunrise of the next day.

Suddenly, the English turned and rode furiously across the river and chased Kinmont down the Scottish bank. Not far from where the rivers Liddel and Esk join forces and run from there to the Solway Firth, the Scottish party was overtaken and overcome. Kinmont was bound to his horse and conveyed, under guard, to Carlisle castle to await a decision on his future from Thomas Lord Scrope, English West March Warden.

Scrope wrote to Elizabeth I, queen of England, asking what he should do with Kinmont. In his opinion, the Border Reiver was such an important prisoner that he needed the ruling of the English monarch as to the course he should take.

Scrope did not receive a reply and thus deemed that it was best that Kinmont should stay where he was, warded in Carlisle castle.

The whole of Scotland—monarchy, lords, and church—were incensed at what they saw as a blatant and expedient exploitation of the Border Law.

Working behind the scenes as the episode unfolded were the premier English Border Reiver family, the Grahams. They were friends with Thomas Carleton, erstwhile Captain of Carlisle castle, who had been dismissed by Scrope because of his double-dealing with the Scottish reivers.

The Grahams requested that Sir Walter Scott of Buccleuch, Kinmont's superior as Keeper of Liddesdale, should meet them to discuss the Kinmont affair. At the meeting, the Grahams ventured the thought that Buccleuch, suitably accompanied with a party of Scottish reivers mainly from the Scottish vales of the rivers Liddel, Ewes, and Annan, should raid Carlisle and force their way into the castle and rescue Kinmont. When the Grahams intimated that there would be not only inside help from members of the garrison of the castle but also a journey south through English territory uncontested by any of the English reivers, Buccleuch warmed to the notion.

On 12 April 1596 the rescue party, about seventy strong, assembled at Mortonrigg, Kinmont's tower in the Debateable Land, and headed south for Carlisle at sunset. Just before dawn, twenty-five or so of the raiders, mainly Armstrongs, were looking across the river Eden, near its confluence with the river Caldew, at the formidable pile of Carlisle castle. Leaving their horses on the north bank, they swam the river, and made their way to a postern gate in the western wall of the castle. The gate was opened from the inside, probably by one of Thomas Carleton's servants still employed there.

Only five of the raiders entered the castle. They knew the exact whereabouts of Kinmont's warding because on the previous day a Graham, on legitimate business, had been told by one of the garrison, sympathetic to the cause, where Kinmont was held.

The weather on the night was horrendous. On the ride south, the rescue party had been buffeted by torrential rain. On entering the castle they were served by the weather as the watch, almost to a man, were under cover, protecting themselves from the worst of the elements. Thus their entry was hardly contested. Only two men attempted to impede their progress to Kinmont's cell, and they were soon dealt with. Another guard, marshalling the entrance to the cell, was badly wounded.

The rescue party, now with Kinmont in their midst, left the castle, swam the river, and were soon on their way home to Scotland. The Irvines and Johnstones, stationed as ambush parties should the Scots be pursued north were soon to swell their numbers.

Scrope was to claim in letters to Lord Burghley that the castle had been attacked by 500 men from the Scottish Borders. In a letter to the Privy Council he wrote:

> *Yesternighte in the deade time therof, Walter Scott of Hardinge* [Harden, south of Hawick], *the chief man about Buclughe, accompanied with 500 horsemen of Buclughes*

and Kinmontes frends, did come armed...unto an outewarde corner of the base courte
of this castell and to the posterne dore of the same-which they undermined speedily...
brake into the chamber where Will of Kinmont was [and] *carried him awaye... The*
watch, as yt shoulde seeme, by reason of the stormye night, were either on sleepe or
gotten under some covert to defende themselves from the violence of the wether....

He was soon to point the finger at his own subordinates for the ease with which the castle
was breached:

And regardinge the myndes of the Lowthers to do villeny unto me, havinge beene
assured by some of their owne, that they woulde do what they coulde to disquiet my
government, I am induced vehementlye to suspect that their heades have bin in the
devise of this attempte, and am also persuaded that Thomas Carlton hath lent his hand
hereunto; for it is whispered in myne eare, that some of his servauntes, well acquainted
with all the corners of this castell, were guydes in the execution herof.

The amity between England and Scotland, even as late as 1596, ploughed an uneven furrow.
The relationship between James VI of Scotland and Elizabeth I of England had been fraught
with confrontation, especially about the state of the Borders. On receipt of a letter from James
to Elizabeth saying she should listen to both sides of the Kinmont affair and that he was not
prepared to hand over Buccleuch as demanded until she did, Elizabeth threatened to discon-
tinue the pension granted to him at the Treaty of Berwick in 1586. Even her fertile mind, however, had not given due consideration to what this action would cause.

The Scottish Council quickly perceived that James could not now conform to the wishes
of Elizabeth. Had he done so and handed over Buccleuch to the English, it would appear to
the people of both nations that he had done so for the pension. In due course, as a result of this,
Elizabeth softened her approach. Elizabeth was to write to James and say:

I beseech you to consider the greatness of my dishonour, and measure his [Buccleuch's] *just*
delivery accordingly. Deal in this case like a King who will have all this realm, and others
adjoining. See how justly and kindly you both can and will use a prince of my quality.

The plea of Elizabeth was initially ignored and she resorted to a firmer approach. *"If the*
king of Scotland...keeping the said offenders in his grace and protection...therefore involves himself in
their guiltiness, leaving the queen to have her remedy by another nature...."

Buccleuch was finally warded in Berwick in October 1597 much to the satisfaction of
Elizabeth, though he was treated with respect and eventually freed.

The Kinmont affair, which had raged for over a year, slowly lost its impetus at a time when
both countries saw nothing to gain by endless confrontation. Thus, it was consigned to history.
It remains to be verified exactly what Elizabeth meant when she spoke of a "remedy by another
nature." Perhaps one day that quandary may be resolved.

"Carrying Away the Booty": Drake's Attack on the Spanish Silver Train

by JENNY BARDEN

In April 1573 Francis Drake attacked the Spanish "Silver Train" near Nombre de Dios in Panama—this was the mule train loaded with bullion from Peru en route to King Philip II's treasury in Spain. The attack was a success, a triumph after almost a year of failed attempts in an enterprise that had been beset by disease and misfortune, including the loss of Drake's two younger brothers and over a third of his crew.

With the exception of the fatal wounding of Drake's ally, the Huguenot Captain Le Testu, Drake suffered very few casualties and the Spanish put up little resistance. Effectively they ran away, leaving Drake and his motley band of pirates, black runaway slaves (the Cimaroons), and French privateers in possession of the equivalent in gold and silver of about a fifth of Elizabeth I's annual revenue.

But what to do with so much bullion? This is where the story of Drake's first great enterprise becomes particularly fascinating because he was left with so great a weight in treasure that he and his men could not carry it all away.

Historians continue to debate over exactly how much was involved. In *Sir Francis Drake Revived*, the best English account of the raid (one which Drake presented to Queen Elizabeth in 1593), the weight of silver seized is stated to have been "near thirty tons". There were 190 mules in total, each carrying the standard load of 300 pounds. But the mules were also carrying much more valuable gold which the Spanish, smarting from the humiliation of the raid and no doubt wishing to play down the loss, put at "more than 100,000 pesos" including 18,363 pesos of fine gold from Popayan "consigned to your majesty."

This weight in gold alone would have been close to half a ton, and most of it would have been in the form of unminted gold discs or "quoits".

Drake had fifteen men with him on the raid, as well as twenty French corsairs and maybe forty Cimaroons. They had attacked the Silver Train about two miles from Nombre de Dios along the *Camino Real*—the "Royal Road" by which Spanish bullion was carried from the Pacific to the Caribbean—and their boats had been left "seven leagues" away at the Rio Francisco (probably the modern-day Rio Cuango twelve miles to the east).

Michael Turner of the Drake Exploration Society has done some excellent research in retracing the route they would probably have taken and calculates that the most they could have carried was sixty pounds each. So, of the thirty tons of treasure, Drake's men could only have taken away just over two tons—and they had to march through a storm that night.

Imagine what those men must have gone through, burdened with as much as they could possibly carry, sure that the Spanish soldiers from Nombre de Dios would be in hot pursuit, scrambling along a difficult trail through thick rainforest known only to the Cimaroons, in the dark, lashed by a tropical storm and without any sleep. Then, when they arrived back at the Rio Francisco, they discovered that the boats which should have been waiting to take them to safety were nowhere to be seen.

With typical undaunted panache, Drake improvised a raft out of driftwood left by the storm, with a biscuit sack for a sail, and set off by sea for his ships moored at a hideout in the Cativas (the modern-day San Blas islands), only to come across the pinnaces intended for the getaway at the mainland point (Punta San Blas). The boats had been driven back by the storm, but that night they returned for the rest of Drake's men and the bulk of the booty.

What happened to most of the silver which they had been unable to carry? In desperate haste, in the immediate aftermath of the raid, all the treasure that could not be carried had been buried under fallen trees, in the sand and gravel of the shallow islands of the Rio Nombre de Dios, and in the burrows of giant land crabs. A vast number of silver bars, each weighing between 35 and 40 pounds, were simply popped into crab holes.

A few days later, a small party of Drake's men returned to the scene of the ambush intent on retrieving this treasure, but they only recovered thirteen bars of silver and a few quoits of gold. The Spanish had found and decapitated Captain Le Testu and then tortured one of the two Frenchmen left with him into revealing where the bullion had been hidden. According to the Spanish, all the buried treasure was recovered, but plainly Drake's men were able to find some that they had missed. Perhaps there is still more waiting to be unearthed....

SOURCES

"Report of the Royal Officials of Panama to the Crown." 9 May 1573.

Sugden, John. *Sir Francis Drake.* Pimlico, 2006.

Turner, Michael. *In Drake's Wake.* Boston, England: Paul Mould Publishing, 2005.

"El Camino Real": A Path Worn through Time

by JENNY BARDEN

WHAT IS LEFT OF *EL CAMINO REAL*? STONES DISAPPEARING INTO THE UNDERGROWTH, lost in darkness, veiled by forest mist. Very little remains, but what does conjures up the shadows of the pack trains that used to traverse this vital road across Panama, bringing bullion from the mines of South America from the Pacific side of the isthmus to the Caribbean by the quickest overland route.

In the sixteenth and seventeenth centuries, *el Camino Real*, "the Royal Road", bore the riches that helped sustain the might of the Spanish Empire and its domination in Europe. It stretched from the city of Panama in the south, across mountains and through rainforest, to Nombre de Dios in the north. Over the stones once laid by some 4000 native slaves under the command of Gaspar de Espinosa in 1517-9, pack trains in convoys, often of two or three together totalling some 200 mules or more, would walk, plod, climb, and struggle over this path until their hooves wore hollows that can still be seen in places today.

The road was never easy. It was only just over sixty miles in length, yet it passed through thick forest and vegetation that proliferated so rapidly the road was in constant need of repair. In the rainy season it became impassable because of the many rivers that had to be forded which turned into torrents once swollen by tropical storms, and even without rain (as I know only too well from experience) the high humidity would soon leave the clothes of any traveller completely saturated.

Those who took the Royal Road had to contend with mosquitoes that carried malaria and yellow fever, and up in the mountains, where drops were precipitous, when a mule lost its footing it would be gone forever. There were other dangers too: the risk of ambush by Cimaroons—bands of runaway African slaves—and towards the end of the sixteenth century there was the very real threat of pirate attack.

Chris Haslam noted some of the hazards in his article "The World's Wildest Walk" for the *Sunday Times* (3/9/2006):

> *Some 300 ft below, the Nombre de Dios river roars through unseen cataracts, a constant reminder of where you end up if you fall. And falling is a constant possibility. The problem is that if you slip, you need to grab something to stop you falling, and if you grab something it will either bite you, spike you or try to tear your hand off. Scorpions, tarantulas and lethal bullet ants lurk in the leaf litter. Deadly eyelash vipers and enormous fer-de-lances lie disguised as branches and roots, and even the flora threatens armed response. Thorns, hooks and barbs shred clothes and skin, causing wounds that*

go septic in hours, and peaceful looking leaves cause cruel and unusual burns. It's hard enough hauling a rucksack around here: imagine driving a stolen mule train.

Francis Drake was the first Englishman to realise the vulnerability of the Spanish bullion supply while it was in transit over the Royal Road, and after several raids along the coast and attacks on shipping for little gain, many setbacks, and a thwarted attempt to ambush the "Silver Train" (as the bullion pack trains were called), he finally achieved a remarkable victory in April 1573 by capturing a convoy carrying almost 30 tons in silver and over half a ton in gold.

This was Drake's first great enterprise—the triumph that began his meteoric rise to fame, fortune, and a place in English history books.

After that attack, the Spanish began to store their treasure at Puerto Bello to the west of Nombre de Dios. (Drake later died of dysentery near Puerto Bello after a failed expedition to raid the City of Panama; he is buried at sea in the bay.)

The *Camino Real* and its offshoot connecting the Chagres river with the City of Panama— *el Camino a Cruces* (part of which still survives as Las Cruces Trail)—continued to be used to carry bullion north and merchandise south for another two hundred years.

In 1671, the buccaneer Henry Morgan used Las Cruces trail to reach the old city of Panama which he then looted and burned to the ground, and in the nineteenth century prospectors used the trail to cross the isthmus on their way to join the gold rush in California. The trail finally came to an end with the construction of the Panama Railroad in 1855. The railway reduced the time needed to cross the isthmus from a minimum of three days, and sometimes several weeks, to only an hour.

With the opening of the Panama Canal in 1914 most of the old road was lost forever, flooded by the damming of the Chagres to form Lake Gatun and by the Madden Dam behind which Lake Alajuela now covers a large part of the old trail. The development of Panama City as a metropolis has obliterated much more, and the forest and rivers have swallowed up the rest.

There are only a few traces left of the highway that once played such an important part in the history of world affairs, traces like the Puente del Matadero in Panama la Vieja, the bridge over which *Camino a Cruces* began.

ENGLISH LADIES-IN-WAITING

BY SANDRA BYRD

HAVING CLOSE FRIENDS IS AN IMPORTANT PART OF MOST WOMEN'S LIVES FROM GIRLHOOD through womanhood. These friends might be especially valuable when the woman's position is exalted, public, and potentially treacherous—such friendships take on an even more important role.

When Oprah Winfrey started her empire she brought along Gayle King. When Kate Middleton was preparing to become Catherine, Duchess of Cambridge, her sister Pippa was her constant companion. And when Anne Boleyn went to court to stay, she took her friends too. Among them was her longtime friend, Meg Wyatt, who would ultimately become her Chief Lady and Mistress of Robes.

Ladies-in-waiting were companions at church, at cards, at dance, and at hunt. They tended to their mistress when she was ill or anxious and also shared in her joys and pleasures. They did not do menial tasks—there were servants for that—but they did remain in charge of important elements of the Queen's household, for example, her jewelry and wardrobe.

They were gatekeepers; during the reign of Elizabeth I small bribes were offered for access to Her Majesty. The Queen was expected to assist her maids of honor in becoming polished and finding a good match; they in turn were loyal, obedient, and ornaments of the court. Married women had more freedom, better rooms, and usually more contact with the Queen.

In her excellent book, *Ladies in Waiting*, Anne Somerset quotes a lady-in-waiting to Queen Caroline as saying, *"Courts are mysterious places.... Intrigues, jealousies, heart-burnings, lies, dissimulations thrive in (court) as mushrooms in a hot-bed."* This is exactly the kind of place where one wants to know whom one can trust. Somerset goes on to tell us that,

> *At a time when virtually every profession was an exclusively masculine preserve, the position of lady-in-waiting to the Queen was almost the only occupation that an upperclass Englishwoman could with propriety pursue.*

Although direct control was out of their hands, the power of influence, of knowledge, of gossip, and of relationship networks was within the firm grasp of these ladies.

Appointment was not only by personal choice of the King or Queen, but was a political decision as well. Queen Victoria's first stand took place when her new Prime Minister, Robert Peel, meant to replace some of the ladies in her household to reflect the bipartisan English government and keep an equal political balance. According to Maureen Waller in, *Sovereign Ladies*, Victoria was adamant.

> *"I cannot give up any of my ladies,"* she told him at their second meeting.

"What ma'am!" Peel queried, "Does Your Majesty mean to retain them all?"

"All," she replied.

Keeping a political balance was a concern during the Tudor years too. Ladies from all of the important households were appointed to be among the Queen's ladies, though she held her personal friends in closest confidence. Queen Katherine of Aragon understandably preferred the ladies who had served her for most of her life right up till her death. Queen Anne Boleyn numbered both Wyatt sisters among her closest ladies as well as Nan Zouche.

Henry told his sixth wife, Queen Kateryn Parr, that she might, *"choose whichever women she liked to pass the time with her in amusing manners or otherwise accompany her for her leisure."*

Many Queens, like Elizabeth I, regularly surrounded themselves with family members, in her case, often those through her mother's side, hoping that they could trust in their loyalty and perhaps, like all of us, because they most enjoyed the company of those they loved best.

CHILDBIRTH IN EARLY MODERN ENGLAND

BY SAM THOMAS

WHEN WE THINK ABOUT THE DIFFERENCE BETWEEN THE PAST AND PRESENT, OUR MINDS often turn to medicine, and with good reason. Who in their right minds would want to return to a world of leeches and blood-letting, of pregnancy without doctors and high death-rates for both mothers and children? But as so many of the writers on this blog have made clear, there is far more behind the history than modern stereotypes, and childbirth is no exception.

If you were to peek in on a woman in labor (or "in travail" as she might have said), the first thing you might notice is the people in the room. There would be a midwife rather than a doctor, of course, and you'd not find her husband—until the eighteenth century at the very earliest, childbirth was the business of women.

Rather than doctors, nurses, and bright lights, the mother would be surrounded by her female friends and neighbors—her god-sibs or gossips—who came to help, socialize, to see and be seen, and at a more general level, just to make sure that everything went right.

(Before we join hands and start to sing *Kumbaya*, it's worth noting that sometimes gossips argued with each other, with the midwife, and even with the mother. Imagine if your own mother were present—and giving you advice—when you were in labor.)

Unlike today, when most women deliver while lying on their backs (good for the doctor, not so good for the mother), early modern women gave birth in a more upright position, either held by two of her gossips or sitting on a birthing stool, or both. While other women could participate in the delivery of the child, only the midwife had the right to touch the mother's "privities."

Once the child was born, the midwife would cut the umbilical cord (for boys, the longer the cord, the longer his, um, equipment; for girls, the shorter the cord, the tighter her privities), swaddle the child, and hand her over to the mother.

The question of maternal mortality has been much discussed, and our best guess is that 5-7% of births ended in the death of the mother. In some cases, death might be caused by an obstructed birth, but more often mothers died some weeks after delivery, usually of puerperal fever, a bacterial infection contracted during childbirth. Thus, while individual incidents of maternal death were not terribly common, most women would know a woman who had died in labor.

After giving birth, the mother would enjoy a period of lying-in. During these forty days, she would be confined to her room, free from the demands of household labor. During this time, her neighbors would visit, but she would not go out into public. At the end of her lying-in, the mother would go to her parish church and give thanks to God for her survival, and resume the heavy work of a wife and mother.

Mother Mourning: Childbed Fever in Tudor Times

by SANDRA BYRD

*B*LACK DEATH. THE GREAT PESTILENCE. PLAGUE. SWEATING SICKNESS. THE VERY WORDS THEMselves cause us to shudder, and they certainly caused those in centuries past to quake because they and their loved ones were often afflicted by those diseases. But when we survey the physical ailments that afflicted sixteenth century women, there is one death that caused the deepest fear among women: Childbed Fever, also known as Puerperal Fever and later called The Doctors' Plague.

Medieval and Tudor medicine centered around both astrology and the common belief that all health and illness was contained in balance or imbalance of the four "humours" of bodily fluids: blood, black bile, yellow bile, and phlegm. Therefore, the letting of blood or sniffing of urine were common practices to address or diagnose illness.

Although it seems ludicrous to us today, this understanding of medicine had reigned supreme for nearly 2000 years, coming down from Greek and Roman philosophical systems. It's been said that perhaps only 10-15% of those living in the Tudor era made it past their fortieth birthday. Common causes of illness leading to death? Lack of hygiene and sanitation.

Decades before the germ theory was validated in the late nineteenth century, Hungarian physician Ignac Semmelweis noticed that women who gave birth at home had a lower incidence of Childbed Fever than those who gave birth in hospitals. Statistics showed that, *"Between 1831 and 1843 only 10 mothers per 10,000 died of Puerperal Fever when delivered at home...while 600 per 10,000 died on the wards of the city's General Lying In Hospital."*

Higher born women, those with access to expensive doctors, suffered from Childbed Fever more frequently than those attended by midwives who saw fewer patients and not usually one after another.

In 1795, Dr. Alexander Gordon wrote, *"It is a disagreeable declaration for me to mention, that I myself was the means of carrying the infection to a great number of women."* Although they did not realize it at the time, it was, in fact, the sixteenth century doctors themselves who were transmitting death and disease to delivering mothers because the doctors did not disinfect their hands or tools in between patients.

Because illnesses are often transmitted via germs, doctors (and busy midwives) could infect the young mothers one after another, most often with what is now known as staph or strep infection in the uterine lining. Semmelweis discovered that using an antiseptic wash before assisting in the delivery of the mother cut the incidence of Childbed Fever by at least 90% and perhaps as much as 99%, but his findings were soundly rejected.

Infected women had no antibiotics to stop the onslaught of familiar symptoms once they began: fever, chills, flu like symptoms, terrible headache, foul discharge, distended abdomen, and occasionally, loss of sanity just before death.

This kind of death was not only no respecter of persons, as mentioned above, but it perhaps struck the highborn more frequently than the lowborn. In fact, fear of Childbed Fever is often mentioned when discussing Elizabeth I's reluctance to marry and bear children.

In the Tudor era, Elizabeth of York, the mother of Henry VIII, died of Childbed Fever as did two of Henry's wives, Queen Jane Seymour and Queen Kateryn Parr. Parr's deathbed scene is perhaps one of the most chilling death accounts of the century, beheadings included.

Although Semmelweis was outcast from the community of physicians for his implication that they themselves were the transmitters of disease, ultimately, science and modern medicine prevailed. Today, in the developed world, very few of the newly delivered die due to Puerperal Fever. Moms no longer need fear that the very act of bringing forth life will ultimately cause their own deaths and therefore can happily bond with their babies instead.

THE TRUTH ABOUT HALLOWEEN AND TUDOR ENGLAND

BY **NANCY BILYEAU**

I HAVE A PASSION FOR 16TH CENTURY ENGLAND. MY FRIENDS AND FAMILY, NOT TO MENTION my agent and editors, are accustomed to my obsession with the Tudorverse. For me, all roads lead back to the family that ruled England from 1485 to 1603. Could it be possible that Halloween, one of my favorite days of the year, is also linked to the Tudors?

Yes, it turns out, it could.

The first recorded use of the word "Halloween" was in mid-16th century England. It is a shortened version of "All-Hallows-Even" ("evening"), the night before All Hallows' Day, another name for the Christian feast that honors saints on the first of November.

But it's not just a literal connection. To me, there's a certain spirit of Halloween that harkens back to the Tudor era as well. Not the jack o' lanterns, apple-bobs, and haunted houses (and not the wonderful Christopher Lee "Dracula" movies that I watch on TCM network every October, two in a row if I can). It's that mood, frightening and mysterious and exciting too—of ghosts flitting through the trees, of charms that just might bring you your heart's desire, of a distant bonfire spotted in the forest, of a crone's chilling prophecy.

In pre-Reformation England, the Catholic Church co-existed with belief in astrology and magic. It was quite common to attend Mass regularly *and* to consult astrologers. *"The medieval church appeared as a vast reservoir of magical power,"* writes Keith Thomas in his brilliant 1971 book *Religion and the Decline of Magic.*

Faithful Catholics tolerated the traditions of the centuries-old Celtic festival of Samhain ("summer's end"), when people lit bonfires and put on costumes to scare away the spirits of the unfriendly dead. In fact, an eighth century pope named November 1 as the day to honor all Catholic saints and martyrs with an eye toward Samhain.

Nothing shows the merger of Celtic and Christian beliefs better than "soul cakes." These small, round cakes, filled with nutmeg or cinnamon or currants, were made for All Saints' Day on November 1. The cakes were offered as a way to say prayers for the departed (you can picture the village priest nodding in approval) but they were also given away to protect people on the day of the year that the wall was thinnest between the living and the dead, a Celtic if not Druid belief. I am fascinated by soul cakes, and I worked them into my first novel, *The Crown*, a thriller set in 1537-1538 England. Soul cakes even end up being a clue!

In the early 16th century, Halloween on October 31, All Saints' Day (or All Hallows' Day) on November 1, and All Souls' Day on November 2 were a complex grouping of traditions and observances. Life revolved around the regular worship, the holidays, and the feast days that constituted the liturgy. As the great Eamon Duffy wrote: *"For within that great seasonal cycle of fast and festival, of ritual observance and symbolic gesture, lay Christians found the paradigms and the stories which shaped their perception of the world and their place in it."*

Henry VIII changed the perceptions of the kingdom forever when he broke from Rome. A guiding force in his reformation of the Catholic Church was the destruction of what he and his chief minister Thomas Cromwell scorned as "superstition." Saints' statues were removed; murals telling mystical stories were painted over; shrines were pillaged; the number of feast days was sharply reduced so that more work could be done during the growing season. *"The Protestant reformers rejected the magical powers and supernatural sanctions which had been so plentifully invoked by the medieval church,"* writes Keith Thomas.

The story in *The Crown* is told from the perspective of a young Catholic novice who struggles to cope with these radical changes.

Yet somehow Halloween, the day before All Saints' Day, survived the government's anti-superstition movement, to grow and survive long after the Tudors were followed by the Stuarts. It's now a secular holiday that children adore (including mine, who are trying on costumes four days early). As for me, I relish the candy handouts, costumes and scary movies—and I also cherish our society's stubborn fondness for bonfires and charms and ghosts and sweet cakes, for in them can be found echoes of life in the age of the Tudors.

Tudor Christmas Gifts

by DEBORAH SWIFT

In Shakespeare's Day it was more usual to give gifts at New Year, but if you were lucky you might receive one at Christmas. Christmas gifts were known as Christmas Boxes and were usually given by a master to his servants, or an employer to his apprentices or workmen. They were a mark of appreciation for work done over the previous year. New Year's gifts were a more equal exchange between friends or relations.

So what might you expect in a Tudor Christmas stocking? Maria Hubert in her book *Christmas in Shakespeare's England* suggests that Shakespeare might have enjoyed receiving paper as it was very expensive, a new quill pen, or a knife with which to sharpen it.

In Shakespeare's play *The Winter's Tale*, a pedlar is selling:

> *Lawn as white as driven snow,*
> *Cyprus black as e'er was crow,*
> *Gloves as sweet as damask roses;*
> *Masks for faces and for noses,*
> *Bugle bracelet, necklace amber,*
> *Perfume for a lady's chamber;*
> *Golden quoifs and stomachers*
> *For my lads to give their dears.*

Elizabeth herself had a liking for candies and sugar fruits. The Sergeant of the Pastry (what a great title!) gave her a Christmas *"pye of quynses and wardyns guilt"*, in other words a gilded pie of quince and plums.

Everyone in her household was expected to give her a gift for the New Year, the more lavish the better since your gift indicated your status. The gifts are well documented and include a gift even from her dustman, who gave her "two bolts of camerick" (cambric) in 1577. In the same year, Sir Philip Sidney gave her *"a smock of camerick, wrought with black silk in the collor and sleves, the square and ruffs wrought with venice golde"*. It seems the dustman's gift was somewhat outclassed!

Other gifts she received were *"eighteen larkes in a cage"* in 1578, and a fan of white and red feathers from Sir Francis Drake in 1589 which was included in her portrait. The portrait also shows her wearing an amber necklace like the one described in Shakespeare's verse and carrying embroidered gloves. Were any of them Christmas gifts I wonder?

For the artisan and lower classes it was the custom to send foodstuffs to your lord or master who owned the land you tenanted. Typical gifts included pigs, fowl, eggs, dried apples, cheeses, or nuts and spices such as nutmegs and almonds.

But what about the man in your life? Well, socks, of course. Or hose to be more precise.

THE ELIZABETHAN
GARDENING CRAZE

BY M.M. BENNETTS

W E TEND TO ASSOCIATE THE TUDORS WITH LOTS OF THINGS—MOST OF THEM OF THE bloody, messy, power-struggle variety. Which is not necessarily an inaccurate picture. But it's only a fragment of the tapestry that was 16th century England.

Because what we don't necessarily consider when thinking about the Tudors is that they—for all their many wives and/or courtiers falling in and out of favour—gave England something it had not had for centuries: domestic peace and tranquillity.

Yes, there were the uprisings against Henry VIII's Dissolution of the Monasteries, and there was Northumberland's attempt to seize power and the crown with an army (which famously melted away) from Mary...but for the most part the country was rebellion-free and troop-free. And this long period of peace gave rise to all sorts of growth.

There were fewer than 3 million people living in England in 1500. But that figure had nearly doubled by 1650, to 5.25 million.

Then too, in 1520, the Church owned roughly one-sixth of the kingdom. By 1558, when Elizabeth ascended the throne—roughly twenty years after the Dissolution of the Monasteries—three-fourths of that land had been sold off, primarily into the hands of the gentry and the increasingly monied middle class. And this substantial change in land ownership brought with it equally substantial shifts in political, cultural, and economic power within the kingdom.

Translated into plain English, there was now a land-owning gentry and burgeoning middle class who found themselves able to spend more of their resources on pleasures and comforts, rather than on self-defence and necessities as they previously would have done.

So rather than the conversation between husband and wife going something like, "I see York is getting resty. I think we really should build another defensive tower and a moat..." the conversation now could go something like, "Hmm, I fancy having a garden over on the south side of the house. With a rose pergola. What about you?"

And this shift in attitude was most particularly true of the second half of the century, during the reign of Elizabeth I.

For just as this forty-five year period of domestic tranquility saw a flowering of the arts, of music and literature, so too, gardening. And it wasn't just gardening for the aristocratic few. For in this latter half of the 16th century, the English really came into their own as gardeners and plant collectors. It was, without question, the first English gardening craze. (It's been going on ever since.)

They had the disposable income. They had the time. They weren't worried about marauding armies. They had the estates. And their international trade and exploration was bringing back seeds and cuttings from the farthest reaches of the globe, daily expanding the already wide variety of plants available.

And within this culture of burgeoning energy and self-confidence, the garden became a symbol of the nation's flowering under Elizabeth's stewardship. Flowers were everywhere in her reign. They were her symbols.

And this was the time too that the garden began to take on a distinctly modern flavour.

Whereas initially, most gardens and plant collecting had been directed toward the herbal and medicinal arts, now flowers were valued for pleasure's sake alone—for their intrinsic beauty, for their scents, for their rarity...and the pleasure garden became an element of Elizabethan status.

Always the gardens of the period were walled or enclosed in some way—by walls, hedges, fences, or even moats—and generally built off the house, often accessible only from the family's main room or parlour.

Enclosing the space ensured a measure of protection from wild animals (hungry deer) or thieves, but it also protected the plants from prevailing winds and provided a warmer microclimate. Then too, in plans of Elizabethan manor houses, one will occasionally find several unconnected walled gardens leading off from the different rooms in the house—some for pleasure, others for the medicinal herbs or vegetables, still others with their walls covered in espaliered apples, figs, and pear....

Also, Elizabethan gardens were always laid out formally, geometrically designed and as often as not symmetrically, with knot gardens being the most common feature of the late 16th century garden. Indeed, one could rightly call the knot garden a very English passion. (They were little known in France or Italy.)

Knots (yes, the name is taken from the knots one makes with string or rope) were made up of square or rectangular patterns created by the use of one of more different types of plant, usually clipped box or santolina. The lines of the knot were interlaced so that they appeared to weave in and out of each other, with greater or lesser complexity. Often, the beds were then filled with sand or grass or gravel of different colours to emphasise the overall pattern of the knot—especially when viewed from an overlooking window or gallery. Sometimes too the enclosed beds contained flowers—clove pinks were a favourite choice.

From the outset of this Elizabethan horticultural boom, London was the centre of taste and innovation. For as well as being the centre of all financial and economic activity, London had citizens with the education, knowledge, and the European contacts to indulge in this growing demand for garden innovation and exotica. (Middle class London houses of the period had attached gardens.)

It was from London's nurserymen, and via their contacts in Vienna, Italy, France, and the Netherlands, that the population ordered their seeds and cuttings. In 1604, if one wanted a pair of garden shears, one ordered them from London. The wealthy Banbury family traded in seeds and plants at Tothill Street in Westminster from probably 1550 to 1650.

And the newly discovered species continued to pour in from all over the globe—African marigolds from Mexico, apples and pear and apricot trees from France and the Netherlands, Clematis viticella from Italy, Oriental planes from Persia. By the 1570s, there were tulips, daffodils, and hyacinths from Turkey—arriving via the circuitous route of Vienna and the Brabant. All of which expanded the already large variety of imported plants and seeds available: Madonna lilies, lupins, snowdrops, cyclamen, hollyhocks, lily of the valley, peonies, ranunculi, anemones, polyanthus.... The list was enormous and is quite unlike the monochromatic green palette to which we imagine Elizabethan gardeners were limited.

Yet perhaps the most surprising of the horticultural innovations of the period was the demand for fruit and vegetables—given that contemporary medicine was adamant in proclaiming that eating vegetables was dangerous and resulted in melancholia and bodily flatulence.

As early as the previous century, there had been those who'd praised the virtues of veg. But just as the list of available flowers grew yearly, so too did the list of vegetables available for cultivation—artichokes, cucumbers, lettuce, parsnip, endive, leek, cress, cabbage, rocket, turnips....

Fruit-growing too had long been popular, and even the poorest in the land had had access to apples. For those with more money, figs, pears, plums, and cherries were a regular part of the diet. But the gardeners of this period now consciously sought out better cultivars and a greater variety.

Sir John Thynne, when obsessing about his garden at Longleat, wrote to his steward to *"send me word how my cherry stones, abrycocks, and plum stones that I brought out of France do grow."* Equally, Sir Phillip Sidney ordered cherry and quince trees from Brabant for his orchard at Penshurst. Robert Cecil, the first Earl of Salisbury, (a passionate gardener and plant collector) sent John Tradescant the Elder to travel in the Netherlands and France to buy fruit trees for Hatfield.

Interestingly too, it's here that one can see the Elizabethan concept of gender differentiation—the flower and kitchen gardens were the province of the women; the orchards were for men. John Tradescant the Elder was paid £50 per annum for the job of laying out the garden at Hatfield House; the Earl of Leicester paid his head gardener £20 per annum; yet weeders—who were always female—were paid threepence a day.

Into this market of enthusiastic and energetic gardeners and plant-collectors, jobbing writer and journalist (and sometime astrologer) Thomas Hill launched the first gardening book ever written. Before his work, there had been herbals, yes. But they were nothing like *The Gardener's Labyrinth*, first published in 1577, which he wrote under the pseudonym of Didymus Mountaine.

For *The Gardener's Labyrinth* was the first practical hands-on, how-to gardening manual, and every page is suffused with the infectious pleasure Hill obviously took in gardening himself. The book was a runaway best-seller and a new edition was published the following year, with four more editions published over the next 75 years.

And while Hill borrowed heavily (some might think annoyingly) from classical writers like Pliny, Palladius, and Cato, and he cobbled together bits that he'd obviously garnered from other sources, even though he often strayed into astrology or his theory that the germination of seeds is governed, like the tides, by the phases of the moon, and even though his pest control remedies read like witches' brew, still, at the same time, in his work, there is this genuine love of getting his hands into the soil. There are diagrams for laying out a knot, there's his advice on how to blanch vegetables, on keeping the beds well-dunged; advice on how to water, how to build a rose arch or how to lay a fast-growing rosemary hedge, how to ensure a regular supply of fresh herbs, all of which still hold true today.

And all of it was written in an engaging conversational tone—quite unlike that used by his contemporaries—it's the voice of a practicing down-to-earth garden writer—a Geoff Hamilton, an Alan Titchmarsh, or the much-missed Jim Wilson.

It was Hill too who summed up the gardening spirit of the age:

> *The life of man in this world is but thraldom, when the Sences are not pleased and what rarer object can there be on earth...than a beautifull and Odoriferous Garden plot Artificially composed, where he may read and contemplate on the wonderfull works of the great Creator, in Plants and Flowers; for if he observeth with a judicial eye, and serious judgement their variety of Colours, Sents, Beauty, Shapes, Interlacings, Enamilling, Mixture, Turnings, Windings, Embossments, Operations and Vertues, it is most admirable to behold and mediate upon the same.*

Stuart Period
(1603–1714)

THE THREE WEDDINGS OF JAMES VI AND I (BUT ONLY ONE WIFE)

BY MARGARET SKEA

MOST OF US ONLY GET MARRIED ONCE (TO THE SAME PERSON). THINGS USED TO BE DIFferent—for royalty at least....

Some of us may have written a poem to our beloved (not guilty). That's something that hasn't changed.

Here is a poem written by James VI to Anne of Denmark in 1589:

> *What mortal man may live but hart*[1]
> *As I do now, suche is my cace*
> *For now the whole is from the part*
> *Devided eache in divers place.*
> *The seas are now the barr*
> *Which makes us distance farr*
> *That we may soone win narr*[2]
> *God graunte us grace…*

Born in 1566, James became king of Scotland at the age of one, following the forced abdication in 1567 of his mother, Mary, Queen of Scots.

In 1589, now 23, negotiations for a suitable marriage, which had been a matter of primary concern to court and country alike since his 16th birthday, were finally concluded.

His choice, Anne of Denmark, was one that pleased him—she was young and handsome. It pleased his subjects—it reinforced the already important trade links with Denmark. And, he said, it pleased God—who had "*moved his heart in the way that was meetest*".

Whether James' understanding of God's will was influenced more by the fact that Anne was eight years younger than himself, while the other candidate, Catherine of Navarre, was eight years older and reputedly looking her age, than by the earnest prayer he claimed, is a moot point. The contract was made, and his chosen proxy, George Keith, Earl Marishchal, was charged not only with taking James' place at the marriage ceremony, but also with the task of bringing the new queen home.

On 1 September 1589 a small fleet left Denmark heading for Scotland.

It was to be an ill-fated voyage. Storms battered the ships, the queen's life was endangered

---

1 without love

2 near

by cannons which broke loose from the their mountings, and when prayers failed to calm the seas, Peter Munk, the Danish Admiral, concluded that the storms were the work of witches and sought safe haven in Norway.

Munk's belief that witches played a part in the storms that threatened the ships was one which James was ready to accept, and witch trials followed in both countries, including the infamous North Berwick trials of 1590.

Unwilling to wait until the following spring, James resolved to send ships from Scotland to bring Anne home. But when his Lord Admiral, the Earl of Bothwell, told him how much such a venture would cost, he quickly changed his mind. In fairness, though James had a reputation of being canny—especially where money was concerned—he probably couldn't afford it.

Enter Maitland, Lord Chancellor of Scotland, who volunteered to send ships at his own expense—an offer that James was quick to accept.

James then made what would be the most impulsive and foolhardy gesture of his life. Disregarding the increased dangers of winter seas, he decided to accompany the fleet to Norway. Knowing it would not please his council, however, he took care both to ensure that word of his intention did not leak out until it was too late for them to stop him and also to leave detailed instructions for the governance of the country in his absence. He was to be away for more than six months.

Fortunately for James, the journey which Anne's ships had struggled to make for almost a month, took just six days, and he arrived in Norway at the end of October.

There followed wedding No. 2 in Oslo, conducted in French by a Scots minister who had accompanied James, and finally, in January 1590, for the benefit of the Danish royal family, wedding No. 3 at the castle of Kronborg in Denmark.

Thoroughly married, by both Scots and Lutheran rites, the royal couple and their entourage caroused the winter away in Denmark, finally leaving on 21 April 1590. They arrived at the port of Leith, just outside Edinburgh, on 1 May 1590, to a tumultuous welcome from a populace eager for a young and healthy king and queen.

It was a marriage that lasted thirty years until Anne's death in 1619, and though the initial happiness did not last, they had eight children—three sons and five daughters. Their firstborn, Henry, died in 1612, and it was their second son Charles who succeeded James. The marriage of their only surviving daughter, Elizabeth, to Frederic V, Elector Palatine and King of Bohemia, eventually led to the Hanoverian succession to the British throne.

A Witch's Lair Found
Buried under a Mound

BY DEBORAH SWIFT

D ARKEST DECEMBER IN 2011—A GROUP OF WORKMEN UNEARTH A SPOOKY FIND....
Near Lower Black Moss reservoir, close to the village of Barley in England, workmen were digging a trench for a new water main. That was until they suddenly struck rock, and began to find the outlines of walls and doorways.

Beneath a grassy mound in the shadow of Pendle Hill, they found a remarkably well-preserved 17th century building. United Utilities' workers were amazed to find a witch's-style cottage, complete with a mummified cat sealed into the walls. Immediately, links were made to the famous Pendle Witches, who were tried for witchcraft 400 years ago in 1612. The fame of the Lancashire Witches in England is similar to that of the Salem Witches in the United States, so excitement was running high.

Simon Entwhistle, an expert on the Pendle Witches said, *"Cats feature prominently in folklore about witches. Whoever consigned this cat to such a horrible fate was clearly seeking protection from evil spirits."* His view was that the cottage could even be the famous Malkin Tower, the site of a notorious meeting between the Pendle witches on Good Friday in 1612.

The cottage is said to be in remarkable condition although most of the objects unearthed seem to have been from the 19th century—artefacts such as crockery, a cooking range, and a bedstead, so whether this is really anything to do with the Lancashire Witches is purely conjecture. Still, the Lancashire Witches have such a hold on the local imagination that it is tempting to ascribe any find in this area to those times.

"In terms of significance, it's like discovering Tutankhamun's tomb. We are just a few months away from the 400th anniversary of the Pendle witch trials, and here we have an incredibly rare find, right in the heart of witching country," Mr. Entwhistle said.

In the year 2012, we reached the 400th anniversary of the trial of the Pendle Witches, when ten people were hanged accused of the deaths of other villagers by witchcraft. They were executed at Lancaster on the twentieth of August, 1612, for having bewitched to death *"by devilish practices and hellish means"* no fewer than sixteen inhabitants of the Forest of Pendle. All over Lancashire events were organised to commemorate the women who died, unjustly condemned to death on the hearsay of their neighbours.

The Demdike family and the Chattox family were the main victims of the witchhunt. Their story was well-documented in *A Discoverie of Witches*, a pamphlet of the time. The full story is a complicated one, but almost everything that is known about the trial is in a report written by Thomas Potts, the clerk to the Lancaster Assizes, completed by 16 November 1612.

At the end of the 16th and into the 17th century, Lancashire was regarded by the authorities as a wild and lawless region, an area *"fabled for its theft, violence and sexual laxity, where the church was honoured without much understanding of its doctrines by the common people"* (Hasted). In addition, James I was obsessed with daemonology and witches, and only fuelled the nation's enthusiasm for finding witches where none existed.

It is from these dark times and this grim northern environment that the two sisters, Sadie and Ella Appleby in my novel, *The Gilded Lily*, go on the run. Ella has been involved in a Witch Trial, the story of which is told in *The Lady's Slipper*. The girls hope to re-invent themselves and find glitter and glamour in fashionable London.

As for the mummified cat—concealing things in old buildings was very common in the 17th century. One of the most common things found in old buildings is shoes. Nobody knows why, but it was supposed that a shoe trapped the spirit of the wearer, and some 1,700 concealed shoes have been found—not just in Britain, but also in Germany, Australia, Canada, and the United States.

Pirate Extraordinaire and Friend to the Crown

By KATHERINE PYM

Sir Henry Mainwaring began life in Shropshire around 1587. He was born to a gentry family and educated as a lawyer at the Inner Temple of London. In 1612, he was given the post to escort the English ambassador to Persia. It would be in an armada-type convoy as a protection against the pirates who lurked around the Strait of Gibraltar. However, Spain and Venice did not trust the armada. They believed the English would turn to piracy as soon as the fleet entered the Mediterranean.

This irritated Mainwaring. In a ship purchased for £700, he set out to the Mediterranean where he turned pirate. He harassed the Spanish, and any other ships not English for a period of several years. He had a fleet of approximately six ships and considered himself the scourge of the Mediterranean. But he did not center around there.

By 1613, he set his base in Ma'amura on the Atlantic coast of Morocco, at the mouth of the Sebou River, about 150 miles south of the Straits. It was a popular pirate stronghold in the early 1600s, a "place of rendezvous" for as many as forty ships and 2000 men. Mainwaring used this base to harass Dutch shipping, as well as the Spanish, French, and Portuguese. His only firm promise was never to attack an English ship, even though he could have amassed a fortune. His countrymen's vessels carried goods from the Levant Company which included spices, fabrics, and unique goods.

In 1614, Mainwaring left the Ma'amura foothold, which was fortuitous. After he'd left, a Spanish armada of 99 ships and thousands of men took hold of the mouth of the Sebou River, and settled in the area, declaring it a Spanish territory. Mainwaring had been saved from destruction by the skin of his teeth.

Now, his main goal was to pester the fishing fleet off Newfoundland. He took ships (though not English ones), their munitions, food, and men. He told King James I one day these men were "many volunteers, many compelled." When King James I asked how this was, Mainwaring replied many men wanted to become pirates, but they were afraid once a vessel was caught, they'd be hanged for piracy. They wanted to enjoy the fruits of these labors without the threat of such brutal and ignominious punishment. A man hanged for piracy was left in the noose until three tides washed against him then dispersed before being cut down. If families didn't claim the bodies, they'd be taken to be dissected.

After plaguing the fishing fleet off Newfoundland, Mainwaring's travels became blurred. He drifted back toward the Mediterranean until in 1616, King James I pardoned him with the seal of England.

He settled in England, wrote a book titled *Discourse of the Beginnings, Practices, and Suppression of Pirates*. He presented it to King James I and received a knighthood in return.

He sat in the House of Commons in the 1620s, supported the Crown during the Civil Wars, and went into exile in France during the Commonwealth, where he died in poverty.

SOURCE

Tinniswood, Adrian. *Pirates of Barbary: Corsairs, Conquests and Captivity in the Seventeenth-Century Mediterranean*. New York: Penguin Group, 2010.

General George Monck
and the Siege of Dundee

by BRIAN WAINWRIGHT

In the late summer of 1651, Scotland's fortunes were at a very low ebb indeed. Her field army had suffered a decisive defeat at the hands of English Commonwealth forces at the battle of Dunbar (3 September 1650) and the nearest thing she had to a government, the Committee of Estates, had been captured at Alyth in Perthshire during the night of 27/28 August by Colonel Alured at the head of a party of 8,000 English horse. King Charles II had led his army out of Scotland and into England at the end of July, and only a few scattered garrisons remained to defend the country.

Although Oliver Cromwell had led the bulk of the Commonwealth forces in Scotland south in early August in pursuit of Charles II, a substantial English army remained behind under the command of General George Monck. These men did not stand idle after the capture of the Committee of Estates, but set about reducing the remaining strongholds that were still held by the Scots in the name of Charles II.

Stirling Castle fell on 14 August, surrendering on terms after a brief siege. By August 23 Monck was at Perth, where his troops received supplies of cheese, biscuits, and other essentials sent by ship from England.

On 26 August, Monck formally "summoned" Dundee—in other words, he invited the defenders to capitulate on terms. However, the Royalist Governor, Sir Robert Lumsdaine, not only refused, but suggested that instead Monck and his army should lay down their arms and accept the King's grace. (It must be remembered that Charles II was still in the field in England at this time, and his comprehensive defeat at Worcester on 3 September 1651 was still a thing of the future.)

Dundee was a well-fortified, walled town, which had previously seen off an attack by the Marquis of Montrose. The Governor's confidence is therefore understandable.

The rules of war at this time were harsh, and were to remain unchanged well into the 19th century. If a garrison surrendered immediately on summons, it could usually expect generous terms. If it resisted for a time and then yielded, it might still receive reasonable terms. However, if it resisted and was eventually taken by storm, any mercy shown was purely at the discretion of the victor. Men taken in arms might lawfully be shot or put to the sword, and although civilians were nominally protected, it was the usual custom to allow the victorious troops to loot and rape to their hearts' content for at least twenty-four hours. Obviously if a civilian male picked up a weapon to defend his family he was likely to be killed without question. In an age when uniforms were by no means standardised, even where they existed at all, it was not always straightforward to distinguish between a soldier and a civilian anyway.

This may seem barbarous, but the intention was to encourage garrisons to yield before a "practicable breach" had been made in their defences. The storming of a fortification was an horrendous business for the attackers as well as the defenders. Many of them would inevitably be killed or badly wounded and it was necessary to provide them with "incentives". Some might hope to be promoted, but for the majority the prospect of several hours looting a town without restraint was reward enough.

By 29 August, siege guns, including mortar pieces, were in place and the following night, amid wet and stormy weather, they were "played upon the town".

Late on 31 August, Monck was reinforced by two regiments of horse who had been out on patrol (and defeated 400 Scottish cavalry while they were about it) and was now in a position to storm the town. The next day began with a heavy exchange of artillery fire, lasting some two or three hours until large breaches were made in the fortifications. At 11 o'clock the English, with their field cry "God with us" broke into the town in two separate places.

Hand-to-hand fighting continued for half-an-hour, when some of the Scots retreated into the church. They were overtaken by the English, and at least five hundred soldiers and townsmen were killed, including the Governor, compared to around twenty English killed. The large disparity strongly suggests that many, perhaps even the great majority, were cut down in the rout. When the English reached the market-place, quarter was given to another five hundred Scots.

One source I came across claimed that 2,000 were killed, including 200 women and children—it is hard to be definitive about such matters at this date when the losing side inevitably magnified casualties for propaganda purposes. The 500 dead can perhaps be taken as a minimum.

Although the English soldiers were given an "official" twenty-four hours to plunder the town, attacks on inhabitants and their possessions went on for a *further fortnight* despite Monck's attempts to stop them. Given that the New Model Army was one of the most professional and disciplined armed forces in Europe, this was completely inexcusable, even by the standards of the time.

I have a long-standing interest in the Civil War in the Three Kingdoms, but until very recently, I had never heard of the massacre of Dundee, which is very odd when the whole world, his wife, and his cat knows about the similar events at Drogheda for which Oliver Cromwell is held responsible. I have difficulty in accounting for this discrepancy, except to point out that in 1660 General George Monck was instrumental in restoring Charles II to his throne, after which nothing bad could be said about him. Whereas, after 1660, nothing was too bad to say about Cromwell.

For anyone who would like to know more about events in Scotland at this time I strongly recommend *Cromwellian Scotland* by Frances Dow, the book which first brought the sad events at Dundee to my notice.

So You Say You Want
an Execution...

BY **SAM THOMAS**

Writers of historical fiction love executions.
From Hilary Mantel's *Wolf Hall*, to Nancy Bilyeau's *The Crown*, to my own *The Midwife's Tale*, authors cannot resist the lure of the gallows or (even better) the stake. Such moments provide drama and tell the reader something important about the world our characters inhabit.

Unlike today's executions which usually take place in a private (and bizarrely medical) setting, early modern executions had all the trappings of a civic ritual. Prayers were said, sermons preached, speeches delivered, all with the goal of setting the world right after a terrible murder. The blood of the victim cried out for justice—an eye for an eye—and the executioner provided it.

But the symbolism went further than this. In many cases, a murderer was executed not at the prison, but at the very scene of the crime. In 1668, Thomas Savage murdered his fellow servant, and after his conviction, he was hanged from a gibbet built in front of the house where he'd committed the crime. What better way to close the book on a murder?

Executions thus were morality plays in which the Crown saw justice done and overawed its subjects with the power of life and death. Given this public setting, it was important that everyone played their part. The condemned was supposed to confess to his crime and confirm that the execution was just. The crowd were supposed to bear witness to justice and the power of the government.

If this was the goal of the play, however, in many cases the actors or the audience went off-script and improvised an entirely new drama, with a much more opaque meaning. The first place that the meaning of an execution could go wrong was with the crowd, for many executions had all the dignity of a three-ring circus. Peddlers strolled through the crowd crying their wares, and many in attendance treated the execution as an opportunity for eating, drinking, and socializing.

One pamphlet from 1696 shows a preacher delivering an execution sermon, while behind him one can see not only the condemned offering up his last prayers, but a magician performing on an adjacent stage. (In this case, it seems better to be the opening act than the headliner.) In other cases, government officials explained their decision to publish the condemned prisoner's final words by saying that the crowd was too loud for anyone to hear him.

If a festive crowd (and magician) could get an execution off on the wrong foot, the condemned could make things worse. In many cases, Catholics condemned for treason proved the most difficult to control. Some Catholics claimed to die as martyrs of the Church (rather than traitors to the Crown—a vital distinction at the time), kissing each step of the ladder as they climbed it, and in one case kissing the executioner himself! Once on the scaffold, they would use their final speeches not to affirm the justice of their execution, but to defend the Catholic Church.

In cases such as these, the crowd or even the presiding officials could get involved, once again robbing the event of its solemnity. In 1591, Judge Richard Topcliffe attacked one prisoner saying, *"Dog-bolt Papists! You follow the Pope and his Bulls; believe me, I think some bulls begot you all!"* Not to be outdone, the condemned replied, *"If we have bulls* [for] *our fathers, thou hast a cow to thy mother!"* Other prisoners taunted the crowd (who naturally gave as good as they got), or even engaged in raucous religious debates.

If executions were meant as awe-inspiring ceremonies that demonstrated the government's power, many did not get the message, and we can only wonder what those involved made of such events.

Religious Upheaval during 17th Century England

by KATHERINE PYM

MANY CENTURIES PLOD ALONG WITH NOT MUCH HAPPENING. BUT WHEN YOU COME INTO the 17th century, it is a minefield of tempestuous action—all due to religion.

From the initial fears that James I might harbour Catholic sympathies to the hostility toward Charles I—a Protestant, but too popish—the century jogged at a furious pace toward religious revolt. Churches were gutted of their musical pieces, their gilded altars, and their stained-glass windows as the country descended into three civil wars and a king's beheading, before settling for a quiet moment into the staid, dark Commonwealth years.

During this decade of Cromwellian rule, color all but disappeared. Men, women, and children wore black with no lace or ribbons. Mayday was no longer sanctioned. Bartholomew's Fair and bear baiting could not be stopped, but drama, song, and dance were. Theatres were closed and Shakespeare's Globe Theatre was pulled down.

Under the Commonwealth, the *Book of Common Prayer* was outlawed as being too popish. Ministers in the Church of England lost their vocations. Many ended up in debtor's prison.

Religious intolerance sidestepped for a moment when King Charles II returned from exile. He wiped the slate clean with the Declaration of Breda, and people of all faiths breathed a sigh of relief. The king would bring a state of sensibility to England.

They were misguided.

Within months of King Charles II's coronation, new laws were put into place that switched the tide from Anglican suppression to Presbyterian suppression. A group of restrictive statutes called the Clarendon Code (which Clarendon did not author) took effect during the years of 1661-1665 that intended to strengthen the power of the Church of England. Within these five years, the Cavalier Parliament rejected the Solemn League and Covenant of 1643 and quelled all nonconformist activity. To hold office, you had to prove you supported the Church of England and take Holy Communion.

By mid-1662, the Act of Uniformity installed the *Book of Common Prayer* back into church services. Those Presbyterian clergy who refused to use it were cast out of their vocations. In an event known as the Great Ejection, two thousand Presbyterian ministers walked away from their pulpits. Many ended up in debtor's prison as their Anglican counterparts had done before them.

In 1664, the Conventicle Act disallowed more than five Presbyters to meet at one time for unauthorized worship. In 1665, the Five Mile Act forbade nonconformist ministers to come within five miles of any incorporated town, nor were they allowed to teach in schools.

While London burned during a conflagration in September 1666, Frenchmen were accused of being papists and setting the town afire. Several were hanged from lampposts throughout the city. The king and his brother had to ride out amidst people burned out of their homes to reassure them the French did not start the fire. God's hand did it.

In 1678, Titus Oates set forth an early version of McCarthyism with the Popish Plot where, in a fit of frenzy, innocent men and women accused of being Catholic were imprisoned or executed.

King Charles II did not let slip that he converted to Catholicism, but his successor, King James II, broadcast it the width and breadth of England. After the Glorious Revolution, James was drummed out of the country, and finally, after so much angst and shedding of tears, his daughter and son-in-law—devoted Protestants—were brought to England as joint ruling monarchs.

England finally set a calmer course toward religion.

For more information on Anglican ministers going to debtor's prison, please see my historical novel, *Viola A Woeful Tale of Marriage*. For Catholics in London, please see *Twins*, a 2012 EPIC finalist. And for more on the Act of Uniformity, please see *Of Carrion Feathers*. All these novels are set in London during the 1660s.

Prophecy and Polemic: The Earliest Quaker Women

by SUSANNA CALKINS

In 1659, over seven thousand women across England, proclaiming themselves "*THE handmaids and daughters of the Lord*," signed Mary Foster's petition to Parliament. "*It may seem strange to some that women should appear in so public a manner,*" she explained, "*but because the blood of our brethren hath been spilt, and also many thousands have had their goods spoiled and taken away, and many of them imprisoned to death…you* [must] *keep the nation from the plagues and judgments of God.*"

The signatories belonged to the newly formed Religious Society of Friends, a non-conformist sect known for "*quaking in the presence of the Lord*" that emerged during the tumultuous Civil Wars. The members, embracing the derogatory name "Quakers," became known for their exuberant religious expression and for respecting the spiritual equality of their female members.

Like many seized by the millennial fever that gripped England in the waning years of the Protectorate (1658-1660), Quakers urged the people and government of England to repent their sins, to embrace the teachings of God, and to take the biblical teachings of justice and retribution to heart.

Emulating the ancient biblical prophets, early Friends openly preached and harangued passers-by, disrupted church services, and shouted out what often seemed to their listeners to be blasphemous declarations and warnings. Dramatically expressing their "Inner Light," both male and female Quakers shrieked, cried, sang, cast off their clothing and "*ran naked as a sign,*" and otherwise buoyantly proclaimed the word of God in the streets, taverns, marketplaces, prisons and, most provocatively, in Anglican "steeplehouses."

Not surprisingly, the earliest Quakers from the mid-1640s through the 1660s elicited controversy, harassment, and popular contempt wherever they traveled. Although Oliver Cromwell initially supported the idea of an all-inclusive state church in the 1650s, in practice both local and state authorities did not welcome the frenetic and disruptive activities of the early Quakers. Most early Friends faced physical and verbal assault by villagers and townspeople (often after being incited by local clergymen).

When Cromwell died in September 1658, the Quakers clamored for the restoration of the monarchy, believing they could convince the Stuart king to establish a broadly tolerant policy concerning religion.

Although King Charles II promised toleration with the Declaration of Breda (1660), thousands of Quakers were imprisoned when they refused to take the Oath of Allegiance to the King. Shortly after, the conservative Cavalier Parliament passed the Act of Uniformity (1662), the Quaker Act of 1664, and the Conventicle Acts, legislation designed to quash religious dissent among the Quakers and other riotous "schizmatics."

While intermittent periods of toleration in the form of Declarations of Indulgence (1662, 1672, 1687, and 1688) occurred within the years of persecution, these moments were usually short-lived. Even after the Act of Toleration (1689), Friends continued to face imprisonment and loss of property throughout the 1690s for refusal to pay tithes to the Church of England.

While many female Friends shouted their apocalyptic visions on the street corners, others furiously composed their admonitions in hastily prepared tracts addressed to Parliament, Cromwell, the king, local and royal authorities, and "the world." Although women in the sect could not take the same steps as their male counterparts—most notably, they could not vote in elections or hope to be elected to Parliament—they could petition government, seek to sway public sentiment in their favor, speak their minds publicly, and publish their views in political and religious tracts, despite the repercussions. While female Quakers only wrote 220 tracts of 3855 before 1700, as a group they wrote more than any other English women before the eighteenth century.

In a period when the monarchy and Parliament fought colonial authorities and themselves, Quaker women recognized and positioned themselves within these larger contests of power—physically, spiritually, and intellectually—allowing them to participate in the political community in ways that women usually could not.

Article excerpted from Calkins, S. (2001) Prophecy and Polemic: Quaker Women and English Political Culture, 1650-1700, *unpublished dissertation, Purdue University.*

SOURCES

Braithwaite, William C. *The Beginnings of Quakerism.* Cambridge: Cambridge University Press, 1955.

Barbour, Hugh. *The Quakers in Puritan England.* New Haven and London: Yale University Press, 1964.

Carroll, Kenneth. *Quaker History* 2 (1978): 69-87 and "Singing in the Spirit in Early Quakerism," *Quaker History* 73 (1984): 1-13.

Forster, Mary. *These Several Papers was [sic] sent to the Parliament the twentieth day of the Fifth Month, 1659.* London, 1659.

Gargill, Anne. *A Brief Discovery of That Which is Called the Popish Religion.* London, 1656.

_____. *A Warning to All the World.* London, 1656.

Moore, Rosemary. "Leaders of the Primitive Quaker Movement." *Quaker History* 85 (1996): 29-44.

Penney, Norman, ed. *Extracts from State Papers Relating to Friends.* London: Headley Brothers, 1910.

Reay, Barry. *The Quakers and Early Restoration Quakerism.* New York: St. Martin's Press, 1985.

Russell, Elbert. *The History of Quakerism.* Richmond, IN: Friends United Press, 1979.

The First Actresses: Nell Gwyn to Sarah Siddons

by KAREN WASYLOWSKI

As many know, before the Restoration of the Monarchy in England women's parts in plays were performed by men. When the first professional actress (no one knows her name) stepped out as Desdemona, the prologue leered:

I saw the Lady dressed!
The woman plays today! Mistake me not;
No man in gown, or page in petticoat;
A woman to my knowledge, yet I can't
(If I should die) make affidavit on't.
Do you not twitter, gentlemen?

It was the year of our Lord December 8, 1660, and through an edict by Charles II, women were finally allowed to legally perform, on stage, in public. During his exile in France, the King had seen females on stage, had enjoyed the view, and, he noted, there had been no outcry or panic in the streets because of it. So a new career path was created for British women and a new job title was born: British Actress.

These women became the Dame Judi's and Dame Helen's of their day.

In the beginning, there was the teenage bombshell, the orange seller, the one and only Nell Gwyn, or "Pretty Witty Nell" as she was known then, the first recognizable celebrity in British pop culture. She was sexy and funny; she was even the mistress of the king. Simon Verelst's two portraits of her demonstrate her playfullness, her use of the "wardrobe malfunction" to enhance her notoriety. In one portrait her top exposes just a bit of nipple, another portrait exposes everything. Nell was the original "pin-up" girl and a definite show stopper as seen in a recent exhibition, "The First Actresses," held at London's National Portrait Gallery. It is not her obvious charms that surprise people, however—we see more skin that this most evenings on cable television—no, it is her obvious charisma, her calm, regal, shameless stare, her "right back at you, buddy" confidence.

By the mid-eighteenth century, the Theatres Royal at Drury Lane and Covent Garden were thriving, but standing unfortunately amidst other businesses, those of a questionable sort and not quite so inspiring. The brothels of London surrounding the theatre district increased the connection between theater and sex, acting and prostitution, despite the fact that many actresses sought legitimacy.

Further feeding the sexual frenzy was the new popularity of "cross-over" or "breeches" roles for women. The actresses Peg Woffington, Frances Abington, and Dorothy Jordan all gained great popularity, and notoriety, with their comedic turns in a man's breeches. The line between performer and person began to blur with the women now being associated with the roles they played. For example, in the 1770s the actress, Mary Robinson, was often known as "Perdita" after her role in Shakespeare's play *The Winter's Tale*. Critics became obsessed with actresses' personal lives, their fashion sense, and their stage outfits.

In 1768, Sir Joshua Reynolds founded The Royal Academy of Art, with its exhibition of portraiture one of the most popular genres. Theatre owners such as David Garrick, among others, sought to bring a greater legitimacy, attain a more reputable status to their theatres, and a bond was formed between the arts. This alliance provided us with many large scale paintings of, among others, the great Sarah Siddons in her famous pose as Tragic Muse. Full length portraits by famous artists provided a dignity, a positive image of their roles and their acting ability. It was also great advertising.

A refined, gentle, sort of eighteenth century Paparazzi mentality had begun.

Francis Hayman, Johann Zoffany, and James Robert, among other artists, became well known for portraits of the actress in their most famous roles. Paintings of actresses depicted center stage became wildly popular, glamorizing the women and associating them with certain parts in the minds of the populace such as Roberts' portrait of Abington in the famous library scene in Richard Sheridan's play *The School for Scandal*, first performed in 1777. A new enthusiasm began from this—the amateur theatrical.

Certain members of the aristocracy built private theatres in their country homes, rehearsing and giving plays for each other, and having their amateur dramatics immortalised on canvas, such as the famous painting of a production of *Macbeth*, where the three witches are none other than Elizabeth Lamb, Viscountess Melbourne, the famous beauty Georgiana, Duchess of Devonshire, and Anne Seymour Damer.

Secret Service, Spies, and Underhanded Dealings during the 17th Century

BY KATHERINE PYM

As historian Violet Barbour wrote in the biography, *Henry Bennet, Earl of Arlington* (published 1914), *"The ministers of Charles II were not chosen for their honesty…"*

This did not make Charles II a stupid man, but one who had gone through years of hardship. His life had often been in peril. Men conspired against him or tried to rule him. This left its mark. To watch for underhanded dealings during his reign, he sought out men who would meet toe-to-toe those who threatened the king and his court.

On the one hand, Charles II filled his court with frivolity. He played, danced, and allowed his spaniel dogs to soil the palace. He and his brother, the Duke of York, loved the theatre, and supported their own troupes. Charles II allowed women on stage.

On the other hand, Charles II inherited a land filled with restless and bitter malcontents whose very existence had shattered at the fall of the Commonwealth. Rarely opening up to anyone, Charles did not trust easily. He *expected* attempts on his life or efforts to overthrow his monarchy.

During the rule of Cromwell, John Thurloe was the head of espionage. As Secretary of State under Cromwell, he sent out spies to cull the plots from within the Protectorate's government. His spy network was extensive. He also employed men—and women—who were, on the surface, stalwart royalists. His spies could be located in every English county, overseas (i.e., in Charles II's exiled court), in the Americas, and the far Indies.

Thurloe compiled lists, sent spies into enemy camps, and had men tortured and killed. One such fellow, Samuel Morland, an assistant to Thurloe under Cromwell, confessed to having witnessed a man being "trepanned to death" at Thurloe's word. (A trepan, according to Dictionary. com was *"a tool for cutting shallow holes by removing a core."*) Not a nice way to go.

Thurloe orchestrated the Sir Richard Willis Plot, wherein the king and duke were intended to be lured out of exile to a meeting on the Sussex coast. Once the brothers disembarked, they would be instantly murdered. Thankfully, we know this plot failed.

Commonwealth spies infiltrated homes, churches, and businesses to destroy the enemy, and under Charles II's rule, his government did the same. Their goal was to destroy nonconformists, or "fanaticks". Depending on who was in power, plots were a part of political life.

After the Restoration, Thurloe was dismissed, but not executed, for crimes against the monarchy. He was released in exchange for valuable Commonwealth government documents.

During the king's exile, Sir Edward Nicholas held the position of Secretary of State, but he was old, nearly age 70. Within two years of the Restoration, Charles II replaced him with Sir Henry Bennet, who took charge of the Crown's espionage.

Joseph Williamson worked for Bennet as the undersecretary. Williamson was born for this work. He took the bull by the horns and enhanced the processes Thurloe had begun. Williamson built a brilliant spy network. He enlisted informers who, for money, turned on their associates. He used grocers, doctors, and surgeons, anyone who would inform him of persons against the king. Informants were everywhere. He obtained ambassadorial letters and had them opened and searched for underhanded deceit. He had men overseas watching for any plots.

His tools were numerous. He loved ciphers and cipher keys. Doctor John Wallis was an expert in this who worked under both Thurloe and Bennet. The man could crack a code in nothing flat.

Williamson, known as Mr. Lee in the underworld, used London's Grand Letter Office for ciphered messages to pass back and forth between the undersecretary's office and his informants and spies. He expected to be kept apprised by ciphered letters, passed through the post office, at the end of each day.

Under Thurloe's stint as Secretary of State during the Commonwealth, the secret service received £800 per year. Under Bennet, the money doubled. Most of the annual budget was spent on spies and keeping them alive.

For more reading on spies and espionage during the reign of King Charles II, see my novel *Of Carrion Feathers* which is set in London, 1662.

Desperate Measures in 17th Century Medicine

by DEBORAH SWIFT

IN THE 17TH CENTURY IF YOU WERE ILL, IT WAS MUCH MORE DANGEROUS TO EMPLOY A PHYsician than to use your local herbalist. The richer you were, the more likely you were to die if you became ill. Not from the disease, but from the treatment! When Charles II became ill, and the best doctors in the country were summoned, a courtier was heard to say, "*It is dangerous to have two doctors, to have fifteen is fatal.*"

No wonder, as the physicians immediately took 16 ounces of blood from him. An emetic of antimony followed, and then a Spirit of Blackthorn purgative, and then a white vitriol enema. The king's head was shaved and blistered and plasters applied to his feet. Is it any wonder he died? The same fate awaited poor George Washington, who was bled of about half the blood in his body before he finally begged to be left alone in peace to pass away, which he promptly did.

Fortunately, most poor people could not afford the expensive attentions of a physician and relied on a local herbalist or cunning woman to administer plant remedies. Plant remedies were much gentler than any treatment offered by a physician, and so the patient had a much better chance of recovery.

Many of the herbal remedies were from common plants such as nettles which were used to combat anaemia and as a blood tonic. Modern research has shown they are rich in iron. Nettles were not only used as a pot herb in spring, but also they could be used to make rope. The fibres were widely used in weaving, producing a flax-like cloth more durable than linen. It was also used as a hair lotion and produced a good yellow dye. The local village herbalist was skilled in all aspects of plant lore.

When I was researching the lady's slipper plant I discovered it had been over-collected in the 17th century because of its use as a nervine or sedative. I also discovered that if taken with alcohol the plant could induce numbness and hallucinations—a very unpleasant cocktail altogether.

But you'll have to read my book *The Lady's Slipper* to find out what happened to Sir Geoffrey Fisk when he used the herb to try to cure his eczema.

> *The lady's slipper*
> *Government and virtues ~ A most gallant herb of Venus, now sadly declined. A decoction is effectual to temper and sedate the blood, and allay hot fits of agues, canker rash and all scrophulous and scorbutic habits of the body. The root drank in wine, is its chief strength, to be applied either inwardly or outwardly, for all the griefs aforesaid. There is a syrup made hereof excellent for soothing restlessness of the limbs, hence oft times goes by the name of Nerve Root.*

Vices ~ Be wary of this herb, for surfeit of it calls forth visions, fancies and melancholy. Take it not with strong liquor. If giddiness, sickness of the stomache, dullness of the senses ensue, or drowsiness withal ending in deep sleep, straightway desist. In women and children, safer it being tied to the pit of the stomache, by a piece of white ribband round the neck.

SUPERSTITIONS AND BODILY HEALTH

BY DIANE SCOTT LEWIS

BEFORE MODERN MEDICINE, LAY PEOPLE AND SOME PHYSICIANS HELD THE BELIEF THAT transferring the ailment to another object could cure you of disease. Since antiquity and well into the eighteenth century, people believed that men reflected aspects of the natural world. It was a dominant strategy that explained the mysteries beyond the ken of the science of the day.

A man in the late seventeenth century, Somerset, claimed that his brother was cured of a rupture by being passed through a slit cut in a young ash tree three times on three Monday mornings before dawn. When the tree was later cut down, his brother grew ill again.

To cure jaundice, you took the patient's urine, mixed it with ashes, and made three equal balls. These were put before a fire, and when they dried out, the disease left and the patient was cured.

In Devon, to cure the quartan ague, you baked the patient's urine into a cake then fed the cake to a dog who would take on the disease.

Even Richard Wiseman—a Barber Surgeon—who wrote *Chirurgicall Treatises* during the time of Charles II, believed that to remove warts you rubbed them with a slice of beef, then buried the beef.

Color, as well, played a part in how health was viewed. "Yellow" remedies were used to cure jaundice: saffron, celandine with yellow flowers, turmeric, and lemon rind. John Wesley, who wrote *Primitive Physick* in the mid-eighteenth century, suggested that sufferers of this illness wear celandine leaves under their feet.

Health was also governed by astrological explanations. Manuals intended for physicians and apothecaries included this "otherwordly" advice. Nicholas Culpeper detailed which herbs were presided over by which planets in his famous health text *Culpeper's Complete Herbal*. For example, if a headache was caused by the actions of Venus, then fleabane (an herb of Mars) would cure the malady.

However, the *Vox Stellarum*, the most popular almanac in the eighteenth century, took a more moderate view: *"Men may be inclin'd but not compell'd to do good or evil by the influence of the stars."* Yet this same almanac, in 1740, listed which diseases were prevalent in certain months—a vestigial form of astrological medicine.

Thank goodness more enlightened physicians, such as brothers William (a leading anatomist and renown obstetrician) and John Hunter (one of the most distinguished scientists and surgeons of his day) in the eighteenth century, came along to bring medical thinking into the modern world. Though superstition among the lay people remained....

SOURCE

Fissell, Mary E. *Patients, Power, and the Poor in Eighteenth Century Bristol*. Cambridge: Cambridge University Press, 1991.

THE DEATH OF KING CHARLES II

BY KATHERINE PYM

FIRST A LITTLE ABOUT HIM....

King Charles II lived a life full of sex and sport. During his youth, he learned to keep his own counsel. He was kind-natured, only allowing his need for revenge against a few of the regicides. Cromwell was one of these, even though already dead and buried.

Charles took a long time to come to a state decision. He'd put it off with a wave of his hand and play with one of his women. He loved Cavalier King Charles spaniels, as they're now known, and always had several romping in his private chambers, soiling the floors so that no one could walk across the room in a straight line.

Even though he reigned in a Protestant country, while on the run in 1651 after his defeat at the Battle of Worcester, Charles was protected (at their peril) by Catholics. For a few hours, Charles hid in a priest hole, very snug and claustrophobic, while Parliament men searched for him. By the end of his trek through England and into exile, Charles had gained a high regard for Catholics and Catholicism.

But I digress.

While Charles reigned, he did not confide in many. He was considered an enigma by both his contemporaries and those today who study him. He had a kind heart. His nature made people comfortable. They confided in him and wanted to be near him. But when Charles wanted to be alone or was tired of the subject, he'd pull out his watch. Those who knew of this would quickly state their business, for soon their king would walk away.

Charles loved reading (not political or religious). He initiated great strides within the theatre sector, and he enjoyed science.

In 1660, he approved a charter for The Royal Society. The group of great minds, Isaac Newton for one, met at Gresham College in London City. Experiments took place there, including draining the veins of a dog into the veins of another dog. The results amazed those curious people.

So, we come to his death....

"He fell sick of a tertian fever," but the official cause of death is: Uraemia (Dictionary.com definition—*"a condition resulting from the retention in the blood of constituents normally excreted in the urine."*), chronic nephritis. Syphilis.

On the evening of February 1, 1685, Charles went to bed with a sore foot. By early morning, he was very ill with fever. His physician, Sir Edmund King, tended to his foot whilst a barber shaved his head. Suddenly, the king suffered an apoplexy. His physician immediately drew sixteen ounces of blood. Sir Edmund took a big risk and could have been charged with treason. The protocol was to get permission from the Privy Council prior to a bloodletting.

For several days, Charles was tormented by his physicians. As a private man, this must have been difficult. Surrounded by more physicians than could comfortably fit into the chamber, he lay in agony while these men attempted to remove the "toxic humours" from his body.

He was bled and purged. Cantharides plasters were stuck to his bald pate; these caused blistering. They attached plasters of spurge to his feet, then applied red-hot irons to his skin. Besides the large number of physicians crowding around his bed, His Royal Highness' bed-chamber was filled to the walls with spectators (family members and state officials).

They gave the poor king,

> *enemas of rock salt and syrup of buckthorn, and 'orange infusion of metals in white wine'. The king was treated with a horrific cabinet of potions: white hellebore root; Peruvian bark; white vitriol of peony water; distillation of cowslip flowers; sal ammoniac; julep of black cherry water (an antispasmodic); oriental bezoar stone from the stomach of a goat and boiled spirits from a human skull.*

After days of this, he apologized for taking so long to die, then added, *"I have suffered much more than you can imagine."*

Finally, on February 6, 1685, *"the exhausted king, his body raw and aching with the burns and inflammation caused by his treatment, was given heart tonics, to no avail. He lapsed into a coma and died at noon on February 7."*

His death is considered by historians as "iatrogenic regicide".

SOURCE

Lamont-Brown, Raymond. *Royal Poxes & Potions: The Lives of Court Physicians, Surgeons & Apothecaries*. Sutton Pub Limited, 2003.

Lloyd's: Lifeblood of British Commerce and Starbucks of Its Day

BY LINDA COLLISON

S HIPS HAVE ALWAYS PLAYED A MAJOR ROLE IN THE IMPORT AND EXPORT OF GOODS; EVEN today, ninety percent of world trade travels by sea. Yet there are obvious risks to be assumed when deep water and Mother Nature, pirates and enemy ships are involved.

The concept of maritime insurance is as old as civilization. Thousands of years ago Chinese river traders minimized their risk by deliberately spreading their cargo throughout several ships. The Babylonians practiced *bottomry*, an arrangement in which the ship master borrowed money upon the *bottom* of his vessel, and forfeited the ship itself to the creditor, if the money with interest was not paid upon the ship's safe return.

About 600 A.D., Danish merchants began forming guilds to insure their members against losses at sea, and merchant cities such as Venice and Florence started using a form of mutual insurance recorded in documents. The Lombards brought the concept of marine insurance to northern Europe and England in the 13th century where the Hanseatic League further developed the means to protect their joint economic interests.

Permit me to fast-forward four hundred years to the 17th century—the rise of English merchants and the search for new markets abroad. Let's pop in to visit London, now an important trade center, and walk along the waterfront....

Lloyd's of London began as a coffee shop on Tower Street, founded by Edward Lloyd in 1688. His establishment, located near the waterfront, soon became a popular meeting place where ship owners and merchants could meet with financiers to discuss ways to match the risks they faced at sea with the capital needed to insure them.

Coffeehouses were then enjoying a great popularity in London and many other European cities. By 1675 there were more than 3,000 of them throughout England. Coffeehouses were social places where men with similar interests met to exchange news and do business, while enjoying the stimulating brew. Much like your corner Starbucks where friends surf for jobs on their laptops while sipping Frappuccinos and interviews are conducted over Venti Iced Skinny Mochas, 17th century Londoners did business while getting buzzed on the bean.

Lloyd's was never an insurance company, *per se*, but instead was a *market*—a regular gathering of people for the purchase and sale of provisions or other commodities. At Lloyd's coffeehouse merchants and shipmasters caught up on the latest shipping news, bid on cargos of captured prizes, and obtained insurance for their ventures. The underwriters, wealthy men referred to as "Names," were the individuals who pledged their own money to insure a particular voyage.

In 1691, Edward Lloyd relocated his coffee house from Tower Street to Lombard Street, where a blue plaque hangs today. The business carried on in this location until 1774 when the participating individuals moved to the Royal Exchange on Cornhill and called themselves the Society of Lloyd's. An Act of Parliament in 1871 gave the business a sound legal footing, incorporating it. Although Ed Lloyd died in 1713, his name remains and is eponymous with the insurance of one-of-a-kind treasures, including Betty Grable's legs and Bob Dylan's vocal cords.

The present Lloyd's building, designed by architect Richard Rogers, was completed in 1986 on the site of the old Roman forum on Lime Street. In the rostrum hangs the original Lutine Bell. Back in the days of the coffee shop, one of the waiters would strike the bell when the fate of an overdue ship became known. If the ship was safe, the bell would be rung twice and if it had gone down, the bell would be rung only once, to stop buying, or selling of "overdue" reinsurance on that vessel. (To see an early Hollywood recreation of Lloyd's, watch the 1936 movie *Lloyd's of London*, with Tyrone Power in his first starring role.)

In his book *The Romance of Lloyd's*, Commander Frank Worsley (of the Shackleton Expedition) sings the praises of Lloyd's, crediting the association with various philanthropic efforts, including the development of the lifeboat service in Britain. In 1802, Lloyd's members voted a donation of one hundred guineas to Henry Greathead, the inventor of the first practical lifeboat and set aside two thousand pounds for the provision of lifeboats on English and Irish coasts.

Lloyd's was also instrumental in the creation of a Patriotic Fund in 1803, granting bounties or annuities to wounded men and the dependents of those killed in battle. Lloyd's headed the fund with twenty thousand pounds, although the record shows that laborers, servants, schooled children, soldiers and sailors, sent their pence and more. Officers and men of the Army and Navy contributed sums ranging from one day's pay to a whole month's. A provisional committee was appointed to manage the Fund, which became a national institution.

On a much darker note, Lloyd's was heavily involved in insuring ships in the slave trade as Britain became the chief trading power in the Atlantic. Between 1688 and 1807, when slave-trading was abolished, British shipping carried more than 3.25 million people into slavery. It may be argued that the individual men who underwrote slave ships acted within the laws of the time and reflected the values of the society in which they lived, yet descendants of black American slaves have accused the Lloyd's of London insurance market (and two United States companies) of profiting from the slave trade in a lawsuit seeking billions of pounds in damages. The past can indeed come back to haunt us.

Lloyd's has always worked closely with the Royal Navy to the benefit of both. Historian Steven Maffeo relates how the insurance market and the British Post Office were important to the Navy's intelligence-gathering throughout the Napoleonic Wars, the news of the victory at Trafalgar being posted at Lloyd's even before the London newspapers broke the story. During the 18th century Lloyd's developed a unique system of maritime intelligence of arrivals and departures which was sent immediately to the Admiralty, who in turn forwarded convoy and other useful information to Lloyd's.

Convoy, the practice of escorting groups of merchant ships by a naval warship, was common practice during the war years of the 18th, 19th, and early 20th centuries, to reduce the loss of ships and cargo to the Enemy. At the beginning of my novel, *Barbados Bound,* the merchant ship *Canopus* is carrying gunpowder and traveling in convoy from England to Madeira during the Seven Years' War. From Madeira, *Canopus* must strike out alone across the Atlantic to deliver the gunpowder on time—and of course Murphy's Law intervenes. Shipmaster Blake says that his ship's guns are his insurance, though of course they would be no real match against a French privateer, hungry for prize.

Lloyd's Register is filled with stories of profit—and disaster. The sinking of the "unsinkable" Titanic in 1912 represented one of Lloyd's biggest losses, along with other major catastrophes such as the 1906 San Francisco Earthquake, the attack on New York's World Trade Center, Hurricane Katrina, Asbestos damage claims, and the 2011 Tohuku earthquake and tsunami. The history of Lloyd's is a fascinating one, and still evolving. Wherever there is risk and money to be made, you'll find the name Lloyd's.

THE HISTORY OF GINGERBREAD

BY GILLIAN BAGWELL

HERE IN AMERICA, WE ASSOCIATE GINGERBREAD WITH CHRISTMAS IN THE FORM OF GIN-gerbread men and decorated gingerbread houses. But gingerbread has a long history. The word "gingerbread" comes from the Old French word "gingebras", which comes from the Latin word "zingiber", meaning preserved ginger. Eventually gingerbread came to mean either biscuits or cake made with ginger and other spices.

The first documented trade of gingerbread biscuits was in the sixteenth century, when they were sold in pharmacies, monasteries, and town square farmers' markets. In Shakespeare's play *Love's Labour's Lost*, Costard, the country fool, tells little Moth, *"And I had but one penny in the world, thou shouldst have it to buy gingerbread."* Some early recipes had more of a kick than we're used to, calling for pepper or mustard. In Shakespeare's play *Henry IV, Part One*, Hotspur mentions "pepper gingerbread."

The town of Market Drayton (then Drayton) in Shropshire, England became famous for its gingerbread biscuits, which were traditionally eaten dipped in port. Possibly gingerbread (and perhaps port!) were responsible for the Great Fire of Drayton in 1641. It started in a bakery and raged through the half-timbered buildings with thatched roofs and destroyed seventy percent of the town.

The other type of gingerbread traditional in England is a dense, moist cake, usually baked in a square shape or loaf. It is traditionally eaten on Bonfire Night, the Fifth of November's annual commemoration of the foiling of the plot by Guy Fawkes and his accomplices to blow up the Houses of Parliament in 1605.

Perkin or parkin (both diminutives of the name Peter) is a kind of gingerbread typically made with oatmeal and molasses, originally made in Northern England. It keeps well, and is traditionally not eaten fresh.

Below are two quite different English gingerbread recipes. The first is from Sir Hugh Platt's *Delights for Ladies*, published in 1608, for gingerbread biscuits. The original and updated recipes are from *A Taste of History: 10,000 Years of Food in Britain*. The second recipe, from October 1907, is the parkin variety of moist gingerbread cake. *The Guardian* newspaper printed it in 2007 and noted, *"Back then parkin sold for eight old pence a pound."*

1608 GINGERBREAD

To make gingerbread: Take three stale Manchets and grate them, drie them, and sift them through a fine sieve, then adde unto them one ounce of ginger beeing beaten, and as much Cinamon, one ounce of liquorice and aniseedes being beaten together and searced, halfe a pound of sugar, then boile all these together in a posnet, with a quart of claret wine till them come to a stiff paste with often stirring of it; and when it is stiffe, mold it on a table and so drive it thin, and print it in your moldes; dust your moldes with Cinamon, Ginger, and liquorice, beeing mixed together in fine powder. This is your gingerbread used at the Court, and in all gentlemens houses at festival times. It is otherwise called drie Leach.

Translation:

2 cups (225 g.) fresh white breadcrumbs

1 tsp. (5 ml.) ground ginger

1 tsp. (5 ml.) cinnamon

1 tsp. (5 ml.) aniseed

1 tsp. (5 ml.) ground liquorice (if available)

¼ cup (2.5 g.) sugar

½ cup (150 ml.) claret

Dry the breadcrumbs under the grill or in the oven (but without browning), and add to the remaining ingredients in a saucepan. Work the mixture over a gentle heat with a wooden spoon, until it forms a stiff dough. Turn the dough out onto a wooden board dusted with ground ginger and cinnamon and roll it out to about ¼ inch (5 mm.) in thickness. It may then be impressed with a small stamp, a 1 inch (2.5 cm.) diameter butter press being ideal for this purpose, and cut into small circles, using a pastry cutter. If antique gingerbread molds are available, then they should be dusted with the ground spices before the slab of dough is firmly impressed into their designs. Then, after the surplus has been trimmed off with the knife, the gingerbread can be removed by inverting the molds, and gently knocking their edges down onto the table. Like most early gingerbreads, this version released its flavors gradually, the gentle aniseed being slowly overwhelmed by the fiery ginger.

Neither of the recipes mentions baking, but I think this might be a mistake. Based on modern recipes, I would bake the gingerbread at 375F/190C for about 8-10 minutes.

1907 GINGERBREAD

2 cups (225g) plain flour

3½ tsp (17.5 ml.) ground ginger

¾ tsp (3.75ml.) ground nutmeg

½ tsp (2.5 ml.) bicarbonate of soda

A pinch of salt

1½ cups (125g) medium oatmeal

½ cup (100g) unsalted butter, softened

2/3 c. cup (125g) light soft brown sugar

Zest of ½ lemon

¼ cup (100g) treacle or molasses

3 tablespoons (75g) golden syrup or corn syrup (or you could use all molasses)

3 ½ tablespoons (50ml) milk

¼ cup (50g) mixed peel, finely chopped

Butter a deep 8-inch (20cm) square cake tin and line the base with nonstick baking parchment. Heat the oven to 350F/180C (160C fan-assisted/gas mark 4). Sift the flour, spices, soda, and salt into a bowl, then stir in the oatmeal. In another bowl beat the butter, sugar, and zest until light and fluffy. Add the treacle and syrup, beat again until creamy and smooth, then add the milk and the dry ingredients, and beat quickly until smooth once more. Fold in the mixed peel, then spoon the mixture into the tin. Cover the top with foil, bake for 40 minutes, then remove the foil and bake for a further 20 minutes, until a skewer comes out clean.

SOURCES

Brears, Peter C. D. et al. *A Taste of History: 10,000 Years of Food in Britain.* London: English Heritage in association with British Museum Press, 1993.

Schmidt, Alexander. *Shakespeare Lexicon and Quotation Dictionary: A Complete Dictionary of All the English Words, Phrases, and Constructions in the Works of the Poet.* USA: Dover Publications, Inc., 1971.

17TH CENTURY RECIPES

BY KATHERINE PYM

FROM THE BOOK *SAMUEL PEPYS' PENNY MERRIMENTS, BEING A COLLECTION OF CHAPBOOKS, FULL of Histories, Jests, Magic, Amorous Tales of Courtship, Marriage and Infidelity, Accounts of Rogues and Fools, together with Comments on the Times*, selected and edited by Roger Thompson of the University of East Anglia at Norwich, 1977.

Whew, what a mouthful! Our titles these days are much shorter, with fewer syllables, easier to remember. To remember this, I simply refer to it as *Penny Merriments*, a tome I found in a bookstore and considered a great find. It has all sorts of wonderful information, like recipes to make one beautiful, or a recipe for the newest way to roast a hare. It sends me right back into the era of my choice....

17th century England opened with traders going to far distant shores, but the cost was enormous. Spices were gathered through the Levant Company (owned by noblemen and gentlemen of quality) and the fledgling East India Company. As the century progressed, their ships went to lands already taken by the Spanish and Portuguese.

The Dutch East India Company (VOC) began at about the same time as England's, but they weren't hampered by the religious upheaval and civil wars England endured during the first half of the century. The Dutch VOC had a leg up on English merchant shipping until Cromwell decided enough was enough and went to war with Holland in what is known as the First Anglo-Dutch War (1652-54), and which was fought entirely at sea. These wars were over trade and who could monopolize which ports in the East and West Indies.

With that said, the recipes below show an inordinate number of spices which were very costly. During the reign of King James I, a fight to near death took place between VOC and English Merchantmen in the South Seas that decimated the crops of nutmeg on Pulo Run Island in the Banda archipelago.

Through the Levant Company, citrus fruits, dates, pepper, cotton cloth, and other fruits and spices were trekked across the desert sands to ports the Levant Company held in the Mediterranean, then imported via ship to London. (I won't even mention the pirate contingent that upped the cost of goods.) Once these commodities hit the London markets, they proved expensive for the middling English household.

The below recipes can only come from later in the 17th century, and were directed to the more well-to-do. Middling folk who could read, enjoyed the thoughts of these though....

To Roast a Shoulder of Mutton with Oysters the best way.

Take one not too fat nor too lean, open it in divers places, stuff your oysters in with a little chopt penny-royal [of the mint family], *baste it with butter and claret wine,* then serve it up with grated nutmeg, yolks of eggs, ginger, cinnamon, butter and red wine vinegar.

To Stew a Leg of Lamb the best way.

Slice it and lay it in order in your stewing-pan, seasoned with salt and nutmeg, adding a pound of butter, and half a pint of claret, with a handful of sliced dates, and the like quantity of currants, and make the sauce with the yolk of two eggs, a quarter pint of verjuice [acid juice from sour or unripe fruit—very sour], and two ounces of sugar. Boil them up, and put them over the meat, serving up hot together.

The Art of Beautifying the Hands, Neck, Breast and Face: Harmless and Approved, with other Rare Curiosities.

To make the hands and arms white, clear and smooth. Take a quarter of a pound of sweet almonds, blanch and bruise them, with a quarter of a pint of oil of roses, and the like quantity of betony-water [plant of the mint family]: heat them over a gentle fire; and then press out the liquid part, and it will serve for either hands or face anointed therewith.

To take away Freckles, Morphew (scurfy skin) or sunburn.

Steep a piece of copper in the juice of lemon till it be dissolved [can copper dissolve?], and anoint the place with a feather morning and evening, washing it off with white wine.

To take off any scurf from the hands and face.

Take water of tartar, that is, such wherein calcined [burnt to a powder] tartar has been infused, anoint the place, and wash it as the former [with white wine].

And now, for the final and most excellent recipe....

To sweeten the Breath, and preserve the Teeth and Gums.

Boil a handful of juniper berries, a handful of sage, and an ounce of caraway seeds in a quart of white wine, til a third part be consumed: strain it and wash your mouth with it morning and evening, suffering a small quantity to pass down: you may whiten the teeth by rubbing them with pumice stone.

So, who wants to try one of these recipes and let me know how it works? I'd especially like to know the results of whitening your teeth with pumice stone. Or should I do a disclaimer? Don't do this without the guidance of a professional!

THE SCENT OF LAVENDER

BY LAUREN GILBERT

I HAVE LOVED THE SCENT OF LAVENDER SINCE I WAS A TEENAGER IN THE '60s WHEN YARDLEY'S English Lavender became a popular fragrance (at least, it was new to me!). Light, fresh, clean and sweet, lavender has an ageless appeal. It is almost impossible to pick up a Regency novel without a mention of lavender, whether it is scenting the hero's immaculate white linen (a suitably masculine blend, of course), or wafting ever so subtly from the heroine's lace-edged handkerchief.

Lavender is an ancient herb, long associated with healing. Its Latin name *Lavandula latifolia*, appears to be derived from the Latin verb *lavare*, meaning "to wash" and the Romans used it to deter flies and sweeten the air, as well as to clean and dress wounds. The ancient Egyptians used lavender in embalming and in scented unguents.

It was widely used in Tudor England, where lavender was placed in linens (not only making them smell sweet but discouraging insects!); sewn into little bags, it could be tucked amongst clothing or into one's bosom. Queen Elizabeth found lavender tea soothing for migraines and used lavender perfume as well.

In the Georgian era, the perfumers D.R. Harris made a popular lavender water for gentlemen, and Floris used lavender in potpourris and perfumes for ladies. (Both are still in business today.)

Down through the centuries, lavender has been long considered something of a miracle herb. In Nicholas Culpeper's herbal (1653 edition), he says it cures *"all griefs and pains of the head and brain that proceed of a cold cause…"* and also recommends its use for dropsy, heart ailments, liver and spleen obstructions, tooth ache, and more.

Even today, herb guides discuss its antiseptic and painkilling attributes. (Mine says it can be used to soothe insect bites, burns, sore throats and headaches, and is a relaxant when used in the bath, among other medicinal uses!) I know from personal experience that it works wonderfully to deter moths and other insects from my linen closet and pantry—how many modern insect repellents work well, smell wonderful, and have no poisonous effects?

Among many old recipes including lavender that I ran across, two seemed good to include. The first is not adapted for modern preparation, other than the list of ingredients:

LAVENDER WINE (1655)

1 bottle of Sack, 3 ounces of sugar, 2 ounces of lavender flowers, and ambergris

Take 2 ounces of dried lavender flowers and put them into a bottle of Sack, and beat 3 ounces of Sugar candy, or fine Sugar, and grinde some Ambergreese, and put it in the bottle and shake it oft, then run it through a gelly bag, and give it for a great Cordiall after a week's standing or more.

—Derived from a recipe from *The Queen's Closet Opened,* by W.M., Cook to Queen Henrietta Maria. (From *A Sip Through Time,* by Cindy Renfrow)

The next recipe contains the old version, and an adapted version so that one can make it if desired:

MARTHA LLOYD'S ENGLISH LAVENDER WATER

To one quart of the best rectified spirits of wine put 3/4 oz. of essence of Lavender and 1/2 a scruple of ambergris; shake it together and it is fit to use in a few days.

Modern Equivalents:

To make Lavender water, put 3 handfuls of dried Lavender flowers into a wide necked screw top jar and add 1 cup of white wine vinegar and 1/2 cup Rose water.
Leave the mixture in the dark for 2-3 weeks and shake the bottle frequently.
If flowers are not available, use essential oils. Mix 25 drops of essential oil (traditionally lavender, rose or neroli) with 2 fl oz (50ml) ethyl alcohol (or isopropyl or vodka). Shake them together in a screw-top bottle. Leave the mixture to settle for 2 days then shake again. To store, pour into a dark bottle with a tight fitting lid and leave almost no air space.

—This recipe is from the Jane Austen Centre Bath website, posted by Laura Boyle 1/3/2002, in its entirety. This is a fascinating website, and well worth a look!

SOURCES

Boyle, Laura. "English Lavender Water." Posted January 3, 2002. *Jane Austen Centre Bath.* http://www.janeausten.co.uk/english-lavender-water/

Bremness, Lesley. *Herbs.* New York: Dorling Kindersley, 1994.

Culpeper, Nicholas. *The Complete Herbal* (1653 edition). Bibliomania. http://www.bibliomania.com/2/1/66/113/frameset.html.

The Georgian Index. "Merchants: Sellers of Perfumes and Other Toilettries." *Georgian London Street and Business Index.* http://www.georgianindex.net/London/l_merchants.html.

Lavender Enchantment. "History of Lavender." http://www.lavenderenchantment.com/History_Lore/history.htm

Lavender Farm. "The History of Lavender." http://www.lavenderfarm.com/history.htm

Renfrow, Cindy. *A Sip Through Times: A Collection of Old Brewing Recipes.* USA: Cindy Renfrow, 2008.

MARRIAGE IN 17TH CENTURY ENGLAND

BY KATHERINE PYM

MARRIAGE IN ENGLAND DURING THE 17TH CENTURY WAS CONFUSING. DUE TO THE VARious governments playing musical chairs for much of the century, the rules continually changed. Ministers who were safe one moment were tossed out of their vocations the next. These inconsistencies brought about corruption and fraudulent marriages. They left honest couples in doubt.

During the reign of Charles I, marriage ceremonies in the Church with the *Book of Common Prayer* prevailed. Under the Commonwealth, couples were to be married by their local JP, but too many did not consider this proper or binding. These couples married clandestinely in a home, tavern, prison, and even brothels with an Anglican minister and the forbidden *Book of Common Prayer*. The couple spoke their vows in the present tense, for to do otherwise could provide a loophole for an unhappy spouse to later invalidate the marriage.

The rules of incest were also confusing. An apprentice could not marry his master's daughter. A woman could not marry her brother-in-law after her husband died. The laws declared they were family within the fourth degree.

Due to these conflicting rules, good folk joined under the king's reign did not know if their marriage was legal under the Commonwealth, and vice versa. This doubt gave way to excuses, and unhappy couples separated to marry another. Bigamy was rampant and perjury in the courts flagrant.

In the 1640s clandestine marriages multiplied due to suppression of the Anglican Church. Marriage shops called Peculiars popped up all over London to accommodate this new vogue. Anglican ministers who lost their professions under the Commonwealth and were in debtor's prison, set up a marriage shop in Fleet Prison chapel. "Ministers" would fill in names of the couple on the certificate otherwise already completed and signed. For a small tip, clerks were called in to witness, the spaces already filled in with names more than likely not their own.

These clerics never asked the couple questions: (1) if they were already married, (2) if one or the other was an in-law, or an apprentice. If the person presiding over the ceremony *said* he was a member of the clergy, and if the vows were stated in the present tense, the couple considered themselves newly joined in marriage—which only time or a change of heart could put asunder.

In 1660 after Charles II returned from exile, the sanctioned religion again became the Church of England, but the Ecclesiastical Courts were in ruins. It took a while for the churches to reintroduce Anglican accoutrements, and clandestine marriages continued unabated.

The reinstated Anglican officials tried to stop the clandestine marriages but failed. Marriage shops sent criers with fistfuls of ready-made marriage certificates to markets to promote the inexpensive, quick unions that only money could dissolve.

While the Ecclesiastical Courts gathered order and strength, unhappy marital unions would be dissolved by desertion, or public sales of the wife—the price most of the time already settled between the old and new spouse. This marriage auction publicly announced the new union.

The least expensive and easiest way of marriage dissolution was by mutual agreement. The couple would then go their merry way to remarry, again, possibly to another who lived not far away.

Before the Ecclesiastical Courts could gain momentum, the formal method of marital dissolution was at King's Bench in Westminster. It provided legal separation, but it almost always went harshly for the wife.

Still at Westminster, a less honest practice was to seek out "straw-men". They lingered in the Hall with straw sticking out of their shoes, showing anyone with a purse of coin they'd perjure themselves during the court proceedings. They would stand before the judge and say anything the purse holder wanted them to say.

This behavior continued through the century. In the 1690s the Crown imposed a Stamp Tax of five shillings for licenses and marriage certificates. It was soon realized (by the lack of income to the Crown) that clandestine marriages continued to prevail. As a result, a series of acts were implemented to shut down the clandestine marriage shops.

As the English government settled into a more comfortable relationship with the Church of England, so too did the marriage market, but it wasn't until the Marriage Act in 1753 that it was finally put under control.

For more on this, please read my historical novel, *Viola, A Woeful Tale of Marriage*, set in London, 1660.

SOURCES

Stone, Lawrence. *Broken Lives: Separation and Divorce in England, 1660-1857*. Oxford University Press, 1993.

_____. *Uncertain Unions: Marriage in England 1660-1753*. Oxford University Press, 1992.

Fabulous Fabrics of the 17th Century

by DEBORAH SWIFT

In the 17th century all yarn for fabric was combed and spun by hand using a drop spindle and then woven into cloth. The immense amount of work that went into this process is often forgotten. Linen, wool, and silk were all spun and combined in different ways to give different effects.

Coloured fabrics were usually called "stuffs" and were very popular after the Restoration and the end of Puritan rule when bold colours could be worn again. Many English fabrics sought to imitate those of France and Italy and were characterised by elaborate finishing techniques such as glossing, hot-pressing, and watering. Weaving and finishing was a specialised craft operated typically by one or two journeyman-weavers in small, independently owned workshops. At this period blue was not very fashionable as many servants were uniformed in blue. Orange and yellow were in vogue for women's clothes. Some fabrics were woven and then cut with decorative slashes. Each slash had to be buttonhole-edged by hand to achieve the effect.

Very desirable too were fabrics embroidered by hand, with what came to be known as "crewel" work, the more opulent the better, as long as you were not in servitude to somebody else, in which case you had to obey the "sumptuary laws" and dress according to your station.

A fabric from a 1630s jacket in the V&A museum features a fanciful bird woven in red wool on a linen twill. Later this sort of work was more often seen on furnishings and draperies for the house.

A linen jacket made in about 1610 was lined with coral silk taffeta. The embroidery includes spider-knots, stemstitch, chainstitch, and buttonhole stitches. The edging is silver gilt bobbin lace. Uniquely, on the V&A website you can see a picture of the jacket being worn in a portrait of the wearer (http://collections.vam.ac.uk/item/O11095/jacket/).

Even handkerchiefs, purses, chemises, and shoes were embroidered, not to mention household linens and drapes for beds and windows.

In portraits too you can see women teaching young girls the art of embroidery and lace-making. One of these displays a lady with a lace-maker's pad as she is working the pinned individual threads into lace.

Embroidered shoes—I do not know if they embroidered the fabric first and then made up the shoes, or did it the other way around. In any case, they are lovely. I used the shoes as part of the inspiration for my book *The Lady's Slipper*, which features beautiful embroidered shoes like the ones in the Northampton Shoe Museum.

PARTY CLOTHES IN THE 17TH CENTURY

BY DEBORAH SWIFT

I WONDERED IF MY 17TH CENTURY EQUIVALENT WOULD OPEN HER CLOSET AND SIGH THE WAY I did when someone invited me to a party and I couldn't decide what to wear. So just what would the fashionable woman about town be wearing in the 17th century?

At the beginning of the 17th century, a woman wore a farthingale and whalebone corsetry beneath her clothes to emphasise a small waist and large hips. So she was probably not as comfortable as she looked. The large amount of gorgeous lace would be hand-made as Elizabethan ruffs gave way to expensive lace collars. Fancy embellished petticoats were now revealed as skirts were hooped back to display them. After the Restoration of the monarchy, women's clothes were elegant and colourful and made from costly fabrics such as satin and silk.

But what accessories might you choose on your night out—perhaps dining with a courtier, or attending a concert?

Well one of the oddest 17th century accessories was the mask or "vizard". These were commonly worn by women to protect their skin from the sun when they went outside, particularly for horse-riding or on carriage journeys. Women also wore masks to maintain their mystery or to keep their identity secret, although not many masks survive, and those that do are in poor condition.

A vizard was found during the renovation of an inner wall of a 16th-century stone building. The nose area is strengthened to stand out and form a case around the wearer's nose. The outer fabric is black velvet, the lining of silk, and inside it is strengthened by a pressed-paper inner. A black glass bead attached by a string to the mask was used to hold the mask in place—the wearer would hold the bead tightly in her mouth. This of course made speaking impossible, so I don't think I would have worn mine for long!

An excerpt from Phillip Stubbes' *Anatomie of Abuses*, published in 1583, says:

> When they use to ride abrod, they have invisories, or masks, visors made of velvet, wherwith they cover all their faces, having holes made in them against their eyes, whereout they look. So that if a man, that knew not their guise before, should chaunce to meet one of them, he would think hee met a monster or a devil; for face hee can see none, but two brode holes against her eyes with glasses in them.

So now you have your dress and your vizard—what else might you need? Well, fans made from silk and decorated paper were widely used by wealthy people during the 17th century and were the most essential accessory for women during the Stuart period. And without being able to speak you would definitely need the "language of the fan".

But I feel we are lacking a bit of glitz and glamour, don't you? So how about embroidered petticoats and a bit of twinkling jewellery?

There was a passion in this period for floral fabrics and jewellery, so it was likely you would put on your earrings by looking in a mirror with an engraved or enamelled back, decorated with floral motifs. You might be tempted to have your dressmaker make a gown, or under-dress, from flower-inspired fabric made in India for export to the English market.

Cosse-de-pois (pea pod) shapes and later flowers became very popular, and many designs in this fashion were produced. Exotic flowers were immensely popular, and botany became a study in its own right.

In *The Lady's Slipper*, my main character, Alice Ibbetson, is a botanist and artist. Like many ladies of this era, she was fascinated by new varieties of flowers.

The intensification of the trade with the near East brought flowers and bulbs to Europe which had never been seen before, and a true craze for flowers suddenly sprang up. The Tulipomania of 1634 is a well-documented example. Flora had been fashionable in embroidery since the end of the 16th century but was now adopted by jewellery designers as well. From the 1650s on, engraving in metal was another, and later preferred, way of depicting flowers. Other popular jewellery designs were the three droplets, or "girandoles", called this as they resembled the branches of a lit candlestick.

If you were going to go outside, then the latest fashion was for Venetian "chopines"—a type of sandal or stilt designed to keep your shoes protected from the filth and dirt of the city streets, and for short ladies, to add a little height.

Constructed from carved wood and silks, they must have been as uncomfortable to wear as modern platform soles, but twice as difficult to keep on. Chopines apparently caused an unstable and inelegant gait. Women wearing them were generally accompanied by a servant or attendant on whom they could balance themselves, and even to put the chopines on was a little like climbing onto stilts, so they were usually put on with the help of two servants. Some chopines could be as high as 50 cm, and their height became symbolic of the status of the wearer.

So now, in whalebone reinforced black dress, gripping my vizard between my teeth, ears heavy with floral gems, I shall totter on my chopines to my sedan!

17th Century Garden
Design for Women

by DEBORAH SWIFT

WILLIAM LAWSON IS CREDITED WITH MAKING GARDENING POPULAR FOR WOMEN WITH his book *A New Orchard and Garden,* which was printed together with the first horticultural book written solely for women, *The Country Housewife's Garden.* Beautifully illustrated with charming woodcuts, it tells the 17th century woman everything she needs to know to have a productive and visually attractive garden.

The concept of a "pretty" garden would have been anathema to most women of the 17th century, as gardens were primarily about producing food and herbs, unless you were very wealthy, in which case the gardening was left to your servants. The 17th century author of *The English Housewife,* Gervase Markham, claimed the "complete woman" had:

> *skill in physic, surgery, cookery, extraction of oils, banqueting stuff, ordering of great feasts, preserving of all sorts of wines…distillations, perfumes, ordering of wool, hemp and flax: making cloth and dying; the knowledge of dairies: office of malting; of oats… of brewing, baking, and all other things belonging to a household.*

Guess that did not leave much time for planting pretty flowers!

Because kitchen gardens were about supplying the table, and as much ground as possible was covered with edible plants, every garden was different, planted according to the whims of the women of the household. William Lawson's book for the country housewife was designed to be read in conjunction with his *New Orchard and Garden,* thus giving women access to the idea of garden design, in print, for the very first time.

William Lawson lived from 1553 to 1635 and was the vicar of Ormesby, a country parish in Yorkshire. No doubt his gardening passion led him to be so long-lived in an age where most people did not reach fifty. Gardening was a national passion in the 16th and 17th centuries, as more species came from abroad, and an interest in subjects concentrating on the useful qualities and medical virtues of plants became popular.

But the war against garden pests was just as hard then as now—Lawson calls them the "*whole Army of mischiefs*" and says that "*Good things have most enemies*". The enemies in his Yorkshire Garden were apparently deer and moles.

Lawson's garden plan included long walkways, a maze, and even a bowling alley. Its rectangular shape is split into six sections over three terraces, with flights of stairs and paths to go from one to the other. Its design demonstrates the vogue in the 16th and 17th century for symmetry and patterns. In the top left square he planned to have topiary, signified by a man with the sword and a horse. A river runs at the top and bottom of the garden where he says *"you might sit in your mount and angle a peckled trout, sleighty eel or some other daintie fish"*.

In my novel, *The Lady's Slipper*, Alice Ibbetson is an obsessive gardener—a pioneer, if you like, testing out the knowledge handed down from her father who was a plantsman much like William Lawson. She finds relaxation in communing with nature. Her maid Ella, featured in *The Gilded Lily*, would try to avoid garden work if at all possible. Her sights are set on becoming a fine lady, just like Alice Ibbetson, and leaving manual labour behind for good.

SOURCE

Lawson, William. *A new orchard and garden: or, The best way for planting, grafting, and to make any ground good, for a rich orchard: particularly in the North and generally for the whole kingdom of England.* London: J. H. for F. Williams, 1626. http://www.biodiversitylibrary.org/bibliography/16493#/summary.

GOSSIP IN EARLY MODERN ENGLAND

BY SAM THOMAS

IN TODAY'S WORLD, WHETHER IT IS USED AS A NOUN OR A VERB, THE TERM "GOSSIP" HAS universally negative connotations. Gossips spread rumors of dubious veracity and are often considered the very opposite of what a friend should be.

But such was not always the case, for in early modern England "gossip" had additional and sometimes contradictory meanings.

According to the *Oxford English Dictionary*, the earliest recorded use of the word "gossip" comes from 1014, but its meaning would have no resonance today, for "gossip" referred to a child's godmother or godfather. The spiritual kinship between the child and the godparent extended to the child's birth parents as well, making them "siblings in god."

And here is where things get really cool: "gossip" is short for "god-sib" which is itself an abbreviated form of "god sibling." Thus your gossips were the women and men you chose as godparents for your child—gossips were your closest friends.

According to the English, the Irish chose wolves as their gossips. As one historian noted, this idea is as interesting if it is false as if it is true. Intriguingly enough, this meaning of the word—including its inclusion of men as gossips—endured into the late 19th century.

In the seventeenth century, "gossip" began to refer to the women who attended a woman during labor and delivery of a child, or at her recovery (or lying-in) afterwards, and here we can begin to see the word taking on its negative connotations. Prior to the eighteenth century, childbirth was women's business and a central occasion for women's sociability. A woman gave birth not in the presence of doctors and nurses (whom she knew not at all), but her friends and neighbors.

Such gatherings of women made some men very nervous, and they spilt a great deal of ink voicing their anxiety. In *'Tis Merry When Gossips Meet* (1602) and its sequel *A Crew of Kind Gossips* (1609), Samuel Rowlands describes the meeting between a widow, wife, and spinster in which the three women exchange complaints about their husbands and the widow offers the other women advice on how to manipulate their spouses.

While there is no denying Rowlands' misogyny, his description may not have been entirely off the mark. Writing later in the century, Margaret Cavendish, Duchess of Newcastle, describes just such a gathering in terms Rowlands would recognize:

> *...as is Usual at such Gossiping Meetings, their Discourse was most of Labours and Child-beds, Children and Nurses, and Household Servants...at last they fell into a Discourse of Husbands, Complaining of Ill Husbands, and so from Husbands in General, to their own Particular Husbands.*

When Cavendish—ever the defender of patriarchy—reprimanded the women for their disrespectful carriage, they turned their guns on her:

> ...the ladies being before Heated with Wine, and then at my Words, with Anger fell into such a Fury with me, as they fell upon me, not with Blows, but with Words, and their Tongues as their Swords, did endeavour to Wound me...it hath so Frighted me, as I shall not hastily go to a Gossiping-meeting again, like as those that become Cowards at the Roaring Noise of Cannons, so I, at the Scolding Voices of Women.

This episode also makes clear we should not imagine these gatherings as occasions for sisterly resistance against patriarchal oppression. Rather, they were the scene of as much infighting and competition as characterized society in general.

In the early modern period then, the term "gossip" could refer to any number of things, ranging from a child's godfather, to a woman's closest female friends, to a woman who spread scurrilous rumors about her neighbors. While some might find such imprecision frustrating, to my mind it simply speaks to the richness of early modern English and the ability of the common folk to define words in terms that were useful to them.

What Was Old in the Olden Days?

by SAM THOMAS

If people know one thing about the early modern period, whether it is Tudor England or Puritan New England, it is that people died young. At some point they saw a statistic saying that the average lifespan was forty years and they leave it at that.

While technically true, this view of early modern life misses quite a bit about the past, not least because talk of an "average" hides the fact that high infant mortality rates skew things considerably. If a pair of twins is born in 1600, and one dies at birth while the other lives eighty years, their average life-span is forty years—but neither twin came remotely close to that number!

The strange thing is that the people of early modern England knew perfectly well that people—lots of people—grew old. In the late seventeenth century, a government commissioner named Gregory King (1648-1712) wrote a report called *Natural and Political Observations and Conclusions upon the State and Condition of England*, in which he estimated the population of England and broke down these numbers based on age as well as social and marital status. According to King, 10% of the population was over sixty.

Remarkably, modern demographers found that King was off by only a single percentage point: at the end of the 17th century, 9% of the population was over the age of sixty.

Put another way, if a girl made it past her fifth birthday—by which time childhood diseases had done their worst—it was not unreasonable to expect that she would live to a relatively old age, even by modern standards.

The question that this raises, however, is what being old *meant* in the past.

In the modern world we mark age in ways that are peculiar to our time and place: we get a driver's license when we turn sixteen, vote at eighteen, drink at twenty-one, receive full retirement benefits at sixty-seven, etc. But obviously none of these markers would have made sense to people living any time before the 20th century. So what mattered to them?

As King's estimate indicates, turning sixty was a big deal—in the minds of many people, that was when you became old. A Presbyterian minister named Oliver Heywood (1630-1704) made a habit of writing annual reflections on his birthday. When he turned fifty-nine, he noted: *"I bless the Lord, I am as fit for studying and preaching this day as ever I was in all my life."*

The next year—despite continuing good-health!—he adopted a rather more dramatic tone:

> *Oh my dear Lord, I am now arrived at the 60th year of my age, and not one amongst a thousand live to this age, and I have passed many changes and revolutions in the course of my pilgrimage.... how soon are these 60 years of my life past, like a tale that's told, a dream when one awakes, its but t' other day that I was an infant, a child, a school*

boy, and now I am grown of the older sort, and anon I shall not be here my place will
know me no more.

"Why sixty?" you ask. In addition to being a comfortingly round number, it had religious significance, for it was when the great Apostle Paul died. Heywood wrote of, *"having passed to the sixtieth year of my Life,* [the date of the life of Paul the Aged] *within a few days; and my Lord only knows how soon my sun may set."*

Intriguingly enough, early modern men and women considered sixty-three to be another year-of note. When Thomas Jolly noted the death of a fellow minister, he added the note, *"he dyed in the close of his great climactericall year* [63], *which is accounted most dangerous."*

This is all well and good, and thank God for demographers who crunch the numbers so we don't have to, but the other half of this question remains unanswered. How did growing old *feel* in the world before modern medicine and the social safety net?

Perhaps the most interesting thing about old age in the early modern period is that one could "grow old" several times. The first phase of old age was known to contemporaries as "green old age." This was a time, usually, when a person was in his fifties or sixties. While the body might have begun to decay, it was a time of generally good health and continuing activity.

In his sixty-first year, the aforementioned Presbyterian minister, Oliver Heywood, traveled over 1,000 miles on horseback over extremely difficult terrain, delivered 135 weekday sermons, and attended forty religious fasts. When he was sixty-eight, he logged 700 miles, eighty-two sermons, and another forty fasts. Other men and women had a similarly pleasant experience of old age, as their children married and started lives of their own, or they found spiritual peace that had eluded them in their youth.

It is here worth noting that an individual's experience of old age is closely tied to wealth and gender. A man who spent his entire life working in the fields would grow old much sooner (and more painfully) than a gentleman or aristocrat. Part of what allowed Heywood to enjoy his green old age was that (by lucky accident) he'd inherited an estate in Lancashire, so he did not have to worry about money.

Thanks to their role bearing children, many women also aged earlier than men, regardless of their social status. In contrast to the popular image of labor being fraught with peril, a woman had only a 6-7% chance of dying in childbirth (over her lifetime, not per birth). But the fact is that in the pre-modern era, a woman might become pregnant a half-dozen times and this could take a terrible toll on her body.

Whatever a person's social status, green old age faded to brown and the elderly grew weaker, sicker, and less likely to recover from illness. In extreme old age, physical decay became a central fact in a person's life, as it became more difficult to see, hear, breathe, and walk. Along with these physical challenges, many elderly people suffered from memory loss and melancholy. In 1699, at age sixty-nine, Heywood described his condition in touching detail:

My wind grows exceeding short, any little motion puts me out of order—my chapel is
near me, but when I walk to it (as yesterday) my wind so fails me that I am forced to

stand and get new breath, before I go into my pulpit. When I go up to my chamber, my breath cuts, that I am forced to sit a season in my chair to breath me. When I lay down in my bed I pant a considerable time and cough and oftimes my waters come from me with motion.

An individual's ability to cope with the challenges of extreme old age varied with social status. The wealthy obviously lived in greater comfort than the poor. A few years after this, Heywood found himself unable to walk the few steps to his chapel, so he paid two men to carry him in a specially-built chair. Obviously, this was a luxury which most of his neighbors could not have afforded.

But old age was not just a physical event. For some in early modern England (particularly the Puritans), it could be seen as an event of cosmic significance.

Early Georgian Era (1715–1800)

Mary Delany, Artist and Personality

by LAUREN GILBERT

Born Mary Granville on 14 May 1700 in Wiltshire, England, Mary was the daughter of a Tory aristocratic family who were supporters of the Stuart crown. From the age of eight, she lived with her aunt and uncle, Lord and Lady Stanley, who were close to the court. Lady Stanley had hopes of Mary's becoming a Maid of Honor and educated her accordingly. Lady Stanley brought Mary into close contact with court circles. Unfortunately, the death of Queen Anne in 1714 ended those hopes with the introduction of the Hanoverian line with King George I.

Skilled in painting, needlework, and other crafts and an ardent music lover (she became acquainted with Handel through Lady Stanley), Mary was an accomplished young woman when she went to live with her uncle Lord Landsdowne at Longleat. She was described by Edmund Burke as *"a woman of fashion for all the ages."*

Lord Landsdowne was an intimate friend of Alexander Pope and Jonathan Swift. Because of her parents' financial straits and Lord Landsdowne's political aspirations, at the age of seventeen, Mary was forced to marry Alexander Pendarves, who was 60 years old and a member of Parliament.

Mr. and Mrs. Pendarves moved to London in 1721, where Mary was able to renew her friendships at court and in society. Unfortunately, the marriage, which had not been good to start with, deteriorated as Mr. Pendarves became a heavy drinker and very jealous of attention paid to his young wife. He died in 1724, leaving Mary a young widow with only a few hundred pounds per year on which to live and no home of her own.

But Mary's widowhood actually brought her a greater freedom of movement than she could have had as either an unmarried or a married woman. She was able to socialize, attend concerts, and basically please herself. She lived with her aunt, Lady Stanley, again, as well as with other friends, particularly Margaret Bentinck, Duchess of Portland. She travelled to Ireland, where she became acquainted with Dr. Patric Delany, an Anglican pastor.

She hoped for an appointment to the royal household, which did not come to pass, but became a close and loyal friend of the royal family. She was unsatisfied with choices available to women; she was against marriage as a necessity, and felt that marriage should be a matter of choice only. She engaged in a massive correspondence writing about her interests. She also had a relationship with Lord Baltimore, which ended in 1730, after she came to feel he was trifling with her affections.

In 1743, Mary married Dr. Delany, whose wife had died, and lived with him for the next 25 years in Dublin, where her focus was on gardening and her botanical interests, shell art, needlework, gilding, and many other crafts, and she continued her voluminous correspondence. Sadly, Mr. Delany died in 1768 and with his death, Mary lost interest in her other pastimes. Then in 1771, she combined her interest in botany and crafts by creating what she called "paper mosaicks". These were extremely intricate, detailed, and botanically accurate pictures of plants and flowers, made of tiny pieces of paper cut and pasted in layers.

In these later years of her life, Mary had a house near Queen's Lodge at Windsor, given to her by King George III and Queen Charlotte who also visited her there, and she spent at least half the year with the Duchess of Portland. Her eyesight failed in 1782 and she died in 1788.

She left ten albums of her mosaics, *Hortus Siccus,* which ultimately went to the British Museum in 1897. Although she was a woman of parts, noted for her botanical knowledge and artistic abilities in many areas, her wit, and her charm, ultimately it is her paper mosaics which have kept her fame alive.

SOURCES

British Museum. "Mary Delaney (Biographical Details)." http://www.britishmuseum.org/research/search_the_collection_database/term_details.aspx?bioId=127351.

Cariati, Christine. "Flora Delanica: Art and Botany in Mrs. Delany's 'paper mosaicks.'" *Venetian Red,* December 4, 2009.
http://venetianred.net/2009/12/04/flora-delanica-art-and-botany-in-mrs-delanys-paper-mosaicks/.

Paston, George. *Mrs. Delany (Mary Granville) A Memoir.* London: Grant Richards, 1900. Via Internet Archive http://archive.org/details/mrsdelanymarygra00past.

The Peak of Chic. "Mary Delany and Her Paper Mosaicks." *The Peak of Chic: Musings on Stylish Living,* September 4, 2008. http://thepeakofchic.blogspot.com/2008/09/mary-delany-and-her-paper-mosaicks.html.

Port, Andy. "Now Showing: Mary Delany a Force of Nature." *New York Times Magazine Blog.* September 29, 2009.
http://tmagazine.blogs.nytimes.com/2009/09/29/now-showing-mary-delany-a-force-of-nature/.

Women and the Garden. "Mary Granville Pendarves Delany 1700-1788." *Women and the Garden,* April 28, 2011. http://womenandthegarden.blogspot.com/2011/04/mary-granville-pendarves-delany-1700.html?utm_source=BP_recent.

The Rise and Rise of the English Landscape Garden

by M.M. BENNETTS

Throughout the early part of the 17th century, under James I and Charles I, English gardens continued to develop along the lines discussed previously in The Elizabethan Gardening Craze.

But with the onset of the Civil War in 1642 and the subsequent Protectorate under Oliver Cromwell, gardening, such as it had been, ground to a halt for many different reasons. Armies tramping across the countryside, particularly armies of Levellers, aren't good for the preservation of gardens. Taxes were high and remained very high under Cromwell which meant substantially less disposable income.

Also, many of the keen gardeners and plantsmen had been Royalists. And they, like the famed garden writer John Evelyn, chose to spend the decade of Cromwell's rule on the Continent studying gardens, or travelling, often to stay close to Charles II in exile, or further afield, even plant collecting in the Americas.

Which is not to say that Cromwell's period in power didn't have a marked effect on the countryside as a whole. For during the Protectorate, huge swathes of forest, particularly in the Midlands, had been chopped down. As Daniel Defoe wrote of Theobalds, King James's former palace: *"...it has suffered several depredations since that, and in particular in the late Time of Usurpation, when it was stript, both of Game and Timber..."* And in the place of pleasure gardens, Cromwell and his advisers encouraged, both on moral and economic grounds, the planting of vast orchards.

With the Restoration of Charles II, the idea of a pleasure garden was once again permitted. But now, after their experience on the Continent, the large landowners and fashionable gardeners sought to recreate versions of the most splendid garden of their age: Versailles. And this formal style, full of grand canals, classical statuary, fountains, and extensive geometrical beds edged in box, held sway into the early years of the 18th century.

But vast, formal gardens are very expensive to maintain—they are not only labour intensive, they also take up so much land that might be otherwise profitably employed. And it was the garden writer and designer, Stephen Switzer, who suggested a cheaper alternative in his *Ichnografia Rustica*, published in 1718. He was writing mainly for the owners of villas—successful businessmen mostly—whose smallish estates were near London.

His proposal was that one should open up the countryside so that one might enjoy *"the extensive charms of Nature, and the voluminous Tracts of a pleasant County...to retreat, and breathe the sweet and fragrant Air of gardens."* He went on to suggest that the garden be *"open to all View, to the unbounded Felicities of distant Prospect, and the expansive Volumes of Nature herself."*

Switzer examined costs and expenses; he proposed that the designs be more rural and natural and relaxed, that garden walls were an unnecessary expense, etc. In short, Switzer proposed the landscape movement which would transform the gardens of England.

But garden taste—the same as everything else—is never the work of a single individual. There are always many other motives and forces which contribute in some proportion or other to the evolving result. And several other significant influences must be cited here, all of which come into play to a greater or lesser extent over the next century.

The first, perhaps, is the rise in popularity of the Grand Tour. The 18th century was the century when "taste" mattered, when demonstrating one's qualifications as a gentleman meant being a collector or connoisseur—of books, of art, of music, of gardens. And where did one acquire the polish that gave that aristocratic and classically educated sheen? Italy, of course.

So off troop our young Englishmen of the era, with their tutors, to Italy. Where they study the paintings of Renaissance masters, the glories of classical antiquity in Rome, the elegance of Tuscan gardens, the refinements of Venetian music? Well, yes and no.

If one believes the pious letters they wrote home, then yes. If one reads the despairing accounts of their tutors and their Italian hosts and their letters to each other, then the view leans a little more heavily towards Carnivale, carousing, and wenching with their fellow Englishmen. And in their last weeks picking up a few "souvenirs" in the form of lesser Italian artists—often copies of 17th century Italian landscapes—which, yes, do present the soon-to-be idealised vision of Nature is Art.

Yet Englishmen abroad rarely behave as do Englishmen at home.

So the 18th century Englishmen—without a centralised, all-powerful royal court in which to play politics and power, such as was at Versailles—created their own recreational playgrounds.

The play is still about power, prestige, and status, but here it's married to a cultivated aesthetic as well as to forestry, farming, economy, and sport—riding, shooting, fishing, hunting—a gentleman's concerns and country pursuits, whether he is a Whig grandee or a gentry landowner of the Tory persuasion.

And the acquisition of land (and more land), with all the rights, privileges, and status it conferred, gives these landholders the scope to create these gardens which still hold the visitor rapt. Whether for the *nouveaux riches*—the titans of commerce such as Henry Hoare who was buying his way into the landowning gentry and created Stourhead—or for the greatest of all Whig aristocrats, like the Duke of Devonshire at Chatsworth, these gardens become a expression of a unified landed class based on "good taste", political power, and economics.

Thus, as the eighteenth century progressed, influenced by their experiences of the Grand Tour, by writers such as Pope and Walpole, and by visiting other gardens, England's landed classes began to favour a less formal and more naturalistic approach to landscape design. In developing the uniquely English concept of the landscape garden, William Kent, Lancelot ("Capability") Brown, and the other great landscape architects of the period were responding to a complex assortment of social and aesthetic ideals among their clients.

As well as the integration of forestry, farming, and sport into the landscape, the ambition was in many respects to create an almost "natural" appearance, where trees, water, open grassland, and carefully placed structures (bridges, temples, and monuments were popular) created a carefully balanced microcosm of the English countryside.

Capability Brown is widely regarded as the most influential figure in eighteenth-century landscape design. Born in Northumberland in 1716, he moved south in 1739 and worked as an assistant to William Kent at Stowe, before embarking on what arguably became the greatest career in the history of landscape design.

Brown was more hands-on than Kent; he would always make a personal visit to a new client's estate, evaluating the constraints and opportunities it presented, before sending an assistant to undertake a detailed survey. His remarkable achievement was his ability to bring common ideals and design principles to bear on the specific topography, geology, and prevailing climate of a client's estate.

Above all, there is a sense of effortlessness in Brown's designs, a sense that the park and garden have grown organically out of their surroundings, requiring little or no human intervention or management (though the opposite was, of course, the case).

And it is in these respects that the "new" landscape movement grows out of the mediaeval and Tudor deer park which was the archetypal symbol of status. Even at this late period, venison is still proscribed on the open market; it is still a sign of favour or wealth.

The creation of the "ha ha" in the late 17th century made it possible to have the expansive views—how to wow your guests, who believed, as you did, that *a gentleman should own his view*—without having the deer or cattle coming right up to the Dining Room windows.

It must be said that the concept that a gentleman should own his view, deeply engrained in the psyche of England's landed classes, sometimes led to surprising results. At Wallington in Northumberland, the seat of the Trevelyan family, the main public road passes relatively close to the house, but was sunk to a depth of several feet so that it was invisible from the house!

Likewise, the effortlessness that typifies Brown's landscapes finds a parallel in his architecture, particularly at Claremont in Surrey, where his mansion sits atop its hill in splendid isolation, with no visible tradesmen's entrance to spoil the view on any side. (The tradesmen's entrance is in fact through a tunnel, the entrance to which is concealed in a stand of trees to the north-east of the building.)

And to this day, in many people's eyes, these gardens, landscapes, and houses still encapsulate all that is quintessentially and timelessly English. They stand as a record of our social history; they record the ideals of landowners, great and small, through a period of quiet yet profound social and economic evolution—each estate its own ensample of Shakespeare's vision of "this scept'red isle".

DOGGETT'S COAT AND BADGE: THE WORLD'S OLDEST ROWING RACE

BY **GILLIAN BAGWELL**

Doggett's Coat and Badge is both the name of and prize for the oldest rowing race in the world, which has been held in London every year since 1715. It is believed to be the oldest continually staged annual sporting event in the world and has a colorful and unlikely history.

Thomas Doggett, an Irish actor and comedian, was born in Dublin in about 1640, and made his first stage appearance in London in 1691 as Nincompoop in Thomas D'Urfey's *Love for Money*. He became popular, and when Thomas Betterton opened the new theatre at Lincoln's Inn Fields in 1695 with William Congreve's comedy *Love for Love*, Doggett delighted the crowds playing Ben, a role the playwright had written for him.

While he continued a successful acting career, Doggett also became one of the managers of the Theatre Royal Haymarket and the Theatre Royal, Drury Lane, which is another London institution with a very long history. It's where Nell Gwynn got her start selling oranges when the first theatre opened in 1663, before she began acting.

Doggett lived in Chelsea, and since the river was a principal way to get about London in those days, he was a frequent patron of the Thames watermen. There is a story, apparently apocryphal, that one day Doggett fell into the water and that a waterman rescued him from drowning.

In any case, he had a fondness for the watermen, and in 1715 he set up a contest in which watermen raced the four miles between the Swan Pub near London Bridge and the Swan Pub in Chelsea, rowing the four-seated wherries in which they regularly carried passengers. Watermen had been authorized by the crown since 1510, and were members of a company, which regulated the trade. They wore a uniform—a red coat with a silver badge, and the prize for Doggett's race was such a cap and badge.

Doggett was *"a great Whig in politics"* and an ardent Hanoverian, and the race was held on August 1 to commemorate the date of George I's accession to the English throne the previous year. The badge given to the winner featured the word "Liberty" and the horse representing the House of Hanover.

Incidentally, George I was the son of Sophie of Hanover, the daughter of Elizabeth of Bohemia and granddaughter of James I. He succeeded because Charles II had no legitimate heirs and was succeeded by his Catholic brother James II, who was ousted in favor of his Protestant daughter Mary and her husband and cousin William of Orange. When they had both died, Mary's sister Anne came to the throne. Sophie would have succeeded her, but died only months before Anne did. Charles II had at one point wanted to marry his cousin Sophie. It's too bad he didn't as it would likely have averted the succession crisis, the Jacobite uprisings, and the destruction of Scotland. But I digress....

Doggett organized the race each year until 1721, the year that he died, and his will provided:

> *for procuring yearly on the first day of August forever…Five Pounds for a Badge of Silver weighing about Twelve Ounces and representing Liberty to be given to be rowed for by Six Young Watermen according to my Custom, Eighteen Shillings for Cloath for a Livery whereon the said Badge is to be put…all which I would have to be continued yearly forever in Commemoration of His Majesty King Georges happy Accession to the Brittish Throne.*

The Fishmongers' Company has set the regulations since 1769, and there have been some changes since Doggett's day, when the race helped attract trade for the Watermen. The contestants originally battled against the outgoing tide, but since 1873 they have rowed with the incoming tide.

The original wherries, which took about two hours to row from London to Chelsea, were succeeded by various other craft. Now the race is held on a Friday in late July, and the contestants use contemporary single racing sculls and complete the course from London Bridge to Cadogan Pier in Chelsea in about thirty minutes. The record, set by Bobby Prentice in 1973, was 23 minutes and 22 seconds.

Originally, only professional watermen could compete, but since 1950 amateurs have been allowed to take part, though they do not accept monetary prizes. Claire Burran was the first woman to compete, in 1992. Modern contestants all receive a miniature of the silver badge, and the Fishmongers' Company still hands out the prize money to the winners and the competing rowing clubs.

SOURCES AND FURTHER READING

Ackroyd, Peter. *Thames: The Biography*. New York: Doubleday, 2009.

Parish Register. "Watermen and Lightermen." Docklands Ancestors Ltd. http://www.parish-register.com/watermen_and_lightermen.html.

Weinreb, Ben, et al. *The London Encyclopaedia*. UK: MacMillan, 1983.

THE ORIGINAL JACK THE LAD: JACK SHEPPARD, 1702-1724

BY **MIKE RENDELL**

Had you been around in London on 16 November 1724, there is a one in four chance that you would have been in the procession (some two hundred thousand strong) wending its way in a carnival atmosphere towards Tyburn Hill where the empty gallows were being prepared for a hanging. One in four, because the crowd represented at least a quarter of the capital's population at the time, and they were all there to "honour" one man: the diminutive Jack Sheppard.

Daniel Defoe is presumed to have been hard at work scribbling the final touches to a biography which was on sale "hot from the press" by the time of the execution. And the twenty-two-year-old Jack, his cart escorted by uniformed guards, paused long enough at the City of Oxford Tavern in Oxford Street to sink a pint of sack (sherry), no doubt bemoaning the fact that one of his prison guards had discovered a pen-knife secreted about his person and thereby scotched his chance of escape. And escaping was what Jack was good at, and why the crowds had turned out in their thousands.

There is a series of three scenes engraved by George Cruikshank in 1839, over a hundred years after Sheppard died, to illustrate the serialised novel *Jack Sheppard*, by William Harrison Ainsworth. For there was no doubt that the baby-faced Jack Sheppard was a thief and was getting his just rewards from a legal system designed to protect the wealthy. But over and over again, he had thwarted justice with his daring escapes, and no doubt the throng wanted to see if he could pull off the final escape, the big one, from Death itself. There was to be no such luck, and the lad finally went to meet his Maker that day nearly three centuries ago.

Sheppard had been born in 1702 into abject poverty in the deprived area of Spitalfields. His father died when he was young and his mother had little choice but to send him to the workhouse when he was six years old. Jack was lucky—eventually he was placed with a draper on The Strand called William Kneebone as a shop-boy. Kneebone took the lad under his wing, taught him the rudiments of reading and writing, and encouraged him to become apprenticed as a carpenter (a seven year indenture, which was signed in 1717 when Jack was fifteen). His master was Owen Wood whose premises were in Covent Garden.

All went well for five years—Jack was an exemplary pupil who showed every aptitude for carpentry and hard work. Then, well, he went off the rails.

Maybe it was too many visits to The Black Lion off Drury Lane; maybe it was the blandishments of the young whore, Elizabeth Lyon (otherwise known as Edgeworth Bess), whom he met there; or maybe it was the company he fell into while frequenting the establishment, and in particular the notorious Joseph "Blueskin" Blake or the duplicitous Jonathan Wild (who styled himself the Thief-Taker General, though in reality he was a thief himself, but one who turned in his acquaintances whenever it was opportune to do so).

Whatever the reason, the fact was young master Jack turned himself to a life of petty crime, and soon there was no way back. For a while it was pilfering, helping himself to odds and ends from people's houses while on carpentry errands. But by 1723 he had jacked in his apprentice-ship and set up home with Mistress Bess.

Naturally she wanted to be spoiled rotten; naturally she was not content with the proceeds of minor shop lifting; she wanted Jack to show her the good life. He turned to burglary (an offence which carried the death penalty). Mistress Bess was arrested after they moved to Picca-dilly from Fulham; Jack broke in to the jail and rescued her!

Jack and his brother Tom, aided by Bess, embarked on a series of robberies until Tom got caught. The previous year he had also been apprehended (and suffered the painful penalty of being branded on the hand). This time he shopped his brother Jack to save his own skin, and a warrant for Jack's arrest was issued.

Knowing this, and anxious to get his hands on the forty pounds offered as a bounty, Jon-athan Wild betrayed Jack to the constables, and he was arrested and locked up in the very prison from which he had rescued Elizabeth. Within hours of his incarceration he had cut a hole in the ceiling (leg irons notwithstanding), climbed onto the roof, and dropped down to join a crowd who had gathered when news of his escape became known. Diverting attention by announcing that he could *"see someone on the roof over there"*, he calmly shuffled off in the opposite direction....

In May 1724, Jack was arrested for a second time—caught while in the act of lifting a pocket-watch from a gentleman in what is now Leicester Square, and was taken off to Clerken-well prison, where he was locked up with his mistress. A few days passed while Jack, active with a file, cut through the manacles which chained them both and then removed one of the iron bars on the prison window. He lowered himself and his buxom Bess down to the street on a knotted bed-sheet (no mean feat given his lack of stature) and off they went into the darkness.

Things escalated—they tried their hand at highway robbery and burglary, stooping so low as to break into the home of his old employer and helper, William Kneebone, but the greedy Jonathan Wild was closing the trap. He found Elizabeth Lyon, plied her with alcohol to loosen her tongue, and by this means established where Jack was staying.

Again he was arrested, again he was sent to prison—this time to the notorious Newgate, and guess what, he escaped from there as well!

On 30 August a warrant for his death was being brought to the prison from Windsor—but by the time it arrived it was discovered that Jack had escaped. Aided and abetted by Bess, he had removed one of the window bars, dressed in female clothing brought into the prison by his accomplice, and made good his escape via boat up the river to Westminster.

By now he was renowned for his escapades. He was every Cockney's hero, Jack the Lad, whom no bars could hold. After all, he hadn't killed anyone, he was the ultimate cheeky chappy who always got away from the law in the nick of time. Added to that, he was good looking in a baby-faced sort of way, young, strong, and very agile. This was the stuff of which legends would be made....

Jack laid low for a few days but was soon back to his old tricks and on 9 September was captured and returned to the condemned cell at Newgate. His fame meant that he was visited by the great and the good—gawpers who wanted to say that they had met Jack Sheppard. All this time he was not just in leg-irons, but chained to iron bolts in the floor of the cell.

Cheekily, he had demonstrated to his guards his ability to pick the padlocks with a bent nail and they in turn had increased the security by having him not just hand-cuffed but bound tightly as well. Having trussed him up like a turkey, they retired for the night...and Jack set to work.

He couldn't get rid of the leg-irons but he could free himself from the other restraints. He managed to break into the chimney, where his pathway was blocked by an iron bar. This he dislodged, using it to break a hole in the ceiling and as a crow bar to open various doors barring his way. At one point he went back to his cell to retrieve his bed clothes, as he needed these to drop down onto the roof of a building next to the prison. He waited until midnight, let himself into the building via the roof, and calmly walked out the front door (still in his leg-irons).

The lad must have had a fair amount of chutzpah, because after lying low for a couple of days he was able to persuade a passer-by that he had been imprisoned elsewhere for failing to maintain an illegitimate son—and would he mind fetching some smithy tools? The passer-by obliged, and within a few hours Jack had broken his fetters and was off to taste a freedom which was to last all of a fortnight.

It was at this point that the journalist Daniel Defoe was brought in to pen Jack's story, which he did anonymously as *The History of the Remarkable Life of John Sheppard*.

On the night of 29 October, Jack Sheppard broke in to a pawnbroker's shop in Drury Lane, helping himself to a smart black silk suit, a silver sword, rings, watches, a peruke wig, and other items. He then hit the town, dressed in style, and passed the next day and a half drinking and whoring. Finally, in a drunken torpor, he was arrested on 1 November, dressed *"in a handsome Suit of Black, with a Diamond Ring and a Cornelian ring on his Finger, and a fine Light Tye Peruke"*.

Back he was taken to Newgate, imprisoned in an internal room and weighted down with iron chains. His celebrity status meant that he was visited by the rich and famous, and had his portrait painted by James Thornhill, painter to his Majesty King George I.

There was a clamour for his release, but the authorities were adamant: Jack must pay the price for his notoriety. And so it was that on 16 November 1724, a huge and happy crowd escorted Jack to the gallows, where he did what prisoners were supposed to do—hang. After a quarter of an hour he was cut down, rescued from any attempt by the vivisectionists to claim his body, and buried in the churchyard at St. Martin's-in-the-Fields.

That was the end of Jack Sheppard but not the end of his story. Pamphlets, books, and plays were written, all singing the praises of this swash-buckling hero. His name quickly became an icon, and his story inspired John Gay to write *The Beggar's Opera* in 1728. It was hugely popular.

Others piled into print and for the next one hundred years the tales based on Jack's exploits were legion. It got so bad that at one stage the Lord Chamberlain's office banned the production of any play containing Jack Sheppard's name in the title—for over forty years—for fear that it would encourage lawless behaviour.

Let us remember Jack Sheppard—a twenty-two-year-old who went to the gallows for offences which today would merit little more than a slap on the wrist or a spell in a Young Offenders Institutiion. The boy did wrong, but his memory lives on in our collective consciousness, kept alive by every tale of "the lovable Cockney rogue" and every mention of behaviour being that of "Jack the Lad".

IN THE WAKE OF JAMES COOK

BY LINDA COLLISON

WHEN WE IMAGINE THE HISTORY OF GREAT BRITAIN, WE THINK OF THE SEPARATE classes of people—peerage, gentry, the middling sort, and the servants—as being very static. To a large degree that was the case. Yet unlike many nations, in England some degree of upward mobility was possible (at least historically!).

James Cook, one of five children born to the wife of a Scottish farm laborer in Marston, Yorkshire, was not born a gentleman with title or income, but he made the most of his talents and the most of his opportunities in life. Young James went to sea as a teenager, working aboard a collier out of Whitby, hauling coal from Newcastle. When the Seven Years' War began, Cook joined the Royal Navy where he rose to the rank of captain on his merit.

A self-taught cartographer, Cook's talents were put to use making detailed maps of New-foundland in battles against France which gained him the recognition of his superiors and also the recognition of the Royal Society. He was given command of the *Endeavour*, a re-named converted collier sent on a secret mission to look for a lost continent and to observe the transit of Venus, a measurement needed to estimate the distance of the earth from the sun.

Captain Cook would command three scientific voyages of exploration across largely uncharted or poorly charted areas of the planet, making better maps and astronomical observations in great detail. He would not find the mythical continent geographers of the day thought existed nor would he find the Northwest Passage, but his explorations and his detailed charts were important to Britain, and the entire Western World.

In the 18th century scurvy killed more sailors than did battles. Scurvy would not be fully understood until 1932 when ascorbic acid was identified. Yet none of Cook's crew died from scurvy, in spite of prolonged voyages. Cook took a shotgun approach to prevention, ordering his crews to drink malt and spruce beer which he believed to have anti-scorbutic properties.

Although these particular substances are now known to have no real effect in preventing the vitamin deficiency, what probably contributed greatly to the relative good health of his men was Cook's insistence that the crew eat fresh, local foods at every opportunity (he was a "local-vore" way ahead of his time!). For a good scholarly article on 18th century ideas of scurvy remedies, see Brett Stubbs' *Captain Cook's Beer: the anti scorbutic use of malt and beer in late 18th century sea voyages.*

For his contribution to the greater body of scientific knowledge, Captain James Cook was inducted as a fellow of the Royal Society, a rare honor in those days for the son of a farm laborer to achieve.

By most accounts James Cook was a fair and humane captain, a superb navigator and cartographer, a dedicated explorer, and an all-round exemplary naval officer. He was a husband and father of six children, though absent for years at a time. Elizabeth Batts Cook, wife of James, lived into her nineties.

Cook's ships were not warships, and with few exceptions they were welcomed by most of the Island Nations, who were quick to embrace Western friendship and technology. But on his third voyage and circumnavigation, a string of misunderstandings and poor decisions led to a skirmish during which the famed navigator was killed by the Hawaiians. The event did not lead to war. On the contrary, the Kingdom of Hawaii remained on good terms with the British, incorporating the design of the Union Jack into its own flag.

In October of 1999, my husband Bob and I had the opportunity of a lifetime. We signed on as voyage crew members aboard His Majesty's Bark *Endeavour*, an Australian-built replica of the famed Whitby converted coal carrier, for a three-week crossing from Vancouver to Hawaii. The *Endeavour* replica is a floating museum that circumnavigated the globe twice, stopping at many ports along the way. She is now berthed in Sidney, Australia, where she occasionally circumnavigates the continent that Cook painstakingly charted.

My three weeks living the life of an 18th century seaman led to a renewed appreciation for Captain James Cook, a man who was born without title, fortune, or influence but made the most of his life and changed the world.

Three weeks as an 18th century seaman also inspired my first historical fiction novel *Star-Crossed*, published by Knopf, and my second book *Surgeon's Mate* published in 2011 by Fireship Press.

RIGHT-ROYAL COMINGS AND GOINGS AT WEYMOUTH, 1794

BY MIKE RENDELL

CARVED INTO THE LIMESTONE NEAR THE TOWN OF WEYMOUTH IN DORSET, SOME 300 feet above sea level, is a picture of a man on horseback, 280 feet long. Not just any man, but reputedly King George III, and for over two centuries he has been there, commemorating the fact that the monarch used to visit the town regularly over a fifteen-year period.

George III started his visits in 1789, encouraged by tales about how beneficial the sea air (and indeed sea water) would be to his fragile health. Year after year he came back, his final visit being in 1805. The figure was carved three years afterwards, so George never saw it. That hasn't stopped all manner of stories about the King being offended because it shows him riding away from his beloved Weymouth, rather than entering it....

The carving has been spruced up this year to coincide with the fact that Weymouth plays host to the Olympic Games sailing competition, and not before time as His Majesty has been looking decidedly grey of late!

I thought it would be fun to look out the records of just one of His Majesty's visits, to see exactly what he got up to. This may help any aspiring writers out there who would like to include a reference to the goings-on in the Royal household. Fortunately the records in the *Gentleman's Magazine* for 1794 are really very detailed and give a fascinating picture of the Royal court "on tour".

The record starts by announcing that on August 15,

> *at an early hour in the morning, after a slight refreshment of tea, coffee &c the King, Queen, Prince Ernest and the six Princesses left Windsor in two post chaises with the most loyal effusions of good wishes from the inhabitants for their safe return.*

Weymouth turned out to welcome the Royal party later that day: broadsides were fired by the sloops of war off the coast, while a cannon was fired on the Esplanade by way of a Royal salute.

> *A melancholy accident happened to the two men firing the cannon, owing to their not sponging the gun properly, the cartridge took fire, by which one of the men had his hand blown off, and the other lost one of his eyes and was otherwise most hurt. The cloaths of the latter were set on fire, and were with much difficulty torn off time enough to save him from being burnt to death.*

Not the most auspicious of starts....

The next day, a Saturday, saw the King take an airing on the Dorchester Road, while Her

Majesty and the Princesses walked on the Esplanade and regaled Mr. Wild and his family, of Lulworth Castle, with a great share of her conversation.

Sunday 17 August saw the King make an early start—by seven o'clock he was walking to the Look-out, getting back for his breakfast two hours later. The Royal party went to Melcombe Church to hear a sermon by the Rev'd Groves—they always attended church there, much to the dismay of the Princesses who found the atmosphere inside horribly warm and stuffy, on account of the great press of onlookers. By the evening, rain had set in and the King went for a damp walk, leaving his wife and children behind in their rooms.

The fun started in earnest the next day at seven—His Majesty had a quick dip in the briny "in his old machine" before taking an airing on the road to Wareham. A replica of the bathing machine has just been restored and on 1 June was put back on the sea front. Rumour has it that when the King went for a swim a small orchestra was concealed in the next-door bathing machine so that they could strike up "God Save the King" as His Majesty emerged, like King Neptune, from the tumultuous waves!

19 August saw Princess Augusta brave the sea while her father walked along the Esplanade. He then decided to ride out along the road to Dorchester while the Queen and five of her daughters "took an airing in the carriage" before returning to "the Dukes Lodge" for dinner. The Dukes Lodge was owned at that stage by the King's brother the Duke of Gloucester.

A year or two later the King purchased Gloucester Lodge and used it for all subsequent visits. Later years saw it converted into a hotel. A disastrous fire in the 1920s caused the Lodge to be altered with the addition of an extra storey and a huge porch—and it remains as luxury apartments with splendid sea views.

Things settled down to a routine of bathing, walking, riding out, and trips to the theatre (apparently often to see the same play…). On the evening of 21 August, the whole party traipsed up to see the Army Camp "and saw the men go through their exercises. His Majesty paid the Marquis of Buckingham many compliments on their different manoeuvres" and in return was rewarded with a "21 gun salute and the men gave three huzzas".

The next day—a quick swim and then they assembled at the pier at ten to be taken on board the frigate *Southampton* for a trip round the bay. That was just the Dress Rehearsal, since the next day they repeated the exercise in order to review the fleet from on board the *Southampton*. The Prince of Wales turned up at half past three, and at seven the entire family and its entourage headed for the theatre "which was full and brilliant."

Sunday saw a return to Melcombe church, and in the afternoon the Queen and the Princesses "took an airing in the Sociable on the sands." Apparently they brought at least two of these open carriages with them since they all paraded in the Sociables over the next couple of days. The full title of the vehicle was a sociable barouche, and consisted of two double seats facing each other, usually drawn by one but sometimes two horses.

More visits to the theatre followed in the next few days, to see *The Chapter of Accidents* and *The Romp*. If it wasn't the theatre, they stayed in and played cards, but if *She Stoops to Conquer* was on, they invariably went to see that, or *Animal Magnetism* starring Tony Lumpkin as "the Doctor"….

The days dragged by into September with little to alter the routine. On 8 September,

Princess Augusta bathed while her father walked the esplanade prior to an airing on horseback upon the Dorchester road. It was their Majesties' Wedding Anniversary, so the guns of the frigates and sloops in the bay thundered out their salute, answered by a salvo from the shore battery. There was a ball and supper that night *"in honour of the day"*.

On 9 September His Majesty bathed (no longer in his old machine: the new one had been brought into commission). *"This afternoon his Majesty held a Privy Council at Gloucester Lodge."* The meeting broke up at half past four leaving the King time for an afternoon stroll. That evening the Queen had a concert and a card party, and the next day looked to be a repeat of all that had gone before—bathing, promenading, taking the air, and *"the Royal Family intended to honour the theatre with their presence; but were prevented by the arrival of an express with news of the death of Her Majesty's sister."*

The Prince of Wales, who loathed these family gatherings (and anyway far preferred the more fashionable company to be found in Brighton), was able to escape on 12 September, going on *"a shooting party to Mr. Churchill's seat near Blandford."*

Those remaining went to see the Sencible Cavalry, where Farmer Enfield had generously *"donated an ox roasted whole. The spectators were numerous"*. The Sencibles appear to have been a sort of Home Guard, intended to protect the country as opposed to being sent overseas. General Tarleton stated in Parliament that:

> he could not see the least public utility—he never saw a corps of sencibles that answered his idea of military excellence: they were well enough adapted for young gentlemen to display their equestrian graces and military prowess in country villages but the expense [half a million pounds in 1796] was enormous.

And so they strutted around, doing their stuff, and munching on roast ox....

Another day, more swimming, more games of cards, more airings in the Sociable. I was interested to see that at this stage the Queen had not actually gone into mourning for her sister—official mourning started on 14 September, four days after the death, when it was reported that *"This day the Royal Family and the nobility here went into mourning for the Queens sister"*. That didn't preclude His Majesty and Prince Ernest going bathing, nor going on board the *Southampton* for a spot of dinner, nor indeed going to the theatre.

The 16th was a trifle unfortunate for some: the royal party went to watch the Buckinghamshire Militia be put through their paces—*"His Majesty paid the Marquis a very high compliment on the men being so well disciplined"* before sitting down *"to a cold collation in the Lord Chancellor's marquee. On leaving the camp a royal salute was fired; when a melancholy accident took place—one of the gunners belonging to the artillery had his arm shot off, and expired soon after."*

A trip to Maiden Castle to view the Sencible Cavalry took place the following day, and no doubt His Majesty, taking dinner at Gloucester Lodge, was able to observe the commotion as *"Mr Farrow and his two daughters, in the company of two naval officers, were coming on shore at the pier when the boat ran foul of a post buried under the water and was overset."*

On 18 September, *"Princesses Mary and Elizabeth bathed in the Floating Machine"*. Prince

Ernest and the Duke of Gloucester also had a quick dip before a huge thunderstorm occurred and a gale swept across Weymouth Bay. *"About nine the Sunflower, being driven from her anchor, fired two guns of distress…the longboat from the Southampton with great difficulty saved them from going upon the rocks."*

The Royals stayed indoors until the storm abated and then went out in the evening to the theatre. It stayed rough and wet for the next few days but the twenty-second was the anniversary of the King's coronation so *"the troops fired a feu de joie, which was answered from the batteries. At one the ships fired a royal salute, and were all dressed on that occasion."*

In the coming days there were hunting parties and much drinking of tea at Lady Powlet's as well as more trips to the theatre. But all good things must come to an end, and I dare say that the Royal Princesses were well pleased when the sixteenth of September came and they could all spend the entire day packing and preparing for departure—no swimming, no riding, no promenading, and no theatricals.…

An early start on the day of departure (18 September) saw everyone set off at five in the morning. They paused for an hour at Salisbury, came through Hartford-bridge, and reached Windsor at half past six. *"A general illumination took place in the evening, bells ringing and guns firing, amid the acclamation of the whole town."*

So there you have it—five weeks by the seaside, very much *en famille*. It certainly helped put Weymouth on the map!

THE BLUE STOCKING CIRCLE

BY **LAUREN GILBERT**

AFTER THE DEATH OF QUEEN ELIZABETH I (A VERY SCHOLARLY WOMAN), EDUCATION FOR women declined. Gentlewomen in the early 18th century England were not encouraged to be educated. For many, reading, writing, and a little arithmetic were the most they could hope for (useful skills for acquiring religion and running a household)—and maybe a little French, drawing or painting, and some music, for social accomplishments.

For most women of lower classes, even that much education was not possible. Ideally, women should be content with whatever fathers and husbands chose for them to know. As Alexander Pope wrote in 1720:

> *In beauty and wit*
> *No mortal has yet*
> *To question your empire has dared;*
> *But men of discerning*
> *Have thought that in learning*
> *To yield to a lady was hard.*

However, not every woman was satisfied to be uneducated, confined solely to domestic interests or placated with empty compliments. Even without the kind of formal education provided to young men, there were women who learned at home, acquired knowledge, and wanted to be able to use and enjoy it.

I should begin by saying that this article is an introduction, a broad and general overview, to a group of well-to-do, mostly married, society women in the mid-18th century, who wanted to do more than dance and play cards for recreation. They were women of some education who met informally to discuss literature, the arts, education, and similar topics. They did not allow politics and scandal as topics for discussion. These meetings, or "conversations," were similar to the French *salons* and were held in the women's homes.

The two most noted hostesses were Elizabeth Vesey and Elizabeth Montagu. Other women who participated included Fanny Burney (Madame d'Arblay), Hannah More, Mary Delany, Catherine Talbot, and Elizabeth Carter. Each of these women is worthy of a blog post of her own.

Several of these women were authors or artists themselves. (Elizabeth Montagu contributed to Lord Lyttleton's *Dialogues of the Dead*. Hannah More and Fanny Burney were both novelists. Mary Delany produced hundreds of letters and her own works of art.) Some provided encouragement to those who did write, study, and create. Individually, members of the group provided financial assistance to artists, writers, and others who were in need.

Interestingly, the participants at these meetings were frequently fairly evenly divided between men and women right from the beginning. (This was not about men vs. women; these were women who wanted to be involved on an even level with men.) Elizabeth Vesey was the first important hostess of these gatherings, and her husband participated in her events. He himself was interested in literature and was considered an excellent host.

The hostesses invited educated men to participate and mixed society figures with writers and artists. The male guests included David Garrick, Horace Walpole, James Boswell, Dr. Samuel Johnson, Sir Joshua Reynolds, Lord Lyttleton, and Samuel Richardson. Science, music, art, literature, and education itself were all represented at these meetings and were widely discussed. Sometimes, one particular speaker would dominate the event; other "conversations" might consist of small groups conversing among themselves.

Where did the term "Blue Stocking" come from? There are several theories, but the most accepted indicates that the term was coined as an affectionate nickname for Benjamin Stillingfleet, botanist and poet, who had given up society. He originally declined his invitation to Mrs. Vesey's "conversation" because he did not have formal evening wear, which included black stockings. She told him not to mind, just to come in his blue stockings (his usual everyday wear) and he did; he was very popular and was called "blew stockings" afterwards.

According to Boswell, *"Such was the excellence of his conversation, that it came to be said, we can do nothing without the blue stockings, and thus, by degrees, the title was established."* This term was gradually applied to the women members of the group as a good natured nickname. Hannah More wrote a poem "Bas Bleu" (French for Blue Stocking) celebrating the group. The term seems to have begun as an informal, affectionate nickname within the group that later was applied in derision by outsiders. Ultimately, to be called "blue" or "bluestocking" became a negative term for an earnest or priggish woman who likes to show off her knowledge.

Today, the "Blue Stocking Circle" is considered an early feminist movement. Personally, I find it difficult to apply the modern term "feminist" to these women. They were women of their time. Their positions and resources allowed them certain freedoms that other women did not have; although they clearly supported intelligent women and education, there is nothing to show they sought a radical change in social structure.

Politics were not a subject for their "conversations," and there is no indication that they were actively discussing significant changes on a societal or political level in relation to the position of women in general. In fact, they were not always tolerant of those who did flout certain society standards.

For example, Hester Thrale was friends with Elizabeth Montagu and Fanny Burney. However, Mrs. Montagu and Miss Burney couldn't accept Hester's second marriage to an Italian music teacher named Gabriel Piozzi, and the friendships ended. Clearly, even though they were willing to mix elements at their "conversations," there were still conventions to be upheld.

They were generous with their support, but there is no indication they tried to change the world in which they lived. However, these women clearly showed that females could hold their own with men in intelligent conversation, that women were capable of enjoying literature and learning about science and the arts as well as how to embroider and draw. Their group was the most well known, but by no means the only group involving women in discussion; debating societies were very popular. In a very real sense, their "conversations" and similar groups contributed to people thinking about the issues that ultimately became feminism.

SOURCES

Byers, Nina. "Overview of Women's Education in England and the United States 1600-1900." December 4, 1999. *Contributions of 20th Century Women to Physics.* http://cwp.library.ucla.edu/articles/WL.html.

Drabble, Margaret, Jenny Stringer, and Daniel Hahn, eds. *The Concise Oxford Companion to English Literature.* Oxford University Press, 2003.

Heape, R. Grundy. *Georgian York.* London: Methuen & Co. Ltd., 1937.

Hilton, Boyd, *A Mad, Bad, and Dangerous People? England 1783-1846.* New Oxford History of England. Oxford: Clarendon Press, 2006.

Hodge, Jane Aiken. *Passion and Principle: The Loves and Lives of Regency Women.* London: John Murray Publishers Ltd., 1996.

Ward, A.W. and A.R. Waller, eds. *The Period of the French Revolution*, Volume XI of *The Cambridge History of English and American Literature in 18 Volumes.* http://www.bartleby.com/221/.

ROBIN HOOD, AGINCOURT, AND GENDER EQUALITY?: ARCHERY IN LATE GEORGIAN ENGLAND

BY J.A. BEARD

FROM THE LEGEND OF ROBIN HOOD TO THE GALLANTRY OF THE ARCHERS AT THE BATTLE of Agincourt, archery has long been a part of the English's cultural identity, even if some of their Saxon ancestors didn't think much of it for war.

Alas, in England, as in so many other places, the superior lethality and ease of training associated with firearms caused the practical-minded English to adopt the newer weapon over bows and arrows. Over the centuries, the proud tradition of English archery sank into near irrelevance.

In the closing decades of the Georgian period, a growing fascination with many things from the medieval past led to the rebirth of the English archery tradition. Many gentlemen of means were gentlemen of leisure. Indeed, it was a mark of pride to not have to work for one's living. They had more time to devote to non-vocational pursuits (though, I suppose, gambling can be a vocation of sorts). Among other things, though, this meant that many gentlemen also had time to devote their attention to sporting activities.

It was this context that in 1781 led Sir Ashton Lever to form an archery society in London, the Toxophilite Society. There were some earlier societies formed, but they would lack the influence of Sir Ashton's society. The men of this society were interested in archery as both a sport and as another way to socialize. This particular society also would gain a powerful patron in the form of the Prince of Wales (later the Prince Regent and ultimately King George IV). The Toxophilite Society became the Royal Toxophilite Society, which, incidentally, still exists today.

The royal boost and success of the Royal Toxophilite Society helped inspire archery clubs and societies throughout England. These societies and clubs typically had rules and uniforms. That being said, actual serious attention to mastering archery was far from universal. While many archery societies did their best to lay the groundwork for a sport of skill and dedication, many other societies used archery as just a flimsy excuse to throw lavish parties and get drunk with the sports aspect barely a consideration. So, in that sense, these Georgian fellows were not that different from many amateur sports clubs in modern times.

Although Western target archery has grown and evolved over the decades, many basics of the sport are still heavily influenced by the influence of these earliest archery societies.

Those who have seen the Gwyneth Paltrow version of *Emma* may remember an archery scene where Emma Woodhouse shoots off a few arrows. Though Austen's novel contains no references to Miss Woodhouse practicing archery, this scene is otherwise not anachronistic.

In contrast to the gender differences that marked many other activities in the late Georgian and

Regency periods, archery was considered not only an acceptable pastime for women, but even an acceptable pastime for proper ladies, including a gentleman's daughter such as Emma Woodhouse.

At the time, most sports were effectively barred, via social condemnation, from women as they were considered that most horrible of things for Georgian ladies: unfeminine. Archery was considered an activity in which women could demonstrate their grace and "feminine form" in a way that the people of the time didn't consider vulgar. While archery was not the only permissible sport (some other examples included the badminton precursor, shuttlecock, and lawn bowling), it was unusual in its relatively quick acceptance of women into the fold for an activity that started as male only.

The initial men-only archery societies allowed female guests of members to visit to shoot, and many (though certainly not all) soon allowed full female members. In 1787, the Royal British Bowmen were the first archery society to allow full women members.

Besides the satisfaction that comes with mastering an activity of skill, co-ed archery societies could also help facilitate useful social interaction as they provided excellent opportunities for aristocratic men and women to mix.

To be clear though, it's important to note that the Bowmen's interest in adding women was likely considerably less influenced by such social considerations. They had a reputation as one of the most serious archery clubs of the period and often frowned upon the partying and drinking that interfered with the practice of the sport. For them, archery was a sport, not an excuse to party.

ELIZABETH LINLEY SHERIDAN: LADY OF FANTASY AND TRAGEDY

BY **WANDA LUCE**

As a passionate author and reader of Regency-era fiction, I have often wondered if any real persons actually experienced the kind of romance that I and other Regency authors portray in our books. Those who share my partiality for the Georgian/Regency genre most probably love it because they find themselves transported into a world of idyllic romance and glorious endings.

Unlike real life, Georgian and Regency-era novels carry the reader blissfully along through a multitude of ups and downs to a satisfying ending in which the hero and heroine at last form a deep alliance between soul mates. The reader expects and even anticipates that this love match, so beautifully brought to its desired zenith, will in like form continue so long as both partners shall live.

As I searched for a real life story like the fictional ones I create, I discovered a lady whose life seemed stamped from the ideal, until I read about what transpired in her life beyond what in my novels is the final scene. Her life prior to marriage was a pattern card for a Jane Austen spin-off, but afterward? Well, I hope you will take a moment to honor her by reading my short summary of her life.

Elizabeth Ann Linley Sheridan was one of the great beauties of the late 18th century. She was born the second of twelve children to composer Thomas Linley and his wife Mary Johnson on September 7, 1754. Thomas Linley taught his children musical skills, but of the seven who at length had musical careers, Elizabeth, or Betsy as she was called by her friends and family, possessed the greatest talent.

As a child, Elizabeth stood outside the Pump Room in Bath and sold tickets to her father's concerts, but by the age of fourteen, she was a stunning Soprano who drew her own crowds. From an early age, her dark hair, slim, tall figure, and porcelain skin drew the attention of men. Artist Thomas Gainsborough painted many portraits of her out of a desire to depict her exceptional beauty.

Elizabeth began her vocal training at an early age and gave her first performance at Covent Garden when only twelve. Over the next few years, she transformed from a lovely girl with an extraordinary voice into a beautiful young woman whom a great many men desired to court. Her singing enchanted the public wherever she went, and her ability and beauty became famous.

In spite of the many marriage proposals Elizabeth received, her father pressured her into an engagement with Walter Long who was about four times Elizabeth's age. Although she found the idea of marrying him repugnant, her father desired the wealth Mr. Long would bring to the family. Mr. Linley also hoped Elizabeth's marriage to a man of wealth would prevent her from pursuing a career on the stage. Long, however, broke off the engagement, sending wild rumors flying that she had cried off. On 26 June 1771, a comedy about her life, called *The Maid of Bath*, opened at the Haymarket Theatre.

Shortly after the drama of Elizabeth's broken engagement, Richard Brindsley Sheridan, the playwright, one of Elizabeth's most ardent admirers, swept her off her feet, and on 18 March 1772, the two eloped to France. Unfortunately, the marriage was invalid while both of them were underage. Although neither father approved of a union between Elizabeth and Sheridan, Elizabeth's father eventually capitulated and granted his consent in an effort to save his daughter's reputation. On 13 April 1772, Elizabeth at last married Sheridan in Marylebone, London.

Over the course of their marriage, Elizabeth was plagued with poor health and suffered many miscarriages, but in 1775 at the age of twenty-one, she finally delivered a son, Tom.

In spite of Sheridan's initial passion for Elizabeth, he soon sought his pleasure in other women's beds, particularly those of the Devonshire set including the Duchess of Devonshire's sister, Harriet, and consigned Elizabeth to years of despair and loneliness over his unfaithfulness. Though they began to live quite separate lives, the two occasionally appeared in public together.

Elizabeth's beauty soon caught the eye of the handsome Lord Edward Fitzgerald in whose arms she eventually sought the affection now absent in her marriage. Unfortunately, the affair produced a daughter and exposed Elizabeth's infidelity, but the most terrible consequence was the serious effect the pregnancy had on her health. Overcome with guilt for his affairs and neglect, her husband helped her through the difficult pregnancy.

After the delivery, Elizabeth developed tuberculosis. In an effort to improve her health, Sheridan took her to Bristol to soak in the hot wells, but to no avail. One night, he discovered Elizabeth at her piano, crying, the tears dripping down her thin arms. Her suffering and his guilt nearly drove him to madness.

On 28 June 1792 Elizabeth passed away. So great were the crowds in the street that the carriage could barely edge its way to Wells Cathedral. Her husband adored the daughter Elizabeth had conceived by Lord Fitzgerald and took her in as his own, but only months after her mother's death, the infant daughter also passed away.

Imagine for a moment if Richard had remained faithful, adoring, and attentive how different Elizabeth's life might have been. Just a thought.

GRACE DALRYMPLE ELLIOTT:
A VERY HIGH FLYER INDEED!

BY **LAUREN GILBERT**

GRACE DALRYMPLE ELLIOTT WAS A COURTESAN, AND A VERY FAMOUS (OR SHOULD I SAY, notorious?) one. Intelligent, educated, and witty as well as beautiful, Grace was known for making her own choices and living her life on her own terms, or at least as much her own as a woman of her time was able.

Documentation about her is spotty: her marriage record, divorce records, daughter's christening record, an obituary, a death certificate and a will all exist. However, they tell us little of the woman herself. She is mentioned in a few letters, gossip columns in *The Rambler, Town and Country Magazine, Matrimonial Magazine*, and similar "tabloid" type journals, but (again) the real woman eludes us. Even her own memoirs, *Journal of My Life During the French Revolution*, were altered.

No letters to or from Grace herself, no account books, no diary have yet surfaced. However, what we do know about Grace is fascinating.

Grace Dalrymple was born about 1754 to Hew (Hugh) Dalrymple and his wife Grizel (Scottish variation of Grace) in Scotland. Her father was of respectable family, possibly connected to Scottish aristocracy. Her parents were separated before she was born. She was sent to a convent boarding school in either France or Flanders at approximately age eleven, when her mother died. She remained there for about five years before joining her father in London.

His profession and finances at that point are not clear; however, he was working on establishing himself. Grace was tall for her time (possibly as tall as 5'7"), slender with excellent posture, a heart-shaped face, and brown hair (worn powdered, per her time).

Two portraits by Gainsborough, and a miniature, possibly by Cosway, show a very attractive woman. She attracted Dr. John Eliot, a Scottish-born physician, who was short, unattractive, and about fourteen years older than she. He was successful, having come under the patronage of Sir William Duncan, who attended King George III.

Dr. Eliot attended many members of the *ton*, including the Prince of Wales, and was constantly working on improving his practice and earning more money. He spent time and made friends with people in high society. He would have been considered an excellent match. They were married in October of 1772 by "special license".

The doctor was very busy, working in his practice, becoming known for his bed-side manner (especially with his women patients), leaving Grace to socialize on her own. Apparently, they were quite different persons: she was very young and enjoyed society, while he was much older and preferred to stay home when not occupied with his work or his own pursuits. Grace socialized with Dr. Eliot's friends, who in turn introduced her to other people. A young wife was generally not chaperoned, so here was a very young woman on her own in a very fast crowd. Gossip columns of the day suggest Grace had multiple lovers, but her affair with the married rake, Arthur Annesley, eighth Viscount Valentia, made her notorious. It is unclear when the affair began, but Grace and Valentia made the gossip columns in 1774 and 1775.

At the same time, her marriage to Dr. Eliot degenerated to the point that they couldn't stand each other. Dr. Eliot had servants and paid informants spy on her. Grace was stubborn, reckless, and didn't understand that her middle-class background required a level of discretion to which the higher born members of Society didn't have to attain. Grace and her husband stopped sharing a room, and she was apparently sent off to the country for nine months to be sure she was not pregnant with a child of questionable paternity.

Dr. Eliot filed divorce papers in 1774. After going through ecclesiastical court for the legal separation and civil court for the damages for criminal conversation, the final bill for divorce was presented to the House of Lords in Parliament in 1776, and King George III signed off on it. Dr. Eliot got the right to remarry and damages; Grace got an annuity of 200 pounds per year.

Interestingly, years later, bequests in his will to his illegitimate children by multiple women indicate that Dr. Eliot was quite the womanizer himself! Dr. Eliot became Sir John Eliot in 1776, but (thanks to the divorce) Grace was never Lady Eliot.

This is the first point at which Grace could have sunk without a trace. Disgraced and homeless (her father was dead, her sister basically disowned her), Grace was in a difficult situation. However, amongst all the gossip, there is no hint that Grace ever walked the street or was associated with a brothel. She acquired "protectors," weighed her options, and generally traded up. Grace was linked with a number of men, and her relationships frequently seemed to overlap. We will consider three of her most advantageous.

In January of 1776, her relationship with George, Marquess of Cholmondeley, an extremely wealthy and powerful man of the Prince of Wales' set, became public. Lord Cholmondeley was tall and good looking. He was nicknamed "Lord Tallboy," while Grace was known as "Dally the Tall." They were apparently a handsome couple, well suited personally as well as physically.

There is every indication that they sincerely loved each other and that Grace hoped to marry him. Rumors about a possible marriage between them surfaced in 1776 and in 1778, but nothing happened. Grace chose to go to France about May of 1779. She and Cholmondeley were reunited as lovers 1781-1784, but their relationship had changed. Ultimately, in 1795, Cholmondeley married Charlotte Bertie (an heiress from an old, powerful, distinguished family).

From 1779-1781, Grace was in France, again in high society, and her name was associated with several court figures, including the Comte d'Artois and Philippe, Duc de Chartres (later Duc d'Orleans). However, in 1781, Cholmondeley made a visit to Paris with another woman. Grace returned to England, following Cholmondeley in early June, and they reunited briefly.

During the summer of 1781, possible in June, Grace had a brief affair with the Prince of Wales. Over in a short time, possibly a matter of weeks, this affair was important because Grace became pregnant. Her daughter was born March 30, 1782, and Grace stated that the father was the Prince of Wales.

The child was christened Georgiana Augusta Frederica Elliott for the prince, and the christening record (which still exists) shows the prince as her father. Although the Prince of Wales didn't deny the child, he did not acknowledge her either. However, the christening record was left intact, and the prince paid Grace an annuity from at least 1800 until her death. (The annuity may have started earlier—the prince's accounts are not complete.)

Multiple candidates for the child's paternity arose, however, and Lord Cholmondeley was a prime consideration. He was involved with Grace at the right time. Georgiana was placed with him and his family; he raised her and took responsibility for her. While this might have been a matter of tidying up the situation for the Prince of Wales (always a good move), it could have been achieved with much less personal involvement.

Georgiana became known as Georgiana Seymour, made a most advantageous marriage, and continued as a member of Cholmondeley's family. Grace and Cholmondeley maintained contact, and he helped her with money periodically. He also paid for her funeral. One way or another, they remained connected for almost fifty years, until her death.

Grace left England for France in the late summer of 1784 with Philippe, Duc de Chartres. Philippe was charming, generous, very rich, and married; he provided Grace with her house in Paris and a cottage in the country. She was sincerely attached to him, as he was to her, but he was serially unfaithful. She remained in France during the prelude to the Revolution and during the Terror. This was the period of her life described in her memoirs, written in 1803. During this horrifying and exciting time, she supposedly carried messages on behalf of Marie Antoinette to various loyalist groups in France and to the Austrian government in Brussels in 1790. She saw the royal family returned to Paris after their attempted escape in 1791, saw various atrocities, and was questioned and imprisoned in various prisons under great hardship with other well-known figures, including Josephine de Beauharnais. She was finally released from prison, possibly in 1794.

There are indications that, during this time in France, she also provided information to British officials, possibly spying for her country. There are many questions about the accuracy of her *Journal,* as there is little supporting documentation and there are noticeable discrepancies. However, there is no doubt that she was present and involved.

Available information indicates that Grace went back and forth between France and England from this point until she finally returned to France in 1814. After this, there is no further record of her until the end of her life. The last two years of her life, she was a paying lodger in the home of M. Dupuis, the mayor of Ville d'Avray. There are indications that she suffered debilitating health problems, possibly stemming from her time in prison, that resulted in a slow death. She received last rites from a Catholic priest.

Although she died alone, there is no indication she was poor—she had two annuities, and left a will. She was approximately 69 years old and living in retirement at the time of her death. However, Grace had lived an exciting life, in the thick of the highest society and stirring world events, determined by her own choices. She showed herself to be a strong and courageous person, who chose her path and stayed with it.

Her granddaughter, Georgina Cavendish-Bentinck (Georgiana's daughter), had Grace's manuscript of *Journal of My Life during the French Revolution* published by Richard Bentley in 1859. She (or someone) provided him with anecdotal information (sources unknown), which he included. He wrote a prologue and epilogue, containing a number of his own opinions and inaccuracies, divided the work into chapters, and made other alterations, resulting in serious errors. Unfortunately, since the original manuscript has disappeared, there is no way to sort out his changes and errors from what Grace wrote herself. No one knows how Georgina came by the manuscript.

SOURCES

Drake, Sylvia. "Grace Dalrymple Elliott's Journal de ma vie: Originally a pro-revolution memoir?" Jan. 29, 2010. *Under the Sign of Sylvia.* http://misssylviadrake.lifejournal.com/15492.html. (Article includes the Oxford Dictionary of National Biography article about Grace by Martin Levy in its entirety.)

Great Scotswomen Blog. "Grace Dalrymple Elliott." http://www.firstfoot.u-net.com/Great%20Scot/graceeliot.htm.

Manning, Jo. *My Lady Scandalous.* New York: Simon & Schuster, 2005.

Sir John Soane: At Home with an Eccentric Genius...or *"Padre Giovanni Has Come to Visit."*

by GRACE ELLIOT

I RECENTLY HAD THE PLEASURE OF VISITING THE SIR JOHN SOANE'S MUSEUM, HOWEVER I went alone. Despite my best efforts, I totally failed to convince my teenage sons to come with me. The trouble was I approached things from the wrong angle. When my youngest asked, "Who was John Soane?" to encourage him along I tried the hard sell.

"John Soane was the famous Georgian architect who designed the Bank of England."

My son remained blank faced so I tried again.

"He was a famous collector and eccentric who filled his home with classical artefacts and fabulous paintings."

To his credit my son tried to look disappointed as he excused himself by saying he needed to bathe his bearded dragon (which in all fairness, he did then do)—so I went alone.

But on my return it was a different story as I gushed with enthusiasm over what I had seen.

"It was an amazing place; Soane built light-wells into the house and used stained glass in orange and yellows, so the rooms appear to glow."

My elder son, an art student, perked up and started to listen, as I explained in more detail.

Numbers 12-14 Lincoln's Inn Field were the home of influential Georgian architect, Sir John Soane (no, don't switch off, I promise it will get more interesting), and what I hadn't realised before my visit was just how excitingly eccentric the great man was. I went unprepared for the sheer scale of the collection crammed into his home. Artefacts press in from all sides, no wall space or flat surface unoccupied, and yet everything is in perfect harmony and order. The sheer weight of marble cornices, capitals, friezes, and plaques mounted on the walls set me wondering about the danger of collapse.

Soane, his wife, and their two sons lived in the house/museum much as it appears today: Greek and Roman marbles lining the stairwells, a full sized Egyptian sarcophagus in the basement, a room of Hogarths mounted on hinged walls. In the basement, Soane created an atmosphere reminiscent of catacombs or Roman burial chambers, of which the centrepiece was the magnificent Egyptian sarcophagus of King Seti I, bought by Soane when the British Museum refused to pay 2,000 pounds for it. With hieroglyphics yet to be deciphered in his time, Soane celebrated the arrival of this important antiquity with three evening parties, illuminated by three hundred oil lamps and attended by nearly a thousand people.

Mrs. Soane must have had the patience of a saint to put up with the stamp of her husband's overwhelming personality, but by all accounts they were a happy couple. A mark of Soane's eccentricity was his "Monk's Parlour." This was a downstairs room designed in a gothic fashion, with dark, sombre colours and heavy furniture to illustrate the importance of light (or lack of it) in creating atmosphere.

What is even more delightful is that when Soane wanted to be alone he would claim: *"Padre Giovanni has come to visit,"* and disappear into the Monk's Parlour to take tea. However, since Padre Giovanni was fictitious—actually a play on Soane's own name "John"—his visits were an excuse to enjoy solitude.

The moral of this story is that sometimes the plaudits of history can blind us to the personalities who create it. No dry as dust exhibition of worthy achievements can ever set the imagination alight to the wonders of the past quite so much as a glimpse into the mind of the people who inspired them.

Child's Play...or Is It?:
Georgian Era Nursery Rhymes

by LUCINDA BRANT

Nursery rhymes are the first poems and songs children learn, generally before they go to school. They help broaden vocabulary, teach counting, and sharpen memory. They are nonsense and hold no more meaning than what is intended within the rhyme. Nonsense? That's all well and good for children to believe, but we adults know better, don't we? Or do you?

Of course, they are not meaningless, nor are they nonsense (not if you are the intended target). In this post I'll focus on several nursery rhymes from the Georgian era.

Humpty Dumpty

Humpty Dumpty sat on a wall,
Humpty Dumpty had a great fall.
All the King's horses,
And all the King's men
Couldn't put Humpty together again!

There are several theories as to the origin of *Humpty Dumpty* and from my research the most popular is that Humpty Dumpty was a large cannon used during the Civil War to defend the town of Colchester. A walled town with a castle and several churches, it was a Royalist stronghold. The Parliamentarians (Roundheads) aimed at the wall on which Humpty Dumpty sat and caused the Royalist cannon to fall, and eventually the Royalists were beaten. The Siege of Colchester lasted for eleven weeks from 13 June to 27 August 1648.

However, the rhyme wasn't published until 1810 in *Gammer Gurton's Garland*, where there is no mention of the King's men or his horses:

Humpty Dumpty sate [sic] *on a wall,*
Humpti Dumpti [sic] *had a great fall;*
Threescore men and threescore more,
Cannot place Humpty dumpty as he was before.

This first published version leads to the more obscure theory (I can't find a reference anywhere, and I would like to claim it as my own, but, alas, I think one of my history teachers told me) that Humpty Dumpty is not a cannon at all but a specific person. I believe it refers to King George III and that the rhyme is about his mental illness.

Humpty Dumpty sits on a wall—this makes him higher than anyone else, alluding to his royal status. There was no one higher in England's Georgian society than the King. He has a great fall—George III had several bouts of mental illness. Threescore men and threescore more —that's 120 men!—come. This suggests that it made no difference to the King's condition how many men were called to attend on him. They *"cannot place Humpty dumpty as he was before"*— the King's mental illness cannot be cured and thus he can no longer rule as king.

Life will never be the same again for King George or his subjects. As a consequence of the King's mental illness, the Prince of Wales became Prince Regent. The date of the rhyme's first publication, 1810, is significant because this was the year the Regency was discussed in Parliament, and the Prince of Wales became Prince Regent by law in early 1811.

George III was not the only one in his family to be represented in a nursery rhyme. His second son, Prince Frederick, the Duke of York and Albany, was also the subject of a rhyme that satirized his abilities as a military field commander.

The Grand Old Duke of York

The Grand old Duke of York
He had ten thousand men
He marched them up to the top of the hill
And he marched them down again.
When they were up, they were up
And when they were down, they were down
And when they were only halfway up
They were neither up nor down.

Of course, there are those who contend that it is not Frederick the nursery rhyme is about but another old Duke of York, Richard, claimant to the English throne and Protector of England during the Wars of the Roses, and the march referred to is the Battle of Wakefield on 30 December 1460. Richard marched his army to his castle at Sandal, built on top of the site of an old Norman motte and bailey fortress. Its massive earthworks stood 33 feet (10m) above the original ground level, and so *"he marched them* [his soldiers] *up to the top of the hill."*

Then, in what many scholars believe to be a moment of madness, he left his stronghold in the castle and went down to make a direct attack on the Lancastrians and so *"he marched them* [his soldiers] *down again."* Richard's army was overwhelmed and he was killed.

The theory I prefer involves Prince Frederick, Duke of York and Albany, the second and favorite son of George III and Commander-in-Chief of the British Military throughout the Napoleonic Wars. The grand old Duke of York is said to refer to his fighting in Flanders in 1793. The Duke won a cavalry conquest at Beaumont in the April of 1794 and then was roundly defeated at Turcoing in May and recalled to England.

The "hill" in the rhyme is the township of Cassel, built on a mount that rises 176 meters (about 570 feet) over the otherwise level lands of Flanders in northern France. Though he was a bad field commander, Frederick was a competent military organizer who raised the professional level of the army, playing a significant behind-the-scenes role in the Duke of Wellington's victories in the Peninsular War. The grand old Duke of York also founded Sandhurst College.

Georgie Porgie

Georgie Porgie pudding and pie,
Kissed the girls and made them cry
When the boys came out to play,
Georgie Porgie ran away.

There are two contenders for the title of Georgie Porgie. The first is George Villiers (1592-1628), Duke of Buckingham, the bisexual lover of James I. George was a very good-looking gentleman with highly suspect morals. He did not confine his sexual favors to the king but had affairs with many of the ladies at court, as well as the wives and daughters of powerful nobles.

It is also believed he used his privileged position with the King to force his attentions on unwilling ladies. He *"kissed the girls and made them cry"* and managed to avoid prosecution or retaliation—*"when the boys came out to play, Georgie Porgie ran away"*.

Villiers' notorious affair with Anne of Austria, Queen of France, injured both their reputations and was written into Alexander Dumas' novel *The Three Musketeers*. Villiers' liaisons and political scheming were questioned in the English Parliament who finally put a stop to James I intervening on his young lover's behalf.

The second contender for the title of Georgie Porgie, and the one I prefer, is none other than the last of the Hanoverian Georges—"I'm the Fat One" (to quote *Horrible Histories*)—the Prince Regent, and subsequently George IV (1820-1830).

In later life, George was not just fat, he was grossly obese. He gave huge banquets and drank to excess. Although he was described as the "First Gentleman of England" and is credited with championing the Regency style of clothing and manners and was considered clever and knowledgeable, *Georgie Porgie* highlights his worst traits. His laziness and gluttony led him to squander his abilities.

He spent whole days in bed and his extreme weight made him the target of ridicule, hence the reference to "pudding and pie". By 1797 he weighed in at 245 pounds (111kg) and by 1824 the waist of his corset was 50 inches (127cm).

George had a notorious roving eye. His checkered love life included several mistresses, illegitimate children, and bigamy. Beautiful women invited to dine with the King were warned not to find themselves alone, for George was not above taking liberties with his female guests. He *"kissed the girls and made them cry"*. He was also considered a coward by those who knew him well; thus, *"When the boys came out to play, Georgie Porgie ran away."* A senior aide to the king recorded in his diary that, *"A more contemptible, cowardly, selfish, unfeeling dog does not exist.... There have been good and wise kings but not many of them...and this I believe to be one of the worst."* The Times once wrote, George preferred *"a girl and a bottle to politics and a sermon."*

Jack and Jill

Jack and Jill went up the hill
To fetch a pail of water;
Jack fell down and broke his crown,
And Jill came tumbling after.

Kilmersdon, a village in Somerset, has claimed this rhyme as its own, and there is a set of stone tablets along a path up to a well at the top of the notorious hill. The village claims that during 1697, a young unmarried couple courted up on a hill, away from the prying eyes of the village. Fetching a pail of water was a ruse. Jill became pregnant and just before she gave birth, Jack *"fell down and broke his crown"*; he was killed by a hit to the head from a rock. Days later *"Jill came tumbling after"*, dying in childbirth.

This could well be true, and could only help boost tourist numbers to Kilmersdon. However, the rhyme was not published until the 1700s. While 1760 is touted as the year of publication, there are those who contend the actual date was closer to 1795. The latter date would tie in nicely with the theory that the protagonists Jack and Jill are in fact the ill-fated French royal couple Louis XVI and his Queen Marie Antoinette who were both guillotined in 1793.

"Up the hill" is said to represent Louis XVI's ascension to the French throne in 1774. Jack falling down is reference to the French Revolution and Louis being arrested and charged with treason. He "broke his crown" when he was guillotined in January 1793, and Marie Antoinette (Jill) soon followed when she "came tumbling after" and was guillotined in October of the same year.

There Was an Old Woman Who Lived in a Shoe
There was an old woman who lived in a shoe
She had so many children, she didn't know what to do;
She gave them some broth without any bread;
Then whipped them all soundly and put them to bed.

The old woman is said to refer to the English Parliament and the shoe itself is England. It is said that if you look at a map of Great Britain and turn it 90 degrees clockwise it resembles a shoe. By the mid 1700s England is considered an "old woman" by its colonies, particularly the American colonies, set in her ways and intractable. Her many children are said to represent the English colonies, young, growing, and inquisitive.

"Some broth without any bread" and then a whipping before bed, refers to the piecemeal and violent way the English Parliament dealt with colonials and their problems—in the same way a harsh parent treats a child considered wayward and naughty. The dismissal and subsequent harsh treatment of the very real problems faced by the American colonists eventually led to the American Revolutionary War.

Jack be Nimble
Jack be nimble,
Jack be quick,
Jack jump over
The candlestick.

There is consensus amongst historians as to the identity of Jack being the notorious pirate Black Jack Smatt who lived at Port Royal, Jamaica during the latter half of the 17th century. Port Royal was known as "The Wickedest City on Earth", until razed by an earthquake in 1692, at which time Jack and his fellow pirates were heard of no more. Yet, his legend lived on well into the eighteenth century and the printing of the first Mother Goose nursery rhymes.

Jack Smatt was nimble and quick—he evaded capture by the British authorities, and he was never tried for piracy because he had the knack of getting himself out of a "hot spot" (represented by Jack jumping over a candlestick). Black Jack Smatt lives on in the 21st century consciousness as the eighteenth century pirate Captain Jack Sparrow of the *Pirates of the Caribbean* movies, fabulously portrayed by the wonderfully talented Johnny Depp.

Who Killed Cock Robin?

"Who killed Cock Robin?"
"I," said the Sparrow, "With my bow and arrow, I killed Cock Robin."
"Who saw him die?"
"I," said the Fly, "With my little eye, I saw him die."
"Who caught his blood?"
"I," said the Fish, "With my little dish, I caught his blood."
"Who'll make the shroud?"
"I," said the Beetle, "With my thread and needle, I'll make the shroud."
"Who'll dig his grave?"
"I," said the Owl, "With my little trowel, I'll dig his grave."
"Who'll be the parson?"
"I," said the Rook, "With my little book, I'll be the parson."
"Who'll be the clerk?"
"I," said the Lark, "If it's not in the dark, I'll be the clerk."
"Who'll carry the link?"
"I," said the Linnet, "I'll fetch it in a minute, I'll carry the link."
"Who'll be chief mourner?"
"I," said the Dove, "I mourn for my love, I'll be chief mourner."
"Who'll carry the coffin?"
"I," said the Kite, "If it's not through the night, I'll carry the coffin."
"Who'll bear the pall?
"We," said the Wren, "Both the cock and the hen, we'll bear the pall."
"Who'll sing a psalm?"
"I," said the Thrush, As she sat on a bush, "I'll sing a psalm."
"Who'll toll the bell?"
"I," said the bull, "Because I can pull, I'll toll the bell."
All the birds of the air fell a-sighing and a-sobbing,
When they heard the bell toll for poor Cock Robin.

Finally, there is my all-time favorite nursery rhyme, *Who Killed Cock Robin?* There is no mystery here, no rhyming for the sake of it as with other children's rhymes we would recite without really knowing what they were about. The sparrow confesses at once, and those animals gathered around poor dead Robin offer in one way or another to help with his burial. There are versions of *Who Killed Cock Robin?* in German and Norwegian, and some scholars suggest that the poem is a parody on the death of William Rufus, who was killed by an arrow in the New Forest (Hampshire) in 1100.

The earliest written record for this rhyme is in *Tommy Thumb's Pretty Songbook*, which was published c.1744, with only the first four verses being printed. Speculation is that "Cock Robin" refers to the political downfall of Sir Robert Walpole, Robin being a diminutive of Robert. Walpole was First Lord of the Treasury and England's first Prime Minister, and his government was toppled in 1742. Walpole had many enemies and *Who Killed Cock Robin?* was a taunt at his downfall.

The extended edition wasn't printed until 1770, and it's this extension of the poem which has led to speculation that *Who Killed Cock Robin?* in its entirety was written to inform the eighteenth century child as to what occurs after someone dies, so that they are familiar with the burial process. After all, at this time, most burials occurred at night when most people, particularly children, were in their beds so that there was no fear of the spread of disease as the body was transported to the graveyard.

The relationship between nursery rhymes and actual historical events or persons is considered by many to be apocryphal but whether you believe there is a political connection or not, it is always fun to speculate!

SOURCES

Alchin, L.K. "Nursery Rhymes: Lyrics, Origins, and History." *ChildhoodHeritage.org.* http://www.childhoodheritage.org/.

Baker, K. "George IV: a Sketch." *History Today*, 2005 55(10): 30–36.

Clarke, John. "George IV," in *The Lives of the Kings and Queens of England*, edited by Antonia Fraser, 225. Alfred A. Knopf, 1975.

Collcutt, Deborah. "Why does the Weasel go Pop?—The Secret Meaning of Our Best-Loved Nursery Rhymes." *MailOnline*, 16 August 2008. http://www.dailymail.co.uk/femail/article-1045841/Why-does-weasel-pop---secret-meaning-best-loved-nursery-rhymes.html.

Harrowven, Jean. *The Origins of Rhymes, Songs and Sayings*. Kaye & Ward, 1977.

"Jack Be Nimble." *Nursery Rhymes from Mother Goose.* http://nurseryrhymesmg.com/rhymes/jack_be_nimble.htm.

McSmith, Andy. "Grand Old Duke: The Greatest Scandal Never Told." *The Independent*, 1 January 2009. http://www.independent.co.uk/news/uk/politics/grand-duke-the-greatest-scandal-never-told-1220042.html.

Miss Cellania. "Who Was the Real 'Georgie Porgie'?" *Neatorama*, 3 August 2011. http://www.neatorama.com/2011/08/03/who-was-the-real-georgie-porgie/.

NPR. "The Real Meaning of Nursery Rhymes." Interview with Debbie Elliott and Chris Roberts. *NPR*, 2005. http://www.npr.org/templates/story/story.php?storyId=4933345.

CELEBRATING BURNS' NIGHT

BY M.M. BENNETTS

O NE OF THE GREAT MYSTERIES OF LIFE TO NON-SCOTS IS HAGGIS. DID I SAY HAGGIS? SORRY. What I meant to say was, today is the birthday of the great Scots poet and national hero, Robert Burns, born in Alloway, Ayrshire, in 1759, the elder of two sons of a tenant farmer.

Although as a lad, Burns had little in the way of formal education—probably two to three years in the local school—he was taught by his father and grew up devouring whatever books came his way, reading all of Shakespeare, Milton, and the Bible. He learned some French. Significantly too, he learned firsthand the traditional ballads, legends, and songs of Scotland.

At this period, Scotland was very much under the thumb of England, with many repressive laws prohibiting expressions of Scots culture—the wearing of tartan was banned and the use of Scots Gaelic had been outlawed, for example—all in response to Bonnie Prince Charlie's failed rebellion in 1745-6. There was a heavy presence of troops quartered on the population, and anti-Scots sentiment ran very high among the English overlords—English slang of the period refers to Scotland as Scratchland.

Nevertheless, our lad, Rab, grows up, starts falling in love with pretty girls (a life-long habit), goes off briefly to study surveying in Kirkoswald, then moves with his family to a farm near the villages of Tarbolton and Mauchline...and by 1783, begins writing poetry.

A couple of flings and a farming failure later, he's being urged by a friend to write for publication. He also meets Jean Armour and things get serious. Jean's father doesn't think much of him, denies that they're married, and eventually has the pair of them publicly reproved in open church for their relationship. Nice. Still, in that same year, 1786, Burns' first book, *Poems Chiefly in the Scottish Dialect*, is published in late July, and in September, Jean gives birth to twins.

So, instead of emigrating to Jamaica as he had planned, Burns visits Edinburgh to arrange for a second edition of his book. There, he finds himself the toast of the Edinburgh literati.

Edinburgh in the late 18th century was at the heart of the Scottish Enlightenment, and was known throughout the western world as a centre of intellectual culture. It's not just that it was home to such writers and thinkers as David Hume or Adam Smith, it also had one of the world's top medical universities, and it had—despite the onerous anti-Scots laws of the age—a vibrant literary salon culture, one conversant with the recent success of the American Revolution and the works of the radical, Thomas Paine. And Burns, for all that he was a peasant's son (and yes, he did make clanking social mistakes and occasionally was too blunt-spoken for anyone's comfort) was seized upon by this crowd of intelligentsia as the voice of the genuine Scots.

He wasn't the first to write in the Scots vernacular (he wrote in Lowland Scots, a.k.a. Lallans)—there had been Allan Ramsay and Robert Fergusson before him. But in a way, Burns and his work embodied the 18th century enlightened ideal of the nobility and honesty of the "natural man" as expressed by Jean-Jacques Rousseau, the French philosopher and author.

Burns' poetry is vibrant, often funny, a celebration of the world of the "people", running the gamut of emotion from alehouse humour to profoundest love. Though not unlettered, he is wholly without the "steeped in classical tradition" artifice that characterises much of the literary work of other 18th century British poets.

He doesn't idolise or worship the natural world; it's just part of life. He's scathing in his attacks on the rigid fundamentalism of the Presbyterian elders of the Kirk (*Address to the Unco Guid* [uncommonly good]). He mocks pretension and hypocrisy wherever he encounters it. Others may write of high sentiment; he writes *To a Louse, on seeing one on a lady's bonnet at church*.

And when he writes of love, which he does frequently (he had a lot of practice), his is the voice of all the longing, beauty, lust, and tenderness combined together. We may think *"My love is like a red, red rose…"* sounds twee or clichéd today, but within the context of the 18th century, its undiluted purity of tenderness and affection stopped readers short, redefining the vocabulary of love for at least the next century.

The Edinburgh edition of Burns' *Poems* was published in April 1787, earning him £500. And this enabled him to tour the Borders and the Highlands.

And, whilst he was travelling about (falling in and out of love), he started collecting Scottish songs—often Scottish fiddlers' songs for which he wrote memorable lyrics—and which he contributed to *The Scots Musical Museum*, a publication which over the next few years printed some 200 of Burns' contributions. So in a very real sense, he preserved Scotland's folk and musical heritage which without him would most certainly have been lost….

In 1788, he acknowledged Jean Armour as his wife, and she gave birth to a second set of twins.

By 1791, his inventive narrative poem, *Tam o' Shanter*, had been published, and Burns had given up farming to move with his family to Dumfries to work as an exciseman.

Burns is probably best known for his poems or songs such as *Auld Lang Syne, My Luve is Like a Red, Red Rose* and *Tam o' Shanter*. But he also wrote the anthems of Scots national pride, *Scots Wha Hae wi' Wallace Bled*, and *Is There for Honest Poverty* with its oft-repeated line, *"A man's a man for a' that"* (which incidentally is just a kind of compilation of French Revolutionary slogans—and for which he was investigated by the authorities and nearly lost his position with the Excise and Custom).

In July 1796, Burns died of a rheumatic heart condition. He was only 37.

But the story doesn't stop there, because his work was taken up by the fledgling Romantic movement of William Wordsworth and Samuel Taylor Coleridge. It also became a powerful element in the Scottish fight-back against Anglicisation as led by Sir Walter Scott in the early years of the 19th century. Defying the law, the gentry and aristocracy started wearing plaid again. Deliberately. And having their portraits painted wearing the kilt and clan badges.

Gradually though, Burns' work was subsumed into the cult of the tartan and genteel Scottiphilia of the Victorians as led by Queen Victoria and Prince Albert, and Burns wasn't fully recognised until the end of the 19th century. In 1885, there were only eight affiliated Burns Clubs. By 1911, there were 200 of these clubs and Burns was seen as the antidote to the romanticised history of Scotland, and the voice of the ordinary Scots.

Which brings us back to the haggis…because every year, as befits the national poet and hero,

Burns' birthday is celebrated with a fierce national fervour throughout Scotland and abroad with a traditional Burns' Supper—a meal designed to commemorate his humble beginnings as a ploughboy laddie.

(Although the "observance" used to be stricter—it used to be men only—now it's slightly more relaxed, though many of the elements remain the same.)

The meal is made up of three courses and they're traditional "peasant" fare: cockie-leekie soup (chicken and leek soup), followed by haggis (Burns wrote a cheeky poem, *Address to a Haggis*), mashed neeps (mashed turnips) and bashed tatties (mashed potatoes), with oatcakes and cheese to finish.

In between each two plates, all around the table, a single bottle of whisky is placed to be shared.

(And before I tell you what haggis is and how it used to be made, may I point out that 18th century Scotland was a poor country, and farmers were desperately poor throughout Europe anyway. Hence, unlike today when we throw lots of everything away, they didn't. They used every part of a slaughtered animal. They couldn't afford not to.)

200 years ago then, haggis was made up of the less than desirable parts of a sheep—the brains and whatever else was left. This is ground and mixed with oatmeal and spices (usually a lot of pepper). The whole is then put into a sheep's intestine and boiled until cooked through. Nowadays, with EU health and safety legislation, it's no longer the off-cuts, but regular mutton that's used. And most local butchers have their own closely guarded secret recipes for the spices.

So that's the menu. The men wear their kilts. Obviously. When the haggis is brought in from the kitchen on a platter, it's accompanied by a piper and piped in. Then comes the solemn honour of piercing the haggis-beastie—which I've seen done with a sword.

Once everyone is served, another of the evening's traditions begins: during the meal, each of the guests is required to recite a Burns poem. Or sing it.

Now the most sensible of guests requests early the privilege of saying grace—and it's Burns' own Selkirk grace which is used. "*Some hae meat and canna eat, and some wad eat that want it, but we hae meat and we can eat, sae let the Lord be thankit.*" And then he settles back to enjoy his meal and his whisky as over the course of the evening, the recitation of the poetry and songs becomes more and more uproarious (due to the quantities of whisky consumed).

And truly, it's a meal and an evening's entertainment where, should Burns himself wander in, he'd find himself most at home.

Finally, as befits a host of one of these fine gatherings, I'd like to recommend a rendition of my most favourite of Burns' songs: *Ca' the Yowes* [Call the Ewes, as sung by Andy M. Stewart: https://www.youtube.com/watch?v=h0rpv9vxbU8]. It's a modest poem, mostly talking about the herding of sheep actually, but in Burns' hands, this is turned into the most heart-felt of love songs, ending with the verse: "*Fair and lovely as thou art, Thou hast stown my very heart: I can die—but canna part, My bonnie dearie.*"

Slainte!

PRONUNCIATION: EIGHTEENTH CENTURY STYLE

BY MIKE RENDELL

IT IS FASCINATING TO CONJECTURE WHAT OUR ANCESTORS WOULD HAVE SOUNDED LIKE—how they spoke, and whether they had a strong accent. We can read what they wrote down, but we can never be sure what their pronunciation was in the era before tape recorders and gramophones! I recall seeing learned articles suggesting that Shakespeare may have spoken with an American accent. (And why not? The accent must have derived from something, somewhere—why not the English Midlands in the 16th century?)

Of course it is difficult to draw conclusions from one indicator—then, as now, there would have been huge variations based upon origin, background, education, and wealth. But I can comment upon how my ancestor Richard Hall chose to speak, or at least, how he aspired to speak, in the 1700s because he wrote down those words which might otherwise trip him up.

The fact that he wrote them down shows how important it was to "speak proper English"—how vital it was to appear different from all those migrants heading into the capital in the middle of the eighteenth century. London's deaths exceeded births, yet the population in London still increased every year, thanks to the drift of men and women seeking work, looking for the streets paved with gold. They came from the villages and towns up and down the country and brought with them the regional accents, colloquial expressions, and slang from their own region. If my 4x-great-grandfather was to succeed in business, he needed to sound the same as his wealthier customers, not the same as a yokel from the shires!

To modern ears some of the pronunciation sounds a bit twee and precious, but think for a minute how accents and pronunciation changes. Think of Her Majesty, who in the sixty years she has adorned the British throne, has altered enormously in the way she pronounces the "Queen's English." Fashions change.

Where the spelling differed from the pronunciation, Richard Hall jotted down the reminders: so, we get "shaze" for "chaise", "dimun" for "diamond", and even "crownor" for "coroner".

I was also intrigued to see that "gold" was pronounced "gould", farthing as "fardun" and daughter was "dawtor" and nurse was "nus". Yes, some of the examples are obvious ("yot" for "yacht"), but on the whole he does come across as a tad affected by modern standards!

Place names and proper nouns were obviously not the same as now: I can just about remember people calling "Cirencester" by the name of "Sissester" and the Somerset village of Congresbury being pronounced "Coomsbury", but although we still talk of "Brummies", we don't call the city "Brummijum" any more. Bartholomew is not, so far as I am aware, pronounced "Bartolomy". And even in Richard's time "Brighthelmstone" was being abbreviated to match the way it was pronounced—"Brighton".

I suppose it boils down to the fact that pronunciation, like spelling, changes over the centuries, as well as from locality to locality. But it does make you think, when a well-educated man like Richard speaks of "hartichokes" rather than "artichokes", and calls his cucumbers "cowcumbers". Step back in time and I might have quite a problem being accepted in polite company as I rather think my ancestor would have fallen about laughing at *my* strangled vowels and plummy pronunciation! Wristband was pronounced "risban", waistcoat was "wescote", and if you were sitting at the table doing your toilet (i.e. attending to your wig, powdering your nose, applying a little white lead to the forehead, and rouge to the cheeks...) you would of course remember to pronounce it "twaylet" or even "twilight".

In some ways you can brand Richard a snob—he cultivated the way he presented himself because he was desperate to be accepted.

The story of Richard's life, how he married an heiress, how he built a shop at One London Bridge, how he fell out with his family and retired to become a gentleman farmer in the Cotswolds, is told in my book, *The Journal of a Georgian Gentleman.*

Steal a Book, Seven Years' Hard Labor Overseas: Transportation as Punishment in the 17th-19th Centuries

BY J.A. BEARD

ENGLAND, LIKE MANY SOCIETIES THROUGHOUT HISTORY, HAS HAD TO STRUGGLE WITH what to do with its criminal population. For a good chunk of English history, punishment was harsh and severe. Executions were common for a number of offenses. The fundamental question of how justice is best served has been explored throughout English history and influenced by shifts in historical, philosophical, and religious beliefs.

With the expansion of British colonial holdings in the 17th century, another option arose: transportation. The idea was simple in concept if occasionally more complicated in execution. Transportation at its core was exile. Instead of local imprisonment, execution, or another punishment, an offender was sent to a distant overseas holding. In this way the home country depleted its criminal population and minimized the resource impact of a growing criminal population.

Transportation was not reserved for the most heinous of offenses such as murder. A variety of crimes, both major and relatively minor, could end up with a criminal being sentenced to transportation. For example, in 1723, one man was sentenced to transportation and an accompanying seven years of labor for stealing a book.

Initially, many criminals were transported to colonies in continental North America and the West Indies. The American Revolution complicated things and ended North America as a popular choice for transportation even for non-rebellious areas. By 1787, British transportation was focused instead on Australia and some other smaller colonial holdings.

Transportation may have been exile at its core, but it was also supposed to serve the needs of the home country beyond that. In addition to the restrictions one might expect, such as the death penalty for those returning from transportation, these sentences typically carried with them a hefty labor requirement. The services expected from the convicts might be directed toward what we'd now call public works projects, or the convicts might end up as indentured servants to free citizens in a colony.

As one might expect, sending people thousands of miles away and never allowing them to return home was going to predispose them to even more anti-social behavior than whatever got them in trouble initially. If they had no hope of any sort of normal life, it would only contribute to the kind of instability and revolts one witnessed with completely enslaved populations. One way of combating this, and also serving the general idea of some form of semi-merciful justice, was to limit the main criminal penalty period to a defined number of years. After the prisoners served their sentences, they would not typically regain all of their rights, but, at minimum, would have enough that they could live a semi-normal life.

Related to the exile of general criminals, a variation on transportation was also used to sell people directly into slavery. Though your standard-issue English criminal probably would end up an indentured servant on a plantation or digging a canal or what not, hundreds of thousands of Irish and Scottish political and war prisoners taken during the 17th century ended up being sold into slavery in the West Indies and this, in some cases, continued in some forms even until nearly the end of the 18th century. Please note that in most cases these were, for all intents and purposes, true slaves and not simple indentured servants.

The interbreeding of Irish and African slaves (who were initially considerably more expensive than Irish slaves) in the West Indies became so extensive that by the end of the 17th century, specific laws were passed to prohibit it. Admittedly, the issue with the Irish and Scottish was more an offshoot of war (and rebellion) between England, Scotland, and Ireland, and even many of the laws concerning their handling were distinct from the various transportation acts passed to cover non-political/war-offenses.

Given our modern view of a more rehabilitative justice system, transportation may seem cruel. Indeed, even being a child did not necessarily protect one from a transportation sentence, though age and size (tiny laborers aren't efficient, after all) were somewhat taken into account. There are, however, documented cases of children as young as seven years old being transported to Australia. It is important to keep in mind, though, that by the standards of the time, transportation was often considered somewhat more lenient than the more common punishments: execution or being sentenced to a disgusting and overcrowded prison on land.

Then, as now, the building of more prisons to give convicted criminals more space wasn't high on the list of societal priorities. In addition, the general English (or general world) attitude toward punishment from the 17th through 19th centuries could more generally be defined as retribution-based rather than rehabilitation-centered. There were such severe issues with prison space that even more disgusting and overcrowded prison ships were used as supplements.

That being said, it's hard not to notice the national self-interest served by thousands upon thousands of cheap laborers being available to help develop new colonies. Transportation would linger, as a punishment, officially until 1868, but for several reasons, including socio-economic and geopolitical changes, it had *de facto* ended years before.

A Shocking Catalogue of Human Depravity: Patrick Colquhoun and the Cataloging of 18th Century London Crime

BY J.A. BEARD

For the bulk of English history, organized and centralized law enforcement was conspicuously lacking, even in London, a city hardly free from crime. Even as the population of the city in the mid-18th century grew to over a half-million souls, policing was a scatter-shot and limited affair due to various cultural factors, including the English population's inherent distrust of the concept of centralized and organized police forces.

In the social, legal, and cultural struggles that led to the rise of these forces, those who wanted more organized police forces first had to persuade the populace, and those in positions of influence, that such groups were even needed. One key player in that task was Patrick Colquhoun.

Colquhoun was, among other things, a former Lord Provost of Glasgow, a businessman, and a trader. Toward the end of the 18th century, he became particularly interested in the issue of crime and became a magistrate in London. During this time he explored the links between crime and socio-economic factors. One of his chief concerns was the idea of preventative policing. He felt that the mere presence of more professional police, particularly in areas around people associated with crime, would contribute to a reduction in crime. While many, if not all modern police forces, make heavy use of this concept, at the time it was considered a bit radical in England.

It's not necessarily that the English didn't believe in the idea of preventative policing or think it couldn't work, but more that they were very concerned the cost to personal liberty would not be worth it. The English of the time distrusted the idea of centralized and organized police almost as much as they did large standing armies. The French had such a system, which also included heavy spying on the public, something that did little to raise the esteem of the concept among the English public.

Colquhoun's studies led him to write several works on the subject, the most influential of which was his *Treatise on the Police of the Metropolis*. In this work he strongly argued for the need for centralized police authorities. While that concept was not unique at the time or pioneered by Colquhoun, his book was unusual in that it attempted to bolster his argument by giving detailed statistics on the state of crime of London. Indeed, he referred to the *Treatise* as a *"shocking catalogue of human depravity"* and hoped that his data would show that police reform wasn't just a good idea but a necessity to save a city sliding into moral decay.

The *Treatise* didn't just give simple numbers of criminals. It broke down crimes into specific categories to let the full range of criminality be known. For example:

> *1. Professed Thieves, Burglars, Highway Robbers, Pick-Pockets and River Pirates, who are completely corrupted; —many of whom have finished their education in the Hulks, and some at Botany Bay: N.B. There will be an increase of this class on the return of Peace, now estimated at about: 2000.*

Hulks, incidentally, were prison ships. Botany Bay was the name of an Australian penal colony (even though the actual colony ended up being located elsewhere).

Everything from gambling foreigners to gin-drinkers were included. Some categories are a bit uncomfortable for modern readers in that they may be more reflective of the prejudices of the time than objective presentations of criminality, such as counts of *"itinerant Jews…holding out temptations to pilfer and steal."* Of course, the world's oldest profession was included: *"20. Unfortunate Females of all descriptions, who support themselves chiefly or wholly by prostitution: 50,000."*

In total, he came up with 115,000 people who were *"supposed to support themselves in and near the metropolis by pursuits either criminal—illegal—or immoral."* The population of London at that the time was a little over 950,000. He also included detailed information on the estimated losses to the public from theft, fraud, robbery, et cetera. For example, he claimed that Thames-related thefts alone totaled over 500,000 pounds a year, which, depending on what estimate of inflation one uses, would be between 40-400 million in today's pounds.

The numbers, both crimes and monetary losses, shocked the public. Many people dismissed them and claimed Colquhoun was exaggerating. It's hard for us to judge the accuracy of the figures. He was attempting to do a systematic analysis, but various modern tools, such as advanced statistical sampling and population error analysis, weren't available to him.

Colquhoun based his numbers mostly on sampling from his time as a magistrate. He even went so far to suggest that his numbers were actually low-ball estimates as he excluded certain classes of "delinquency" that might still account for a significant number of people.

Whether or not Colquhoun's numbers were completely accurate, they had a tremendous impact. Many people began to see more of a need for police. That being said, the culture was still very much against centralized policing. A strong and centralized police force, it was feared, would ride rough-shod over the rights and freedoms of the citizens. Although various additional social factors, government bureaucracy, and the war with Napoleon pulled attention and effort away from the idea of strengthening, organizing, and centralizing police by the government, merchants worried about river thefts took notice.

Colquhoun, with the aid of influential utilitarian philosopher Jeremy Bentham and John Harriot, a Justice of the Peace and mariner, secured funding in 1797 to form a professional Thames River Police force to help curtail the rampant cargo theft afflicting the Thames and merchants.

While it might seem odd on first brush that a philosopher was involved in the formation of the police force, it's important to note that utilitarian ideas concerning cost-benefit analysis of moral and ethical issues, along with its emphasis on careful analysis, were very influential on

Colquhoun's approach to criminology. Bentham himself was considerably interested in social reform, and the reform of crime and punishment was part of that.

The River Police were based heavily on the ideas of preventative policing. Although this police force met with extreme resistance and even violence on occasion, they were successful enough that the government would eventually take control of them and make them into a public policing entity by 1800. The influence of the *Treatise* itself would be cited in later decades as more generalized, centralized, organized public police forces were formed.

BRITAIN'S CROSS-DRESSING WOMEN

BY LINDA COLLISON

WOMEN PRETENDING TO BE MEN CROP UP REGULARLY IN ENGLISH AND IRISH LITERA-
ture and contemporary dramatic productions. A recent film starring American actress
Glenn Close as Albert Nobbs is based on a short story by 19th century Irish writer George Moore.

Albert Nobbs is the story of a nineteenth century British woman of illegitimate birth who
portrays herself as a man in order to get work. The movie has been Glenn Close's passion project
for fifteen years and was released in January 2012. You can watch trailers of it on the Internet.

Women passing as men are tantalizing archetypes as old as the Cheviot Hills. Most real
women who dressed as men did so primarily for economic opportunities. I believe it may have
been more common than we know, back in a time when a woman depended upon a man for her
livelihood and her legal status.

Most of us have heard of Anne Bonny and Mary Read, infamous British pirates of the early
18th century. These two didn't actually pretend to be men but dressed in trousers and lived the
rough life of pirates alongside their partners and lovers, the most ruthless of men. (Although,
Mary Read was raised as a boy, so she may have had some gender issues....)

Less well known is Christian Cavanagh, an Irish-born mother who disguised herself as
a man and operated under several aliases including Welch, Welsh, Jones, Davies, and Mother
Ross. Daniel Defoe, an author with empathy for women as evidenced by his 18th century
novels *Moll Flanders* and *Roxanna, the Fortunate Mistress*, chronicled her life in *Mother Ross: The
Life and Adventures of Mrs. Christian Davies, commonly called Mother Ross on Campaign with the
Duke of Marlborough*. No pirate, she!

After the disappearance of her husband, Christian left her children in the care of her
mother and a nurse and pursued him into the army. Dressed as a man, she first volunteered
as a foot soldier and fought at the Battle of Laden during the Nine Years' War, where she was
wounded, captured, and exchanged without being discovered as female. She later re-joined
another campaign as a trooper of the 4th Dragoons where she served from 1701 to 1706 when
she was wounded in action again—and this time discovered.

Hannah Snell was a young Englishwoman who also went in search of her man who had run
off. She ended up serving as a soldier and as a marine for a many years until she too, was wounded
and found out. Hannah was honorably discharged and granted a pension in 1750 (increased in
1785), a rare thing in those days. A good account of Hannah Snell and two other women who
served in the British Navy can be found in *Lady Tars* (a Fireship Press reprint). There may have
been many more such women who never were detected because they were never wounded.

Patricia, natural daughter of an 18th century Barbadian cane planter, poses as *Patrick* in the
fictional Patricia MacPherson Nautical Adventure Series. Inspired by *Star-Crossed*, originally published by Knopf/Random House and republished by Fireship Press, the idea for the character came

to me in the middle of the Pacific Ocean aboard the *HM Bark Endeavour*, a replica of Captain James Cook's famous vessel, on which I served as a voyage crew member in 1999.

While climbing the rigging to make and furl sail, heaving on hempen lines as thick as my wrist in unison with my mates, and taking my turn at the helm, I discovered a woman really could perform the same work as a man aboard a ship during the age of sail. But why would she, I wondered? And how might she pull it off? Answering these questions has led to many years of research about the Royal Navy during the 18th century and other aspects of colonialism.

Romance and adventure aside, in a man's world some women chose to become men rather than turn to the poorhouse or prostitution. It must've been a tough choice but not without its rewards.

THE WIG BUSINESS WAS BIG BUSINESS IN 18TH CENTURY FRANCE

BY LUCINDA BRANT

IT IS OFTEN ASSUMED THAT THE WIG OF THE 17TH AND 18TH CENTURIES WAS THE PRESERVE of the aristocracy, *"an aristocratic ornament of Old Regime Europe"*, a marker of high birth and status worn by the privileged few. Indeed, at the French Courts of Louis XIII and Louis XIV, wigs were very much part of the display of power and status.

(Wig here refers to the wigs worn by men. Women's hair is not discussed in this post.)

The full-bottom wigs worn by Louis XIV of France required ten heads of long human hair to achieve one luxuriant wig with an over-abundance of flowing locks. Cost consideration aside, how to wear such an article in everyday life made it prohibitive to all but the most aristocratic, fashion-conscious courtier.

Yet, by the end of Louis XIV's reign in 1715, the wearing of wigs had spread throughout France. Surprisingly, wigs were not the exclusive preserve of noble courtiers but had *"tumbled down the social hierarchy"*, so far down, in fact, that by the mid 1700s wigs were upon the heads of tutors, bakers, messengers, servants, cooks, and shopkeepers. All wore a wig, and often owned two—one for every day and one for Sunday best.

The Marquis of Mirabeau lamented,

> *Everyone* [in Paris] *has become a Monsieur. On Sunday, a man came up to me wearing black silk clothes and a well-powdered wig, and as I fell over myself offering him compliments, he introduced himself as the oldest son of my blacksmith or saddler; will such a seigneur deign to dance in the streets?*

The male wig became big business in the 18th century. It was no longer an aristocratic affectation or worn only by certain non-aristocratic professional groups such as judges, lawyers, and clergymen. The wig was not confined to men in the city but spread to towns and villages. As well as every town having a wigmaker or three, estimates put the number of journeymen who trudged the roads of rural France selling wigs at 10,000.

The account books of French wigmakers attest to a customer base that included not only the wealthy merchant citizens of the town but also priests, petty clerks, and shopkeepers, and in the death inventories of middle class citizens, wigs figured as prominent possessions. The wig was such a universal object of consumption by mid-century that it became synonymous not with luxury but with convenience.

Wig advertisements stressed comfort and appeal as most important when considering the purchase of a wig. Wigmakers were keen to emphasize the free movement of the head of the 18th century wig. Unlike its predecessor, the full bottom wig, which restricted its wearer's movements and peripheral vision, an 18th century wig permitted the wearer to carry out his daily life as if he was wearing his own head of hair, not someone else's.

The Parisian wigmaker Neuhaus asserted that wearing a wig was far more convenient than looking after natural hair. Well, he would, wouldn't he? He's in the business of selling wigs! But he went to great lengths to ensure his customers felt comfortable in their wigs. He announced the invention of a new *"elastic skin that grips the wig"* without any irritating loops or garters, and *"this skin has the softness of velvet, and does not at all inconvenience the head."*

In some respects, Neauhaus's assertion regarding the convenience of the wig over a natural head of hair was true, given the prevalence of head lice, the lack of shampoo and intermittent bathing practices. It was far easier for a man to have his head shaved and wear a wig than to groom his own hair, particularly when, for a small fee, he could have his barber maintain his shaven head and have his wig serviced by his local wigmaker.

With wigs being the universal male consumer product of the 1700s, and everyone from shopkeeper to king wearing one, men were spoiled for choice. While a shop boy might only be able to afford one wig, and thus had to choose wisely and for durability, those of the one percent of the population, the nobleman and the wealthy merchant, could afford to own dozens of wigs. If they considered themselves to be a leader of fashion, were eccentric, or merely had the money to indulge a whim, they could purchase wigs that others could only dream of owning (or not, as the case may be!).

It has often been assumed that every man wore a powdered wig, but this was not so. For everyday wear and for most occasions, men wore their wigs in their natural state, which was unpowdered natural hair. Only on the most formal of occasions, when the nobility attended court or a formal function, were wigs powdered.

Another misconception is that because wigs looked like wigs (you could tell it was a wig!) then the wig must have been made from horsehair. Not so. All the evidence—portraits, surviving wigs, engravings, documents, letters—suggest that less than half of all wigs consisted of hair from horses, and from such animals as goats and cows. Most wigs were made from human hair. For the shop boy, however, the "horse-hair tie wig" was probably his only option.

There were a small number of wigmakers who were prepared to experiment with other materials, and often because of this found themselves ostracized by their fellow wigmakers. Yet, the experimental wig attracted the eccentric, the dandy, and the jaded gentlemen. Looking for something different to make them stand out in the crowd or as a mark of their wealth, these gentlemen were not afraid to parade about society and garner the stares of amazement, incredulity, and puzzlement of others about the hairpiece atop their heads.

Horace Walpole, that great 18th century letter writer and gossip, who collected fascinating tidbits about Society, wrote in a letter dated 1751, about Edward Wortley Montagu's odd manner of dressing, commenting *"that the most curious part of his dress, which he has brought from Paris, is an iron wig; you literally would not know it from hair...."*

Naturally, I just had to give one of my characters an iron wig and so the eccentric poet Hilary Wraxton in *Salt Bride* gets to wear one at a recital, causing hilarity and disruption to an afternoon's entertainments.

Made from iron wire turned into spiral curls, such a wig could also be made of copper. While Edward Wortley Montagu may have thought he cut quite a figure in English society parading about in his iron wig, one wigmaker advertised an iron wig as being economical because it can *"withstand rain, wind and hail, and all without causing discomfort to the wearer."* (I wonder about that final claim.)

Feathers were also used in the making of wigs, particularly sporting wigs. Wigs made from the tails of mallards or drakes were said to be not only durable but could also fight off the wet. Some parsons' wigs employed feathers at the front and were known as "feather tops". One can imagine the congregation doing its best to keep a straight face with a parson at the pulpit in a fine feather top wig delivering the Sunday sermon.

Most sectors of male society succumbed to the wearing of a wig in 18th century France. Testament to the wig's universality was its necessity. Without a wig, a gentleman's outfit was incomplete; he could not go about his daily business out in the world without his wig—just as in the 21st century, a man's business suit is not complete without a tie. An 18th century bewigged gentleman wished to project an air of elegance and refinement, no matter his station in life, and this is evidenced in the many portraits that survive of handsome chaps in frock coat, breeches, and perfectly fitted wig. Whether as part of a family group or in a singular pose, the wig helped make the man. As to the many styles created for the gentleman's wig, that requires a whole other post!

SOURCES

Bender, A. "Hair and Hairdos of the Eighteenth Century." http://www.marquise.de/en/1700/howto/frisuren/frisuren.shtml.

Briand, Pablo and Gustavo Briand. "The Hair at the Eighteenth Century." *The History of the World of Hair.* http://thehistoryofthehairsworld.com/hair_18th_century.html.

Cunnington, Willet and Phillis Cunnington. "Handbook of English Costume in the Eighteenth Century." *The English Century Garb Homepage.* http://www.theweebsite.com/18c-garb/1750.html.

Kwass, Michael. "Big Hair: A Wig History of Consumption in Eighteenth-Century France." *American Historical Review* 111 (June 2006).

Walpole, Horace. *The Letters of Horace Walpole*, Vols. 1-4. Edited by Charles Duke Yonge. London: Putnam and Sons, 1890.

Woodforde, John. *The Strange Story of False Hair.* London: Routledge and Kegan Paul, 1971.

GORGEOUS GEORGIAN METROSEXUALS, OR HOW TO STRUT YOUR METROSEXUAL STUFF IN GEORGIAN ENGLAND

BY **LUCINDA BRANT**

THE TERM "METROSEXUAL" WAS COINED BY MARK SIMPSON TO DESCRIBE A MAN (ESPE-cially one living in an urban, post-industrial, capitalist culture) who spends a lot of time and money on his appearance. *Urban Dictionary* definition number 5 states: *"A straight guy who's so cool, smart, attractive, stylish, and cultured, that everyone thinks he's gay. But he's so secure in his masculinity that he doesn't care."* Both these definitions can be applied to wealthy men in the 18th century who had time and money to spare.

Throughout English (and French) history there have been men such as this, but it wasn't until the 1700s when the aristocracy and the upper echelons of the wealthier merchant middle class had the time and money that the metrosexual truly came into his own. Men aspiring to be gentlemen spent as much time and money fussing about their looks and what to wear as did women, and the evidence is there in their clothes, daily practices, and accoutrements.

With minor modification to *Urban Dictionary's* definition of what it is to be a metrosexual today, here is my list (not definitive) of what it took for a gentleman in 18th century England to be classified as a Gorgeous Georgian Metrosexual.

You were "metrosexual" if:

You employ a French hair stylist instead of a barber, because barbers don't do pomade and powder.

You own at least twenty pairs of shoes, just as many pairs of shoe buckles—some diamond encrusted—half a dozen pairs of gloves (in every shade), and you always carry in your frock coat pocket an enameled snuffbox and a quizzing glass.

You aren't afraid to use padding in your stockings, if necessary, to enhance your male attributes. Strong, large calf muscles are a must. (What were you thinking I meant?)

You cultivate white hands and polished nails; so necessary when taking a pinch of snuff and standing about showing off your calf muscles in mixed company.

You would never, ever be seen in public without your cravat; same goes for hair powder when attending balls and routs.

You know and care just as much about dress fabrics, color, and weave as your wife and are not afraid to share your expert opinion with anyone.

You don't rise before 11 a.m., and then you sit around in your embroidered silk banyan and matching turban half the day sipping chocolate and sorting through cards of invitation.

You can't imagine life without your valet.

Despite being flattered (even proud) that gay guys hit on you, you still find the thought of actually getting intimate with another man unappealing.

Thus, for all your peacocking, you are quintessentially male. You carry a sword and know how to use it, are good with your fists, love blood sports, shooting, horse racing, and playing cards at your club with male chums.

Dressed in a salmon pink silk embroidered frock coat with matching silk breeches, old gold embroidered silk waistcoat, lace ruffles at your wrists to showcase your white hands, white clocked stockings to set off your massive calf muscles, an elaborately tied lace cravat, powder in your hair, a mouche at the corner of your mouth and wearing diamond buckled shoes with a heel, you watch women swoon at the sight of you! Why? Because underneath that gorgeous metrosexual exterior is a real man just waiting to get his gear off!

Flip, Shrub, and Other Drinks Favored of Georgian Londoners

by TIM QUEENEY

WHILE RESEARCHING MY NOVEL *GEORGE IN LONDON*, SET IN 1751, I CAME ACROSS MANY intriguing types of food enjoyed by Londoners of the Georgian era. Among the most colorful of these were the names of popular drinks. From small beer and perry to flip and shrub, the drinks of 18th century London often carried names whimsical to our modern ears.

Take rum fustian, for example. It's a wonderfully old-fashioned name. Not one you're likely to hear today. If it was, you might at least expect you were getting a rum drink. But you would be wrong. Rum fustian was made with a quart of strong beer, a pint of gin, a bottle of sherry, and twelve eggs, smoothly mixed and flavored with nutmeg, lemon, and sugar.

The key element in the fustian was gin. A distilled liquor that uses juniper berries for flavoring, gin was a wildly popular drink in Georgian London, so popular and so cheap—you could buy a large quantity for only a penny—there were fears that English society would collapse due to the drunkenness, illness, and death brought on by widespread gin abuse during the Gin Craze.

Artist William Hogarth's engraving "Gin Lane" shows the state of alarm many people felt about the Gin Craze. Gin consumption was rampant from the 1730s to roughly 1750 when the Gin Craze began to taper off. As Rosamond Bayne-Powell writes in *Eighteenth Century London Life*, "*...working men went into gin shops on Saturday night, and were found lying dead drunk on the pavement the next morning.*"

Along with gin, the other widely consumed drink in London was beer. In 1725, Londoners drank 1,970,989 barrels of strong beer. London had, by one eighteenth century count, 207 inns, 447 taverns, 5,875 beerhouses and 8,659 brandy shops dispensing beer and other drink. If that prodigious amount of strong beer was imbibed, what was small beer? As its name suggests, small beer had a low alcohol content and was considered fit for servants and children. This dispensing of beer to children, while alarming by modern standards, wasn't quite as callous as it sounds. Water supplies in the eighteenth century were often dangerously contaminated. The alcohol in small beer was usually sufficient to kill deadly micro-organisms.

Wine was also popular. Since Britain was often at war with France in the eighteenth century, French wine could be hard to come by. The solution was Portuguese wine, including wines shipped from the city of Oporto, hence the name "port" for wine from Portugal.

The 1725 numbers had London consuming 30,000 tuns of wine. A tun was a large barrel holding roughly 256 gallons or about 960 liters. Thus, the 30,000 tuns equaled about 7,680,000 gallons of wine.

What about the other colorful drink names? Perry was a drink made from pears, much as hard cider was made from apples. Shrub was a drink made with a "shrub" or concentrate of orange or lemon juice mixed with sugar and rum. Toddy was hot black tea to which was added sugar or honey, cloves or cinnamon, and whiskey. And porter was a type of dark beer brewed with dark malts. It was from porter that stout evolved.

Perhaps the quaintest name for an eighteenth century drink enjoyed by Londoners is flip. Flip was made by mixing ale with sugar, adding eggs and a spice such as nutmeg or cinnamon, and pouring in a liberal portion of rum or whiskey. Then the liquid was made to "flip" or froth by immersing a red-hot poker from the fire. This was a popular drink with sailors, and Darius Attucks, the mariner who accompanies young George Washington on his adventure in London in my book *George in London*, would likely have had flip often.

During George and Darius' adventure in London, they attend a gala ball at the house of George's patron, the Baron Mowenholtz. Darius describes the refreshments for the guests:

> *The back hall nearest the kitchen was provided with several long tables and lit by four candelabras. Across the tables was arrayed a rich selection of sweet meats, roasts of beef, quails, pigeon pie, cold mutton, veal chops, Colchester oysters, ox palates, pickled whiting, turtle soup, peas, boiled potatoes, leeks, apples, oranges, plums, cheeses both white and yellow, loaves of bread, cakes, syllabubs, Atholl Brose, fruit pies and tarts. To drink were bottles of cherry wine, a bowl of brandy punch, fustian punch, mulled wine, French claret, Madeira Sack, heavy port wine, porter, ale, gin and rum—as this last was a sailor's spirit, I fancied the baron had provided it for my benefit and so availed myself aplenty.*

A Midnight Masquerade
in 18th Century London

BY **LINDA COLLISON** *(DISGUISED AS A SHIP SURGEON'S MATE)*

"**D**O YOU KNOW ME?" THE BLACK DOMINO, A MASKED FIGURE WEARING A FULL LENGTH hooded cloak, croaks as we present our tickets and enter the Haymarket masquerade in our costumes. We exchange glances; indeed, we do not know if the cloaked figure is a friend or a stranger. Yet the domino seems to know *us* (or is he or she just bluffing?) Feeling bold in our disguises, we answer flirtatiously and dart away, losing ourselves in the crowd. The great theater is filled with *masks* (an 18th century figure of speech for people wearing masks). Many liberties will be taken and much mischief will happen here tonight, mark my words!

The English word "masquerade" is of foreign origin and had come into common usage by the second decade of the 18th century when the masquerade as a commercial entertainment became established in London. Advertised in newspapers, the event required attendees to purchase a ticket. Count Heidegger is credited with the development of the public masquerade in England as a capitalist venture. Stylized and commercialized, these urban masquerades were a vestige of the ancient carnival.

In one form or another, ritualized disguise has been around for a very long time and is an important part of many cultures. The 18th century masquerade, like those of Renaissance-era Venice, allowed the different levels of society to mix and mingle. When in costume, one is free to say and do things one wouldn't ordinarily do. There was a lot of excitement associated with these masquerades, as well as license taken. They were an excuse to speak one's mind, express one's secret self, flirt, fondle, or be carried away. Masquerades brought out the exhibitionist or the voyeur in all who attended.

"I love a masquerade," wrote Harriette Wilson in her memoir of the period, *"because a female can never enjoy the same liberty anywhere else."*

Rooted in medieval English and Celtic festivals such as May Day, Midsummer's Eve, All Hallows' Eve, and the Christmas Gambol, the Masquerade developed into an urban phenomenon in 18th century England, influenced by the carnivals of Venice.

The 18th century London masquerade enjoyed both popularity and reproof throughout the 1700s. Many novelists, including Henry Fielding, Francis Burney, Maria Edgeworth, and Daniel Defoe all made use of the masquerade as a setting for intrigue. Sometimes shocking things happened at masquerades, including prostitution and rape, and many essayists and religious reformers railed against them.

Three types of costumes predominated in London's 18th century masquerades. The "domino" was a neutral costume, a great hooded cloak that totally enveloped the body. Worn with a mask or a hood, it was a complete disguise but a generic one. "Fancy dress" was the second general category, including a wide array of character types (milkmaids, clerical figures, military officers, exotic foreigners such as Turks, Orientals, or pirates). The third type were costumes meant to portray a particular character, a specific individual. The goddess Diana, Van Dyke, Rubens and his wife, Harlequin and Punch, Don Quixote, Henry the VIII, Mary, Queen of Scots, and Old Harry himself were ubiquitous characters at London masquerades of the period.

"There is something inherently appealing in the idea of the masquerade—an ineluctable charm in the notion of disguising oneself in a fanciful costume and moving through a crowd of masked strangers," writes historian Terry Castle in *Masquerade and Civilization: The Carnivalesque in Eighteenth-Century English Culture and Fiction.* This excellent scholarly work is a must for students of the 18th century British novel.

Personally, if I weren't an author I would surely be an actress. I love the adventure of putting on a disguise and pretending to be someone else, exploring the world in someone else's shoes. Come to think of it, that might explain why I am compelled to write fiction....

I have not yet employed the public masquerade in my novels, but the theme of disguise figures prominently into my historical fiction.

Feeling a Little Flushed, Dear? (The Invention of the Flush Toilet)

BY **MIKE RENDELL**

I HAVE ALWAYS WANTED TO WRITE A TRULY LAVATORIAL POST FOR THIS BLOG, AND THIS IS it—the story of the flush toilet!

Its origins lay back in Elizabethan times when in 1596 Sir John Harington came up with his mighty Ajax (his name for a flushing privy). His invention was therefore the very first "john". The Ajax closet (a pun on the fact that "a jakes" was the medieval name for a toilet) consisted of a seat perched over a brick tank with a cistern of water which could be directed by means of a valve being opened. Once a week it was necessary to empty the contents of the closet into a cesspool. Harington made two, one for himself and one for his godmother, who happened to be Queen Elizabeth.

Harington published a book entitled *The Anatomy of the Metamorphosed Ajax* giving builders details of how to build his privy. The Frontispiece reads: *"How unsavoury places may be made sweet, noysome places may be made wholesome, filthy places made cleanly"*. Harington never got over the ridicule and scorn heaped upon him for his invention, and in particular for having written a book about it, and it never caught on.

People continued to use the "close stool", and it appears in all its glory in a number of Gillray's cartoons. It was perfectly acceptable to show a caricature of the monarch (George III) sitting next to his Queen on a toilet, while courtiers rushed to and fro!

By the second half of the 18th century the world was finally ready for the flush toilet. The saviour had come in the form of Alexander Cumming, a watchmaker who in 1775 patented his design. This consisted of a pan with a sliding valve at the bottom called the Strap, which could be released by the user at the same time as water was delivered from a cistern operated by a separate tap.

Around this time a young locksmith and cabinet maker called Joseph Bramah appeared on the scene. He was working with a Mr. Allen, installing closets based upon the Cummings patent, when Mr. Allen decided on a few improvements aimed at stopping the water freezing in cold weather. He replaced the Strap with a hinged flap which sealed the base of the bowl.

To Allen should go the credit, but to young Bramah went the patent. He opened a factory in Denmark Street, St. Giles, and throughout the next century the Bramah factory poured out the new-fangled sanitary ware. They were generally housed in fine mahogany furniture, and there is a particularly fine example to be seen in Kew Palace, and another at the residence of Queen Victoria at Osbourne House on the Isle of Wight.

It wasn't long before potters like Josiah Wedgwood got in on the act. Wedgwood designed his first decorated closet pan in around 1777. Small wonder they became status symbols with their beautiful designs. Mind you, there was no sewerage system to go with them, so "the problem" of the effluent was merely moved further downstream, so to speak.

Fortunately, another design improvement hit the market in 1782 when the stink trap was introduced by John Gallait. This consisted of a water trap (similar to a modern bottle trap). Unfortunately, it was impossible to keep clean…but at least it was a step in the right direction.

And what of Thomas Crapper, widely believed to have invented the flush toilet? Well, he wasn't even born until 1836 and, in fact, what he invented was the ballcock. And no, he didn't give his name to the human waste we all associate with his name—"crap" had been in use for some time, although quite possibly it became fashionable because of the association with his toilets.

The story has it that American servicemen, visiting these shores in the First World War, popularised the phrase "going to the Crapper" because that was the name in the bowl! Try telling that to the compilers of the *Oxford English Dictionary*, who point out that the word was in use in its modern sense by 1846, probably deriving from the Old French "crappe" meaning waste.

Post script: "spending a penny"? Look no further than the Great Exhibition of 1851 where visitors wishing to avail themselves of the facilities (known as Monkey Closets and designed by George Jennings) were obliged to part with one penny for the privilege.

So there you have it: if the characters in your novel need to visit the "smallest room", you know what was historically accurate!

A Time to Reflect—on Mirrors

By MIKE RENDELL

It is interesting that when my ancestor Richard Hall was writing in 1781 about a mirror it was the old frame which got thrown away, to be replaced with a "New Carv'd Gilt frame"—while the actual glass was kept. Why? Because mirrors were extremely costly.

Mirrors had of course been around for several thousand years, originally using polished bronze or similar materials. But in the sixteenth century, Venetian glassmakers on Murano found a way of coating the back of a sheet of glass with silver mercury.

Rivals stole the method of production and brought it to France, Germany, and particularly England, so that by the 1700s London had a thriving mirror-making industry.

Cheap it was not—and it was also highly dangerous, since mercury is an extremely unstable and dangerous chemical to work with.

The process was quite complicated. First you needed a stone table which was completely level (so that mercury would not run off when poured), but the table had to be capable of being tilted gently. Then you needed a completely flat sheet of tin, moulded to give a gulley running all round its four sides(to catch the mercury as it drained). The tin was tied securely to the table. A small amount of mercury would then be spread across the surface and rubbed gently into the surface of the tin (traditionally using a hare's foot).

The next stage was to pour mercury over this prepared surface to a depth of between three and six millimetres. It needed to be as evenly spread as possible. Then came the difficult part—lowering the glass sheet onto the mercury so that it floated. The weight of the glass would force the mercury out to the gulley running round the tin sheet where it could be collected and used again. A blanket would be placed over the glass and weights used to press down the glass. The stone table would then be tilted, and the whole shebang left to dry for three weeks. The critical moment would come when the glass was lifted from the table—apparently even a loud noise could cause the mercury to run off from the back of the glass, with potentially fatal consequences. Death by inhalation of mercury fumes was not uncommon in factories where mirrors were made.

Small wonder therefore that a mirror or looking glass was an expensive item, certainly one which it was worthwhile for Richard to spend one pound eleven shillings and sixpence to re-frame (perhaps nearer a hundred pounds in modern terms).

The chemical process of coating a glass surface with metallic silver was not discovered until thirty years after Richard's death. The actual inventor is a matter of dispute, but one candidate is the German, Justus von Liebig, who published an article in 1835 remarking that *"...when aldehyde is mixed with a silver nitrate solution and heated, a reduction is formed, as a result of which the silver settles itself on the wall of the vessel, forming a superb mirror."*

In Richard's time, mercury-backed mirrors came in all shapes and sizes. The woodcarver

Grinling Gibbons made intricately carved frames to go with his mirrors, but in the eighteenth century the adornment to the frames was often painted rather than carved. They became part and parcel of the design of the fireplace. Designers such as Robert Adams would produce schemes for fireplaces with a matching mirror and frame above it, sometimes reaching to the ceiling.

Mirrors designed to go above a fireplace were known as chimney glasses, while those intended to go between two sets of windows were called pier glasses. It became fashionable in the eighteenth century to have mirrored sconces—wall fittings to hold a candle but with a mirror at the back to reflect light back into the room. Later in the century cheval glasses came into fashion. According to *Encyclopaedia Britannica*:

> *The cheval glass was first made toward the end of the 18th century. The glass could be tilted at any angle by means of the swivel screws supporting it, and its height could be adjusted by means of lead counterweights and a horse, or pulley, from which the name was taken. Thomas Sheraton in the 1803 edition of The Cabinet Dictionary, included a design with a nest of drawers at one side and another with a writing surface. When wardrobes were fitted with mirrored doors, the cheval glass became unnecessary in bedrooms.*

Meanwhile, my great-great-great-great-grandfather Richard Hall would have sat at his dressing table in his bedroom, attending to his toilet (or perhaps, as he would have said, his "twaylit") using his tilting adjustable mirror (which I still use). It makes you ponder on the transient nature of an image to think it was once his visage which reflected in the looking glass, and now it is mine!

CURRENCY IN THE SECOND
HALF OF THE 18TH CENTURY

BY MIKE RENDELL

IT IS ONE OF THE MOST BASIC OF EVERYDAY OCCURRENCES: YOU NEED TO PAY FOR SOMETHING, using cash. But what coins would have been in the purse of your average hero or heroine in the second half of the 18th century? If you want to be authentic, it may help to look at what was, and was not, in circulation.

First, it is interesting to look at inflation during the period 1750 to 1800 to see what buying power money would have had. A useful instant conversion giving the "value" of, say, one hundred pounds in different years is shown at the National Archives website: www.nationalarchives.gov.uk/currency/results.asp.

£100 in **1750** would have the buying power of £8500 (as of 2005 values).

By **1780** this had been whittled down to £6285.

By **1790** it had dropped to £5603.

In **1800** (with the effect of the war with France firing up inflation) it was £3217.

This demonstrates that "the pound in your pocket" had slumped in value by well over fifty per cent in half a century.

Where were the coins made? At the Tower of London. It may seem odd to us, but the public were actually allowed into the Tower to see the Royal Mint in operation. This was the only place in use as an official Mint, all the earlier provincial mints having been abandoned. Hence my ancestor records, *"April 25, 1771, went with General Whitmore, Mr and Mrs Snooke, Mr Gifford and my Wife to see the Mint at the Tower"*.

Put to one side the question of bank notes. Although they had been introduced by the Bank of England a century earlier, they were only used in high denominations. For instance, from 1725 onwards there were notes of 20, 25, 30 and upwards in multiples of ten pounds to a hundred pounds, and then in multiples of a hundred to five hundred pounds. Above that there was a note having a value of a thousand pounds.

These were huge sums, and although the really wealthy might have access to these notes, they were never in general use. Indeed, the public wanted to "feel the value" and expected their currency to equate to the inherent value of the metal their money was made from.

For centuries there had been no problem: gold was worth twenty times its equivalent weight in silver, and silver was worth 12 times that of humble copper. These relative values were reflected in the age-old division of the pound into twenty shillings, and the shilling into a dozen pennies. But these divisions came under huge strain with the inflationary pressures—particularly affecting the price of silver.

A shortage of that precious metal marked the second half of the century. The silver mines in the Southwest of England had become exhausted, the Seven Years' War had cut off supplies from the continent, and the price of silver rocketed. The Royal Mint knew it could not reduce the size of the silver coins as they were already tiny—a silver penny weighed just half a gram and was only a few millimetres across. The public had never liked the idea of a debased coinage, so the Mint took the easy option: it didn't make any silver coins, year after year after year!

During the period 1760 to 1800, it would, therefore, be quite wrong to refer to a "newly minted" crown (5/-) or half-crown (2/6d) because they weren't made at all.

My ancestor specifically refers to holding on to "a Carolus" (Latin for Charles), meaning a crown coin from the reign of Charles II. I still have the coin, and it is so worn that the portrait is barely discernible.

And so it was with all the coins—those in circulation got older and more indistinct, making it easy for forgers to issue silvery metal blanks as counterfeits. No shillings were issued (other than a special batch designed for Ireland) apart from in 1787 when coins to a face value of £50,000 were issued in shillings and sixpences. For the rest of the time—virtually no silver at all. Gold was coined fairly regularly, mostly "spade guineas" having a face value of 21 shillings. These were frequently counterfeited, using brass gaming tokens of the identical size and similar design.

The spade guinea and the worthless gaming token with a completely impossible date of 1701 (George did not become king until 1760) might easily confuse the public—particularly if offered in change after dark or by candlelight in the gloom of a counting house at the back of the shop.

In the first half of George III's reign there were no pound coins (twenty shillings), but a quarter guinea appeared for a year in 1762, and a third of a guinea coin (seven shillings) appeared in 1797. By then, the Bank of England had introduced one and two-pound notes, but it is worth remembering that a pound was still a lot of money.

My ancestor records paying his barber Edward Slatter "for shaving this whole year two guineas" (plus a shilling paid to the barber's son as his Christmas Box). Shaving was of course a whole-of-head task (i.e. not just the face) to enable a wig to be worn comfortably.

In 1797, one pound also represented six months' school fees paid for educating both of his children, or the amount spent on soap in an entire year. It would cover his wine bill for six weeks or, alternatively, a fortnight's worth of meat from the butcher. Coal cost him about a pound a month (at between ten and fifteen shillings a ton delivered to his house). A pound was also what he paid by way of taxes for nearly six months (that was to change in 1800 with the introduction of the hated Income Tax, when he was suddenly faced with a bill for £36 p.a.).

My ancestor's diaries show that on Valentine's Day every year he gave each child in the local school one penny ("*98 Boys and Girls one penny each i.e. Eight shillings and two pence, plus a penny for the post boy*").

War with France resulted in the issue of paper notes, and these gradually became acceptable to the public, meaning that the Royal Mint was able to stop making gold guineas between 1797 and 1813. The smaller items of currency were, however, still left in desperately short supply.

To get round the silver shortage, various alternatives were tried including over-stamping

Spanish 8 reales coins with King George III's head in the centre, using the goldsmiths' hallmark. In monetary terms they were given the curious value of 4/9d. The Bank of England (as opposed to the Royal Mint) then issued dollars of five shillings between 1804 and 1811 along with a token currency of three shillings, and its half (eighteen pence). None of these were particularly common.

The 8 reales silver coins of the king of Spain over-stamped in the centre with the head of George III were not much liked, giving rise to the comment, *"they may have the heads of two kings but they are not even worth a crown"*.

Copper coins were also far from plentiful in the early years of the reign of George III. Pennies and halfpennies were minted in the first half of the decade in the 1770s—and then nothing until 1797 with the introduction of the "Cartwheel" coinage. All of the cartwheel coins are dated 1797, regardless of the year of issue.

These giants, containing respectively a penny and two-pence worth of copper, were unique in having the inscription impressed on to the surface as opposed to being raised up. They demonstrate the power of the newly introduced steam-powered presses. Using pure copper, which is soft and easily worn, meant that whereas vast numbers of these coins were minted, comparatively few remain in really good condition. They cannot have been too popular with the public—they weigh one ounce and two ounces respectively, so carrying a stack of them would ruin the stitching in anyone's purse!

Instead, the public got used to using smaller tokens often issued by traders in a particular town or area, satisfying the local need for pennies, halfpennies, and farthings. (As an aside, my ancestor diligently wrote down a reminder that it was proper to pronounce the word farthing as "fardun"). The problem with these tokens is that they were technically illegal (breaching the monopoly granted to the Royal Mint by the Crown) and could often only be exchanged in the town of issue.

Things did not get back to a sensible footing until the whole coinage was overhauled in 1816. This coincided with the move of the Royal Mint from its old headquarters in the Tower of London to new and more spacious premises nearby, where mechanisation was more practicable. This involved the new steam presses supplied by Boulton and Watt.

It was decided to allow silver and copper to be representative, i.e. without equivalent intrinsic value, and from then on the coinage was based solely on the gold standard. Out went the 21 shilling guinea and in came the twenty shilling pound (using 22 carat gold) with its multiples in two and five pounds. Also in 1816, back came the silver crown and half crown. Back came the shilling and the sixpence, along with the smaller silver denominations (4d i.e. groat, 3d, 2d and 1d).

In conclusion, the issue of coins other than for higher values was a complete mess in the period 1760 to 1816. Partly this was caused by inflationary constraints, partly by the limited space available within the Tower of London to bring in new machinery. The results were chronic shortages, poor quality coins in circulation, and an increase in forgeries—even though counterfeiting carried the death penalty.

The problems existed because we were wedded to a dual standard (i.e. both gold and silver), and the problems went away "overnight" in 1816 when the coinage was completely re-vamped.

Prior to that date the public had to endure fifty years of confusion and inconvenience, as well as the financial loss caused whenever anyone unscrupulous or dishonest palmed off inferior foreign coins, forgeries, or blanks. It must have been a rotten time to be in business, and my ancestor's diaries reflect this damaging uncertainty.

Travel in the Second Half
of the 18th Century, or
What Would Jane Austen's
Earliest Heroes Have
Packed for the Weekend?

BY **MIKE RENDELL**

Apparently Jane Austen wrote her first novel *Love and Freindship* (sic) in 1789 when she was 14. It is classed as part of her *Juvenilia*—one of 29 stories bound up into three manuscript books. So, if she had her hero pay a visit for the weekend, what would he have packed in his bags? Well, I can say what Richard Hall would pack for a weekend away, because he noted it in his diary in May 1784. (He was my great-great-great-great-grandfather.)

Some of the entries are hard to decipher but it appears to start off with shirts—first a couple of night shirts, then what appears to be two "neck shirts" including a "new fine plain" one. He packed two Ruffles plus "One fine Holland Ditto" as well as three pairs of silk stockings. One piece of gauze, three pairs worsted (stockings, presumably) went into the case along with a couple of night caps made of "linnen".

"W. shoes" may have referred to walking shoes but I cannot be sure, and I have been unable to decipher the following line apart from seeing that it involved *"one Blue Ditto and One Silk"*.

He needed a cloth coat and waistcoat (he called it "cloath") as well as a silk waistcoat and a white dining waistcoat. Silk breeches and five stocks were packed as well as "muffatees". Sadly, I have no record showing what these were made from—they were fingerless gloves or wrist bands, often knitted but sometimes made of elasticated strips of leather, or even fancy ones made of peacock feathers. They remained popular for many years—even Beatrix Potter has Old Mrs. Rabbit earning her living by knitting rabbit-wool mittens and muffatees in *The Tale of Benjamin Bunny*.

One knitting site called *Dances with Wolves* states:

> *In the days before central heating, keeping warm in winter was a major challenge. We think we know about dressing in layers, but most of us don't have to resort to wearing coats and hats and gloves indoors. But heavy layering was necessary. Working with your hands in mittens is clumsy at best. The solution? Wear muffatees.*
>
> *Muffatees are tube-like, fingerless mitts that cover wrist and hand up to the middle of the fingers, usually with an opening along the side for the thumb. The simplest, and*

possibly earliest form was comprised of the cuff or leg of a worn-out stocking, minus the foot. But in the 18th and 19th centuries, many pairs were sewn from warm cloth, or simply knitted of wool in plain or fancy patterns.

Several sites give patterns—and incidentally, Richard often called them wrist bands (pronounced "risbans" according to the one of the entries in his diary, at the same time as remembering that "waistcoat" was pronounced "wescote").

They were thought to work on the basis of keeping the blood warm at the point where the pulse is felt at the wrist, but leaving the fingers completely unfettered.

For longer journeys Richard would then record how many items of luggage were needed. For a trip lasting a fortnight (travelling the 264 miles from Bourton on the Water to Weymouth and Lulworth Castle and back) he needed seven items, all of them charged separately by the coachman. And then as an afterthought Richard showed an eighth item—his steam kettle! This would have gone on board along with the Great Trunk, the blue box, the wainscot (i.e. wood-panelled) box, his green bag, his great coat, his shoes and his wig box.

The actual cost of travel was considerable. Richard shows a coach journey from Bourton to Evesham of 41 miles costing over one pound eleven shillings. This would have been the equivalent of perhaps a hundred pounds (around 150 dollars) today. This included his dinner at four shillings and ten pence (equivalent to a buying power of perhaps 22 dollars today); the waiter was paid a sixpence (a couple of dollars); the horsler (i.e. ostler) a shilling (four dollars); and turnpikes one shilling and sixpence (six dollars).

The actual coach fare came to a guinea (getting on for a hundred dollars nowadays), and these figures have to be seen in the light of farm labourers having to get by on ten shillings a week!

Why the turnpikes? Their frequency increased as a direct result of the Duke of Cumberland's campaign against the Jacobites in 1745/6. Moving troops north to meet the rebels was handicapped by the dreadful state of the roads, and in the wake of the Duke's criticism, Parliament encouraged local communities to form Turnpike Trusts. In return for filling in potholes and re-surfacing and maintaining the roads, each Trust was entitled to levy a toll.

Within a couple of decades roads had improved dramatically—to the extent that some coach operators were able to run throughout the night. Think Georgian carriage lamps and think of a coach-and-four thundering through the darkness! The result was a dramatic decrease in journey times. The cost of travel in turn came down, as the operators reduced their overheads by cutting out the need to stay overnight, for instance on the journey between London and Bristol.

Stand and Deliver...
Your Tolls?: The Rise and
Fall of the Turnpikes

BY **J.A. BEARD**

Of all the benefits of modern industrialized civilization, roads are perhaps one we take the most for granted. Perhaps quality roads and ease of transport seem not all that worthy of special attention. Many ancient civilizations, after all, had developed fine road networks. At the dawn of the Georgian age, however, the quality of many roads in England left much to be desired.

First, let's take a step back and consider many roads prior to the 18th century. During this period, the resources and funds for road maintenance were maintained mostly at the parish level. Paving of any form certainly was limited. This was adequate for making sure various local roads were decent, but the system didn't do much to maintain the quality of distant roads and the intermediate roads connecting various far-flung locales.

The net result was a haphazard system of road improvements of varying quality. Wheeled travel was often unpleasant and dangerous. Rugged road conditions and holes could easily lead to accidents.

Inclement weather only made things worse, and England is far from an arid country. It was somewhat difficult to drive a coach through a muddied mess. Riding a horse was more manageable, but not necessarily comfortable or practical depending on one's circumstances. Economic improvements, along with the accompanying transportation of heavier amounts of goods, also contributed to wear and tear on many a poor-quality road.

Even if the Georgian-era traveler ignored the poor quality of the roads and the difficulties associated with weather, there also was the unpleasant issue of highwaymen. The increase in traffic and trade travel, particularly in the environs of London, hadn't been lost on the criminal element. The lack of an organized police force, let alone anything akin to a highway patrol, only contributed to the problem. A swift, mounted criminal could wave a pistol and demand that someone, "Stand and deliver!" often with impunity despite the threat of execution or transportation to Australia.

Things began to turn around for the often poor, sad, and unsafe roads of England at the beginning of the 18th century because of the Turnpike Acts. Following up on earlier parliamentary acts, in 1696, the first Turnpike Act was enacted, the first of many to follow.

So what were these Turnpike Acts, why did they have to pass so many, and what did they have to do with road quality and highwaymen?

These acts established Turnpike Trusts. These trusts were granted the responsibility of

| *Castles, Customs, and Kings*

taking care of a certain portion of a road and were also granted several legal tools to do this, including two of particular importance: the right to collect tolls and the right to control access on roads through the use of both gates and men. The name turnpike itself comes from gate designs that involved pike-like constructions on crossbars that could be rotated, though not every tollgate necessarily had such a design, and now, of course, the word turnpike has evolved into just a general term for toll road.

The trusts could each handle their various roads and road sections as they saw fit, so many would farm out the actual administration of the trusts to other enterprising people. These sort of trust subcontractors, as it were, would then do their best to efficiently run the trusts for a profit.

In the early years of the system, the various turnpike roads weren't necessarily all that much better maintained than before, but technichal advances led to general quality improvements, particularly in the latter half of the 18th century, which, in turn, fueled a massive expansion of the system, with a general slowing of expansion with the coming of the 19th century.

While the trusts, in general, contributed to road improvements that helped reduce transport times and the general quality and safety of travel, they also improved general security. Although there were some other contributory factors, the rise of the turnpike system, particularly on high traffic roads, greatly contributed to the decline of highwaymen. The presence of so many guarded gates made post-robbery escapes far more difficult.

Although there were nearly one thousand trusts in place by the end of the Regency, and thus the tail end of the Georgian era, in 1820, it's important to note that the majority of roads in England were still maintained by parishes and other local entities. That being said, many major important roads were under the control of turnpike trusts.

Although, like so many things, the decline of the turnpike system was multi-factorial, the most fundamental contributory factor was the rise of a swifter and more efficient means of mass transit: the railroads. By the end of the 19th century, a stronger central government, municipalities, and county councils took down the gates and took over the responsibility of maintaining the roads. Only a smattering of smaller private roads, tolled bridges, tolled tunnels, and the newer M6 Toll remain as the descendants, direct and indirect, of the extensive system that once covered tens of thousands of kilometers.

Top Ten Tourist Attractions in London, 1780

by MIKE RENDELL

Look at a current list of the most popular tourist attractions in London and you would probably come up with a Top Ten which would include the British Museum, the Tate Modern, the National Gallery, the Natural History Museum, the London Eye, the Science Museum, the V&A, Madame Tussaud's Wax Works, the National Maritime Museum, and the Tower of London. Throw in St. Paul's Cathedral and Westminster Abbey and you have a dozen of the most popular sites in the capital, visited by millions of people every year.

But sight-seeing is not new, and it begs the question: what would that list have looked like if it had been prepared 250 years ago? Which museums had opened their doors? Where were the popular art galleries? Would it have been that different from our modern list?

Of course, I do not have admission figures for the Georgian era, but what I do have is my great-great-great-great-grandfather's diaries, and in these I can see what he liked to visit—and perhaps the results are not so different from today's tourist attractions. Sure, we didn't see the London Eye in the 1780s, but we did have something else which gave panoramic views of the city before skyscrapers and tower blocks interrupted the scene. My ancestor Richard Hall may not have had the Tate Modern, but he had other galleries and exhibitions to look at, and here follows my own Top Ten from the 1780s—a personal selection of places to visit if the hero or heroine in your novel is coming to London.

THE TOWER

It may no longer have been the home of the Astronomer Royal, but it did have lots of other things—the Royal Regalia, the Royal Menagerie, and the Royal Mint.

It may come as a surprise that tourists could call round and watch the coins being minted, but that is exactly what my ancestor Richard Hall did in 1771. The Tower was only a few hundred yards from his shop and home at One London Bridge. He and his friends would have seen half guineas being minted (small gold coins worth ten shillings and sixpence—the equivalent of perhaps £45/$70 in terms of current buying-power).

They bought three pence worth of macaroons (almond-based sweets) and ate them as they wandered around, and they paid the driver to keep the horse-drawn carriage waiting outside so that they could avoid the rain on the journey home. Richard bought a pamphlet listing the royal regalia. It cost him an entrance fee of one shilling a head to view the coronation jewels, etc. because he went in a group (the rate went up by half as much again for solo visitors).

THE BRITISH MUSEUM

The British Museum opened in 1759 and Richard went to see it the following year. Visitor numbers were strictly controlled—you ordered a ticket some days in advance and were given a fixed time and date to call. Visitors were accompanied by a guide and taken round in groups of a dozen.

The original museum was housed in Montagu House, pulled down in the 1840s. Entry was free and given to "*all studious and curious Persons*" and included the chance to see the vast collection of natural curiosities (shells, fossils, insects, and natural phenomena) built up by Sir Hans Sloane, as well as the magnificent bequest from George II of the old Royal Library.

THE MONUMENT

202 feet high, the Wren-designed Monument is exactly 202 feet from where the Great Fire of London broke out in Pudding Lane in 1666. The 311 steps up the winding staircase led to an amazing panoramic view of the city. Richard would have been able to look immediately below him and see his shop next to St. Magnus the Martyr Church, and at London Bridge crossing the Thames over to where he had been brought up as a youngster in Southwark.

If he turned round and faced north, he would have observed how the rapidly expanding city had swallowed up farmland in the aftermath of the Great Fire, as far as the eye could see. The climb to the top was not for the fainthearted: there was no safety cage at the top until 1842, and there were several instances of people falling or jumping to their death.

THE ROYAL ACADEMY

Richard bought an engraving showing "*the back front of the New Royal Academy*" when he visited it in 1780. The building opened twelve years before, and by 1781 some 547 paintings were displayed. By 1801 the number had almost doubled, and in accordance with the taste of the day, paintings were displayed closely together, from floor to ceiling.

PICTURES AT SPRING GARDENS (OTHERWISE KNOWN AS VAUXHALL GARDENS)

For his one shilling admission in 1780 Richard would have been able to see all levels of London life. The gardens were frequented by anyone who was anyone (the Prince of Wales and his aristocratic buddies were regular visitors) as well as by the lowest of the low. Promenading gave the opportunity to see and be seen, and as darkness fell, the place was illuminated with oil lamps, music was played, and guests took their seats in the fifty or so supper boxes. Each was adorned with a different painting, and in the daytime these were available for the general public to view.

COX'S MUSEUM

James Cox was a jeweller who made fabulous bejewelled automata (i.e. items with clockwork moving parts). At one stage he claimed to have a thousand silversmiths and jewellery workers in his employ, turning out objects for places such as the Imperial courts in Russia and China.

He opened a museum at Charing Cross to display some of his wares. Entrance was not cheap (Richard would have paid ten shillings and sixpence per head to go in—and then forked out the same again for the official catalogue). But what a spectacle! He would have been greeted by a gold dais, surmounted by giant paintings of King George II and his Queen, painted by the court painter Zoffany. From there he would have been led through a succession of salons, each exhibiting things such as full sized tigers and elephants made of silver and gold, studded with precious stones. He may have seen the gorgeous life-sized silver swan, with its articulated neck which enabled it to bend forward and appear to pull a silver fish from the water (still in working order today, and nowadays to be seen at the Bowes Museum at Barnard Castle).

Time and time again Richard went back to see the display, taking a succession of guests with him throughout the 1770s.

DON SALTERO'S

Don Saltero was in reality John Salter, and he ran a coffee house by the side of the Thames in Chelsea. He thought a Spanish variant of his name gave a little added colour—and his was no ordinary coffee shop. It was a veritable treasure trove of tat—a museum where display cabinets filled every space and exhibits hung down from the ceiling. Natural curiosities, holy relics, fossils, shells, coins, and medals—anything and everything was displayed. Entrance was free as long as the visitor bought a cup of coffee—or, as in Richard's case, the visitor purchased an exhibit. Thirteen shillings appears to have been paid for shells, and I still have Richard's collection today.

MRS. WRIGHT'S WAXWORKS

Before Madame Tussaud came to London (and got trapped here because of the war with France) there had been a succession of wax-works. The one Richard favoured was in Pall Mall and was run by an American woman called Mrs. Wright. She created a sensation with her models of the Great and the Good, and reportedly enjoyed playing tricks on people by arranging her models in life-like poses on a settee, and watching as the visitors tried to strike up a conversation! Mrs. Wright later sought a pension from the U.S. Government, claiming that she had in fact been acting as a spy while in England, sounding out politicians about their plans during the War of Independence and smuggling notes back to America, rolled up inside the wax effigies which she had made.

THE LEVERIAN (HOLOPHUSICON)

Writing in 1780, Richard Hall mentioned that he went with *"Wife, Daughter, son Francis and Sophy to see Sir Ashton Lever's Museum of Natural Curiosities—and curious they indeed are! Dined afterward at a steakhouse."*

The Leverian as it was called (when it wasn't going by the weird name of the Holophusicon) had opened in 1775 and entertained visitors for over twelve years. Inside were a small sample (well, 25,000!) of Sir Ashton's vast collection of fossils, shells, and animals (birds, insects, reptiles, fish, monkeys and so on).

Richard would have paid over twenty five shillings (equivalent to perhaps a hundred pounds or 150 dollars) for his party to explore the exhibition at Leicester House, and for this they would also have been able to marvel at some of the curiosities brought back by Captain James Cook from his Pacific voyages.

THE ROYAL HOSPITAL

Richard Hall noted in his diary that he and Martha (his daughter) went by boat to Greenwich and ate whitebait. He would have marveled at the beautiful buildings making up the Royal Hospital for Seamen at Greenwich (subsequently the Royal Naval College). Designed by Sir Christopher Wren and constructed in various stages throughout the first half of the century, the buildings could accommodate up to 1500 sick and injured sailors. When the Baroque Painted Chapel in the King William Court was finished, it was deemed far too grand for the sailors and it became a tourist attraction.

What comes across from my ancestor's diaries is how much time (and money!) he was prepared to spend entertaining friends and showing them the sights.

SIR SIDNEY SMITH AND THE SIEGE OF ACRE, 1799

BY M.M. BENNETTS

ONE OF THE PERENNIAL FEATURES OF BRITISH HISTORY FROM TUDOR TIMES ONWARDS IS the rivalry with France for maritime power and influence and colonial possessions. This had already proved an economically crippling policy for France during much of the 18th century—it had spurred the Seven Years' War during which France lost both her North American colonies and her navy, and it prompted the financing of the American Rebellion against Great Britain, which had ultimately bankrupted France and brought on the Revolution of 1789.

Still, the French strategy of the day seemed to be, why abandon a losing game?

In 1798, the young General Bonaparte convinced the Directory that conquering Egypt was just the ticket to curb Britain's overseas expansion. It would give them a foothold in the eastern Mediterranean, and they could wallow in their lust for ancient Oriental splendour and knowledge. What could be better? The Egyptian government was weak, disorganized, and corrupt and therefore easy to topple, and their overlords, the Ottomans, weren't paying much attention anyway. Right?

Plus, with a charismatic leader like Napoleon, they could forge on up through the countries of the Middle East and seize Constantinople, thus bringing liberty, fraternity, and all those good things to the enslaved peoples of the Ottoman Empire. And from there, press on in the footsteps of Alexander the Great all the way to India and challenge British influence there.

Yes, it would be the biggest land-grab in history, but what of that?

The Directory were delighted with the prospect of removing young Bonaparte from Paris (let him go off and be someone else's headache for a while)—he was getting too popular and he had the support of the army too. So they sanctioned the expedition.

There was of course the now-famous chase around the Mediterranean by Admiral Nelson and the Fleet which ended with the Battle of the Nile, during which Nelson destroyed the French fleet, thus marooning the French army in Egypt. For which victory Lord Nelson became the ultimate national hero. But I don't want to talk about that.

The person I want to talk about is Captain Sir William Sidney Smith (1764-1840), an Englishman of extra-ordinary cunning and intelligence. He was said to be *"of middling stature, good-looking, with tremendous moustachios, a pair of penetrating black eyes, an intelligent countenance, with a gentlemanly air, expressive of good nature and kindness of heart."*

He was a naval officer, yes, of great daring and flamboyance—his raids on the French coast are the stuff of legend. (He and Nelson were rivals.) But he was also a fine intelligence agent and in 1798, he was incarcerated in the high-security Temple Prison in Paris (running his spy ring from his cell there) at exactly the time Napoleon was gaining permission from the Directory for his Egyptian expedition.

On a panel of wood in his cell, Smith inscribed this, by Rousseau:

> *Fortune's wheel makes strange revolutions, it must be confessed; but for the term revolution to be applicable, the turn of the wheel must be complete. You are today as high as you can be. Very well. I envy not your good fortune, for mine is better still. I am as low in the career of ambition as a man can well descend; so that, let this capricious dame, fortune, turn her wheel ever so little—I must necessarily mount, for the same reason you must descend.*

But Smith then made it personal for Bonaparte, and wrote:

> *I make not this remark to cause you any uneasiness, but rather to bring you that consolation which I shall feel when you are arrived at the same point where I now am—yes! at the same point where I now am. You will inhabit this same prison—why not as well as I? I no more thought of such a thing, than you do at present, before I was actually shut up in it.*

On 24 April 1798, Smith escaped, courtesy of a daring raid by French Royalists.

Once free, he returned to Britain, and was dispatched to Constantinople in October 1798 (his brother was ambassador there), given command of the 80 gun battleship, *Tigre*, and full powers to command the effort against Napoleon in the Levant. Sultan Selim, in response to the incursion into his territory, had declared war on France. He also admired Smith very much and put him in charge of the sea and land forces being assembled for the purpose of driving the French out of the Levant.

So, fast-forward to January 1799.

Bonaparte and his French troops have conquered, so to speak, Egypt. He has set up a government to suit himself. He has robbed the place of as many antiquities and treasures as he can manage. He's ordered the slaughter of the Al-Azhar mosque and neighbourhood in response to their insurrection against him. The place is under martial law.

His troops have been decimated by disease and dehydration. He has no transport to get his men back home. Clearly it's now time to swing into action up the east coast of the Mediterranean to take Constantinople and/or open up an overland route to India. Preferably both.

Up the coast the 13,000 French troops march, across the Sinai desert with little food and less water.

First stop Jaffa. Which they storm and take in an orgy of slaughter, killing civilians and soldiers alike, at the beginning of March. Once in control, the French provision themselves, but they also come into contact with bubonic plague (again).

Nevertheless, from there, they march up around the eastern edge of the Mediterranean, arriving at Haifa on 17 March from which the citadel of Acre—long fought over during the Crusades—is visible by telescope.

And across that stretch of blue water, Napoleon sees something he had not planned on: British battleships and Turkish gunboats in the harbour. (Their total control of the sea-lanes also meant his transport ships carrying all his heavy siege guns were seized and he was wholly deprived of news from home or from base-camp in Egypt.)

Yet still, determined to fulfill his destiny as the new Alexander (yes, he really did believe that!), Napoleon presses on, and on 18 March, the French take up their position before the walls of Acre.

The citadel at Acre is built on a promontory, with only one side facing land—the rest surrounded by water—and possessing a very neat little harbour.

Now the Governor of Acre had for the past 25 years been Pasha el-Djezzar. (Djezzar translates as either Butcher or Cutter—a soubriquet more than earned by his treatment of his enemies.) He had certainly talked big, and threatened all manner of savagery against the French when they were in Egypt, but he was rather inclined to abandon Acre once the chips were down. Smith talked him into staying on.

With one of the Royalist spies who had rescued him from the Temple—an engineer who had shared a desk with Napoleon at school, Louis-Edmond Phelippeaux—Smith and Djezzar had reinforced the walls and land-facing towers.

Still, under the constant battery of guns, the French dug their trenches and opened siege on 28 March with their field guns. They also sent an army officer under a flag of truce to demand surrender, but Djezzar threw him into prison.

When a breach was opened in the walls of one of the towers, the French were not only repulsed but also ran into a dry moat and found their scaling ladders were too short; hence they retreated under fire. Within days, they were running out of ammunition, so Napoleon offered rewards for cannonballs.

Djezzar offered a bounty for enemy heads.

By early April, the French had launched another assault which had failed, but more worryingly, the sappers had dug their trenches almost to the walls and were attempting to mine one of the towers.

A sortie by the British drove them off, but by mid-April they were back driving the mine under the tower. On the 24th, the mine was blown, but they'd miscalculated the position and only the front wall of the tower's lower storey had collapsed. French troops stormed the breach, but again were driven back.

Meanwhile, the Turks were sending reinforcements both by land and sea, and Napoleon had to dash off to scatter the reinforcements in a series of skirmishes and battles, most notably the Battle of Mount Tabor. There is no doubt that here, the French fought bravely against overwhelming (but rather disorganised) odds.

Another mine had now been dug under the same tower (which they called the Cursed Tower). Yet again, the tower only partially collapsed and the storming French troops were pelted with rocks and grenades and finally repelled with powder kegs filled with burning mixtures of gunpowder and sulpher—they're known as stink pots, these missiles, for the clouds of acrid smoke they give off.

At last, the replacement siege guns which Napoleon had requested sent overland arrived at the end of the month. Though it took them six days to set them up, Smith was expecting defeat and wrote to tell the Admiralty so.

On 7 May the newly installed French siege guns began pounding away, and it seemed an end was inevitable.

But again, British seapower came to the rescue and that evening, ships carrying supplies and reinforcements arrived.

Napoleon, seeing this, and never a patient man, stepped up the bombardment, and French troops finally occupied the the second storey of the Cursed Tower. But not for long.

In the morning, Smith himself led a party of Marine reinforcements and took back the breach, holding it until more reinforcements arrived. (This act of heroism shamed Pasha Djezzar, and he ordered his own troops to stand and fight, which they did with rather frightening gusto.)

Meanwhile, Napoleon had been busy spreading propaganda—he was a master of it. And he'd had printed two sets of pamphlets, one for Christians and one for Muslims. For the benefit of the Christians, he claimed he was the natural successor of those great men, the Crusaders, and a defender of Christian faith. To the Muslims, he declared that he had already destroyed the power of the pope in Rome and the Knights of St. John in Malta and that he was the true defender of Islam.

Smith got hold of these. And ordered them distributed amongst the opposite factions of those for whom they were intended. Local goodwill dried up to parching.

He also had bundles of leaflets dropped into the French trenches offering on behalf of the Sultan a free passage out of Syria for any soldiers wise enough to lay down their arms.

Napoleon was incandescent, and wrote, *"Smith is a crazy young man...."*

Having survived the latest assaults and secure in the knowledge that the garrison was reinforced and supplied, Smith sat back (if you can call it that) and watched with enjoyment as the effects of his propaganda war took hold. The French position was now untenable.

Still, Napoleon was determined to have one more go—he'd never been defeated before—and on 10 May, in the full glare of a sweltering Middle Eastern sun, the final French assault was launched. Though Napoleon wanted to lead it himself, he was persuaded not to. General Kleber led the assault, while Smith led the defence.

The French were beaten to a standstill and Kleber ordered a retreat.

And Smith, cheeky as ever, wrote to Napoleon:

> *General, I am acquainted with the dispositions that for some days past you have been making to raise the siege; the preparations in hand to carry off your wounded, and to leave none behind you, do you great credit. This last word ought not to escape my mouth—I, who ought not to love you, to say nothing more: but the circumstances remind me to wish that you would reflect on the instability of human affairs.*
>
> *In fact, could you have thought that a poor prisoner in the cell of the Temple prison—that an unfortunate for whom you refused, for a single moment, to give yourself any*

concern, being at the same time able to render him a signal service, since you were then all-powerful—could you have thought, I say, that this same man would have become your antagonist, and have compelled you, in the midst of the sands of Syria, to raise the siege of a miserable, almost defenceless town? Such events, you must admit, exceed all human calculations.

Believe me, general, adopt sentiments more moderate, and that man will not be your enemy, who shall tell you that Asia is not a theatre made for your glory. This letter is a little revenge that I give myself.

Napoleon was beaten.

He cut his losses and on 20 May began the retreat to Egypt with his exhausted and ill troops, over a third of his original force either dead or disabled. Although he claimed victory when he returned to Cairo, by the end of August, he had abandoned his troops in Egypt, hurried back to France alone, proclaiming his venture a success, taking charge of the army, and before long, the nation.

In 1808, he ordered the demolition of the Temple prison—he said, because it had become a place of Royalist pilgrimage as both Louis XVI and Louis XVII had been held there. Others maintained it was so that Smith's prophecy could never come true and he would never be incarcerated there.

Madness in Their Method: Water Therapy in Georgian and Regency Times

by LUCINDA BRANT

Using water to treat illness, known today as hydrotherapy, is a practice dating back to Ancient Egypt. Greek and Roman historians also mention the use of water in the treatment of muscle fatigue, hydrophobia, and fever. Using water therapy as a psychiatric tool is attributed to Jean Baptiste Van Helmont's massive medical tome the *Ortus Medicinae* published in 1643 and translated into English by John Chandler in 1662.

Van Helmont advocated water immersion therapy in the treatment of mental illness. The patient was fully immersed in cold water until the point of unconsciousness and thus at the point at which the patient could drown, because he believed near death immersion in cold water could "kill the mad idea" which caused mental derangement.

Naturally, this was a very dangerous technique and never became widespread. However, Van Helmont's staunch belief in using water as a treatment for mental illness was taken up by various medical institutions and practitioners across Europe so that by the 18th century, the "water-cure" in its various forms became one of a number of standard treatments used by physicians and insane asylums when dealing with all manner of psychiatric conditions.

The two main types of water cure were the *douche* or cold shower and the *balneum* or bath. The douche required cold water be poured over the patient's head or sprayed at the patient's body to cool the heat of madness if insane or rouse the depressed if suffering from melancholia. The bath was used to calm overwrought nerves and to encourage sleep.

In the early years of this type of therapy, most cures were performed out of doors near a source of water—the sea or a pond. This allowed for public viewing. However, as asylums, both public and private, became more widespread in the 18th century, water cures were moved indoors. Inside and away from the public eye and an immediate source of water, institutions and their practitioners developed inventive ways and a wide variety of apparatuses to deliver water therapy to the mad and melancholic.

There were cold shower rooms, bath boxes that shut patients in, shower contraptions that delivered water at intervals via a system of pulleys and levers, dunking devices that immersed patients at regular intervals into small ponds as the device rotated and turned on giant cogs, and there was the simple ladder and bucket method that involved the patient sitting in a wooden barrel while behind a screen attendants ran up and down ladders with buckets of water that they poured onto the patient's head from a great height.

And then there was "the chair". Benjamin Rush wrote in a letter:

I have contrived a chair and introduced it to our [Pennsylvania] *Hospital to assist in curing madness. It binds and confines every part of the body. By keeping the trunk erect, it lessens the impetus of blood toward the brain. By preventing the muscles from acting, it reduces the force and frequency of the pulse, and by the position of the head and feet favors the easy application of cold water or ice to the former and warm water to the latter. Its effects have been truly delightful to me. It acts as a sedative to the tongue and temper as well as to the blood vessels. In 24, 12, six, and in some cases in four hours, the most refractory patients have been composed. I have called it a Tranquillizer.*

This water therapy was used by some physicians as a means of treating married women who had become "mildly distracted" and had opted out of their marital responsibilities (i.e. didn't want to have sex with their husband). One such practitioner who used the method to sadistic effect was Patrick Blair.

Blair had his female patients blindfolded, stripped, and strapped to a bathing chair. The woman was then subjected to 30 minutes of water being sprayed directly into her face. When the woman refused to agree to return to the marital bed, Blair went one step further and repeated the treatment for 60 minutes, then 90 minutes, and when she promised obedience Blair allowed her to sleep.

Yet, the next day, sensing the woman was "sullen" and probably had only agreed because of the treatment, he again had her strapped to the chair and subjected to the treatment at intervals over the next two days. Finally, exhausted after such physical and mental torture, the woman succumbed and agreed to become a *"loving and obedient and dutiful wife forever thereafter"*. To make certain she did, Blair visited her at her home a month later and was happy to report *"everything was in good order"*.

Patrick Blair is the model for Sir Titus Foley in my novel *Autumn Duchess*, a dandified and well-respected physician whose medical forte is treating females for melancholia.

When Antonia, Dowager Duchess of Roxton, is seen to be excessively melancholy and is still wearing mourning three years after the death of the Duke, her loving son is at his wits' end, and he instructs Sir Titus to treat his mother, little realizing that part of his treatment is the use of water therapy.

Thankfully, Blair's sadistic treatment of his female patients was not the norm. Yet, most physicians, indeed most people in the 18th and early 19th centuries, viewed water therapy in its various forms as an acceptable means of coercing, treating, and hopefully curing patients with various mental, melancholic, and recalcitrant afflictions.

By the mid-18th century water therapy had become a standard treatment in the "mad doctor" medical bag. Yet, in this Age of Enlightenment, when many people came to view the shackling of the mad as inhumane, there were those physicians who advocated the use of water therapy not only as a cure but as a more humane means of coercion, thus doing away with the need for physical restraints. Thus water therapy was not only used on the mad and those suffering from depression, it was used by some physicians in the good-natured belief that it would persuade patients who had veered from the path of what society viewed as "normal" behavior to "get back on track".

SOURCES

"Annual Report to the Friends (July 2005-June 2006)." *The Institute for the History of Psychiatry.* Cornell University, New York.

Porter, Dorothy and Roy Porter. *Patient's Progress: Doctors and Doctoring in Eighteenth-century England.* Stanford, CA: Stanford University Press, 1989.

Porter, Roy. *Blood and Guts: A Short History of Medicine.* London: Allen Lane, 2002.

Rush, Benjamin. *The Letters of Benjamin Rush: 1761-1792.* Edited by Lyman Henry Butterfield. Princeton University Press, 1951.

Scull, Andrew. *Social Order/Mental Disorder: Anglo-American Psychiatry in Historical Perspective.* Berkeley: University of California Press, 1989.

STOURHEAD: PAINTING WITH NATURE

BY M.M. BENNETTS

STOURHEAD. HOME TO THE FAMOUS HOARE FAMILY—BANKERS TO CATHERINE OF BRA-ganza, Vanbrugh, Lord Byron, and Jane Austen.

Along with Wilton and Longleat, it is one of the great houses—surrounded by gardens, of course—of south Wiltshire. And it has been a must-see destination for garden visitors for over two centuries.

In 1717, Henry Hoare, the son of the man who'd founded Hoare's Bank, bought Stourton Manor and promptly had the crumbling half-derelict mediaeval-Tudor pile pulled down.

Then, with Colen Campbell (champion of the newest thing in architecture) as his architect, he set about rebuilding a new Palladian villa, which he would call Stourhead, on an adjacent site. Yet, unlike so many of their contemporaries who sought land-owning respectability and the political power that came with it, the Hoares did not disengage from the business which had made the family rich. Rather the family continued on doing that which they did very well—banking and making money...even as they turned their excess profits into land and Parliamentary influence.

Upon the first Henry Hoare's death in 1725, his son, also called Henry, completed the work of house-building.

And it was he who, until his death in 1785, made the house and garden what it is today. Well-travelled and well-read—he was travelling and/or living on the Continent until 1738. It wasn't until 1741 that he finally made his home at Stourhead.

After the death of his wife in 1743, and even as he continued to work on the house and purchase paintings and sculptures for it, he began work on the garden—but again, unlike his contemporaries, he didn't hire a master gardener like Capability Brown.

No, Hoare did it himself.

And basing his work on the idealised landscapes he loved by Claude Lorrain, Poussin and especially Gaspar Dughet, Hoare made his garden by painting with nature. *"The greens should be ranged together in large masses,"* he wrote, *"as the shades are in painting: to contrast the dark masses with the light ones, and to relieve each dark mass itself with little sprinklings of lighter greens here and there."*

He had the vast lake that is such a striking feature still today created in 1754 by damming a small stream. (For the trivia seekers among you, the lake is the source of the River Stour—one of five rivers in England so named—which flows through Wiltshire and Dorset, reaching the English Channel at Christchurch. In at least one early map of Dorset, it is shown as the River Stower, as it is pronounced to this day. Stourton, on the other hand, is pronounced "Sterton".)

Writing of the garden in 1755, Hoare said:

Whether at pleasure or business, let us be in earnest, and ever active to be outdone or exceeded by none, that is the way to thrive.... What is there in creation [at Stour-head]*...those are the fruits of industry and application to business, and show what great things may be done by it, the envy of the indolent, who have no claim to Temples, Grottos, Bridges, Rocks, Exotick Pines and Ice in Summer.*

Like many of his class, Hoare sought to illustrate his classical education and erudition through classical references and allusions in his building and the decoration of the garden. So he had a Pantheon built that same year based on the Pantheon in Rome, and the whole trip around the lake—it feels like a good two to three miles up and downhill—was based on the journey of the classical hero, Aeneas.

Within a few years, the garden was renowned, not only for Henry Flitcroft's temples around the lake, but for the wide range of plants which had been gathered from around the world and coaxed into growing in this very English landscape.

Indeed, visiting Stourhead became such a late 18th century craze among polite society (similar to visiting Derbyshire and Chatsworth) that Hoare had an hotel built, the Spread Eagle, only a few hundred yards from his gatehouse. Though when Mrs. Libby Powys—a prolific garden visitor and arbiter of garden taste—came for a visit in 1776, she found the inn full....

Over the years, the house was expanded—notably by Henry Hoare's grandson, Richard Colt Hoare (1758-1838) who became a noted county historian and an omnivore of a collector. It was he who had built the two side wings—the one to house his library and the other to house his Picture Gallery. It was he also who employed the younger Chippendale to make furnishings for the two new wings and invited a young unknown watercolourist, J.M.W. Turner, down to Wiltshire to paint.

Today, the house and gardens too have seen many changes. The house was gutted by fire in 1902—though because it was slow to spread, the furnishings and paintings from the ground floor were able to be rescued. And within months, it was being rebuilt.

More distressing still to the then owner, the 6th Baronet, Henry Hugh Hoare, was the death of his only son in 1917, while he was serving in Palestine. Thus, by 1938, Hoare had decided to give the house and gardens to the National Trust, and in 1946, he did so.

And thus Stourhead, the great visitor attraction of the eighteenth century, came full circle. The Spread Eagle now serves excellent pub lunches; Hoare's estate workers' cottages now provide holiday lets. And the landscape garden designed by a banker, now moulded timelessly into Wiltshire's landscape, continues to paint with nature as season gives way to season.

THE PURSUIT OF THE PICTURESQUE

BY M.M. BENNETTS

Eh? The picturesque? What's that twaddle, you say? Let me explain....

The *Oxford English Dictionary* defines picturesque as *"like or having the elements of a picture; fit to be the subject of a striking or effective picture; possessing pleasing or interesting qualities of form and colour (but not implying the highest beauty or sublimity): said of landscapes, buildings...."*

Furthermore, the OED tells us that the word didn't enter the English language until 1703 (which is quite late). But by the mid-18th century, the picturesque was well on its way to being all the rage, and the concept would hold British society rapt until well into the 1830s...which is a very long time for matters of taste and style.

The whole concept can be traced—sort of—to the Italian landscape paintings of Claude Lorrain, Salvator Rosa, and Nicolas Poussin—these same painters who were so influential in formulating the ideal of English Landscape Gardening. Yet these painters and their works also wholly engaged the imaginations of two 18th century British poets, James Thomson (1700-1748) and John Dyer (1699-1757).

It may seem hard to believe, but before these two, poetry just wasn't about nature. It didn't extol the beauties of nature, and the idea of poetically rendering the sights, scents, or colours of the natural world—well, you can just forget that.

But these two changed all that—these men were landscape painters in verse, displaying all the delights of sunrises and sunsets and panoramic views as much as if they'd been daubing oils on canvas.

And this change in poetic emphasis and vision played into the 18th century Enlightenment ideal of the purity and goodness of the natural world as extolled by authors such as Jean-Jacques Rousseau. Which in turn fed into the nascent Romantic movement and the works of William Wordsworth and Samuel Coleridge Taylor.

Hence nature, once just there and untameable, was now viewed as if it might be an infinite sequence of subjects that would make up *"a striking or effective picture"* with paint, poetry, or in the case of the landscape gardeners, plants and "picturesque" ruins.

Here's Wordsworth's offering from *Lines Composed a Few Miles above Tintern Abbey* (written July 1798).

> *...Once again*
> *Do I behold these steep and lofty cliffs,*
> *That on a wild secluded scene impress*
> *Thoughts of more deep seclusion; and connect*
> *The landscape with the quiet of the sky.*
> *The day is come when I again repose*

Here, under this dark sycamore, and view
These plots of cottage ground, these orchard tufts,
Which at this season, with their unripe fruits,
Are clad in one green hue, and lose themselves
'Mid groves and copses. Once again I see
These hedgerows, hardly hedgerows, little lines
Of sportive wood run wild; these pastoral farms,
Green to the very door; and wreaths of smoke
Sent up, in silence, from among the trees!

And reading about it, reciting it, viewing the paintings of these landscape painters, all encouraged the 18th century population to look at nature and to embrace the landscape with an artistic eye and a new-found sense of gusto.

So what do they do? They start touring the country like mad...some visit the many famous landscape gardens, some make walking tours of the Lake District (Wales was popular too), and some travel farther to see the beauties of Scotland as did Dr. Johnson.

Obviously, it's not just the landscape of Great Britain which has travellers so entranced—up until 1789 the beauties of France, Italy, and Greece are well within the well-heeled tourists' reach. But with the coming of the French Revolution in 1789, and France's rapid descent into turbulence and war, the natural wonders of the Continent cease to be viable destinations, and the British travellers turn inward, their journeys confined to their own little island.

Jane Austen writes of Elizabeth Bennet and her Aunt and Uncle Gardiner visiting the Peak District of Derbyshire, an activity many of her readers would have considered quite normal. She likewise sends Anne Elliot down to Lyme Regis to visit the seaside and walk along the Cobb to view the seething grey waves of the Atlantic coast. What are they doing? They are indulging in a very British pastime; they are—like everyone else of taste and discernment—indulging their passion for the picturesque.

And so much a part of the English psyche was this hobby of seeking out the lofty peaks, cascades, cliffs, woods, ruined castles by midnight, and other such scenic prospects, that beginning in 1809, William Combe and Thomas Rowlandson published a verse parody with pictures of the whole pastime in *The Poetical Magazine*, called *The Tour of Dr. Syntax in Search of the Picturesque*.

The verse story tells the tale of Dr. Syntax—a down-at-heel scarecrow of a curate and schoolmaster in a rusty black suit and scratch wig—who conceives of a trip round England. Penny-pinched and hen-pecked, he aims to make money out of recording his experiences and the sights he encounters. As Syntax describes his plan:

I'll make a TOUR—and then I'll WRITE IT.
You well know what my pen can do,
And I'll employ my pencil too:—
I'll ride and write, and sketch and print,

And thus create a real mint;
I'll prose it here, I'll verse it there,
And picturesque it ev'ry where.
I'll do what all have done before;
I think I shall—and somewhat more....

Syntax's subsequent adventures bumbling through the English countryside on Grizzle, his equally dubious horse, make Don Quixote look like James Bond. The illustrated comic poem was a runaway success.

Still, even amidst the well-aimed mockery, the fashion for the picturesque was far from running its course. On the contrary. The new generation of Romantic poets—Keats, Scott, Shelley, and Byron—were busily adding to the picturesque canon in poetry.

And the new star of the artistic firmament, J.M.W. Turner, capitalised on the craze, embarking on painting a series of commissioned watercolours for *Picturesque Views of the Southern Coast of England* (completed in 1826). In 1818, he was again commissioned to paint a series of watercolours of Italian subjects for *A Picturesque Tour in Italy.*

Still later, from 1827-1838, he painted another 96 views for *Picturesque Views in England and Wales.* And all of the above were turned into engravings, which sold in their thousands—making Turner a very rich man...though this last group of works really signalled the end of the dominance of the picturesque.

Britain had a new, young queen, and, it would seem, a new outlook. Wordsworth, Coleridge, Keats, and Rowlandson were old hat, remembrances of a bygone age. So at last, the craze that had captivated generations was at an end.

(Except, of course, we're still at it...just ask to see the visitor numbers of the National Trust or English Heritage....)

The Must-have Garden Accessories for the Rich and Richer? A Glasshouse and Pineapples!

by M.M. Bennetts

Oranges and lemons first made their way to the English plate and palate sometime during the reign of James I. They were the preserve of the rich. Obviously. Unsurprisingly, within a very short space of time, these citrus fruits—which we take quite for granted—were *the* status symbol.

In order to grow the fruits then, small conservatories were built to protect the potted trees over the cold English winter months. And they weren't called conservatories. They were known as orangeries or orange houses.

They had solid roofs because the plants are dormant in the winter months anyway, and featured glass windows (or French doors as we'd call them) along one side—usually the south side—so that the sunshine through the windows from February onwards would help restart the growth until the trees could be taken out into the garden once danger of frost had passed.

Queen Henrietta Maria had such a structure built at Wimbledon Manor House in the 1630s.

By the 1650s, despite the deteriorating political situation which might have taken their attention off such frivolities, the well-heeled were for the most part installing heating into their orange houses, usually in the form of free-standing charcoal-burning stoves. Which occasionally proved unreliable and sometimes poisoned the plants with charcoal fumes.

So the famed garden writer John Evelyn suggested a new kind of stove—this was fixed outside the glasshouse and the heat was conducted into the conservatory through pipes. It sounds obvious to us, but to them, this was innovation! Not only that, but Evelyn was the first to call these orangeries "conservatories".

Within fifty years, even as the range of plants and fruits to be grown in them had expanded, so too the technology had advanced. In 1710, the Duke of Chandos' new conservatory was heated by flues, with the central glass section flanked by two walls into which were built coal fireplaces.

Which meant that through the winter months, the tables of the rich and nobles featured not only the citrus fruits, but a wide range of vegetables. And, as well as stocking their conservatories with other plants such as jasmines and pomegranates, they were producing the ultimate symbol of status—largely because they did require a conservatory and were so difficult to grow—the pineapple.

Which incidentally weren't just eaten. Generally, for at least a fortnight or so before eating, the pineapple would be on display on the dining table as part of a centrepiece.

But, by this time, the conservatory had outgrown its simple original function and was being viewed more as an architectural accessory rather than a horticultural one. They were garden features now and were often being built as a focal point in a garden, rather like the Tudor banqueting houses had once been. Hence, they now often contained a degree of furnishing and, like at Dyrham Park near Bath, were used during the summers as an extra room, when all the plants were outside.

Lady Hertford wrote in 1739 of the Earl of Bathhurst's greenhouse at Riskins in Buckinghamshire, describing it as *"a very agreeable room; either to drink tea, play at cards, or sit in with a book, in a summer's evening..."* for it was filled with a *"collection of orange, myrtle, geranium, and oleander trees"*.

As the range of available seeds grew, so too did the building of specialist greenhouses. By the early years of the 19th century, it was not unknown for larger households to have a specialist "melon house" which was also used for growing cucumbers, strawberries, and salad greens year-round in raised hot beds.

The technology for heating the glass structures continued to advance, though it remained somewhat experimental. And by the end of the 18th century (due to the wars with France), glass was heavily taxed, so on the whole glasshouses remained prohibitively expensive.

Yet the true test of a skilled horticulturist remained his ability to grow pineapples. (It was also a measure of one's wealth that one could afford the wages of a head gardener who could grow pineapples.) So in addition to the melon houses and the conservatories which were now attached to the house and used as a summer room, special "pineries" were built.

In 1777, *"two hothouses full stocked with pine apples and plants"* were built at Knole for the sum of £175.

By 1805, garden designer and painter Humphry Repton was outlining his plans (in paint) for vast greenhouses for Woburn Abbey which he called "The Forcing Garden" and that promised fresh exotic fruit and vegetables throughout the winter. It was also Repton who suggested that the conservatory should be connected to or built off the library (which was by the early 19th century the most used public space of a house) as a natural transition between the house and the garden outside. And it was this which gave rise to the Victorian tradition of building conservatories for the next several generations as garden rooms attached to libraries.

Still, the prize for the greatest pineapples—and thus the greatest conservatory building and the most lavish spending—probably goes to the Marquess of Hertford in 1822. For it was his gardener, Thomas Baldwin, who sent several pineapples to an anniversary dinner of the Royal Horticultural Society—the largest of which weighed 8lbs 14oz.

Late Georgian and Regency Era (1800-1837)

THE EXTRAORDINARY CLANDESTINE ACTIVITIES OF A NINETEENTH CENTURY DIPLOMAT

BY **MAGGI ANDERSEN**

PART DIPLOMAT AND PART SPY, RELATIVELY LITTLE HAS BEEN WRITTEN ABOUT CHARLES Stuart, Lord Stuart de Rothesay, later 1st Baron Stuart de Rothesay (1779-1845). In his book *Private & Secret,* Robert Franklin writes:

> *Headstrong, daring and never lacking personal courage or conviction, Charles Stuart*
> *was in many respects a product of his age, but in others he, and his like, also helped to*
> *shape that age, and consequently the face of Europe as we know it today.*

Sir Charles Stuart, as he was known from 1812 to 1828, was no ordinary diplomat. His story is also the story of the British intelligence service coming of age in the modern era. Although as old as time itself, and reaching unparalleled sophistication under Walsingham in the late 16th century and again under Charles II in the 17th, Britain's modern secret service came of age in the 19th century, when it was developed as a key weapon against French power in both politics and war.

It's not difficult to understand how Stuart chose his profession. His paternal grandfather, John Stuart, 3rd Earl of Bute, was one of the two Secretaries of State in the days when those great functionaries controlled the country's Secret Service, chiefly through the agency of the Post Office. As Prime Minister, Lord Bute's greatest achievement was to bring the Seven Years' War to an end, bribing Members of Parliament, it's reputed, from secret funds. (All secret service funds were discretionary at this time.)

Charles' father, General Sir Charles Stuart, a distinguished soldier, could not rely on official sources for intelligence as the Army had no official intelligence service until 1803 when the Depot of Military Knowledge was set up. He learned the ways and means of intelligence-gathering when he saw active service in the American War of Independence.

Young Charles was at Eton until sixteen years of age in 1795. Two years later he went up to Christ Church, Oxford. During those two years he traveled with his father and kept a journal: *Travels in Germany and the Imperial Hereditary States, 1795-1797.* At Weimar he sat at the feet of German thinkers, Goethe and Schiller, and penned descriptions of these great men in letters. His letters to his father revealed his burgeoning interest in the political situation:

> *...the Prussians are exceedingly busy in fortifying all their frontier places towards*
> *Galacia in the newly acquired part of Poland. Some people say war is declared; I must*

confess it appears to me very odd that the House of Austria should take such a step after being so weakened as she certainly has been in the French war. Everything in this country has a very war-like appearance though few people seem to know how it will turn out.

His travels left him restless. After a year at Oxford, he moved to Glasgow University. In 1801 his father died. Admitted to Lincoln's Inn, Charles began to read for the Bar, but was unable to settle. He considered politics and proposed himself as Member of Parliament for Poole, in Dorset, a borough that his father had represented for many years. But Lord Hobart found him a place as a diplomat under the auspices of the Foreign Office. He was to be Secretary of Legation at Vienna, seat of the Austrian Empire, but he had time to spare and decided to see something of Russia.

It was the summer of 1801, and Europe was in a state of suspended animation—the French Revolution was over, Napoleon was First Consul, but the Peace of Amiens had not yet come into being.

When the Second Coalition against France crumbled in 1801, England was alone. Charles set out in July traveling through Prussia, Berlin, a partitioned Poland, and on to St. Petersburg. In Vienna, he kept a journal again, *Journal, Northern Europe 1801*, and this time he recorded what he saw and heard as a budding diplomat, rather than a student or the dutiful son of a British officer.

Between 1810 and 1814 he served as Envoy Extraordinary and Minister Plenipotentiary to Portugal and Brazil. In 1812 he was appointed a Knight of the Order of Bath (KB) and was sworn into the Privy Council in 1814.

In 1815 he was made Knight Grand Cross of the Order of the Bath and appointed British Ambassador to France. Stuart is suspected of having been involved in the escape of the Comte de Lavalette from the prison of the Conciergerie in Paris, the day before he was to be executed.

During Napoleon's Hundred Days, he left Paris and was in Brussels at the start of the Waterloo Campaign. After the fall of Napoleon he returned to Paris as the Envoy Extraordinary and Minister Plenipotentiary to Portugal and Brazil. One of the English visitors to Paris, Lady Granville, observed of him: *"He discovers what others are about or would be about to a degree that must be very useful to him in his present situation."*

Sir Charles Stuart felt some responsibility for the safety of the Duke of Wellington and Viscount Castlereagh, the Foreign Secretary—which was made more difficult due to the fact that neither man was over-concerned for himself. There were at least two attempts on Wellington's life during this period, and others may have been prevented by Stuart's vigilance. Nobody was punished for either of the best-known attempts on Wellington's life.

One attempt was carried out by an old soldier, devoted to Napoleon. He was arrested, but was not convicted, despite the fact that there was no doubt of his guilt. The court held that the evidence was not strong enough. Stuart suspected a political motive and sent one of his agents, a man called Darby, to the trial. He took notes, which were sent to Castlereagh, and whether or not on the Foreign Secretary's instructions, he lodged an official complaint.

Two events, one in England and one in France, dominated Stuart's private and secret work during the second half of his first term as ambassador at Paris. In January 1820, George III died, and the accession of the Prince Regent as George IV made his wife, Caroline, Queen of England; in February 1820, the Duc de Berri, second in line of succession to the French throne, was assassinated, and public reaction brought the ultra-royalists to power. Stuart also had to contend with Castlereagh's death in 1822, when George Canning became Foreign Secretary again. Neither George IV nor Canning was well known or trusted by the sovereigns and statesmen of Europe.

The Prince of Wales' marriage to Caroline of Brunswick had been a disaster from the first, and the Princess had been living a peripatetic existence in Europe for several years. Now that they were king and queen, George wanted to divorce her, but his ministers were anxious to avoid a divorce—as much mud would stick to him as to her, and the Monarchy would suffer. Sir Charles was drawn into the affair officially as one of the King's ministers abroad, and unofficially as a private investigator.

When Caroline returned to England and proved to be more popular than the king, Stuart worked to bring to light Caroline's sexual relationship with her servant, Pergami, but he failed. He had several agents working on the case, and there was no doubt that Pergami had lived with the lady, but they found no evidence that she had provided him with more than board and lodging. The trial duly took place, but it had an inconclusive ending. The bill was withdrawn; Caroline was never given the recognition that she craved, and she died less than a year later.

Charles was created Count of Machico in 1825 and Marquess of Angra in Brazil in 1825.

In 1825, the Portuguese King John VI named Stuart his plenipotentiary with powers to negotiate and sign with Brazil a Treaty on the recognition of that country's independence. Invested with those powers, Stuart signed the treaty recognizing Brazilian independence on 29 August 1825, and on 15 November of the same year the Portuguese King ratified the treaty.

In January 1828 he was once again appointed Ambassador to France and was raised to the peerage as Baron Stuart de Rothesay of the Isle of Bute at the same time. He continued as Ambassador to France until 1831. In 1841 he was made Ambassador to Russia, a post he held until 1844.

Lord Stuart de Rothesay married Lady Elizabeth Margaret, daughter of Philip Yorke, 3rd Earl of Hardwicke, on 6 February 1816. They had two daughters: the Hon. Charlotte Stuart (1817-1861), wife of Charles Canning, 1st Earl Canning; and the Hon. Louisa Anne Stuart (1818-1891), wife of Henry Beresford, 3rd Marquess of Waterford.

Between 1831 and 1835 Lord Stuart de Rothesay constructed Highcliffe Castle at Highcliffe, Dorset.

With his wife at his side, de Rothesay died there, most likely from cerebro-vascular disease in November 1845, aged 66, when the barony became extinct. Lady Stuart de Rothesay remained a widow until her death in June 1867.

SOURCE

Franklin, Robert. *Private & Secret: The Clandestine Activities of a Nineteenth-Century Diplomat.* Book Guild, 2005.

11 May 1812: The Death of a Statesman

by M.M. BENNETTS

IT HAD BEEN A HELLISH KIND OF A DAY ALREADY. AND IT WAS ONLY GONE FIVE IN THE AFTERNOON. First on the agenda had been the bruising debate over the Conduct of the War in the Peninsula, with the Whigs and Radicals joining forces like some verbal artillery unit.

And in less than an hour, there would be yet another stormy session in the Royal Chapel of St. Stephen, where the House of Commons met—this time over the repeal of the Orders in Council, which the Government had announced they intended to do on 29 April. That at least ought to please the pro-American radical factions on the opposition benches. And one trusted it would stop this silly to and fro-ing with the Americans over impressment. Because what England did not want was a war with the Americans. Not at this time. Not when they were utterly dependent on wheat and flour from New England to feed Wellington's troops in the Peninsula.

But the debate finished, Brougham having finally closed his gob for the moment, and MPs were pouring out through the lobby doors and into the stone hallway...many of them on their way to the necessary chamber, no doubt. It was the usual crowd. Lord Osborne, General Gascoyne, Smith, the MP for Norwich...and emerging from a side door which stood adjacent to a stone staircase, known chiefly for its worn treads, the Prime Minister and Chancellor of the Exchequer, Sir Spencer Perceval, deep in conversation with Lord Osborne.

It was just a normal Monday afternoon. The afternoon of 11 May 1812.

John Bellingham had been a merchant and, with his wife, had travelled to Russia. There, his business had failed and he, owing many roubles, had been placed under house arrest. He'd finally been freed and the debt forgiven on the understanding that he would leave Russia.

Upon his return to England, he'd taken to writing letters to various Government officials accusing the Russian envoy of ruining his business and demanding restitution—which letters had eventually all been passed to the Treasury to be handled by the Chancellor. But over a period of three years, the Chancellor had given him no joy—despite the hundreds of letters and petitions he'd written.

Angry and resentful over his ill-treatment, for the past several months, he'd taken to sitting in the gallery of the House of Commons, assessing its weak points, learning to identify the various Honourable Members. He'd also sent threatening letters informing the Chancellor that as he'd failed to dispense justice, Bellingham felt at liberty to execute justice himself. But no one paid much heed—it's doubtful his letters were even read. Most probably they were just added to the already overladen pile of his ceaseless correspondence.

Now, armed with a pair of pistols, at just gone five in the afternoon, as the members were streaming from the chamber, he had hidden himself in the shadow of the stone stairs, just behind the folding doors. And as the Prime Minister emerged into the lobby, Bellingham stepped forward, aimed for Perceval's heart, and fired.

The shot reverberated through the closed stone corridor, deafening all.

The Prime Minister, his hand clutched to his breast, reeled backwards and fell, murmuring, "Murder!" (Or as other eyewitness accounts have it, "I am murdered!")

Smith, with Osborne's help, struggled to raise the fallen man. Someone cried, *"Oh my God! It's the Prime Minister!"*

Someone else called for a doctor.

Smith, Osborne, and a few others lifted him to carry him to the closest chamber, that of the Speaker's Secretary, and there laid him on a sofa.

Back in the hallway, chaos had broken out. There were calls to seal off the doors, shouts that it was a conspiracy and a French conspiracy at that.

A black-coated doctor from Great-George-street arrived and was shown to the small room. He searched Perceval's neck and wrists for any sign of a pulse, then said what they'd all been fearing for the past quarter of an hour: *"It is too late, gentlemen. I am sorry, he is dead."*

(The shot, fired at point-blank range, had passed through Perceval's heart.)

In the hallway, the MPs were milling and congregating in a fury of concern, and there were loud cries of *"Shut the doors, let no one out!"* Then, as the reality of what they had witnessed dawned upon them all, there were exclamations of *"Where's the murderer? Where's the rascal that fired?"*

From out the shadows of the stone staircase, John Bellingham, dressed in an overlarge and worn brown coat, stepped forward and loudly proclaimed, *"I am the unfortunate man!"*

If it had been chaos before, now it became a scene from bedlam. Instantly, Bellingham was seized and searched—in his pockets another primed and loaded pistol, an opera-glass, and a number of papers and bundles of letters. The spent pistol was not found. Upon being questioned why he had done such a thing, he replied, *"Want of redress and denial of justice."*

To which there were calls for him to be hanged or taken out and shot. Clerks were racing through the corridors, locking doors—for if this was part of a conspiracy, who or what was next?

The Speaker of the House banged and banged with his gavel, desperate in his attempts to bring the House to order. But to no avail. Finally, fearing for Bellingham's safety—for the honourable members were now a mob of angry, murderous men—he had no choice but to order that he be removed by the Sergeant of the House to the prison room, by means of a secret passage.

With many doubting that Bellingham had acted alone, and given the Napoleonic state's record in dispossessing European countries of their legitimate rulers, an emergency Cabinet Council was called.

Over the fraught course of that evening, they arrived at a series of measures to prevent further disturbance and panic, and to flush out fellow-conspirators and/or French spies. Sharp-shooters were installed atop government buildings and on the roof of 10 Downing Street. The mail was stopped and all foreign letters opened and scrutinised at the Foreign Letter Office. The Household Cavalry guarding the King and Queen at Windsor and the Prince Regent in London was trebled. The Thames River police were put on high alert and ordered to search vessels for possible conspirators. And the militia was called out to patrol the streets of the capital in force. It was as full-on as any modern government's response to a terror attack.

Taken before the Magistrates that evening, Bellingham denied any personal enmity towards Perceval, expressing great sorrow for his death and insisting he had only taken away the life of the Chancellor of the Exchequer. Despite, or perhaps because of, Bellingham's obvious mental derangement, a verdict of "wilful murder" was returned by the Coroner. At last bound over for trial, at 1.00 a.m., Bellingham was escorted, manacled, from Westminster to Newgate Prison by a company of the Light Horse.

The next day, 12 May, the Foreign Secretary, Viscount Castlereagh, addressed the Commons on the proposal to award Perceval's widow and children a handsome annuity in recognition of the great sacrifice he had made on behalf of his country. But as he paid tribute to his friend and colleague, Castlereagh broke down, sobbing, before the assembled MPs and had to be helped back to his seat—to strong sympathy from the House.

John Bellingham was tried for murder on 15 May at the Old Bailey before Lord Chief Justice Mansfield, with the Duke of Clarence, the Marquis Wellesley, and almost all the aldermen of the City of London occupying the bench. The jury took fourteen minutes to return a guilty verdict.

The following Monday, the 18th, Bellingham was hanged before the Debtor's Door of Newgate Prison.

Sir Spencer Perceval was buried in the family vault of St. Luke's, Charlton on 16 May. A memorial to him was placed in Westminster Abbey in June 1812.

Spencer Perceval remains the only Prime Minister to ever have been assassinated in British history. Though that's not the only reason he should be remembered. He had been a good man and a good Prime Minister and Chancellor of the Exchequer, respected by his contemporaries to a remarkable degree. He had steered the country through a most volatile and dangerous period, both domestically and abroad.

Yet saddest of all, like his mentor, the great William Pitt, he did not live to see the fruition of his work to defeat Napoleon. Indeed, he didn't even know that at the moment of his death, the tide was at last turning against the Napoleonic juggernaut.

His murder, although generally overlooked today, summoned up the same fears for national security as we have suffered in our generation. This is perhaps best seen in a letter written by his step-mother to Lord Castlereagh shortly afterwards:

What a catastrophe, my dearest Castlereagh, are you condemned to witness, and what privation has the country suffered in this tragedy of Mr Perceval's murder. Never since the Duke of Buckingham has such a daring assassination been attempted in England; but what a difference in men; one justly an object of public jealousy and contempt; the other admirable in all his attributes and every day obtaining more confidence. Some deep plot must be at the bottom of this desperate act. I can never credit that a lunatic alone conceived and executed it. I now tremble for your life.... There is a conspiracy against everything good and great. I hope you do not despise caution in your own person.

Perceval's assassination and the subsequent private and political turbulence form the cornerstone of my novel, *May 1812*. The above account, as well as that in the book, is drawn from several eye-witness accounts found in the newspapers and journals of the day.

LONDON IN THE EARLY
19TH CENTURY

BY M.M. BENNETTS

WE LIKE TO THINK OF LONDON IN THE EARLY 19TH CENTURY—AT THE TIME OF JANE Austen or the Regency—as this almost magical place. One where the traffic-less streets and squares are lined with graciously proportioned brick or Bath stone mansions, inside which ladies clothed in beautiful muslins and gentlemen in cravats flirted discreetly while sipping their ratafia. Right? And it all ends happily in marriage.

Whereas dramas purporting to shew mid-18th century London offer a robust, even rambunctious, view of the city with all classes and trades rubbing coat-tails in a Hogarthian panorama, the early years of the 19th century are presented as one of an ordered, elegant, static society operating within this hermetically-sealed neo-classical environment of pristine paintwork and pilasters...with, if I may say so, nary a sniff of reality.

For the reality is quite, quite different.

In 1800, London was the greatest metropolis in Europe, with a population of 1.1 million souls. Great Britain itself had a population of some 11 million. So roughly one-tenth of the population lived within the city boundaries of London and Westminster.

And, like all cities during all periods of history, London in the early 19th century was a place of transition, never static. It was a city in flux, a product of the Tudor, Restoration, and Georgian building, development, and neglect, a rambling amalgamation of the centuries which was only starting to give way to the ideas of the new century—ideas of adequate housing for the poor, proper sewage and drainage, safety....

The London fog—which is not a product of Sir Arthur Conan Doyle's imagination, but rather the effect of burning coal for domestic heating—was pervasive, even in summer, an acrid, dull grey blanket hanging perpetually over the city, obscuring the dome of St. Paul's, even often making it impossible to see across the street.

Gas-lighting in the streets wasn't really introduced until 1814 and thereafter. The roads and streets were rarely cobblestone, but rather clay poured onto grit which turned to a glaucous soup of sludge during heavy rain—and would have been covered in horse muck. (As in Dickens' day, there would have been sweeps, who, for a small fee, stood ready to clean the way across the road for pedestrians.)

There were somewhere around 30,000 vehicles in London in 1813, including 1100 hackney coaches for hire and about 400 sedan chairs. Some 400 coaches departed London each day for destinations all over the country too—most of them from Charing Cross. So London was a place of perpetual comings and goings, of bustle and hub-bub.

And the noise of it—all the people and horses and carriages and drays, the industry, the docks and dockworkers—was immense, unimaginable even. *"A universal hubbub; a sort of uniform grinding and shaking, like that experienced in a great mill with fifty pairs of stones..."* is how one visitor to the West End described it.

Visitors to the city were often by struck by two things—the beauty and magnificence of the great monuments, such as St. Paul's Cathedral and Westminster Abbey, and the "tumult and blaze", or in other words, the noise and smoke and fog. As in Shakespeare's day, London could still be smelled and tasted on the wind from as far away as 50 miles.

And even that area we associate with Regency society, the West End, was in a state of flux—only half built or only recently completed, and there were building sites and builder's rubbish everywhere. Building in the 18th and 19th centuries was a slow process even at the best of times—builders were often speculators who went bust before completion. And there were, of course, no power tools.

St. James's Square, the ultimate address (Viscount Castlereagh and his wife lived at Number 11), was only completed in 1792, though it had been begun in 1736. Berkeley Square was built and completed in the mid-18th century, as was Chesterfield St. (home to Beau Brummell until 1814). Hay Hill was under construction from 1760 until 1812.

Boodles' Club on St. James's Street was only completed in 1765 and Brooks' in 1778, with some building works unfinished until 1826. So much of St. James's Street was still brand spanking new, though it was, from the outset, a male enclave with all of a gentleman's requirements and desires catered for within just a few minutes' walk in one direction or the other. Hatchard's the bookseller was and is just around the corner on Piccadilly; Lock's, the hatter, still has premises just a few steps down from White's Club. And St. James's Street itself runs directly into King Street, a not-new neighbourhood, well-known for its high-class brothels and gambling hells.

And here, let me say that in the 18th and early 19th centuries, London was the sex capital of Europe. There have been several reprints of the notorious Harris's List—an address book of prostitutes in the capital. The artist, Sir Joshua Reynolds, (founder of the Royal Academy) was known to have had at least one copy. Nor was he alone in this. The small book went into several printings (usually sold out within days)....

And just beyond the permeable boundaries of the West End enclave of the rich and aristocratic, rubbing shoulders with it, jostling it at every turning, the rest of London was not new, not pristine...quite the opposite.

It was Old London, slum after slum of the vilest, most notorious reputation—always well-earned. Or it was home to the industry which had made the city rich. A city of banking and mercantile interests that spanned the globe. Or it was dockland—for London was a great port as well as everything else.

The most notorious slum of Old London was the "Mint", a ten-minute amble from London Bridge (present day Southwark)—a place of uninhabited buildings, unroofed and in ruins, many shored up by great beams propped up in the centre of the road, blackened timber houses, their upper floors leaning precariously over their foundations, or relics of once-fine mansions now falling down and surrounded by narrow courts and alleys—a place of unimaginable squalor where some 3000 families lived in cramped rooms where the sewage bubbled up through the floorboards—home to the most desperate of thieves, beggars, prostitutes, and outlaws.

Near Westminster Abbey was another notorious slum, the Almonry, which lay beside Tothill Fields—though many knew the area as "the Devil's Acre". Near St. Martin-in-the-Fields, at the west end of the Strand, was another warren of squalor. And beyond that, to the west, St. Giles, the most notorious of all, also called the Rookery or Little Dublin because of its predominately Irish population—conveniently located for those who followed thievery as a trade at the east end of Oxford St., which even 200 years ago was a mecca for shoppers. (There was a good reason for taking a tall, strapping footman to attend on one when one went to shop....)

The names of the streets perhaps evoke most effectively this London: Dark Entry, Cat's Hole, Pillory Lane.... Beyond St. Giles lay Seven Dials and beyond that Clare Market—a maze of streets with an evil reputation into which wayfarers were said to vanish and from which they never emerged.

Beyond, to the east, lay Saffron Hill and Chick Lane—washed by the stinking River Fleet—a teeming thieves' quarter with rooming houses where the freshly laundered (stolen) handkerchiefs would be suspended on poles across the narrow streets to ruffle and shimmer in the breeze.

And so it goes. Clerkenwell, which contained Jack Ketch's Warren, leads on to Smithfield with its cattle market, Spitalfields, and another thieves' quarter around Flower and Dean Street, and beyond, Petticoat Lane—the distribution centre for much of the city's stolen goods.... And south of that, Whitechapel with its many slaughterhouses.

South of the river, around Lambeth were the suburbs of labourers—artisans, clerks, and tradesmen. Indeed tradesmen, merchants, warehousemen, and shopkeepers could be found living just about anywhere, for London was a teeming residential city, with many of its workers living "above the shop", even in St. James's.

And beyond? Beyond the city lay not countryside, but wasteland. Or something we don't associate with European cites at all: shanty-towns.

Tomlin's New Town, a vast spread of wooden hovels, had been growing up on what is modern-day Paddington for nearly forty years since the mid-18th century. Elsewhere, animal dealers lived in wagons and huts, surrounded by their dogs, rabbits, fowls, and birds. Over in Battle Bridge (what is now King's Cross) there were *"mountains of cinder and filth"*, thousands of vast piles of horse dung, or the refuse of "waste-grains and hop-husks" dumped there by generations of London ale-brewers.

Amazing, isn't it? And terrifying. And alarming and exciting. This then is the real London of the early 19th century, a roiling sea of humanity, all shouting, hawking, riding, running, buying, selling, banking, dealing, stealing, eating, laughing, praying, all caught up in the business of living in the new century, following all walks of life, from "St. Giles to St. James" as they used to phrase it.

Food for more than one novel, wouldn't you say?

THE HOLE IN THE WALL:
REGENCY DANCING

BY DAVID WILLIAM WILKIN

As noted elsewhere, I have spent some time teaching the dances that were done during the Regency era. I have spent the time doing this because I have found tremendous enjoyment performing them as well as guiding others through them. The advent of devices like the iPod and now our iPhones have allowed me to store some of these tunes on the device and carry them with me, as well as listen to them whenever I wish, even as I write my Regency novels, such as my latest, *Jane Austen and Ghosts.*

Regency dancing has been in vogue here in the U.S.A. for many years now. We owe its acceptance in the United States to the attendees of Science Fiction conventions, specifically the wives of the authors of Science Fiction and Fantasy.

These ladies, bored by not having much to do, took their love of Georgette Heyer's Regency romances and asked one fan who was known for his ethnic dancing to choreograph dances that they had read about. The dances took off. Dancing spread to other venues, where attendees of Science Fiction conventions also were members of reenactment groups, specifically the Society for Creative Anachronism (SCA), which ends its study of previous times in 1600, well before our period.

Those interpreters of history, however, found a resource for dance from John Playford and the *English Dancing Master.* Though published in 1651, it is thought that all the dances he recorded and printed were also done before. A later dance, Hole in the Wall, made its way into many realms, that of the SCA and that of those dancing in the Regency genre at Science Fiction and Fantasy conventions and events solely concerned with the Regency.

Notes say that this dance, presented for you here, is from 1721. The music is from Henry Purcell and published in 1695 as Air VIII Hornpipe. The music was part of the incidental music in the revival of the 1677 tragedy of Mrs. Aphra Behn's *Abdelazer or the Moor's Revenge.* As far as we can tell, the name of the dance has little to do with the play. The orchestration of the music makes this piece related to the music of the French court of the late 17th century.

As mentioned, reenactment societies have taken this dance to the Regency and to the Renaissance. Many of those who dance it from those eras take the time to add embellishments believed to be found at those times. The dance, however, remains the same and is pleasant in any era.

Here is a technical description of the dance:

1) A couple honor each other, cast out and around B couple, meet below, pass through B couple to place; B couple honor each other, cast out and around A couple, meet above, pass through A couple to place.

2) A man, B lady bow and cross by right shoulders, exchanging places. B man, A lady bow and cross by right shoulders, exchanging places.

3) All 4 in set join hands, circle clockwise halfway to place. A couple cast around B's, B's lead up.

And now, let me break this down for you, first by giving you some *definitions*:

Set—The set is the group of dancers. In Hole in the Wall, men line up facing their partners. The first couple at the top of the line is the A couple, the next couple is the B couple, and these two couples are one set. The next couple, the third in the line, are A's once more, and so on.

Honor—An honor would be for the man to give a short bow, and the lady a curtsy.

Cast—Casting out and around means that the A man turns over his left shoulder and walks behind the B man to the place vacated by the next A man in line as he has also cast and moved down the line. The A lady does the same, turning over her right shoulder and walking behind the B lady on her side of the set to the place vacated by the next A lady.

Cross—The cross is when a dancer goes to the other side of the set. In Hole in the Wall the cross is done along the diagonal, so instead of facing one's partner, the dancer faces and crosses with the person of the opposite gender who is standing next to his or her partner.

Hands Round—This is often called as four hands round, though all four people and all eight of their hands (two each) are used. Everyone joins hands in the square, making a circle. The circle now advances a certain number of places; in Hole in the Wall, it is two, or halfway around the circle. In this dance the dancers end up back where they started so this is often called as halfway to place.

Progression—This is the term for how couples move on to dance with new people, for advancing to their next set of partners.

Now that we have some definitions in place, let's move on to the *dance figures*:

THE FIRST PART OF THE DANCE

- The A couple *exchange honors*, which is the man bowing and the lady curtsying.

- The A man *casts* by turning over his left shoulder and walking behind the B man to the place vacated by the next A man in line as he has also cast and moved down the line. The A lady does the same, *casting* over her right shoulder and walking behind the B lady on her side of the set.

- The A's, who are now next to the B's who have not moved, must *meet below and pass through*. This is often done with the active couple (the A's) lightly touching inside hands at shoulder height. They walk back between the B couple and return to the place they started the dance. The entire figure is done without stopping.

- The second part of the first figure is the B couple doing everything the A couple just did.

The B couple is at this time the active couple. This, though, is somewhat the reverse of the A couple. The B couple casts out and walks behind the A couple going up the set to meet above the A couple and then walks between the A couple back to place.

THE SECOND PART OF THE DANCE

- This is now done on the diagonal. The A man *honors* the B lady and she him. They *cross* to each other's place passing right shoulders. Again, many touch the fingers of their right hands to each other in our modern interpretation with a bit of flirtation. When they reach the place that was occupied by the other, they *honor* once more.

- As there was repetition before, so too again. This time the B man and the A lady do what was just done by their partners.

THE THIRD PART OF THE DANCE (THE *PROGRESSION*)

- *All four join hands* and walk in a circle clockwise, halfway. This puts each person in the place where they started the dance.

- As at the beginning of the dance, the A couple *casts* down, but not this time to where the other A's were before. This time they go to where the couple they have been dancing with (the B's) are standing.

- Our B couple must get out of the way, and joining inside hands, as is done now, the B man leads his partner to the place that their A couple has vacated.

- At the end of this, the B's find themselves with a new A couple, and the A's have a new B couple as well.

Please note that at each end of the line, after one time through, there are extra couples. The B couple at the very top of the line has no couple to dance with, and the A couple at the bottom of the line is in the same position. The solitary couples will wait one time through the dance and then return to dance, but this time as they go along the line to the other end, they are now the reverse couple of what they were before. If they started as an A, they are now a B, and vice-versa.

At the Regency Assembly Press pages there is one page devoted to Regency dancing, as you would find at the time and recreated for today.

SOURCE

Keller, Kate Van Winkle and Genevieve Shimer. *The Playford Ball: 103 Early Country Dances 1651-1820*. Country Dance & Song Society of America, 1994.

Almack's: It's Not Quite What You Think...

by M.M. BENNETTS

Almack's. The name conjures up images of a glittering Regency ball attended by ladies in elegant silk gowns and gentlemen in the formal attire of the age, all dancing and bowing together—Mr. Darcy and Elizabeth Bennet, only in polished London setting. Though this, I suspect, may be down to the frequency with which the late Georgette Heyer wrote of the place.

The reality, regardless of the fictional lore, was somewhat different.

Almack's Assembly Rooms were located on King Street, St. James's. The Assembly Rooms themselves had been opened in 1764 by a Scot by the name of MacCall who, allegedly, decided on an approximate anagram of his name for the rooms.

There was a large ballroom—some ninety to one hundred feet long and forty feet wide—which was decorated with gilded columns and pilasters, classic medallions, and very large mirrors. By the late Regency (post 1814-15) it was lit by gas in elaborate cut-glass lustres.

There was a balcony at one end where the small orchestra was seated. Refreshments (such as they were) were deliberately (revoltingly) mediocre: weak lemonade or orgeat or ratafia, dry biscuits, and day-old brown bread and butter. (Although good wine or alcohol was never served on the premises, many gentlemen would have arrived already drunk.)

There was also a dais or raised seat at the upper end, where the Lady Patronesses sat, *"nodding acknowledgment as the invitees arrived."*

Balls were given once a week, on Wednesday evenings, for a twelve-week period during the Season—roughly from the beginning of March until early June. Until 1814, only country dances were permitted. Thereafter, quadrilles and the waltz were introduced to liven things up. No one was admitted after 11 p.m., but frequently the dancing went on well into Thursday morning.

By 1801, the required "uniform" for a gentleman was the look made famous and fashionable by George Brummell: a dark coat (navy or black), white cravat, and black knee breeches and silk stockings or tight black pantaloons with thin shoes (men's black dancing pumps), and chapeau bras. Wider trousers or any introduction of colour were unacceptable and the wearer would be turned away at the door.

Admission to these balls was by ticket only, or by "voucher" (a cardboard square) as they were called, which were on sale on Bond Street.

And the cost of this? Almack's membership fee was ten guineas—around £350 in today's money according to the UK National Archives. One then had to buy one's tickets at a cost of ten shillings each (£17 in today's money).

But these vouchers were only made available to those on the List. And the means for inclusion on this List is among the most important things one needs to know about the place. For Almack's during the early years of the 19th century was an exclusive club. Very exclusive. And it was run by women.

And not just any women. These are ladies of highest birth, fortune, and snobbery. And possibly the last of those qualities is the most important. They are the Lady Patronesses.

In 1812, the Patronesses were:

Lady Emily Cowper: daughter of the Earl and Countess of Melbourne; by 1814, the lover of Lord Palmerston and then his wife; sister of William Lamb and therefore sister-in-law to Lady Caroline Lamb who is the niece of the Duke and Duchess of Devonshire and daughter of the Earl and Countess of Bessborough;

Lady Jersey: wife of the 5th Earl of Jersey, the granddaughter of Robert Childs, a banker, and a considerable heiress; sister to the 11th Earl of Westmorland (and yes, her nickname was Silence because she never shut her mouth);

Lady Castlereagh: wife of Viscount Castlereagh (later the Marquis of Londonderry—he was Foreign Secretary and Leader of the House of Commons from 1812 until his death in 1822), she was the daughter of the 2nd Earl of Buckinghamshire—he'd been the British Ambassador to Russia and the Lord Lieutenant of Ireland;

Mrs. Drummond Burrell: wife of the notable dandy who was enobled so she later became Lady Gwydry and eventually Lady Willoughby de Eresby;

Lady Sefton: wife of the 2nd Earl of Sefton;

The Austrian Ambassador's wife, **Princess Esterhazy**, and after 1814, the Russian Ambassador's wife, **Countess Lieven** (who deserves her own blog as she is one of the most opinionated, odiously officious, haughtiest busybodies ever to breathe oxygen).

Unofficially, until he fled to the Continent to escape his debtors in 1814, Mr. Brummell also wielded a great deal of influence over whom to admit to the List and whom to strike off.

And probably it is this description of those who wielded the power to include or exclude that is most informative about Almack's. Because although politics (and sex, London street riots, and the war) were all forbidden topics of conversation there, these were women at the pinnacle of political power and patronage, influence and wealth, not just in Britain but in Europe itself.

Between them, they weighed and scrutinised Britain's nobility and gentry. And in most cases, found it wanting. Probably some full three-quarters of Britain's aristocracy failed to gain their approbation. Wealth—especially if it "smelled of the shop"—was no guarantee of entry. Nor was birth. Good looks or talent might help. Dancing well, especially if one were male, was a definite asset.

According to Captain Gronow in his *Regency Recollections*:

> Very often, persons whose rank and fortunes entitled them to the entree, were excluded by the cliqueism of the lady patronesses: for the female government of Almack's was a pure despotism and subject to all the caprices of despotic rule.

The travel writer, Major Chambre, in his *Recollections*, wrote of the "Rules of Admission":

No lady or gentleman's name could continue on the list of the same patroness for more than one set of balls. No gentleman's tickets could be transferred; nor could ladies procure them for their female friends, nor gentlemen for gentlemen. A mother might give hers to a daughter, or one unmarried sister to another. Subscribers who were prevented coming, were requested to give notice to the lady patronesses on the day of the ball by two o'clock...that the vacancies might be filled up.

Moreover, having been on the List one year did not necessarily mean one could look to be included in the next year's List. Often too, in what might be described as playfulness (some might call it bitchiness) the patronesses would extend vouchers to a lady, but not her husband. Or vice versa. Particularly if it was felt one had married beneath oneself.

Almack's was, in short, a place wholly given over to the pursuit of sex and marriage—and these are alliances based on property, money, political influence, and prestige. It is not about "love-matches".

In Austenite language (though Jane Austen herself never mentions it), Almack's was a place where Miss Georgiana Darcy could be safely introduced to eligible young men, without her brother or her trustees worrying that she might encounter a fortune-hunter of the stamp of Wickham or Willoughby. Likewise, these eligible young men would be sure that Miss Georgiana Darcy had been vetted by the Patronesses, that she was possessed of the fortune she claimed to have, and that she was suitably well-born.

For those who are devotees of *Downton Abbey*, if I may give another example, Almack's provided one setting where the Lady Mary Crawleys of the age might encounter suitable gentlemen with whom they might form an alliance. It was never a place for ingenues from the country.

It was a hot-house atmosphere of gossip, music, dancing, and repressed sexual tension perhaps, but above all, it was a place where the very rich and very powerful played, partied, and reigned supreme....

In Gronow's words, Almack's was *"the seventh heaven of the fashionable world."*

Dorothea Christorovna Benckendorff Lieven: Princess Lieven

by LAUREN GILBERT

Countess Lieven, later known as Princess Lieven, is a frequent character of Regency-era fiction. Long known as one of the patronesses of Almack's Assembly Rooms, she was the wife of General Count Christophe Lieven (later Prince Lieven) who was the Russian Ambassador to Great Britain from late 1812.

In Georgette Heyer's *The Grand Sophy,* Countess Lieven is mentioned as follows:

> *"I was not aware that you are acquainted with the Countess Lieven," said Miss Wraxton.*
>
> *"Do you dislike her?" Sophy asked, aware of the coldness in Miss Wraxton's voice.*
>
> *"Many people do, I know. Sir Horace calls her the great intrigante, but she is clever and can be very amusing."*

She was a noted hostess, whose salon was famous for society and politics.

Princess Lieven was born December 17, 1785 at Riga. Shortly after completing her education, she married Lieutenant-General Count Lieven in early 1800 in St. Petersburg at age fourteen. Even at that age, she demonstrated significant talent for being a hostess and for conversation. The couple had five children: a daughter who died very young, and four sons.

In 1809, then-Count Lieven became the Russian Envoy to the Prussian Court, which was the Countess' first public position. In 1811, Count Lieven was appointed Ambassador to London, a post he held until 1834.

Both of the Lievens used all of their abilities to restore friendly relations between Russia and Great Britain. Countess Lieven became a leader of fashion and threw herself into society, becoming a prominent hostess whose invitations were highly prized. She was elected a patroness of Almack's sometime in 1814 or earlier, and is credited with introducing the German waltz there.

During the Lievens' time in London, Countess Lieven cultivated friendships with those holding political office who could best further the interests of the Russian government. Countess Lieven was definitely a political animal and contributed significantly to her husband's success as ambassador. In fact, there were very few political events she did not influence to some degree between 1812 and 1857.

Countess Lieven was fully conscious of her own importance and superiority and had a high opinion of her own charms. She did not hesitate to form friendships (sometimes more than friendships) with influential men in a position to influence political matters to suit her. She would drop friends and form new ones as political matters shifted, which did create some hard feelings but did not apparently affect her usefulness.

She is supposed to have had affairs with every major statesman involved in European politics, including the Austrian diplomat Prince Metternich, George IV, and numerous prime ministers—her relationships changing as the members of the Cabinet changed. Her relationship with Metternich is believed to have begun at the Congress of Aix-la-Chapelle in 1819, when Metternich tried to bring Czar Alexander into accord with Austria, and continued until 1825, when (coincidentally?) the accession of Nicholas I caused Russian policy to change.

Excerpts of her letters to Metternich are fascinating reading. In 1825, she was entrusted by Czar Alexander to make a secret overture to the British government. In a letter to Count Nesselrode, his foreign minister, the Czar wrote, *"It is a pity Countess Lieven wears skirts. She would have made an excellent diplomat."*

Count Lieven was granted the title prince in 1826. In 1834, he was recalled to Russia. Soon after the Lievens' return to Russia, their two youngest sons died. Princess Lieven subsequently left Russia and settled in Paris, where she continued to involve herself in politics, forming a close relationship with Francois Guizot. Her Paris salon was known as the listening post of Europe. She died at her home in Paris on January 27, 1857, and was buried at the Lieven family estate next to her two young sons who had died in St. Petersburg.

Regency Era Classified Ads

by **DEBRA BROWN**

TULIPS.—A Gentleman removing to town, has a BED of 100 rows TULIPS to DISPOSE OF: the price will be 1s. each root, and there will be from 1,300 to 1,500 blooming roots: a stage may also be taken if convenient. Apply to Mr. Potts, seedsman, 74 Cornhill.

Punctuation and capitalization is as in the ad.

TURTLE and VENISON.—T.DALE, Northumberland Coffee-house, Charing-cross, respectfully acquaints his Friends and the Public, that he DRESSES a fine HAUNCH of VENISON, THIS DAY, to be ready at 5 o'clock, and every Monday, Wednesday, and Friday, during the Season: fine lively turtle dressed every day, and sent to any part of town. Families supplied with turtle and venison on the most reasonable terms.

Who said they didn't shoot deer?

A LADY may be accommodated with BOARD, a pleasant sitting room, with an airy bed-room, on moderate terms, in a genteel establishment for a few young ladies, 8 miles west of London: there is also a vacancy for a parlour boarder: the house is most pleasantly situate, and the neighbourhood highly respectable. Letters, post paid, addressed to W.M., Miss Wallers, milliner, Hill-street, Richmond, Surrey, will receive due attention.

And better yet…

BOARD and LODGING for Ladies only—A Widow Lady, resident at Highgate wishes to receive Two respectable Ladies into her family, where they will experience all the kind attentions of a liberal and comfortable home, the house is pleasantly situate near the church, has a good garden, and the back windows command a beautiful prospect; the terms moderate. Cards of address at 109, Hatton-garden.

I suppose some of you could see this house for yourselves.

PARTNERSHIP.—A Gentleman engaged in a most RESPECTABLE

PURSUIT, is willing to admit another that unites family respectability with a general knowledge of business: it is expected that the applicant be of active habits, as the party intends to reside much in the country, in consequence of his present state of health; or the whole may be purchased for an adequate consideration: persons influenced by idle and intrusive curiosity need not apply, nor any that cannot command 1,200l. Address, post paid, with name and residence, X.Y.Z., care of Mr. Winbolt, stationer, 48, St. Paul's church-yard.

A PUPIL, of the celebrated Porson, and of great experience in TEACHING the GREEK and LATIN CLASSICS, particularly the former, has simplified the method of acquiring that beautiful and philosophic language, so that it is the work of only a few months. Letters, only, post paid, M.N., Proctor's, 101, Fleet-street, duly noticed.

(What was duly noticed?)

AN AUTHORESS, in immediate want of a sum of money, and anxious to procure it without the delay attending representation, is desirous of DISPOSING of 1 or 2 MANUSCRIPT DRAMATIC PIECES, which, in the hands of a person acquainted with theatrical effect, are capable of being rendered highly interesting and producing ultimately great advantages. Address by letter, post paid, A.B. Brown's circulating library, Marylebone-street, Piccadilly.

AS GOVERNESS.—The Daughter of a Clergyman deceased, who has for many years filled the above situation in families of the highest respectability, would be happy to undertake the CHARGE of TWO or THREE YOUNG LADIES, and instruct them in the English and French languages grammatically, the latter to speak fluently, writing, arithmetic, geography, and music, likewise the rudiments of Italian: the advertiser would much prefer that her pupils should not exceed the age of 10 or 11. Letters addressed, post paid, to D.E.F. at W. Darton's, jun., bookseller, 58, Holborn-hill, will meet with immediate attention.

SELECT ARTICLES FOR THE TOILETTE.—ATKINSON'S AMBROSIAL SOAP prepared by a new process, which divests it of all alkaline and irritating qualities: it prevents the skin chapping, removes freckles, redness, or hardness, and makes it luxuriously soft, white, and even, price 1s. the square; it is also prepared in shaving cakes, and is peculiarly adapted for gentlemen who have strong beards or tender faces; price 9d. 1s., and 1s. 6d.

each. Atkinson's Curling Fluid for the growth of the hair, (founded on the discovery of the causes which occasion baldness,) is a certain regenerator of the hair where it has fallen off from illness, perspiration, change of climate, or hereditary causes, it also keeps it in curl in exercise in dancing or walking, or in damp weather, price 3s. 6d. a bottle. Atkinson's Vegetable Dye changes grey or red hair on the head or whiskers to a permanent brown or black, price 5s. and one guinea. Sold by the proprietor, James Atkinson, perfumer, 43, Gerrard-street, Soho-square; and by most perfumers in the kingdom.

These CHARMING classified ads were taken from *The Times* (in London) of August 18, 1819. The front and back pages of the paper are classified ads of all types. Inside, you will find news articles not enhanced with any drawings.

The paper was sent to me in a lovely gift box by Thomas Walker of Historic Newspapers. Be sure to check out his website for old newspapers from around the world. And now, for a classified ad of my own:

AN AUTHORESS, in immediate want of a sum of money, and anxious to procure it without delay, is desirous of DISPOSING of a NUMBER of copies of a book: suitable for the reading enjoyment of older GIRLS and WOMEN of established and respectable families. Kindly GENTLEMEN have also spoken well of the STORY, entitled, *The Companion of Lady Holmeshire.* Sold by proprietor Amazon, post paid unless bought for purse or pocket on a Kindle device.

Libraries in Georgian and Regency England

by LAUREN GILBERT

IN THE 18TH CENTURY, THE MARKETING OF LITERATURE EVOLVED FROM PRIVATE PATRONAGE to publishing by booksellers. This resulted in writers becoming less entertainers for hire (e.g. in the 16th century, Spenser writing *The Faerie Queene* for the court of Queen Elizabeth) and more independent professionals. This resulted in two new literary forms—the periodical essay and the novel. These forms brought literature into the clubs, coffee houses, assemblies and other public places—out of the universities, private libraries, and churches—exposing it to a wider audience such as merchants and the upwardly mobile.

In the Georgian era, literacy became more widespread among the lower classes as a result of a concern that people should be able to read the Bible for themselves. Money was furnished to the Church of England for this education, and more people were exposed to books and newspapers.

Initially, a library or study was not common—a collection of books (especially with leather bindings) in a private home was a sign of wealth and prestige. A library or study was designed for the use of the master, being a place where *"...typically, a country gentleman would receive his tenants or keeper..."* (Pool, 191).

Until 1861, the tax on paper helped keep books scarce and expensive. The Stamp Act of 1797 levied a tax of sixpence on each copy of a newspaper. This was raised in 1815 to 4 pence, with a separate tax of 3 shillings on pamphlets and 3 shillings sixpence on newspaper advertising (Hughes, 128). Books therefore were expensive and considered luxuries.

At the Jane Austen Society of North America's Annual General Meeting in 2004, held at the Huntingdon Museum, Stephen Tabor lectured on "The Look of the Book" in Jane Austen's time and described the bindings: leather (most expensive), cloth, and paper. For example, when Thomas Creevey, MP, found books too expensive to buy, he lamented when he could no longer access certain volumes of Wellington's Dispatches and had to make do with works available from a different library. The cost factor alone makes Reverend Austen's library of over 500 volumes all the more remarkable.

Because of the cost of newspapers, newspaper societies were formed in local parishes where a group of people each contributed a weekly sum to subscribe to a London newspaper and 2 or 3 provincial papers (about sixpence a week); poorer districts had more subscribers contributing less (about 1 penny a week) to subscribe to a provincial paper. (A total of 5000 of these societies were operating in the 1820s.)

Local printers and booksellers started their own libraries. In London alone, by 1819 there were twenty-eight booksellers which kept circulating libraries and nine with reading rooms. Hatchard's Booksellers which was founded in 1797 in Piccadilly and is still open today was one of the booksellers with a reading room. In 1821, there were approximately 65,000 reading societies in Great Britain providing reading material for annual subscriptions ranging from 1/2 guinea to 2 guineas a year to families.

The cost of books was one factor in encouraging people to join together to form libraries. On November 30, 1814, in reference to a possible second edition of *Mansfield Park*, Jane Austen wrote, *"People are more ready to borrow and praise, than to buy—which I cannot wonder at"* (*Jane Austen's Letters*, 287). Most towns had subscription libraries and circulating libraries where books could be borrowed for an annual fee. Lending libraries of this nature started up in provincial towns and watering places and spread.

Although a large percentage of published material was religious in nature, novels became extremely popular across all class lines. For example, the novels of the Minerva Press, which included *The Mysteries of Udolpho* by Mrs. Radcliffe, were read by all levels of society.

Many of these subscription libraries still exist and are in use in England today. The Association of Independent Libraries was founded in 1989, and the founding members were all institutions which began as independently-funded subscription libraries established between 1768 and 1841. The association now includes libraries of historic foundation not necessarily meeting the original criteria.

The oldest member library is Chetham's Library, founded in Manchester in 1653 as a public reference library by the merchant Humphrey Chetham for the benefit of the people of Manchester. The smallest member library is the Tavistock Subscription Library, founded in 1799 in Tavistock, Devonshire—in 1810, the Duke of Bedford was the president of this library. The majority of the libraries in this association still retain their independence.

SOURCES

Austen, Jane. *Jane Austen's Letters.* Edited by Deidre Le Faye. Oxford: Oxford University Press, 1993.

Hughes, Kristine. *The Writer's Guide to Everyday Life in Regency and Victorian England from 1811-1901.* Cincinnati, OH: Writer's Digest Books (F & W Publications), 1998.

Pool, Daniel. *What Jane Austen Ate and Charles Dickens Knew.* New York: Simon & Schuster Inc., 1993.

Sanborn, Vic. "The Circulating Library in Regency Resorts." *Jane Austen's World.* August 30, 2010. http://janeaustensworld.wordpress.com/2010/08/30/the-circulating-library-in-regency-times/.

White, R.J. *Life in Regency England.* London: William Clowes & Sons, 1969.

Williams, E.N. *Life in Georgian England.* London: William Clowes & Sons, 1967.

Ashes, Tallow, and Turpentine: Coming Clean in the Regency Era

by MARIA GRACE

KEEPING CLOTHES CLEAN HAS ALWAYS BEEN A CHALLENGE. TODAY, WE CAN SIMPLY GO TO the store and buy a specialized product according to whichever stain needs cleaning. In centuries past, the mistress of the house needed to be well versed on what home preparations could be used to keep her household fresh and clean. Some Regency-era solutions are similar to what we use to today, and some were positively stomach churning.

LYE

Plain lye formed the backbone of much of the everyday laundry cleaning arsenal and was fairly easy to obtain. Ashes from household fires were packed into a barrel with holes drilled in the bottom and lined with hay. Water was poured through the ashes and concentrated lye dripped from the holes.

The strength of the solution was critical for its cleaning power. If an egg did not float high enough in the solution it was too weak and would be poured through the ashes again. Lye that was too strong could burn skin and damage fabrics and would need to be diluted. Urine, for its ammonia content might also be added to a lye solution to improve its cleaning power.

Body linen and other garments whose colors did not need to be protected, sheets and household linens were soaked in a vat of lye prior to being boiled on laundry day. The process was called "bucking" and attempted to restore the white or off white color to the laundry.

SOAP

The generous use of soap was a modern advance in dealing with dirty laundry. At first it was used sparingly, only to treat stains. Later, it would be added to the main wash for cleaning.

Though soap could be purchased, what could be made at home often was, especially in areas away from larger urban centers. Soap could be made in several ways. A pail of lye could be added to about three pounds of melted animal fat and boiled all day. To avoid all that boiling and stirring, four pails of lye could be stirred into a barrel of 30 pounds of animal fat. Additional lye was added until it looked "right" to the soap maker. The soap might be used while it was still soft or it might be set up—dried and hardened with warm weather and salt.

Household manuals often contained various specialized recipes for soap with different fats and additives touted as better for one use or another. Individual households would also have their own recipes handed down from mother to daughter.

WATER SOFTENERS

Sodium borate (borax) and sodium carbonate (washing soda) were often added to the water to improve the action of the soap. Borax was preferred to washing soda which would yellow whites and damage their texture. Borax could be added to the soap when it was made to eliminate the need to add it to the laundry water separately.

Both borax and washing soda had to be purchased and might not be available to poorer or more remote households.

STAIN REMOVAL

Stains were as much a problem then as they are now. Different recipes were used for different stains. These included:

- Grease and oil stains: chalk, brick dust, and pipe clay
- Grass stains: alcohol, lemon and onion juice, kerosene
- Blood stains: kerosene, lemon juice
- Wax stains: a hot coal wrapped in a clean rag or wet brown paper
- Urine stains: milk
- Fruit stains: milk, lemon juice, onion juice

OX-GALL

To deal with stains on expensive colored fabrics which would bleach in a lye solution, ox-gall was the favorite solution. Ox-gall was obtained by sending a bottle to the butcher who filled it with the contents of cows' gall-bladders.

BLEACHING

Despite soaking in lye, stubborn articles sometimes required additional bleaching. Human urine and hog manure were often used for this purpose as was lemon juice. Sunshine in combination with lemon juice or lye was a freely available bleaching agent. Some estates and towns set aside areas of mown grass as "bleaching grounds" where articles could be spread on laundry day. The chlorophyll in the grass helped in the bleaching process.

BLUING

Since soap and washing soda often yellowed white articles, bluing would be added to the rinse water to neutralize the yellowing. Blue dye, of various formulations, was placed in a small bag which would be swished through the rinse water and removed leaving a slight blue color behind.

STIFFENING

Like other laundry necessities, starch was made at home. Wheat, potato gratings, and rice were common sources. Wheat starch might be added directly to water. The water used to cook rice or potatoes might be saved for starching. Similarly, grated potatoes could be soaked in water then removed and the water used for starching laundry.

For delicate laces, sugar might be added to the final rinse water rather than starch. Alternately, gum arabic, made from the sap of acacia trees, might be used to stiffen laces and collars.

DRY CLEANING

Silk and woolen clothes never touched water. Several dry cleaning techniques were developed to preserve the fabrics through the cleaning process.

Fullers used fuller's earth, an absorbent clay, and a thistle to clean wools.

Scourers spot cleaned silks once a year. Salt, chalk, or fuller's earth as well as solvents like turpentine, kerosene, gasoline, lemon juice, warm milk, or even urine were used on the fine fabric. The whole garment was never immersed and scrubbed.

Leather breeches were scrubbed with a "breeches ball" made of a mixture of ox-gall and fuller's earth.

Interestingly, because many fine garments were not laundered with harsh lye, scrubbing, and boiling, they remain preserved today. Far fewer examples of body linen survive today because of the harsh measures used to keep them clean.

SOURCES

"The Complexities of Wash Day in the 18th Century." *Woodville Plantation*. http://www.woodvilleplantation.org/Schedule/laundry_day_18th_century1.pdf.

Harris, Kristina. "Victorian Laundry (or, Aren't You Glad You Didn't Live Then?)." *Vintage Collection*. 2002. http://www.vintageconnection.net/VictorianLaundry.htm.

"History of Laundry." *Old and Interesting*. June 13, 2010. http://www.oldandinteresting.com/history-of-laundry.aspx.

"History of Laundry - after 1800." *Old and Interesting*. September 30, 2010. http://www.oldandinteresting.com/history-of-washing-clothes.aspx.

Olmert, Michael. "Laundries: Largest Buildings in the Eighteenth-century Backyard." *Colonial Williamsburg Journal* (Autumn, 2009). http://www.history.org/foundation/journal/autumn09/laundries.cfm.

A Regency Era Lady's Prodigious Layers of Clothing

by WANDA LUCE

Poor darlings! What a production it was for a lady of the Regency era to go from bare skin to polished enchantress. Knowing what must go under that elegant outer gown just makes me itch and turn in my skin. Such a binding set of underclothing must have made escaping it at night a great thing.

Or, maybe I am just a typical 21st century woman who finds modern day clothing too restricting. Well, since you and I are involved in this article for the sole purpose of exploring those far more dreadful early 19th century underclothes, I suppose we might as well get on with the investigation.

The very first layer donned by the fashionable women of the Regency era was the chemise, or shift. It was a thin, full-length cotton garment with short, tight sleeves, a low neckline, and a plain hem. Our present day slip is very similar, though unlike the chemise, a slip is worn over the other layers of undergarments. A chemise provided a barrier between a woman's body and the other layers of clothing and absorbed perspiration.

This first layer bore up under washings with the most stringent soaps, and chemises were often boiled to achieve a high level of cleanliness as well as to remove any stains or discoloration. The transparent muslins and silks of the era were intended to flow elegantly around a lady's form, but without the help of a chemise or shift, society might have been granted far too immodest a display of her private "attributes." In my Regency era novel *Lydia*, my heroine goes for a swim in a private pond wearing only her chemise.

Once the chemise was in place, a woman slipped into short stays, a corset that extended only a short way below the breasts. Those who hoped to appear thin wore long stays.

Drawers, or underpants, were not in common use at this time, though some did wear them. They buttoned at the knee and were open at the crotch. Quite a drafty bit of nonsense if you ask me! Well, the advent of the modern toilet was yet a way off, so the logistics of squatting over a chamber pot necessitated certain "concessions" in the clothing line.

Our modern day sensibilities and cultural delicacies (if we have any left) make the idea sound rather obscene—but so it was. However, consider: while women were anchored lock, stock, and barrel inside so much fabric, at least they enjoyed the cooling free breezes underneath it all. I cannot quite reconcile their rigid morality with the concept of a completely exposed... but, oh well, a great many things in history make very little sense by today's standards.

Although I cannot bear the thought of wearing all that rigmarole, I often envy those ladies that they got to wear such wonderfully feminine clothing. Were I to dress in that way today, the local sheriff would most likely offer me a kind escort to the "sanitarium."

For those who would like the experience of dressing like a lady of the *ton*, several present-day organizations offer Regency-era balls. How I would love to step back in time and mingle, just once, at a London-season ball with the most illustrious members of the "upper ten thousand"! How fun it might have been to be a Miss Elizabeth Bennet.

THE CHANGES IN LADIES' FASHION FROM 1780S TO 1814: TOO MUCH OR TOO LITTLE

BY **MAGGI ANDERSEN**

IN THE 1780S AND EARLY 1790S, SKIRTS WERE FULL AND ROUND AND SLIGHTLY PUFFED OUT at the back, although the wide panniers had gone. Generous fichus covered the bosom. As France's Republican and classical styles spread across the Channel, however, the bulk of the skirt gradually diminished; it took ten yards to make a dress in 1796, but only seven yards in 1801. The number of petticoats diminished too, until some women wore only one or even none at all (to the scandal and shock of moralists and the secret delight of the male population).

Petticoats in the past had been highly decorative and visible—a prominent part of the dress itself. Now, if it showed at all, it was an ornamental band at the bottom of a dress. A ball gown found in 1801 *Gallery of Fashion* is a "robe", a descendant of the open-fronted gown that exposed the petticoat, in the style of the 18th century.

Like the robe, the frock or gown could be adapted with equal ease to morning or evening wear. One 1807 example of an evening frock, has a square neckline, short sleeves, and a relatively smooth front of sprigged muslin; all the fullness is gathered at the back and allowed to cascade down as a train.

An 1808 walking frock, however, has no train and is worn with long gloves, a jacket-like vest, a shawl, and a straw bonnet. This careful covering of almost all exposed skin would have met with the approval of the author of *The Mirror of Graces* (1811), who advised the cautious woman that:

> Morning robes should be of a length sufficiently circumscribed as not to impede her walking, but on no account must they be too short; for...[when] showing the foot or ankle the idea of beauty is lost....

In addition to the petticoat, many women now took to wearing drawers. These were quite long—long enough that Lady de Clifford pointed out to Princess Charlotte that hers were visible every time she got into or out of a carriage. Unimpressed, the princess replied, *"the Duchess of Bedford's are much longer, and they are bordered with Brussels lace."* There was, as the princess implied, little effort taken to hide the drawers, which came into fashion around 1806.

Above the petticoat, a chemise was worn. This was a knee-length linen or cotton shirt, often with a frill of some kind at the neckline and short sleeves. It was usually, but not always, worn beneath a dress. If it were worn, part of it, for example, the decorative neckline, often peeked from underneath the dress.

As the silhouette slimmed, the waistline rose, until it ended just under the breasts. The dress itself was rather loose and pulled into classical folds of drapery, often by drawstrings at the neckline. Beneath this apparent ease and lightness, many women retained the stays they had worn for centuries. These were corsets made of heavy cotton fabric or silk and stiffened with whalebone. They were sometimes assisted in front with a "divorce," a triangular piece of padded metal that separated the breasts.

Necklines were very low and revealed a great deal of the bosom, so many women retained the modesty pieces of earlier decades, tucking a gauzy piece of fabric around the back of the neck and into the top of the gown, sometimes crossing at the front. During the day women wore the morning or walking dress with long sleeves, gloves, and bonnets, which covered all of the skin. Morning gowns were often white.

Evening gowns were exclusively short-sleeved until about 1814. The anonymous author of *The Mirror of Graces* suggested white above all for evening gowns, as "*White is becoming to all characters,*"—but if a large woman, "*a lady of majestic deportment,*" chose to wear colors, she should adhere to "*the fuller shades of yellow, purple, crimson, scarlet, black and grey.*"

After 1814, fichus were discarded and women displayed their low necklines to full advantage.

SOURCE

Olsen, Kirstin. *All Things Austen: An Encyclopedia of Austen's World*, Volume I. Greenwood, 2005.

Ladies' Slippers and Half-Boots in the Regency

BY WANDA LUCE

How essential to every lady's wardrobe are the shoes! While today we romp about in every sort of convention for the foot, in early 1800s England, the choices were vastly more limited. Slippers were ill-suited to extensive walking but served well for the pampered lifestyle of the *haut ton*, the gentry, or the wealthy merchant class.

Call me a muffin-head if you like, but I was quite shocked to discover that the slippers were often fashioned of colored leather. I guess, somehow I doubted their ability to make such beautifully colored leather in that era. As a Regency-era author, I am ashamed to admit I did not know this. I suppose I assumed the slippers were made of any number of available fabrics like sturdy cottons or satins.

The pointed ends look quite dangerous, if you ask me, but I can assure you that they rounded out in the later Regency. Such extreme points on ladies' shoes have enjoyed a hearty revival at various points in time, but they never seem to last for long.

While some slippers were made of leather, some were composed of silk.

Soon, the high-heeled pumps of the 18th century disappeared, as did the stripes and embellished patterns seen at the turn of the century. Regency era shoes were crafted in a variety of colors and often came with ribbon ties. These flat, delicate shoes were little more than ballet slippers and were mainly worn in the evenings or indoors.

By mid-Regency, women enjoyed the greater utility of half-boots, and by 1810, fashionable women wore these flat-soled half-boots for almost every occasion. Although certainly more durable than slippers, they were often made of kid (goat) leather, nankeen, or a denim-like fabric and were not impervious to soaking up water and mud. The thin, pliable kid could be dyed or embroidered but did not stand up well to rough treatment.

Jane Austen, in her manuscript *The Watsons*, wrote:

> *Emma was not inclined to give herself much trouble for his entertainment, and after hard labour of mind,* [Lord Osborne] *produced the remark of its being a very fine day, and followed it up with the question of:"Have you been walking this morning?"*
>
> *"No my lord, we thought it too dirty."* [Unpleasant, stormy]
>
> *"You should wear half boots." After another pause: "Nothing sets off a neat ankle more than a half boot; nankeen galoshed with black looks very well. Do not you like half boots?"*
>
> *"Yes; but unless they are so stout as to injure their beauty, they are not fit for country walking."*

Although still a minority in women's footwear at the beginning of the 19th century, ankle boots would become the dominant style of daytime footwear by the 1830s. Let it here be noted, however, that most of the women in Europe—the women of the lower classes—rarely owned more than one pair of shoes. I cannot but think that their half-boots were far sturdier than those of the upper classes.

Well, though hardly a complicated subject, I think it to have been worthy of this short examination. Certainly, though the history of shoes is not a momentous topic, our feet and those of our ancestors have carried us and them into our successes and follies alike.

How different the world's history would have been if none of us had been born with feet! How much of good and bad alike might never have occurred without shoes on these feet. Thus, how valuable to mankind has been the shoe and no less so in early 1800s England.

I hope you have found my article a little diverting and that you have gained, even if only just a little, more knowledge of our ancestors' foot-trappings. One can be quite certain my heroines were all properly shod in the shoes of the day.

Mr. Darcy Strips Off...

by M.M. BENNETTS

First off, we have a conundrum.

Because, of course, there are two versions of the novel featuring Mr. Fitzwilliam Darcy, set in two sartorially different periods. Do I tell you about Mr. Darcy circa 1796-97 when *First Impressions* was being written? Hmm.

Well, that's easily solved. In 1797 wealthy young men were wearing cravats in the style of the Prince of Wales, which *"were then worn without stiffening of any kind, and bagged out in front, rucking up to the chin in a roll."* Messy. Very messy. Not to say slovenly....

Therefore, a picture of Darcy circa 1813—when the revised novel, *Pride and Prejudice* as it was now called, was published—is no doubt the better choice.

Gentlemen's clothing had undergone a radical change during the early years of the 19th century. The long war with France had isolated Britain from the Parisian trend-setters who had dominated the 18th century, along with their preference for brightly coloured silks and satins. In their place, a new, austere, almost monochromatic aesthetic had taken hold, courtesy of one George Brummell, based on the finest of British tailoring, and drawing its inspiration from the military, from English horsemanship, and from a classical standard of masculinity as seen in the ancient Greek and Roman statuary, most notably the Apollo Belvedere.

And this ideal of *"unity, simplicity and a continuously flowing movement from one part of the body to the next"* is at the core of Regency menswear.

The body beneath must needs be moulded into a figure worthy of the clothes too—hence the daily exercise taken by gentlemen at the many boxing saloons, such as Gentleman Jackson's, or fencing schools about London. Riding is also known to build strong back and shoulder muscles, as well as those of the thighs and calves. Carriage driving also requires very strong shoulders.

So, there's the man and the ideal...but what's he wearing?

Among the essentials of this new neo-classical look were breeches or pantaloons for the day, made either of doeskin or chamois leather or a soft stocking-like fabric. (If made of soft leather, often the wearer first wore them dampened, allowing them to dry to his physique so that they more closely resembled a second skin—they weren't called bum-clingers for nothing.) Both had corset lacing at the back, a fall front fastened by side buttons over the stomach, and were held up with braces to maintain the severe and fitted line over the thigh.

They were also cut wider on one side at the top of the thigh, and higher on the other, to accommodate the family jewels, in a custom known as dressing to one side. Beneath the knee, button fastenings kept the fabric taut down the length of the leg.

Evening breeches or pantaloons were made of sheer black silk jersey, knitted cashmere, or a stretchy silk-stockinette imported from India, made with only one seam per leg and that along the outside—though this was sometimes embroidered or "clocked" down the length of it—all of which was intended to frame the muscles of the thigh.

For summer, the breeches would be cut the same, but made of stout pale or white linen or nankeen, a heavy twilled cotton.

Just as important was a gentleman's fitted waistcoat, which would have been made of white or skin-toned fabric—the idea being that if a gentleman were to remove his coat, in his shirt-sleeves and from a distance, he would resemble nothing so much as a naked Greek god, muscular, beautiful, carved from marble or stone.

Coats were now made of dark matte fabrics such as wool Bath cloth or "superfine", sculpted through the back and shoulders, with a high collar to provide a contrasting frame to the whiteness of the starched cravats. Our Mr. Darcy has several specialist tailors from whose work to choose: John Weston's at No. 34 Old Bond Street, or even Mr. Brummell's favourite, Schweitzer & Davidson on Cork Street.

Beneath it all, the shirt of white linen, plain and lightly starched, with collars *"so large that, before being folded down, it completely hid* [the] *head and face..."* with tiny buttons at the neck and cuffs. Cuffs were worn long—a good inch or two longer than the coat sleeve to emphasise the fact that the gentleman did not work.

About Mr. Darcy's neck was his starched cravat.

Made of fine Irish muslin, a triangle was cut on the diagonal from a square yard of fabric, with its edges plainly stitched. This triangle was then folded twice and wrapped carefully about the neck, with the ends tied in one of several manners before the wearer lowered his chin to create a neat series of folds which were either rubbed into place by a day-old shirt or pressed with a hot iron. (I favour the day-old shirt method myself...less danger of frying the larynx.)

Footwear? Highly polished Hessian boots with spurs by day and thinly-soled black pumps for evening.

Underwear? Very little was worn and then only rarely—it being pretty much a thing of the 18th century, although it was still in use (in cold weather, for example) and referred to as "summer trousers". In this look of careless, casual, sensual arrogance, there was no room for lumpy knickers or rucked up shirt tails. However, due to the transparency and cut of the tight kneebreeches and pantaloons, a lining of either flannel or cotton was sometimes incorporated into the garments.

Mr. Darcy would have dressed some three or four times during the course of a normal day.

He would also have required, per week, in addition to the usual *"20 shirts, 24 pocket handkerchiefs, 9 or 10 summer trousers, 30 neck handkerchiefs, a dozen waistcoats, and stockings at discretion"*, a chintz dressing gown and Turkish slippers for taking his breakfast.

He would also have several driving coats and/or greatcoats, caped, and made of a heavier wool worsted or "Norwich stuff" for colder, rainier weather (every day from September to May and most of June).

Like Brummell and other gentlemen of his class and station, Darcy would have bathed every part of his body every day, and in hot water. He would have used no perfumes (they were considered very 18th century!) but would have smelled instead of very fine linen and country washing.

So there he is—drab greatcoat emphasising the width of his shoulders, thigh-hugging doeskin breeches, pale waistcoat, dark coat (navy, grey, or black being the preferred colours), and pristine white cravat and collarpoints outlining the strength of his jaw. Polished Hessians are on his feet.

Does he not look fine? Every inch a god?

So now...let's take it off.

His high-crowned bevor, his cane, his gloves, and his greatcoat he has, fortunately, left with the footman belowstairs. The door is shut.

His boots (with or without horse muck on them) have been left at the door or really anywhere but in the bedchamber, if at all possible. There are two reasons for this. One, this may be a good idea at a time when there are no Dysons or Hoovers. But also, the method of removing one's boots generally required the backside of another person, and gentlemen didn't much care for bootjacks as it was said to break down the back of the boot. Equally, the reason a gentleman did not *"sit down in all his dirt"* was a pungent one.

So shoes are a better bet. Easier to slip off.

And it all starts this way: with the the kissing...this could go on for a long time. A very long time. Because the most important thing is always that his Eliza feels and knows that her wishes and desires are paramount to his.

Then, the coat comes off. It's easier, I'll be frank, if she'll slips her hands upward from his chest toward his shoulders and lifts it away from him. But assuming she's not forward and that he doesn't have his coats cut so as to make removing them akin to peeling an obstreperous orange, he shrugs the thing off, first one shoulder, then the other, all the while still kissing her.

Then, the waistcoat. Button by tiny button. All eleven or so of the things. More than that if the waistcoat is double-breasted. And with each button, a sensation of incremental yet greater sensual liberty is attained.

The waistcoat now on the floor with the coat, Darcy slides his index finger into the front of that knot of white linen at the base of the throat and pulls. An index finger into the remaining tied-bit and pulls. And freedom. And the end of the cravat is yanked and pulled off and discarded onto the floor.

Then he takes down his braces, first one, then the other.

And finally, he undoes the small Dorset buttons at his neck and cuffs. But being not a little impatient, he pulls the shirt off over his head without unbuttoning it all the way.

But the removal of the shirt only happens when she wishes it to happen. For all the time, his removal of his clothes is secondary to touching her, kissing her, telling her in every wordless way that her beauty blocks out the sky and the stars and is all that he sees.

And that's how he did it.

"To teach thee, I am naked first..."
—John Donne

UNREQUITED LOVE: JANE AUSTEN AND AMERICA

BY LAUREN GILBERT

JANE AUSTEN HAD LITTLE TO SAY ABOUT AMERICA, AND THAT LITTLE WAS NOT GOOD. IN her letter to Martha Lloyd on September 2, 1814, she did not reflect a positive view of the new United States, writing *"…I place my hope of better things on a claim to the protection of Heaven, as a Religious Nation, a Nation in spite of much Evil improving in Religion, which I cannot believe the Americans to possess."*

The ideals of democracy espoused by America, and later in the French Revolution, were a more direct and positive influence on earlier authors with whom Jane was familiar such as Edmund Burke and Charlotte Turner Smith, but suffered an eclipse when, in France, the Terror erupted and the King and Queen were executed.

Park Honan wrote that, in *The Loiterer*, Jane's brother James printed a story reflecting the Tory view of France and America, in which a Scottish soldier fighting against Washington becomes a democratic fool, loses his values, marries a rich, vicious, mean-born widow, and becomes miserable, ruined by the American Revolution. There is a strong probability that Jane would have read the story.

Austen's novels reflect a more prudent Tory approach to advancement than the Scottish soldier in question pursued: her heroines who made advantageous marriages and the men who advanced clearly have worth of their own in terms of character—but also in terms of birth. In *Pride and Prejudice*, Elizabeth Bennet was a "gentleman's daughter", so her marriage to Mr. Darcy was not totally inappropriate. In *Mansfield Park*, Fanny and William Price's mother was Lady Bertram's sister, so there was good blood there (however diluted) to supplement their individual merits. In spite of Emma's improvements, Harriet (born, as we come to discover, the illegitimate daughter of a tradesman) was matched appropriately with the farmer Mr. Martin, and her friendship with Emma evolved into a more suitable relationship.

The War of 1812 (the circumstance under discussion in the letter previously cited) would have been a concern but does not make an appearance in her novels (as with so many other politically-charged events of her time). But it seems clear that America was a negative influence in the world, in Austen's view. She tended to uphold the more traditional values and structures currently in place in England, even while she makes her concerns about women's role and place in those structures apparent.

In considering the West Indies as part of the Americas, the situation and viewpoint are somewhat different but not more favorable. The combination of the West Indies and trade were directly allied to slavery. Her aunt Leigh-Perrot brought a plantation in Barbados with her when she married Jane's uncle. Austen's father, George Austen, was a trustee for a plantation owned by James Nibbs, a former classmate. Austen's brother Charles' naval career included five years in the North American Station, searching ships and interfering with trade between France and the United States. Charles married Fanny Palmer, the daughter of an official in Bermuda while stationed in the West Indies.

The issues of slavery and income mentioned in *Mansfield Park* would have had a great deal of immediacy for her family, as discussions of plantation business matters, including slavery, would have been fairly common. Austen's disgust for slavery was made apparent, however discreetly, by the references in *Mansfield Park*, previously mentioned, as well as in *Emma*.

In *Emma*, Austen's character Jane Fairfax referred to her role as a governess as a form of slavery of the mind, if not the body, and was extremely reluctant to embark on her career. Even the reference to Mrs. Elton's family in Bristol with wealth coming from trade has a dark connotation, due to Bristol having been a significant port involved with the slave trade. (The slave trade was outlawed in 1807, but slave ownership in the British Empire was still legal, during Austen's lifetime.)

I was unable to find any positive references to the Americas in Jane Austen's letters or novels. Even though Austen's novels carry a subtle undertone of the injustices to women in the current English system, the democratic ideals that led to the American and French revolutions clearly did not resonate with her. There is no indication she espoused the radical transformation of her society.

While bearing in mind that the letters remaining are a fraction of what she had written, available information indicates that Austen viewed the Americas as a dangerously radical, unreligious place where people of low birth and poor character could be advanced socially and materially, in spite of their unworthiness. Given the fairly recent loss of the colonies and subsequent revolution and Terror in France, a jaundiced view of America by Austen and her contemporaries would not be unreasonable or surprising. One can only hope that subsequent developments would have found favor with her, especially in view of the continuing popularity of her novels here.

SOURCES

Ellwood, Gracia Fay. "'Such a Dead Silence': Cultural Evil, Challenge, Deliberate Evil and Metanoia in *Mansfield Park*." *Persuasions On-Line*, vol. 24, no. 1 (2003). http://www.jasna.org/persuasions/on-line/vol24no1/ellwood.html.

Honan, Park. *Jane Austen: Her Life*. New York: Ballantine Books Edition, 1989.

Hubback, J. H. and Edith C. *Jane Austen's Sailor Brothers*. http://www.tilneysandtrapdoors.com/mollands/etexts/jasb/jasb7.html.

LeFaye, Deirdre. *Jane Austen: The World of Her Novels*. London: Frances Lincoln Ltd, 2002.

_____, ed. *Jane Austen's Letters*, Third Edition. Oxford: Oxford University Press, 1997.

MacDonagh, Oliver. *Jane Austen: Real and Imagined Worlds*. Avon, UK: 1991.

Mitton, G. E. *Jane Austen and Her Times, 1775-1817*. New York: Barnes & Noble, Inc., 2007.

Ray, Joan Kilingel, PhD. *Jane Austen for Dummies*. Hoboken, NJ: Wiley Publishing, Inc., 2006.

Sheehan, Colleen A. "To Govern the Winds: Dangerous Acquaintances at Mansfield Park." *Persuasions On-Line*, vol. 25, no. 1 (2004). http://www.jasna.org/persuasions/on-line/vol25no1/sheehan.html.

Tomalin, Claire. *Jane Austen: A Life*. New York: First Vintage Books Edition, division of Random House, 1999.

CLASS DISTINCTIONS IN REGENCY ENGLAND

BY PHILIPPA JANE KEYWORTH

TODAY I WANT TO WRITE ABOUT A WELL-KNOWN PRIMARY SOURCE, *THE MIRROR OF GRACES*, by A Lady of Distinction. This book was first published in London in 1811, and, presumably due to its popularity, it was subsequently re-printed in New York in 1813 and 1815, in Edinburgh in 1830 and then again in Boston in 1831.

The copy that I own is an enlarged photo-reprint and spans some 239 pages or more. At such a length, I can hardly say that this article will cover the entirety of the book or will be a full analysis of the source. However, I wanted to share a little something about this captivating text which I am currently studying.

Specifically, I have been drawn to the passage entitled "On the Peculiarities of Dress, with Reference to the Station of the Wearer". It strikes me that when reading a Regency romance and even when writing one, we tend to focus on the positives of class divides. Who can resist a classic *Pride and Prejudice*-esque storyline that follows the romantic attachment of a man and woman divided by class who eventually overcome it?

What we sometimes fail to see is, as John Tosh describes it, *"The gulf between past and present."* We don't give complete gravity to the social divides of the time and instead we romanticize them. In truth, while reading this passage from *The Mirror of Graces*, I wasn't sure whether to laugh or to frown in comprehension. The peculiarities of dress A Lady of Distinction refers to are the fashions of the time, and she sets us straight from the beginning by describing the danger of lower and middle classes dressing fashionably:

> It is not from a proud wish to confine elegance to persons of quality that I contend for less extravagant habits in the middle and lower orders of people: it is a conviction of the evil which their vanity produces that impels me to condemn in toto the present levelling and expensive mode.

And before this statement of her conviction she declares the propriety of corresponding your dress with not only your season of life, character, and figure but also with your station. She speaks of this matter so: *"This is the subject not less of moral concern than it is a matter of taste."*

Yes, that's right, you've got it. She believes that dressing for your station is not just about taste but actually your moral obligation. Well, doesn't this just put a new spin on the classical fashions of the Regency!

She differentiates between tradesmen and those with "fortunes of princes". Of course, for those with "fortunes of princes" it is different. They are allowed to array their "fair partner" in "rich produce", but not so for the tradesmen: *"...but I animadvert on our retail shopkeepers, our linen drapers, upholsterers, &c. who, not content with gold and silver baubles, trick out their dames in jewels!"*

Shocking! She even uses an exclamation mark!

And what, pray tell, does she think of the morality of these tradesmen she so heartily attacks for their expensive tastes? *"No wonder that these men load their consciences with dishonest profits, or make their last appearance in the newspaper as insolvent or felo de se!"* Incompetent both in business and morals.

Just wait until she gets onto the working-class women....

> *If the brazier's daughter is taught to sing, dance and play like the heiress to an earldom, we must not be surprised that she will also emulate the decorations of her rival...not able to have hers of gems, foil-stones produce a similar affect...*

So, these women are like those of today who shop in Primark to emulate the fashions of Chanel and D & G.

Is this successful in attracting men (which is one of the purposes of such finery)? The section goes on to say: *"...and when she is thus arrayed, she plays away the wanton and the fool, till some libertine of fortune buys her either for a wife or a mistress."* Harsh words!

So, having devoted four pages to these working-class tradesmen and women, A Lady of Distinction moves swiftly, and unsurprisingly, back to the class she is from:

> *After having drawn this agreeable picture of her who has well-chosen, I will leave this modern daughter of industry to her discreet and virtuous simplicity; and once more turn to her whose fortune and station render greater changes and expence in apparel not only admissible but commendable.*

I found this passage, as I have said, quite humorous, but it was also very enlightening. There is a lot to be learned here.

The author is, as she describes herself, *"a woman of virtue and a Christian"* who does not feel it beneath her dignity to lift her pen on these subjects, so I will therefore assume her to be from the upper echelons of society. It's important to count this information when making any deductions from what has been said above.

What I will deduce from the above extracts are:

- The importance of dress to some women in Regency Society;
- The industrial revolution allowing for the rise of rich tradesmen (note the term she uses, *"this modern daughter of industry"*);
- The ability of the middle and lower classes to buy finer clothing;
- Tradesmen becoming bad businessmen when they buy fine clothing for their female relatives—oh, I love this woman's logic!
- The availability of "mimmick" clothing, jewels, etc.;
- Dress being a clear factor denoting status;

- The status line being questioned and blurred by trade and affluence;
- The "truth" that tradesmen's daughters dressing above their station leads to wantonness and becoming a libertine's wife or mistress;
- Following the fashions and spending money on fashion for women "of fortune" is commendable.

Again, I want to stress that this is a tiny section of this text which I have analysed and there are far more diverse subjects within it which should not be discounted. However, it does provide a valuable window through a contemporary text into opinions advocated by one woman, at least, and embraced by more, most probably, as evidenced by the multiple re-printings of this book.

It is an interesting text, especially as it is written almost twenty years after Mary Wollstonecraft's controversial text, *A Vindication of the Rights of Woman*, which declares the need for women to receive an equal education to men, whereas *The Mirror of Graces* implies the opposite. To gain some insight into the differing views on women and their roles between the years 1792 and 1811, I would highly recommend reading these two contemporary texts. They could not be more different, and yet both contain insights into the mindset of women toward other women and toward their role within society itself.

Which mindset was more prevalent? It would have been amazingly helpful if the rest of the women in Regency England had written a volume cataloging their responses to the views put forth in these two texts—if only!

Vicars and Curates and Livings...Oh My!

by MARIA GRACE

In the 1800s the English laws of primogeniture, intended to preserve the integrity of large landed estates, made it a challenge for younger sons of the landed gentry to establish themselves in life. If their family did not possess an additional estate for them to inherit or they lacked some other relative to provide an inheritance, younger sons had little choice but to make their own way in the world. The question was how.

Traditional "learned" professions—the church, the law, and medicine—had a respectable character as "liberal professions" befitting gentlemen. So these, together with the armed forces, formed the primary options for gentlemen's younger sons. The church was a particularly attractive option if a family had a living they could bestow as they chose. A living meant a guaranteed income and home for the lifetime of the clergyman lucky enough to be appointed to it.

ORDINATION

To qualify for a living, a man had to be ordained. The process started with a standard honors degree from Cambridge or Oxford. Afterwards, the candidate needed a testimonial from his college vouching for his fitness for ordination. He then presented the testimonial to a bishop and made arrangements for an examination to prove his competency in Latin, knowledge of the Scripture, and familiarity with the liturgy and church doctrine as written in the *Thirty-Nine Articles*. Many bishops made only a cursory examination in these areas; only a few took their responsibilities more seriously.

After Japanning (slang for ordination referring to putting on black cloth, from the color of black japanware), a man was qualified to administer the sacraments of the church. His career would begin at age twenty-three, as a deacon, assisting an ordained priest. At twenty-four, he could be fully ordained and eligible to be in charge of a parish and obtain a living.

OBTAINING A LIVING

For all but the luckiest young men, the real challenge began at this point. The surest way of procuring a benefice was to be related to the patron. A well-placed relative might mean a young man could walk into a living immediately after ordination. Less well-connected individuals could wait ten or twenty years for the opportunity.

The right to appoint a clergyman to a living was called an advowson and considered a form of property to be bought, sold, and inherited. Typically an advowson sold for five to seven times the annual value of the living. Instead of selling an entire advowson, a gentleman strapped for cash might sell just the "right of next presentation" as did Sir Thomas Bertram in Jane Austen's *Mansfield Park*. An extremely fortunate clergyman could own an advowson and appoint himself to a living.

Approximately 11,500 benefices or livings existed in England and Wales at the end of the 18th century. This sounds like a sufficient number; however, over half the ordained clergy never received a living.

Oxford and Cambridge colleges controlled nearly 5% of benefices, presenting them as gifts to fellows and masters who wished to marry and leave academic pursuits. Another 10% or so belonged to the Crown, to be presented to government supporters. Bishops and cathedral chapters possessed about 20%. The gentry and aristocracy held the largest share, on the order of 60%. Most great families had at least one or two livings at their disposal.

THE VALUE OF A LIVING

Still, having a living did not guarantee the holder a life of wealth and ease. An 1802 figure suggests a third of the benefices brought in less than £150 a year and some 1,000 of those less than £100. (£50 a year was more or less equivalent to our minimum wage.) A clergyman needed an income of £300-400 per annum to be on the level with the lesser gentry.

Incomes might be increased by serving more than one parish, but this seldom resulted in real wealth. Only a third of all clergy acquired more than one living. Slightly more than one in twenty held more than two benefices and of these, few had as many as four or five.

Additional income might also be found through teaching or cultivating gardens and the glebe (acreage provided by the parish). The amount of land varied by parish; some only had a field, others fifty acres or more. The incumbent might choose to farm it himself or rent it out to a tenant farmer.

ENTER THE CURATE

In the Regency period, once installed in a living, a man was there for life. No one less than the bishop could remove him for cause. A vicar could resign his duties to a curate once he obtained the permission of his bishop. Many hired a curate from the beginning of their incumbency. Others only did so when they had to retire.

A curate was usually a young man just recently ordained, who assisted or sometimes performed the duties of a clergyman. A curate's wages would be paid from the vicar's own pocket and typically were very low, as little as £50 per year, not enough to afford a maid. Moreover, a vicar did not have to give up the parsonage house to the curate. He might continue to live in it himself and leave the curate to find his own living quarters somewhere within an easy distance of the church.

Even at trifling wages, a curacy was not easy to obtain. In the early 1800s curates made up close to half of the clergymen. Even with a position, their future was not secure. The death of the incumbent did not imply the curate would ascend to the living. Moreover, there was no guarantee that the successor would even continue to employ the curate. A curate did not retire unless he had private means of support because the church offered no pensions.

As members of the clergy, curates were regarded as gentlemen. Despite their official standing, the subservient nature of their position and their paltry incomes caused some of the gentry and peers to hold them in disregard.

PARISH DUTIES

The clergyman's duties in the church included holding service on Sundays and holding Holy Communion at least three times a year. Midweek duties included baptisms, marriages, funerals, and visiting the sick.

Outside of the church, the clergyman officiated at parish meetings to discuss local affairs including charity, parish employment, care of the poor, repair and maintenance of the church, and election of the churchwardens. The parish was responsible for the administration of the poor laws and elected Supervisors of the Poor who collected the Poor Rate taxes from the wealthier parishioners. The parish also appointed two Surveyors of Highways to supervise the maintenance and repair of the roads. Thus, whether vicar or lowly curate, the clergyman played a major role in the life of his parish community.

SOURCES

Collins, Irene. *Jane Austen, The Parson's Daughter*. Hambledon Press, 1998.

_____. *Jane Austen & the Clergy*. Hambledon Press, 2002.

Day, Malcolm. *Voices from the World of Jane Austen*. David & Charles, 2012.

Grose, Francis. *Dictionary of the Vulgar Tongue, 1811 ed.* Ikon Classics, 2004.

Le Faye, Deirdre. *Jane Austen: The World of Her Novels*. Harry N. Abrams, 2002.

MacDonagh, Oliver. *Jane Austen: Real and Imagined Worlds*. Yale University Press, 1991.

Mayer, Nancy. *Nancy Mayer: Regency Researcher*. http://www.susannaives.com/nancyregencyresearcher/.

Sullivan, Margaret C. *The Jane Austen Handbook*. Quirk Books, 2007.

A Glimpse of York during the Regency Era

by LAUREN GILBERT

Y ORK IS AN INCREDIBLY ANCIENT CITY. ROMANS AND VIKINGS ESTABLISHED COMMUNITIES here. (The Roman Ninth Legion set up camp there and called it Eboracum, and in 208 A.D., the Roman Empire was governed from York.) A long Christian tradition carried on in York.

A great cathedral, York Minster, was built here, with construction beginning on the earliest incarnation of that monumental work in the 7th century. York Minster was (and is) the seat of the Archbishop of York, the second most powerful churchman in the Church of England. The Normans built onto it. The kings Edward I, II, and III held their parliaments there, and the Courts of Justice were held in York for seven years in the 13th century.

At the end of the Wars of the Roses, the City of York came in squarely on the side of Richard III, recording that:

> ...*King Richard late mercifully reigning upon us was thrugh grete treason of the duc of Northfolk and many othere that turned ayenst hyme, with many othre lordes and nobilles of this north parties, was pitiously slaine and murdred to the grete hevynesse of this citie, the names of whome foloweth hereafter...*

Clearly, York was an important and powerful city, in the thick of things for centuries.

By the Georgian era, things had settled down quite a bit. Although other parts of Yorkshire had industrialized, the city of York did not, possibly due to trade restrictions called the "freedom regulations." However, it remained the county seat and regional administrative center and a center of church matters including an ecclesiastical court.

Natural waterways and canals made trade and travel easier. The turnpike made it easier, and faster, to get to York from London and other cities. It was a military town, having the Cavalry Barracks, and became an important social center with assembly rooms, horse racing, theater, and other social amenities, attracting local gentry and nobility with seats in the county. These county families included those named Fairfax, Scrope, Bourchier, Carr, and Fitzwilliam, some with illustrious titles. These, in turn, attracted friends from out of town. The horse races attracted the Prince of Wales and his set. Book stores, linen-drapers, mantua makers, milliners, boot makers, and other businesses provided the goods and services required by the fashionable.

During the Georgian era, some beautiful buildings were constructed, and Fairfax House, built for Viscount Fairfax, was just one of these buildings. Richard Boyle, third Earl of Burlington, was responsible for the elegant designs of the Mansion House and the Assembly Rooms in York. The city became known as a polite and elegant place to live and to visit and was one of the fashionable escapes of the day.

During the Regency era, theatre, dancing, and other entertainments continued to be very popular in York, as elsewhere, and there was an active social season. Mrs. Jordan (mistress of the Duke of Clarence) performed in *The Country Girl* in 1811; Edmund Keane performed at the Theatre Royal in 1819.

The Assembly Rooms (also known as the Burlington Rooms) had their balls, where country dances, quadrilles, and cotillions were still popular, even as the waltz was coming into fashion. If dancing wasn't one's preference, one could gamble in the Round Room. In their way, the Assembly Rooms were the Almack's of the north, as young people were there to see and be seen, to meet and mingle. Madame Tussaud also appeared in York with her wax sculptures in a travelling exhibition during this era. A beautiful tree-lined walk of approximately a mile along the River Ouse, called the New Walk, was a popular place to take the air.

The York Races were especially popular. Even though the Prince of Wales was no longer interested in horse racing by 1807, many of the nobility and gentry still came to York in May for races and the festivities surrounding them, including the Race Ball held in the Assembly Rooms. Buying and selling of race horses, and gambling on the races themselves (and in the Round Room after the races), made the races an especially costly form of entertainment.

Unfortunately, the lack of industry that made York such a polite and elegant city in which to live or visit resulted in a decline. By the 1820s, the assemblies were down to six winter meetings and a few special event assemblies. By the 1830s, the races and theatres were in decline, and the city itself was no longer the important social center it had been. The population declined somewhat, and the nobility and gentry that had patronized the racing and social scene were spending more time elsewhere. It wasn't until later in the 19th century that things improved again.

SOURCES

Bebb, Prudence. *Life in Regency York.* York, England: Sessions Book Trust, 1992.

Donnelly, Shannon. "Regency Horses." *Rakehell Blog.* January, 2003. http://rakehell.net/article.php?id=152&Title=Regency-Horses.

"Fairfax House." *York Civic Trust.* http://www.fairfaxhouse.co.uk/?idno=4.

Heap, R. Grundy. *Georgian York: A Sketch of Life in Hanoverian England.* London: Methuen & Co. Ltd., 1937.

"History of York: Timeline." *York Museum Trust.* http://www.historyofyork.org.uk/timeline.

Lang, W. Andrews and Elsie M. *Old English Towns.* London: Bracken Books, 1965.

Tillott, P.M. ed. "A History of the County of York: the City of York." *Victoria County History* (1961): 266-8. http://www.british-history.ac.uk/report.aspx?compid=36358.

"Transcription of page from York City House Book containing death entry of Richard III." *Society of Friends of King Richard III.* http://www.silverboar.org/deathentry.htm.

Nom nom nom: Regency Style

by M.M. BENNETTS

With much of the western world so indisputably in the grip of culinary multi-culturalism, it can be hard to imagine an age in which mealtimes weren't dominated by a need for ready-meals, speed-eating, 24-hour electrical supplies, ease of world transportation, or advertising.

But so it was in early 19th century Britain.

To begin with, there was no ready supply of electricity or gas to fuel either household lighting or a stove or open hearth for cooking and baking. Instead there were candles, made of beeswax or tallow, oil lamps, wood and coal—all of which were immeasurably more expensive comparatively than our modern equivalents.

Hence the beginning of one's day, obviously depending on social class, came with the rising sun and daylight. Within the prosperous middle class, the gentry, and aristocracy this was probably somewhere between seven and eight.

The first meal of the day was generally taken at ten. It lasted for about an hour and it was a good solid English breakfast. "Morning" itself then lasted until dinner at perhaps three or four in the afternoon. Dinner went on for about two hours.

And it's important to note that the hours at which these meals are served also provide for the greatest amount of natural light in the kitchen for the preparation of the food, and also, the least number of candles required, both upstairs and down.

London society of the Beau Monde dined at five o'clock, or even later, and generally had their tea or a light supper sometime late in the evening, after returning from the theatre or in the middle of a ball...But in the country, one kept "country hours", and thus mealtime was dictated by the hours of light and also by the fact that traveling at night was often inconvenient and certainly hazardous even on a moonlit night.

Dinner, then....

First off, this is the moment to drop those preconceptions about how many courses served one after another—five or seven or nine—was a sign of wealth and breeding. Because English service didn't have many courses, one served after another.

For the most part, there were two courses, often called removes, plus dessert. And the servants didn't serve each individual from a tray onto their plate either.

Oh, and there was no allotted placement either, with the exception that the host would be the first into the room, escorting the "senior" lady, and taking his place at the foot of the table, while the hostess sat at the upper end of the table and the guest(s) of honour sat near her.

When the family or family and guests walked into the dining room, the table would already be spread with an array of dishes of every kind of food—soup, fish, game, poultry, meat, pies, sauces, pickles, vegetables, puddings both sweet and savoury, jellies, and custards. Depending upon the occasion, there might be anything from five to twenty five different dishes, all arranged symmetrically around a centre dish.

Initially, it was the host who would supervise the serving of the soup and/or carve the joints of meat that might be brought in once the soup tureens were removed. A kind of balance was also maintained with fish—usually with salmon at one end of the table and perhaps turbot at the other.

After the meat—saddle of mutton, haunch of venison, sirloin of beef—had been carved, the gentlemen at the table helped themselves from the nearest dishes and each offered it to his neighbour, or else a servant was to fetch a dish from another part of the table.

It does sound like a great deal of food, yes. But generally, one didn't eat one's way through everything. It seems to have been more a case of choosing three or four things that one liked from amongst the array.

To wash it all down, ale, beer, wine, as well as soda water would have been served, though some gentlemen are recorded as having preferred port, hock, or sherry with their food. And importantly—for dining was a very social element in their days—once the soup had been served, both ladies and gentlemen would start drinking everyone's health round the table—"taking wine" with each other as it's called.

Once the family and guests had eaten as much as they wished from that first selection, an intermediate course of cheese, salad, raw celery, and suchlike might be brought round. Then the table was cleared, and a second remove of an equal quantity of different dishes was brought in and arranged on the table, with, just as previously, both sweet and savoury dishes included.

Finally, the guests and family having eaten their fill, the table would again be cleared and the cloth removed to reveal either the polished table surface or another cloth lying beneath, and the dessert would be laid out. This dessert consisted of fruits and nuts, perhaps ice-cream or sweetmeats. And this was usually accompanied by port or Madeira.

Once the company had sat over dessert for about a quarter of an hour, the ladies would leave the dining room and retire to the drawing room, where they would embroider, chat, play the fortepiano, or read aloud for about an hour. After which point they would order their tea and coffee to be brought in, and the gentlemen, having discussed the war, the government, the iniquitous price of wheat, their efforts at sheep-rearing, and other such thrilling topics over their wine, would join them.

Louis Simond, a Franco-American with an English wife, visited England in 1810-11 and left this record:

> *There are commonly two courses and a dessert. I shall venture to give a sketch of a moderate dinner for ten or twelve persons—First course* [included] *Oyster sauce, Fish, Spinage, Fowls, Soup, Bacon, Vegetables, Roast or Boiled Beef, Vegetables. Second course* [included] *Creams, Ragout a la Francaise, Pastry, Cream, Macaroni, Cauliflowers, Game, Pastry. Dessert* [included] *Walnuts, Apples, Raisins and Almonds, Cakes, Pears, Oranges.*

Phantasmagoria: Getting Your Fright On in Late Georgian England

by J.A. BEARD

T HE LADY AND HER GUESTS HAVE GATHERED IN A SITTING ROOM. ONLY THE LIGHT OF A few candles fights off the choking darkness.

Suddenly, a rattling chain and the scratching of unearthly talons echo through the room. A skeleton appears, then a ghost! The terrified audience holds their hands in front of them in a feeble attempt to shut out the creatures.

The English of the late Georgian era appreciated a good fright just as much as we do. The rise of Gothic literature and related novels of fright provided a giddy thrill for many readers, but reading about a phantom lacks the impact of actually seeing one. Though the people in this era lacked television and movies, they did have their own way of experiencing the visceral thrill of laying their eyes on the macabre and supernatural: the phantasmagoria.

Before we discuss the actual show, we need to discuss the primary tool used for it: the magic lantern. Though historians aren't completely sure, the magic lantern seems to have been invented in either the 15th or 16th century in northern Europe.

The magic lantern is a fairly simple device. It is basically just a concave mirror that is placed in front of a light source. The set-up allows the gathering up of light. In the magic lantern, the concentrated light is then passed through a glass slide with an image on it toward a lens. The lens then projects a larger version of the slide image onto another surface. So, what they really had was a simple slide projector.

In the earliest magic lanterns, candles or a conventional (non-magic as it were) lantern provided the necessary light. As the centuries passed, improved illumination technologies were integrated into the magic lantern to provide for brighter images. Though various types of images were projected when the devices were first introduced, dark images of supernatural creatures were popular from the earliest years. Skilled performers made use of multiple magic lanterns, sound effects, smoke, and other such elements to create a thrilling experience.

The magic lantern had a history on the Continent before its arrival in England. The quick summary version is that during a period of heightened interest in spiritualism and all things dark and supernatural, particularly toward the end of the 18th century, a well-positioned magic lantern could do a lot to convince people that something supernatural was indeed present, especially in a time where people would rarely encounter such technology.

By 1801, the phantasmagoria was firmly established in England. At this point, many showmen began to be a bit more honest about the non-supernatural nature of their shows. It's important to note that not everyone believed they were witnessing supernatural goings-on even before the lantern men fully committed to honesty, but there was enough belief in it to occasionally attract the attention of authorities.

Coming clean, among other things, also allowed for better integration of other theatrical elements such as live music and guided narration. The displays by this point made use of multiple wheeled projectors. The mobility allowed for the ghosts, devils, and other assorted creatures to move, grow, or shrink during the performance as needed.

The shows grew in popularity just before and during the Regency period (1811-1820). The Prince Regent, never one to pass up a good time in whatever form, was known to entertain guests and himself with phantasmagoria displays on occasion (along with regular non-horror themed shows as well).

The magic lantern and phantasmagoria would remain popular through the end of the Georgian era and well into the Victorian era.

THE GREAT FROST FAIR OF 1814

BY M.M. BENNETTS

Boxing Day, 1813. Like a blanket of lambswool, heavy fog lay over southern England as the temperature plummeted.

That afternoon, piled into two travelling carriages, the Foreign Secretary, Viscount Castlereagh, and his family had drawn away from their house in St. James's Square, heading for Colchester in Essex on their way to Harwich from which they were to depart for the Continent. As his niece wrote, they left London *"in a fog so intense, that the carriages went at a foot's pace, with men holding flambeaux at the head of the horses."*

Though deep frosts, gales, and deeper snows, blizzards even, had marked the last decade of the old century, the cruel bite of this mini-Ice Age had seemed to lessen in the opening years of the 19th century. Though Boxing Day three years previous had seen such severe temperatures that the Thames had frozen as Londoners huddled inside their houses, trying to keep warm.

A heavy frost began the next day, 27 December 1813, followed by two days of a continuous heavy snowfall—the heaviest recorded snowfall for nearly 300 years. The upper reaches of the Thames froze too.

A day later came a slight thaw, and the ice at Wey Bridge began to break up and to float downstream, only to crash and jam into a jagged and solid mass—like some scene from the Polar icecap—between Blackfriars and London Bridges.

And the frost returned, harder and colder than previously—probably due to the covering of deep snow that coated the land. The fog too still hung heavy over London, stranding travellers, slowing or halting the mails, while great ice floes continued to break off and to drift down the waterway.

By the 30th, the fog had finally cleared—whipped off by a Northerly gale.

But by now, the tidal stretch of the Thames had frozen so solid that people were walking across the river to the other bank. And the watermen, unable to make a living rowing people across the water, demanded a toll of these brave pedestrians.

And still the cold held, gripping the land as the temperatures continued several degrees below freezing. By 4 January 1814, the Great Frost Fair had begun.

Stalls and tents, decorated with *"flags of all nations, streamers and signs"* began appearing on the ice to create what they called "City Road", among them kitchens or rapidly constructed "furnaces" selling roasted geese, lamb, rabbits, and sausages to the public. Gin and beer were also on sale.

In the middle of the river, a marooned barge was converted into a "dancing room".

Contemporary accounts from *The Annual Register* and Hone's *Every Day Book* provide the most vivid and wonderful stories of the winter in London that year and of the Fair itself.

21 January 1814: *"In London the great accumulation of snow already heaped on the*

ground, and condensed by three or four weeks of continued frost, was on Wednesday increased by a fresh fall, to a height hardly known in the memory of the oldest inhabitants. The cold has been intensely severe, the snow during the last fall being accompanied with a sharp wind and a little moisture. In many places, where the houses are old, it became necessary to relieve the roofs, by throwing off the load collected upon them, and by these means the carriage-way in the middle of the streets is made of a depth hardly passable for pedestrians, while carriages with difficulty plough their way through the mass."

27 January 1814: *"Yesterday the wind having veered round to the south-west, the effects of thaw were speedily discernible. The fall of the river at London Bridge has for several days past presented a scene both novel and interesting. At the ebbing of the tide huge fragments of ice were precipitated down the stream with great violence, accompanied by a noise equal to the report of a small piece of artillery. On the return of the tide they were forced back again; but the obstacles opposed to their passage through the arches were so great as apparently to threaten a total stoppage to the navigation of the river."*

1 February 1814: *"The Thames between Blackfriars and London Bridges continued to present the novel scene of persons moving on the ice in all directions and in greatly increased numbers. The ice, however, from its roughness and inequalities is totally unfit for amusement, although we observed several booths erected upon it for the sale of small wares, but the publicans and spirit-dealers were most in the receipt of custom.*

"The whole of the river opposite Queenhithe was frozen over, and in some parts the ice was several feet thick, while in others it was dangerous to venture upon, notwithstanding which, crowds of foot passengers crossed backwards and forwards throughout the whole of the day. We did not hear of any lives being lost, but many who ventured too far towards Blackfriars Bridge were partially immersed in the water by the ice giving way. Two coopers were with difficulty saved."

2 February 1814: *"The Thames this day presented a complete frost fair. The grand mall or walk extended from Blackfriars to London Bridge. This was named the city road, and was lined on each side by persons of all descriptions. Eight or ten printing-presses were erected, and numerous pieces commemorative of the 'great frost' were printed on the ice."*

3 February 1814: *"The number of adventurers increased. Swings, book-stalls, dancing in a barge, suttling-booths, playing at skittles, and almost every appendage of a fair on land appeared on the Thames. Thousands flocked to the spectacle. The ice presented a most picturesque appearance. The view of St. Paul's and of the city, with the white foreground, had a very singular effect; in many parts mountains of ice upheaved, resembled the rude interior of a stone quarry."*

4 February 1814: *"Each day brought a fresh accession of pedlars to sell their wares, and the greatest rubbish of all sorts was raked up and sold at double and treble the original cost. The watermen profited exceedingly, for each person paid a toll of twopence or threepence before he was admitted to the fair; and something also was expected for permission to return. Some of them were said to have taken as much as six pounds in a day. Many persons remained on the ice till late at night, and the effect by moonlight was singularly novel and beautiful. The bosom of the Thames seemed to rival the frozen climes of the north."*

Then, finally, on 5 February, an incoming tide brought about a sudden shifting in the mass of ice.

Booths which had only a few hours previously been secure were suddenly floating downstream and several people had to be rescued from the broken-off floes. Further down, the great jagged floes crashed into ships and boats, damaging them.

By 7 February, the sensational event was finished: *"The ice between London Bridge and Blackfriars gave way yesterday, in consequence of the high tides. On Saturday, thousands of people walked on the ice from one bridge to the other notwithstanding there were evident signs of its speedy breaking up, and even early yesterday morning some foolhardy persons passed over from Bankside to Queenhithe. About an hour after this the whole mass gave way, and swept with a tremendous range through the noble arches of Blackfriars Bridge, carrying along with it all within its course, including about forty barges.*

"The new erections for the Strand bridge impeded its progress and a vast quantity of the ice was there collected, but the strong current on the Somerset House side carried everything before it, and the passage of the river became at last free."

Quite simply amazing, don't you think?

ENTERTAINMENT TONIGHT: REGENCY STYLE

BY M.M. BENNETTS

IMAGINE IT. OUTSIDE THE TEMPERATURE HAD DROPPED SO LOW THAT THE THAMES WAS freezing; hoar frost had coated, white and deep, the red-tiled roofs of London's houses and churches. It was so bitter that even the city's notorious foists had taken the night off—perhaps their fingers were too stiff with cold for pinching purses?

Yet from the large windows of one building at least—Covent Garden—a mellowed golden light shone out into the night and the sounds of a packed house of some 3000 people, all laughing, rose and fell. For inside, the cold forgot, the atmosphere rich with the smell of orange peel and burning wax, the crowd were entranced by the new pantomime they'd all come to see—*Harlequin Asmodeus or Cupid on Crutches*.

Nor was it the first of that evening's entertainments on Boxing Day 1810.

To begin there had been a performance of Shakespeare's *As You Like It*. Then they had been treated to a tragedy, a dismal thing called *George Barnwell*. (The critic Hazlitt called it *"a piece of wretched cant."*) And now, six hours into the evening's entertainment, now, out came the clown they'd all been waiting for—Grimaldi, known to them all as "Joe"—about to fight a bout of fist-icuffs with a pile of animated vegetables...or rather, a pile of vegetables which he had assembled into a kind of person which then, somehow, at the tap of a sword, had come to life.

Magic!

And the night was still young. For after the mock fight which would see Grimaldi chased off the stage by the vegetable man, would come the pantomime, *Harlequin Asmodeus*, with its traditional story—generally speaking, two lovers kept apart, usually by unspeakable rivals or cruel parents, but who find happiness in each other's arms after the completion of a quest—and an equally traditional cast—Harlequin and his love, Columbine, and their enemies, the elderly miser, Pantaloon, and his servant, Clown.

It would be explicit, satirical, and energetic, and set against a background that would feature many of the common sights of the metropolis itself, all of which would be transformed by a touch of Harlequin's wand into something different (by means of ingenious stagecraft)—just like the vegetable man—a sedan chair into a prison, for example.

Welcome to a night out at the theatre, Regency style.

London, during the early years of the 19th century, had three main theatres: Drury Lane, Covent Garden, and Sadler's Wells in Islington. And during that period perhaps as many as 20,000 Londoners attended the theatre every night.

That number doesn't include the various concert halls or pleasure gardens such as Vauxhall

Gardens either. The Theatre Royal in Drury Lane and Covent Garden confined their "seasons" to the autumn and winter. Sadler's Wells filled in the gap during the spring and summer.

Long programmes, as described above, especially those with grand, jaw-dropping spectacles—plays starring dogs, elephants, children, the lines between comedy and tragedy blurred—were the order of the day. And ever since war had broken out with France, there'd been a kind of national fervour on which the theatres played.

Reenactments of sea battles were especially popular—this was the day of the great hero, Lord Nelson, and all of England was navy-mad—so Sadler's Wells staged a recreation of Nelson's victory at the Nile called *Naval Pillars*. Later, they put on a recreation of the Franco-Spanish siege of Gibraltar—and for this, the management converted the theatre's cellars and stage into a vast water-tank and had the replicas made of the fleet of ships, using a one inch to one foot scale, and working miniature cannon.

Nor were grand tableaux all that drew the oohs and ahs of the packed houses, all sitting there amid the atmosphere of orange-peels and smoke, heckling, cat-calling, and flirting, as other play-goers drifted in and out of their boxes or pushed onto the benches of the pit, all chatting and laughing during the long evenings' performances.

Among the other great draws was William Betty, a thirteen year old boy, also known as Master Betty or the "Child of Nature" (he was very beautiful), who made his debut at Covent Garden on 1 December 1804 in the happily forgotten drama, *Barbarossa*. (He was paid fifty guineas a performance.)

Tickets for that first performance were sold out in seven minutes, the cavalry were called out to lift fainting women from the crowd in the Piazza and carry them to safety, and in the hours before his first entrance, the audience had been roaring. Then he came on and an absolute hush fell over the auditorium.

Master Betty appeared at both Covent Garden and Drury Lane, went on to play Romeo, then Richard III and even Hamlet, and the audiences were wild for him with women fainting and crying...all of which lasted until his voice broke a couple of years later. (The tragedienne, Sarah Siddons, managed to be out of town or otherwise engaged for most of his London run.)

The downside to all this excitement, of course, was fire.

In the early hours of 20 September 1808, smoke and flame were seen coming from the Theatre Royal at Covent Garden. But by the time the Phoenix Fire Company arrived, the interior was already destroyed. Twenty-three people died in the fire, many of them the firefighters, and the adjacent homes were also destroyed. John Philip Kemble, its owner, had lost everything.

But raising money, Kemble saw the foundation stone for a new Theatre Royal laid by the Prince Regent in December and the theatre reopened on 18 September 1809. To riots.

For Kemble and his financiers had decided that in order to pay for the rebuild, they'd put up the price of seats. Until after two months of riots—where insignias marked with OP for Old Prices were worn by growing numbers of Londoners—they gave way and brought back the lower fees.

But not far away, Drury Lane was levelled by fire on 24 February 1809 while its proprietor, Richard Brinsley Sheridan, watched from the window of the House of Commons. The theatre where Mrs. Siddons had captivated audiences was no more. And because of his own financial instability, Sheridan was unable to raise the funds to rebuild, so it didn't reopen for another three years....

And theatre itself was in a kind of a revolution, as the stilted declamatory style and tragic poses of 18th century actors gave way to a more natural, more intimate performance, such as that of Edmund Kean, changing old style caricatures into authentic, credible characters. Kean opened his London stage career on 26 January 1814, playing Shylock to a packed house at Drury Lane and doing nothing as it had been done for the past hundred years.

Kean's Shylock was a human being, a man of genuine emotion—the critics were wowed, the audience stunned. His subsequent performances as Richard III, Hamlet, Othello, Macbeth, and King Lear transformed performance. Previously, many of these Shakespearean tragedies had only been performed in their Bowdlerised versions—think *King Lear* with rhyming couplets and a happy ending.

And in between the tragedies featuring Kean, or the comedies which showed off a long-legged Mrs. Jordan in breeches-roles, the entr'acte ballets with their lovely limbed female dancers drew the young men of the pit, all ogling and hoping for more than a glimpse of ankle or perhaps a tryst arranged in the Green Room.

All this, and Grimaldi's antics too—a walking, tumbling, leaping, bawdy, animated version of a Rowlandson or Gilray cartoon.

Victorian Era (1837–1901)

THE VICTORIAN TECHNOLOGICAL REVOLUTION: TRANSPORTATION

BY GARY INBINDER

THE VICTORIAN ERA (1837-1901) WAS A PERIOD OF GREAT TECHNOLOGICAL PROGRESS, especially in the industrialized West. Consider the lives of the average Europeans—country folk, townspeople, or city-dwellers—between 1600 and 1800, and the changes won't seem that dramatic. On the other hand, the difference between 1800 and 1900 was profound.

In the fields of transportation and communication, progress that had plodded along for centuries kicked into high gear in the 19th century, especially following the Napoleonic Wars. Steamships replaced sail, cutting the trans-Atlantic crossing from weeks to days. Railways reduced a day's journey to hours. The telegraph—and later the telephone and wireless—made communications over long distances instantaneous.

I'm in my early sixties, so I've lived through a period roughly equivalent in time to Queen Victoria's reign, and I've seen many changes. Take just one example. I remember our family's first television, a twelve-inch, black and white console. You had the choice of five channels: the three networks and two local stations. We had a rabbit-ear antenna that, to put it mildly, didn't produce the best reception, and my father was constantly changing burned out vacuum tubes, fiddling with the controls, and experimenting with different antennae.

The set lasted a few years before it gave up the ghost and we lived without TV for a couple of years before replacing it. Fast forward, and consider the progress—solid state circuitry, color, ever larger screens, computerization, cable and direct TV, hundreds of channels from which to choose, high definition flat screens, and all the bells and whistles of contemporary home entertainment. That will give you some idea of the sort of technological change the Victorians experienced between the 1830s and the turn of the last century.

The complete story of Victorian technological progress far exceeds the scope of this post; therefore, I'll limit myself to a brief overview of some major improvements in transportation and communications.

SAIL TO STEAM

Steamboats and steamships first appeared in the early nineteenth century, but their rapid development and dominance is associated with the Victorian era. In 1838 the steamers *Great Western* and *Sirius* raced across the Atlantic, establishing the Blue Riband competition for the fastest trans-Atlantic passage by passenger ships. *Sirius* crossed first, in eighteen days, about twenty-two days better than the average for a sailing packet.

However, *Great Western* left England four days after *Sirius* and almost caught her, arriving in New York just one day after her rival. The competition stiffened when Samuel Cunard entered the picture. In 1840 his first ship, the *Britannia*, crossed the Atlantic from Liverpool to Halifax, Nova Scotia in a record eleven days and four hours. While the increased speed was impressive, Charles Dickens, who crossed the Atlantic on the *Britannia*, was not enthusiastic about the accommodations:

> *Before descending into the bowels of the ship, we had passed from the deck into a long narrow apartment, not unlike a gigantic hearse with windows in the sides; having at the upper end a melancholy stove, at which three or four chilly stewards were warming their hands; while on either side, extending down its whole dreary length, was a long, long table, over each of which a rack, fixed to the low roof, and stuck full of drinking-glasses and cruet-stands, hinted dismally at rolling seas and heavy weather.*
>
> –Charles Dickens, *American Notes* (1842)

From the 1840s to the 1890s ships became faster, larger, safer, and more comfortable. By the late 1870s the average Liverpool to New York crossing had been reduced to approximately ten days, with seven day record runs. By 1900, ships like White Star's 17,274 ton, steel hulled, twin screw liner *Oceanic* were regularly making the crossing in five days. First and Second Class passengers crossed in relative comfort, and even the immigrants in Steerage fared better than passengers on the early steamers.

COACHES TO TRAINS AND AUTOMOBILES

The earliest years of Queen Victoria's reign saw the beginnings of a railway boom. The early railways were short lines begun in the 1820s, but they really got up a head of steam in the late 1830s and 1840s, with track spreading out across Britain. In 1840 there were approximately 1,500 miles of track, in 1850 more than 6,600, and by 1900 approximately 22,000 miles carried millions of passengers and immense quantities of freight. Speed, safety, and comfort improved significantly during that period.

Novelists noted the change and not necessarily with admiration. For example, Dickens used the railways as a metaphor for the dark side of progress, comparing the speed of the locomotive to the onward rush of life toward its inevitable end:

> *Away, with a shriek, and a roar, and a rattle, from the town, burrowing among the dwellings of men and making the streets hum, flashing out into the meadows for a moment, mining in through the damp earth, booming on in darkness and heavy air, bursting out again into the sunny day so bright and wide; away, with a shriek, and a roar, and a rattle, through the fields, through the woods, through the corn, through the hay, through the chalk, through the mould, through the clay, through the rock, among objects close at hand and almost in the grasp, ever flying from the traveller, and a*

deceitful distance ever moving slowly within him: like as in the track of the remorseless monster, Death!

–Charles Dickens, *Dombey and Son* (1848)

Artists also used the railways of that era as subjects for their paintings, most notably J.M.W. Turner's *Rain, Steam, and Speed—The Great Western Railway.*

The development of the automobile had been retarded in Britain by a law that set a 4 mph speed limit for "locomotives" driven on the roads and required the "locomotive" to be preceded by a man on foot carrying a red flag. The Locomotive Acts (or Red Flag Acts) had been passed to control heavy steam driven road vehicles that were considered dangerous and damaging to the roads when driven at speeds in excess of a walk.

In 1896, the speed limit was raised from 4 mph to 14 mph for "Light Locomotives" and the requirement of the man on foot was abolished. The change is celebrated in the annual London to Brighton run for veteran cars. With the change in the law, motoring became popular among the British upper classes including the Prince of Wales, the first member of the Royal Family to own a car, a 1900 Daimler.

TELEGRAPH, TELEPHONE, AND WIRELESS

Many believe that electric telegraphy began in 1844 in the United States when Morse opened a line between Baltimore and Washington, D.C. However, in 1837 the English inventors William Cooke and Charles Wheatstone devised an electric telegraph that used magnetic needles to transmit messages. Their first telegraph linked Euston station and Camden town, and from there it spread through the burgeoning British railway system, carrying messages and controlling signals, improving efficiency and safety.

The first cable crossed the Channel in 1851, followed by others across the Irish and North Seas. In 1866, Isambard Kingdom Brunel's giant steamer, *The Great Eastern*, laid the first successful trans-Atlantic cable. The electric communications revolution spread, and by the late 1870s, the whole world was connected by a great telegraphic web.

In 1876 the telephone was pioneered and patented in the United States by Alexander Graham Bell. The new invention became a "hit" at the Philadelphia Centennial Exposition when the Emperor of Brazil remarked, "My God, it talks!"

The first London telephone directory (1880) listed 255 names. That same year there were approximately 30,000 telephones in the entire United States. However, there were more than 25,000 phones in use in Britain by the late 1880s, and more than 200,000 in the U.S. by 1890. The novelist Theodore Dreiser took particular note of the new technological wonder by referencing the pay telephone in a dramatic scene:

At the first drugstore he stopped, seeing a long–distance telephone booth inside. It was a famous drugstore, and contained one of the first private telephone booths ever erected. "I want to use your phone a minute," he said to the night clerk.

–Theodore Dreiser, *Sister Carrie* (1900)

Marconi's Wireless Telegraph Co. formed in London (1897) established radio communications between England and France (1898), and in 1901, the last year of Queen Victoria's reign, succeeded in sending and receiving signals across the Atlantic. Thus, the Victorian telecommunications revolution laid the foundations for the global communications network of today.

In 1873 Jules Verne wrote *Around the World in Eighty Days*, taking into account all the recent advances in transportation and communications, including the completion of the U.S. Transcontinental Railroad, the Suez Canal, and the extension of the Indian railway system. His fictional traveller, Phileas Fogg, could plan his journey based upon reliable steamship schedules and railway timetables, and he could also take advantage of improved communications provided by the worldwide telegraphic network.

To demonstrate the viability of Verne's hypothetical journey, in 1889 *New York World* reporter Nellie Bly made the globe circling trip in seventy-two days. Her feat would have seemed as incredible at the beginning of Queen Victoria's reign as a manned lunar landing to folks watching their twelve-inch black and white, vacuum tube televisions in the early 1950s. Like a Victorian, I have seen Science Fiction become Science Fact within the span of my lifetime.

For better or worse, technology took off like a rocket in the Victorian era, and it's been streaking its way to the stars ever since.

Sir Goldsworthy Gurney and His Steam Carriage

BY GARY INBINDER

On a warm summer day in Southwest England during the ninth year of the reign of His Majesty King George IV, a handsome couple—I'll call them Mr. and Mrs. Darcy—were out for a breath of air, dashing through the verdant countryside along one of Mr. McAdam's new roads. They travelled in a jaunty red curricle drawn by a matched pair of high-stepping grays. Pale sunlight streamed through a stand of trees lining the turnpike. A mild wind rustled the leafy branches, barely raising a dust-cloud on the newly laid roadbed.

As they whirled along, the Darcys noticed a strange dark object looming on the horizon. From a distance, it appeared to be a large carriage of some sort, shimmering in the heat waves and moving toward them at a great rate of speed. The horses sensed it coming; skittish, they broke stride and started to gallop. It required all Mr. Darcy's strength and skill to rein them in.

The unidentified vehicle bore down upon the Darcys; its features soon became distinguishable. Could it be the Royal Mail Coach out of London led by a galloping team, on its way to Bath? They could see no horses.

Instead, they spotted a coachman, or more appropriately a "driver" perched on a seat over a single wheel. He was dressed in top hat and red coat; instead of holding reins, he grasped a large handlebar attached to a steering mechanism. Passengers, both ladies and gentlemen, sat above and behind the driver on a dragon-like contraption that belched smoke and cinders and hissed steam from every orifice. There were no familiar sounds of pounding hooves, the slapping and rattling of leather straps and fittings, but rather a mechanically rhythmic thumping, puffing, and chuffing and a grinding of wheels on macadam as the monster rumbled forward at a blazing twenty miles per hour.

Mr. Darcy steered the jolting curricle to the roadside where they came to an abrupt halt beside a drainage ditch. He tried to quiet his horses as they snorted, whinnied, and stomped the turf with restless hooves. The "thing" chugged by in a cloud of steam, soot, and dust. Presently, Mr. Darcy turned to his wife with a scowl: "I say, Lizzy, I'm deuced if it ain't Gurney's blasted steam carriage!"

Mrs. Darcy frowned and nodded in silent agreement. She lowered her parasol, then shook and dusted off her white muslin dress. The rumbling subsided; the steam carriage vanished in the distance, leaving a thin trail of smoke in its wake. Mr. and Mrs. Darcy continued their journey in a decidedly less jolly mood following their confrontation with the monstrous progeny of the Industrial Age.

My sketch of an encounter with the steam carriage is fanciful, but such an incident might have occurred on an English road prior to the passage of the Locomotive Acts (aka Red Flag

Laws) that reduced speed limits for "locomotives" to 4 mph in the country and 2 mph in towns and cities and required a man carrying a red flag to precede each vehicle. These laws retarded the early development of the automobile in Great Britain and their repeal (in 1894) is celebrated in the annual London to Brighton run for veteran cars.

The steam carriage was the brainchild of Sir Goldsworthy Gurney, one of those extraordinary self-taught "gentleman inventors" who seemed to flourish in the 19th century. There were other steam road vehicles at the time, but Gurney's was among the first and arguably the best.

Gurney was born in Cornwall in 1793 into a well-to-do family, studied medicine and practiced as a surgeon, but is best known for his practical inventions including the oxyhydrogen blowpipe, a high-pressure steam jet for extinguishing fires in mines, the Gurney burner, and Gurney light.

Gurney was knighted in 1863 for improving the lighting and ventilation of the House of Commons. But of all his scientific achievements, he is chiefly remembered for building a steam carriage that in 1829 travelled from London to Bath at an average rate of 15 miles per hour.

The steam carriage owed its success to another Gurney invention, the "steam-jet" or blast system that produced greater power in a considerably lighter engine. Interestingly, Gurney's improvement was incorporated by George Stephenson into his highly successful track locomotive Rocket that made railway travel practical.

For a time, Gurney was associated with the great Scottish civil engineer, Thomas Telford. Telford's roads had foundations better able than McAdam's to bear the weight of the steam carriages. He envisioned a British highway system open to steam powered traffic that would compete with the existing canal system and the new railways. There was some interest in Telford and Gurney's schemes. For example, the famous London to Bath journey was made at the request of the army.

But there were powerful lobbies against the development of the steam carriage, and they had some good arguments on their side. Mining and industry were financially committed to the railways; Stephenson's improved engines and a faster and cheaper method of producing wrought-iron rails made the fixed track system more efficient and cost effective. The Stockton-Darlington railway (1825) was a commercial success, and that led to the building of the ambitious Liverpool-Manchester line (1830) where passenger trains could run at speeds of 35 miles per hour.

Following Gurney's successful demonstration of the steam carriage, Sir Charles Dance, using Gurney's design, initiated a regular service between Gloucester and Cheltenham, the nine mile distance being covered in about 45 minutes. This service ran for three months in 1831. Dance also financed a Gurney-designed "drag and omnibus" (the engine pulled the omnibus, an attempt to overcome passengers' objections to sitting over a boiler) that ran from London to Brighton and made a demonstration run on London streets in 1833.

But by that time the light road locomotive was already doomed by commercial and political opposition and the railway's success. The railways had the mining and manufacturing interests on their side; they were joined by the toll road owners and the mail coach lobby. This combination persuaded Parliament to raise tolls on the steam carriages, effectively driving them out of business.

Thomas Telford died in 1834; his vision of a British highway system built for motorized traffic would not be fully realized until the next century. Goldsworthy Gurney went on to other projects and would be honored for his achievements. By the time Gurney died in 1875, Siegfried Marcus in Austria and Etienne Lenoir in France had experimented with vehicles powered by internal combustion engines. These automotive pioneers were followed by the Germans—Daimler, Maybach, and Benz—who began marketing his gasoline powered automobiles in the late 1880s. Almost sixty years after Gurney's steam carriage journeyed from London to Bath, the age of the automobile had begun.

THE REBECCA RIOTS

BY ANITA DAVISON

Genesis XXIV:60—"*And they blessed Rebekah and said unto her, let thy seed possess the gates of those which hate them...*"

O N THE NIGHT OF 6 JUNE 1839 THE TOLLGATE AT YR EFAIL WEN [EFAILWEN] WAS destroyed and the tollhouse set on fire by men dressed in women's clothes with blackened faces for the second time. These incidents marked the start of the Rebecca Riots which spread to many communities in Pembrokeshire and Carmarthenshire.

In the early 19th century, farming was the main industry in Wales, where life was both hard and primitive. Only a few people could read and write. Wales had seen a population increase which increased competition for land and jobs, thus adding to unemployment and poverty. Wet summers ruined corn harvests, forcing farmers to buy corn at famine prices to sustain themselves, their animals, and their families.

Rents remained static, as did the turnpike tolls, so seeing themselves as victims of "tyranny and oppression", farmers and their workers took the law into their own hands to rid themselves of these unjust taxes.

The first institutions to be attacked were the hated toll gates, which were controlled by Turnpike Trusts, comprised of wealthy businessmen who owned most of the main roads. They decided on how many tollgates (turnpikes) could be built and what charges they made to those using them. The tolls were intended for maintenance and improvement of the roads; however, many trusts charged extortionate tolls and diverted the money to other uses.

Most people in rural Wales made their living on small tenant farms they rented from wealthy landlords and relied on the roads to take their produce to market. They were also burdened with having to pay tithes, payments for the support of the Anglican parish church payable in crops or wool. Their landlords were members of the Anglican church who mostly spoke English, whereas in the 1830s, eighty percent of the population of west Wales was Welsh-speaking and Non-Conformist. Thus they resented having to pay tithes to a church that was not their own.

Farmers collected lime to improve the quality of the soil, but the Tollgate Trust set a toll of five shillings (25p) to move a cart of lime eight miles inland. Eleven different Turnpike Trusts operated around Carmarthen, each with several gates, and each time people passed through the gates with produce or lime carts, they had no choice but to pay the toll.

Harvests in 1837 and 1838 were poor, increasing shortages. Smallholders could barely afford to take their goods to market, and in addition they were being charged high tolls for using the roads.

In 1839, a group of toll-renters, led by Thomas Bullin, an Englishman, increased toll rates and installed side-bars, simple forms of gates set on side roads to catch any traffic that had attempted to bypass the main toll booths. These side-bars dramatically increased the cost for farmers carting lime to their fields and almost ruined them.

This precipitated the first attack on Yr Efail Wen, [Efailwen], the attackers calling themselves Merched Beca (Welsh for Rebecca's Daughters) or merely the Rebeccas. The Whitland Turnpike Trust rebuilt the gate, but a week later, a crowd of three hundred people destroyed it for the second time with the battle cry "Rebecca".

The disturbances started again in 1842 when the Whitland Trust built a new gate at The Mermaid, on the lime road at St. Clears in Carmarthenshire. This was destroyed in November, as were the tollgates at Pwll-trap and Trevaughan. The gates were rebuilt, but by early December all gates in St. Clears had been destroyed. The government refused to send soldiers, and so the magistrates called in the marines from Pembroke Dock and the Castlemartin Yeomanry Cavalry. The rioting continued.

In the village of Hendy on 7 September 1843, a woman gatekeeper named Sarah Williams had been warned not to collect any more tolls and that rioters were on their way, but she refused to leave. That night she was heard shouting *"I know who you are,"* by a neighbouring family. The rioters set fire to the tollgate and Sarah ran for help, but when she returned, she was shot dead.

By October 1843, the riots stopped, and the government was forced to call a Commission of Enquiry to explore the grievances of the Welsh farmers. This also resulted in the Turnpikes Act of 1844 which consolidated the trusts and simplified the rates as well as reducing the hated toll on lime movement by half.

The wearing of women's clothes was an established feature of traditional Welsh justice; the Ceffyl Pren, wooden horse, bears many similarities to the Rebeccas, with men wearing female clothing, blackening their faces, and conducting mock trials. Miscreants were sentenced to ride the Ceffyl Pren through the streets to punish members of a community for marital infidelity or informing on a neighbour.

Dylan Thomas wrote the screenplay for a film, *Rebecca's Daughters*, which was published as a novel of the same name in 1965, though the film was not released until 1992, and starred Peter O'Toole, Paul Rhys, and Joely Richardson.

FOURTEEN YEARS' HARD LABOUR

BY **PRUE BATTEN**

I F, LIKE ME, THE GENERATIONS OF ONE'S FAMILY IN TASMANIA CAN BE TRACED BACK TO SET-
tlement, then it is a fair enough assumption to believe there exists a convict somewhere in
the family tree. My great-great-grandfather was such a man.

William Owen Millington was born on 10 June 1810. Where in England is not known
precisely, but given that he married his first wife, Mary, in Chipstead in 1836 and that he was
tried and found guilty of his crime in Chichester in 1837, one must draw a circle around those
areas and assume he and his family lived within that circle.

I rather like the description of Chipstead in the *Domesday Book*, its assets being three hides,
seven ploughs, one mill, and woodland worth five hogs. I'm sure if William had realised that
the whole of the Chipstead estate had been worth so little in the *Domesday Book* that he might
not have followed the path he took so many years later. But then we know, don't we, that value
is a relative thing?

What price starvation though?

As a carpenter William was unable to provide as he may have wished. At the age of twen-
ty-seven, he stole two sheep for the sustenance of his growing family. Found guilty of the theft,
he was tried and sentenced to transportation to the penal island of Van Diemen's Land (Tasmania), where fourteen years' hard labour was to be completed. His marriage with Mary, like
that for all transported convicts, was effectively annulled as he left.

Sentences were in blocks of seven years—whether it was for a kerchief or a loaf of bread—
and the age of the perpetrator meant nothing. In William's case, two sheep equalled fourteen
years. In addition, under British civil law, a man could be declared dead after seven years of
absence. In effect, this made it possible for families left behind to move on with their lives. It
also enabled any convict who lived to work out his pardon, the chance to remarry in the colonies
without the charge of bigamy.

So William was transported from Southampton on the *William Bentick* and after sailing in
miserable hulk conditions to the other side of the world, arrived in Hobart on the twenty-sixth
of August, 1838.

Tasmania as a penal colony had been in existence for some 30 years at this point; the town
of Hobart had been established, and outlying settlements were growing with the opening up
of valuable agricultural holdings. The town of Bothwell in the Central Highlands of Tasmania
was one such and it was William's good fortune that he was a competent carpenter and was sent
there to serve his time, indentured to a resident vicar.

Bothwell was a town that served large pastoral estates of cattle and sheep graziers. In the
first two decades of its settlement, churches, a school, soldiers' barracks, and hotels were built,
so there was scope for William to earn his pardon.

No convict could work for money; it was a condition of the sentence. At best, he had minimal shelter, clothing, and sustenance and could expect no more, so one wonders why my great-great-grandfather could have been so ill-advised as to present an invoice for his work to the vicar.

He was of course lashed, how many times we are unable to ascertain, but enough to make sure he trod the straight and narrow through the hot highland summers and freezing winters that Bothwell offered, until he became a free man in 1851.

I always wonder why he didn't hasten then to the goldfields of Ballarat and Bendigo on the mainland for what is euphemistically called the Great Australian Goldrush—and where, it is often claimed, the true Australian identity began to form. Instead, with the desire for major wealth no doubt beaten out of him, he settled in Hobart and married again—to a widow called Elizabeth in Saint David's Church of England, later Hobart's Saint David's Cathedral. He continued his carpentry trade, but as often happened with carpenters historically, also became a Hobart undertaker.

William Owen Millington was lucky to be sent to Bothwell as an indentured convict rather than be shipped to the misnamed "model" (meaning humane) prison of Port Arthur, lucky too that the infamous hell hole of Sarah Island in the far west had ceased operations in 1833. In both instances he may well have been fortunate to survive at all. His trade was a gift, the opening of pastoral lands with towns close by a godsend, and he lived to tell the tale.

As members of the family have tried to track down William's descendants in England, it has become obvious that many don't know that "lost" William was in fact a convict. Perhaps there remains the need to ignore such skeletons whereas here in the colonies, one knows one has truly "made it" if one can show such a thing in one's own ancestry.

What I find most astonishing is that this many years later, William's great-great-great-grandson, my own son, is a qualified joiner and carpenter but also, ironically, a working member of a family of sheep farmers.

Scotland Yard and a New British Mystery

BY **MARY LYDON SIMONSEN**

LONDON HAS ALWAYS BEEN A CITY OF HAVES AND HAVE NOTS WITH MANY UNSAVORY NEIGH-borhoods abutting some of London's poshest addresses. If you walk the streets of Mayfair, you might admire the shiny black wrought-iron gates that surround many of the properties. However, they were not put there for decoration, but, instead, were used to keep the less fortunate from becoming more fortunate at the expense of London's well-heeled by smashing a window and gaining entrance to the townhouse.

Despite having a significant criminal element, London did not have an organized police presence until 1749 when the Bow Street Runners were founded by Henry Fielding, the author of *Tom Jones*, who was also a magistrate, and his blind brother, John (aka the "Blind Beak"), who reputedly could recognize 3,000 criminals by the sound of their voices.

Fast forward to 1829 when Parliament passed an act introduced by Home Secretary, Sir Robert Peel (who gave his name to the "Bobbies"), in which the first true London police force was organized under the direction of Commissioners Colonel Charles Rowan and Richard Mayne. The men occupied a private house at 4 Whitehall Place, the back of which opened onto a courtyard: the Great Scotland Yard. The Yard's name was inspired by its site, a medieval palace which housed Scottish royalty on their visits to London.

The police were originally viewed by the public as "spies," but their role in several important cases cemented their reputation with the citizens of London. Inspector Charles Frederick Field became good friends with Charles Dickens, who occasionally accompanied constables on their nightly rounds. Dickens used Field as a model for the all-knowing Inspector Bucket in his novel *Bleak House*.

Following a major scandal in 1877, the Metropolitan Police was reorganized, and the Criminal Investigation Department (CID), a respected unit of plainclothes police detectives, was born. In 1890, the police force moved to its new building on the Victoria Embankment, retaining its name, but as New Scotland Yard.

During the second half of the 19th century, one of Scotland Yard's most durable detectives, Frederick Porter Wensley (aka "The Weasel"), began his 40-year career and investigated cases including the murder of thirty-two-year-old French woman Emilienne Gerard. On the morning of November 2, 1917, street sweepers found Gerard's torso along with a note reading: "Blodie Belgium." (This was during the First World War.) Wensley questioned Louis Voisin, Gerard's lover, asking him to write "Bloody Belgium." Voisin made the same spelling error, establishing his guilt.

With the setting of narrow streets and a London encased in a dense fog, the year 1888 saw the first appearance of Jack the Ripper, who was responsible for five murders between 1888 and 1891 in the Whitechapel area of London. More than 160 people were suspected of being the Whitechapel murderer, including Lewis Carroll, the author of *Alice in Wonderland*, and painter William Richard Sickert. Two letters received by the Yard gave detailed facts and were signed "Jack the Ripper." With no more leads or murders, in 1892, the Ripper case was officially closed.

In 1967, the police force moved once again to its present location, a modern 20-story building near the Houses of Parliament. Today, Scotland Yard has roughly 30,000 officers patrolling 620 square miles occupied by 7.2 million citizens.

Although I am the author of several Jane Austen re-imaginings, when I read for pleasure, I like to kick back with a good mystery. After having achieved some success with my Austen novels, I decided to try my hand at writing a mystery. In *Three's A Crowd*, Patrick Shea, a young detective sergeant serving at a police station in Greater London, has his eye on a position with a murder investigation team at New Scotland Yard. Part of Scotland Yard's attraction for Patrick is an organization steeped in history. If you are a fan of the television series *Law & Order UK*, you will enjoy *Three's A Crowd* and its sequel, *A Killing in Kensington*.

THE GREAT STINK OF LONDON 1858

BY DEBRA BROWN

I GREATLY ENJOY LIZA PICARD'S BOOK, *VICTORIAN LONDON*. IF YOU WANT TO READ NUMEROUS great anecdotes, her book is a wonderful source. Her first chapter discusses the smells of London past.

Day and night in Victorian times, she says, London stank. The Thames' "main ingredient" was human waste. Human excrement was sold as fertilizer to nurseries and farms surrounding London by the night-soil men who emptied the cesspits. A chamber pot might be emptied on your head as you walked through the narrow streets, adding to the stench of dead dogs, horse and cattle manure, and rotting vegetables.

By 1841, there were 1,945,000 people living in London and 200,000 cesspits full and over-flowing. Years of waste fermented in miles of sewers in Holborn and Finsbury with no access to the Thames. Even in aristocratic Belgravia, Grosvenor Square, Hanover Square, and Berkeley Square, noxious matter stopped up house drains and reeked. Buckingham Palace smelled from drains that ran below.

Cows were kept in cowsheds all over London in appalling conditions with no space for cleaning. Cattle, sheep, and pigs sold in Smithfield Market walked through London streets leaving behind 40,000 tons of dung a year, and thousands of horses each excreted 45 lbs. of faeces and 3.5 lbs. of urine a day.

A fourteen foot deep pit at St. Bride's Church was reopened every Wednesday to take in carcasses of dead paupers until it could hold no more. The whole neighborhood stank.

Coal gas stank, and gas mains leaked. In Bermondsey, skins and hides were tanned using a process including dog turds. Refuse from hospitals, fish market washings and offal, slaughter-house offal, glue-makers, candle-makers, bone dealers, dye works, dead rats, dogs and cats and even—the January 1862 journal *The Builder* said—dead babies stank.

Finally, there was a breakthrough (right?) when water closets became a normal part of a house. By 1857 there were 200,000 of them all duly sidetracking the cesspits and emptying straight into the Thames via the sewers. The result was the Great Stink of 1858.

This at last precipitated actions which helped to turn things around.

The Harlot Who Was Dickens' Muse, or Even Greater Expectations

by KATHERINE ASHE

This is the story of a British author's inspiration. It happens his muse was an American woman. She fits into the history of British letters for she was the inspiration for Miss Havisham, the bitter spinster jilted at the altar who is the central character of *Great Expectations* by Charles Dickens. Just how far may a novel depart from the facts of its inspiration? Very far indeed.

Granted, Dickens met her when she was an old woman, a wealthy dowager living in a mansion in New York City's then fashionable Harlem. She was Madame Jumel, widow of the wealthy French liquor importer, Stephen Jumel, and even wealthier in her own right, for she had cornered the Manhattan real estate market just as farms were being divided into the blocks now demarcated from 14th Street to 34th Street. She was, by her own effort, the richest woman in the western world.

She entertained Charles Dickens during one of his American tours. And astonished him by showing him her dining room, festooned with cobwebs, scattered with green and rock hard crumbs. For the room was her relic of the night she entertained Joseph Bonaparte, the Emperor of France's elder brother.

Also, in her household was a little girl, actually her sister's granddaughter, who she was training to entrance men with her charms. A little boy was even provided for the child to practice upon. Thus Eliza Jumel came to inspire the character of the raddled, embittered, jilted-at-the altar Miss Havisham of *Great Expectations*.

Dickens noted what he saw, and wrote the story that sprang to his mind. But the truth of Madame Jumel could not have been further from Miss Havisham.

We know the actual details of Eliza's life because, after her death, the son, George Washington Bowen, whom she left in Providence, Rhode Island, to be brought up in the brothel of Mother Freelove Ballou, sued to gain her estate. There were a parade of witnesses, from her own servants in New York to the Governor of Rhode Island himself who, from his childhood, remembered her as Betsy Bowen, the tart of the dockyards.

The revelations left New York scandalized, titillated, entranced. Madame Jumel was eccentric, yes. A few years before her death, she had offered charity to homeless men during an economic crash. The men found themselves dressed in uniforms (designed and paid for by Madame) and drilled daily by the lady herself astride her charger. She was preparing to invade

Mexico and make herself an empress. If this sounds like utter madness, it wasn't quite. She was carrying forward the plans of her second husband, Aaron Burr.

What was Madame's heritage? She was born Eliza (Betsy) Bowen, the daughter of a servant girl who, very unfortunately, previously had become pregnant and was cast into the streets of Providence. There she was first rescued by a brothel owner named Solomon Angel (one would not dare to make these names up) who handed her on to Mother Freelove.

In 1775, the now confirmed harlot, Phoebe, attracted the attention of a gentleman visiting Providence, and he took such an interest in her that he gave her enough money to stay off the streets for a while. During her time of absence from her profession, Phoebe discovered she was pregnant, and the child she bore was Eliza. The father, she informed Eliza, was none other than George Washington.

While still sheltered from life on the streets, Phoebe married a fisherman named Bowen, and the baby Eliza was given his name. But Bowen soon fell from his boat in a drunken stupor and was drowned.

Phoebe and Eliza were back at Mother Freelove's, where Eliza, or Betsy as she was being called, grew to be a lively beauty and a great asset to the establishment. That is, until a French sea captain named DelaCroix, finding her not only winsome but quite intelligent as well, lured her to France. There he taught her French, and she joined several of his other protégées in his remarkable business.

Betsy, speaking French now, was set up by Captain DelaCroix in New York City and passed off as his wife. The aim was to entrap rich men into affairs with this lonely, lovely French wife. Then the captain would appear in the midst of a *scene flagrante* and the fearful lover would find himself the victim of blackmail. Charming, *n'est-ce pas?*

New York City was prosperous and merry in these early years of the 1800s, and Eliza's victims included the very best people. But there were two men who escaped being her victims: Alexander Hamilton and Aaron Burr. Hamilton, because gossip had it he was a love-child of George Washington's—hence Eliza may have considered him her brother—and she did have some standards, you know. Burr, because she fell in love with him, and he got rid of Captain DelaCroix for her and set her up in a career in the theater.

On the stage she was not nearly the success she had been in the boudoir, but she did well enough to dazzle an acquaintance of Burr, the liquor importer Stephen Jumel, a Frenchman with his own fleet of ships. Her French was sufficiently convincing even to fool him.

Soon Eliza gave up the stage and was installed as Jumel's mistress, with the clothes, the coach, the house—all the accoutrements of a wife except the legality.

Why did Burr give her up? He was pursuing a political career. A career that would bring him repeatedly into tied vote with Thomas Jefferson for the Presidency of the United States. He couldn't afford a woman with Eliza's reputation. But there's every indication that he loved her, and her acquisition by Jumel may have done nothing to slow him down—at first.

Secure and rich, Eliza now set her sites to the next step up: official marriage to Jumel. The businessman was frantically summoned to return at once from a trip to Washington. What he found was Eliza, pale, coughing her last, attended by his doctor and a priest. History has it that, in tears, he begged his mistress if there was anything he could do for her in these, her last moments, and she murmured, "Yes, Stephen, make an honest woman of me." The priest was there, the rite was performed, and Eliza leapt from her deathbed screaming, "I'm Mrs. Jumel!"

Jumel was known for his practical jokes. He took this one in good part and married Eliza again, properly in a church.

It was about this time that Burr found his access to his beloved curbed. The doors of the Jumel house were mysteriously closed to him. And it was at this time that his exchange of letters with Alexander Hamilton, which led to their fatal duel, commenced.

The letters show Burr being vague in his complaint. He had withstood Hamilton's politically aimed slanders for years without wincing, but now he was implacable—although rather vague. Hamilton tried every means to appease his opponent, until at last Burr accused him of having irreparably impaired his private life. He demanded Hamilton "give satisfaction," and the duel took place on the cliff at Weehawken, New Jersey.

Was the cause Eliza? Had Hamilton hinted to Jumel of an ongoing relationship that caused Burr to be banned from the Jumel house?

After the duel, which brought on Hamilton's slow death, Burr retreated to Washington to serve out his term as Vice-President of the United States. He had been the runner-up in the Jefferson/Burr presidential election and Vice Presidents then were the number two winner.

Dueling was of course illegal. Officially, Burr had murdered Hamilton, but in Washington, so long as he was serving in office, Burr couldn't be touched by the law. His term finished, he fled west—to found an army to invade Mexico and establish a dominion for himself. Unfortunately, Jefferson took fright, imagining the army was intended to abduct *him*. The law was sent after Burr, and he was brought back ignominiously (he was a small man) tied on a lawman's saddlebow. But accusations didn't stick and Burr ended up exiled to France.

What was Mrs. Jumel doing all this time? Finding herself in such happy circumstances, she went to Providence hoping to rescue her sister. Their mother was dead by this time—shot as a squatter in an illegal shack. The sister, Eliza discovered, was also dead, found floating in Providence's harbor. But she had left a little girl, also named Eliza, who was beginning the cycle of their family's sad history again, as a servant. Madame Jumel bought little Eliza out of servitude and made her an adoptive daughter.

Then she set about creating what was probably the first historical restoration in the United States, now known as the Morris Jumel Mansion. (It claims to be the oldest house in Manhattan and can be can be visited: http://www.morrisjumel.org.)

Why did Eliza do this? Built in 1765, this magnificent home of a royalist, Roger Morris, had been abandoned as the Continental Army moved into New York, and it came to serve as George Washington's headquarters. After the war, it had degenerated into a country inn. Eliza persuaded Jumel to buy it, then spared no expense in restoring it and magnificently furnishing its octagonal ballroom—for this was to be the occasion of her entry into New York high society.

It was a grand event, no doubt. But it backfired. A guest brought a friend who was none other than the Governor of Rhode Island, who remembered Eliza as Betsy of the dock and streets, and he told Jumel a bit of his wife's early history.

Years later, the servants reported how Jumel confronted Eliza—and how she fought back. Had she not been a good wife? A good mother to their adopted daughter? How dare he take the word of a stranger above what he knew of her himself! And she brought from her capacious skirt's pocket the little pistol he had given her. Jumel was reduced to tears, begging her not to shoot. Indeed, how could he have been so foolish? So cruel? Could she forgive him? If she only would forgive him, he would take her and little Eliza on a trip to France on his flagship named for her, the *Eliza*.

Eliza relented and put away her gun. And the Jumels went to France on the *Eliza*.

But nothing in Eliza's life could be so ordinary as a shopping trip to Paris. Approaching her port of La Rochelle, the *Eliza* was battered by storms and driven south, taking shelter in the Gironde, near Bordeaux, to make repairs. There, a boat filled with magnificently uniformed French officers hailed them and asked to come aboard.

It seemed that Napoleon had just lost the Battle of Waterloo. He was intending to flee to America but his ship was trapped at La Rochelle, unable to leave harbor because of the storm. The American ship had been seen trying to beat her way in, then turning south. The Emperor's aide de camp, Lelande, had been sent to see if that American ship could be found, and if it would be willing to rescue Napoleon and take him to where he might start a new life. The vanquished Emperor hoped to retire to a farm in New Jersey.

Of course the Jumels agreed. But by the time Lelande reached La Rochelle, the British had closed off the harbor. In despair, Napoleon had surrendered. In thanks, he sent Lelande back to the Jumels with a gift—his coach and his personal effects, all that remained of his earthly possessions.

The Jumels entered Paris in the Emperor's wreath-emblazoned coach—and they were the only ones who knew what had become of Napoleon. Soon they were deep in efforts to free the Emperor, and Eliza was the darling of the Paris aristocracy. Forget about those parvenu snobs in New York City!

But soon the Jumels were near bankruptcy, attempting to fund the Emperor's restoration.

There was the house in New York and Stephen's warehouses—they were worth something. Eliza insisted that only she knew the mansion's worth, so she should return and see to its sale, while Stephen remained, seeing to their interests in Paris.

In New York, the first person Eliza contacted was Aaron Burr, who was returned from his French exile and had a small law practice now in Lower Manhattan. Burr advised Eliza to keep the house and rent it, and instead sell the warehouses. He would guide her in her investments of the proceeds. Thus Eliza got into the business of real estate speculation. How much was Burr's work and how much Eliza's will never be known, but in a few years she could move from her miserable room in a Long Island farmhouse back into her mansion with riches to spare.

Stephen returned from France. Life was idyllic; the mansion's hilltop lands stretched down on each side to the Hudson and the East River, and the view from the master bedroom's balcony reached (with a spy glass) to the harbor. Stephen, elderly now, loved his land, and rode the hay wagon up to the house with the last load of haying. He slipped off, broke his arm, the arm became gangrenous, and soon he died.

Eliza was a very rich widow. Burr wasted little time. He brought a clergyman to visit. Aaron

Burr and Eliza Betsy Bowen Jumel were married. During their divorce proceedings, which happened fairly soon afterward, she said he had forced her and embarrassed her into marrying him. And she accused her hasty husband of infidelity already.

It seemed that Burr, still entranced by the opportunities out West, had sold one of Eliza's carriages and its fine team of horses and given the proceeds to a woman who was leading a group of settlers westward. In a terrific argument in the mansion's hall, Eliza insisted the woman was his mistress. He swore she was not, and then and there suffered a stroke. Crippled, barely able to speak, Burr insisted on being taken from the house, down the length of Manhattan to his office.

Paralysed, poverty-stricken, unable to pay his office's rent, he ended up living at the mercy of a kind woman innkeeper on Staten Island. It was there that Eliza's lawyer, Alexander Hamilton Junior, handed Burr the final papers of divorce. Burr took the documents, saying, *"I have always loved women…"* and died. One might say he died at the hands of his victim Hamilton's son.

Did Eliza regret her actions? She took up Burr's project of invading Mexico and made it her own. But she died in her bed, composing a polite letter to a friend.

Madame Jumel, the inspiration for Miss Havisham, was a far cry from a jilted and embittered spinster.

Cameos, Silhouettes, and *Cartes de Visite*

By DEBRA BROWN

Once upon a time there were no cameras, but people wanted images of their loved ones or of themselves to share. No doubt sketches and carvings were made from earliest times on whatever materials could be obtained. The likeness of the person would depend upon the skills of the artist and other factors, such as materials.

One early form of likeness is the cameo. Ancient cameos were often made from semi-precious gemstone, usually onyx or agate, where two contrasting colors meet. Less expensive cameos are made from shell or glass. Artistic cameos were made in Greece as far back as the 3rd century B.C. They were very popular amongst the Augustus family of ancient Rome.

Revivals in popularity of the cameo have occurred periodically. The first such revival in Britain was during the reigns of George III and later his granddaughter, Queen Victoria, to the extent that they were being mass produced during the latter half of the 19th century.

French Finance Minister Etienne de Silhouette cut black profiles as a hobby. The cuttings were originally called profile miniatures or shades. The name silhouette was in use by the early 19th century. These provided family members with a likeness that was much less expensive than a painted miniature, and it is thought that Silhouette's name became associated with them because of his severe economic policies. The likeness could be cut by a skilled artist in minutes using paper and scissors. At times, gold accents and colored paint were used to add interest. The cost of a silhouette could run from a shilling to more than a guinea. A silhouette might be done, along with a poem, to remember a departed loved one.

Resort and spa towns came to have at least one silhouettist. The daughter of King George III, Princess Elizabeth, was an amateur in the field. Materials used included paper, wax, glass, or plaster. More costly silhouettes were framed. A famous English artist was John Miers (1756-1821), who began his career in Liverpool and then moved to a London studio at No. 111 Strand in 1788. He charged a guinea per silhouette. Some that he did on ivory came to be used in rings, lockets, and bracelets.

A proliferation of unskilled artists took up the lucrative trade, decreasing its popularity. Then another advent threatened the silhouette medium: commercial photography.

In 1854, a Parisian photographer named Andre Disderi patented a multi-lensed camera which produced eight small likenesses on one large glass negative. The resulting print was cut, the portraits were trimmed, and they were then mounted on cards measuring two and a half by four inches. This was the usual size of a visiting card, and so these photos were dubbed *cartes de visite.*

In 1859, Napoleon III had his photograph made up in this manner, initiating a craze throughout Europe, and then in America, called cardomania. The craze reached England in 1861 when J.E. Mayall took *carte de visite* portraits of the royal family. Soon, studios opened in every town. A photographer in Bath reportedly sold between sixty and seventy thousand cards in a single year.

By the third quarter of the 19th century, hardback, leather-covered photograph albums with stiff cardboard pages, often decorated with drawings, were to be found in most Victorian parlors. *Cartes de visite* featuring famous personalities were added to these family albums with crowds gathering whenever shop windows displayed the latest. Actors and society, political, clerical, and military figures and especially the royal family were in great demand. When the Prince Consort died, not less than seventy thousand of his *cartes* were ordered from Marion and Company of Regent Street. *Cartes de visite* were eventually made in larger, cabinet print size.

Thomas Stevens introduced something new in 1879—the silk-woven picture or Stevengraph. Two scenes of local interest were woven on a loom. These sold for a shilling, with new pictures being issued once a month. Portraits were later done in this manner, featuring members of the royal family, sportsmen of the day, and so on. By the early twentieth century, even silk-woven postcards portraying famous passenger liners were sold as souvenirs to passengers aboard the ships.

THE HUMBLE ENVELOPE

BY MIKE RENDELL

Scene I: 1770, London; Arabella sits down at her writing desk, extracts the envelope which she placed in the drawer earlier, and fingers trembling, inserts the paper-knife and cuts eagerly across the top of the envelope, pulling out the beautifully written letter and starts to read....

FACT OR FICTION? ALMOST CERTAINLY FICTION, SINCE THE USE OF ENVELOPES WAS ALMOST unheard of at that time! Why? Because envelopes did not make a significant appearance until Rowland Hill's reform of the Post Office in 1840. Prior to that date, only the very wealthy, or terminally stupid, would have used envelopes (which would have had to have been made by hand). The reason was that postal rates were fixed not by weight but by the number of sheets of paper.

Why use an envelope, which counted as a separate sheet, when the address could be written on one section of the main letter, and folded into place?

Known as "entires" by modern collectors, these letters, usually of a single sheet of paper, would be folded into three, then the "wings" tucked in at the back so that the address could be written clearly on the face of the entire. Unfolding it, the writer would then fill every part of the letter, often turning it sideways to fill in the inside of the wings. Once the letter was finished, it would be sealed across the back so that the wings could not be opened up. The seal, made of wax, was known as a wafer.

The address on the entire would sometimes be marked "via London" because roads between the towns were slower than the much longer journey via the capital. Letters to London were usually sent by reference to nearby public buildings (the local church, or public house, etc.) and although the 1765 Stamp Act introduced street numbering throughout the City, it was some years before this caught on. My ancestor, who lived at One London Bridge, was still receiving letters addressed to him "opposite St. Magnus Church" (rather than "Number One London Bridge") well into the 1780s.

Rowland Hill published his paper "Post Office Reform: Its Importance and Practicability" early in 1837. Here was a crusader for reform who in his own words admitted, *"I had never been inside the walls of a Post Office"*.

Untramelled by historic considerations, he was able to take a completely fresh look at mail deliveries and come up with some startling proposals, which led almost immediately to the development of the machine-made envelope. He examined the cost of delivering a carriage-full of letters from London to Edinburgh and, having apportioned the cost per letter, he concluded that we needed a system which had a uniform rate for a letter of moderate weight, regardless of the distance it was to cover and "without reference to the number of enclosures".

One of the people called to give evidence to the Select Committee on Postal Reform in

1838 was the paper maker John Dickinson. He referred to *"the new fashioned envelope with the four corners of the paper meeting under the seal"*. In other words, at that stage envelopes existed but were not in widespread use.

The upshot of the parliamentary deliberations was that Hill's proposals were largely accepted. Gone was the idea of the recipient paying for the letter. Instead the sender would pay a uniform rate of one penny. Gone was the need to count sheets of paper, or to frank the envelope, and the cost of delivery was drastically reduced because Hill was convinced that this would result in a massive increase in volume which in turn would bring down the cost to the Post Office of delivering each item.

The result was the commissioning of the country's first postage stamp, a gummed "Penny Black" with a portrait of the eighteen-year-old Queen Victoria based on the design for her coinage by William Wyon. It also led to the design of a penny wrapper—an envelope which people could buy which already had the postage paid.

A prize of £200 for the best design of the penny wrapper was awarded to William Mulready after a competition held in 1840. He came up with a flamboyant design with Britannia seated on a lion, dispatching post to the four corners of the globe via winged messengers. The public hated it, and the Mulready envelope was quickly withdrawn. However, the stamps, and the new postal system, were hugely popular.

In the very first year, no fewer than 68 million Penny Blacks were moistened and stuck down onto envelopes which had the advantage of completely concealing the contents. Even Queen Victoria was delighted with the stamp—so much so that she refused to countenance a change to her portrait, meaning that her youthful face was still adorning her stamps some 60 years later! Arguably, our postage stamp designers are flattering to a similar degree with our present monarch, although she has been allowed to age gradually as time goes by.

Before long, in back offices up and down the country, it was customary for a clerk to laboriously cut out an envelope-shape on paper, using a tin template. He would cut through perhaps two dozen sheets at a time, using a craft tool or sharp knife. The cut-outs would then be passed to another clerk for folding, and then to another for the side triangles to be glued together. The result: an envelope which ensured that the contents remained secure, private, and protected from the elements.

The first envelope-folding machine in this country resulted from a collaboration between Rowland Hill's kid brother Edwin and Warren de la Rue in 1840 (i.e. almost immediately after the postage stamp was introduced, when it quickly became apparent that handmade envelopes could not keep pace with the new demand). Various other people came up with design improvements, and by the mid 1850s the modern envelope was being churned out by the million.

There is a rather nice story as to why Rowland Hill was so passionate about reforming the postal system. He explained to a parliamentary committee that he was inspired by the plight of a poor servant girl who was observed receiving a letter. Unable to pay the required fee of one shilling, she turned the letter round in her hand for a few seconds before returning it to the postman, declining to accept it because of the not inconsiderable cost. Horrified that such a potentially valuable and important missive should go unread for the sake of twelve pence, the gallant Rowland dashed forward and paid the fee, expecting gushing thanks from the grateful servant.

Not so, for she seemed not to care one way or the other. When challenged as to her indifference, she replied that she knew who it was from and when looking at the marks on the outside of the envelope could quite readily work out the contents, and had no need to pay a fee. It reminds me of the time when phone calls from a public phone box gave the caller a chance to Press Button A or B—and in that time you could just about shout a brief message for free down the line before being cut off!

Addendum: The window envelope? Patented 1902 by an American (what else could he be) called Americus Callahan. And airmail? The first mail to be delivered by air was in January 1785 in a cross channel balloon flight from Dover to Calais, carrying a letter from William Franklin addressed to Benjamin Franklin's grandson. The first aerogramme (i.e. an envelope specifically designed for the purpose and which opens up to become a letter) is surprisingly modern—it was first issued in Iraq in 1933.

Black edged mourning envelopes? Popular immediately after the Penny post was introduced, as a way of preparing the recipient for "news from the grave" contained in the letter within. Dickens in *Nicholas Nickleby* (1839) and Thackeray in *Vanity Fair* (1848) both refer to the black edged envelopes as bringing news of a bereavement. The mourning envelope became part of the ritual of coping with death, and would be used by the family of the bereaved for up to twelve months (except for business letters which were always on plain white paper).

While we are on the subject of bereavement, for me, the saddest letters I came across when researching *The Journal of a Georgian Gentleman* were the ones detailing the illness and death of my ancestor Richard Hall's sister-in-law from smallpox in 1769. Not only were the letters sent at almost hourly intervals to Richard from his brother-in-law as the disease progressed, but by a remarkable coincidence, they have all survived. Not only do I have all the letters which Richard received—I also have copies of the ones sent by him by way of reply! Read the book for the story of an extraordinary event which happened 250 years after the letters were written, whereby the whole correspondence was re-united!

Popular Pigeons and Slanderous Psittacines

by GRACE ELLIOT

I N Victorian times, bird keeping was a popular hobby amongst city communities. Native birds such as thrushes, bullfinches, and goldfinches were trapped at night in country villages and sent by train to the suburbs to be sold in markets at Greenwich, Hounslow, and Woolwich.

Bullfinches and goldfinches were especially popular, since they could be trained to sing and fetch a high price, several shillings each, whilst larks sold for six to eight pence apiece. There was even a market for dowdy birds such as house sparrows—once they were disguised with paint—but sadly when they preened they died of lead poisoning.

Even more unpleasant was the craze in the 1890s for "flying" greenfinches. These birds were sold for half a penny each, with a cotton thread tied to a leg. The idea was to bet on which bird could fly in circles longest before it dropped dead of exhaustion.

Keeping caged birds was widespread, even amongst prisoners held at the Tower of London. One prisoner wrote *An Epitaph on a Goldfinch*, on the death of his pet bird: "*Buried June 23, 1794 by a fellow prisoner in the Tower of London.*"

The Spitalfields weavers of the 1840s also prized their birds. The breeding of fancy pigeons and canaries, Almond tumblers, Pouting horsemen, and Nuns, was taken very seriously. Bird shows were highly competitive, matching the fashion amongst wealthier classes for dog shows. It could be a dodgy business—the prize winning pigeons at a show in Islington had had their throats stitched back to improve their appearance—the perpetrators were found out and prosecuted.

London's pigeons are descended from those that escaped from dovecotes in medieval times to roost amongst the city's ledges and towers. In 1277, a man is recorded as falling from the belfry of St. Stephens, Walbrook, whilst trying to raid a pigeon's nest, and in 1385, the Bishop of London complained of "malignant persons" who threw stones at pigeons resting in city churches.

One parrot owner was W.S. Gilbert, who wrote the words to accompany Sir Arthur Sullivan's music. He owned a particularly fine parrot, reputedly the best talker in England. When a guest commented on the appearance of a second parrot in his hallway, Gilbert replied: "*The other parrot, who is a novice, belongs to Doctor Playfair. He is reading up with my bird, who takes pupils.*"

However, pet birds were not popular with everyone. George Bernard Shaw was given a caged canary which he heartily disliked, calling it a "little green brute." He was delighted when the bird was stolen and equally disappointed when a friend replaced it. His comment was: "*I'm a vegetarian and can't eat it, and it's too small to eat me.*"

THE POOR ALWAYS AMONG US

BY **PHILLIP BROWN**

THE NINETEENTH CENTURY SAW A HUGE GROWTH IN THE POPULATION OF GREAT BRITAIN. By the end of the century, there were three times more people living in Great Britain than at the beginning. Families were getting larger, children began to survive infancy better, and immigration, particularly from Ireland, swelled the inner cities.

In the cities, jobs were scarce. Large numbers of both skilled and unskilled people were looking for work, so wages were low, barely above subsistence level. If work dried up, or was seasonal, men were laid off, and because they had hardly enough to live on when they were in work, they had no savings to fall back on.

In his book *The Victorian Underworld*, Kellow Chesney gives a graphic description of the conditions in which many were living:

> Hideous slums, some of them acres wide, some no more than crannies of obscure misery, make up a substantial part of the, metropolis.... In big, once handsome houses, thirty or more people of all ages may inhabit a single room.

As the century progressed, the middle and wealthy classes, through a mixture of fear of the underclass (sounds familiar today) and genuine compassion, founded numerous societies to give aid and help, particularly to the "deserving poor". A popular hymn still showed the distance to be travelled, however:

> The rich man in his castle,
> The poor man at his gate,
> God made them, high and lowly,
> And order'd their estate.
>
> —The third verse of "All Things Bright and Beautiful", first published in 1848 in Hymns for Little Children (London: Joseph Masters, 1848), by Cecil Frances Humphreys. In modern versions of this hymn, the third verse is omitted.

In earlier periods, Victorian artists had typically portrayed the poor of the countryside in rather a jolly way (where in reality, starvation was a shadow that stalked many rural workers—hence the flight to the cities).

But by the 1870s and 1880s, more realistic portrayals began to emerge in response to Dickens and other writers who were more hard hitting about the challenges faced by the poor. Yet even in *From Hand to Mouth—He Was One of the Few Who Would Not Beg* by Thomas Faed, you still felt that people knew their place, and of course such pictures were intended for the middle class patrons, who didn't want poverty on their walls in its utmost reality. But at least the subject was being discussed and portrayed, and a few artists like Luke Fildes went as far as they dared.

Another attempt to bring problems to light was in the reforming journal *The Graphic*, edited by the social reformer William Luson Thomas, who believed strongly that art could bring about social reform. John Millais recommended him to Dickens who used him to illustrate *The Mystery of Edwin Drood*.

> *A brilliant morning shines on the old city. Its antiquities and ruins are surpassingly beautiful, with a lusty ivy gleaming in the sun, and the rich trees waving in the balmy air. Changes of glorious light from moving boughs, songs of birds, scents from gardens, woods, and fields—or, rather, from the one great garden of the whole cultivated island in its yielding time—penetrate into the Cathedral, subdue its earthy odour, and preach the Resurrection and the Life. The cold stone tombs of centuries ago grow warm; and flecks of brightness dart into the sternest marble corners of the building, fluttering there like wings.*
>
> —Charles Dickens, *Edwin Drood*

In 1888, William Powell Frith portrayed what is almost a photograph of a typical London street, where the rich and poor did intermingle freely.

Herbert von Herkomer (born in Bavaria but settled in Bushey, Hertfordshire where he built Lululaund—named after his third wife—which was important in the British film industry) captured the real rural poor…though in the later *Eventide: A Scene in the Westminster Union* (1878) the finished picture was carefully "polished" to show the old age paupers happily drinking tea and content.

Domestic labour is seldom seen in Victorian art, though photography picked it up, particularly the fascinating if bizarre work of Arthur Munby, who photographed his future wife Hannah Cullwick as a scullery maid.

A governess was in an awkward position in the Victorian household, neither quite a servant nor a member of the family. As a sign of this social limbo, she often ate in isolation. She had a middle class background and education, but she was paid and not really part of the family. Being a governess was one of the few legitimate ways an unmarried middle class woman could support herself in that society. Her position was often depicted as one to be pitied.

Bordering constantly on poverty (and by popular repute, prostitution), the overworked seamstresses were the next level down if education did not allow them to seek a governess position. After several reports, distressed seamstress became something of a *cause celebre*. The public was barraged with newspaper articles, pamphlets, novels, short stories, poetry—the most famous of which is Thomas Hood's "Song of the Shirt" from 1843:

> *With fingers weary and worn,*
> *With eyelids heavy and red,*
> *A woman sat, in unwomanly rags,*

Plying her needle and thread—
Stitch! stitch! stitch!
In poverty, hunger, and dirt,
And still with a voice of dolorous pitch
She sang the "Song of the Shirt."

Popular literature was full of stories of a happy, healthy, and virtuous young woman leaving her home in the countryside to become a seamstress in the big city where she encounters an evil employer and/or seducer, and begins an irreversible decline leading to death and/or prostitution.

This brings me to the last and perhaps the best of the great Victorian painters who dealt with the final end of such women as in *Found Drowned*, the painting by George Frederic Watts of 1867. (Charles Dickens wrote *The Chimes* to highlight the issues.) This was by no means uncommon. Newspapers listed drownings from London bridges each morning.

I could go on to mention the *Past and Present* triptych of Augustus Egg and the importance of photography in documenting what is to us now a vanished world. But for anyone wanting the feel of the poor of London, just read Dickens or *London Labour and the London Poor* by Henry Mayhew (the founder of *Punch*).

THE HIGHER EDUCATION OF WOMEN IN THE VICTORIAN ERA

BY LYNNE WILSON

UNIVERSITY EDUCATION FOR WOMEN UP UNTIL THE VICTORIAN ERA IN BRITAIN HAD BEEN impossible, however this was a topic of great discussion at the time with divided opinion on the subject. It was from the mid to late-19th century that real progress began to be made, as a range of women's issues were at the forefront at this time. However, there were still few who saw education as a way of changing women's lives and giving them opportunities, with many supporters at the time believing a higher education was necessary simply to make women more effective wives, mothers, and teachers.

An article in the *Glasgow Herald* newspaper highlights the problem:

> *It may be questioned if the present age is destined to make its mark in history by anything more deeply than its earnest effort to raise the ideas of the sphere and duties of woman, and to elevate the character of her education in accordance with those new ideas.... Every day brings fresh evidence of the genuineness and growth of this demand for a higher culture than can be met by the traditional and conventional arrangements for female education.*

As university education for British women had been fairly unheard of in this era, the application of a prospective female medical student, Sophia Jex-Blake, in1869, to attend lectures at the Edinburgh medical school, caused quite a storm of controversy. The subject was greatly debated, and, encouragingly, it seemed that there was a reasonable amount of support for this amongst the academic community of Edinburgh.

A report in the *Edinburgh Evening Courant* newspaper showed an example of some of that support:

> *Lady Doctors—"On Saturday night, Mr J A Bevan delivered a lecture at the Hanover Square Rooms on "Women Doctors.".... Mr Bevan could not understand why women should not be allowed to practice as doctors. He pointed out which, in his mind, they were well fitted."*

The education of another budding female doctor, Elizabeth Garrett, was thrust into the spotlight at this time as an example of a success story resulting from female education. Elizabeth Garrett had tried some years prior to Sophia Jex-Blake to gain entry to the Edinburgh medical school and had been refused admission. *The Scotsman* newspaper reported on this story:

Miss Garrett, who seven years ago strenuously endeavoured to induce the Universities of St. Andrews and Edinburgh to admit her to study for a degree of Doctor of Medicine, but in vain—who subsequently passed the examinations, and became a licentiate of the Apothecaries' Company of London—and who has now for several years been in successful practice of her profession in the Metropolis, has, we learn, just been admitted by the Faculty of Medicine of Paris to examination for a degree of M.D.... It is curious to have to notice Miss Garrett's continued success in other quarters at the very time at which we have also to record that another lady applicant is now knocking at the gates of our Scottish Colleges.... It may well be that public opinion has now so far advanced in this matter that Miss Jex-Blake's application to the Medical Faculty of the University will not be refused at all.

Subsequently, many persons in both in the Medical Faculty and Senatus voted that Miss Jex-Blake should be admitted to the summer classes at least as a tentative measure. Unfortunately, however, this did not come to fruition, due to an outcry against the impropriety of "mixed classes". The idea of women learning about male and female Anatomy whilst in a classroom filled with men was just too much for prim Victorians to bear.

In the meantime, however, several other women, on hearing about Sophia Jex-Blake's fight and the discussions taking place in Edinburgh, came forward as prospective students, and, as a result, a second petition was presented to the Senatus Academics. Finally, there was light at the end of the tunnel, albeit, with some conditions, as this article in *The Scotsman* newspaper showed:

On the recommendation of both the Medical Faculty and Senatus, our University court has given its sanction to the matriculation of ladies as medical students on the understanding that they pass the usual examinations, and that separate classes are formed for their instruction.

However, despite the efforts of Sophia Jex-Blake and other supporters for women's education, women, although being allowed to begin medical study in this year, were not permitted to graduate from Edinburgh University at the end of their study. The protesters against female medical education gathered near Surgeons Hall in November 1870, where the women were due to take an examination in Anatomy, and heckled and threw rubbish at them. The incident became known as the "Surgeons Hall Riot".

Then in 1873, the Court of Session ruled that the University had the right to refuse the women degrees. Sophia Jex-Blake moved back to London and established the London School of Medicine for Women in 1874, and later returned to Edinburgh in 1878, setting up practice at Manor Place in the New Town. She also opened a clinic for poor patients, which is now Bruntsfield Hospital. The other members of the "Edinburgh Seven" who had attempted education at Edinburgh gained their qualifications elsewhere, with the exception of Isabel Thorne, who gave up on her plan to practice as a doctor. Edinburgh University eventually admitted women as undergraduates in 1892, after an Act of Parliament had been passed.

Flirting With Fans: A Victorian Tradition

by KAREN V. WASYLOWSKI

WITH SO MANY RESTRICTIONS REGARDING PROPER BEHAVIOR BETWEEN A LADY AND THE gentleman of her choosing during the Victorian Age, how was a girl ever to express her interest in a young man? The Regency era and its overt sexual freedoms were a thing of the past (supposedly); nice young ladies no longer could dampen their gowns (tell me another one) to show off their lovely figures, nor could they rouge their nipples (perhaps).

Pity the poor Victorian lady. Without the allurements allowed in the past, these pioneering women were reduced to using props. Parasols, gloves—anything with which to flirt; these sisters of ours were desperate.

And the most interesting, the most useful of all, was the fan. Position, posture, and pressure—the three keys. Flirting with fans was an artform dating all the way back to 17th century Italy. It should be reinstated and pursued during our lifetime. I wonder if Snookie ever considered one...?

Here are some of the popular fan signals and what they mean. Perhaps one can practice at home on husbands?

> The fan placed near the heart: "You have won my love."
> A closed fan touching the right eye: "When may I be allowed to see you?"
> The number of sticks shown answered the question: "At what hour?"
> Threatening movements with a fan closed: "Do not be so imprudent."
> Half-opened fan pressed to the lips: "You may kiss me."
> Hands clasped together holding an open fan: "Forgive me."
> Covering the left ear with an open fan: "Do not betray our secret."
> Hiding the eyes behind an open fan: "I love you."
> Shutting a fully opened fan slowly: "I promise to marry you."
> Drawing the fan across the eyes: "I am sorry."
> Touching the finger to the tip of the fan: "I wish to speak with you."
> Letting the fan rest on the right cheek: "Yes."
> Letting the fan rest on the left cheek: "No."
> Opening and closing the fan several times: "You are cruel."
> Dropping the fan: "We will be friends."
> Fanning slowly: "I am married."
> Fanning quickly: "I am engaged."
> Putting the fan handle to the lips: "Kiss me."

Opening a fan wide: "Wait for me."

Placing the fan behind the head: "Do not forget me."

Placing the fan behind the head with finger extended: "Goodbye."

Fan in right hand in front of face: "Follow me."

Fan in left hand in front of face: "I am desirous of your acquaintance."

Fan held over left ear: "I wish to get rid of you."

Drawing the fan across the forehead: "You have changed."

Twirling the fan in the left hand: "We are being watched."

Twirling the fan in the right hand: "I love another."

Carrying the open fan in the right hand: "You are too willing."

Carrying the open fan in the left hand: "Come and talk to me."

Drawing the fan through the hand: "I hate you!"

Drawing the fan across the cheek: "I love you!"

Presenting the fan shut: "Do you love me?"

If there are too many here to remember I propose little cheat sheets...stuffed into white gloves...and the gloves should definitely hold onto a lovely pink parasol!

SOURCE

Gaffney, Micki. "The Language of the Fan." *Books, Belles and Beaux.* July 11, 2009. http://joanne-sliceoflife3.blogspot.com/2009/07/language-of-fan.html.

STRANGE VICTORIAN REMEDIES

BY LYNNE WILSON

As 19th century Britain's economy grew, the use of advertising to sell products greatly expanded. Due to the expense involved in a visit to the doctor, one such area in which advertising became popular was with remedies and cures for everyday ailments which people could purchase relatively cheaply and administer themselves.

With very few restrictions on the claims that could be made, many seemingly miraculous cures appeared for sale. Although some of these remedies had some scientific basis, others were, unfortunately for the unwitting buyer, completely useless. On researching my book *A Year in Victorian Edinburgh*, I came across some weird and wonderful examples of both useful and useless remedies in the form of newspaper advertisements from 1869. Here are a few of these examples:

> *THE GREAT SULPHUR CURE, so effectual for Diseases of the Throat and Lungs, may be best used by Inhaling Sulphurous Acid Gas, by means of MACKENZIES INHALERS, Price 3s., Manufactured by J. MACKENZIE, Chemist, 49 George IV. Bridge, Edinburgh.*

Sulphur was thought to cure many ailments, including Cholera, of which there had been several outbreaks previously. Sulphur could be taken in the form above, or alternatively, another popular method in the 19th century was to "take the waters", in the form of visiting spas or drinking mineral waters containing iron, copper, or sulphur to cure common ailments such as rheumatism, arthritis, overindulgence, and respiratory disorders such as asthma.

With all forms of bathing being popular in the Victorian era, many establishments such as the one below opened. "Galvanic baths", which were though to have health-giving properties, were baths in which an electric current was passed through the water and hence, through the body. Turkish baths worked on the principle of sweating out all impurities and then washing them away.

> *The Edinburgh TURKISH, MEDICATED AND GALVANIC BATHS, SCIENNES HILL, Newington. LADIES—Tuesday and Friday, from 10 AM till 4 PM, 2s., Course of Ten Baths, 15s. From 7 till 10 Evenings, 1s., 6d. Course of Ten Baths, 12s. 6d.*
>
> *GENTLEMEN'S days as formerly, from 10 AM to 4 PM, 2s., Evenings, 1s. 6d.*

The use of electricity in treatments was often popular, and another means by which it was utilised was in applying currents to nerve points via a battery and cables, such as the treatment advertised below. It was believed that the "life-giving force" of electricity could relieve lung diseases, inflammation of the brain or liver, rheumatism, small pox, and even cure drunkenness!

Victorian innovators would claim that these illnesses could be cured simply by wearing these electric belts or sitting in a magnetically charged room.

ELECTRICITY IS LIFE. CURE YOURSELF BY THE PATENT SELF-AD-JUSTING CURATIVE AND ELECTRIC BELT. Suffers from Nervous Ailments, Painful Dreams, Indigestion, Debility, Weakness, &c., can now cure themselves by the only "Guaranteed Remedy" in Europe, protected by Her Majesty's Great Seal. Free for One Stamp, by H. JAMES, Esq., Medical Electrician (to the London Hospitals) Percy House, Bedford Square, London.

N.B. Medicines and Fees Superceded. (REFERENCE TO THE LEADING PHYSI-CIANS OF THE DAY.) BEWARE OF COUNTERFEITS to guard against SPU-RIOUS IMITATIONS, I have appointed NO LICENCEES. A TEST GRATIS. SEND FOR DETAILS. ESTABLISHED 1840. (As Medical Electrician to the Hospitals.)

By far the most common type of advertisement however, seems to be aimed at people's insecurity or vanity regarding either loss of hair or greying hair colour. In the *Edinburgh Evening Courant* newspaper in 1869, an advertisement appeared for "Luxuriant and Beautiful Hair":

Miss S. S. Allen's World's Hair Restorer or Dressing never fails to quickly restore grey or faded hair to its youthful colour and beauty. It stops the hair from falling off. It prevents baldness. It promotes luxuriant growth. It causes the hair to grow thick and strong. It removes all dandruff.

Many other advertisements promised equally astounding results.

Although on the face of it, these seem like fairly harmless, albeit utterly ineffective remedies, the reality was that some of these products had ingredients which were toxic to varying degrees, as an article in *The Edinburgh Evening Courant* newspaper shows:

"Poisonous Lotions for the Hair"—Nothing is more extraordinary than the irrational credulity of even educated, intelligent persons, in accepting a tradesman's puff as a genuine warranty. When, for instance, will people be warned against the use of poisonous hair dyes? It can be no secret that white lead is the chief ingredient in the black dyes now so largely sold. Paralysis, in a more or less severe form, is the inevitable consequence of applying these lotions to the hair.

Thankfully, by the end of the Victorian era, things were began to improve, with restrictions on the sale of poisons and more analysis being carried out by reputable retailers such as "Boots the Chemist" to determine the safety of products for sale. However, it wasn't until the start of the 20th century that greater scrutiny of these products came into existence and manufacturers began to be prosecuted for fraudulent claims.

News items courtesy of *The Scotsman* Archive.

GERTRUDE JEKYLL

BY M.M. BENNETTS

S HE WASN'T A QUEEN OR A PRINCESS. NOR WAS SHE A PAWN. SHE WAS DENIED NEITHER EDU-
cation nor legal standing. Yet through her extra-ordinary life, her quietly pioneering work,
and her writings, she has exerted more practical influence over how the 20th century British
viewed their surroundings and what they did with them than any person before or since. And
she was a Victorian woman.

Her name is Gertrude Jekyll (pronounced to rhyme with treacle).

She was born on 29 November 1843 (just five years into Victoria's reign), the fifth of seven
children born to Captain Edward Jekyll, who was an officer in the Grenadier Guards, and his
wife, Julia Hammersley. The family was well-to-do, though not titled, and living at 2 Grafton
Street in Mayfair at the time of her birth.

When she was nearly five, the Jekyll family moved to a sprawling country house near
Guildford in Surrey, called Bramley House. Situated just off the Horsham Road, in the fertile
Wey Valley, the house was surrounded by lush green meadows where cattle grazed in fields
edged and speckled with cow parsley and buttercups.

There, with her many siblings, Gertrude was encouraged to wander first in the garden and
latterly, farther afield, exploring the park with its streams, woods, and mill-ponds, climbing
trees, playing cricket with her brothers, and learning first-hand all about plants, flowers, and the
landscape—studying the outcrops of sandstone, eroded by time, the heaths, the tree roots. She
also had the benefit of good governesses who taught her languages, music, and art, and in this
"age of liberal indulgence" her parents elected for her to continue to study all three.

As she matured into young womanhood, her greatest desire was to be an artist, so in 1861,
her parents enrolled her at the South Kensington School of Art to study painting. Jekyll was
among the first handful of women to be taught at art school—where she studied the works of
great artists, but most especially the work of J.M.W. Turner and his use of colour.

In the autumn of 1863, she travelled to Corfu, Crete, Rhodes, Athens and Constantinople—drawing and sketching.

Upon her return home, she met John Ruskin, and through him came into contact with that
new wave of British artistry, the Arts and Crafts Movement. She visited William Morris, went
to lectures by John Ruskin, met Edward Burne-Jones and Dante Gabriel Rossetti. Through
Morris's influence, she began design and embroidery, as well as beginning to work in metal and
wood. Indeed, her diary for these years mentions frequent meetings with the greats of Victorian
art such as Frederick Leighton and G.W. Watts.

And year after year, she travelled abroad—to France, Italy, or Spain. She spent a winter in
Algiers. She visited the great gardens of Europe and the Near East.

By the time she was thirty, she had gained a reputation for carving, modelling, house-painting, carpentry, smith's work, repousse work, gilding, wood-inlaying, embroidery, gardening, and all manner of herb and flower knowledge and culture.

In 1868, the family had left Bramley Park to move to a house in Berkshire that Edward Jekyll had inherited. But when he died in 1876, the family members who remained at home decided to return to Surrey. They bought land high on Munstead Heath, near Godalming and the Wey valley and hired an architect to build them a house there.

And it was there that Gertrude Jekyll really began to come into her own as she spent more and more of her time creating the garden there at Munstead. Indeed, within four years, the garden was already sufficiently famous to merit a visit from the first President of the National Rose Society, Dean Hole, and from William Robinson, the editor of *The Garden*.

Jekyll then bought a plot on the other side of the lane from Munstead Heath, and there developed the ideas that would transform the gardening culture of Victorian England—from one of formality and carpet bedding, as she called it, to a marriage of colour and contrast, of cool to balance hot, of shape and scent, and year-round beauty.

Over the course of her life, she wrote thirteen books on gardens and gardening, and made plans for or helped to make the plans for some 350 gardens.

Her advice often flew in the face of what had been accepted practice for decades and replaced it with a hands-on love of gardening, of the processes of creating a garden, from double-digging the beds to arranging leaf-shapes to compliment each other, to planting herbaceous perennials in naturalistic drifts of colour as a painter—indeed painting a picture with plants—and using all that she had gleaned from her years studying art.

Among her favourite colour dynamics was the creation of a long and deep border of graduated harmonies that set pink against grey foliage at each end then fused into white flowering plants which bled into pale yellow into pale blue, then into darker blues punctuated by stronger yellows, oranges, and vibrant reds back into the oranges, yellows, and on until the softened misty edges of palest pink against the silvery greys of catmint, stachys, and artemisia. It was a blending and use and understanding of colour worthy of Turner himself.

Jekyll was 46 when she first met the young architect Edwin Lutyens, and their collaboration of house and garden design and decoration is one of the significant partnerships of the early 20th century. Though many of their houses and gardens remain, some having been ruined and then restored, many of them have disappeared, so it is through Jekyll's prolific and delightful writings and garden plans that she is best known to us today.

Always blunt-spoken, never shying from controversy, her writings are practical and witty, honest, engaging, and wry. (She used to refer to the smell of one plant as "housemaid's armpit".) And through them all there runs a theme of looking deeply and well at everything, of learning to look and to see as an artist. Whether it's the shape of a leaf or the vivid contrast of colours or the spill of foliage against crumbling stone, she encourages one to see what's really there, not what habit tells us is there. Is the bark of a tree really brown? Or is it black and tan and crumbling mould and mottled moss?

To learn how to perceive the difference and how to do right is to apprehend gardening as a fine art. In practice it is to place every plant or group of plants with such thoughtful care and definite intention that they shall form a part of the harmonious whole, and that successive portions, or in some cases even single details, shall show a series of pictures. It is so to regulate the trees and undergrowth of the wood that their lines and masses come into beautiful form and harmonious proportion; it is to be always watching, noting and doing, and putting oneself meanwhile into closest acquaintance and sympathy with growing things.

And that seeing, for Miss Jekyll, was the beginning of the magic, the art, and the process that is a garden....

BATTLE OF ISANDLWANA,
22 JANUARY 1879

BY RICHARD DENNING

THE TWENTY-SECOND OF JANUARY IS THE ANNIVERSARY OF TWO BATTLES THAT WERE fought only miles apart—one of which was a great defeat for the British, and the other, the action in which the greatest number of Victoria crosses were handed out.

The Anglo-Zulu war of 1879 started with a great defeat for the British invaders. On 22 January, 20,000 Zulus overwhelmed a force of 1800 British and allied troops on the plain beneath the mountain of Isandlwana and destroyed it. An entire battalion of British Infantry was wiped out to the last man. It was a defeat that stunned a Victorian Britain accustomed to victory and conquest.

This battle, along with the stubborn and heroic defence of Rorke's Drift that night by the British garrison there, has always been of interest to me as it seems to exemplify the heights of human heroism (exhibited by both sides), coupled with the depths of folly and horrors that only war can bring.

BACKGROUND

The origins of the conflict with the Zulus in 1879 have strange parallels with the conflicts in the Gulf and the Middle East. In recent times, the U.S. and allies' interventions in the Gulf have been seen by some as spurred on by a concern about access to oil. Whether that is true or not of the present day, the British government in Cape Town in 1879 did not take much of an interest in the interior of South Africa, and much less in Zululand, until diamonds and other resources were discovered there. Then, suddenly, efforts and policies were introduced aimed towards confederation of the various colonies under a strong British rule.

Amongst the territories brought under the British Crown were Natal and the Boers' homeland of Transvaal. The Boers' main enemy and rival was the strong and powerful independent nation that had arisen under Shaka Zulu in the 1830s. A nation that could put 25,000 warriors in the field was a threat to the security of Transvaal and ultimately all of South Africa. Or at least that is the way that Sir Henry Frere—the British governor—looked at it.

Frere sent Cetshwayo, the Zulu king, a series of demands and ultimatums insisting that he disband his army and allow a British governor into his capital Ulundi. Frere knew that Cetshwayo would never agree to that, and when the Zulu king declined his demands, the British General Chelmsford was ordered to invade.

Chelmsford's original plan envisaged splitting his army into five columns which would invade and converge on Ulundi. Chelmsford himself accompanied the central columns (II and III). They marched to the mission station at Rorke's Drift and on 11 January began the invasion.

It would have been better to have waited a few weeks as in January there was heavy rain and as a result moving a large army with baggage and artillery would take a long time. However, Frere was eager to have the matter resolved and so the British went in. The result was that it took many days for the central column to assemble fully inside Zululand at a base Chelmsford had established beneath an odd shaped mountain called Isandlwana.

WHAT HAPPENED

Cetshwayo heard of the invasion soon after it had begun and on 17 January ordered 24,000 men to move towards Isandlwana, although some 4000 split off to move towards Column I. On 21 January the Zulu Impi had arrived near the British camp. Chelmsford's scouts had seen it approach but could not fix its location precisely, so on the twenty-second, Chelmsford decided to take half his force away on a march to try and locate the enemy.

This left Major Pulleine, a staff officer and administrator, in the base with his 1700 men. Chelmsford had refused to order the camp to form into a laager—a reinforced camp with wagons around the outside, trenches, and thorn bushes to impede attack. He did not feel it was necessary and was scathing of the threat posed by the Impi.

This mistake would prove to be costly, for the Zulu commander had outmanoeuvred Chelmsford, and whilst the British general was chasing around trying to locate him, the Impi moved forward in readiness to fall on Pulleine.

The crunch happened when a patrol of Natal mounted troops attached to the British command moved out of the camp to scout some valleys to the north east. There, in a valley within a couple of miles of the camp, was the entire Zulu army. The Zulus rose up as one and attacked the fleeing horsemen and followed them up and out onto the plain.

Pulleine formed the 24th Foot up into firing lines, and the British Infantry began pouring volleys from their Martini Henry Rifles into the enemy ranks. The Zulus fell in droves but still came on—massing and waiting to charge. Actually the redcoats held the vast numbers away for a long time but then something went wrong.

Around 1:15 p.m. that day, the Natal irregular companies out on the British right wing were outflanked and fell back. More or less at that moment, Pulleine was ordering the Regular companies to pull back to shorten their line. There was also a shortage of ammunition reaching the forward companies. There was a vast supply in the camp but for some reason it was not being handed out quickly enough. A combination of these factors meant that the previously pinned Zulu Impi was able to charge the British line.

Gaps appeared in the companies; then the gaps widened as the warriors surged through them. In a matter of fifteen minutes the Zulu army overwhelmed the British and the wings of the Impi swung in to deny escape to all save a lucky 80 or so men. The colour party with the regimental and the Queen's flag wrapped the flags around the chests of two officers who made a bid to reach the Buffalo River and Rorke's Drift. Their bodies were later found in the river, where they had fallen.

It was all over in a flash, and the British had suffered a huge defeat.

AFTERMATH

Cetshwayo had ordered that the Impi should not invade Natal and should stop on his side of the border. However, about four thousand Zulus who had not fought at Isandlwana decided to attack the British base at the mission station of Rorke's Drift. Throughout the night of the twenty-second to the twenty-third of January, they led repeated attacks against a single company of about 100 British who fortified it. Eleven Victoria crosses would be handed out for the bravery of officers and men in the 24th Foot stationed there. The Zulus broke off the attack in the morning.

Cetshwayo had missed two opportunities to inflict a decisive defeat. His Impi had neither attacked the column under Chelmsford nor captured Rorke's Drift. As a result, the war was not yet over.

News of the defeat at Isandlwana reached London on 11 February and caused an uproar. It literally stunned the nation, and even the Queen demanded to know why her soldiers were fighting the Zulus. It is small wonder then that the subsequent news of Rorke's Drift arriving hot on the heels of the disaster was greeted with enthusiasm.

Nevertheless, the defeat led to a calling off of the January invasion. It would be June before the British army would be in a state to resume the war, and July before the Impi were defeated at the Battle of Ulundi. Cetshwayo was captured by the British in August but, perhaps in recognition of the bravery of his army, was treated pretty well and became something of a celebrity in London where he was allowed to live on a pension for the rest of his life. His kingdom, however, was absorbed into the British Territory of South Africa.

So then, a terrible battle and a tragic outcome for a brave warrior people, the Battle of Islandwana remains a dramatic moment in history. In my novel, *Tomorrow's Guardian*, Edward Dyson, an officer in the 24th, is believed to have perished in the battle. Tom and his companion Septimus travel back in time to rescue him and bring him to the present day.

Twentieth Century

Downton Abbey and the Fight for Irish Freedom

by TIM VICARY

In the marvelous TV series, *Downton Abbey*, one theme that will surely develop further is the relationship between the youngest daughter of the house, Lady Sybil, and Tom Branson, the Irish chauffeur. Despite the strong disapproval of her parents the young couple fall in love and elope to Dublin to get married. This marriage is a very shocking and traumatic event for Lady Sybil's parents, the Earl and Countess of Grantham, and it is clear that Sybil's married life with her husband is going to be far from easy.

There are three major problems which the young couple will have to face: class, religion, and nationality. Class is the biggest: as the youngest daughter of wealthy English aristocrats, Lady Sybil has committed a colossal social blunder. There is no way that she and her new husband can possibly be accepted in the social world in which she has grown up; she may occasionally meet her sister and parents, but otherwise she has surely cut herself off forever. Her father has settled a little money on her, but she will still have to accustom herself to managing on that and her new husband's wages—much, much less than she has previously taken for granted. Let's hope their love is strong; it will need to be.

When my wife, then aged nineteen, agreed to marry me, a graduate with no obvious prospects, her grandmother had similar misgivings. "*When money comes in the door, love flies out the window,*" she wrote, in a forceful letter that could easily have come from the Dowager Countess of Grantham!

Since I was twenty-one and unemployed at the time, the old lady had a point! But at least my wife and I were both English, of a similar religion. Sybil's new husband is a Catholic Irishman, at a time when religion and ethnicity are of crucial significance. In 1919, they elope to Dublin, straight into a cauldron of terrorism, murder, and police repression, a two-year campaign of violence which will result, after many deaths, in the creation of the Irish Free State.

So what, exactly, is going on? Her husband will understand it, but to Sybil all this may come as a nasty shock. Few English people know much Irish history, and she is surely no different. Well, here is a little of what she will need to learn.

When the First World War began, thousands of Irishmen, both Protestant and Catholic, joined the British Army, just like many men from Downton. There was no conscription; they were all volunteers. Like the men Sybil nursed at Downton, many of these Irish soldiers suffered horrific, life-changing injuries while fighting for what they still considered to be their country.

But not all Irishmen saw it like this. Some Irishmen, taking the view that "*England's difficulty is Ireland's opportunity*", decided that their real enemy was not Germany at all, but England. So they tried (unsuccessfully) to get guns from Germany and rose up in armed rebellion. On

Easter Monday 1916, on the steps of the General Post Office in Dublin, Padraig Pearse read out a declaration of Irish independence. Ireland, he said, was no longer part of the United Kingdom; it was now a sovereign, independent state. Behind him, several hundred armed Republicans raised the flag of an Irish Republic.

They had no chance of success. The British government was recovering from the disaster at Gallipoli and planning for the Battle of the Somme; it had no sympathy for Irish rebels who had tried to get guns from the enemy. A week later, after a battle in which 450 people were killed, mostly by soldiers of the Royal Irish Regiment, the rebels surrendered. Pearse and thirteen other leaders were convicted of treason and executed. Their followers were imprisoned in North Wales for six months and then released.

Pearse's death made him a martyr. As the poet W.B. Yeats wrote, *"a terrible beauty is born."* In the general election of 1918, Sinn Fein, the party of Pearse's supporters, won 73 out of 105 seats in Ireland. One of these was won by the first ever woman MP, Constance Markeiwicz. But instead of going to Westminster, the Sinn Fein MPs declared themselves the new Parliament of Ireland, Dail Eireann. A state of war existed, they said, between England and Ireland.

Thus, when Lady Sybil arrives in Dublin with her new husband, she will find herself in the middle of a civil war. Ireland in 1919 was blessed—if that is the right word—with two governments, each of which had politicians, soldiers, and tax collectors. The new Irish Republic had its own army, the Irish Republican Army (IRA) led by Michael Collins. His men began to kill policemen, particularly intelligence officers. They were very good at it. Not surprisingly, the British government disliked this. As far as they were concerned, men like Michael Collins were terrorists. They wanted to capture him, dead or alive. But it was not easy. No one knew where Collins lived, or even what he looked like.

From what we know of Sybil's husband, Tom Branson, it seems likely that he will be more in sympathy with the IRA than the British Army. Sybil's father, the Earl of Grantham, and her sister's new husband, Matthew Crawley, will surely have no sympathy for this. Matthew was fighting in the trenches while men like Michael Collins were skulking at home, conspiring to get arms from the Germans. So what will happen if Tom Branson joins the IRA and kills some British policemen or soldiers? Lady Sybil will have a hard time explaining that to her family!

She will need new friends in Dublin, and given her social background, she may well come across another strong-minded young woman of her own age, Lady Catherine Maeve O'Connell-Gort. Lady Catherine, like Lady Sybil, is a fictional character, the heroine of my novel, *The Blood Upon the Rose*. Like Sybil, Catherine is torn between two worlds; both of her brothers have been killed in the war, and her father is a British Army Colonel in charge of Military Intelligence. It is his job to kill or capture Michael Collins. But his daughter Catherine—just like Lady Sybil—is in love with a young Irishman who is fighting for Irish freedom. Not surprisingly, her father, just like the Earl of Grantham, is appalled.

I think the two young women should meet! Catherine has grown up in Ireland, so she understands the background much better than Sybil; but the pair would certainly have a great deal to talk about!

I wonder if it will happen?

You can read more about Catherine O'Connell-Gort in The *Blood Upon the Rose,* available in Kindle. In case you're wondering, it was first published by Simon & Schuster UK in 1992, long before *Downton Abbey* hit the screens.

THE LOST HOUSES OF ENGLAND

BY **MAGGI ANDERSEN**

THE BBC SERIES *DOWNTON ABBEY* FEATURED AN ARISTOCRATIC FAMILY STRUGGLING TO survive through the First World War and chronicled the changes to society that war caused. Because I write about houses such as these in my novels, I was interested to find out more about the fate of England's great houses.

The past hundred years have seen the loss of many historical houses due to the government's taxing laws, death duties, fire, and the pervasive bombing during the Second World War. The consequence of social changes such as divorce took its toll too, making it impossible for many families to continue the upkeep of these expensive estates. War time requisitioning left many houses in need of costly repair. With the end of the First World War, British society changed irrevocably when the people who staffed the big houses chose a different life than one in service.

Magnificent houses have been broken up, their contents dispersed, and their structures demolished. Underlying the destruction of many, was the fading perception that the continued existence of a specific landed family in a country house was still important to British society.

The only hope for many of these houses, unable to be sustained by family fortunes, was to hand them over to the National Trust.

From 1759, Weald Hall, Essex had been the property of the Tower family who also owned Huntsmoor Park, Buckinghamshire. Robert Adam remodeled the dining room for Christopher Tower in 1778. The core of the Weald Hall was a Tudor block, probably built by Sir Anthony Browne who bought the property from the Crown. It was remodeled around 1720, possibly by the architect Giacomo Leoni.

Neither Huntsmoor Park nor Weald Hall was large. In 1883 Weald Hall estate was 2,481 acres and brought in an income of 4,092 pounds.

Passing down from son to son, Weald Hall was transferred to Christopher Cecil Tower on his marriage in 1913. But Christopher Tower's enjoyment was brief. He was killed in action in 1915 and the Hall was never lived in again. The Hall's situation between Romford and Brentwood made it unappealing for a home, and it was placed in the hands of caretakers and a shooting syndicate.

During the Second World War, the park was used for military purposes and the house badly damaged by fire. In 1946, the 2,000 acre Weald Hall estate was sold by its owner, Captain C.T. Tower, who was going abroad. In 1951 the house was demolished. Its former park is now a public recreation area.

The 1950s were years of crisis for country houses. At least forty-eight were demolished in 1950 alone. The country houses seemed irrelevant, white elephants threatening to drag families down. Many were handed over to the National Trust, others found an institutional use for their houses, but many were pulled down. Ancient medieval seats and great piles created by wealthy Victorian industrialists were demolished with impunity.

The demolition of country houses continued steadily throughout the first half of the 1960s, but their tragic history was brought to the public's attention by *The Destruction of the Country House* exhibits at the Victoria & Albert Museum in 1974. Since then, the battle for preservation has focused on houses that have been abandoned for many years, particularly those where speculators were hoping to profit by letting the houses they owned fall into decay so that they could be pulled down.

It is now legally impossible to demolish a country house of any significance. Today the main risk to country houses is, once again, fire.

For more details on the history behind the loss of these enormous and often breathtakingly beautiful houses, I recommend *England's Lost Houses: From the Archives of Country Life* by Giles Worsley (Aurum Press Limited, 2011).

ELLIS ISLAND AND BRITISH IMMIGRANTS TO THE USA

BY VINCENT PARRILLO

MOST PEOPLE DO NOT THINK OF BRITISH IMMIGRANTS IN CONNECTION WITH ELLIS Island. In fact, most historical photographs of the place depict southern, central, and eastern Europeans, easily recognizable by their kerchiefs, folk costumes, or dark-haired, dark-complexioned countenances. In fact, in my own public television (PBS) documentary, *Ellis Island: Gateway to America*, I utilized many of those same images.

However, many British immigrants also went through Ellis Island. For example, in the 1890s—the period in which my historical novel, *Guardians of the Gate*, begins its tale of the people and events occurring there—nearly 329,000 emigrants left the United Kingdom for the United States. Some were first and second-class passengers and therefore processed on board ship and not at Ellis Island.

Most, though, were the lower and working classes traveling in steerage, and their first steps on American soil were on the Island. (Included in my novel, for example, is the true incident of the deportation of a Scottish family.)

Earlier, between 1870 and 1889, about 1.3 million British immigrants arrived. Ellis Island did not exist then, so they were processed at a state-run immigration station called Castle Garden, which previously had been a concert hall, and its walls still stand in Battery Park at the southern tip of Manhattan.

That impressive number was lessened somewhat by the hundreds of thousands of British subjects who left, disenchanted with what they had found in America. Perhaps, as Charles Dickens complained after his visit in 1842, they found Americans too rude, arrogant, anti-intellectual, prone to be violent, and hypocritical.

His was a harsh judgment, indeed, but it didn't stop other Brits from coming. Between 1900 and 1929, another 1.2 million British migrated to the United States. Again, most were first processed at Ellis Island to gain clearance for entry.

Just because they were British didn't ensure these immigrants would breeze through Ellis Island. For example, among my weekly blogs that relate true immigrant stories is the firsthand account of a Scottish teenager arriving in 1921 with her family, showing the hunger and other tribulations they experienced there. Another blog gives the account of an English minister, whose 1911 detention on Ellis Island so disgusted him that he testified before a Congressional committee on the abysmal conditions he encountered.

Ellis Island was also a transit stop for several notorious or otherwise prominent British subjects. In 1903, anarchist John Turner was detained at Ellis Island and then deported to England because of his political opinions. Her political views kept English suffragette Emmeline

Pankhurst detained on the Island in 1913 until she was also ordered deported by a Board of Special Inquiry on the grounds of "moral turpitude." A public outcry prompted President Woodrow Wilson to reverse that decision two days later.

Sir Auckland Geddes, British ambassador to the United States, inspected Ellis Island in 1922, and his report criticized its lack of cleanliness, its inefficiency in handling appeals, and the smells and wire cages. The controversial report strained relations between the two countries for a while.

Among some of the well-known British immigrants arriving in the Port of New York (although not all went through Ellis Island) were writer Rudyard Kipling (1892), comedian Henny Youngman (1906), comedian Bob Hope (1908), comedian Stan Laurel (1912), conductor Leopold Stokowski (1912), actor Cary Grant (1920), actor Leslie Howard (1921), and author Joseph Conrad (1923).

Born in London to an English-born cabinet maker of Polish heritage and an Irish-born mother, Stokowski presented what an Ellis Island inspector thought was a good opportunity. He told the future conductor that his name was "foreign" and he would give him a new name. *"Thank you very much,"* said Stokowski, *"but my name is Stokowski."* His voice rising more and more, he added, *"It was my father's name, and his father's before him, and it will stay my name!"* The inspector, accustomed to intimidating immigrants by his presence, was taken aback and quickly withdrew the offer.

Other prominent British expatriates who settled in the United States include model and actress Mischa Barton, musician Peter Frampton, labor leader Samuel Gompers, movie director Sir Alfred Hitchcock, actor Anthony Hopkins, actor Peter Lawford, and preservationist John Muir.

On average, about 17,000 British immigrants continue to arrive annually in the United States. These not-so-famous arrivals—mostly known only to their family, friends, and co-workers—settle in many states, but Southern California, particularly the Santa Monica region, has become the permanent home of several hundred thousand first-generation British Americans, who maintain their pubs and traditions among the surfers and rollerbladers.

A Prince, a Prophet, and a Peer: Sir Samuel Hoare

by JOHN B. CAMPBELL

Sir Samuel Hoare, 1st Viscount Templewood, and his wife Lady Maud Hoare, Dame Commander of the Order of the British Empire, Viscountess Templewood, demonstrated how to live a life of engagement and purpose. And they did so in the dramatic days of the early 20th century.

Samuel John Gurney Hoare, 1st Viscount Templewood, more commonly known as Sir Samuel Hoare, offset his relatively small stature with athleticism and a dynamic (though not precisely charismatic) personality. Critics thought him to be narcissistically ambitious while others admired his drive, political savvy, and concern for the greater good. The Machiavellian climate of the British government in those troubling days of anarchists, socialist campaigns, fascism, and Nazi aggression created as much in-court-intrigue as that seen during the reign of Julius Caesar. Would Sir Samuel's early years of training prove adequate?

In 1935, while Hoare served as Secretary of State for Foreign Affairs, a crisis arose when the Italians invaded Ethiopia. Hoare felt he understood the psyche of Benito Mussolini, whom he had gotten to know while previously serving with British overseas intelligence, and sensed diplomatic conflagration on the horizon. He thus felt the need to prevent the Italians from forming an alliance with the ever-menacing Adolf Hitler, were Anglo-Italian relations to become strained.

In Hoare's estimation, it seemed a good idea to join with Pierre Laval, the prime minister of France, in hopes of resolving the dilemma via a secret agreement. Their venture came to be known as the Hoare-Laval Pact, and it outlined how Italy would be allotted two-thirds of the African territory it had conquered. In return, Ethiopia would be allowed to keep a narrow strip of territory with access to the sea. In those late days of the Empire, Hoare felt their solution was generous as well as prudent.

The details of the secret pact, however, mysteriously leaked to the press on December 10, 1935. The pact became widely denounced by the members of Parliament who sat in different camps from Hoare. Prime Minister Stanley Baldwin, being one such, rejected the plan and demanded Hoare's resignation.

Sir Samuel Hoare's resignation speech created one of those "moments" film directors would love to recreate. Reportedly, Hoare stood up and presented a narrative so powerful it, in a flash, engendered a wave of sympathy. With sincerity and fervor, he told his story, explaining how by means of his negotiations *"not a country, save our own, has moved a soldier, a ship or an aeroplane as a result."* Hoare was described by Henry Channon as a Cato defending himself, and Channon added that Sir Samuel, for 40 minutes, had held the House breathless. When Sir Samuel sat down, however, he burst into tears.

From that account alone, we glean a measure of the gentleman's complexity of nature, his talents, and his vulnerability.

Earlier, Sir Samuel got his diplomatic feet wet in—talk about some colourful training—Czarist Russia. In 1916, he was assigned to a British intelligence team, comprised of Oswald Rayner, Cudbert Thornhill, John Scale, and Stephen Alley. Leading them was Mansfield Cummings who had been appointed head of the British Secret Intelligence Service in Petrograd.

Sir Samuel Hoare, as I'd mentioned, was viewed by some as pompous. Whether it was pomposity or boldness, he served as the right kind of front man, from the right class, for Cummings' purposes while the rest of the team worked behind the scenes, focusing their sights on the sinister clog to Russia's international relations—Grigory Rasputin.

Hoare became friendly with Vladimir Purishkevich, the leader of the monarchists in the Duma, and in November of that year, he learned of the man's interest in "liquidating" the *"drunken debaucher influencing the Czarina and Russia's policies."* Hoare later recorded that Purishkevich seemed so casual in his tone on the topic that such talk appeared as mere wishful thinking rather than an actual plot in motion.

At the end of 1916, after Purishkevich joined Prince Felix Yusupov, along with the Grand Duke Dmitri Pavlovich Romanov, Dr. Stanislaus de Lazovert, and Lieutenant Sergei Mikhailovich Sukhotin, they carried out their part in having the Tsarina's special advisor killed.

Afterward, Hoare took issue with—of all people—Tsar Nicholas II (maybe Hoare was a bit pompous) who suggested a sole instigator behind the assassination: Hoare's colleague, British agent Oswald Rayner. Whatever Hoare understood of the intrigue, he had had enough of caviar and vodka and was grateful to leave the icy shark tank behind after getting reassigned to Rome.

Sir Samuel Hoare was literate and widely read in several languages, which had served him well in his demanding work in Russia and Italy during that early phase of his life. Later, timing served him well in that he was part of the wave of young Conservatives in 1922, which propelled him into increasingly senior Cabinet positions for the next eighteen years, a bumpy ride, as we noted at the outset with the account of the Hoare-Laval Pact, but an all 'round successful run.

Sir Samuel Hoare played a particular role that drew him to my attention while I was researching the era for my novel. As Foreign Secretary in 1935, he was instrumental in securing government approval for the British rescue effort on behalf of endangered Jewish children in Europe: Kindertransport.

It was in 1909 that Sir Samuel married Lady Maud Lygon, daughter of Frederick Lygon, 6th Earl Beauchamp. Her title took precedence over that of her husband until he was created a viscount in 1944.

Lady Maud intrigues me. I am still looking for more information on her. She earned her title, Dame Commander of the Order of the British Empire (DBE), in the 1920s, as a result of being the first woman to fly a great distance—12,000 miles plus—as she inaugurated, along with her husband, the London-Cairo-Delhi air service.

You can watch a clip of the lady on the British Pathé site, which features a garden party she held for thalidomide children in or around 1963. Therein, fashionably dressed, she is down on her knees, interacting with the children.

Lady Maud traveled widely with her husband (at one point he was ambassador to Spain). She launched ships (the *Ark Royal*) and inaugurated airports (Croyden/London). This adventurous humanitarian peer makes a cameo appearance in my novel *Walk to Paradise Garden*.

Together, Sir Samuel and Lady Maud endeavored to make a marked difference in the world. How I'd love to time travel and be a guest at a dinner party with them. Wouldn't you?

THE MEN ARE AWAY AT WAR

BY **PETER ST. JOHN**

JUST OVER SEVENTY YEARS AGO, HITLER'S NAZI GERMANY LUNGED AGGRESSIVELY OUT, seeking to set up a "thousand year" rule over the territory and culture of other nations. The momentous world conflict which ensued is now history, but there remain those who survived and who remember....

The men in Britain, except for the aged, the unfit, and those with essential civilian occupations, are away at war. The women at home, wait, watch, and work. Poland falls, then France, and the Netherlands too. Hitler's invasion of England waits on the Luftwaffe gaining supremacy in the air. Britain's fate hangs perilously on the skill and determination of a handful of fatigued fighter pilots and on the engineering excellence of their Spitfires and Hurricanes. London is terror-bombed. The citizens, unsubdued, send their children to the shelter of the countryside and joke about the gang of Nazi thugs.

The siege of island Britain is at its fear-filled height in 1941. The Nazi enemy prowls at the gate. The United States of America sends supplies and a few volunteers, but is not otherwise a combatant. At this time, just after the marvellously prodigious evacuation of British troops from Dunkirk, Britain stands alone with deaths, injuries, and destruction. Belts are tight round nervous, taut bellies. Rationing is in force, and all is scarce. And yet, with faith and unity the people stand together.

Many have chickens in their backyards and they grow vegetables. Public parks are ploughed up to produce cabbages and potatoes. Anti-aircraft guns and barrage balloons also sprout from open spaces. Solidarity among the citizens holds, its bonds strengthened under the stress of war by the courage of King George VI and the firm leadership of Prime Minister Winston Churchill.

Suffering, songs, and secrets are shared in gloomy air-raid shelters. Fêtes and fairs are organised to raise money to buy Spitfire aircraft or finance war production. There's no orange juice for babies, so contests are set up in the autumn to gather rose-hips to make vitamin C syrup for babies. The WWI Women's Land Army is revived to train women for farm work to replace the men called up for the army. A ramshackle yet determined Home Guard, formed of the aged and unfit, prepares to defend each town and village. Lone air-raid wardens patrol at night to warn those who violate the blackout, and stand by to rescue when the bombs fall. Don't forget to carry your gas mask. Everyone bears in mind the slogan "careless talk costs lives".

My six *Gang* books employ the perplexities and predicaments of a youthful evacuee to explore a small part of what it meant to be involved in the great conflict of 1939-45. The focus is on "ordinary" people in everyday life, in an English village at war. They have their loves and hates, friendship and enmity, loyalty and betrayal. This is no history of the Second World War, even less the story of any famous or infamous person. It is rather a tale of real people doing real things, in a real historical situation. The setting is English. The story is fiction based solidly on fact. As to whether it is "English Historical Fiction", is for the reader to decide.

Historical Tidbits Across the Ages

THE ROYAL COAT OF ARMS

BY DEBRA BROWN

THE ROYAL COAT OF ARMS OF THE UNITED KINGDOM OF GREAT BRITAIN AND NORTHERN Ireland. Heraldry. Officially the Coat of Arms of the British monarch, currently Queen Elizabeth II. The Coat of Arms is used by the Queen as monarch and is officially known as her Arms of Dominion.

Many images and symbols make up the Coat of Arms, and each represents something specific.

At the bottom is a white ribbon or banner which reads *Dieu et Mon Droit*. This is French, and translates as "God and my Right." French was the language of the Royal Court at the time of the introduction of the words by Edward III in the 14th century. At the time, it was believed that the monarchs were answerable only to God.

This motto is not required on the Coat of Arms, and although most monarchs used it, there were a few that did not. Queen Anne used *Semper Eadem*, which means "Always the Same."

Originally, mottoes may have been associated with badges or war cries, but they usually expressed loyal or pious sentiments or a play on the name of the bearer. Henry IV was apparently the first monarch to adopt a motto on the Royal Arms with *Souverayne*, which meant "Sovereign."

Behind the banner on the Royal Arms, a grassy mound incorporates the plant emblems of Scotland (thistle), Ireland (shamrock), and England (rose).

The shield has evolved in shape from its Medieval long "kite" shape in the late 1100s into the "flat iron" shape used today. This mirrors the change in actual shields. The kite-shaped shields were large, covering almost half of the bearer's body. As armor became more sophisticated, shields became smaller until they were about a third of the size of the bearer.

It wasn't thought appropriate for the arms of a woman to be shown on a shield connected with warfare; therefore, they are always shown on a lozenge or diamond-shaped shield.

The first and fourth quarters of the shield of the current Royal Arms (at the top left and bottom right): In both, there are three golden lions, one above the other on a red background representing England. They walk facing out with flexed blue claws and tongues sticking out.

The second quarter (at the top right): There is a red lion on a gold background representing Scotland. Standing on his hind legs, he faces forward with blue flexed claws and his tongue sticking out. There is a double border decorated with fleur-de-lis alternating in direction.

The third quarter (at the bottom left): A golden harp with silver strings is sitting on a blue background representing Ireland. The Harp has been the symbol of the Kingdom of Ireland since the early 1200s. The harp is on 8th and 9th century stone crosses and manuscripts and is said to represent the Biblical King David. This possibly explains why harpists have always been a favorite in Ireland. Added in 1541 to the Royal Arms, it now represents only Northern Ireland.

Around the shield you will find the Order of the Garter. It is a French Royal blue "belt" with the motto *Honi Soit Qui Mal y Pense*, meaning *"Shame on him who thinks evil of it."* The

Order of the Garter, founded by Edward III in 1348, was inspired by King Arthur and the Knights of the Round Table. It is a symbol for one of the oldest and most senior orders of chivalry. Though the order was founded by Edward III, it was King Henry VIII who added the symbol to the Royal Arms.

The fleur-de-lis at the bottom of the garter appeared first on the French Royal Arms in the 1100s and was included on the English Royal Arms in 1340. It existed as an emblem long before its use on heraldry when it appeared on the top of the scepter and as on ornament on crowns. Its origins have been widely debated.

The helmet, or helm, sitting atop the shield is based on real helmets that were worn in battle. The shape was originally a simple, cylindrical steel design with a flat top and, at times, gold embellishments. This evolved into more elaborate designs which would never have been used on a real battlefield, but looked more convincing.

During the reign of Elizabeth I, a unique style of helm was designed for the Royal Arms—gold with a barred visor, facing the viewer. This has been used ever since. From the 17th century stylized forms of the medieval helm have been depicted to indicate the rank of the bearer: the melee helm for a peer; the barriers helm for baronets and knights; and the tilting helm for gentlemen.

Tied to the helmet atop the shield is the mantling, a cloth of gold trimmed with ermine fur. The mantling is based on the small cloak that hung from a knight's helmet over his shoulders to protect him from the elements. Often torn or jagged from the cuts and slashes it had received in battle, it would have greatly enhanced a knight's reputation on his return home.

The mantling is usually in the principal colors (tinctures) and metals of the shield. Generally a color on the outside and metal or fur in the lining is depicted; however, the Royal Arms is a rare exception to this as it uses a metal and a fur and no color. It was originally a red cloth lined with ermine fur, but Elizabeth I altered it.

The crest is a group of symbols atop the helmet. The royal crest is a stately lion standing on the crown facing us and wearing a gold crown himself.

Real crests were attached to a knight's helmet so he could be easily recognized in battle. Originally a practical object, the crest degenerated into a farce when it became a drawn formality, rather than worn. Crests appeared in the shape of enormous monsters, odd ships, or clouds, for example, which would have considerably hampered a knight had they been worn.

The supporters of the shield are the animals that stand on either side to hold and guard it. On the left, the most important side, is a crowned, gold lion looking towards us, representing England. Lions represent great strength, ferocity, and majesty—the king of beasts. Though very few people in Europe had ever seen one, the symbol was used. The first actual lion arrived in England during the reign of Henry I (1100-1135) to be kept in his zoo at Woodstock.

In the early days of heraldry, to emphasize their fierceness, lions were shown as rampant or passant. Many people wanted to have lions on their coats of arms, and it became necessary to have sixty or more different positions so that no two coats of arms were alike.

On the right is a silver Unicorn with a gold horn, a mane, beard, and hooves, representing Scotland. Chained to the compartment, he has a coronet around his neck with alternating crosses and fleur-de-lis.

Unicorns were well known through classical Greek and Roman texts and medieval bestiaries. They were described as large and very fierce. Thus they were chosen to guard the Royal Arms, and and it explains why they are always shown chained up. A unicorn's whiteness symbolized purity and chastity, later leading to them being seen by some as symbols of Christ and his incarnation.

In England, supporters were not integral originally to the Royal Arms and were subject to frequent change. Only in the 15th century did their use became consistent. Since then, various imaginary and real beasts have been used. Examples include the hart, greyhound, dragon, and bull.

My information in this article comes from the Churches Conservation Trust who contacted me to share this information near the time of the Queen's Diamond Jubilee. Please visit their website (http://www.visitchurches.org.uk/). There's so much history to be seen! I hope you have enjoyed the symbolism that they have worked so hard to share.

An Englishman and His Dog...

by M.M. BENNETTS

Whether it's Fielding's Squire Western with his Horses, Dogs, and Bottle, or Austen's Sir John Middleton with his dogs, or Bronte's Mr. Rochester with his dog, Pilot, Siegfried Farnon, the vet from *All Creatures Great and Small*, or James Fleet's character in *Four Weddings and a Funeral* with his beloved black Lab, Englishmen are known for their close relationships with their dogs. And never more so than in the past.

Englishmen have always had dogs, haven't they? Yes, of course, they have. They're mad about the creatures. But the stereotypical image we have today of the Englishman with his Labrador retriever or his Jack Russell terrier is actually quite a recent phenomenon, dating only back 150 years or so.

The short-coated Labrador retrievers (which are ubiquitous in the country) didn't originate in Labrador, but in Newfoundland, and the first mention of them there is in 1822, when a traveller there wrote of "small water dogs", commenting that:

> *The dogs are admirably trained as retrievers in fowling, and are otherwise useful.... The smooth or short-haired dog is preferred because in frosty weather the long-haired kind become encumbered with ice on coming out of the water.*

Subsequently (sorry I can't find a date for it), the Earl of Malmesbury saw one of these animals which had been brought home by some English fishermen and instantly decided to have some imported.

By 1830, a sportsman by the name of Colonel Hawker was writing of them and calling the St. John's breed of water dog, saying they were:

> *by far the best for any kind of shooting. He is generally black and no bigger than a Pointer, very fine in legs, with short, smooth hair...is extremely quick, running, swimming and fighting...and their sense of smell is hardly to be credited.*

But it isn't until a letter, written in 1887, by the Earl of Malmesbury, that they're given the name by which we know them today:

> *We always call mine Labrador dogs, and I have kept the breed as pure as I could from the first I had from Poole, at that time carrying on a brisk trade with Newfoundland.*

The Jack Russell terrier, such as those which travel about with HRH, the Prince of Wales, is equally modern.

John Russell (1795-1883), known as Jack, was a sporting mad young man, studying at

---

Oxford prior to taking holy orders, when he encountered a little white terrier bitch. According to a memoir by E.W.L. Davies, published in 1883, the meeting went like this:

> *It was a glorious afternoon towards the end of May, when strolling round Magdalen meadow with Horace in hand, but Beckford in his head, he [Jack Russell] emerged from the classic shade of Addison's walk, crossed the Cherwell in a punt, and passed over in the direction of Marston, hoping to devote an hour or two to study in the quiet meads of that hamlet, near the charming slopes of Elsfield, or in the deeper and more secluded haunts of Shotover Wood.*
>
> *But before he reached Marston a milkman met him with a terrier—such an animal as Russell had as yet only seen in his dreams; he halted, as Acton might have done when he caught sight of Diana disporting in her bath; but, unlike that ill-fated hunter, he never budged from the spot till he had won the prize and secured it for his own.*
>
> *She was called Trump, and became the progenitress of that famous race of terriers which, from that day to the present, have been associated with Russell's name at home and abroad—his able and keen coadjutors in the hunting-field....*

In later life, John Russell became known as The Sporting Parson, and the line of dogs he bred from Trump live on in the flat-coated or wire-haired Jack Russell terrier—full of spunk and personality, the very best ratters one could hope to find, and generally, a beloved nuisance.

So...what's the novelist to do when writing about pre-Victorian times. What kinds of British dogs would have been common in the homes of the gentry or aristocracy? In the homes of farmers?

Spaniels are and were always popular. They're brilliant gun-dogs—and that in any age when shooting was a means of putting food on the table would have been essential. Spaniels in some form or other date back at least to 1368 and these dogs come to be referred to as either land spaniels or water spaniels.

Brittany spaniels, for example, probably date back as far as the 3rd century. But the first records that really pin down an actual Brittany-type spaniel are in 17th century tapestries and paintings.

Perhaps the best known though are what we now call Cavalier King Charles spaniels. These small companion dogs are direct descendents of the small Toy spaniels that were popular throughout the 16th, 17th, and 18th centuries and are often seen in the paintings of those eras. (Madame de Pompadour had one.) Even in Tudor times, they were popular as pets with court ladies. But it was the Stuart kings, particularly Charles II, who gave them their name and reputation.

The diarist Samuel Pepys accompanied Charles II from exile. Here are a few of his comments from his Diary for the date 25 May 1660—the date King Charles landed back in Britain:

> *About noon (though the brigantine that Beale made was there ready to carry him) yet he would go in my Lord's barge with the two Dukes. Our Captain steered, and my Lord went along bare with him. I went, and Mr. Mansell, and one of the King's footmen, with a dog that the King loved (which [dirted] the boat, which made us laugh,*

and me think that a King and all that belong to him are but just as others are), in a boat by ourselves, and so got on shore when the King did, who was received by General Monk with all imaginable love and respect at his entrance upon the land of Dover.

Here, though is an even more interesting morsel of trivia from Pepys' diary, a note about the dogs:

Charles II.'s love of dogs is well known, but it is not so well known that his dogs were continually being stolen from him. In the "Mercurius Publicus," June 28-July 5, 1660, is the following advertisement, apparently drawn up by the King himself: "We must call upon you again for a Black Dog between a greyhound and a spaniel, no white about him, onely a streak on his brest, and his tayl a little bobbed. It is His Majesties own Dog, and doubtless was stoln, for the dog was not born nor bred in England, and would never forsake His master. Whosoever findes him may acquaint any at Whitehal for the Dog was better known at Court, than those who stole him. Will they never leave robbing his Majesty! Must he not keep a Dog? This dog's place (though better than some imagine) is the only place which nobody offers to beg.

Anyway. These dogs fell out of fashion during the reign of William III, who preferred pugs (usually accompanied by a small black page boy). And it wasn't until the late 18th and early 19th century that again they resurface, bred by the Duke of Marlborough at his home, Blenheim Palace. (Which is why the chestnut and white coloured variety are referred to as "Blenheims".)

Other breeds which are surely old enough to figure into the lives of earlier generations of dog-loving Brits include Mastiffs, which Caesar described in his account of the invasion of Britain in 55 B.C.

The Scottish Deerhounds and Irish Wolfhounds were originally one breed, but by 1576, the Deerhound was recognised as different, and highly valuable for the pursuit and killing of deer—a most coveted sporting occupation. Both animals, although technically hounds, are rarely kept as kennel dogs because of their affectionate natures and love for human companionship.

And then of course, there are the packs of hounds—foxhounds and beagles, both of which are used for hunting and are kept in kennels and hunt in packs.

And yes, we love them all. Truly, madly, deeply, and forever....

THE ISLE OF ANGLESEY

BY JOHN WHEATLEY

THE ISLE OF ANGLESEY STANDS IN THE IRISH SEA, SEPARATED FROM THE WELSH MAINland by the beautiful Menai Strait, once described—with its treacherous tides and unpredictable currents—as the most dangerous waterway in the world.

Wherever you go on Anglesey, you find stories.

When the Romans were fastening their iron grip on Britain, two legions under Suetonius Paulinus crossed the strait to *Insula Mona* to destroy the Anglesey stronghold of Druid culture, and by all accounts the bloodiest of slaughters took place. In ensuing centuries, as the emergent kingdom of Wales defended its freedom against powerful enemies, Anglesey was the retreat of the Princes and a royal household was established at Aberffraw.

Ancient historical and cultural ties with neighbouring Ireland were consolidated when, after the Act of Union, 1800, Holyhead on Anglesey was chosen as the final stage of the mail route to Dublin, and it was this which led to the building of the Menai Bridge, completed in 1826.

My first Anglesey novel, *A Golden Mist*, was inspired by the story of the loss of the *Royal Charter*. Returning, in 1859, from Melbourne, with a company of 500 men, women, children, and crew, and laden with bullion from the Australian gold fields, the *Royal Charter* was only thirty miles from her destination, the port of Liverpool, when she was wrecked in hurricane conditions on rocks close to Moelfre, a fishing village on Anglesey's northwest coast. Only forty people survived.

The sad evidence of the *Royal Charter* disaster is still to be found in remote and scattered churchyards along that stretch of coast, and it is said that many of the drowned, reluctant to lose the fortune they had gained on the far side of the world, went to their death weighed down with pockets full of gold. Many stories, too, are told of villagers from Moelfre who grew mysteriously rich in the aftermath of the disaster!

In *A Golden Mist*, Saffy Williams, visiting the UK from South Africa, finds evidence that one of her ancestors lived in Moelfre at the time. Through her quest, and two fictional contemporary narratives, the diary of Sophia Davis on board the *Royal Charter* and the memoir of Richard Williams, a young man living in Moelfre in 1859, I tell the story of the lost treasure ship and the lives and passions of people associated with it.

In 1770, "the great discovery" on Parys Mountain, near Amlwch, on Anglesey's north coast, was the uncovering of rich copper deposits, and it led to a furious mining operation, lasting fifty years, which turned Amlwch from a tiny coastal village into a busy and tawdry industrial town—the copper capital of the world. My second Anglesey novel, *Flowers of Vitriol*, is a moody story of love, betrayal, jealousy, and vengeance set during this early chapter of Britain's industrial revolution.

Baron Hill, the fabulous neo-Palladian mansion set on the hillside, above Beaumaris, and overlooking the celebrated castle—one in the chain of fortifications by which Edward I attempted to subjugate the Welsh—represents the wealth and influence of the Bulkeley family, who provided statesmen in the courts of Elizabeth I and James I, and who played a vital role in Anglesey politics from the Civil War to modern times.

When I found, in my research of Baron Hill, a true story of love and adultery leading to an almost Oresteian tragedy of family vengeance and self-destruction, I chose this as the subject for my third Anglesey novel, *The Weeping Sands*. Over the centuries, Baron Hill played host to many distinguished guests, including royalty, but the Bulkeley family quit the mansion in 1926. Troops were billeted there during World War II, and after substantial fire damage, the house was finally abandoned. It now stands, a derelict and awe-inspiring ruin, camouflaged by trees, on the hillside above Beaumaris.

Mottisfont: The Evolution of an English House

by M.M. Bennetts

IN THE BEGINNING THERE WAS A MAN AND THE MAN'S NAME WAS WILLIAM BRIWERE.

A sketchy history of this man, Briwere, suggests he was a successful businessman who went on to be a rather savvy administrator for the Plantagenets. First as a judiciary left in charge of the kingdom when in 1189 Richard Lionheart embarked on the Third Crusade. Then latterly when he was made a baron, and became a trusted advisor to King John.

In return for his loyalty and service to the crown, he was awarded considerable lands upon which he was permitted to levy taxes. And upon some of this land, he founded four religious institutions: Dunkeswell Abbey and Torres Abbey in Devon, the Hospital of St. John in Somerset, and the Priory of the Holy Trinity at Mottisfont in Hampshire.

Was he trying to buy his way into heaven after a lifetime of financial gain and dubious piety? I can't tell you. I don't know.

The Priory at Mottisfont was founded in 1201 and it housed not monks but Augustinian priests (known for their black hoods), who numbered among their duties ministering to those in need, preaching to the community, and welcoming pilgrims passing on their way from Canterbury to Winchester, or even those on their way to the far-off shrine of Santiago de Compostela in Spain.

Throughout the 13th century and into the 14th, the Priory remained prosperous, supported as they were by the Briwere family and their descendants. And even throughout the modern-day property, there remain traces of this first house at Mottisfont—there's the vast cellarium which was the giant larder for the community as well as traces of the mediaeval church.

But in 1348, the Black Death swept over the country, killing over a third of the population and, in some cases, wiping out entire villages. The Mottisfont cellarer, Walter de Blount, fell victim in 1349. Robert de Bromore and Richard de Caneford, his two successors, died too, in quick succession. And like the rest of the land, Mottisfont was caught up in the subsequent civil and economic hardship of the age.

(An earthquake in Hampshire in 1457 didn't help matters any. William Westkarre, the then Prior, recorded that this had "greatly crushed and loosened" the buildings.)

Still, a generation later, though, things were looking up. Henry VII now sat on the throne and he initially planned to change the priory's status, making it a Collegiate Church. But that was never enacted. Instead, Mottisfont became a subsidiary of Westminster Abbey, before gaining, in 1521, a new patron—Henry Huttcroft.

Then in 1536, Henry VIII ordered the dissolution of the monasteries.

They made quick work of it, for Mottisfont had been sold by June of that same year to

William, Lord Sandys, (the king's Lord Chamberlain for five years) who at once set about transforming the place into a grand new Tudor dwelling.

Now Sandys was one of those energetic and savvy Tudor apparatchiks. He'd been a diplomat during the reign of Henry VII, and subsequently became a staunch supporter of Henry VIII and his new queen, Catherine of Aragon. He was Treasurer of Calais and made a Knight of the Garter in 1518, and was one of the velvet-tongued-talkers who arranged for the meetings between Henry VIII and Francois I of France at the Field of the Cloth of Gold. He also already owned another substantial property in Hampshire—this one near Basingstoke and called The Vyne—where he'd received Henry and Catherine in 1510, and Henry and Anne in 1535.

Sandys was 66 when he set about transforming the priory with its ruined outbuildings, using the structure of the massive church as the spine of his new great house. Four years later, when he died, the house was nearly completed—the main part of the house, the Great Chamber, created out of the church nave.

And again, things looked good and the prosperity of the place seemed a certainty: Elizabeth I visited Mottisfont in September 1569 and again in 1574.

But...and it's a big but...by the middle of the 17th century, England was engulfed in Civil War, and Henry, the 5th Baron Sandys, like so many other Hampshire landowners, fought on the side of the king. He died at the Battle of Cheriton in 1644. Within ten years, the family could no longer afford to keep both houses going, so they sold The Vyne.

Finally in 1684, the 8th Baron, Edwin, died childless. The title expired and Mottisfont was left to Sir John Mill, his nephew.

Then in the 1740s, it was one of Sir John's sons, Sir Richard Mill—Member of Parliament, Sheriff of Hampshire—who demolished much of the Tudor building, then rebuilt and transformed the house, adding a pedimented three-storey extension onto the the old Tudor house, transforming the place into the Georgian home that is seen today. Though interestingly, much of the mediaeval structure was retained, hidden behind the new walls of the new rooms of the south front.

(By 1791, the park had been turned into a fashionable landscape garden. While sometime in the late 18th/early 19th century, an Ice House was built not far from the house—aka a Regency Refrigerator—to be filled with ice during the spring, keeping it cold enough to store winter game, etc. into the summer months.)

And for another century, the Mills family lived and flourished at Mottisfont. In 1835, the estate passed to the Reverend John Barker (a cousin) who instantly changed his surname to Barker-Mill.

Sir John Barker-Mill, besides being a reverend gentleman, was a keen rider to hounds and a racing man. In his time, he replaced the old stables with something more suitable for his fine hunters and his stud-farm, and founded Reverend Sir John Barker-Mills Foxhounds. He also was known for his cherry-coloured cravats and his loud check trousers.

Barker-Mill died childless in 1860, but his widow lived on at the house into the 1880s, founding the first school to be built in Mottisfont village.

The new owner of Mottisfont in 1884 was a Mrs. Marianne Vaudrey (who later changed her name to Vaudrey-Barker-Mill) and she decided to let the house to a family with ten children, the Meinertzhagens, on the condition that they altered nothing in the house and most particularly did not install either electric lighting or any kind of central heating!

Their rent was £320 a year, and they loved it there. Mrs. Meinertzhagen was the sister of social reformer, Beatrice Webb, she who also co-founded the London School of Economics, and the house was frequently visited by the social reformers, politicos, and intellectuals of the day, including George Bernard Shaw, Cecil Rhodes, Charles Darwin, and Henry Stanley, of Stanley and Livingstone fame.

In 1898, following the death of their eldest son in 1898, the Meinertzhagens left Mottisfont, and Mrs. Vaudrey-Barker-Mill set about removing the central heating which had been installed, contrary to her wishes, and spending a considerable fortune, some £40,000 (roughly £3 million in today's money) restoring the old place.

A keen follower of The Gothic, she wished to bring out the monastic history of the place. She removed a parapet on the north side to reveal the roof of the Tudor Great Chamber; she had stucco removed to reveal the mediaeval masonry and arches. She had the Long Gallery redecorated. And when the work was complete in 1908, she let the house for shooting parties. However, in 1932, she had the contents of the house sold.

Whereupon in 1934, the house was bought by a merchant banker and his wife, Gilbert and Maud Russell, who wanted a country house for weekend parties and where they could raise their young family. Another fortune was now spent modernising the house, adding electric lights, and rooms were redecorated and reconfigured once again.

The artist Rex Whistler was commissioned in 1939, to help transform the old, dark entrance hall into a large saloon, and his *trompe l'oeil* murals, painted in gothick style in keeping with the house's origins, were his last and perhaps most beautiful completed work before he was killed in France in 1944, while on active service.

During WWII, along with many other big houses up and down the country, Mottisfont was requisitioned—the Long Gallery became a hospital ward with up to eighty patients at any one time, and children who'd been evacuated from London lived in converted accommodations in the Stable Block. And it wasn't until after the war that Mrs. Russell was able to make Mottisfont her home.

Finally, in 1957, Mrs. Russell gave the house and the estate to the National Trust, though she continued to live there for another fifteen years.

In 1972, Graham Stuart Thomas, the Trust's Garden Adviser, settled on the Walled Garden (formerly the Kitchen Garden and orchard—they grew pears, pine-apples, grapes, figs and vegetables for the house...) as a perfect home for his collection of historic (pre-1900) roses—there are hundreds of them—and it was he who laid out the Rose Garden with such flair and all-consuming love, planting the shrub and climbing roses amongst mixed perennial borders of foxglove, delphinium, iris, and clipped box.

Today, without a doubt, it is the Rose Garden—Britain's national collection of old roses—which attracts visitors from all over the world to Mottisfont in June. And it's no stretch either to understand why, or to say that Thomas saved the old roses for posterity—they were considered very unfashionable and uncool when he began collecting them.

At times, and in certain places in the garden, the scent of roses and clove pinks is almost too fragrant to bear. And there is no direction in which one may look which is not nature at her sweetest, most bountiful perfection, harmony for all the senses....

THE LOST PALACE OF RICHMOND

BY ANITA DAVISON

WHILST RESEARCHING THE ROYAL PALACES THAT ONCE LINED THE RIVER THAMES, I have always wondered about the "lost" ones, those that were left to become ruins, or destroyed long before photographs could tell us what they looked like. One which interests me particularly is Richmond, a royal residence that once dominated the ground between Richmond Green and the River Thames.

In medieval times, Richmond Green was used for grazing sheep, archery, jousting tournaments, and pageants. The earliest recorded cricket match between Surrey and Middlesex was played there in June 1730, which Surrey won, though the score is not known.

The green is surrounded by substantial Regency and Georgian houses which change hands for jaw-slackening amounts, and where locals and dreamers sit at The Cricketers pub and at pavement cafes to watch the cricket and attend fairs in the summer. However, in Tudor times, the houses round the Green existed to serve the Royal Palace, and clues still exist as to its former splendour in the names of the streets that radiate on the west side of the Green, like "Old Palace Gate", "Friars Lane", "Old Palace Yard", and "The Wardrobe". The only remaining section of the palace that remains today is a red-brick gatehouse which still bears Henry VII's coat of arms.

The manor of Shene contained a manor house since Henry I's time, held by a Norman knight before being returned to royal hands. Edward II owned it, and after his deposition it passed to his wife, Queen Isabella. After her death, Edward III turned the manor house into the first "Shene Palace", where he died in 1377.

His grandson, Richard II, came to the throne as a boy, and while still a teenager, married Anne of Bohemia. Shene was their favourite home and when Anne died of the plague at the age of 27, Richard, stricken with grief, *caused it to be thrown down and defaced.*

Henry V began construction on a new castle-like building, though the work halted at his death in 1422. Building resumed for the new king, Henry VI, who was only eight years old when he was crowned.

Edward IV gave Shene Manor to his queen, Elizabeth Woodville, who handed it over to the new Henry VII after his victory over Richard III, who subsequently married her daughter, Princess Elizabeth of York.

The wooden buildings were destroyed by fire when the king and his court were there celebrating Christmas in 1497. In 1500, the name of Shene was changed to Richmond, in honour of the title, Earl of Richmond, which Henry VII held when he won at Bosworth Field.

Built of white stone, the new palace had octagonal or round towers capped with pepper-pot domes that bore delicate strap work and weather vanes. It had three stories set in a rectangular block with twelve rooms on each floor round an internal court. This area contained staterooms and private royal apartments, while the ground floor was entirely given over to accommodation for palace officials.

A bridge over the moat, surviving from Edward III's time, linked the Privy Lodgings to a central courtyard some 65 feet square, flanked by the Great Hall and the Chapel and with a water fountain at its centre. The Great Hall had a buttery beneath. The Chapel ceiling was of chequered timber and plaster decorated with roses and portcullis badges, underneath which were extensive wine cellars.

The middle gate that opened into the Great Court was turreted and adorned with stone figures of two trumpeters, and to the east was situated the palace wardrobe where soft furnishings were stored. There was also a moat, a Great Orchard, public and private kitchens, and a Library. The palace gardens were encircled by two-storey galleries, open at ground level and enclosed above, where the court could walk, play games, admire the gardens, watch the tennis.

Richmond Palace became a showplace of the kingdom, and the scene of the wedding celebrations of Henry VII's eldest son, Prince Arthur, to Catherine of Aragon. Also, the betrothal of Princess Margaret to King James of Scotland took place at Richmond in 1503.

Henry VII died at Richmond in 1509, and the following year, his son, Henry VIII, married his brother's widow, Catherine of Aragon. In 1510 Catherine gave birth to a son, Henry, at Richmond, whose lavish christening celebrations had barely finished when the baby died a month later.

Henry VIII's jealousy of Wolsey's palace at Hampton Court led to him confiscate Hampton Court, giving Wolsey Richmond in exchange. Richmond became home to Mary Tudor, who stayed for a few months before being moved to Hatfield House. Then the palace was given to Anne of Cleves as part of her divorce settlement from Henry VIII.

In 1554, when Queen Mary I married Philip II of Spain, Richmond was where they spent their honeymoon, and within a year, Mary had imprisoned her sister Elizabeth there.

Queen Elizabeth was particularly fond of Richmond as a winter home—and loved to hunt stag in the "Newe Parke of Richmonde" (now the Old Deer Park). It was here she summoned companies of players from London to perform plays—including William Shakespeare's. She also died there in 1603.

James I gave Richmond to his son, Henry, Prince of Wales, as a country seat, but before any refurbishment could be done, Henry died and it passed to Prince Charles, who began his extensive art collection, storing it at Richmond.

In 1625, King Charles I brought his court to Richmond to escape the plague in London, and he established Richmond Park, using the palace as a home for the royal children until the Civil War.

After Charles I's execution, the Commonwealth Parliament divided up the palace buildings and had them extensively surveyed, in which the furniture and decorations are described as being sumptuous, with beautiful tapestries depicting the deeds of kings and heroes. The brick buildings of the outer ranges survived; the stone buildings of the Chapel, Hall, and Privy Lodgings were demolished and the stones sold off.

By the restoration of Charles II in 1660, only the brick buildings and the Middle Gate were left. The palace became the property of the Duke of York (the future James II) and his daughters, Mary and Anne, grew up there. Their only surviving half-brother, Prince James Edward (the "Old Pretender"), was nursed at Richmond, but the restoration work, begun under the auspices of Christopher Wren, ceased in the revolution of 1688 when James II fled to France.

The surviving buildings were leased out, and in 1702, "Trumpeters' House" was built, replacing the Middle Gate where two statues of trumpeters stood. These were followed by "Old Court House" and "Wentworth" in 1705-7. The front of the Wardrobe still shows Tudor brick-work as does the Gate House. "Maids of Honour Row" built in 1724 is a uniform terrace built for the maids of honour of Caroline of Anspach, the wife of George II. These replaced most of the buildings facing the Green in 1724-5 and the majority of the house now called "Old Palace" was rebuilt in about 1740.

Traces of the elaborate gardens are still there, having been incorporated into private res-idences. The view from the river is still beautiful, and as you pass in a barge and squint a little, maybe you can still see the "pepper pots" and turrets of the old palace where kings and queens once lived.

FAVERSHAM, KENT

BY LAUREN GILBERT

FAVERSHAM IS A FASCINATING PORT TOWN IN KENT. SOME YEARS AGO, MY HUSBAND AND I had the pleasure of attending the Hop Festival there. It's a lovely town, compact and walkable. Its history goes back to before 811, and it was known to be settled by the Romans.

Part of the ancient royal demesne, Faversham is mentioned in the Domesday Book, and it also possesses an early Cinque Ports charter (considered to be the oldest in existence) and was linked to Dover. King Stephen founded Faversham Abbey in 1147 and was subsequently buried there with his wife Matilda and son Eustace. The abbey was dissolved by Henry VIII and now nothing remains but ruins. The beautiful parish church, St. Mary of Charity, still remains.

As a port city, Faversham had a customs house, and fishing was an important industry. (The oyster beds were particularly important.) The town has an association with medieval queens and a fascinating history. Queen Elizabeth I endowed a grammar school here.

However, I am going to focus on a specific point of interest: gunpowder.

Advances in weaponry and military activity created a need for gunpowder, and Faversham was peculiarly suited to meet this need. The ingredients for gunpowder, especially charcoal and sulphur, were readily available. The site was perfect for factories, with a stream for watermills, and the continent was easily accessible from the port. The earliest gunpowder works was established in the 16th century. The original small factories were joined together as the Home Works.

Home Works was ultimately nationalized by the British government in 1759. Another factory, Oare Works, had been built nearby in Davington parish in Kent in the 1680s. A third factory, Marsh Works, was built by the government in 1787. These mills provided gunpowder to the East India Company and the military, supporting the war effort. It is interesting to think of the powder from these factories possibly being used by Nelson's ships at the Battle of Trafalgar and by Wellington's troops at Waterloo!

Gunpowder from these factories was also used for blasting for canals and tunnels (especially important for railway expansion). These plants continued in operation, and produced explosives during World War I.

In 1916, a horrible explosion killed over 100 employees. In 1934, the gunpowder factories were closed due to fears that the area would be vulnerable to invasion or attack if war with Germany was declared.

The site of Home Works was redeveloped in the 1960s except for Chart Gunpowder Mill, which is an historic site. The Marsh Works became a site for mineral extraction which is still in operation. Oare Works is a county park, featuring conserved process houses, trails, and a visitor center.

SOURCES

Hasted, Edward. "The Parish and Town of Faversham." Originally located in *The History and*

Topographical Survey of the County of Kent, Vol. 6, 1798. *British History Online*. http://www.british-history.ac.uk/report.aspx?compid=62974.

"History of Faversham, Kent." Kentfind.Co.UK. http://www.kentfind.co.uk/about/faversham/history.php.

Percival, Arthur. *Old Faversham*. Rainham, Kent: Meresborough Books, 1988.

Turcan, Robert. *Faversham through Time*. Stroud, Gloucestershire: Amberley Publishing, 2010.

THE GROSVENORS

THE FIRST GROSVENOR, A NEPHEW AND FAVORITE OF WILLIAM THE CONQUEROR, WAS Gilbert d'Avranches. He accompanied William across the Channel to the Battle of Hastings in 1066.

(Many histories state that the first Grosvenor was actually Hugh d'Avranches, but the Grosvenor Estate professes Hugh was a relative of Gilbert, and not the nephew of William the Conqueror. I would have gone with "Hugh" but I figured the Grosvenor Estate knows its own family....)

As a result of his dedication to William, Gilbert received the Earldom of Chester, but he had to fight for it. It was very close to the Welsh border and a Saxon stronghold—Gilbert dealt with those who refused to be conquered in such a brutal manner that he became known as Lupus (wolf). One story holds he tortured and killed a young gypsy boy for poaching on his land. After he killed the young gypsy boy, the gypsies cursed Gilbert, saying *that no son would follow father in the succession to the earldom."*

Along with the name of Lupus, Gilbert also received the nickname le Gros. Extremely fat, he loved wine, rich food, and women. He's known to have sired upwards of twenty illegitimate children. Finally marrying Ermentrude of Clarement, he had a legitimate son, Richard, and a daughter, Matilda.

His real passion was hunting, however, and this is how Gilbert came to receive the name by which he would be known henceforth. Gilbert gained the name *Gros Veneur*, French for "Large Huntsman." (The Grosvenor Estate translates it as: Chief Huntsman.)

Since Gilbert was obese, and later needed a hoist to set him onto the saddle for the hunt, one can say he was very "gros" or truly gross (boo, hiss, bad humor). He spent many hours in the saddle and had little humility or reverence before his Lord God. During one hunt, he kenneled his hounds in a church for the night. In the morning they were all found dead.

Toward the end of his life, Gilbert repented. Due to his gluttony, he had a difficult time walking. Afraid he would go to Hell for his debauchery, he *"founded the Benedictine Abby of St Werburgh, where the monks were to spend their lives in solemn prayer for the soul of their patron."*

In partial fulfillment of the gypsies' curse, Gilbert's son, Richard, succeeded him but died in 1120 without an heir. The Grosvenor curse continued to crop up again over the years.

The family did not play a prominent part in English history until 1385. There is mention that Sir Robert Grosvenor went with Richard II to fight the Scots. He was known to John of Gaunt and Henry IV.

In 1617, James I created Sir Richard Grosvenor a baron, and the "red hand" was added to the Grosvenor coat of arms. Despite this, Sir Richard resided in debtor's prison for many years. He had cosigned a brother-in-law's loans that went unpaid.

It was not until Sir Thomas Grosvenor (1655-1700), 3rd Baronet, that the family came closer to the household name we know today. Sir Thomas married Mary Davis, daughter of a scrivener, who had inherited 500 acres in the west end of London. It was considered a wet meadow, an area which we know as Mayfair, Pimlico, and Belgravia, now called the London Estate.

By the time of Sir Thomas, the Grosvenors had built a robust estate. They owned coal and lead mines and stone quarries in Wales. Sir Thomas had built and moved his family home from a castle-like affair with a moat to a large house on the present site of Eaton Hall.

But the Grosvenor curse continued. Thomas' son, Sir Richard, 4th baronet (1689-1723), died without issue. Sir Thomas, 5th baronet (1693-1733), died in Naples unmarried.

Several Grosvenor generations avoided the curse even as their wealth and status grew, marking them Baron, Earl, then Marquess.

Hugh Lupus (1825-1899), created 1st Duke of Westminster, continued this streak of good fortune, but the curse was believed to have returned when in 1909 the four-year-old son of the 2nd Duke died. Even though the 2nd Duke married several times, he never sired another son.

William Grosvenor, the 3rd Duke of Westminster, was born brain damaged, *"and so small he was fed milk through a fountain pen filler"*. He died 1963 without an heir. The 4th Duke held the dukedom for only 4 years. He died of wounds received during combat in WW2.

The current Duke is Robert, 5th Duke of Westminster, and his wife, the Hon. Viola Lyttelton. They produced two male children, thus finally breaking the Grosvenor curse...hopefully for good.

Back in the 17th century...London at the time of Sir Thomas Grosvenor was exciting and full of motion. His prime of life was during a period when so much changed forever in England. For more on London (1662), please read my *Of Carrion Feathers*, a tale of espionage during the reign of King Charles II.

SOURCES

The Grosvenor Estate. http://www.grosvenorestate.com/.

Sexton, Carole. *Tales of Old Cheshire*. Countryside Books, 2011.

TIME: A TIMELINE OF CLOCKS

BY DEBORAH SWIFT

WHEN WRITING HISTORICAL FICTION, AS WELL AS GOING BACK IN TIME TO THE PERIOD I am writing about, I often have to consider that the notion of how time was measured in previous times is very different from my own. In the 17th century poorer people still used sand-glasses or hour-glasses, and not everyone could afford a clock in their house. Churches rang the bells so that people had some sense of the time passing, but in general people were much less fixated on exact times than we are today.

The first clock was of course the sun, and the position of the stars in the night sky. The first recorded mention of the sun dial was in 742 B.C. There is, however, evidence of use of the sun dial as early as 2,000 B.C.!

By 330 A.D., sand-glasses were thought to be in use, although this is disputed because the hand-blown glass was very fragile, and no examples have survived. Sand-glasses used to be made in different sizes to measure different amounts of time. Some would be large enough to stand on the ground and require servants to lift and turn them.

Candles with the wax scored to mark the time were widely used in poorer households who could not afford a sand-glass, or sometimes candles were fixed to a marked plate. There is evidence that Alfred the Great used a candle clock in 885 A.D.

In 1490 the mainspring was invented by Peter Hele, or Henlein, a locksmith of Nuremburg. About this time the small domestic or table clock made its appearance, but these were expensive items and the previous more homespun methods of measuring the time continued to be used by most people.

Clocks gradually became more elaborate. A "masterpiece" clock (a requirement for admission to the guild of master clockmakers in Augsburg) struck the hours and quarters and displayed no less than three systems of counting hours: French hours (I–XII), Italian hours (1–24, beginning at sundown), and Nuremberg hours (divided into daylight and night hours, which vary in number according to the season of the year). Complex!

In 1541, an astronomical clock was fixed in one of the towers of Hampton Court Palace, and by 1610, glass was able to be moulded to form a protective cover for watch dials.

In 1657, Christiaan Huygens, a Dutch Physicist, made the first pendulum controlled clock, and grandfather clocks began to make their appearance in wealthier homes. The two kinds of movements are 30-hour and eight-day, which indicates how long before the clock has to be wound with a key. The melody, bell, chime, or gong sounds on the hour in the eight-day clocks and on the hour and half hour in the 30-hour clocks.

By 1765 the centre Second hand became common. A lovely eight-day mahogany long-case clock dated around 1835 has a decorated arch dial. Often the painted dials depicted mythological scenes or the four seasons. The Met Museum has some nice examples (http://www.metmuseum.org/toah/hd/clck/hd_clck.htm).

Around the middle of the 1800s, the spring-powered movement developed, paving the way for a variety of smaller clock cases. Many different materials were used in clocks. Wood was popular, including mahogany, oak, pine, walnut, and cherry.

In 1858 the British Horological Institute was founded—an association of Clock and Watch Makers for the purpose of advancing their art, and *The Horological Journal*, the oldest periodical dealing with the craft, was started.

Greenwich Mean Time became the standard time for the whole of the United Kingdom in 1880.

Oh my word! Is that the time? Two thousand years has gone by and I hardly noticed. Must get on with some writing!

And just in case you're interested in the English Civil War, orchids, obsession, adventure, and romance, my book *The Lady's Slipper* is out now, featuring the turning of many sand-glasses, the occasional church chime, and the loud tick of a pendulum clock.

September in British History

by KAREN WASYLOWSKI

GIVE US BACK OUR ELEVEN DAYS!

Did you know that absolutely nothing happened in Britain from 3 September to 13 September, 1752? It is a fact. Nothing.

The reason is pretty simple. The calendar used during this period was the Julian Calendar, based on a solar year of 365.25 days. Problem was, it ran a little over time and eventually the calendar fell out of line with the seasons.

The solution: Britain decided to dump the Julian Calendar and adopt the more favorable Gregorian Calendar, and September 3 instantly became September 14. Eleven days were gone, eliminated, abolished. People protested in the streets believing their lives would be shortened. They chanted: "*Give us our eleven days back!*"

SEPTEMBER 24

September 24 was traditionally the start of the harvest time in medieval England and a lovely ceremony, a race to harvest, called "Calling the Mare." As the very last of the crops were being brought in, the farmers would hurriedly fashion a straw horse then go to a neighboring farm that was still rushing to finish and throw the straw mare over his hedge. They would taunt "Mare, Mare," and that farmer would gather his final crop and do the same to any other farmer still trying to harvest. The last man to finish had to keep the straw mare all year and have it on display to show he was the slowest of them all.

SEPTEMBER 29

And when the tenauntes come
To paie their quarter's rent,
They bring some fowle at Midsummer
A dish of fish in Lent
At Christmas, a capon,
At Michaelmas, a goose,
And somewhat else at New Yere's tide
For feare the lease flie loose.

—George Gascoine, English poet, 1577

Michaelmas is the feast day of St. Michael the Archangel, the patron saint of the sea and boats, horses and horsemen. Michaelmas Day is the final day of the Harvest Season, and it was also the first day of the winter night curfew and the church bells would ring once for each night of the year until that point. The bells are still rung to this day in a city called Chertsey from Michaelmas Day, 29 September, to Lady Day, 25 March.

There are traditionally four "quarter days" in a year—Lady Day (25 March), Midsummer (24 June), Michaelmas (29 September), and Christmas (25 December). They are spaced three months apart, on religious festivals, usually close to the solstices or equinoxes. They were the four dates on which servants were hired, rents were due, or leases begun.

It used to be said that harvest had to be completed by Michaelmas, almost like the marking of the end of the productive season and the beginning of the new cycle of farming. It was the time at which new servants were hired or land was exchanged and debts were paid. This is how it came to be for Michaelmas to be the time for electing magistrates and also the beginning of legal and university terms. Some Michaelmas superstitions include:

- The devil stomps or spits on bramble bushes, so don't pick blackberries after Michaelmas.
- Victorians believed trees planted on this day would grow really well.
- In Northern England and Ireland, if you eat goose this day you will have good luck for the rest of the year.
- In Ireland, if you found the ring hidden in the Michaelmas pie you would soon marry.

FIRST MONDAY AFTER SEPTEMBER 4

In a town called Abbotts Bromley in Staffordshire a colorful tradition takes place. Six men carrying long sticks with horns attached to the top march down the street. Two sets of three men each, their horns painted blue on one team and white on the other, charge each other as if to fight, then they retreat, people dance, Maid Marion is there also, along with a boy with a bow and arrow, a triangle player, a musician, and a Fool.

SEPTEMBER 14

On Holy Rood Day (rood is another name for cross) children were traditionally freed from school to gather nuts.

OTHER NOTABLE DAYS IN HISTORY

- September 2-6, 1666—The Great Fire of London
- September 7, 1533—Queen Elizabeth I born
- September 9, 1087—William the Conqueror dies
- September 28—St. Wenceslas Day
- September 29, 1758—Nelson is born

TWELFTH NIGHT

BY LAUREN GILBERT

TWELFTH NIGHT CELEBRATIONS HAVE TAKEN PLACE SINCE MEDIEVAL TIMES. A RELIGIOUS holiday initially, it celebrated the coming of Epiphany, the arrival of the Magi at Jesus' birthplace. It is the culminating festival of Christmastide, the twelve days of Christmas.

The English traditions of Twelfth Night are what most of us think of when the name "Twelfth Night" is used: food, especially an ornate cake and great feasting, drinking, games, plays, dances and masked balls, and other fun times.

Shakespeare's play, *Twelfth Night*, is supposed to have been written to perform on Twelfth Night.

Although the Christmas tree was a 19th century custom imported from Germany, decorating with greenery, such as rosemary, ivy, mistletoe, holly, bay, and laurel was very popular over centuries, from pagan times. Christmas fires, Yule logs, and candles were also part of the celebration. Even Oliver Cromwell was not able to completely stamp out all vestiges of Christmastide and Twelfth Night during his Puritan rule, and the festivities revived again under Charles II.

Traditionally, Twelfth Night is celebrated on either the fifth or the sixth of January (depending on how the twelve days are counted, which varies somewhat from one tradition to another). The Twelfth Night tradition still seems strong in Great Britain (witness the many pictures of the mummers' parades, the Holly Man, and other festivities found with the simplest Google search), Hispanic cultures still celebrate Three Kings' Night, and there are surviving traditions in the other western European countries.

However, in the United States, Twelfth Night is no longer celebrated commonly in the traditional sense. Twelfth Night was once widely celebrated in the colonies, especially those settled by the English. The colonists brought their traditions with them and adapted them to their new environment. George and Martha Washington were married on Twelfth Night in 1759, and entertained on Twelfth Night throughout the day each year; Martha's papers include a recipe for an enormous Twelfth Night Cake. Christmas wreaths decorated with fruit (apples, oranges, etc., which were considered delicacies) were hung on doors, as can still be seen in Colonial Williamsburg.

The Twelfth Night Cake is customarily a ring-shaped cake with currants, candied fruits, and nuts (or any combination) baked into it. Also baked into the cake was a coin, a carved or cast-metal baby (representing the Christ Child), or a bean and a pea. Whoever got the coin or baby was the king; in the case of the bean or pea, the man who got the bean was king, the woman who got the pea was queen. The king and queen ruled the festivities. Later, the king's privileges included providing the next year's cake.

This cake may be elaborately iced and decorated, often with one or two crowns, or may be light and decorated with colored sugars. (This tradition still lives in the United States in some of the Mardi Gras customs; some Twelfth Night cakes are decorated with the colors now associated with Mardi Gras: purple, green, and gold or yellow.)

Wassailing was also a tradition during Christmastide and on Twelfth Night. Wassail (your health) involved toasting with a hot mulled cider and/or ale and was very popular in southern England from about the 14th century on. One custom was wassailing the apple trees, which involved pouring a little wassail on the trees to ensure a good harvest and good cider the next year.

One important footnote: it was essential to remove the greenery before midnight on the sixth of January. If left up, the greenery could attract goblins or cause bad luck in the New Year, so it was traditionally taken down and burned. In America, the fruits used to decorate the wreaths were eaten as part of the celebratory feasts.

SOURCES

Beckford, Martin. "Christmas Ends in Confusion Over When Twelfth Night Falls." *The Telegraph*, 1/6/2009. http://www.telegraph.co.uk/news/religion/4126725/Christmas-ends-in-confusion-over-when-Twelfth-Night-falls.html.

Boyle, Laura. "Twelfth Night." *Jane Austen Centre*. http://www.janeausten.co.uk/twelfth-night/.

Doe, Martha. "The Puritan Ban on Christmas." *TimeTravelBritain.com*. http://www.timetravel-britain.com/articles/christmas/ban.shtml.

Levins, Sandy. "Understanding Twelfth Night: The Holiday That Time Forgot." *Camden County Historical Society*, 1/3/2005. http://historiccamdencounty.com/ccnews93.shtml.

Miller, Amy, "What Is The Twelfth Night Christmas Season?" *ShareFaith*. http://www.faithclipart.com/guide/Christian-Holidays/twelfth-night.html.

BE MY VALENTINE!

BY MARIE HIGGINS

When love is not madness, it is not love.

—Pedro Calderon de la Barca

Many are the starrs I see, but in my eye no starr like thee.

—English saying used on poesy rings

Loving is not just looking at each other, it's looking in the same direction.
—Antoine de Saint-Exupéry, *Wind, Sand, and Stars,* 1939

Gravitation is not responsible for people falling in love.

—Albert Einstein

Oh, if it be to choose and call thee mine, love, thou art every day my Valentine!
—Thomas Hood

I claim there ain't Another Saint As great as Valentine.

—Ogden Nash

Must, bid the Morn awake!
Sad Winter now declines,
Each bird doth choose a mate;
This day's Saint Valentine's.
For that good bishop's sake
Get up and let us see
What beauty it shall be
That Fortune us assigns.

—Michael Drayton

"Be My Valentine..."

Who was Saint Valentine...and why do people celebrate his name by writing sonnets, giving flowers, or candy to those they love?

Here is what I researched about our dear *Saint Valentine.* Several articles were written about the "legend" of Saint Valentine....

There were many different Saint Valentines who were martyred during the days of ancient Rome. Little is known about the one whose feast day is celebrated on February 14, except that he is said to have been buried on that day on the Via Flaminia north of Rome.

One of the articles talked about a priest who served during the third century in Rome.

When Emperor Claudius II decided that single men made better soldiers, he outlawed marriages for young men. The priest—Valentine—realized the injustice, defied the emperor, and continued to perform marriages for young lovers in secret. When Valentine was discovered to be going against the emperor, Claudius ordered the priest be put to death. On the eve of his execution, Valentine wrote a letter to his lover (some believed it was the daughter of one of the jailers). Valentine signed this letter, "from your Valentine". Eventually, the Catholic Church canonised Valentine.

It wasn't much later until this day became associated with "love". During the Middle Ages, it was commonly believed in France and England that February 14 was the beginning of birds' mating season.

Valentine greetings did not become popular until the Middle Ages. The oldest known valentine still in existence today was a poem written in 1415 by Charles, Duke of Orleans, to his wife while he was imprisoned in the Tower of London following his capture at the Battle of Agincourt.

When I think about my favorite Valentine's Day, only one comes to mind. I had just met my future husband, but at the time, I was dating his best friend. Little did I know that my future husband was secretly wishing I would love him and not his friend. Anyway, it was my future husband's idea to get some red spray paint and spray a big heart on my snow-covered lawn. That morning when I pulled out of my driveway on my way to work, I saw the heart and inside it the words "Be Mine". Ah…that's been the most memorable Valentine's Day gift!

THE ORIGINS OF APRIL FOOLS' DAY

BY RICHARD DENNING

HAVE YOU BEEN TRICKED ON THIS DAY BY A PRANK OR JOKE? MAYBE YOU RECALL SOME famous tricks in the past. The BBC once broadcast a documentary of farmers in Italy picking spaghetti from bushes and trees after a bumper harvest. Thousands were tricked. In the USA, Taco Bell announced it had purchased the Liberty Bell and renamed it the Taco Liberty Bell.

When though did this tradition start?

The suggestion, recorded in *The Country Diary of Garden Lore*, is that 1 April was the day that Noah sent a rook out looking for land as the flood waters subsided, but where that comes from I cannot find out.

One explanation links it to ancient festivals such as the Roman Hilaria, celebrated at the end of March when people would dress up in disguises. There are theories that this time of year with its variable weather—sometimes cold, sometimes hot—tricks men and makes us fools.

A more substantial explanation related to 1582, when France switched from the Julian calendar to the Gregorian calendar. This changed the start of the year from the last week of March/1 April as it used to be to January 1. Because it took a while for this fact to become known and accepted, people who celebrated the New Year on 1 April were ridiculed. A paper fish called a "poisson d'avril" would be stuck to their backs to show they were fools. This is still part of present day French culture.

In England, the celebration came in about 1700 becoming more popular as the century went on. The British changed calendars in 1752 themselves, which may have encouraged the tradition. The Scots celebrated a two day event (how come they often manage to get two days out of something we English get one day from!) Hunting the Gowk Day involved sending folk on wild goose chases or false errands, whilst Tailie Day involved pinning tails or notices to people's backsides.

This morning my father recreated the spaghetti hoax in a picture he emailed me to show my son. Have you thought up any good ones? Or have you been the butt of an April fool?

MayDay, MayDay, Mayday!

BY MIKE RENDELL

AND NO, THE INTERNATIONALLY RECOGNIZED DISTRESS SIGNAL HAS NOTHING WHATSO-ever to do with the first day of May: it is a deliberate corruption of the French expression *venez m'aider* ("come and help me"), having been chosen in 1923 by a senior radio officer by the name of Frederick Stanley Moxford. He wanted a word that would indicate distress and would easily be understood by all pilots and ground staff in an emergency at his local airport (Croydon). It was soon picked up and is now the accepted distress call for planes and ships alike.

A less well-known call sign is "Pan-pan" (from the French *panne*—meaning a breakdown) which is used in less serious incidents such as mechanical problems which are not life-threatening. As with "Mayday" it is repeated three times to ensure clarity and to prevent confusion.

But I digress: what of May Day, the first day of May and the first day of summer? Traditionally, this was always celebrated in Northern Europe as a chance to say farewell to winter and an opportunity to have a celebratory bonfire (in some parts of Ireland it is still known as Bonfire Night, whereas the English save that expression for 5 November, being Guy Fawkes' Night).

It is also the subject of some lovely customs, many of which lasted longer where the Celtic traditions remained strong, rather than elsewhere. Take the charming custom of washing your face with May dew. The 1652 book by Dr. Gerard Boate entitled *Irelands Naturall History* says this of the custom:

> *The English women, and gentlewomen of Ireland…did use in the beginning of summer to gather good store of dew, to keep it by them al the year after for several good uses both of physick and otherwise, wherein by experience they have learnt it to be very available.*

The collecting of dew would take weeks of preparation. In April, May, and into June the girls would get up before the dawn, go to the green fields (wheat was best), and harvest the dew—either with their bare hands, or more especially by spreading a sheet out over the moist grass, and then wringing it out and collecting it in a glass jar. This would be topped up every day, and for the whole year would sit in the sunlight by a suitable window.

Every few days the concoction would be purified by carefully straining off the water so as to leave behind any sediment, dirt, or other impurities. And so, after nearly a year in which the freshest of fresh waters was imbued with sunbeams, it could be splashed on the face! Dr. Boate's book opined, *"The dew, thus thoroughly purified, looketh whitish, and keepeth good for a year or two after."*

The distillation was at its most powerful if applied before sunrise on 1 May, and in an age when we consider it beneficial to rub avocado extract into our hair or spread unmentionable products over our skin to prevent wrinkles, who is to say that a spot of early morning dew water is not just as magical in its properties?

The practice gave rise to the riddle:

I washed my face in water
That had neither rained nor run,
And I dried it on a towel
That was neither woven nor spun.

The answer lay in the fact that having washed your face in dew, you always allowed it to dry in the fresh air—you would hardly go to all that trouble and then wipe it off afterwards!

This custom was by no means limited to the uneducated country poor—it was also favoured by ladies of fashion and has in some cases been transported, and lives on in at least one household in the United States. One woman tells a story that goes back several generations of how in one particular family the girls always set their alarms for six in the morning on May 1 so that they could run outside and rub their faces in the morning dew on the lawn!

Among the anticipated benefits of applying dew to the face (or even better, naked dew rolling!) was that it would prevent freckles, sunburn, and wrinkles. It could prevent headaches, and even walking barefoot through the dew would ease bunions and callouses as well as preventing corns! For some reason it also enabled the person concerned to have greater dexterity in untangling nets, ropes, or freeing knots from string and thread. (Memo to self: get up early 1 May and roll around in the buff on the neighbour's lawn—I don't have a lawn, so his will have to do!)

Ireland, in particular, had many other May Day traditions, including cutting down a thornbush and putting it up outside your house and decorating it with ribbons. Another custom was to keep the brightly coloured egg-shells left over from Easter, and then string them together as a loop to hang around the tree.

But tree-rustling was such a problem that a law was passed in the reign of George III (1775) stating:

> *every person who shall put up any Maybush opposite or near to his or her house or suffer*
> *any Maybush to be so put up or to remain for the space of three hours opposite or near*
> *to his or her own house…not being a person lawfully possessed of trees or woods or not*
> *having lawfully obtained the same…shall forfeit and pay such sum not exceeding forty*
> *shillings* [two pounds—the equivalent today of perhaps $220].

Another tradition was putting up a Maypole at a crossroads. The tallest was reputedly at the Strand in London, near the present St. Mary-le-Strand Church. It was erected shortly after the Restoration of the Monarchy in 1660 (all such practices having been banned under Cromwell's Protectorate) and was over 130 feet tall. It stood there until a storm blew it down twelve years later.

The tradition of putting up maypoles caused our legislators to impose controls (presumably because of the risk of serious injury to road users from collapsing poles). An Act of Parliament dated 1792 was passed to *"Improve and keep in repair the Post roads of the Kingdom"*. Amongst other things it stated that *"If any person…shall erect any sign-post or maypole or maybush on any part of the said roads…every person so offending shall forfeit the sum of twenty shillings."*

The Irish had a similar tradition of putting up maypoles at cross-roads, but whereas the English seemed content to tie ribbons round the poles and dance around them, the Irish came up with some splendid alternatives. There were two famous crosses in Dublin at Harold's Cross and Finglas, and they would be smothered in soap until slippery. A succession of prizes having first been tied to the pole, the young men would then be challenged to climb the slippery pole and claim the prize—a hat, a pair of breeches, or an old watch.

It was also often an occasion for dancing and carousing, as well as traditional activities such as sack races, gurning (making contorted facial expressions through horse collars), wrestling, chase-the-pig, and so on. In Tralee in 1785, an eccentric landowner called Miss Cameron introduced the custom of men racing each other with sacks of coal or flour draped around their necks—a spectacle giving rise to much rejoicing and revelry.

Some of the traditions date from the fact that May Day in Ireland was the traditional day for hiring agricultural labourers. It was also the day when rent was due. In some places such as Limerick, it was customary for the farm workers to parade through the main streets of the town, complete with ploughs, scythes, and other agricultural implements.

In England many of the celebrations are limited to a specific town or village. Padstow in Cornwall has its hobby horse (or rather, "obby-oss"), while many places reckon that May Day is the start of the Morris Dancing season (cue much waving of hankies and banging together of stout poles). Across the country there may be people rushing into the North Sea, or attending festivals, or jumping off bridges! And that is quite apart from those who regard the day as International Workers' Day.

800 Years of Christmas in England

by KATHERINE ASHE

CHRISTMAS TREES, SANTA CLAUS, AND HEAPS OF PRESENTS: NONE OF WHAT WE NOW TAKE for Christmas traditions are indigenous to old England. The indoor, decorated tree is German, appearing first at the Georgian Court and in noble English households as a branch of yew set with candles, introduced by Queen Charlotte. By 1800 Charlotte had enlarged her display to a whole potted yew, and aristocratic families were starting to imitate the beloved queen's custom.

Yet the popularization of the Christmas tree dawdled until 1840 when Prince Albert's decorated trees were much lauded in the contemporary press. These first English yew boughs and trees had candles and paper cones filled with candies for the children. And small presents were set out beneath them. But there was no Santa Claus or Father Christmas.

Santa, in his quasi-Lappish outfit with his reindeer sleigh and predilection for chimneys, is purely American, birthed in the lovely poem *The Night Before Christmas*, credited to Clement Moore but now thought to have been written by Henry Livingston, Jr. Santa is a demigod of Plenty, like the Roman Ops, fat and opulent and merry, and a total stranger to ancient Christmas ways.

There was of course, Saint Nicholas, Bishop Nicholas of Myra, in what is now Turkey, whose feast day is December 6. He is famed for giving a great gift, but what he gave had nothing to do with Christmas: it was bags of money to provide three virtuous but penniless sisters with dowries. During the Reformation, as the interest in saints waned, Sinter Klaas remained a favorite in Holland, filling children's shoes with sweets and toys on Christmas Eve. It is this Dutch manifestation that has become Santa Claus. If he arrived in England with William and Mary, he seems not to have taken root, but in New York, where the old Dutch families still reigned in Society in the 19th century, he inspired the shy Mr. Livingston with his icon-making verse.

Christmas gift giving, in old English tradition, has neither to do with Saint Nicholas nor even Christmas day. It recalled the gifts the three Magi brought to the Christ child, and the proper day was Epiphany or Twelfth Night, January 6.

If all we do is really not so very old, how was Christmas celebrated in times long gone by?

Christmas, in well-to-do households, from the twelfth into the nineteenth centuries, was the time of liveries: the giving of clothes to the servants. In noble establishments the liveries would be new and in the lord's heraldic colors. And the clothes given at Christmastide were to last all year. In poorer homes, the clothes would be the master and mistress' used garments, presumably their every-day ones. Their finer clothes would be turned, cut up, and reused as long as there was any use left in the fine fabrics.

Children, parents, spouses, and lovers exchanged gifts at Epiphany in recollection of the gifts the Magi brought to the Christ child.

Washington Irving, traveling in England on business in 1814-15, bemoans the loss of the ancient customs, Protestant solemnity, which by his time, had long since been replaced by urbane carousing in the cities. Dancing, feasting, winter revels such as those in which Lady Caroline Lamb cavorted wildly to attract young, beautiful, lame George Gordon, Lord Byron, were far too heady for an old church holiday still tainted with Calvinist sobriety.

In the countryside, Irving writes of the survival of the ancient traditions. Fiction or not, his *Old Christmas* is redolent of how Christmas was celebrated in English noble households from the Middle Ages onward to last flickers in the 19th century.

The oldest customs centered upon the church and the fief. In convents, ancient lullabies, sung by nuns for their own joy, celebrated the birth of the Christ child, who was husband to them all in the mystical wedding of their vows. A few churches developed reenactments of the arrival of the shepherds and the Three Kings. Caroling grew—contrapuntal, melismatic, rondelled or in simple chant.

From convents and the choirs of high clergy to country churches where villagers with the best voices were pressed to serve, the music of Christmas moved from the church loft into the roadway, and caroling from door to door became a custom to be met with hot cider, milk punch, and cakes. In cities, the poor turned caroling into a means of earning a pittance in the cold and holy season when charity, Dickens tells us, was most meet.

And on the fiefs? In the village church, during the modest twelfth and thirteenth centuries, the villeins attended a very early Mass, then went to the lord's hall, where a great feast, the high point of the year, was held, with beef and braun and beer for the folk, a boar's head, wine, and dainty dishes for the noble family at the table on the dais. Music, by strolling trouveres, or a talented tutor in the lord's household, or a villager with a flare for song with simple flute or drum, was the entertainment, with round dances for the young.

Until the dance was interrupted by the Bean King. As in the ancient Roman Lupercalia, Christmastide was a time for reversal of roles: villein became master, maid became man, man became housewife, and clergy became…able to tell ribald jests. And over all ruled the Bean King: king for a day, since he or she had found—and nearly broken a tooth upon—the hard, dry bean baked in the cake. The finder reigned in a topsy turvy world of merriment.

When the dancing and buffoonery waned from tiring spirits and beer befuddled brains, it was time for the story teller: the wandering trouvere intoning his tales of Arthur, Tristan, or more recent heroes to the plucked rhythms of his harp; or the village reeve or witten recounting the more humble doings of Wayland and a threatening fairy land. Finally, sodden with beer and overspent spirits, the villagers one by one crumpled to the lordly hall's floor, to sleep a snoring, whickering, dream-filled sleep in a deep litter of hay scented with mint and lady's bedstraw.

Feasting, though simple and hearty for the commoners, was remarkably elaborate for the table on the dais. Kitchen labor was abundant, and Christmas preparations could take many days. Minced meats with fruit and spices were baked in pastry coffers—ancestors of mincemeat pie. Not only was sweet and tart a favored combination, but also sweet and salt. Since Roman times for health's sake high cuisine observed a balance of the "humors." Thus meat could be stuffed with fruit.

Turkey, an American bird, was Scrooge's Christmas present to the Cratchets, though goose was the more common bird for feasts, and at grand tables swan was served, or peacock pie enrobed with the bird's brilliant feathered skin and tail, the noble head wired erect.

But what of the mummers and the Morris dancers, you say. Mumming seems to have a divided history: holiday enactments by masked courtiers can be traced to the fourteenth century, developing into professional performances by the sixteenth. Shakespeare's *Twelfth Night* might be considered a prime mumming, with its Lupercalian reversal of roles, its typical counterpoint of virtuous (Viola, Olivia, and the Duke) and base motivation (Sir Toby, Sir Andrew, Malvolio) and its theme of miraculous resurrection (Sebastian and Viola saved from the sea)—a perfect model of the themes of early mummings.

Mumming as it has more recently come to be known in Britain, where villagers in costumes and disguises would beg fees for their performances, is a late arrival to Christmas, first appearing, so far as documentary evidence can reach, only in the eighteenth century. Here the chief characters are usually Saint George, the Turk, and the Doctor who resuscitates Saint George. These plays would appear to have more in common, in regard of text, with the paladin puppet plays of Italy than old English enactments. Some scholars hold that mumming of this sort springs from very ancient folkways in Ireland.

Less organized and more common perhaps were "mummings" such as Washington Irving portrays when he has the children of Bracebridge Hall raiding the attics for the finery of ancestors and appearing costumed in antique garb, declaring themselves to be Dame Mince Pie or the lord and lady of a long past chivalry. There is no play per se in this spontaneous "mumming," but a striking of attitudes and much dance.

And the Morris Dancers? Those hearkeners back to Robin and Maid Marion who leap and batter with staves? They too are not so very old—so far as current scholarship can tell. "Morris" is a term used as early as the mid-fifteenth century but, in the way of non-standardized spelling, may refer to the Spanish moresca, which seems to have something to do with Moors.

Is the Morris Dance perhaps a survival of a pre-Christian ritual? Possibly, as Robin Hood may have been a member of the triumvirate of Cunningman, lady-in-white and dying god, according to the researches of archeologist Margaret Murray, but modern scholarship likes neither Margaret Murray nor the notion of the survival of pre-Christian customs, and certainly not at Christmas time.

Teams or "sides" of Morris Dancers are a part of present day British Christmas celebrations and derive from the work of Cecil Sharp who, in 1899, viewed a traditional Morris Dance at Headington and set about recording and reviving the custom. Washington Irving knew the Morris Dance as well. But between the 19th century and the old Spanish sword dance said to have been performed for Ferdinand and Isabella to celebrate their conquest of the Moors, there are wide gaps. How did a Spanish sword dance come to be associated with Robin Hood, or choreographed combat with staves come to keep company with Christmas?

As Santa and reindeer, trimmed trees and stuffed turkeys, Morris Dances and mumming are our present ways to celebrate, so the biblical gifts of the Magi, the legend of the medieval Jongleur de Notre Dame who, having nothing but his song and dance, offered those to the Christ child, form a slowly changing continuum in the spirit of giving what we can give, in Christianity's celebration of the birth of Jesus.

Made in the USA
Lexington, KY
21 December 2014